REVISIONARY PLAY

REVISIONARY PLAY

STUDIES IN THE SPENSERIAN DYNAMICS

HARRY   BERGER,   JR.

*With an Introductory Essay
by Louis Montrose*

UNIVERSITY OF CALIFORNIA PRESS

Berkeley   Los Angeles   London

University of California Press
Berkeley and Los Angeles, California

University of California Press, Ltd.
London, England

Library of Congress Cataloging-in-Publication Data
Berger, Harry.
    Revisionary play: studies in the Spenserian dynamics / Harry
Berger, Jr.; with an introductory essay by Louis Montrose.
    p. cm.
    Bibliography: p.
    Includes index.
    ISBN 0-520-05683-3 (alk. paper)
    1. Spenser, Edmund, 1552?–1599—Criticism and interpretation.
2. Spenser, Edmund, 1552?–1599. Faerie queene. I. Title.
PR2364.B397   1989
821'.3—dc19   87-32618

Printed in the United States of America   1   2   3   4   5   6   7   8   9

I wish to thank the following editors, journals, and publishers for their permission to reprint all or part of these essays:

"The Spenserian Dynamics," *Studies in English Literature (1500–1900)* 8 (1968): 1–18.

"Archaism, Immortality, and the Muse in Spenser's Poetry," *The Yale Review* 58 (1969): 214–31.

"Spenser's *Faerie Queene*, Book I," *Southern Review* (Australia) 2, no. 1 (1966): 18–50.

"*Faerie Queene*, Book III: A General Description," *Criticism* 11 (1969): 234–61.

"The Structure of Merlin's Chronicle in *The Faerie Queene* III (iii)," *Studies in English Literature* 9 (1969): 38–51.

"Spenser's Gardens of Adonis: Force and Form in the Renaissance Imagination," *University of Toronto Quarterly* 30 (1961): 129–49.

"The Discarding of Malbecco: Conspicuous Allusion and Cultural Exhaustion in *The Faerie Queene* III.ix–x," *Studies in Philology* 66 (1969): 135–54.

"Busirane and the War between the Sexes: An Interpretation of *The Faerie Queene* III.xi–xii," *English Literary Renaissance* 1 (1971): 99–121.

"Two Spenserian Retrospects: The Antique Temple of Venus and the Primitive Marriage of Rivers," *Texas Studies in Literature and Language* 10 (1968): 5–25.

"A Secret Discipline: *The Faerie Queene*, Book VI," in *Form and Convention in the Poetry of Edmund Spenser*, ed. William Nelson (New York: Columbia University Press, 1961), 35–75.

"The *Mutabilitie Cantos:* Archaism and Evolution in Retrospect," in *Spenser: A Collection of Critical Essays*, ed. Harry Berger, Jr. (Englewood Cliffs: Prentice-Hall, 1968), 146–76.

Parts of "The Moral Eclogues" first appeared in "Mode and Diction in *The Shepheardes Calender*," *Modern Philology* 67 (1969): 140–49.

"The Mirror Stage of Colin Clout" reprinted from "The Mirror Stage of Colin Clout: A Reading of Spenser's *Januarye* Eclogue," *Helios* 10 (1983): 139–60.

Parts of the last four chapters reprinted from "The Aging Boy: Paradise and Parricide in Spenser's *Shepheardes Calender*," in *Poetic Traditions of the English Renaissance*, ed. Maynard Mack and George deForest Lord (New Haven: Yale University Press, 1982), 25–46.

"Orpheus, Pan, and the Poetics of Misogyny: Spenser's Critique of Pastoral Love and Art," *ELH* 50 (1983): 27–60.

For Maggie

CONTENTS

ACKNOWLEDGMENTS

Because I recently completed the acknowledgments for another volume of essays published by the University of California Press, I considered slotting new names into its formulas. But then I realized that there were no formulas there; and I thought better of myself. Also, some of the same names would happen again. It would be insincere and insulting, for example, simply to repeat what I said before about Doris Kretschmer, who refused time and again to let me back out of what we both laughingly called my contractual obligations to the University of California Press. It isn't that I couldn't have finshed putting this volume together without her; it's that I wouldn't have, which made her job tougher and her strategies of containment more impressive. What would Charlotte Cassidy say if I were to blame her as I did before, "not because she has been typing and copyediting my manuscripts for more than twenty years but because the form of her fair copy was so much more beautiful than the content of my foul papers that I was often reluctant to disturb it with revisions that would undoubtedly have made this a better book"? And would my research assistant Beth Pittenger like it if instead of taking the trouble to think up something new I were once again to record my gratitude to her "for the meticulous care with which she prepared the manuscript, helped me reconstruct the footnotes, and retyped [many of] them in printer-ready form"? I suspect that if I took the lazy way out and thanked the Committee on Research at the University of California, Santa Cruz, "for their willingness to believe my promises and for their good sense in supporting my research," they would stop believing and supporting, and who could blame them? How would Barbara Ras feel if I should merely paraphrase the words I used to thank her for the care with which she oversaw the complex production process that translated a manuscript into a book?

And were I to repeat that she successfully oversaw the complex cooptation process that translated an authorial mental case into a willing collaborator, that would be giving her more credit than she deserves; I was easier to deal with the second time around. These are, after all, thanks and acknowledgments, not letters of recommendation. If I thank Amy Klatzkin for the patient and skillful copyediting that cleaned up almost 500 pages of uneven prose, I want people to believe I mean it. But if she asked me, I would gladly write her a letter of recommendation.

Mere repetition and flattery, then, can't do justice either to their contributions or to my gratitude. The occasion calls for a fuller, more inventive, more exacting expression of the sweet wound of obligation the recipient bares in acknowledging gifts and givers. And I plan to produce that expression soon. But now more pressing business gets in the way as a host of new names, new acknowledgments, jostle forward and demand to be recorded.

There are, for example, those members of the faculty life-support system in my college locally known as the Cowell Steno Pool where for twenty-two years I have taken my problems large and small, material and spiritual, to be solved, or analyzed, or, best of all, scoffed at: Sharon Overgaard, Phyllis Halpin, Marianna Alves, and especially Wallie Romig, who teaches me how to read everything (but chiefly my own text) with utmost suspicion.

There are all those friends with whom over the years I have talked, agreed, disagreed, and sometimes argued. These conversations were not necessarily about Spenser, but their recurrent outcome—to persuade me that I didn't know what I was talking about—made it possible for me to keep moving on, if not always toward better ideas, then at least toward different ones. I think fondly and gratefully of John Pope, W. K. Wimsatt, Jr., Angus Fletcher, Richard B. Young, Mary and Martin Price, Richard Sylvester, Thomas Greene, Michael Holahan, Paul Alpers, Stephen Greenblatt, John Lynch, Page duBois, Jay Farness, Thomas Vogler, H. Marshall Leicester, Jr., and more graduate and undergraduate students than I can remember, though the Spenser graduate seminar I taught at The University of North Carolina in 1967 stands out vividly in my mind. Finally, it gives me great pleasure to thank Louis Montrose not only for his introduction to this volume but also for his friendship, his support, his always astute and sympathetic criticism, and the remarkable set of essays—already classics in the field—which have shown (and continue to show) me how to think more responsibly, more reflexively, about Spenser in particular and critical practice in general. It was chiefly his work that enabled me to return to *The Shepheardes Calender* and see it afresh.

This volume is gratefully dedicated to Maggie because, when I was working on the essays during the fifties and sixties, she was there, and I couldn't have gotten through them, or other things, without her help.

INTRODUCTORY ESSAY

by Louis Montrose

> Plato treats Critias and his Atlantis very much as More treats
> Hytholoday and his Utopia, as Spenser treats Faerie, Sidney poetry
> and Shakespeare the green world. All are useful only if they pro-
> claim their hypothetical status, and are understood to have literal
> existence not in space or time but solely, as Spenser puts it, "deepe
> within the mynd." They should not be approached as exemplars to be
> copied but rather as hypothetical models—guides, not commanders,
> as Jonson put it. However much they attract us in and for them-
> selves, their ultimate purpose is to lead us beyond them. Models
> exist to be emulated, not imitated; the interpreter's aim is to render
> his models in a certain sense obsolete, by becoming a model himself.
>
> —*Harry Berger, Jr., "The Renaissance Imagination"*

I

For more than a quarter century, Harry Berger has been a model for
interpreters of the Renaissance imagination. In such intellectually bold
and influential essays of the 1960s and early 1970s as "The Renaissance
Imagination: Second World and Green World," Berger gave to a generation of students and scholars new conceptual tools for working with a
variety of Renaissance cultural texts—philosophical discourses and paintings as well as poems and plays. In insisting that such cultural texts are
sites of seriously playful intellectual work—imaginative spaces within
which cultural paradigms may be formulated, tested, evaluated, and revised or discarded—Berger implicitly affirmed the status of imaginative

My thanks to Page duBois, Roxanne Klein, and Lisa Lowe—and, of course, Harry
Berger—for their encouragement and criticism of this essay.

1

forms as modes of ideological production that do not merely reflect social reality but actively shape it. He thus helped to lay the groundwork for current attempts to reconstrue the object of analysis in Renaissance literary studies as the whole range of discursive practices by which early modern European society and its subjects are constructed.[1] No critic of English Renaissance literature in Berger's generation has had at once so formative and so liberating an influence upon how we read that literature; and surely none continues today, with such daimonic energy, to engage the work of others and to renew his own.

The past decade has seen a second flowering of Berger's career. This prolific body of recent and ongoing work is remarkable for its intellectual range and for its combination of analytical subtlety and rhetorical force. His recently published essays on Platonic dialogues, classical and Renaissance pastoral, Shakespearean drama, and cultural theory enact Berger's coming to terms with both the current scholarly literature and the debates on theory and method in several disciplines. At the same time, they manifest themselves as the latest stages of a vast evolving intellectual project focused on "the ecological interaction between *homo faber* and his environment—that is, the conscious and nonconscious productive processes by which man makes his history and by which he continually re-creates himself and the world in which he finds himself."[2]

The opening essay of this volume is entitled "The Spenserian Dynamics"; each of the essays, however, manifests "the Bergerian dynamics": a readiness to entertain and to appropriate whatever in the shifting currents of cultural studies may be usefully reshaped to his own ends, and a ceaseless rethinking and rewriting of what he has made in the past. What I admire most about Berger and his work—in this case the project and

---

[1] Perhaps the single most important influence on this reorientation in the field of English Renaissance literary studies has been Stephen Greenblatt, *Renaissance Self-Fashioning* (Chicago: University of Chicago Press, 1980). Among subsequent reviews and critiques of this so-called New Historicism, see Jonathan Goldberg, "The Politics of Renaissance Literature: A Review Essay," *ELH* 49 (1982): 514–42; and Jean E. Howard, "The New Historicism in Renaissance Studies," *English Literary Renaissance* 16 (1986): 13–43. Also see my early review essay on Greenblatt's book, "A Poetics of Renaissance Culture," *Criticism* 23 (1981): 349–59; and my more recent statement, "Renaissance Literary Studies and the Subject of History," *English Literary Renaissance* 16 (1986): 5–12.

[2] Harry Berger, Jr., "Naive Consciousness and Culture Change: An Essay in Historical Structuralism," *Bulletin of the Midwest Modern Language Association* 6 (1973): 1. Reprinted in Berger, *Second World and Green World*. I must note the androcentric bias of Berger's language here, a bias he has since acknowledged and repudiated.

the person, the subject and the method, strike me as inseparable—is their apparently inexhaustible capacity for what he himself, characterizing Spenser, has called re-vision. Throughout his work, and apropos of every human activity and experience, Berger insists upon the temporal and the temporary, upon the tentative status of all resolutions, all syntheses, and upon the necessity for perpetual open-ended dialogue. He steadfastly resists all forms of intellectual foreclosure.[3]

II

Commencing with *The Allegorical Temper* (1957), a monograph on Book II of *The Faerie Queene* that was based upon his doctoral dissertation, Berger has found in the poetry of Spenser both a model and a subject for his own interpretive activity. Throughout his career, Spenser's Faerie has discovered to him a landscape "deepe within the mynd" that is at once increasingly familiar and irreducibly strange; a heterocosm whose textual places may be periodically revisited, reexperienced, and revised in new texts of his own. Berger's characteristic methods and working habits, and the idiosyncratic pattern of his career, are duly registered in the occasion of the present book and in the disposition of its parts. Part I is composed of previously published essays on Spenser's poetry in general and on *The Faerie Queene* in particular. All were originally published between 1961 and 1971 and appear here unrevised, except for the correction of errors and the excision of redundancies. Berger's preeminence as an interpreter of Spenser is grounded upon this

[3] As I was drafting this introduction, I received the Winter 1987 issue of *Representations*, containing Harry Berger's latest publication, "Bodies and Texts" (*Representations* 17: 144–66). The opening pages of the essay, on the interpretation of *King Lear*, are italicized to signify that they are "cited from a lecture . . . delivered to different audiences during the last few years" (p. 145). In coy self-deprecation he confesses, "I have never been overly swift in making connections between what I was talking or writing about and the way I was talking or writing about it. My reflexive or metacritical faculties have atrophied from years of New-Critical sedentism" (p. 146). Needless to say, this strategic confession is the transition between the cited earlier text and the essay proper, which is an extended metacritical re-vision and re-grounding of the entire academic debate of "text versus performance" within which the earlier paper had been conceived: "My purpose here is to suggest that the controversy itself (including my share in it) has been ill founded, poorly grounded, and myopic, and to explore some of the basic structural forces and cultural changes of which it is a superficial symptom" (p. 146). What follows is a brilliant and wide-ranging engagement with the "problematic of speech versus writing" (p. 146) and with Poststructuralist theories of the text. The whole essay—as text and as performance—epitomizes the latest and most complex phase of the evolving Bergerian dynamics.

body of work, which has been continually cited and quoted since its initial, piecemeal, appearance in print over the course of a decade.[4] Teach-
ers and scholars in the field of English Renaissance literature have frequently expressed the wish to see these studies brought together and
made more readily accessible to them and to their students. The long
delay in realizing such a project is caused largely by Berger's construing
his publications as merely provisional readings, as working papers fixed
in print only to be left behind. His personal imperative is to be always
writing—to write and, having written, to move on. This is why his
characteristic medium has remained the essay: his thinking will not keep
still long enough for him to "finish" a book. Most of the essays in part I
are in fact quarried from a large manuscript on the central books of *The
Faerie Queene* that was never readied for publication; this project, like
the complex narrative poem that is its subject, is thus marked by the
perpetual deferral of ending. Because all of these essays are representative of a particular stage of Berger's interpretive activity, they have
been arranged here not in the largely circumstantial chronology of their
initial publication but rather as a sustained reading of successive books
and episodes of the poem. The fundamental Spenserian and Bergerian
themes and strategies sketched in the first two essays are unpacked and
exemplified in the nine that follow. With part II the situation is different. Here Berger presents a monograph-length study of *The Shepheardes
Calendar,* only parts of which have previously appeared in print.[5] Thus
the study of the earlier poem here follows the study of the later one because it constitutes Berger's retrospective, revisionary encounter with
Spenser's beginnings.

Berger's attribution to Spenser of "a radically historical consciousness" ("The *Mutabilitie Cantos,*" 243) depends upon his own complex
use of the concepts of "evolution" and "retrospection." These are so central to Berger's way of reading the Spenserian text as to require a re-

---

[4]There are four published pieces on Spenser from this period not reprinted here:
Berger's introduction to the anthology of critical essays on Spenser that he edited for the
Twentieth Century Views series (Englewood Cliffs: Prentice-Hall, 1968), 1–12; "The
Prospect of Imagination: Spenser and the Limits of Poetry," *Studies in English Literature*
1 (1961): 93–120 (itself a prospectus for the larger project); "Spenser's 'Prothalamion':
An Interpretation," *Essays in Criticism* 15 (1965): 363–80 (which did not make a comfortable fit into the plan of the present volume); and "Mode and Diction in *The Shepheardes Calender,*" *Modern Philology* 67 (1969): 140–49 (which has been revised and
subsumed by part II of this volume).

[5]Part II of this book is in fact a revision and integration of work produced during
two distinct phases of Berger's career: the earlier work was composed between 1959 and
1968; the later work during 1979–80.

hearsal here. Let me begin by quoting at length from the opening pages of the concluding essay in part I of this collection—Berger's fullest exposition and exemplification of what he construes as "the Spenserian dynamics":

> The objective character of Spenser's vision is *evolutionary*. . . . We may find in Spenser's poetry an overall developmental pattern in which three vectors coalesce: from lower to higher, from simpler to more complex, and, of course, from earlier to later. These vectors run parallel courses in the history of the individual psyche and in that of culture or civilization. . . .
>
> The subjective mode of Spenser's historical vision is retrospective: he looks back into the past from his own *here and now*. In his early or archaic world, action is caused for the most part by the large-scale play of forces which, though psychic as well as cosmic, operate outside any individual will or consciousness. . . . As psyche and culture develop, this collective and determined mode of behavior gradually yields to the more active and original assertions of individual souls. When the center of will, decision, and activity is located in the individual consciousness, archaic determinism gives way to retrospective determinism as the dominant organizing mode.
>
> When cosmic and primitive influences dominate, the forms of existence tend to be at once unstable and universal (that is, recurrent and generic or archetypal). When psychic and rational influences dominate, the forms tend to be personal, unique, and potentially more stable; at the same time, the forms of discord, evil, danger, and temptation are subtler and therefore less easily located and contained. Fundamental to this model is Spenser's conviction that no moment of union or reconciliation, of relief or triumph, is to be construed as absolute—absolute either in the sense of being final or in the sense of being totally one-sided. Every triumph or resolution at a lower level of existence or an earlier phase of experience releases new and different problems at a higher level or a later phase. . . .
>
> The full vision of the pattern I have been describing is seldom attained by characters within the Spenserian world, while its complex and articulated unity is a condition attained by soul, state, or culture only in relatively advanced phases of its career. And only in such phases does the imagination double back to activate the tacit or latent elements . . . of experience to set the present moment within its developmental context. . . . Spenser presents the latest form of experience both *in* his work and *as* his work. The historical sense which is the defining mark of that work asserts itself in his effort to locate the various elements of his poetic *discordia concors* at their proper temporal distances from the present. His poetry thus represents in its complex form all the phases which preceded it and which it, in effect, supersedes. This representation is achieved by means of the technique of *conspicuous allusion:* the depiction of stock literary motifs, characters, and genres in a manner which emphasizes their conventionality, displaying at once their debt to

and their existence in a conventional climate—classical, medieval, romance, and so on—which is archaic when seen from Spenser's retrospective viewpoint. ("The *Mutabilitie Cantos*," 243–45)

Synthesizing materials from a variety of intellectual traditions, Berger constructs a paradigm—more immediately recognizable as neo-Hegelian than Neoplatonic—that he both applies to Spenser's text and ascribes to Spenser's consciousness.[6] The model is doubly homological in that it interrelates collective and individual histories both at the highly abstract level of Culture and Psyche and at the specifically literary level of Tradition and Career. It seeks to explain simultaneously the narrative content of the poem, the foregrounding of the poem's relation to antecedent cultural texts, and the poem's status as a record of the growth of a poet's mind. It attributes to the text an extraordinary degree of reflexivity and to the writer an extraordinary degree of historical and cultural self-awareness, of critical detachment.

This model—which stands so much apart from earlier and contemporaneous dominant paradigms in Spenser studies—produces many brilliant observations concerning the narrative, stylistic, and thematic organization of the Spenserian *oeuvre* and of its constituent parts. Berger's readings of specific books and episodes of *The Faerie Queene* are never less than suggestive and are often persuasive. (The model itself pre-

---

[6] At one point Berger explicitly identifies what he characterizes as the Spenserian dynamic with "the Hegelian dynamic of sublation (*aufheben*): the new context and usage confer on earlier, simpler forms a destiny more inclusive than their own, a more universal and organic function, so that they may transcend themselves in a manner not possible to them in their first isolated push toward fulfillment" (*"Faerie Queene,* Book III," 117). Berger's way of representing the evolutionary model of consciousness that he attributes to Spenser has interesting affinities with Erich Neumann's contemporaneous Jungian model of parallel mythological-psychological "archetypal" stages in the histories of culture and psyche:

> In the history of mankind as in the development of the individual there is an initial preponderance of transpersonal factors, and only in the course of development does the personal realm come into view and achieve independence. The individualized conscious man of our era is a late man, whose structure is built on early, pre-individual human stages from which individual consciousness has only detached itself step by step.
>
> The evolution of consciousness by stages is as much a collective human phenomenon as a particular individual phenomenon. Ontogenetic development may therefore be regarded as a modified recapitulation of phylogenetic development. (Erich Neumann, *The Origins and History of Consciousness*, trans. R. F. C. Hull, Bollingen Series 42 [Princeton: Princeton University Press, 1954], xx)

Whatever its affinities, Berger's use of an evolutionary paradigm seems to me open to charges of anachronism.

cludes the possibility that these or any other readings could be definitive.) In readings as specific as that analyzing the description of Sylvanus and the satyrs in *Faerie Queene* I.vi or as general as that characterizing the ethos of Book III, the model deployed in the essays collected here has had a fundamental influence upon the ways in which we read, teach, and write about the poetry of Spenser.

What today strikes us—perhaps I should say, what now strikes me—as conspicuously unrepresented in this model is a dimension of historical experience that is tangibly sociopolitical: there is little explicit or sustained acknowledgment of the poet as a gendered and classed subject acting and acted upon in a particular society, or of the poem's production—its writing, dissemination, and reading—as a social act. Our current concern to address this dimension cannot be dismissed as a fashionable anachronism; on the contrary, it is a preoccupation of Spenser's society, a preoccupation that strongly marks his text. The silences in Berger's own text—and my concern with those silences—mark the interpretation of Spenser's poetry as itself a historically determinate social act. Any reading of the Spenserian text is necessarily partial—by which I mean incapable of offering an exhaustive description, a complete explanation, but also incapable of offering any description that is itself impartial, disinterested. The interpretive activity of the critic of Renaissance literature is, like its object, a production of ideology. By this I mean that it does not merely bear the traces of the critic's values, beliefs, and experiences—his or her socially constructed subjectivity—but actively instantiates them; that it is a vehicle for the critic's partly unconscious and partly calculating negotiation of disciplinary, institutional, and societal demands and expectations; that to the degree that it is an inscription of cultural priorities and a medium of professional advantage, its pursuit of knowledge is inevitably impure. As professional readers of the Spenserian text, we have investments—overdetermined investments that will always remain at least partially obscure to ourselves—in those versions of "Spenser" represented and produced in our texts.

If they have tended to avoid direct confrontations of sociopolitical issues, Harry Berger's writings have nonetheless always manifested a contestatory stance toward the prevailing critical orthodoxies. Any explanation for the absence of a historically specific sociopolitical dimension in his writings on Spenser must surely take into account that at the time these essays were written the prevailing mode of historical scholarship in American literary studies had for generations been almost wholly positivistic; the sociopolitical study of Spenser was epitomized by the pursuit of topical identifications or the cataloguing of commonplaces—

activities that merely impoverished the text. In his introduction to an
anthology of Spenser criticisms that, like many of the essays in part I,
was published in the late 1960s, Berger states that

> in this editor's opinion, much recent Spenser commentary has suffered from
> the conservative influence of literary iconography and intellectual history,
> solid and important though these forms of inquiry be. This conservatism
> perhaps develops in reaction to the tendencies of some "new-critically"
> trained readers to see "modern" complexities in a Renaissance poet. Literary
> interpretation seems indeed of late to have drifted farther away from the
> arms of the more hard-headed historical disciplines; it has opened itself to
> breezes from psychology, epistemology, anthropology, existentialism, and
> phenomenology, also to impulses from the approaches to cultural history de-
> riving from Hegel, Dilthey, Cassirer, and others. (*Spenser: A Collection of
> Critical Essays*, 2)

The imputation of "conservatism" and "reaction" to the practices of
iconography and intellectual history, the repudiation of "hard-headed"
empiricism for tough-minded theorizing: Berger's vocabulary tacitly
acknowledges that he and his colleagues are engaged in a politics of
scholarship that is related, in however mediated a fashion, to the larger
cultural politics of the society in which they live. Berger has never sym-
pathized with the endemic intellectual and ideological conservatism of
Spenser studies. His work eschews the tendencies evident in much modern criticism to celebrate Spenser's poetry either as a repository of those
traditional religious and social values to which the critic remains deeply
committed, or as the representation of an idealized past with which the
critic nostalgically identifies. Having been a graduate student in the preeminent Yale English Department during the postwar decade, and for
the next decade an untenured member of its faculty, Berger was indeed a
"new-critically" trained reader—though by no means merely another
New Critic. It may be that the experience of social and ethnic difference
from the genteel Protestant and Anglo-Saxon ethos that pervaded and
still pervades Spenser studies both produced in him a sense of cultural
exclusion and provided the vantage point for his appropriation of a text
and a tradition that were not his cultural birthright.[7]

---

[7] In a metacritical analysis of "the shift of focus, in recent Renaissance scholarship
produced in the U.K. and U.S., from ideas to relationships of power as the fundamental
units of historical analysis and interpretation," Don E. Wayne argues persuasively that
"for scholars of the immediate post-war period, many of whom were first-generation
Americans of non-English ancestry, a fundamental political problem was to establish
an entitlement to the role of critic with respect to English culture" ("Power, Politics,

The "conservatism" of which Berger complains was "in reaction" against precisely that tendency in Spenser commentary that he himself, more than anyone else at the time, was actively pursuing. In part it is a capacious yet critical openness to a variety of intellectual "breezes"—an audacious refusal to maintain disciplinary decorum—that distinguishes his earlier work sharply not only from that of orthodox literary historians but also from that of orthodox New Critics. I have already suggested that a central element in Berger's iconoclasm, in his repudiation of what he calls "the conservative influence of literary iconography and intellectual history"—and tacitly of the Christian Humanist apologetics embedded in much of this criticism—has been the resolutely secular humanist orientation of his work on Spenser. Berger invariably prefers philosophical to theological modes of exegesis. Throughout these essays his paradigm for human creative activity is not Christian caritas but rather Platonic eros; the latter better serves his conception of a "Spenserian dynamics." Such an orientation is manifest, for example, in his resistance to a version of Spenser that emphasizes the continuity in his work of medieval stylistic, intellectual, and spiritual traditions and a medieval mode of cognition. Thus he goes out of his way to contrast the dominant vertical axis of Dante's narrative with the radical horizontality of Spenser's:

> Spenser's world and its places are not actualized in advance like an obstacle course waiting to steer its assayers toward their preordained goal. They emerge out of the problems and actions of his characters. . . .
>
> Since his "world picture" exists primarily as a function of the changing psychic development of the major characters, it would be more appropriate to substitute the temporal concept of *dynamics* for the more static and spatial concept of *world picture.* . . .
>
> . . . Temporal and cosmogonic explanation is detached from the world and applied to human behavior and experience. Its main reference is social, ethical, psychological, and phenomenological. ("The Spenserian Dynamics," 23, 25)

While necessarily acknowledging the antiquarian, melancholic, and pessimistic strains in Spenser's poetry, Berger consistently emphasizes what he sees as its dominantly evolutionary, progressive, and optimistic char-

---

and the Shakespearean Text: Recent Criticism in England and the United States," in *Shakespeare Reproduced*, ed. Jean E. Howard and Marion O'Connor [London and New York: Methuen, 1987]). I have benefited from reading this essay and am grateful to my colleague for allowing me to see it in typescript.

acter. He represents the Spenserian worldview as anthropocentric, its dynamics as mundane and temporal, its mode of "human behavior and experience" as individual and interpersonal.

Among the essays of the 1960s reprinted in part I of this collection, that subtitled "Force and Form in the Renaissance Imagination" most fully expounds the humanist tradition of Renaissance cultural historiography, extending from Burckhardt to Cassirer, within which Berger reads Spenser. Among its characteristics are the projection of what Berger calls "second worlds," circumscribed imaginative spaces within which to experiment with the possibilities of human experience and action and to test their limits; a great diversification of the modes of textual and iconic representation and an increasingly sophisticated reflection upon the unstable referentiality of symbolic forms; and a heightened consciousness of historical change and cultural diversity, with a concomitant sharpening of historically and culturally specific self-consciousness. This paradigm of the Renaissance Imagination can be put to use, for example, to clarify the function of the cycle-of-months episode in the *Mutabilitie Cantos:*

> We must not confuse Spenser's picture of the medieval mind with what are often thought of as Spenser's medieval habits of mind. . . . If this vision is particularly attractive to Spenser, it is not because he is uncritically traditional or unconsciously medieval. The medieval mind may have believed in this vision as a divine and providential work, a panoramic picture of God's real order of nature. But Spenser employs the technique of conspicuous allusion in this canto not only to distance that vision in terms of cultural time, but also to emphasize its artistic and artificial quality. The essence of the order is so clearly dependent upon and communicated by its artistic organization . . . that we are impressed primarily by the synoptic power of the human poet's imagination. ("The *Mutabilitie Cantos,*" 268)

Berger's Spenser is not a residual medievalist inscribed within a divinely ordained and perfected cosmos but rather an emergent modernist actively engaged in constructing the imperfect world in which he dwells.

Most important for Berger's study of Spenser, and for the larger study of cultural change that has evolved from it, is a humanist emphasis upon the individual and collective capacity of *homo faber* for fashioning both the world and the self:

> The forms of human vision came more and more to be felt as creations of the human mind in response to a God who manifested himself chiefly in process, force, and relation.

. . . [The Renaissance constituted] an intellectual climate in which the visible forms of the real are no longer felt as external or given but are created and stabilized through the experience of the individual soul and the creative effort of the individual imagination. . . . If all forms are in a sense mind-made . . . then the forms created by the mind, and the experience through which they are created, assume a new and urgent reality of their own. . . .

. . . the poem was conceived not merely as a report of prior experience but as the unfolding experience itself. . . .

This revisionary play can only have come about at a time in history when the concept of *self* was in flux: disengaging from the more objective concepts of *soul* and *person* and moving toward the notion of *experiencing subject*. ("Spenser's Gardens of Adonis," 132, 134–35, 135–36)

Without a clearly countervailing perspective on the limitations and illusions that make problematic any claim for human agency, Berger's analyses are sometimes in danger of lapsing into affirmations of a humanist ideology from which they have not yet fully emerged. Throughout his essays of the 1960s, Berger foregrounds the unique human subject—"the experience of the individual soul and the creative effort of the individual imagination"—as the locus of meaning and value. As I have suggested, what remains insufficiently articulated in these earlier writings is that *what* and *how* "the experiencing subject" experiences are always already subject to the pervasive shaping and constraining power of sociocultural codes and categories, institutions and practices.[8] As Berger's own recent work fully acknowledges, the "intellectual breezes" blowing today have decentered the subject so that "the individual soul" now appears to be an effect rather than a source of culture.

---

[8] The absence of this articulation may become more conspicuous if the quoted passage is contrasted with a passage from the epilogue to Greenblatt's *Renaissance Self-Fashioning*, published a decade and a half after Berger's essay:

When I first conceived this book several years ago, I intended to explore the ways in which major English writers of the sixteenth century created their own performances . . . to understand the role of human autonomy in the construction of identity. It seemed to me the very hallmark of the Renaissance that middle-class and aristocratic males began to feel that they possessed such shaping power over their lives, and I saw this power and the freedom it implied as an important element in my own sense of myself. But as my work progressed, I perceived that fashioning oneself and being fashioned by cultural institutions—family, religion, state—were inseparably intertwined. . . . The human subject itself began to seem remarkably unfree, the ideological product of the relations of power in a particular society. . . . If there remained traces of free choice, the choice was among possibilities whose range was strictly delineated by the social and ideological system in force. (p. 256)

A generation younger than Berger, though of similar ethnic and academic background, Greenblatt is obviously more able and more willing to foreground his own stake in his

III

Part I of this collection, concerned largely with the erotic central books of *The Faerie Queene*, Spenser's Legends of Chastity and Friendship, was written a generation ago, in an earlier phase of Berger's own life and career. Most of part II, concerned with *The Shepheardes Calender*, the text that inaugurated Spenser's profession of poetry, is the production of a more recent and later phase of Berger's life and career. In the former, Berger's analysis of "the Spenserian dynamics" is appropriately inflected toward the dialectic of male and female; in the latter, toward the dialectic of age and youth.

Throughout the essays in part I, Berger remains as wary of ecstasy as of apocalypse:

> The concord proper to human beings turns not on the hope for complete union but on the awareness that such a hope is deceptive: since two lovers are neither able to melt into one nor likely to live happily ever after if they expect to melt into one, they must acknowledge their differentness or separateness and accept their differences. . . . This concord is not founded on the desire of absolute union but on the discipline of tempered *com*munion. ("The Spenserian Dynamics," 22)

It seems to me that in such passages as this Berger gives a contemporary inflection to the historically emergent model of companionate marriage operative in Spenser's text; at the same time, however, he suppresses the contradictions in this erotic and domestic model, its conservation of hierarchical power relations in both social and discursive practice. In the dynamic evolutionary principle of eros that Berger sees as impelling Spenser's allegorical narrative,

---

intellectual project, to demystify any pretense of scholarly disinterestedness. What is recognized and acknowledged here, albeit reluctantly, is that the human subject is always already inscribed in ideology, that individual acts of creation are inevitably marked by "relations of power in a particular society." (Note that even in its earlier, unproblematically humanist, form—at least as Greenblatt characterizes it here—the Renaissance subject of self-fashioning was not generically Man but was already classed and gendered as a bourgeois or aristocratic male.) Throughout *Renaissance Self-Fashioning*, however, gestures of Foucauldian antihumanism remain in tension with a powerful fiction of individual autonomy that the writer can no longer wholly embrace yet cannot wholly relinquish. Indeed it is as the record of an unresolved struggle for Greenblatt's own authorial self-fashioning that his text achieves a metacritical consonance with the texts it interprets. Greenblatt's writings sometimes appear to recuperate traditional humanist categories of Self and Art in the very process of subverting them.

the most complex form of love is that which is fulfilled and symbolized by marriage—not simply love of friends, not simply attraction between male and female, not an affair of souls without bodies or of bodies without souls, but the richer and more difficult love between masculine and feminine *persons*. In this *discordia concors* the opposition of contrary sexes is mingled with a crucial similarity, namely, that the lovers are separate, equal, and unique selves. ("The Spenserian Dynamics," 34)

I do not think that such an unequivocal declaration of equality and unique subjectivity, whether of characters or persons, can be sustained by *The Faerie Queene*, or perhaps by any other extant Elizabethan text. (Even if Berger is anachronistic here, his misreading of Spenser can be read against tendencies in the sociocultural ambience of the later 1960s, when many of these essays were published: tendencies toward erotic mysticism and primitive communism, on the one hand, and toward political repression and military aggression, on the other.) Within the narrow furrow of Spenser studies, Berger's critical tack provided a salutary corrective to romantic readings of the poem's ambivalent representation of symbolic hermaphroditism. More important, it was perhaps the first serious and sustained confrontation and theorization of the recurrent deferral of narrative closure in *The Faerie Queene*.[9]

The enlightened male critic of the late twentieth century represents the enlightened male poet of the late sixteenth century as capable of an unproblematic identification with, and representation of, his female Other:

> In his epic as in his minor poetry Spenser sets himself the task of realizing the otherness and complex reality of woman by seeing life from the feminine point of view. The traditional vision of relationship must be transformed into a new and personal vision, and it is entirely in accord with his own conceptions of poetry and love that he *displays* the act of revision as part of the content of his poem. ("*The Faerie Queene*, Book III," 92)

Berger seems here to essentialize the notion of a "feminine point of view" and to suggest that Spenser can "see" it with an objectivity transcending his own gendered and historically specific subject position. Any attempt to claim Spenser as a proto-feminist, however, is undermined by the obvious strategies of authorial mastery by which he constructs and voices his female characters, by which he inscribes them within nar-

---

[9]The most important subsequent study—which gratefully acknowledges a debt to Berger's essays—is Jonathan Goldberg, *Endlesse Worke: Spenser and the Structures of Discourse* (Baltimore: Johns Hopkins University Press, 1981).

ratives that subject them to the whims of Fortune, to the wills of male heroes and villains, or to the transpersonal imperatives of Historical Destiny. Readers—women as well as men—must ask of themselves as of Spenser if it is possible to distinguish the effort of sympathy from the project of appropriation, if the act of understanding otherness is not in fact synonymous with the act of constructing it.

In his earlier studies of the central books of *The Faerie Queene*, Berger's ethical-psychological focus is upon "the discipline of tempered *com*munion," the difficult necessity that lovers "acknowledge their differentness or separateness and accept their differences"; in his later studies of *The Shepheardes Calender*, that focus is upon the difficult necessity that the individual accept and endure "the natural course of life itself" ("'An Hoor Heed and a Grene Tayl'," 441), the vicissitudes of temporality and mortality, change and loss. An axiom of Berger's interpretive practice here is that he is not engaged in deconstructing Spenser's text but merely in explicating its own strategies of deconstruction; the claim is that the poem already constitutes a reflexive critique of its own sources, genre, and content:

> Spenser's *Shepheardes Calender* is self-amused pastoral, a critically and comically squint reenactment of attitudes, topics, and norms characteristic of a traditional literary mode. If it is "about" the limits of conventionally defined pastoral assumptions and points of view, it is equally "about" forms of sensibility and responses to life restricted enough to fit within those narrow bounds. The fundamental object of Spenser's criticism is the longing for paradise as the psychological basis of the pastoral retreat from life. He presents this longing in dialectical form, inflected either toward wish-fulfilling fantasy [the recreative attitude] or toward bitter rejection of the world that falls short of such fantasy [the plaintive attitude]. These two inflections are causally interdependent and mutually intensifying. . . .
>
> I shall refer to this recreative/plaintive dynamic as the "paradise *principle*." ("Introduction to *The Shepheardes Calender*," 277–78)

Berger's argument in this second part of the book is complex and subtle—not least in its ways of engaging other critics of the poem and turning upon their pastoral criticism the metapastoral critique that Berger attributes to the poem itself. This metapastoral critique has three aspects: "the motivational critique of the system of values embedded in the psychology of withdrawal . . . the intertextual critique of the way pastoral conventions idealize their literariness along with the psychological experience they represent . . . the reflexive critique, by any particular work, of its own commitment to the genre" (p. 320). Evident in this recent work on Spenserian pastoral are both the continuity and refinement of Berger's earlier concerns and an engagement—on his own terms—with some of the central concerns of "New Historicist" critics: the active role of texts in the production and inculcation of norms and values and in the formation and re-formation of subjectivity; the historical constitution of the category of Literature and the scope of its ideological functions; the degree to which, and the means by which, a text may open an internal distance toward the structures of power and knowledge within which it has been written or is being read.

Today neither the "old New Critic" he calls himself ("Bodies and Texts," 147) nor quite a fellow traveler of the "New Historicism," Harry Berger remains *sui generis*, an intellectual *senex-puer* of cultural studies. The fruits of his New Critical training have been, and continue to be, his subtlety and brilliance as a close reader (especially of texts that, like *The Faerie Queene*, are usually analyzed at a middle distance), his sensitivity to tonal nuance, his teasing out of etymological and paronomastic possibilities, his powerful sense of verbal ambiguity. His earlier work displayed a New-Critical delight in the multivalent play of language. His more recent work—including the monograph on *The Shepheardes Calender* published here as well as several articles on Shakespearean drama—has been characterized by an increasingly ironic conception of surplus meaning. In such studies, he performs trenchant anatomies of language as the medium through which characters involuntarily speak their darker purposes—their duplicities, complicities, and self-deceptions.[10]

In these more recent writings, Berger's New-Critical tendencies have begun to modulate into Poststructuralist ones. If this modulation remains as yet tentative, it is because Berger tends in these essays to construe linguistic indeterminacy as the means by which the limitations, contradictions, and tacit collusions within the imaginative community of

[10] On Shakespeare, see "*King Lear:* The Lear Family Romance," *Centennial Review* 23 (1979): 346–78; "The Early Scenes of *Macbeth:* Preface to a New Interpretation," *ELH* 47 (1980): 1–31; "Marriage and Mercifixion in *The Merchant of Venice:* The Casket Scene Revisited," *Shakespeare Quarterly* 32 (1981): 156–62; "Text against Performance in Shakespeare: The Example of *Macbeth*," *Genre* 15 (1982): 49–79; "Against the Sink-a-Pace: Sexual and Family Politics in *Much Ado About Nothing*," *Shakespeare Quarterly* 33 (1982): 302–13; "Sneak's Noise: Rumor and Detextualization in *2 Henry IV*," *Kenyon Review*, n.s., 6 (Fall 1984): 58–78; "Text against Performance: The Gloucester Family Romance," in *Shakespeare's "Rough Magic": Renaissance Essays in Honor of C. L. Barber*, ed. Peter Erickson and Coppélia Kahn (Newark: University of Delaware Press, 1985), 210–29; "Psychoanalyzing the Shakespearean Text: The First Three Scenes of the *Henriad*," in *Shakespeare and the Question of Theory*, ed. Patricia Parker and Geoffrey Hartman (New York: Methuen, 1985), 210–29.

the text—the collective ideology by which the characters are spoken—is exposed to the readers' scrutiny by the rhetorical-ethical strategies of the writer. In other words, at the same time that Berger's analysis of the text places the autonomous and unified speaking subject into question at the level of character, Berger tacitly recuperates such a subject in the person of the poet who has "created" the text and/or in the person of the critic who interprets it. The latter re-creates the poem in his or her own text, itself a kind of "second world" in which the interpreter enjoys a "freedom to probe for subtexts and collate structural ironies" ("Text against Performance in Shakespeare," 61). By adapting to his present purposes a strict New-Critical distinction between the writer and his characters, Berger's essays strongly imply that such linguistic slippages are not so much a general condition of discourse as manifestations of the author's ironic mastery over the imaginative world of his text—a mastery that the critic expounds and thereby shares. Much of Berger's work—and the essays collected here are no exception—is characterized by a methodological equivocation between his own powerfully appropriative acts of interpretation and the critically conservative representation of those acts as an exposition of authorial intention. Despite the pervasive presence of Berger's distinctive voice and angle of vision in his readings of Spenserian texts, he has until recently remained reluctant to foreground explicitly in his writings his own instrumental role in the production of the meanings that he attributes to "Spenser." If I suggest then that the text in which Berger represents Spenser is also the text in which Spenser represents Berger, I hasten to add that such a dialogue is the necessary condition of substantive critical activity. This volume amply testifies to the imaginative power and fertility of Berger's Spenser, and of Spenser's Berger.

Some readers may think me churlish, or at least impolite, to criticize the author in my introduction to his work. In the case of this author, however, mere encomium would itself be indecorous; it would be an affront to Harry Berger's own sense of his enterprise. An ongoing process of engagement, critique, appropriation, and revision: this is the way in which Berger characterizes Spenser's stance toward his cultural heritage and poetic precursors and also toward the corpus of his own poetry; such a process could just as well be said to characterize Berger's stance toward his critical heritage and also toward the corpus of his own Spenser criticism. By the protean character of his writings, by his self-positioning at the margins of the academic "scene," Berger resists closure, resists cooptation. "I try to be a moving target," he once told me. Any interpreter of Spenser would do well to emulate (not imitate) the model of Harry Berger.

PART ONE

The Faerie Queene

The Spenserian Dynamics

I

SPENSER'S VIEW OF experience is based on an old and familiar topic, the *discordia concors*, though what he does with it is new and unique, and in some important ways quite modern. In the second stanza of *Faerie Queene* IV.ii he alludes to Menenius Agrippa, "that prudent Romane" who reconciled rebellious factions with the fable of the belly and the members. The familiar burden of this fable is that the less fortunate members strive against the more fortunate without realizing the necessity of diversified functions for the health of the whole system. In the blindness of their ignorant (or innocent) self-assertion, they strive to break away from the whole and thus jeopardize themselves as well as the system on which they depend. The implied moral is that the existence of each part depends on the whole for which it exists, while its power derives from the particular function which differentiates it; from this also springs its weakness and dependency, its need of others. In such a system, a certain amount of discord is essential. Where there is no opposition there can be no true concord. When the idea of otherness, of equal and independent and unique character, is not kept firmly in mind, the

The text of Spenser's poetry used in this volume is *The Poetical Works of Edmund Spenser*, vol. 1, *Spenser's Minor Poetry*, ed. Ernest de Sélincourt (Oxford: Clarendon Press, 1910); vols. 2 and 3, *Spenser's "Faerie Queene,"* ed. J. C. Smith (Oxford: Clarendon Press, 1909).

bonds of friendship or cooperation are scarcely possible. In the proper vision of concord, a diversity of many produces an overarching unity of one only so long as diversity and unity are sustained together in equilibrium.

In his study of Books III and IV Thomas Roche rightly identifies this theme as the central impulse of Spenser's thought and shows how his poetry reveals "the emergence of order from chaos and of friendship from enmity" in numerous forms and contexts.[1] Roche assumes that the primary impulse behind Spenser's *discordia concors* is the drive toward union, the resolution of conflict and reconciliation of opposites in Happy Ending. But a glance at a key passage in *Faerie Queene* IV.x will show that this is only one of two dominant forms which the *discordia concors* assumes in Spenser's poetry and that the two forms are set against each other in a dialectical relation.

In the porch of the temple of Venus sits an un-Venerean figure, sober, womanly, and richly dressed:

> On either side of her, two young men stood,
>> Both strongly arm'd, as fearing one another;
>> Yet were they brethren both of halfe the blood,
>> Begotten by two fathers of one mother,
>> Though of contrarie natures each to other;
>> The one of them high *Love*, the other *Hate*,
>> *Hate* was the elder, *Love* the younger brother;
>> Yet was the younger stronger in his state
> Then th'elder, and him maystred still in all debate.
>
> Nathlesse that Dame so well them tempred both,
>> That she them forced hand to joyne in hand,
>> Albe that *Hatred* was thereto full loth,
>> And turn'd his face away, as he did stand,
>> Unwilling to behold that lovely band.
>> Yet she was of such grace and vertuous might,
>> That her commaundment he could not withstand,
>> But bit his lip for felonous despight,
> And gnasht his iron tuskes at that displeasing sight.
>
> *Concord* she cleeped was in common reed,
>> Mother of blessed *Peace*, and *Friendship* trew;
>> They both her twins, both borne of heavenly seed,
>> And she her selfe likewise divinely grew;
>> The which right well her workes divine did shew:

---

[1] *The Kindly Flame* (Princeton: Princeton University Press, 1964), 17.

For strength, and wealth, and happinesse she lends,
And strife, and warre, and anger does subdew:
Of litle much, of foes she maketh frends,
And to afflicted minds sweet rest and quiet sends.

By her the heaven is in his course contained,
And all the world in state unmoved stands,
As their Almightie maker first ordained,
And bound them with inviolable bands;
Else would the waters overflow the lands,
And fire devoure the ayre, and hell them quight,
But that she holds them with her blessed hands.
She is the nourse of pleasure and delight,
And unto *Venus* grace the gate doth open right.

(x.32–35)

Stanza 34 describes concord as an active control which resolves hostility and tension, a control which brings good things of nature and fortune, peace of mind, an end to anger and enmity. Stanza 35 describes concord as the continual tempering of opposites; the ambiguous syntax shifts power from the Almighty's "inviolable bands," which suggests determinism, to Concord's "blessed hands," which suggests a more precarious and ongoing effort of control. The concord of stanza 34 is restricted to the sphere of human activity and relations, while that of stanza 35 is cosmological. The first concord is essentially focused on a *moment*, the moment of reconciliation in which peace and friendship are born. The second concord is not fixed on the happy resolution of trouble but is a sustained process of control which can never stop. The moment of happiness is not enduring on this earth, and the final line of stanza 34, in stressing the psychological value of concord as relief, may remind us that "sweet rest and quiet" can be as dangerous as they are necessary. We shall see that Spenser treats the elemental and cosmic tendencies of stanza 35 as influential aspects of the human organism, aspects of both psyche and society, and this is an important cause of the disruption by which human peace and friendship are perpetually threatened. For this reason Concord as a human personification—orderly and amiable but "of very sober mood"—shares with God the control of the subhuman universe.

Roche's "emergence of order from chaos" is neither the only nor the most important pattern of concord. Spenser sees this urge to resolution as a hazardous lure, for the only moment which resolves all troubles with finality is the moment of death. To fix all one's hopes on a single moment, a single effort, a single blow for eternal freedom, ease, or pleasure, is to deceive oneself. The Concord of IV.x is ultimately an instrument of Venus Genetrix whose aim is to bring opposites together in the recurrent moment of union which replenishes the earth. The model of this subhuman ideal is the marriage of rivers: when two streams flow together, they become indistinguishable. Spenser frequently shows the futility of the desire of two lovers to become one, to merge in absolute and perfect union. The model of merging rivers is not adequate for human relationships, and this is perhaps why the marriage of Thames and Medway in IV.xi takes place in the house of Proteus, a house of oceanic flux and death. The aim and function of Venus Genetrix is but one aspect of human relationship, therefore human lovers, urged by Venus to achieve this aim, must partly resist.

Unlike Venus, who self-sufficiently contains opposites within herself—"She syre and mother is her selfe alone, / Begets and eke conceives, ne needeth other none" (IV.x.41)—Concord both joins and separates opposites existing apart from herself. The tableau described in stanzas 32 and 33 is curious because Concord mediates Love and Hate in such a way as to keep Hate from being defeated: since Love is stronger, it is the intervention of Concord which saves Hate from total defeat, and his antipathy to Concord is therefore self-destructive. The concord proper to human beings turns not on the hope for complete union but on the awareness that such a hope is deceptive: since two lovers are neither able to melt into one nor likely to live happily ever after if they expect to melt into one, they must acknowledge their differentness or separateness and accept their differences. Guarding against the world, against themselves, against each other, they must become reconciled to the importance of maintaining barriers and accept that the happy ending lasts only a moment and must be continually reaffirmed. This concord is not founded on the desire of absolute union but on the discipline of tempered *com*munion. The harmony of Heraclitus comprises the tension of the bow as well as that of the lyre: though Spenser sees this clearly, Roche and many other commentators are like Plato's Eryximachus in wanting to dispense with the bow.

Spenser presents the theme of concord briefly and explicitly in a number of loci, though his treatment varies according to context. In V.ii.34–35 and 39–41, for example, Artegal makes a statement vaguely similar to Concord's, but he attributes the conservation of order to a stern Artegal-like Maker who not only created all things "in goodly measure" but also

> *maketh* Kings to sit in soverainty;
> He *maketh* subjects to their powre obay;

> He pulleth downe, he setteth up on hy;
> He gives to this, from that he takes away.
> For all we have is his: what he list doe, he may.
>
> *(italics mine)*

In this context *maketh* connotes force as well as creation and, along with the echo of *make* in *may*, indicates an absolute, even repressive, male power—the kind of god necessary in a world of primitive force and justice, a world without love, such as Artegal seems to encounter. Concord, by contrast, is a maternal figure who tempers extremes on the Isle of Venus. A third version of the *discordia concors* theme, occurring in *An Hymne in Honour of Love* and *Colin Clouts Come Home Againe*, will be discussed in the following section after the theme has been set in a more inclusive framework.

II

Ideally, a view of the *discordia concors* motif in Spenser's poetry should include a synoptic description of the Spenserian "world picture." The trouble with this is that there is no Spenserian "world picture"—at least not in the sense that there is a Dantesque "world picture." Nor (as Robert Ellrodt has shown) can we easily and uncritically impose on his work the various forms of Neoplatonic cosmology. Spenser is not interested in cosmology per se, and nowhere except in the heavenly hymns does he present cosmological details like those we find in Dante. We need only compare the treatment of landscape in *Faerie Queene* I, often called "medieval," with the treatment of landscape in the *Divine Comedy* to see the great difference. Spenser's world and its places are not actualized in advance like an obstacle course waiting to steer its assayers toward their preordained goal. They emerge out of the problems and actions of his characters. Spenserian landscape for the most part evolves from the projection of inscape. And where Dante's obstacle course is literally vertical, Spenser's, as it materializes, is for the most part "horizontal": where Dante's cosmos is hierarchically organized in terms of *up* and *down*, the dominant Spenserian vectors are *in* and *out*, and these vectors control both the psychic, or allegorical, and the topographic (plains, forests, houses) elements of experience.

Since his "world picture" exists primarily as a function of the changing psychic development of the major characters, it would be more appropriate to substitute the temporal concept of *dynamics* for the more static and spatial concept of *world picture*. There is certainly a distinct and characterizable Spenserian dynamics which is, in its most general form, ancient and familiar. Many of the notions touched on above may be found in a primitive and widely diffused cosmogony, described in the following passages by F. M. Cornford:

> The world began as an undifferentiated mass, without internal boundaries or limits—an *apeiron*. This mass separated into two parts, which were opposed or 'contrary'—male and female. Finally, the male and female were united by Eros, the contraries were combined, and gave birth to individual existence—to Gods, or to things. . . .
>
> The coming into existence of individual things is variously attributed by the early cosmologists to love or harmony, and to feud, strife, or war. The two representations are, as Heracleitus insisted, not so irreconcilable as they seem to be at first sight. They are only two ways of conceiving the meeting of contraries. The two contraries are antagonistic, at perpetual war with each other. It is a war of mutual aggression—each seeking to invade the province of the other. But this very invasion involves a mixing of the two elements—a reconciliation, or marriage, in which both combine to produce a compound, the individual thing. Earth and Heaven are essentially the female and male principles in Greek cosmology. In the 'gap' between their sundered forms appears the winged figure of the cosmic Eros, whose function is to reunite them. In the more primitive cosmogonies, which make the world begin with the hatching of an egg, whose two halves form Sky and Earth, Eros is the bird with golden feathers who comes out of the egg.[2]

In such later and more sophisticated thinkers as Aeschylus and Plato, the primordial disorder—whether it is thought of as chaos, *apeiron, ananke, moira, ate,* or something else—is treated not merely as a beginning but as a permanent element in the constitution of the world:

> The philosophic poet and the poet philosopher are both consciously concerned with the enthronement of wisdom and justice in human society. For each there lies, beyond and beneath this problem, the antithesis of cosmos and chaos, alike in the constitution of the world and within the confines of the individual soul. On all these planes they see a conflict of powers, whose unreconciled opposition entails disaster. Apollo and the Furies between them can only tear the soul of Orestes in pieces. The city of uncompromised ideals, the prehistoric Athens of Critias' legend, in the death-grapple with the lawless violence of Atlantis, goes down in a general destruction of mankind. . . . the way to peace, for Plato as for Aeschylus, lies through reconcilement of the rational and the irrational, of Zeus and Fate, of Reason and Necessity, not by force but by persuasion.[3]

[2] *From Religion to Philosophy* (New York: Harper Brothers, 1957), 68, 70.
[3] Cornford, *Plato's Cosmology* (New York: Humanities Press, 1952), 363–64.

Chaos originally referred to the yawning gap or abyss created by the separation, but in later usage (exemplified by Cornford in the above passage) it was applied more generally to any primitive state of disorder, less order, or preorder.

Cornford and many others have elaborated the hypothesis that this primitive view of the world was developed by projection and extension of a social model, the norms of tribal organization providing a language for explaining etiologically the structure of the world. When Plato and Aristotle affirmed that the world had no beginning, cosmogonic explanation was recognized as ancient superstition. Plato felt that such myths could legitimately be revived only in the heuristic manner employed in the likely story of the *Timaeus*. Plato's tentative way of advancing cosmological hypotheses and positing ontological hierarchies was abandoned by the time of the late antique philosophers. In Plotinus and Proclus the "Platonic" world view had hardened unambiguously into *the* hierarchic structure of the universe, and this structure was in the main an unguarded projection of logical categories such as those exemplified by the famous tree of Porphyry. A hierarchic order of the Plotinian sort is most conventionally symbolized by spatio-visual relations which stress its underlying stability and timelessness, and it was Plotinus who stated as a principle that cosmogonies and other narrative myths translate timeless relations into temporal representations, for example, conveying logical priority by temporal sequence (*Enneads* III.v.10). Thus if there is any truth to the anthropological hypotheses, the progressive rationalization of the world from primitive to Christian times involves a gradual and continual projection from self to other, from society to cosmos, from the local and familiar to the remote and unfamiliar, from inner experience which (as Kant pointed out) is felt primarily in terms of time, to the experience of the environment which we see around us in space.

When we turn to Spenser we shall find the lines of force moving in the other direction. Cosmology is not, as I suggested before, his main interest. Temporal and cosmogonic explanation is detached from the world and applied to human behavior and experience. Its main reference is social, ethical, psychological, and phenomenological. Spenser might have detected this tendency in the Neoplatonism which derives from Ficino, but he carries it much further. For example, lines 57 – 118 of *An Hymne in Honour of Love* can be read not only as a watery restatement of the old cosmogony but also as a myth about the development of consciousness. The mind first confronts experience under the aspect of chaos, or primal ocean, an undifferentiated flux, and it does not even do this until aroused from an inertial womblike innocence:

> ere this worlds still moving mightie masse,
> Out of great *Chaos* ugly prison crept,
> In which his goodly face long hidden was
> From heavens view, and in deepe darknesse kept,
> Love, that had now long time securely slept
> In *Venus* lap, unarmed then and naked,
> Gan reare his head, by *Clotho* being waked.
>
> And taking to him wings of his owne heate,
> Kindled at first from heavens life-giving fyre,
> He gan to move out of his idle seate,
> Weakely at first, but after with desyre
> Lifted aloft, he gan to mount up hyre,
> And like fresh Eagle, make his hardie flight
> Through all that great wide wast, yet wanting light.

The goddess who presides over this waking of desire is not Beauty, as in the *Symposium*, but simply Clotho, the youngest Parca, connected with the moment of birth; this suggests the necessary and more or less negative quality of this birth. Only after the mind is faced toward the "wild wildernesse" does Cupid's mother "lend him light" so that he may find his way through "the world that was not till he did it make." Then follow the phases of differentiation: First desire or eros separates the "sundrie parts . . . / The which before had lyen confused ever" in Chaos. This leads to the alignment and conflict of contraries:

> The earth, the ayre, the water, and the fyre,
> Then gan to raunge them selves in huge array,
> And with contrary forces to conspyre
> Each against other, by all meane they may,
> Threatning their owne confusion and decay:
> Ayre hated earth, and water hated fyre,
> Till Love relented their rebellious yre.

Elemental phenomena and tendencies are not to be dissolved or resolved into a homogeneous unity; their differences are essential to organic articulation; their blindly destructive and suicidal efforts to preserve their integrity are to be constrained and rechanneled. Cupid compels them to serve broader and higher interests, binding them in life-preserving systems of whose complexity and organization the elements themselves are unaware:

> He then them tooke, and tempering goodly well
> Their contrary dislikes with loved meanes,

> Did place them all in order, and compell
> To keep them selves within their sundrie raines,
> Together linkt with Adamantine chaines;
> Yet so, as that in every living wight
> They mixe themselves, and shew their kindly might.
>
> So ever since they firmely have remained,
> And duly well observed his beheast;
> Through which now all these things that are contained
> Within this goodly cope, both most and least
> Their being have, and dayly are increast,
> Through secret sparks of his infused fyre.

The *HL* thus suggests an evolutionary process from elements through composite organisms to animals and men, a process which is more clearly defined in *Colin Clouts Come Home Againe* (839–70): Eros reconciles the elemental enemies until they begin to feel a little love for each other, and "So being knit, they brought forth other kynds / Out of the fruitfull wombe of their great mother." The "other kynds" are various, complex, and new: heaven, day, earth, living creatures—animals, birds, fish, man. Unlike the essentially conservative force of the lower Venus, whose aim is to generate more of the same by pairing and re-pairing, masculine eros embodies a restless dialectical thrusting toward more highly organized forms.

As these remarks suggest, Spenser's conception of concord and his use of the traditional dynamics are themselves dynamic: the movement from lower to higher is often coordinated with two other vectors, those from earlier to later and from simpler to more complex. In spite of Spenser's frequent interest in depicting interruptions, failures, countermovements, and counterstatements (such as the myth of decline from golden antiquity), this evolutionary model remains fundamental in his thought, at least as a theoretical ideal which eros at all levels of existence tries to actualize. Evidence from various parts of his work may be assembled to focus Spenser's basic attitude, namely, (1) at any moment in the history of a culture, nation, or individual, a cross-section of the temporal continuum would reveal a *concors* more or less appropriate to that phase of development; (2) the optimal character of concord may increase as time goes on; (3) this does not mean that problems will be solved for all time at some millennial point in culture or personal history but rather that as they change—and even change for the worse—the tests of experience will have improved the general quality, increased the potentiality, of the personal, national, and cultural organism. This implies of course that no

moment of union or reconciliation, of relief or triumph, is to be construed as absolute—absolute either in the sense of being final or in the
sense of being totally one-sided. Every triumph or resolution at a lower
level of existence or an earlier phase of experience releases new and different problems at a higher level or a later phase.

III

As Spenser presents it, development might be seen in Hegelian terms as
a movement from consciousness to self-consciousness, or in Platonic
terms as a movement from the cavebound autistic state of *eikasia* up the
divided line toward the greater enlightenment—ethical as well as intellectual—of *dianoia* and *nous*. But the systematic application of this dynamic model is not limited to the life span of the psyche. It may be applied to particular forms of experience, like poetry and love, and also, as
suggested above, to the larger development of cultural and literary history. In other words, the early-to-late pattern is a theoretical model—
something like a general set of equations—specific versions of which
may be found in all the areas of experience which Spenser's poetry
depicts.

A central aspect of this model is quickly grasped by inverting Haeckel's
famous and now discredited first law of biogenetics, "Ontogeny recapitulates phylogeny." The inversion would read, "The development of
the race recapitulates the development of the individual." This is simply
the historical and dynamic analogue of the notion, first elaborated by
Plato in the middle and later dialogues, that the structure of the world is
isomorphic with the structure of the soul—a notion found in various
forms in the work of Aristotle, Virgil, and Augustine and in the general
assumptions of classical and Christian cosmology. To view the development of a culture—for example, from Homer to Plato, from pagan to
Christian, or from pagan through medieval to Renaissance—in terms
derived from the study of the development of the psyche is an obvious
way of organizing the whole of existence on a rational model scaled to
human concerns.

In the passages from *HL* and *CC* quoted above, eros seems to represent a process inherent less in the parts than in the whole, a process
which guides the *concors* creatively through a number of phases tending
ideally toward a "higher," or more complex, form of organization. In its
ancient cosmological context the notion of eros as *desire* is a metaphor
transferred from the area of human consciousness and used to suggest
the imperfection or lack of fulfillment which keeps things in motion,

straining toward the future. Eros is thus ambivalent, though its ambivalence is sequential: since the elements must repel each other in order to emerge from Chaos, "hate"—the elder brother in the porch of Concord—is the first phase; since the elements must be "reconciled" and combined in diverse mixtures to sustain their elemental functions, "love" is the second:

> For how should else things so far from attone
> And so great enemies as of them bee,
> Be ever drawne together into one,
> And taught in such accordance to agree?
> Through him the cold began to covet heat,
> And water fire; the light to mount on hie,
> And th'heavie downe to peize; the hungry t'eat
> And voydnesse to seeke full satietie.
> So being former foes, they wexed friends,
> And gan by litle learne to love each other:
> So being knit, they brought forth other kynds
> Out of the fruitfull wombe of their great mother.
>
> *(CC* 843–53)

Psychologically, eros is always felt at first as an affliction, a pain-giving force which disturbs equilibrium and fills the soul with violent longing or frustration. It is this eros which assaults the world and Britomart in the early cantos of Book III and which distracts Colin Clout in the *Shepheardes Calender*. If it is hateful and plaintive, it is also a necessary experience, for it drives the soul of lover or poet out of its childhood— out of its self-enclosed, self-delighting idyll of innocence, a garden state in which, like Clarion in *Muiopotmos*, it would otherwise degenerate. The soul may resist natural process; it may fear to risk its autonomy or to commit itself to the uncertainty and pain which threaten it. This phase of resistance is embodied in an extreme form in the regressive "chastity" of Marinell, whose oceanic power remains destructive of self and of others so long as his mother keeps him prisoner. But Marinell's hate turns violently into its opposite in IV.xii, and this is characteristic of eros in primitive and in degenerate phases during which it is not directed or harnessed by rational consciousness: whether in the world or the soul, what Leonardo da Vinci calls the "spirit of the elements"—the force emergent from chaos—leads first to blind self-assertion, then to extreme instability and loss of control. To be obsessively reduced to a single passion, humor, or element and to be driven restlessly from one to another in continual flux are the contrary modes of behavior in this phase.

Spenser exemplifies these modes in describing Ate's four victims in
Faerie Queene IV.ix.21:

> *Druons* delight was all in single life,
> And unto Ladies love would lend no leasure:
> The more was *Claribell* enraged rife
> With fervent flames, and loved out of measure:
> So eke lov'd *Blandamour*, but yet at pleasure
> Would change his liking, and new Lemans prove:
> But *Paridell* of love did make no threasure,
> But lusted after all, that did him move.
> So diversly these foure disposed were to love.

Druon figures the too stern abstention of Marinell and Artegal before
they were afflicted by Cupid; Spenser seems to have modeled this excessive withholding of self, this innocent and foolhardy self-reliance, on
Chaucer's Troilus. The syntax implies that Druon's delight is the cause
of Claribell's contrary rage ("The more was Claribell . . ."). Each of
the four is reduced to the simple erotic disposition he exemplifies, and
Spenser presents this elemental state not merely as an allegorical function
but also as degenerate and obsessive behavior in the examples, who are
products of psychic breakdown. Their warfare is compared to the strife
of elements two stanzas later:

> As when *Dan Æolus* in great displeasure,
> For losse of his deare love by *Neptune* hent,
> Sends forth the winds out of his hidden threasure,
> Upon the sea to wreake his fell intent;
> They breaking forth with rude unruliment,
> From all foure parts of heaven doe rage full sore,
> And tosse the deepes, and teare the firmament,
> And all the world confound with wide uprore,
> As if in stead thereof they *Chaos* would restore.

Druon means "oak," and oak leaves are frequently symbolic of early
pagan culture. Spenser associates oak with two related aspects of primitive
violence in Book IV, that of Artegal in his early savage state (IV.iv.39) and
that of the figure Lust (IV.vii.7), who represents a nightmare distortion
of Artegal—a feminine nightmare of what might happen to the chastely
loving woman who both wants and fears to submit. Another kind of
primitivism and violence is embodied in Book I in the figure of Orgoglio,
who supports himself "Upon a snaggy Oke, which he had torne / Out
of his mothers bowelles" (I.vii.10). A *Geant* born of "Earth his uncouth

mother" and "blustring Aeolus his boasted sire," Orgoglio represents the carnal pride which prevails when elemental forces in the psyche break free from the will's control: a "monstrous masse of earthly slime, / Puft up with emptie wind, and fild with sinfull crime" (I.vii.9). His birth has been associated with an earthquake (S. K. Heninger), and this suggests again the cataclysmic upheaval of chaos forces "breaking forth with rude unruliment" in nature and in soul. Blind and stupid, unaware of the true implications of his genealogy, connected in his ignorance to the forces of Night and more particularly to Aveugle's three sons, the Sans- brothers ("his stature did exceed / The height of three the tallest sonnes of mortall seed"), Orgoglio is destructive of those higher motives on which his existence depends:

> So growen great through arrogant delight
> Of th'high descent, whereof he was yborne,
> And through presumption of his matchlesse might,
> All other powres and knighthood he did scorn.
>
> *(I.vii.10)*

His porter and foster father is Ignaro, "an old old man" whose "eye sight him failed long ygo" and whose wrinkled face was turned backward (I.viii.30–31). This particular form of carnal pride is nurtured by just that form of ignorance and innocence which undid Redcross during the first six cantos, and Orgoglio's victims are not the evil rulers found in Lucifera's dungeon but rather "guiltlesse babes, and innocents trew," "true Christians . . . / And holy Martyrs often doen to dye, / With cruell malice and strong tyranny" (I.viii.35–36). Theirs is an innocence which cannot cope with carnal pride or a zeal which has been overcome by Orgoglio in the world, perhaps because martyrs were misguided by the tyrannic Orgoglio lurking unknown in their own souls. The appearance of Orgoglio signifies not only the moment of Redcross's imminent psychic breakdown but also his paralyzing consciousness of this moment (I.vii.11).

One of the characteristics to which Spenser frequently points in his depictions of primitive and regressive behavior is the ambivalence suggested in the tableau of Concord. In the confusion of Book III, where distinctions and relations are only beginning to emerge from an amorphous or polymorphous chaos, characters find it hard to differentiate martial from erotic wounds and motives, just as it often does not seem to matter whether the object of one's hostility or desire is of the same or the opposite sex. Once the elemental, sexual, and psychic contraries have emerged from chaos, have been stabilized in simple primary form, and have confronted each other, the problems of concord arise. One form taken by these problems in Books IV and V is that of the conflict between exclusively erotic and anti-erotic attitudes. The latter are exemplified by the conventional and repressive "morality" of the Stoic censors criticized in the second stanza of the proem to Book IV:

> Such ones ill judge of love, that cannot love,
>   Ne in their frosen hearts feele kindly flame:
> For thy they ought not thing unknowne reprove,
>   Ne naturall affection faultlesse blame,
>   For fault of few that have abused the same.

Stoic censors are defective either because of age or because of niggardly dispositions. They might well be thought of as druidic, bound by ancient convention or superstition, but insofar as *druid* is related to primitive oak-culture (old because ancient, and therefore young) the reference might be extended to a second kind of "moral" anti-eroticism, that of Druon, Marinell, and Artegal before he saw Britomart ("rebellious unto love" and formerly "wont to despise" all women). Such early impulses of the psyche to remain pure and simple must be superseded. The rationale which Spenser applies to lecherous knights also touches stern knights and Stoic censors: all of them hold themselves back from true love, from the natural demands and limits of life; all rely too much on themselves, feel too little sympathy for others, rigorously lock themselves up within themselves, and, like closed elemental systems, resist the processes of concord and nature.

This resistance to change and chance, this primitive fury to keep pure, simple, and eternally the same, becomes one of the dominant themes of Book V. In the proem Spenser adopts the perspective of a utopian moralist who, appalled by the disorder of the actual world around him, retreats into the rationalizations of the Golden Age, namely, that the beginning of time was the best of times and that history is one long fated decline or degendering until all things "arrive at their last ruinous decay." He then objectifies this view in the pristine justice of Astraea, Artegal, and Talus with its a priori rules, its savage force and lack of sympathy, its schematic rigor. Talus, who is "made of yron mould, / Immoveable, resistlesse, without end" (V.i.12), embodies in its pure form the Astraean element imposed on Artegal's consciousness when she brought the hero

> Into a cave from companie exilde,
>   In which she noursled him, till yeares he raught,
> And all the discipline of justice there him taught.
>
> There she him taught to weigh both right and wrong
>   In equall ballance with due recompence,
>   And equitie to measure out along,
>   According to the line of conscience,
>   When so it needs with rigour to dispence.
>   Of all the which, for want there of mankind,
>   She caused him to make experience
>   Upon wyld beasts, which she in woods did find,
> With wrongfull powre oppressing others of their kind.
>
> *(V.i.6–7)*

Talus is both ludicrous and sinister, a grotesque image of the Stoic censor's wish fulfillment, expressive indirectly of his fear of weakness and contamination. His law has some points of similarity with the *lex talionis*. As a parody of the desire for total, easy, and immediate control, Talus represents a violent reaction to the panic syndrome which Spenser with some detachment presents as a threat to himself when he adopts the utopian perspective.

The sudden reversal of an elemental state to its opposite takes place in Artegal during the Radegund episode when his martial fury is momentarily overwhelmed by "ruth of beautie" and he succumbs to those very forces (the law of ocean, fortune, and passion) which Astraea had commissioned him to suppress. As in his encounter with Britomart, Artegal's duel with Radegund resonates with erotic suggestions. Jolted out of his pre- or anti-sexual innocence he is forced to recognize previously hidden aspects of his psyche, to discover that erotic and feminine traits are included within his male nature. A similar discovery is forced on Redcross in the opening cantos of Book I when, awakening to lust under the aegis of Archimago, his chivalric view of Una as Princess and Damsel-to-be-saved is replaced by an equally one-sided view of Una as whore. And in the early phases of the *Amoretti*, as in the first of the four hymns, the poet-lover's attitude is shown to oscillate between two extreme and simplistic responses: the urge to lust, projected in the Petrarchan tyranness, and the urge to worship or idealize, represented by the Neoplatonic Idea, angel or saint.

The dynamics of the *discordia concors* appears in more pervasive and structural patterns which may only be touched on here: We find it in the root concepts of the first two books of *The Faerie Queene*, holiness (wholeness) and temperance (understood as *krasis*, or blending). The "elements" in these books are psychic and spiritual as well as cosmological and physical; various forms of division, fragmentation, and regression are explored in the experiences of Redcross and Guyon, most of which center on the discord between the order of the macrocosm and the order perceived by the microcosm (psyche), and on the interior discords which cause or result from this disrelation. A different embodiment of the theme appears in the love poems and in the presentation of character in Books III, IV, and V. The harmony of love is composed of diverse relations: love of self, of God, of friends, of family, of pleasure, of generation. The most complex form of love is that which is fulfilled and symbolized by marriage—not simply love of friends, not simply attraction between male and female, not an affair of souls without bodies or of bodies without souls, but the richer and more difficult love between masculine and feminine *persons*. In this *discordia concors* the opposition of contrary sexes is mingled with a crucial similarity, namely, that both lovers are separate, equal, and unique selves.

Spenser further articulates the parts of this concord by his usual method of analyzing and dramatizing the structure of the individual soul, a method based on the distinction between British and Elfin or Faerie characters. The Britons—Arthur, Redcross, Britomart, and Artegal—are relatively complicated, ambiguous, continually changing and developing figures whose destinies lie beyond Faerie in the historical world. Elfins and Faeries, by contrast, are restricted to Spenser's fairyland. They are *ideal* not only because they are exemplary but also because they may personify aspects of human nature. In the middle books of *The Faerie Queene* Belphoebe, Florimell, and Amoret come by a process of allegorical assimilation to represent conflicting aspects of the feminine psyche in general and of Britomart's psyche in particular; the same holds for the relation of Timias, Marinell, and Scudamour to Artegal. Belphoebe, Florimell, and Amoret are elements of the psyche in the same way that fire, earth, air, and water are elements of the physical cosmos. Each has her own environment and is almost entirely secluded from the other members of her team; she does not in fact know she is on a team. Each asserts the elemental claims of the function she embodies; all continually if unconsciously help or hinder each other. They personify determined or deterministic functions of feminine life. Because they are ideal they do not undergo interior development but appear fixed and childlike and are always described as perfect. Their trouble is that they are perfect in too limited a manner, or limited because too perfect.

When they follow their own natures they throw themselves and others into confusion. Their diverse impulses must be felt, faced, coordinated, and guided by a freer, more aware, and more inclusive consciousness, that of real woman in general and of Britomart in particular.

Spenser carries this development of self-consciousness and control through a series of phases, articulated by the major divisions of Books III, IV, and V. To move from Chastity to Friendship and Justice is to move from problems of concord within the self to problems of concord with others. Ideally, the development is founded on chastity, in which one keeps oneself from reducing other selves to mere objects of appetite or, conversely, in which one restrains the tendency utterly to escape from or to surrender to others in order to relieve the painful tensions caused by fear or desire. Chastity should lead to and be fulfilled by that equilibrium of separate selves Aristotle called friendship, which in turn cannot be properly maintained without the help of justice. Justice tempers one's attitude toward others so that their otherness—their differentness, independence, or even natural hostility—may be properly acknowledged and accepted. It is finally on this basis that the subtler and more personal problems classified under "courtesy" are given play in Book IV, for these are modern and sophisticated problems. The atmospheric change from V to VI is clearly from a mythic panorama of European regression (as suggested in the name *Geryoneo*, the New Archaism) to a muted vision of socio-personal failures of trust, intimacy, respect, and communication. The antique and heroic failures of modern political society in Book V fuse in odd, indirect, and powerful ways with the contemporary and "pastoral" failures of moral fiber in Book VI.

Archaism, Immortality, and the Muse in Spenser's Poetry

SPENSER'S HISTORICAL CONSCIOUSNESS affects basic notions about poetry and experience found in his work. "Historical consciousness" is by now a commonplace of Renaissance scholarship, a defining characteristic attributed to the "period" and its thinkers by way of distinguishing them from their predecessors. The tendencies which Spenser's historical consciousness displays share many of the features ascribed to his contemporaries, but its overall form is perhaps more familiar to scholars of the nineteenth century. The form is epitomized in the following statement by A. N. Whitehead in *Process and Reality:*

> In principle, the animal body is only the more highly organized and immediate part of the general environment. . . . But the transition from without to within the body marks the passage from lower to higher grades of [actuality]. . . . The higher the grade, the more vigorous and the more original is the enhancement from the supplementary phase. Pure receptivity and transmission gives place to the trigger-action of life whereby there is release of energy in novel forms. . . . [What is transmitted is] enhanced in relevance or even changed in character by the passage from the low-grade external world into the intimacy of the human body.[1]

[1] *Process and Reality: An Essay in Cosmology* (New York: Social Science Bookstore, 1929), 182–83.

The objective character of Spenser's historical vision is evolutionary; its subjective mode is retrospective. I shall discuss each of these poles in turn, but I would like to remark here that Spenser presents his poetry as itself a "supplementary phase" of the processes of experience and development which the poetry depicts. The processes comprise a continual "transition" not only "from without to within the body"—from cosmos to psyche—but also from past to present; *The Faerie Queene*, for example, is the latest, the most highly organized, and the most novel form of energy released in the evolutionary process.

By evolutionary, I mean that his poetry exhibits an overall developmental pattern in which three vectors coalesce: from lower to higher, from simpler to more complex, and of course from earlier to later. These vectors run parallel courses in the history of the individual psyche and in that of culture or civilization. The normal and normative growth of human consciousness and conscience is from a relatively narrow, simplistic, or elementally "pure" perspective to a broader, more complex, and comprehensive perspective. In early or in regressive stages, for example, distinguishable areas tend to blur or overlap, as when the mind fails to perceive or respect the boundaries between itself and the world, man and God, self and other, love and hate, heaven and earth, the divine and the chaotic or natural sources of energy. The other side of the reciprocity of psyche and culture is the effect of the microcosm on any phase of the larger order: here Spenser agrees with Plato, Virgil, and others in depicting the institutions and products of "early" culture as dominated by, expressive of, those tendencies of the psyche which are usually described as childlike, autistic, superstitious, sensuous.

The subjective mode of Spenser's historical vision is retrospective: he looks back into the past from his own *here and now*. In his early, or archaic, world action is caused for the most part by the large-scale play of forces which, though psychic as well as cosmic, operate outside any individual will or consciousness. Book III of *The Faerie Queene* is especially ordered to suggest how entirely independent actions and episodes occurring in widely separated places and moments of the Spenserian world can produce a meaningful coalescence whose import could not possibly be grasped by any of the figures involved, except perhaps by gods and prophets (and even their perspectives are limited in ways to be discussed later). The driving purpose of this organic system of forces is beyond its conscious members because both system and purpose are retrospectively fashioned by the poet and only tentatively, temporarily, fulfilled in his own time. The possibility of prophecy is founded on deterministic presuppositions, and a leading characteristic of Spenser's "primitive" age is the manifest domination of behavior by extra-human forces whose influence tends to conserve or restore an archaic state of affairs. As psyche and culture develop, this collective and determined mode of behavior gradually yields to the more active and original assertions of individual souls. When the center of will, decision, and activity is located in the individual consciousness, archaic determinism gives way to restrospective determinism as the dominant organizing mode.

The full vision of the pattern I have been describing is seldom attained by characters within the Spenserian world, while its complex and articulated unity is a condition attained by soul, state, or culture only in relatively advanced phases of its career. And only in such phases does the imagination double back to activate the tacit or latent elements—the primitive and palingenetic factors—of experience to set the present moment within its developmental context. As I suggested before, Spenser presents the latest form of experience both *in* his work and *as* his work. The historical sense which is the defining mark of that work asserts itself in his effort to locate the various elements of his poetic *discordia concors* at their proper temporal distances from the present. His poetry thus represents in its complex form all the phases which preceded it and which it, in effect, supersedes. This representation is achieved by conspicuously alluding to the traditional or conventional or antique character of the forms of culture and experience which appear in the poetry. Spenser places traditional material in historical perspective by quotation and revision: he depicts it as something old, separates those elements which are still valid from those which are inadequate or outmoded, and transforms it into something new.

The process of transformation derives from—in fact, is necessitated by—the peculiar features of memory, whose limits contribute as much to the process as its power. Spenser's most complete analysis of these features in their psychological dimension occurs in the allegory of the three internal senses residing in the turret of Alma's castle of temperance (II.ix.44–58). The three faculties are personified as sages: the young Phantastes is portrayed less as the traditional image-storing capacity than as the purveyor of foresight (he "could things to come foresee") and "idle fantasies"; the second sage, "a man of ripe and perfect age" who "could of things present best advize" probably represents the particular reason or cogitative faculty; the third sage is memory, decrepit and old and in "th'hindmost roome of three," yet most important to the heroes of Book II as well as to Spenser. These faculties belong to the lower reaches of cognitive or conscious functioning; theirs are the more automatic operations of preconscious (or, in the old psychology, sensitive) rationality rather than the more voluntary operations of intellective rationality. They are psychophysical functions specifically connected to a part of the body (the brain) and therefore different from Alma, who, consigned to no special part of her castle, seems to represent the rational or intellective component. She is not the rational soul in general but rather the soul exercising the habit and act of temperance, which involves governing the "lower" parts and powers of the self: her three sages "counselled faire Alma, how to governe well" (ix.48). Robert Kellogg and Oliver Steele observe that "like all the heroines of Book II she is a virgin to show her freedom from earthly passion," and they conclude from her virginity that "she, like all human souls, is betrothed to Christ."[2] A better reason is that she, like most good virgins in Spenser, is in a relatively early, and therefore incomplete, condition: she is threatened by and needs help from the outside world; the soul attentive primarily to its own order and to the egocentric virtues is not yet ready to open itself to chastity in the context of love, or to concord and justice; the feelings which presently occupy her heart are centered on shamefastness and praise-desire (concern for one's own image).

The three sages are fundamentally passive to the data they receive. Phantastes' "foresight" is a kind of irritability, a restlessness impelling him to premature judgment:

> nought mote hinder his quicke prejudize:
> He had a sharpe foresight, and working wit,
> That never idle was, ne once could rest a whit.
>
> *(ix.49)*

His fantasies are a chaos of superstitions and delusions characteristic of ancient mythopoeia, *eikasia*, and the collective inheritance of the vulgar: "Infernall Hags, *Centaurs*, feendes, *Hippodames*, / Apes, Lions, Ægles, Owles, fooles, lovers, children, Dames" (ix.50); "idle thoughts and fantasies, / Devices, dreames, opinions unsound" (ix.51). Finally, and significantly, the youngest and least reliable of the interior senses is connected to foresight, "visions, sooth-sayes, and prophesies," all of which entail the archaic determinism of the primitive mind, its uncritical habit of projection, and its rash but futile effort to control the future.

The murals on which the second sage meditates are structured and solid achievements and therefore contrary in character to those of Phantastes:

---

[2] Kellogg and Steele, eds., *Books I and II of "The Faerie Queene," "The Mutability Cantos," and Selections from the Minor Poetry* (New York: Odyssey Press, 1965), 335.

Of famous Wisards, and with picturals
Of Magistrates, of courts, of tribunals,
Of commen wealthes, of states, of pollicy,
Of lawes, of judgements, and of decretals;
All artes, all science, all Philosophy,
And all that in the world was aye thought wittily.

(ix.53)

The central items are the political analogues of temperance, but all are creations of the human mind which constitute the perceived cultural environment. These are the viable traditions, the institutions which have stood the test of time and are currently in use. As the first and final items suggest, the data available to this sage represent the accumulated wisdom of the elders through which nature has gradually been transformed into civilization. But the fact of historical development is not available to the faculty which advises "of things present." The sage can see the answers but not the questions, the resolutions but not the problems. He need not clarify, select, organize, or revise: he responds to lucid images ("painted faire") of works which have successfully attained "ripe and perfect age." And this is all he does, which accounts both for his attractiveness to the visiting knights and for the brevity of their stay:

There sate a man of ripe and perfect age,
Who did them meditate all his life long,
That through continuall practise and usage,
He now was growne right wise, and wondrous sage.
Great pleasure had those stranger knights, to see
His goodly reason, and grave personage,
That his disciples both desir'd to bee;
But *Alma* thence them led to th'hindmost roome of three.

(ix.54)

—the "ruinous" chamber of memory. For the middle sage is in his own way antihistorical: his "continuall . . . usage" and advice about the present are restrictively determined by the limited range of his evidence; his murals exclude the failures registered by fantasy and memory. Locked in his eternally efficient present (a happy conservative), he can have little awareness of the dangers which have threatened Alma for seven years (ix. 12)—Maleger and his rout of throwbacks, freaks, and "villeins," personifying the sins, vices, and temptations to which the body and its psychophysical functions make the soul susceptible. Though Maleger is something like the "law of the members," he attacks the castle-body from outside, not only because he has so far failed to break in but also because he represents a generic set of evils which are part and parcel of the ethical and social environment created by the soul. If and when Maleger breaches the castle defenses his evils would seem to be most directly channeled to Phantastes' room (cf. xi.8–13, where many of Phantastes' "idle thoughts and fantasies" appear among Maleger's troops).

In the first two chambers the automatic process of programming or sorting-out is too extreme, while the pictorial immediacy with which the sorted data are registered on the walls enforces their acceptance and realization by the faculties in question. A controlling consciousness primarily influenced by the second sage might be tempted to conceive the actual world as exhibiting perfect order, while the evidence from "phantasia" would suggest that the actual world is purely chaotic. These chambers are simple contraries in selectively isolating the products of folly and wisdom. Neither in itself provides sufficient information for the critical acts of judging and comparing. Neither singly nor together could they lead an introspecting reason to infer the historical character of psyche and temperance—temperance as the tempered tempering or blending (*krasis*) of *given* elements through trial and error, fruitful struggle, choice, and revision. Such inference demands a more complete and impartial inventory, and this is provided by Memory, which is contrary to both the first two functions in being unselective. Memory, furthermore, stimulates the mind to engage in critical activity *because* it is inferior to the other functions in selection and vividness.

Memory's power lies in its weakness. Its character as reservoir or matrix triggers the re-forming tendencies of mind because it is so manifestly incomplete. This is what makes it parent to the Muse. Its power also lies in its preservation of records *of* and *from* the antique age, the matrix-time of man. In drawing the mind at once "backward" and "downward" it may appeal to the escape wish of weaker souls or to the more innocent limitations of such figures as Guyon, who finds there a golden chronicle of pure Elfin triumphs which matches his own restricted experience and nature. But this is the risk attending the process by which retrospective determinism operates: in Whitehead's words, "If there is to be progress beyond limited ideals, the course of history . . . must venture along the borders of chaos," a statement which applies to the chronicle Arthur reads and to the general character of memory itself:

> This man of infinite remembrance was,
>   And things foregone through many ages held,
>   Which he recorded still, as they did pas,

Ne suffred them to perish through long eld,
As all things else, the which this world doth weld,
But laid them up in his immortall scrine,
Where they for ever incorrupted dweld.

(ix.56)

His differences from the previous two sages are significant: he is more
passive (they sat, he "in a chaire was set"); they exercise their offices by
responding to data which seem simply to be *there*, automatically given
and recorded; his is the apparently more primitive function of recording
(memory externalized as written history and thus available to future
memories), though actually it is more sophisticated since, as described,
it is a more or less voluntary act of copying/writing, and therefore it is
more closely related to rational than to automatic process. Memory's au-
tomatism is located in the capacity for "infinite remembrance," which is
the specific meaning of "lively vigour" and "minds redoubled forse"
(the older he gets the more he has to remember) in the previous stanza.
Apart from this force, he is like his objects, always on the verge of falling away, declining into nothing. As facts must be *held* in his records, so
memory must be *upheld* and at the same time transcended by the higher
and later powers of rational consciousness. This need is more urgent in
his case since he is less able than the other sages to focus on his data: these
data are written, not pictorial; he is half-blind and "unhable them to
fet"; he tosses and turns them endlessly as if he does not know or cannot
find what he is looking for. That his helper, Anamnestes (the reminder
or re-collector), is a little boy means that neither occupant of memory's
chamber is capable of fully intelligent usage and choice. As in Eliot's
Gerontion, the old man whose mental career spans history and the young
boy who reads to him must both await the third person, the interpreting
mind which alone can draw the pattern from the vanities, the "cunning
passages, contrived corridors / And issues" of history. And as the chron-
icles of Arthur and Guyon reveal, the particular pattern will depend on
the interpreter's mental set, on what he is predisposed to find.

Compared to the powers of reason, will, and rational imagination, the
cognitive processes represented by the three sages are, if not primitive,
then closer to and more determined by the external world. The internal
senses complete the relatively passive and automatic phases of sensory
reception. But what they receive and transmit is not the simple low-
grade world of nature; it is the world of culture and history, the world
already transformed by the continual interchange of nature and psyche at
a level which is "natural" (instinctive) in that volitional or conscious interference scarcely exists. Spenser's allegory stresses the absolutely recip-

rocal play of influences, since so much of what is received by the internal senses consists of phenomena which, for better or worse, originated in the soul and passed thence into the world to become real features of the environment. The environment itself thus "evolves" in a Hegelian sense, that is, its composition is progressively enriched by man-made ingredients which comprise the detritus of Phantastes as well as the accomplishments of the Muses. If reality is dynamic, if under the apparently fixed substantial forms of the perceived world the ceaseless change and interchange of energy follow an evolutionary progression no human view of the world taken from a single moment or standpoint can be total or final. Such a standpoint could well be imposed on a mind which relies too heavily on either of the first two sages, for each is fixed on a single plateau. This is why the historical sense, founded on memory, is so important for Spenser and why he insists on it stylistically and thematically throughout his poetry.

If indeed reality is dynamic and evolutionary, it follows that some of the qualities traditionally ascribed to poetry and the Muses may not seem adequate to Spenser. This deficiency is especially true of the cluster of concepts associated with the term *immortality*. Apart from its metaphoric application to literary fame and its traditional application to the life of souls, angels, and God, *immortality* has some fairly stable areas of reference in Spenser's work: "eternal" recurrence at the level of nature; "timelessness" in the ideal or idyllic fictions of art; the persistence and "everlastingness" of what has already occurred, thanks to memory and its records; the durability of what Spenser calls a "moniment" (monument)—that which has been preserved because of its intrinsic value and its usefulness to posterity as memorial, model, or admonition. Slanted toward the different but often related idea of infinity, immortality may refer either to the universal (that which is everywhere the same) or to the innumerable.

The limiting aspects of immortality may be shown by examining some phrases which describe Memory and are also applied to his children, the Muses: Memory was "of infinite remembrance," he recorded all things that happened and "laid them up in his immortall scrine, / Where they for ever incorrupted dweld," and his chamber was full of "old records from auncient times deriv'd." *Scrine* is from *scrinium*, a chest or casket for manuscripts, and Spenser's use suggests something like a mummy case. The term appears again in the second stanza of the proem to Book I:

> Helpe then, O holy Virgin chiefe of nine,
> Thy weaker Novice to performe thy will,

> Lay forth out of thine everlasting scryne
> The antique rolles, which there lye hidden still,
> Of Faerie knights and fairest *Tanaquill*,
> Whom that most noble Briton Prince so long
> Sought through the world, and suffered so much ill,
> That I must rue his undeserved wrong:
> O helpe thou my weake wit, and sharpen my dull tong.

The implication is that Spenser is "going back" to ancient sources and subjects, as in the opening stanza he referred back both to Virgil and to his own early poetry. "Everlasting scryne" here suggests "a supply always available": public and therefore objective literary possibilities, not yet actualized, in whose forms the poet will unveil his own unarticulated epic. The name *Tanaquill*, renamed *Gloriana* in II.x.76, emphasizes the ancient and pre-Spenserian character of the subject matter he is about to revise. The echo of *Faerie* in *fairest* (or *fairest* in *Faerie*) prepares us for the peculiarly restricted character of the Elfin world and sensibility— timeless and ideal in being both idyllic (withdrawn from history and vicissitude) and totally meaningful (universally applicable).

In the proem to Book V the phrase "the image of the antique world" (Pr. 1) admits of two interrelated meanings: "the image I have (*or* which was transmitted to me) of the antique world" and "the image created by the antique world." The image, whether golden or stony, soft or hard, is too simple and "pure," and the modern mind which passively entertains it may be misled—or entertains it because already misled—about the "state of present time" (V.Pr.1). Again, in VI.Pr.4, the phrase "plaine Antiquitie" may mean "simple and rude Antiquity" or "clear and lucid Antiquity." The present age, however virtuous, is esteemed "all but fayned showes" when "matcht with plaine Antiquitie." The attitude toward the clarifying and simplifying tendencies of imagination is ambiguous: they may arise from the need to abstract clear patterns from the muddy actual world in the effort to make sense of it, or they may arise from the desire to turn away and escape "back" into a better time, which in fact has only one locus: "deepe within the mynd" (VI.Pr.5). Insofar as antiquity provides unchanging models expressive of earlier times and solutions, their very permanence may argue a defect either in the models or in the present user who uncritically resorts to them.

At III.iii.4 Spenser invokes Clio in preparation for Merlin's chronicle:

> Begin then, O my dearest sacred Dame,
> Daughter of Phœbus and of *Memorie*,
> That doest ennoble with immortall name

> The warlike Worthies, from antiquitie,
> In thy great volume of Eternitie:
> Begin, O *Clio*, and recount from hence
> My glorious Soveraines goodly auncestrie,
> *Till that by dew degrees and long protense,*
> Thou have it lastly brought unto her Excellence.

(italics mine)

Since I discuss this passage later, in "The Structure of Merlin's Chronicle," I shall only observe that *pro-tense* as a pun ("before-time," therefore protracted antiquity) reflects back on the "immortall name" with which Clio ennobles "the warlike Worthies, from antiquitie." The functions of Clio in this passage and in *The Teares of the Muses* are identical: "I, that doo all noble feates professe / To register, and sound in trump of gold" (*TM* 97–98); that is, she selects exemplary images of the "good governour"—"the honorable race / Of mightie Peeres" (79–80)—for the instruction of future generations. Unlike Calliope in the same poem, Clio apparently restricts herself to real historical models; her complaint is that through the "bad dooings" of contemporary peers, there is "nothing worthie to be writ, or told" (99–100): "So shall succeedings ages have no light / Of things forepast, nor moniments of time" (103–4). Furthermore, the executive paradigms she memorializes distinguish themselves primarily in physical warfare, which suggests the archaic character of her models:

> In th'eyes of people they put all their praise,
> And onely boast of Armes and Auncestrie;
> But vertuous deeds, which did those Armes first give
> To their Grandsyres, they care not to atchive.

(TM 93–96)

Indeed Clio's chronicle in III.iii is much shorter than that in II.x (where the invocation is not to Clio but to all the "learned daughters of Apollo") because the former is almost entirely concerned with wars and invasions; it excludes all chronicle data which do not bear on martial exploits and warlike worthies.

It is not enough merely to immortalize ancient norms of virtue and behavior or to protend them by slavish imitation. Whoever opens the volume or scrine "of Eternitie" must learn to particularize the archetypes (or stereotypes) which come tumbling out so that they will be truly relevant to the demands of the present. This is of course the familiar attitude Spenser shared with other Renaissance humanists.

To apotheosize the "image of antiquity" is often, for him as for them, the regressive act of an imagination unable to cope with the difficulties of contemporary life. Such an act protracts a habit of mind proper to earlier stages of culture: euhemerism. In V.vii, while describing the Temple of Isis so as to stress the discontinuity between ancient mythopoeia and his own revision, Spenser refers to this habit:

> Well therefore did the antique world invent,
>   That Justice was a God of soveraine grace,
> And altars unto him, and temples lent,
>   And heavenly honours in the highest place;
> Calling him great *Osyris*, of the race
>   Of th'old Ægyptian Kings, that whylome were;
> With fayned colours shading a true case;
>   For that *Osyris*, whilest he lived here,
> The justest man alive, and truest did appeare.
>
>   *(V.vii.2)*

The ennobling function ascribed to the Muse named Clio may be associated with this tendency. Spenser exemplifies the more adequate response in the proem to Book VI, appealing first to the Muses and the example of plain antiquity, then shifting forward to a new Muse and model:

> But where shall I in all Antiquity
> So faire a patterne finde, where may be seene
> The goodly praise of Princely curtesie,
> As in your selfe, O soveraine Lady Queene . . .
>
>   *(VI.Pr.6)*

Thus while Spenser's use of terms like *everlasting* and *records perma-nent* may seem at first glance to be purely honorific, we must take into account the extent to which they are qualified by their association with such phrases as "antique rolles" and "registered of old," for these suggest something fixed early in culture and therefore permanent if not necessarily adequate. His attitude toward the antique imagination and its culture is conditioned by the evolutionary premises of his historical vision. In spite of his frequent interest in depicting interruptions, failures, countermovements, and counterstatements (such as decline from golden antiquity, regression, premature fixation, and protraction or protense of an early structure), the evolutionary model remains fundamental in his thought, at least as a theoretical ideal which all forms of energy and desire try to actualize. And these forms include not only religious, political, social, and erotic experience but also the poetic activity. Spenser views the development of the poet in the parallel perspectives of phylogeny and ontogeny. The first originates in the matrix of nature, the second in the matrix of literary convention. From the first derives the work of ancient bards and sages, which is the creation or reception and transmission of myths. Mythopoeia and mythology are related to superstition in being products of the collective and primitive consciousness. By contrast, the work of the sophisticated individual poet in his early career consists primarily in the reception of the literary commonplaces of thought and rhetoric—the matrix of convention. As the extent and quality of the glosses in *The Shepheardes Calender* (1579) might suggest, the young poet finds that the myth and the convention have much in common. Both are external and traditional impositions—recurrent, universal, and impersonal—which the poet is not simply to transmit in a new wrapping but to transform and revise. The myth no less than the commonplace may be a pressed or artificial flower preserved in the *Elizium*, the *antho-logical* garden, of the Muses. If the poet approaches them as an antiquarian, an aesthete, or a hedonist, this may well be a function of an inadequate response not to poetry but to life; the world proffered by the antique Muses is hardly a copy of the world the poet lives in as a man. Spenser has revealed his awareness of this in a number of poems—most directly in *The Teares of the Muses*—and I shall conclude with a brief discussion of his view of the conventional Muses. But first I should like to glance at some relevant aspects of intellectual background.

We are familiar with two conceptions of the poet, one old and one modern, which prevailed during the Renaissance: in the first, the artist and poet are important because they embellish the actual world; in the second they are important as makers of an imaginary world. One source of the familiarity of these notions is Sidney's *Apology*. Sidney begins by setting forth, with great historical acumen, what might be termed a Horatian or Orphic view of the poet: poetry is primarily rhetoric, "the skinne as it were and beautie" of philosophy and other disciplines. Ancient priests, princes, politicians, and philosophers all spoke in verse. This theory treats the poet as a direct contributor to the culture and civilization of the actual world—what Sidney calls the brazen world when speaking of the new poet's golden world, but what the early humanists, whose opinions are the source of this theory, praised as the repository of man's greatest achievements. They transformed the medieval defense of art as ornament-plus-argument into a praise of man deriving from Latin civic and rhetorical traditions. Medieval and Roman theories have in common a subordination of poetry to the actual world, so that in shifting from the medieval back or forward to the Roman theory the humanists were only shifting emphasis from real heaven to real earth.

In the series of odd reversals produced by shifts of interest in Renaissance thinkers, the Latin influence gave way to "earlier" Greek philosophy and to a new but different sort of cosmic theory. When in the *Apology* Sidney moves from the Horatian to his own different definition of the poet as maker of the golden world, he echoes the historical shift from humanist to Neoplatonist praises of man. The Neoplatonist philosophers extended man's sphere of influence from city to cosmos and viewed the human soul as the dynamic center of the universe, capable of becoming all things, of converting natural objects into symbols and ideas or spiritual substances into images. Parallel to this development was a shift in the theory mainly of those apologists who were artists and poets rather than educators and scholars: if the mind could internalize the world and raise nature to a higher power, then the artist could externalize the world of mental forms in the imaginary space of a panel or the plot of a poem. Sidney, Leonardo, Michelangelo, Tasso, and others look for a significant image of man less in the surrounding world than in the objectified forms of imagination.

When apologists want to emphasize the antiquity and universality of poetry they speak of the Muses as presiding over all learning and culture, and they resort to the older idea of the poet as a learned rhetorician whose distinguishing mark is his gift of language; the poetic function is the expressive component of any cultural act. Here the activity of the Muses may be more appropriately ascribed to the second sage than to Memory, for the Muses inspire "all artes, all science, all Philosophy, / And all that in the world was aye thought wittily."

Sidney's shift from a Horatian to a Neoplatonic-Aristotelian definition seems to serve not only as a historical perspective but also as a contrast which helps sharpen his New-Critical distinction between poetry and other things. Insofar as this is true his theory and Spenser's poetry have a common basis in a relatively sophisticated idea of fiction and the counterfactual. But the polemical context of Sidney's argument leads him astray, and if Spenser took his cue from Sidney's idea of the true poet, he moves considerably beyond him in practice. The essential difference between them lies in the way each conceives of the content of the fictional world. Sidney's distinction of the poetic art from those described above fastens on two qualities: the poet's world is golden, whereas actuality is brazen, and the poet may give relatively free rein to his Phantastes: "Onely the Poet . . . dooth growe in effect another nature, in making things either better then Nature bringeth forth, or, quite a newe, formes such as never were in Nature, as the *Heroes, Demigods, Cyclops, Chimeras,*

Furies, and such like; so as hee goeth hand in hand with Nature, not inclosed within the narrow warrant of her guifts, but freely ranging onely within the Zodiack of his owne wit." True poetry is golden in "fayning notable images of vertues," and therefore *fancy*, whether unreal or impure, is not enough. But Sidney's polemical purpose leads him to push the golden world too far toward that excess of purity and perfection, that mingling of the ideal (what should be) and the idyllic (what could be), which Spenser saw as itself a form of escape: "Poetrie ever setteth vertue so out in her best cullours, making Fortune her welwayting hand-mayd, that one must needs be enamored of her. . . . But the Historian, beeing captived to the trueth of a foolish world, is many times a terror from well dooing, and an incouragement to unbrideled wickednes." [3]

Spenser as poet differs from both the earlier and the more modern conceptions: from the earlier because his is an imaginary world and hence is unique—*his* imaginary world, not an aspect of or contribution to the common actuality of nature and culture; from Sidney's true poet because his Muses reveal *what is* as well as what should or could be. His second world is brazen as well as golden. His Muses may indeed preside over the whole range of learning, but they do so *within* the second world, and unlike Sidney's Muses they utilize the whole range of Memory, not merely the extreme poles of the spectrum represented by the first two sages in Alma's castle. Compared with the theory embodied in Spenser's work, Sidney's idea resembles the humanist and Neoplatonist forms of *laus mentis* in tending one-sidedly toward glorification of the soul's excellence, virtue, learning, productivity, and so on.

Such a tendency is too frequently rooted in the twinned and mutually intensifying impulses of idealism and pessimism, escape and despair. The very perfection over which golden Muses preside testifies to their insulation from life. They have withdrawn from actuality, and especially from the actual world in its historical or evolutionary dimension. It is small wonder that when confronted (as in *The Teares of the Muses*) by contemporary life they break out in excessive and unrelieved complaint. In this poem Spenser allots each Muse sixty lines in which to describe the traditional compartment over which she presides and to bemoan the barbaric state of ignorance which characterizes present-day culture. The poem is intendedly unconventional in that its conventionality is placed in quotation marks and conspicuously affirmed: the individual Muses speak with the voice of antiquity and convention. Their tears are plain-

---

[3] "An Apology for Poetry," in *Elizabethan Critical Essays*, ed. G. Gregory Smith (London: Oxford University Press, 1904), 1:156, 160, 170.

tive, not merely elegiac, for their vision of the golden past and black present is too absolute and pure. Since the Golden Age to which they appeal exists not really in the past but "deepe within the mynd," their longings for and visions of an ideal world are "timeless" and "eternal," and therefore time has passed them by.

The very separateness of the Muses, the traditional classification into distinct genres, poses related problems. The differences Spenser indicates among the Muses of lyric, love poetry, and rhetorical decorum (Euterpe, Erato, Polyhymnia), and also those between Clio and Calliope, are relatively fine and admit some overlapping. Traditional classification demands that minute if real differences be artificially magnified into genres. Nevertheless, any good poem moves freely back and forth across the boundaries and is in effect a concord of limited elements. The simple genre, developed by isolating a single element of theme or style, is too inflexible to present the fluid complexities of life as Spenser knows it, though it may more adequately have served to express forms of experience apprehended by the antique imagination. In his own poetry, the ancient Muses and their artificially discrete genres are united in a "greater Muse," variously identified in *Faerie Queene* I.Pr.2, I.xi.5−7, IV.xi.10, and VII.vii.1−2. The relation of the nine Muses to his greater Muse is that of past to present, or traditional to unique, but it is also that of elemental parts to the complex whole. Personifying a state of mind, the elemental figure which admits of no variety or complication reveals all the negative or obsessive qualities Spenser frequently reads into such notions as pure, timeless, fixed, eternal, and—because of its schematic or emblematic simplicity—universally applicable (archetypal). If the monotony of the Muses' plaintive stance makes for a fairly low-grade poem, and for fairly low-grade poetry, it is yet functional: endless complaint implies willed passivity to the external world as it is (bad as it is). This is what the antique Muses—with their angle of vision, their reservoir of aureate subject matter and expression—do to those minds under their spell. Presiding over convention and inspiration, the Muses properly control but the first moment of poetic action; the remainder, the poet's burden, lies in revision and original response. If I may modify the passage from *Process and Reality* cited in my opening paragraph, Spenser's historical and realistic sense of the world makes it imperative to him that poetry, like all other things, be enhanced in relevance or even changed in character by the passage from the low-grade external world of timeless convention into the intimacy of a unique human imagination.

Spenser's *Faerie Queene*, Book I

Prelude to Interpretation

THE CONTROLLING BELIEF of the first book is the poet's faith in tradition and particularly in the biblical symbolism of apocalypse, a symbolism which unites historical and theological perspectives in a single vision. But since this is a *poet's* faith it entails something more than uncritical respect for the ancient order: there is also faith in the mind's ability to make a hypothetical world in which the old order may be tested. Spenser's language and landscape provide an arena sharply demarcated from the actual world. In this arena the problems of actuality, which are represented at the various "levels" of allegorical reference, are not simply disguised as fictions but are transposed into the forms of serious play so that they can be imaginatively staged, experienced, justified.

The controlling literary form of the first book is that of apocalypse, which means literally a stripping away, a rending of the veil in which "the substance of things to be hoped for" is manifested in its visible embodiments. It is only because falsehood and evil display themselves through the hero's own failings that they can be caught and stripped away, as Orgoglio, Duessa and Despair are purged from the hero, or as his corruption is purged by Amendment in the House of Penance. If we remember that Fidelia's cup with the serpent (x.13) is St. John's symbol and recall the occasion giving rise to the symbol, we shall have a paradigm of the poem's apocalyptic pattern. On Ephesus the poison given to

John by the Emperor Domitian miraculously condensed into a serpent and left the cup. The serpent in Fidelia's cup suggests the need for faith by showing forth the enemy found in the very cup of faith; it also suggests how faith can reveal the poison in its true and primal nature. In the gradual development of a single soul through and toward faith, the scattered evil is gathered together until it is trapped and displayed. Ultimately the dragon of chaos and hell will be manifested in the cup of the universe.

In Johannine theology, apocalypse—the future fulfillment and not the visionary promise—is effected through a historical process, called *krisis*, in which the gradual separation of the good from the evil leads to a final moment of encounter and judgment when, at the end of time, the two armies stand face to face. The life in time is a trial and a touchstone. As St. Augustine described it, the two natures and their corresponding societies were so mingled in the earthly city that the blessed could come to understanding and peace only through experience of the satanic deception at work in self as well as world: no one could be good who was not first of all wicked (*City of God* XV.1). To experience, to recognize, to reject, to draw oneself apart is not only to fulfill oneself, but also to expose the enemy and so help articulate the *concordia discors* of God's plan.

But to *see* the evil is not to conquer it. If the goal of history is the salvation of souls and the fulfillment of persons, the saving of a single soul, however much God presses the whole universe into its service, does not end history. There is a disequilibrium between apocalyptic promise—offered in some embattled *now* of life—and eschatological fulfillment: the adversary continues to flourish in this world; the earthly city swells its population and increasingly flaunts its evil until it demands a showdown at the end of time (Dan. 8.22–25, Matt. 24, Rev. 18). Thus as the good prove themselves the evil power becomes more manifest. But this exposure is ultimately self-deceptive and self-destructive: concentrating itself in a place and shape, pressing for open battle, the adversary can be quelled in a single encounter.

I

This rationale of disclosure informs the narrative of Book I in a number of ways, and these may conveniently be approached by glancing at the opening stanzas of canto i:

> A Gentle Knight was pricking on the plaine,
> Y cladd in mightie armes and silver shielde,
> Wherein old dints of deepe wounds did remaine,

The cruell markes of many' a bloudy fielde;
Yet armes till that time did he never wield:
His angry steede did chide his foming bitt,
As much disdayning to the curbe to yield:
Full jolly knight he seemd, and faire did sitt,
As one for knightly giusts and fierce encounters fitt.

But on his brest a bloudie Crosse he bore,
The deare remembrance of his dying Lord,
For whose sweete sake that glorious badge he wore,
And dead as living ever him ador'd:
Upon his shield the like was also scor'd,
For soveraine hope, which in his helpe he had:
Right faithful true he was in deede and word,
But of his cheere did seeme too solemne sad;
Yet nothing did he dread, but ever was ydrad.

Upon a great adventure he was bond,
That greatest *Gloriana* to him gave,
That greatest Glorious Queene of *Faerie* lond,
To winne him worship, and her grace to have,
Which of all earthly things he most did crave;
And ever as he rode, his hart did earne
To prove his puissance in battell brave
Upon his foe, and his new force to learne;
Upon his foe, a Dragon horrible and stearne.

A lovely Ladie rode him faire beside,
Upon a lowly Asse more white then snow,
Yet she much whiter, but the same did hide
Under a vele, that wimpled was full low,
And over all a blacke stole she did throw,
As one that inly mournd: so was she sad,
And heavie sat upon her palfrey slow:
Seemed in heart some hidden care she had,
And by her in a line a milke white lambe she lad.

So pure an innocent, as that same lambe,
She was in life and every vertuous lore,
And by descent from Royall lynage came
Of ancient Kings and Queenes, that had of yore
Their scepters stretcht from East to Westerne shore,
And all the world in their subjection held;
Till that infernall feend with foule uprore
Forwasted all their land, and them expeld:
Whom to avenge, she had this Knight from far compeld.

> Behind her farre away a Dwarfe did lag,
> That lasie seemed in being ever last,
> Or wearied with bearing of her bag
> Of needments at his backe . . .

The first four lines of stanza 1 and the first six of stanza 2 introduce the archetypal quest, something old, familiar, and by no means fictional. Yet as the disjunction opening stanza 2 suggests, two different perspectives on the quest are offered. The emphasis of stanza 1 is on romance, that of stanza 2 on religious or theological implications. The chivalric and Christian forms of quest are by no means identical; they may, but they need not, be conjoined. Something of their problematical relation is suggested by the third stanza's suddenly narrowing the image of the quest to the limited terms understood by, available to, the hero himself. There is a touch of irony in "deare remembrance, for whose sake, ever him ador'd": this is rather what the hero forgets than what he remembers during the quest. The second stanza thus looks forward to the perfected awareness which he does not yet possess; it reminds us of heroic potentialities which succeeding episodes will reveal as unactualized. Line 8 of the second stanza implies that Redcross is, in modern parlance, something of a "straight man," and the general effect of the opening description is to identify him as the latest of innumerable questers, eager, brave, and innocent. Stanza 3, which enforces the gap between his partial and our more complete knowledge, concentrates the hero's problem in the ambiguous phrase, "his new force to learne"—that is, "to learne the nature and extent of his own untested powers," or "to prove the force of that tested armour, new to him." There is, as we shall see, a confusion in his own mind about the source of his power; perhaps he takes himself too seriously because of the armor he wears. Yet the armor is his by election (Letter to Raleigh), a token of that second nature which God offers him but which will not be truly his until he has earned it. He is still a nameless bumpkin in oversized armor and he has a long way to go before becoming England's patron saint.

By way of convenient oversimplification we might read these three stanzas as introducing three domains of the poem, labeled respectively Romance, Theology, and Faerie. Faerie indicates the imaginary world and landscape treated as entirely literal, as if this were the only world and no other existed. Its character is that of the checkerboard world perfected by wish and perverted by nightmare—the golden world of victorious heroes and vincible monsters. Romance includes Faerie in a mixed world containing symbolic and allegorical landscapes, a world in which some characters are not only independent creatures but also aspects of other characters. In language, manner, and subject matter, Romance formally announces itself as turning away from the pressure and imperfection of the actual world, re-creating experience in new forms within a remote but self-sufficient space. This world contains both Elfins and Britons: Elfins are locked in Faerie and know no other life; they cannot grow because they are already perfect in their own kinds. Britons are only temporarily in Faerie and are being tested, developed, and prepared for historical destinies. The perfected characters of Satyrane, Guyon, Calidore, Belphoebe, Florimell, Amoret, Scudamour, Sansjoy, and so on, are limited and static compared to the more realistic and embattled psyches of Redcross, Britomart, and Artegall.

Spenser's treatment of the imaginary world has much in common with that of Shakespeare and also with the conception of the painted world developed in Italy during the fifteenth and sixteenth centuries and lucidly exemplified in the theory and practice of perspective. By announcing that his world is imaginary, the poet, playwright, or painter simultaneously affirms his limits and asserts his power; he reminds his audience that it is all only play, but it turns out to be serious play. In separating imaginary space from the space of readers or spectators, in establishing controlled lines of communication between the two, in manipulating the two worlds through constantly shifting relations of detachment and involvement, the artist may suggest that the audience will see an image of itself as in a mirror, or an analysis of itself refracted through a prism. At the same time he jealously isolates his own domain, proclaims its autonomy, and demands his audience to attend to the work for its own sake. Spenser might well agree with Hamlet, for whom the purpose of playing was to hold "the mirror up to nature, to show virtue her own feature, scorn her own image, and the very age and body of the time his form and pressure." We may refer virtue's feature and scorn's image to the unreal embodiments of good and evil who inhabit the golden world of Faerie, while the very age and body of the time may be sought in the more complicated depiction of actual human nature focused in Spenser's Britons. In Spenser's mixed mode of Romance, with its serious play, Theology provides the high seriousness and Faerie the pure play: the former isolates the poet's indications of the real, the spiritual, the divine; the latter isolates human ideals which are radically withdrawn from and innocent of actuality.

These stanzas manage to give us a good deal of information about Redcross. We learn something about his quest, his appearance, his character and potentialities, and something also about the limited nature of his consciousness. Yet over against this we are confronted by the patent artifice of the whole situation. The first five stanzas are sharply framed and flattened by the emblematic style of visualization. As has often been pointed out, Spenser is not interested in realistic physical description— if Redcross were *pricking* his horse, Una could scarcely stay astride her ass and lead her lamb by a line. The lamb disappears after being sacrificed to a simile in stanza 5; it is a symbol and not a traveling companion. A sense of distance and visual stasis, a sense also for the miniature or toy quality of the landscape, may be evoked if we try to "see" the opening scene. We may be reminded of the St. George paintings by Uccello (one at Paris, the other formerly at Vienna) which—like his three *Rout of San Romano* panels (London, Paris, Florence)—seem to depict forms of art rather than forms of life. We know how much Spenser's descriptions remind us of artificial or play forms—tapestry, painting, masquing, and such recreative pageantry as the Accession Day Tourney which Frances Yates attributes to the "imaginative re-feudalization of culture" popular throughout Europe at the time.[1] Finally, we should remember the peculiarity in Spenser's choice of motif which William Nelson has pointed out:

> No Renaissance humanist could have thought the legendary life of St. George a respectable literary model. By the sixteenth century accretions of impossible adventure and the buffoonery of village St. George plays must have rendered the story ridiculous; in fact, it had been denounced as apocryphal as early as the fifth. Spenser is able nevertheless to turn it to serious uses because such a legend, however incredible or even absurd it may be, asserts ideals of nobility, love, and holiness which are consonant with his purpose.[2]

We move closer to the rationale of Spenser's presentation if we change Nelson's final sentence to read, "Spenser is able to turn the legend to his own serious uses *because* it may be incredible or even absurd." What he seems to want is the atmosphere of an ideal world, but not necessarily ideal in a Neoplatonic or "supersensuous" manner; ideal rather as imaginary and mind-made, as a special self-enclosed landscape remote from actuality. He presents a golden world, a second nature, which could not be found anywhere but in the oddly treated picture plane of his own poem;

[1] "Elizabethan Chivalry: The Romance of the Accession Day Tilts," *Journal of the Warburg and Courtauld Institutes* 20 (1957): 22.
[2] *The Poetry of Edmund Spenser* (New York: Columbia University Press, 1963), 150.

into this second nature ride his British heroes, bringing with them the problems of real life. And he not only seems to enjoy stressing this play or toy quality of his fairyland, he seems even at times to patronize, to show his amusement, to put on a melodramatic tone smilingly, to reveal his pleasure in the rhetoric of innocence and of malice:

> Soone meete they both, both fell and furious,
> That daunted with their forces hideous,
> Their steeds do stagger, and amazed stand,
> And eke themselves too rudely rigorous,
> Astonied with the stroke of their owne hand,
> Do backe rebut, and each to other yeeldeth land.

> As when two rams stird with ambitious pride,
> Fight for the rule of the rich fleeced flocke,
> Their horned fronts so fierce on either side
> Do meete, that with the terrour of the shocke
> Astonied both, stand sencelesse as a blocke,
> Forgetfull of the hanging victory:
> So stood these twaine, unmoved as a rocke,
> Both staring fierce, and holding idely
> The broken reliques of their former cruelty.

> . . . .
> . . . The flashing fier flies
> As from a forge out of their burning shields,
> And streames of purple bloud new dies the verdant fields.
>
> *(ii.15–16, 17)*

> Sober he seemde, and very sagely sad,
> And to the ground his eyes were lowly bent,
> Simple in shew, and voyde of malice bad,
> And all the way he prayed, as he went,
> And often knockt his brest, as one that did repent.

> He faire the knight saluted, louting low,
> Who faire him quited, as that courteous was:
> And after asked him, if he did know
> Of straunge adventures, which abroad did pas.
> Ah my deare Sonne (quoth he) how should, alas,
> Silly old man, that lives in hidden cell,
> Bidding his beades all day for his trespas,
> Tydings of warre and worldly trouble tell?
> With holy father sits not with such things to mell.
>
> *(i.29–30)*

   when all drownd in deadly sleepe he findes,
  He to his study goes, and there amiddes
  His Magick bookes and artes of sundry kindes,
He seekes out mighty charmes, to trouble sleepy mindes.

  Then choosing out few wordes most horrible,
   (Let none them read) thereof did verses frame . . .
           (i.36–37)

  He then devisde himselfe how to disguise;
   For by his mightie science he could take
   As many formes and shapes in seeming wise,
   As ever *Proteus* to himselfe could make:
   Sometime a fowle, sometime a fish in lake,
   Now like a foxe, now like a dragon fell,
   That of himselfe he oft for feare would quake,
   And oft would flie away. O who can tell
The hidden power of herbes, and might of Magicke spell?
           (ii.10)

  He in great passion all this while did dwell,
   More busying his quicke eyes, her face to view,
   Then his dull eares, to heare what she did tell;
   And said, Faire Lady hart of flint would rew
The undeserved woes and sorrowes, which ye shew.

  Henceforth in safe assuraunce may ye rest,
   Having both found a new friend you to aid,
   And lost an old foe, that did you molest:
   Better new friend then an old foe is said.
   With chaunge of cheare the seeming simple maid
   Let fall her eyen, as shamefast to the earth,
   And yeelding soft, in that she nought gain-said,
   So forth they rode, he feining seemly merth,
And she coy lookes: so dainty they say maketh derth.
          (ii.26–27)

  I, whether lately through her brightnesse blind,
   Or through alleageance and fast fealtie,
   Which I do owe unto all woman kind,
   Feele my heart perst with so great agonie,
When such I see, that all for pittie I could die.

  And now it is empassioned so deepe,
   For fairest *Unaes* sake, of whom I sing,
   That my fraile eyes these lines with teares do steepe . . .
          (iii.1–2)

These touches remind us of the extent to which the poet controls his world and also of his interest and pleasure in it. The pleasure borders on the recreative in quality, since the poet so obviously enjoys his own role playing as well as that of his villains. He delights in playing Archimago as a caricature bogeyman, in having his innocents misapply the limited and too consoling wisdom of proverbs, in sacrificing narrative economy to the rhetorical impulse. An interpretive amplification like the ram simile tells us a great deal about Redcross's psychic condition, about his motives, about his too great similarity to Sansfoy. The pastoral modulation precisely registers the self-reductive tendencies of the combatants. But such a modulation is also comic, and the rhetorical mixing of puns, hyperbolic adjectives, and idiomatic phrases emphasizes its recreative character. We are made to feel that the poet enjoys doing this sort of thing and will take advantage of any opportunity to embroider his narrative. This lends to the entire poem an air of improvisation—one may, for example, see the ram simile as generated by the pun lurking in *rebut*, as if the poet suddenly decided to stop and play with the idea suggested by the word.

As the overstated apostrophe to Una implies, Spenser is never fully or realistically caught up *within* his imaginary world; he stands before it as a painter before a panel, looking at it, adding touches, interpreting to observers, displaying rather than expressing his responses. This, rather than the panel alone, is what we are asked to observe: the poet interpreting between his puppets and us. There is thus very little question of real dramatic suspense, and when Spenser pretends to squeeze the last drop out of so juicy a situation as Sansloy's imminent rape of Una he is scarcely trying to make us crane forward:

> Ah heavens, that do this hideous act behold,
> And heavenly virgin thus outraged see,
> How can ye vengeance just so long withhold,
> And hurle not flashing flames upon that Paynim bold?

> The pitteous maiden carefull comfortlesse,
> Does throw out thrilling shriekes, and shrieking cryes,
> The last vaine helpe of womens great distresse,
> And with loud plaints importuneth the skyes,
> That molten starres do drop like weeping eyes;
> And *Phoebus* flying so most shamefull sight,
> His blushing face in foggy cloud implyes,
> And hides for shame. What wit of mortall wight
> Can now devise to quit a thrall from such a plight?

> Eternall providence exceeding thought,
> Where none appeares can make her selfe a way:
> A wondrous way it for this Lady wrought . . .
>   *(vi.5—7)*

namely, the troop of satyrs whose "rude, misshapen, monstrous" appearance frightened Sansloy away. The operatic parody reminds us that in spite of all the fuss everything is well under control. The world in which Una's cries make stars drop like weeping eyes is run by Spenser's, not God's, providence, and the final three lines serve mainly to alert the reader to Spenser's own inventiveness.

The effect of these techniques is not simply to disparage the fairytale surface of the poem in order to direct us to the more serious business of allegory. Oddly enough, Spenser's devices keep the fairytale world firmly before us: the fabulous narrative is to be taken seriously, not evaporated into ideological correlatives; *but it is to be taken seriously as play.* If it serves a significance beyond itself, that significance cannot be approached except through the poet's make-believe. This is an effect about which Sidney was quite explicit, and we may follow A. C. Hamilton's lead in showing how Spenser may be illuminated by the *Apology:*

> With a tale forsooth he commeth unto you, with a tale which holdeth children from play, and old men from the chimney corner.

> the Poet . . . never affirmeth. The Poet never maketh any circles about your imagination, to conjure you to beleeve for true what he writes. . . . What childe is there that, comming to a Play, and seeing *Thebes* written in great Letters upon an olde doore, doth beleeve that it is Thebes? If then a man can arive, at that childs age, to know that the Poets persons and dooings are but pictures what should be, and not stories what have beene, they will never give the lye to things not affirmatively but allegorically and figurativelie written. . . . in Poesie, looking for fiction, they shal use the narration but as an imaginative groundplot of a profitable invention.[3]

For Spenser as for Sidney, the elements of play and artifice have important ethical, even epistemological, functions: by stylistically articulating those elements the poet simultaneously reminds us that he is inventing what ought to be (rather than affirming what is) and proclaims to us

---

[3] *Elizabethan Critical Essays*, ed. G. Gregory Smith (London: Oxford University Press, 1904), 1:172, 185. See A. C. Hamilton, *The Structure of Allegory in the "Faerie Queene"* (Oxford: Clarendon Press, 1961), chap. 1.

his freedom from criteria of verifiability and correspondence which subordinate the other arts to nature. Thus the Neoplatonic Idea, the humanist's "winning of the mind from wickedness to vertue," and the Aristotelian "what should be" are uniquely founded on the poet's re-creative urge and skill. If fiction and holiday come closer than actuality and everyday to what is real and even holy, it is only because the mind at first withdrew "from pleasure less" to a world of its own making, to a gratuitous delight and indulgence in its own powers.

Ultimately, as we shall see, Book I will move temporarily beyond the play world, but in accordance with the apocalyptic pattern its connections with a reality beyond imagination will only be gradually disclosed. As the interpreter of his world, Spenser keeps us carefully poised between the options of pure Faerie and determinate allegory. Una's background as given in i.5 above, for example, is too general to be pinned down. We cannot be sure, so early in the narrative, precisely what the kings, queens, east, west, and dragon represent, though we are quite sure they represent something. If Redcross's "bloudie Crosse" and the "infernall feend" suggest a religious connection, the armor and dragon seem primarily functions of the romance adventure; this element is enforced by the description of the dwarf which concludes the opening section. Una is on a long trip and is at least real enough to require a fairly heavy "bag of needments." Thus Spenser manages both to suggest meanings beyond or outside the immediate narrative and to leave them in abeyance. The climate of allegory clearly surrounds the opening passage, but there is little indication of what it is and how it relates to the story. Especially during the earlier phases of the adventure, episodes tend to be *dark conceits* to readers as well as to the hero. We, of course, always know more than the hero knows or could possibly know about the world he moves in—though it would be ridiculous to say that the main difference lies in the hero's having less leisure than the reader to interpret the episodes. Since he confronts things where we confront words, and since we have the advantage of being aware that he is in a poem, he does not feel invited to join us in seeing himself in an allegorical landscape. Nevertheless, the darkness in which the hero moves is by no means balanced by the clarity of the reader's understanding. If this were so, we would be less sympathetic toward him than we are. Because Spenser keeps us as well as the hero off balance, we are forced to follow the narrative more intently, and indeed we come to realize that the hero is our scapegoat: he errs, sins, suffers, is alienated from the world of common day *so that* we may interpret.

II

This problematical character becomes clearer when we try to consider the allegory apart from the story: we may in general wonder why, when Redcross has conquered a dragon-lady named Error, he spends nine cantos falling into deeper error? If he overcomes Error, why should he succumb to Hypocrisy? If he abandons Una, why should he then conquer Faithlessness? If he conquers Faithlessness, why should he succumb to Falsehood? In its abstract form the moral dialectic does not work. Only the concrete characters which the abstractions assume in the poem, only their place in the action and their relation to the hero, will make them logical. For example, it is not easy to define the precise relation of Sansfoy to Redcross unless one considers the details of the poetic context and its place in the sequence of events, but even this is inadequate: we must adopt, or at least try out, some general hypothesis about the rationale which informs these allegorical appearances. Whether we think of Sansfoy primarily as Faithlessness or as Infidelity—there is some difference of connotation—will depend largely on the pattern of expectation we have set up in ourselves regarding the way to approach allegorical significance.

In this instance both the sequence and the details offer an economical model of the approach to be adopted here. Redcross has just been deceived by Archimago into thinking Una unfaithful. The magician had first offered him a wanton dream-Una who aroused in the young knight a "great passion of unwonted lust, / Or wonted feare of doing ought amis," and on this "He started up, as seeming to mistrust / Some secret ill, or hidden foe of his" (i.49). His first awakening to lust immediately produces a guilt reaction; *wonted feare* indicates his habitual virtue, the inhibiting power of his chivalric consciousness. But he awakens to see another wanton Una, a disguised spirit which Archimago places before his eyes, and this proves almost too much for him.

> All cleane dismayd to see so uncouth sight
> And halfe enraged at her shamelesse guise,
> He thought have slaine her in his fierce despight:
> But hasty heat tempring with sufferance wise,
> He stayde his hand, and gan himselfe advise
> To prove his sense, and tempt her faigned truth.
>
> *(i.50)*

The uncouth sight becomes the external evidence verifying the dream, the cause of his unwonted lust. The secret ill becomes the no longer hidden foe, Una. In this context "To prove his sense, and tempt her faigned truth" is thoroughly ambiguous; it may refer to his lust as well as to his scruples, and we may also feel the verb *slay* to carry a sexual as well as a repressive implication. The apparition Una has thus become the sensual object, the moral scapegoat, the projected image of his lust; by slaying the apparition he may kill the feeling in himself. Though Redcross appears to weather this storm, he has already lost faith in Una—"Much griev'd to thinke that gentle Dame so light, / For whose defence he was to shed his blood" (i.55). Yet this loss of faith is coincident with the emergence into consciousness of his own sexual desire. Therefore when Archimago next morning shows him the apparition Una making love to another spirit, Redcross "burnt with gealous fire, / The eye of reason was with rage yblent" (ii.5), and getting hastily dressed he runs away, leaving the real Una behind and flying also "from his thoughts and gealous feare" (ii.12).

As the knight sees it, he has run away from his own lust and potential infidelity, now associated with Una in his mind; in this way he has, in his eyes, maintained his chastity and remained faithful to the chivalric ethics of his quest. What *actually* happens has been sensitively analyzed by Kerby Neill, whose diagnosis reveals the close interconnection of ethical with psychological issues:

> we must conclude that the Red Cross Knight is essentially on trial, and furthermore that the power of Archimago and Duessa to deceive him is not great, especially if he remains chaste in feeling and strong in faith. . . . he fails because he is not sufficiently strong in faith nor confirmed in chastity. At the allegorical level he doubts Truth, and at the literal level he burns in wrath and a sensual jealousy that makes him an easy prey to the next temptation of the flesh. In spite of dreams, false apparitions, what appeared the valid testimony of the senses, and the later appeal of what seemed a lady in distress, if the Red Cross Knight had kept passion under the rule of reason, he would not have been started on his way to ruin by the witchcraft of Archimago and Duessa.[4]

His first step in his flight from himself was to have projected his feelings onto Una. In doing so he denied the whole machinery and promise of the quest, the evidence provided by the armor which magically or mystically fitted and by Gloriana's validation of the undertaking. All this, connected with the "substance of things to be hoped for" and the "evi-

[4] "The Degradation of the Red Cross Knight," in *That Soueraine Light*, ed. W. R. Mueller and D. C. Allen (Baltimore: Johns Hopkins Press, 1952), 109–10.

dence of things unseen," is given up before Archimago's powerful evidence of things seen. It is clear that Redcross is to be blamed for this defection, but it is also clear that the cards have been stacked against him; avoiding an overt evil he commits a more serious but less discernible sin. We are shown the difficulty of avoiding sin by one's unaided powers, the cosmic organization of evil forces ready to capitalize on a single slip, the extent to which this organization exceeds consciousness and jeopardizes one's total being.

In turning to Archimago, Spenser shows what his triumph means. Archimago rejoiced to see his guests "divided into double parts" (ii.9). This phrase should be taken literally; not only Redcross divided from Una, but Redcross divided from himself and consequently Una divided into two—the real Una exiled from the hero's consciousness and the false image of Una which has replaced her there. This image will shortly materialize as *Duessa,* Double-being. The phrase comically applied to Archimago has serious application to Redcross: "of himselfe he oft for feare would quake, / and oft would flie away" (ii.10). The description of Archimago donning his new disguise provides an image of the knight's new condition; he is now inhabited and directed by the Archimago within; his armor and consciousness serve those powers within him which are enemies of Una, of truth and reason, of faith and the Christian quest—enemies therefore of his survival:

> But now seemde best, the person to put on
>   Of that good knight, his late beguiled guest:
>   In mighty armes he was yclad anon,
>   And silver shield: upon his coward brest
>   A bloudy crosse, and on his craven crest
>   A bounch of haires discolourd diversly:
>   Full jolly knight he seemde, and well addrest,
>   And when he sate upon his courser free,
> *Saint George* himself ye would have deemed him to be.
>
> But he the knight, whose semblaunt he did beare,
>   The true *Saint George* was wandred far away,
>   Still flying from his thoughts and gealous feare;
>   Will was his guide, and griefe led him astray.
>   At last him chaunst to meete upon the way
>   A faithlesse Sarazin all arm'd to point,
>   In whose great shield was writ with letters gay
> *Sans foy:* full large of limbe and every joint
> He was, and cared not for God or man a point.
>
>   *(ii.11–12)*

This is significantly the first mention of the hero's real name, and the last for some time; we are ironically informed of his true identity at the very moment he is casting it far from him, losing power over his own future. The narrative would seem to indicate a division between the hero's image of what is happening to him and what in fact is happening to him—between his consciousness and his unconscious being, the latter referring to that part of himself and the world now concealed by the passions and perceptions of his vitiated consciousness.

This division suggests that the dominant reference of the allegory is psychological. In this context the meeting with Sansfoy is both logical and peculiar. Allegorically considered, the hero conquers—rejects—overt faithlessness but does so blindly, for the sake of or on the basis of false faith (Duessa). What is peculiar is that this recapitulates the process which just occurred in Archimago's house. The process has been externalized and now confronts him as a threat from the outside, and also as the next episode in the sequence. The dream logic which, as we shall see, prevails in this part of the poem allows interesting consequences to be drawn: until he is rescued by Una and Arthur and brought to the House of Holiness, the hero's condition steadily worsens, but he himself scarcely moves forward at all. The forward progress of the narrative operates in part like a treadmill: insofar as a later episode extends an earlier moment we may see him as trapped in that moment; different aspects, different effects of that single error present themselves, surround him, and enslave him so that he cannot extricate himself until they have worked their own destruction with help from Una and Arthur. Thus the time he seems to move through in the second, fourth, fifth, and seventh cantos, and even in the eighth and ninth cantos, is largely an illusory passage, an interior duration disjoined from external quest time, from normal movement into the future. Against this decelerated tempo the normal rhythm of quest time is developed in those episodes which deal with Una's sylvan exile.

Sansfoy thus appears not simply as faithlessness in the abstract but as the hero's own infidelity. He and Duessa objectify a true version of the hero's *secret ill* and *hidden foe;* they have in effect been given life by Redcross in this poem. An evil condition of psyche, permitted or induced by him, now confronts him as an external enemy. The enemy is both a sign to the reader and a symptom offered to the hero's consciousness. In killing Sansfoy, Redcross not only conquers the enemy but also suppresses the symptom. Since the external foe symbolizes an interior evil, issues are posed which the hero himself could not possibly comprehend. Every encounter of this sort has the double aspect of progress and risk, although, as suggested above, the fact and nature of the progress is not evident until the tenth canto. Committing itself to a place and a shape, the evil can be faced, coped with, and overcome. But its external appearance is a disguise that allows it to continue working within the hero: spiritual and demonic forces of evil, dwellers in his own soul, manifest themselves in such a way as to deceive the knight into thinking that they are not demonic and not inhabitants of self, that he can control them by physical and chivalric deeds. Thus he is forced to face similar evils a second time and in more critical forms, as when he moves from overt to covert error, from the imitations of Una to Duessa, from Lucifera and the Sans- brothers to Orgoglio, from Sansjoy to Despair.

Given such a method of presentation, it is clear that the details of narrative and landscape contribute essential information about the quest. The ram simile, for example, tells us that the two knights are not in full control of their own powers, that they are reduced to bestial forms of consciousness motivated by sex and aggression, elements of animal *pride* (the knights fight for Duessa as rams "for the rule of the rich fleeced flocke"), that Redcross is more like his foe than he thinks, and that he is fighting for Duessa or false faith or divided being even before he is aware of it. Spenser also shows us that even though suppressing the symptom involves self-deception, it is necessary, the lesser of two evils, at this stage of Redcross's adventure. Had he the full knowledge of his faithlessness he might well be reduced to despair. Sansfoy himself seems more knowledgeable about this than Redcross and, as befits an embodied symptom, he offers information which, so far as we know, fails to register on the hero:

> Curse on that Crosse (quoth then the *Sarazin*)
>   That keepes thy body from the bitter fit;
>   Dead long ygoe I wote thou haddest bin,
>   Had not that charme from thee forwarned it:
>   But yet I warne thee now assured sitt,
>   And hide thy head. Therewith upon his crest
>   With rigour so outrageous he smitt,
>   That a large share it hewd out of the rest,
> And glauncing downe his shield, from blame him fairely blest.

> Who thereat wondrous wroth, the sleeping spark
>   Of native vertue gan eftsoones revive,
>   And at his haughtie helmet making mark,
>   So hugely stroke, that it the steele did rive,
>   And cleft his head. He tumbling downe alive,
>   With bloudy mouth his mother earth did kis,

> Greeting his grave: his grudging ghost did strive
> With the fraile flesh; at last it flitted is,
> Whither the soules do fly of men, that live amis.
>
> *(ii.18–19)*

The language describing Sansfoy's death anticipates the pathology of despair which plays so large a part in later episodes; it reveals Sansfoy's essential self-hatred, his suicidal eagerness for death. His reference to the cross reminds us that the hero's defection is not simply infidelity to the damsel and her quest but to the whole Christian context and community. As the Despair episode later shows, it is well that *Redcross* is not now reminded of all this; Despair also offers to "bless" the hero from blame after inducing a most bitter fit. Thus the Saracen's proper allegorical title would seem to be not merely *Faithlessness* but *Consciousness of Faithlessness*; he threatens to disclose to the hero the extent to which Redcross himself has unwittingly become infidel to the very source of his life. Ignorance of anything but his romance conditions is at this point the hero's salvation. False faith is better than no faith as a motive for survival. As an embodied mode of consciousness, Sansfoy represents an element of the hero's psyche which threatens him with immediate, perhaps total, loss of control and joy (Sansloy and Sansjoy). By some instinct of survival this mode of consciousness has been projected outward so that it can be encountered *as* an enemy and suppressed. It is only because of this threat that "the sleeping spark / Of native vertue gan eftsoones revive," native virtue here being sheer animal force, the blind courage needed to stay alive.

The difference between what the hero sees and what interpretation elicits is an important aspect of the poem. Here the difference is great, which suggests how far the hero must go, how much he has yet to learn; so much is concealed from him that it is better for him to remain innocent and let the evil he has unloosed run its course. As the poem proceeds, however, the indications of allegorical meaning will become clearer. Lucifera, Orgoglio, Despair, the House of Holiness, the dragon— their symbolic connections are drawn by the poet with increasing explicitness and precision. Though the reader is always asked to interpret, the cause becomes less the obscurity and more the complexity of the particular episode.

III

In the sequence from dream Una through apparition Una to Duessa, we are shown the gradual objectification of the Morphean dreamworld in which Redcross is placed by Archimago and from which he is not fully released until the hermit Contemplation reveals his identity. The hero's psyche is, in effect, unfolded into an environment. But one might carry this a step further: the poem continually reminds us *that* soul is being unfolded into an environment, and it does this partly through the agency of allegorical names and pointers. The hero's ambience is real but unrealistic, and the very nature of its externality is called into question since we see it being projected from his soul. Archimago's hypocrisy and Duessa's duplicity consist partly in their roles as internal powers masquerading as figures in the landscape. In Spenser's hands, the ancient techniques of allegory, along with the conventions of psychomachia and dream vision, serve to articulate the mode of experience which Bacon later discussed under the rubric of the Idols of the Cave:

> It is a false assertion that the sense of man is the measure of things. On the contrary, all perceptions, as well of the sense as of the mind, are according to the measure of the individual and not according to the measure of the universe. And the human understanding is like a false mirror, which, receiving rays irregularly, distorts and discolours the nature of things by mingling its own nature with it.
>
> The idols of the Cave are the idols of the individual man. For everyone (besides the errors common to human nature in general) has a cave or den of his own, which refracts and discolors the light of nature. . . . So that the spirit of man (according as it is meted out to different individuals) is in fact a thing variable and full of perturbation, and governed as it were by chance. Whence it was well observed by Heraclitus that men look for sciences in their own lesser worlds, and not in the greater or common world. (*Novum Organum* I.xli–xlii)

Heraclitus's observation was more accurately translated by Herrick in a couplet which might well serve as an epigraph to Book I:

> Here we are all, by day; By night w'are hurl'd
> By dreames, each one, into a sev'rall world.

For Bacon, the Idols of the Cave are natural defects which may be corrected or prevented by the true empirical interpretation of nature. For the Spenser of Book I, however, it is precisely *nature* and the *natural* which lead downward to error and must be overcome. His own image of the Idols will be assembled in greatest concentration in the Cave of Night.

The movement of Book I is from the lesser or several worlds of night to the greater or common world of day, from a world projected by a spirit variable and full of perturbation—a world which in its uniqueness isolates its maker—to the holiness, or *wholeness*, of the single shared world created by an Other and disclosed only after the veils of projection have been stripped away. The progress from projection to apocalypse (two forms of image making) may be glimpsed by conceiving the great difference between the pagan visions of Night and of the satyrs and the scriptural vision which emerges as a background to Orgoglio and occupies the foreground of the poem in cantos x and xi. We shall see that Spenser manipulates cantos iv and v to suggest that the House of Pride is a surface whose reality is the Cave of Night—as might be expected from Lucifera's descendence, or rather ascendence, from Pluto and Proserpina. But the cosmology and theology dramatized in the Cave of Night are both ante- and anti-Christian. Night's world is, as it were, an isolated pocket in the Christian universe, an atmosphere which is not translucent glass but rather a false mirror reflecting the vitiated will and understanding of its denizens.

The gradual imposition of this discolored cave on the natural universe may be traced in the changing character of night, which is at first part of the normal rhythm of life even if a potentially dangerous time:

> Now (sayd the Lady) draweth toward night,
> And well I wote, that of your later fight
> Ye all forwearied be: for what so strong,
> But wanting rest will also want of might?
> The Sunne that measures heaven all day long,
> At night doth bait his steedes the *Ocean* waves emong.

> Then with the Sunne take Sir, your timely rest,
> And with new day new worke at once begin:
> Untroubled night they say gives counsell best.

So Una; the problem with night is that Archimago can use the same arguments:

> Right well Sir knight ye have advised bin,
> (Quoth then that aged man;) the way to win
> Is wisely to advise: now day is spent;
> Therefore with me ye may take up your In
> For this same night. The knight was well content:
> So with that godly father to his home they went.
>
> *(i.32–33)*

The antipathy between day and night has increased by the beginning of the second canto:

Phoebus fiery carre
In hast was climbing up the Easterne hill,
Full envious that night so long his roome did fill.

(ii.1)

In the third canto there is still a distinction between the "eternall night" in which blind Corceca lived and the time of "deadly sleepe" during which Kirkrapine performs his "nightly stelths." But when Night appears on the scene in the ancient personification of a "dreary Dame, of darknesse Queene" who "in hell and heaven had power equally" and whose enemy is "Jove, that rules both night and day" but favors "the sonnes of Day," it is clear that the natural world of the opening cantos has become obscured. The pagan habit of anthropomorphic projection has confused landscape and inscape, the great and the little worlds. By this technique Spenser shows how the environment in which his hero moves has been transformed from that of natural creation to that of nightmare fantasy. Transferring their condition from self to world, blaming their helplessness and pain on a hostile divinity, the denizens of night have blinded themselves to the real source and nature of evil. The pagan confusion of human and superhuman powers is seen not only as a perverse extension of the human but also as a deceptive reduction of the supernatural.

Spenser traces the idols of the cave to two sources: the moral gravitation toward false faith associated with both the power of Archimago to deceive the senses and the perversions of revealed knowledge identified with Catholic abuses, and the cognitive gravitation toward partial or imperfect faith associated with Sylvanus, the satyrs, and the innocent nature of pagan consciousness. The difference and similarity between Archimago and Sylvanus is important, for the action which separates them seems to have affected the terms in which Spenser presents the basic issues of the quest. Corceca, Abessa, Lucifera (who connects Christian to pagan perversions), and the pagan world of night may be seen as regressive developments of the process initiated by Archimago. The rationale behind these episodes is clearly stated in the Epistle to the Ephesians, 4.17–22:

Henceforth walk not as other Gentiles walk, in the vanity of their mind,
Having the understanding darkened, being alienated from the life of God through the ignorance that is in them, because of the blindness of their heart:
Who being past feeling have given themselves over unto lasciviousness, to work all uncleanness with greediness.
But ye have not so learned Christ;

> If so be that ye have heard him, and have been taught by him, as the truth
> is in Jesus:
> That ye put off concerning the former conversation the old man, which is
> corrupt according to the deceitful lusts.

Archimago, himself an old man, seems to embody the sophistical image-making power of the unregenerate nature seizing control of the psyche. His name may be divided two ways: Archi-mage, the arch-magician, strongest of the strong, and Arch-imago, the arch-image, weakest of the weak. His necromancy and his age, the power and the insubstantiality of his images, derive from the mortality and finitude of fallen nature. But the implication here is that the false perception for which he is responsible is *un*natural; should man control these wayward powers in his soul, he may well achieve his quest.

The figure of Sylvanus, however, suggests something else. Half goat, half man, a deity of woods and gardens, he is truly a god of boundaries: mere nature emerging into human nature, or, conversely, human nature tending toward its lower origins—the satyrs, as Spenser points out, have "backward bent knees" (vi.11). Nelson's research into the iconography of the Wandering Wood of canto i has great relevance to Sylvanus:

> The fourth-century scholar Servius . . . explicates the word *silva* in *Aeneid*,
> I. 314 as equivalent to the Greek υλη, and like υλη double in meaning:
> forest, specifically a wild, uncultivated forest; and the chaos of elements
> out of which everything is created. Servius' note on the forest of the sixth
> book of the *Aeneid* . . . expands on this idea of the material congeries and
> gives it a moral meaning: "For by forests, darkness, and wilderness he . . .
> signifies that in which beastliness and passion dominate." . . . In Renais-
> sance times his definition of *silva* enters the dictionaries, and Cooper defines
> the word not only as "wood" but also as "store of mattier digested together."
> (Nelson, 159)

Spenser's treatment of the woodgod suggests a possible play on *Silva* and *vanus;* the idle, empty, or fruitless *silva*, the elemental bases of human nature, appear here in their primitive and archaic form. The episode seems related to the original Wandering Wood in which innocence is beguiled by the meandering chaos of experience, the variety of worldly activities and harmless pleasures which divert and then deceive the soul. The woodiness of the satyrs and nymphs echoes the woodiness of Fradubio and Fraelissa, while Sylvanus embodies merely the weaker side of Archimago.

The satyrs are forces of morning and spring, connected with the

round of nature yet exhibiting impulses of social harmony and the rudi-
ments of community and capable of a limited response to truth. They are
ambiguously related to the classical world of night, for it is unclear
to what extent they represent a return from or the origins of that world.
Their saving Una from Sansloy immediately follows the rescue of
Redcross from Pride by Una's Dwarf: warned about the true nature of
Lucifera's house, the hero

> early rose, and ere that dawning light
> Discovered had the world to heaven wyde,
> He by a privie Posterne tooke his flight,
> That of no envious eyes he mote be spyde . . .
>
> *(v.52)*

The satyrs are indeed creatures of "that dawning light" which discovers
earth to heaven and heaven to earth. Una's appearance makes them
"glad, as birdes of joyous Prime," "leaping like wanton kids in pleasant
Spring" (vi.13–14). Spenser's first image of them, before they hear
Una's outcries, stresses their self-contained remoteness, their archaic and
repetitive existence *in medio ligni:*

> A troupe of *Faunes* and *Satyres* far away
> Within the wood were dauncing in a rownd,
> Whiles old Sylvanus slept in shady arber sownd.
>
> *(vi.7)*

Sylvanus, wakened by the confusion which the discovery of truth has
caused, is himself confused by what he sees. He immediately loses the
real Una by projecting upon her "mirrhour rare" his own limited memories and feelings. His vain imaginings, heavy with the inertia of sleep
and dream, gravitate back toward the past, toward the earth, toward
frustrated or perverted love and death:

> towards old Sylvanus they her bring;
> Who with the noyse awaked, commeth out,
> To weet the cause, his weake steps governing,
> And aged limbs on Cypresse stadle stout,
> And with an yvie twyne his wast is girt about.

> Far off he wonders, what them makes so glad,
> Or *Bacchus* merry fruit they did invent,
> Or *Cybeles* franticke rites have made them mad;
> They drawing nigh, unto their God present
> That flowre of faith and beautie excellent.
> The God himselfe vewing that mirrhour rare,

Stood long amazd, and burnt in his intent;
His owne faire *Dryope* now he thinkes not faire,
And *Pholoe* fowle, when her to this he doth compaire.

The woodborne people fall before her flat,
And worship her as Goddesse of the wood;
And old Sylvanus selfe bethinkes not, what
To thinke of wight so faire, but gazing stood,
In doubt to deeme her borne of earthly brood;
Sometimes Dame *Venus* selfe he seemes to see,
But *Venus* never had so sober mood;
Sometimes *Diana* he her takes to bee,
But misseth bow, and shaftes, and buskins to her knee.

By vew of her he ginneth to revive
His ancient love, and dearest *Cyparisse*,
And calles to mind his pourtraiture alive,
How faire he was, and yet not faire to this,
And how he slew with glauncing dart amisse
A gentle Hynd, the which the lovely boy
Did love as life, above all worldly blisse;
For griefe whereof the lad n'ould after joy,
But pynd away in anguish and self-wild annoy.

The wooddy Nymphes, fair *Hamadryades*
Her to behold do thither runne apace,
And all the troupe of light-foot *Naiades*,
Flocke all about to see her lovely face:
But when they vewed have her heavenly grace,
They envie her in their malitious mind,
And fly away for feare of fowle disgrace:
But all the *Satyres* scorne their woody kind,
And henceforth nothing faire, but her on earth they find.

Glad of such lucke, the luckelesse lucky maid,
Did her content to please their feeble eyes,
And long time with that salvage people staid,
To gather breath in many miseries.
During which time her gentle wit she plyes,
To teach them truth, which worshipt her in vaine,
And made her th'Image of Idolatryes;
But when their bootlesse zeale she did restraine
From her own worship, they her Asse would worship fayn.

(vi.14–19)

The tree of death on which Sylvanus supports his aged limbs comes to
life as a mirror of inverted and destructive love (the god for the boy, the

boy for the beast), a love which destroys its own object through ignorance or uncontrol ("glauncing dart amisse") and ultimately destroys the
lover's self. Wine, orgiastic frenzy, and sex, a nymph, a whore, the goddess of love, the goddess of chastity and hunting (Lady of Beasts), a boy:
the presence of truth only sends Sylvanus "far off" into his own wandering wood. Parallels to the condition of Pride and Night emerge: truth
makes the satyrs, like Lucifera, dissatisfied with their own kind and nature yet incapable of reaching or holding on to the truth in *its* own nature. Just as Lucifera is caught between Pluto and Jove—the pagan justicer is as close as she can get to the Christian God ("she claymed for her
syre" Jove "or if that any else did Jove excell")—so the satyrs are caught
between Sylvanus and Una.

Because the Archimagian idol-making of Sylvanus represents the
satyrs' natural mode of ordering or responding to experience, they are
not equipped to respond to Christian truth except in a blindly intuitive
manner. That Una leaves them "on a day when Satyres all were gone, /
To do their service to *Sylvanus* old" (vi.33) is simply the narrative equivalent and consequence of their reducing her to "th'Image of Idolatryes."
The appearance of truth threatens to draw them out of the self-satisfied
round of recreative innocence and into a plaintive situation—threatens
them with pain, strife, restraint and discipline, alienation from nature.
Cyparisse's "anguish and selfe-wild annoy," the Nymphs' "feare of fowle
disgrace" and the satyrs' scorn of "their woody kind" find echoing resonance in the hero's situation: the threat of joylessness put down in Sansfoy,
reawakened in Sansjoy, and fulfilled in Despair. The resonance deepens
when we remember that Una's effect on the satyrs is a concentrated image of her effect on Redcross, who is also called from his recreative state
of clownish and chivalric innocence and exposed to spiritual ardors
which he cannot understand, on which he projects his own wandering
idols, and which in the seventh canto will reveal their plaintive side.

The satyrs are momentarily touched by a reality beyond them, but
under the domination of Sylvanus and the pleasure principle they gravitate back toward their ancient, natural service. Redcross, who responds
similarly to Una, must move forward. The similarity suggests that
Sylvanus and the satyrs embody one source of the hero's nature, behavior, and mode of consciousness. Forces which in the Archimagian context were defined from a Christian perspective as spiritual and perverse
appear in this pagan context as natural and intrinsic though imperfect.
The cooperation of these two sources of danger in the soul is suggested
by the figure of Idleness, who mediates aspects of Archimago with aspects of Sylvanus:

        sluggish *Idlenesse* the nourse of sin;
Upon a slouthfull Asse he chose to ryde,
Arayd in habit blacke, and amis thin,
Like to an holy Monck, the service to begin.

And in his hand his Portesse still he bare,
    That much was worne, but therein little red,
    For of devotion he had little care,
    Still drownd in sleepe, and most of his dayes ded;
    Scarse could he once uphold his heavie hed,
    To looken, whether it were night or day:
    May seeme the wayne was very evill led,
    When such an one had guiding of the way,
That knew not, whether right he went, or else astray.

From worldly cares himselfe he did esloyne,
    And greatly shunned manly exercise,
    From every worke he chalenged essoyne,
    For contemplation sake: yet otherwise,
    His life he led in lawlesse riotise . . .

                         (iv.18–20)

That the innocence and ignorance of pagan inertia blend so easily with profound spiritual evil, that the unnatural and the merely natural may lead to the same loss of life, point to the moral of the book of holiness: the limits of human power and of man's first nature (the Flesh) can be defined only through the trial imposed by the demands of a truth essentially alien to that nature, a truth which leads that nature to commit itself to error, to war against the Spirit, to find and become aware of its limits. The merely natural roots of the human psyche have been in effect *located*, sifted out through the activity of the first six cantos. We are given a new and clarified view of natural innocence, a stripped and diminished view of those vital energies which human society glorifies as heroic and erotic proofs of man's nobility. The way chivalric man evolves, through repression and sublimation, from the satyrs, is articulated in the figure of Satyrane, who will be discussed later. For now it is enough to remember that the satyrs are poised between the lawless lust of Sansloy, regressing from society to the woods, and the "greedy hardiment" of Satyrane, progressing from the woods to society.

    A "return to barbarism," as Ruskin put it, is necessary to set these powers free from the lawless lust of Redcross, which threatens to destroy them as Sansloy destroyed the lion. Allegorically considered, Una's journey through the woods may be seen as a process whereby truth mobilizes the hero's natural powers against his own self-destructive action. Since reviving the Satyrane within him will not prove sufficient against Orgoglio, she must appeal for help from Arthur, a power external to and transcendent of the hero. But in a peculiar sense, the return to barbarism does lead to a fresh beginning in canto vii: for the first time the hero becomes aware of his weakness; something of the great difference between the kind of enemy he thought he was fighting and the kind of enemy he is actually fighting filters into his consciousness. Furthermore, Una not only mobilizes the hero's natural powers, but her presence also evokes and revives the now archaic satyr forces; therefore she is partly responsible for making manifest this reduced image of man's elemental nature. Truth discovers in some outlandish and outmoded region of the psyche the living *silva vanus* whose effort to attain truth produces only idols of the cave. Disturbing the dancing satyrs from their perpetual round and their god from his sound and shady sleep, Una gives them a momentary glimpse of the Good News announced in other parts of the psyche. We see, of course, that Redcross is ignorant of his relation to these forces. We see also that the old Archimago's power is closely connected to the weakness of the old Sylvanus. Sylvanus, like Redcross, is involved in a network of spiritual powers whose depth of evil exceeds his apprehension no less than does the true nature of the good.

We may gloss this by referring once more to the Pauline matrix of Book I, perhaps most generally to Romans 7.7—"I had not known sin but by the law," nor weakness and error but by the light of truth—together with its implicit corollary, "I had not known the law (truth) except by sin." Some verses from Ephesians 2.8–18 have direct bearing on the narrative drift of Book I:

> For by grace are ye saved through faith; and that not of yourselves; it is the gift of God:
> Not of works, lest any man should boast. . . .
> Wherefore remember, that ye being in time past Gentiles in the flesh . . . were without Christ, being . . . strangers from the covenants of promise, having no hope, and without God in the world:
> But now, in Christ Jesus, ye who sometime were far off are made nigh by the blood of Christ.
> For he . . . came and preached peace to you which were afar off, and to them that were nigh.

But of course the most important text contributing to Spenser's argument is the cited armor passage, Ephesians 6.11–17, the first two verses of which are immediately relevant:

Put on the whole armour of God, that ye may be able to stand against the wiles of the devil.

For we wrestle not against flesh and blood, but against principalities, against powers, against the rulers of the darkness of this world, against spiritual wickedness in high places.

Redcross assumed that he *was* wrestling against flesh and blood, however monstrous; though he was dressed in the armor of God from the beginning of the quest, though he may initially have been aware of its significance (a fact for which there is no real testimony), he seems quickly to forget that it is the evidence of things unseen. As the opening encounter with Error suggests, he pays little attention to allegorical meanings: he is aware only of an adventure and a monster, a chance to try his "new force" and give his greedy "hardiment" its head. When Una tries to dissuade him from provoking the monster, he replies, "Vertue gives her selfe light, through darknesse for to wade" (i.12), and she is no doubt aware that only experience will cure him of this attitude, for she reluctantly accedes to his wish. After his triumph she praises him in a statement which, though carefully balanced, ignores the allegorical for the romance implications of the incident:

> Well worthy be you of that Armorie,
> Wherein ye have great glory wonne this day,
> And proov'd your strength on a strong enimie,
> Your first adventure: many such I pray,
> And henceforth ever wish, that like succeed it may.
>
> *(i.27)*

Many such successes—and perhaps also many such trials to discern more clearly what the evil is and where it lies. The hero doubtless now views his accoutrements as literal pieces of armor, symbols not of divine assistance but of his own chivalric power.

IV

If this is a moral failure, however, it is attenuated by the very character of Spenser's fiction. For the first nine cantos are couched in the idiom of romance—to kill a dragon and marry a princess—and there is no reason for the hero, who is unaware of the allegory, to take his adventure in more than its literal sense. Yet this is precisely his problem, since the appeal on these grounds is to the hero as *hero*, to his own glory and self-concern, his greedy hardiment. He cannot be expected to penetrate be-

yond this idiom, though its vision is limited to the goal of earthly fulfillment. His earthly hope is disclosed as a kind of pride, for hope is a true
virtue only in its theological form—only as a hope of something beyond
this life. Thus his first knowledge and first nature are not enough. It will
require new knowledge, new faith, to make the literal surface of Faerie
translucent, and the gradual increase of symbolic radiance (or darkness)
will measure the hero's painful progress from a remote figure of romance to the saint whose quest becomes a pattern for Everyman.

The technique by which Spenser irradiates the Faerie landscape derives from, or exemplifies, characteristic Reformation attitudes. The
Catholic abuses suggested in the early cantos are traced back and reduced
to an archaic pagan sensibility which projects anthropomorphic idols as
if it never received the Word. The historical failure represented as the
Church of the Middle Ages is seen as a betrayal of the original Gospel
experience and as a regression to the inherent tendency of the *silva
vanus*, the Flesh, to resist enlightenment. Spenser's and Bacon's Idols
were anticipated by Calvin:

> Even when . . . forced to the contemplation of God . . . and . . . led to
> form some impressions of Deity, we immediately fly off to carnal dreams
> and depraved fictions, and so by our vanity corrupt heavenly truth. This far,
> indeed, we differ from each other, in that every one appropriates to himself
> some peculiar error; but we are all alike in this, that we substitute monstrous
> fictions for the one living and true God—a disease not confined to obtuse and
> vulgar minds, but affecting the noblest, and those who, in other respects, are
> singularly acute. . . . Every individual mind being a kind of labyrinth, it is
> not wonderful . . . that almost every man has had his own god. To the
> darkness of ignorance have been added presumption and wantonness, and
> hence there is scarcely an individual to be found without some idol or phan-
> tom as a substitute for Deity. Like water gushing forth from a large and
> copious spring, immense crowds of gods have issued from the human mind,
> every man giving himself full licence, and devising some peculiar form of
> divinity, to meet his own views. . . . never did any mortal devise a scheme
> by which religion was not foully corrupted.[5]

Moving through a series of traditional schemes, both medieval and
pagan, Spenser strips away the merely human increments and returns in
the second half of Book I directly to scripture and that original Gospel
experience. This return is conveniently exemplified in the scriptural al-

---

[5] *Institutes of the Christian Religion,* trans. Henry Beveridge (London: James Clarke,
1953), I.v.11–12, 1:59–60.

lusions which frame the Orgoglio incident. A change in symbolic reference occurs which is in effect a turn from projection to apocalypse, from enemies of flesh and blood to spiritual wickedness in high places.

The monster on which Orgoglio places Duessa is usually referred to by Spenser as a beast, never as a dragon. At vii.17, however, he compares it to the Hydra, "that renowmed Snake"; the description of its tail (vii.18, compare the dragon in Rev. 12.4) and of Duessa on its back connect the dragon-lady motif of Book I to the seven-headed beast and scarlet whore of Revelation 17—the whore drunk with the blood of saints and martyrs on Orgoglio's altar (vii.16–18, viii.6, 12–17, 36). In Revelation 13.1–4, "the dragon gave . . . his power, and his seat, and great authority" to such a beast; "all the world wondered after the beast" and "worshipped the dragon which gave power unto the beast." In early Christian theology this bestial antichrist is a kind of dragon substitute whose appearance signifies a penultimate attempt on the world by the forces of evil which control the cities of earth. In him the enemies of Christ and God reach their maximum power, touching off a series of cataclysms (hence Orgoglio's derivation from an earthquake) which presage the end of time and precede the final glory of the Son (Rev. 13–20). When the reign of the beast is ended, the dragon, "that old Serpent, which is the Devil, and Satan," is attached, bound for a thousand years, "loosed a little season" for a final self-exposure, and cast into the lake of fire.

From the standpont of traditional iconography, Orgoglio's symbolic connections are clearer to us than Lucifera's. Though Lucifera's Vices are perfectly self-explanatory in the context from which they derive— the popular literary, emblematic, and homiletic traditions—the context does not explain Spenser's particular use of them in Book I. Their relation to the hero, the Cave of Night, and the satyrs demands an exploration which cannot be undertaken at this point, though one peculiarity might be noted in passing: Spenser presents the patently medieval allegory of Pride and the Vices as an analogue or consequence of the pagan world of Night; Lucifera provides a turning point from an atmosphere predominantly Christian or Catholic to one predominantly classical. The Vices, the cave, and the satyrs all focus on the effects and causes of evil *in human nature;* the pagan vision of gods and cosmic disorder in canto v is not, as we have seen, a view of the real world at all but a macrocosmic projection of human disorder.

The difference between the vices and Orgoglio's mystical companions is that between "flesh and blood" and "the rulers of the darkness of this

world." Unlike the Vices, the whore and the beast are in themselves
complex mystical figures whose meanings are generated by the apocalyptic environment to which they belong. The vision of universal history,
the growth and cataclysmic violence of evil, the *krisis* in which the powers of darkness draw together under Satan, their show of force and imminent defeat—these suggestions are active and alive in the narrative
environment of Revelation which Spenser invokes in Book I. Revelation
is not yet directly admitted into the fiction, as it will be on the Hill of
Contemplation and in the dragon fight; the disclosure is gradual, and in
cantos vii and viii the apocalyptic world stands, so to speak, "behind" the
fictional characters Orgoglio and Duessa. As the immediate effect of the
action of the first six cantos, Orgoglio is still an enemy of flesh and
blood, an aspect of the hero's lower nature, his elemental forces broken
free from his control. But he is now joined by, he leads to, the cosmic
demonic and divine forces of the last six cantos. In suggesting more
clearly the source of Spenser's vision of evil, the beast and the whore
approach the causes of evil in the universe as well as in man. Locating us
at the intersection of Faerie and Revelation, Spenser replaces and indirectly criticizes the poem's previous cosmology—the classical apocalypse
of Night and its counterpart in the Dawn of the satyrs. Furthermore,
Lucifera's vices belong to a relatively humanistic tradition in that they
are man-made or cultural commonplaces, whereas the energy and truth
of apocalyptic symbols were traditionally ascribed to God's word: in cantos iv and v the poetic will produces its disclosure by juxtaposing two
man-made traditions, but in cantos vii and viii the poetry alludes to a
text which was always felt to be beyond the powers of human invention.
And as Faerie becomes translucent, as more of its meaning is supplied
from outside the poem by a biblical vision whose source is supposedly
divine, Redcross is made to confront the ultimate causes of good and evil
which had been hidden under romance and classical veils in the early
cantos.

Spenser's "return" to the Gospel experience and symbolism is actually
a unique reinterpretation, a new argument expressive of his own individual response, subordinate to the particular needs of his poetic fiction.
Like Milton after him, though less assertively, his stylistic emphasis is
less on Scripture itself than on what he has done with it. We might approach the first book in this light as a dialectic between hero and poet:
the knight, through weakness of will and misplaced self-confidence, permits the evil to grow and to dominate the poem; the poet illuminates the
growing evil, catches and controls it as image, through the widening

network of allusion, the delicate modulations of symbolic reference. What happens to the knight becomes clearer as well as more critical. It even seems that Redcross gets worse *in order to* make the evil luxuriate, tempt it to assert itself and so expose its true nature. The triumph of poetic vision lies not only in this exposure but also in the narrative skill whereby the poet has motivated the exposure, explained and justified its causes in the unfolding of a particular human experience. The poet has earned his right to interpret his image of evil in terms of St. John's cosmic vision. By dramatic logic, by the intricate depiction of psychological cause and effect, the sources of human error are developed and revealed.

V

The theological, historical, and actual references of Book I are framed within—though they press momentarily beyond—a patently make-believe world. These allegorical levels are in effect explained or validated by the coherence and persuasiveness of the poet's fiction. At the same time, the contact of Faerie and Revelation seems primarily a justification *of* fiction: what appeared at first to be a *counterfactual* world, a product not only of *the* imagination but of a particular poet's imagination—this is made clear in the proem to Book I—attains for a few cantos the universal and objective validity of revealed knowledge. Fiction is gradually stripped away as the poet's fable or argument converts the figures and episodes of romance into religious archetypes, but this fairy-tale atmosphere is, as we shall see, reestablished in the final cantos, and the Redcross Knight, who was St. George only for the purposes of this book, returns to Gloriana and to further adventures in Spenser's Faerie.

In their new context justifying the work of imagination, the archetypes of scriptural history are themselves justified. Yet this relation to poetry clearly provides a new basis of relevance for the Gospel experience. For the *truth* of the experience is sought less in its correspondence to reality and more in its coherence as myth, less in its historical and more in its imaginative dimension. A more traditional attitude—Dante's, for example—lays greater stress on the historical and cosmological axes along which individual experience locates itself:

> The Christian . . . aspires to dwell both in time and in eternity. He insists with all his might that God works in history, but he knows likewise that in the pilgrimage of his own soul the whole historical drama of salvation is recapitulated. . . . Transcendent reality reveals itself historically to the race and in parallel myth to the individual. Adam fell, and falls in us. God be-

came man but once, yet the Christ-child nestles in every heart touched by the Holy Spirit. . . . This belief in a double manifestation of the divine mind through identical history and myth has been the very core of Christianity.[6]

—or at least of Christianity through the middle ages.

If Spenser's belief in historical revelation was weakened by the world he saw around him so that he had to turn inward and re-create it to see it better, his response assumes a form totally different from Dante's. Dante's model of the universe begins, after all, with a poetic and ends with a scientific vision: his Hell is an acknowledged product of collective imagination—one reason Virgil is familiar with it is that he had a hand in making it. The mount of Purgatory, on which the inwardness and living privacy of the soul emerges, seems a more private creation in the sense of being a uniquely Dantesque idea, modeled no doubt upon the terraced hills of his actual environment; in Purgatory the pilgrim is more immediately involved as a unique person, the poet-citizen Dante, than in the other canticles. And here, as in *The Faerie Queene*, Book I, the poet's landscape becomes at its apex a scriptural place returning to the simplicity of Eden and early Gospel experience, a place dense with symbolic adumbrations of a reality transcending human thought. But where Spenser frames his apocalypse in Faerie, Dante pushes upward: when the blessed descend from the Rose to manifest themselves, the stage whose symbolic possibilities they actualize comprises the sphere of the actual universe. If these celestial spheres were originally devised by Greek astronomers and identified with physical reality through the influence of Aristotle, Dante and his contemporaries assigned them unequivocally to God and considered them among the redeemed phenomena. This movement from collective through personal myth to science, from the imaginary to the real, accords with all the other self- and man-transcending movements in the *Commedia:* from personal to universal destiny, from current events to universal history, from heroic self-assertion to childlike submission, from opaque to translucent images of personality, from image to seal and arrow to bow. Dante's illustrious vernacular justifies the private experience and interior vision by making it give way to that which is public, actual, and divine; his "double manifestation of the divine mind" thus fulfills the mythic in terms of the historical.

By contrast, Spenser's "archaic" language and vision begin with the

    [6] Lynn White, Jr., "Christian Myth and Christian History," *Journal of the History of Ideas* 3, no. 2 (April 1942): 153.

"antique rolles" of the Muse's "ever-lasting scryne" where the secrets of Faerie "lye hidden still" (I.Pr.2) and end in the new landscape of his own personal Faerie, an imaginary world which, by Book VI, surrounds and ravishes the poet. The antique rolls ("Faerie knights and fairest *Tanaquill*") are the public, and therefore objective, literary possibilities in whose forms the poet will unveil his still unarticulated epic. Thus the manifestation of the divine mind will be sought more in the imaginary than in the historical field; what is revealed historically to the race must be recast as individual myth if the poet is to believe that God works in history.

Spenser's vision makes no claims to being mystical or prophetic. The *Commedia* is presented as a mystical vision remembered and imitated in poetry. The Book of Revelation is prophetic—a vision now of the future stripping-away at the end of time. Its radical metaphors depend on the belief in historical fulfillment and in God's double manifestation; Dante, however, telescopes both myth and history, figure and reality, within his visionary poem. In Spenser's work there are many figures but few realities within Faerie. His emphasis is always on the narrative complication into which the figures enter; the final meaning of such figures as Lucifera's vices and Celia's virtues depends on their role in the imaginary experience.

The same tendency is revealed in the adventure of Redcross. There may indeed be references to the history of the Church in England, to the Tudor dynasty, to particular Christian doctrines, and so forth, but these are all secondary to the individual hero's experience. When Una, isolated from Redcross, moves from the lion to the satyrs to Satyrane to Arthur, we may see in this a survey of the evolution of truth in history as the rejected faith mobilizes defenders, each more adequate than the one replaced. But the primary reference would seem to be that of psychic allegory: social environment and cultural institutions are best seen as effects and externalizations of changing states of soul. Like the worlds of Lucifera and Night, the false and true forms of religion may be viewed as structures within the soul productive of structures in the environment. Insofar as the social and historical developments suggested in Book I are clarified by the hero's lonely quest, the problem of Redcross is the problem of the poem: if man is the model and measure of the universe, if soul is more real than society, if historical time is a derivative function of psychic time, how can men—poets as well as heroes—find or impose the limits on the self necessary to reaffirm the validity and otherness of a divinely ordered environment? How can they restore imagination to theocentric belief without sacrificing the powers newly won for and asserted of the mind in the general reaction to medieval culture?

As we have seen, Spenser's general way of handling this problem is to move from projection to apocalypse, from the expansion of self to the revelation of others, from flesh and blood to spiritual wickedness in high places, from the hero's reliance on the "new force" of chivalry to his reliance on the new force of Christ's sacrifice. Thinking himself an Elfin justicer, the hero isolates himself from the common world, ventures into a fairyland largely of his own making, and undergoes experiences which expose the narcissism and insufficiency of the romance idiom in its literal character. He must learn what we already know, that it is the symbolic rather than the literal dimension which justifies the idiom. This means of course that literal chivalry has a useful function, and Spenser can give it a validity which Ariosto, for example, could not, a validity which Malory was at pains to question. What the hero does literally *for* himself he does symbolically *to* himself, both for the edification of the reader and the redemption of Una's parents. He cannot learn he is a British saint with a historical mission until he has been lured by hope of earthly glory to play Knights and Ladies, deceived by his Elfin view of self to think his prowess sufficient and the quest exclusive. Only through this lure, which calls forth all his powers and spurs him to a heroic activism, will he reach—and therefore experience—his limits and come to know his helplessness before cosmic evil, his worthlessness before God:

> No moral achievement can ever give any claim upon God, and no ascending of the ladder of the chain of being can ever unite man with God and make him into God. The very notion of the deification of humanity was to Calvin blasphemous. Man, who is no clod or clay or lump—he has, in fact, all the excellent qualities which the humanists attributed to him—is nevertheless dust and ashes before God the All-High and the All-Holy. Not by achievement but by trust is man saved, and morality itself is only the by-product of religion, the behaviour springing from gratitude to God for his unspeakable gifts.[7]

This characterization of Reformation thought must be altered to apply to Book I: trust *through* achievement (or the lack of it), religion *through* morality (or its failure), the Reformation not as a denial but as a fulfill-ment and stabilization of earlier humanism.

---

[7] Roland Bainton, "Man, God and the Church in the Age of the Renaissance," in *The Renaissance, Six Essays*, ed. Wallace Ferguson (New York: Harper & Row, 1962), 96.

VI

The various cities mentioned in Book I will suggest how Spenser has mapped out the termini of these relations. When Contemplation shows the revived hero the vision of New Jerusalem with its community of saints and angels,

> Till now, said then the knight, I weened well,
>   That great *Cleopolis*, where I have beene,
>   In which that fairest *Faerie Queene* doth dwell,
>   The fairest Citie was, that might be seene;
>   And that bright towre all built of christall cleene,
>   *Panthea*, seemd the brightest thing, that was:
>   But now by proofe all otherwise I weene;
>   For this great Citie that does far surpas,
> And this bright Angels towre quite dims that towre of glas.
>
> Most trew, then said the holy aged man;
>   Yet is *Cleopolis* for earthly frame,
>   The fairest peece, that eye beholden can:
>   And well beseemes all knights of noble name,
>   That covet in th'immortall booke of fame
>   To be eternized, that same to haunt,
>   And doen their service to that soveraigne Dame,
>   That glorie does to them for guerdon graunt:
> For she is heavenly borne, and heaven may justly vaunt.
>
> (*x.58–59*)

Glorytown, the capital of Faerie, is a prefiguration of the New Jerusalem. With its tower, Panthea, it represents the fragile but radiant world where human skill and imagination find their ideal image. Unlike the opaque pantheon of Night and the glittering house of Pride, this structure is both bright and transparent, allowing communication with a source of light beyond itself, though its own brightness first attracts the eye. Cleopolis is the center of a timeless domain, secluded from history, the questing place of the first nine cantos; it is necessary to the goal, but dangerous if misconstrued as a goal in itself. Outside Faerie with its Cleopolis is England with its London, the time-bound community represented in Faerie by questing Britons.

The proem to Book II suggests that Faerie and England may each be construed as a veil half-concealing the other, while Book I suggests that both are veils half-concealing the New Jerusalem. The idea of *half-*concealment is crucial, for without the veils there may be nothing to reveal, or conversely if there is transcendent brightness it may be too close and too blinding. Spenser avails himself of an insight which was first and perhaps most completely developed in Plato's dialectic, especially in the transition from the *Symposium* through the *Republic* to the *Phaedrus:* the Beautiful is an instrumental Form which arouses the soul's desire and leads it beyond itself toward the less intrinsically appealing Forms of Wisdom, Temperance, and Justice (*Phaedrus*, 250b ff.). An object which leads the desiring soul to relax in its attainment is merely pleasurable, not beautiful—an object of *himeros*, not of *eros*. It becomes beautiful when, after arousing the soul to desire it, it turns and points beyond itself—when, that is, it keeps the soul in motion. As Socrates phrased it in the definition which concludes the *Greater Hippias*, "whatever is beautiful is difficult."

Insofar as one of the major reactions of the Reformation both to Renaissance Neoplatonism and to medieval theology was to increase the distance between man and God, between consciousness and Being, this Platonic rationale assumes great importance for Spenser and his contemporaries. The veils need greater attractive power; they also need greater expressive power; it is therefore more important stylistically to assert *that* they are veils. Indeed the Platonic lure may come close to assuming the status of a neo-Kantian symbolic form in which any vision, however transcendent, is reduced to a veil or symbol *because* it presents itself to consciousness. This symbolic status affects even the New Jerusalem, as Spenser describes Redcross's view of that "goodly Citie"

> Whose wals and towres were builded high and strong
> Of perle and precious stone, that earthly tong
> Cannot describe, nor wit of man can tell;
> Too high a ditty for my simple song;
> The Citie of the great king hight it well,
> Wherein eternall peace and happiness doth dwell.

> As he thereon stood gazing, he might see
> The blessed Angels to and fro descend
> From highest heaven, in gladsome companee,
> And with great joy into that Citie wend,
> As commonly as frend does with his frend.
> Whereat he wondred much, and gan enquere,
> What stately building durst so high extend
> Her loftie towres unto the starry sphere,
> And what unknowen nation there empeopled were.

> *(x.55–56)*

The image identifies holiness with wholeness, that is, with the oneness of shared life, of communion and community. Having traveled so long by himself, Redcross now begins to join and to be joined by real others; the sacramental atmosphere of the dragon fight will further prepare him for union and Una, while the image of Eden will suggest the character of wholeness.

Spenser's Eden is not a garden but a city or kingdom. It lies between the first garden and the New Jerusalem, and also between imaginary Cleopolis and historical England. It is not the literal Eden, for that is a memory, an earthly paradise, a recreative nursery irrevocably behind us, luring us backward and inward. Eden as symbolic community may indicate the fallen society as well as the place from which man is permanently exiled, but Spenser's treatment of the twelfth canto suggests an imaginative substitute, a poetic haven in Faerie which yet displays the tokens of sin and history, the knowledge of exile, and the peregrine urge to keep moving toward *una vera città*. Eden is furthermore the culminating image of psychic allegory, for its three main classes—the rulers, the guardians, and the "raskall many" (xii.5–12)—recall the ideal Platonic state, which is an enlarged and externalized version of the soul. In its theological context it also suggests the mystical community of St. Paul, "the whole body fitly joined together and compacted by that which every joint supplieth, according to the effectual working in the measure of every part, [which] maketh increase of the body unto the edifying of itself in love" (Eph. 4.16). Such a harmony, according to Anglican doctrine, was partly effected by baptism and communion, which

> were a means of drawing Christian people together in benevolence and hearty friendship and of uniting believers with Christ and his grace.
>
> Such grace helps to create or deepen the bond of unity between believers, for membership is not merely membership of Christ but membership with others in Christ. This thought appears several times in Hooker's consideration of the relationship between Christ, the believer, and the sacraments. In the Church there must be mutual fellowship and society, and the members are said in one of the "Private Prayers" of the reign of Queen Elizabeth to be "glued and fashioned together with mutual charity" and "knit with the knot of mutual love." This communion or fellowship includes the Church above and below, and the faith of one, though feeble, is increased by that of others, for the grace and gifts of the Holy Ghost are vouchsafed and given unto every member not so much for their own "particular profit and commodity" as for the general profit and benefit of the whole congregation and Church.[8]

---

[8] H. F. Woodhouse, *The Doctrine of the Church in Anglican Theology, 1547–1603* (London: S.P.C.K., 1954), 37.

What the allegory of Book I suggests about Eden is that Redcross joins this community when it has been structured into his soul, for it seems to represent at once the interior harmony of the redeemed hero and the external society he has saved. In this condition of holiness or wholeness, the soul's diverse powers—wisdom, courage, and desire—are ordered into a harmonious unity. But it is a second oneness, not the first: the order of a redeemed soul and city rather than that of a pagan or prelapsarian garden. It is the spiritual integrity embodied in Una, the gift whose possession was at first rejected but is finally assured. Here the soul or microcosm is not only the model of the city or macrocosm; it is assimilated and justified by membership.

The Faerie Queene, Book III

A General Description

THE WORLD OF Book III is limited in a number of ways. The experience of the important characters is primarily one of *inner* preparation, and the events of the book for the most part affect essentially isolated or separated creatures. Relations seem mainly to be those which precede involvement with others at the personal level. The problems of Book III are generic and archetypal—impersonal rather than personal—in that they arise from one's being a masculine or feminine creature rather than a unique individual like Arthur or Britomart. The feminine fears and fantasies which contribute to the power of Busirane are caused not by the particular responses of Amoret or Britomart but by "wavering *wemens* wit" in general. They are the products of tendencies inherent in the female psyche and encouraged by the existing climate of custom, institutions, traditions, and literature. And finally, the problems posed by the opposition of chastity and eros in III seem to be those which can be resolved by happy *sexual* union: chastity has little to do with insight and second sight, with knowledge and consideration of the other person (the beloved) as a second self. Chastity no less than eros aims at the moment of embrace exemplified in the rejected first ending of Book III by the hermaphroditic reunion of Amoret and Scudamour, exemplified also by the reconciliation of Cupid and Psyche (male desire and the feminine soul) in the Garden of Adonis "after long troubles and unmeet upbrayes."

The limited character of this reconciliation is suggested in the child of

Cupid and Psyche, Pleasure, "that doth both gods and men aggrate" by bringing an end to pain. The rewards of chastity for Amoret are the intensity of her relief and the *streightness* of her fusion with Scudamour, who ran to her

> with hasty egernesse,
> Like as a Deare, that greedily embayes
> In the coole soile, after long thirstinesse,
> Which he in chace endured hath, now nigh breathlesse.
>
> Lightly he clipt her twixt his arms twaine,
> And streightly did embrace her body bright,
> Her body, late the prison of sad paine,
> Now the sweet lodge of love and deare delight:
> But she faire Lady overcommen quight
> Of huge affection, did in pleasure melt,
> And in sweete ravishment pourd out her spright.
> No word they spake, nor earthly thing they felt,
> But like two senceles stocks in long embracement dwelt.
>
> *(III.xii.44–45 rej.)*

The next stanza, which compares them to a *marble statue* of the Hermaphrodite, suggests both their desire to freeze eternally into that posture and their urge to melt into unconsciousness. As the goal of a human lover this happy ending is incomplete and illusory, and it is an example of too violent an oscillation: completely separated from and alien to each other in the Busirane experience, they close as if the otherness separating them could be entirely dissolved by the mere act of *physical* embrace. Something like this is implied by the imagery with which Spenser concludes *An Hymn in Honour of Love*. These are Cupid's gifts to chaste and assured lovers:

> There thou them placest in a Paradize
> Of all delight, and joyous happie rest,
> Where they doe feede on Nectar heavenly wize,
> With *Hercules* and *Hebe*, and the rest
> Of *Venus* dearlings, through her bountie blest,
> And lie like Gods in yvorie beds arayd,
> With rose and lillies over them displayed.
>
> *(280–86)*

But the limited nature of this goal is further stressed when the happy ending of which the stanza is part is forcibly imposed as an artificial conclusion, a false reconciliation following hot on what seems an irreconcilable list of lover's pains:

The gnawing envie, the hart-fretting feare,
The vaine surmizes, the distrustfull showes,
The false reports that flying tales doe beare,
The doubts, the daungers, the delayes, the woes,
The fayned friends, the unassured foes,
With thousands more then any tongue can tell,
Doe make a lovers life a wretches hell.

Yet is there one more cursed than they all,
That cancker worme, that monster Gelosie,
Which eates the hart, and feedes upon the gall,
Turning all loves delight to miserie,
Through feare of loosing his felicitie.
Ah Gods, that ever ye that monster placed
In gentle love, that all his joyes defaced.

By these, O Love, thou doest thy entrance make,
Unto thy heaven, and doest the more endeere,
Thy pleasures unto those which them partake . . .
(259–75)

This *hate*, which in Book III is depicted in the experiences of Malbecco, Scudamour, and Busirane, impels the unbalanced psyche too violently in the opposite direction; the triumph of Love over his older half-brother may be too complete unless tempered by Concord.

The general character of Book III is illuminated by C. S. Lewis's insight that Spenser was his predecessor in sketching the history and demise of courtly love. In III, as throughout his poetry, Spenser consciously and conspicuously revises not only a literary and cultural view of love but also a literary and cultural view of woman. The problem he poses for both Britomart and himself is a modified version of the problem confronted by Chaucer's Wife of Bath—how to redress the balance in a culture whose images of woman and love, whose institutions affecting women and love, were products of the male imagination:

Here have I cause, in men just blame to find,
That in their proper prayse too partiall bee,
And not indifferent to woman kind . . .
(III.ii.1)

Where is the Antique glory now become,
That whilome wont in women to appear?
Where be the brave atchievements doen by some?
(III.iv.1)

In his epic as in his minor poetry Spenser sets himself the task of realizing the otherness and complex reality of woman by seeing life from the feminine point of view. The traditional vision of relationship must be transformed into a new and personal vision, and it is entirely in accord with his own conceptions of poetry and love that he *displays* the act of revision as part of the content of his poem.

The world of Book III is composed of a number of fragmented, partial, or elemental landscapes which are not only places in Faerie but also *topoi* of the collective cultural imagination. As this world reveals only hostile or defective forms of love which must be faced and corrected by Britomart in her search for the real Artegal who will fulfill her visionary (and thus too perfect) image, so the literary traditions available to Spenser offer no forms adequate or suitable to the vision he wishes to actualize in poetry. In redressing the balance, however, he does not simply idealize woman or the feminine viewpoint, for this would amount to the kind of withdrawal from reality which he frequently criticizes. Rather he recognizes that feminine nature has its own inherent limits and tensions, and he therefore acknowledges this by representing feminine defects and excesses. In the *Amoretti*, for example, he demands active cooperation from his beloved, yet this cooperation is slow in coming. If he shows during the sonnet sequence that he stands in need of improvement and that his lady's reluctance is a means to improvement, he also shows that he cannot do all the work by himself. It is the lady's fault as well as his that plaints, prayers, and vows reverberate throughout the first fifty-seven sonnets, and the implication is that her reluctance, protracted beyond reason, comes to be perverse and harmful. The lady must be a lover as well as a beloved. If the poet is to improve his own attitudes and images, she must relent, must share herself, must stamp her true impression on his soul.

The relations and experiences of Book III are those which belong to an early precourtship phase. During this period elemental states and figures emerge from a matrix or chaos and move through early confusion toward separation into simple opposites. In this phase eros naturally manifests itself as hate, that is, as martial or erotic aggression—warfare and hostility, the struggle to possess and devour or to break free from possession, the urge to keep one's elemental condition pure and not to mingle or merge with one's opposites except on one's own terms. The natural tendency of the elemental state or figure is toward a one-sided structure of response which obscures the character of self and world. In this phase it is difficult to acknowledge the right of others to be different and equal: opposites are not conceived as genuine *others* standing over against the self but as objects which exist to threaten or gratify the self. The elemental or primitive consciousness substitutes an image—based on need and desire—for the real object and tries then to possess or destroy that object, or to assimilate it by negating its otherness and reducing it to the desired image. Desire may be indiscriminately aroused by and directed toward any number of objects as well as toward different kinds of objects. The result is often a primitive or regressive confusion of drives and functions distinct in more developed stages of experience.

Spenser's frequent references to the antiquity of his story serve to locate it in the qualitatively "early" or archaic world. Antiquity is not merely "a long time ago," not merely a way of defining the imaginary and/or ideal character of the story, but also a particular primitive phase of psychocultural experience. It is a fictional *then* which is—or ought to be—different from the *now* of poet and reader, even though that "antique" experience may represent critical aspects of current or universal human experience. The passages on the antique glory of women quoted above were presented somewhat misleadingly out of context, for the contexts suggest that limited opportunities for expression were *then* available to women. During the early phase depicted in III, when eros was manifested primarily as hostility, women were forced to express themselves on alien grounds and to compete with men in physical warfare:

> Here have I cause, in men just blame to find,
>   That in their proper prayse too partiall bee,
>   And not indifferent to woman kind,
>   To whom no share in armes and chevalrie
>   They do impart, ne maken memorie
>   Of their brave gestes and prowesse martiall;
>   Scarse do they spare to one or two or three,
>   Rowme in their writs; yet the same writing small
> Does all their deeds deface, and dims their glories all.
>
> But by record of antique times I find,
>   That women wont in warres to beare most sway,
>   And to all great exploits them selves inclind:
>   Of which they still the girlond bore away,
>   Till envious Men fearing their rules decay,
>   Gan coyne streight lawes to curb their liberty;
>   Yet sith they warlike armes have layd away,
>   They have exceld in artes and pollicy,
> That now we foolish men that prayse gin eke t'envy.

>Of warlike puissaunce in ages spent,
>   Be thou faire *Britomart*, whose prayse I write,
>   But of all wisedome be thou precedent,
>   O soveraigne Queene, whose prayse I would endite . . .
>   *(ii.1–3)*

As we shall see more fully later, Britomart is not simply the Ideal Woman; she embodies and is constrained by a certain level of psycho-cultural organization. Her virtue is not the only virtue women need: it is fundamental not merely because it is essential, but also because it is rudimentary. Embattled woman, threatened from within and from the outside, needs this militant virtue if she as well as her lover is to be ful-filled. But chastity in the service of love—the chastity of Britomart or Florimell—is presented as an intuitive rather than an acquired habit; the dangers and frustrations which women face in early experience may intensify this self-protective response until it becomes irrational, ob-sessive, and even destructive. By the end of III.iv the problems con-fronting women have become more oppressive, and the stanzas which introduce this canto present feminine warfare in a more strident manner:

>Where is the Antique glory now become,
>   That whilome wont in women to appeare?
>   Where be the brave atchievements doen by some?
>   Where be the battels, where the shield and speare,
>   And all the conquests, which them high did reare,
>   That matter made for famous Poets verse,
>   And boastfull men so oft abasht to heare?
>   Bene they all dead, and laid in dolefull herse?
>Or doen they onely sleepe, and shall againe reverse?
>
>If they be dead, then woe is me therefore:
>   But if they sleepe, O let them soone awake:
>   For all too long I burne with envy sore,
>   To heare the warlike feates, which *Homere* spake
>   Of bold *Penthesilee*, which made a lake
>   Of *Greekish* bloud so oft in *Troian* plaine;
>   But when I read, how stout *Debora* strake
>   Proud *Sisera*, and how *Camill'* hath slaine
>The huge *Orsilochus*, I swell with great disdaine,
>
>Yet these, and all that else had puissaunce,
>   Cannot with noble *Britomart* compare,
>   Aswell for glory of great valiaunce,
>   As for pure chastitie and vertue rare,

> That all her goodly deeds do well declare.
> Well worthy stock, from which the branches sprong,
> That in late yeares so faire a blossome bare,
> As thee, O Queene, the matter of my song,
> Whose lignage from this Lady I derive along.
>
> *(iv.1–3)*

The comically exaggerated gestures of the poet, culminating in "I swell with great disdaine," help define the relation between then and now: thinking and reading about violent man-killers of old, he passionately identifies himself with their cause—much like a youthful reader of Classic Comics caught up in an outmoded and outlandish world and taking sides with his stereotyped heroines. These heroines are immediately passed by in his own revised version, though Britomart is still an example of that early type. Insofar as the *bold* and *stout* warriors represent chastity it is a chastity which has nothing to do with love and everything to do with war—they are at once too masculine in behavior and too misanthropic in feeling. Within the context of Britomart's experience so excessive a response may be caused by the martial and erotic aggression of men or simply by the natural force of her own passion aroused by the image of Artegal. This response appears as an incipient threat during the early cantos of III, but it does not become serious until Book V, when it is embodied in its degenerate form as Radegund. Pointedly associated with Artemis and Belphoebe (see V.v.2–3 and compare II.iii.26–27), Radegund displays the instinctive Belphoeban chastity exacerbated by frustration (V.iv.29 ff.) until it has become pathological. Already in Book III Spenser shows how the Perils of Florimell convert her chaste love of Marinell to irrational fear, a fear which also affects Amoret in Busirane's house, and in the proem to Book IV he refers this problem to his virgin Queen:

> To her I sing of love, that loveth best,
> And best is lov'd of all alive I weene:
> To her this song most fitly is addrest,
> The Queene of love, and Prince of peace from heaven blest.
>
> Which that she may the better deigne to heare,
> Do thou dred infant, *Venus* dearling dove,
> From her high spirit chase imperious feare,
> And use of awfull Majestie remove:
> In sted thereof with drops of melting love,
> Deawd with ambrosiall kisses, by thee gotten

From thy sweete smyling mother from above,
Sprinckle her heart, and haughtie courage soften,
That she may hearke to love, and reade this lesson often.

(IV.Pr.4–5)

The phrasing allows us to read the "use of awfull Majestie" as a defense against love, a defense perhaps prompted by an imperious fear (and not only by the empress's fear). Though masked in the ceremonial rhetoric demanded by this occasion of address, the context of events preceding the proem in III and following that in IV vaguely associates this fear with chastity as a fixation. Yet as a contemporary figure—"of all wisedome . . . precedent" and not merely "of warlike puissaunce in ages spent"—Elizabeth is exhorted to embody a more evolved and flexible form of psychic organization, to move beyond the "early" structure of habits dominated by chastity toward the complex sophisticated structure dominated by wisdom.

I shall devote the remainder of this essay to a discussion of three leading characteristics displayed by eros in early or primitive psychocultural experience: (1) It is a tyrannical and confusing force cutting across such normally distinct forms of affection as those between man and woman, parent and child, friend and friend. (2) It is a pain-giving force felt at first as hate and hostility. (3) It is a regressive force drawing creatures back toward the undifferentiated matrix from which they derive their origins and from which they struggle to emerge.

I

Normal relations come into focus only gradually and with difficulty. Thus although Book IV deals with new ("later") levels of organization, new kinds of relations of elements—those involved in personal and social situations—it is not until the opening stanzas of IV.ix that Spenser explicitly voices the sequence of changes with which the poem has been concerned since the beginning of III:

Hard is the doubt, and difficult to deeme,
    When all three kinds of love together meet,
    And doe dispart the hart with powre extreme,
    Whether shall weigh the balance down; to weet
    The deare affection unto kindred sweet,
    Or raging fire of love to woman kind,
    Or zeale of friends combynd with vertues meet.
    But of them all the band of vertuous mind
Me seemes the gentle hart should most assured bind.

> For naturall affection soone doth cesse,
>   And quenched is with *Cupids* greater flame;
>   But faithfull friendship doth them both suppresse,
>   And them with maystring discipline doth tame,
>   Through thoughts aspyring to eternall fame.

The elemental metaphor (the fire of sexual love quenching the love of kind) separates the first two forms of affection from true friendship, which transcends and redirects them and which depends on a more mature, more disciplined, ethical consciousness. A similar movement is implied in the porch of Concord (IV.x.32–33): Spenser does not *name* Concord until he has named and characterized Hate and Love. The two half-brothers visualize a more primitive, universal, and instinctive pattern of behavior, and they must manifest themselves before Concord can exercise her more strictly human and rational functions of control.

This confusion of drives and functions may be either primitive or regressive, as the following examples will demonstrate: The assault of the woman-eating monster on Florimell in cantos vii and viii comprises an unpleasant mixture of the urges to violate, to devour, and to destroy. Cymoent's excessive concern for her son Marinell, a concern which effactually cripples him, is more than pure parental affection: it is blurred by overtones of maternal narcissism ("Deare image of my self . . . that is, / The Wretched sonne of wretched mother borne," III.iv.36) and also by a vague sense that Cymoent sees in Marinell a surrogate for his father, "the famous *Dumarin*,"

> who on a day
> Finding the Nympth a sleepe in secret wheare,
>   As he by chaunce did wander that same way,
>   Was taken with her love, and by her closely lay.
>
> There he this knight of her begot, whom borne
>   She of his father *Marinell* did name,
>   And in a rocky cave as wight forlorne,
>   Long time she fostred up, till he became
>   A mightie man at armes, and mickle fame . . .
>
>   *(iv.19–20)*

A similarly blurred situation is hinted at in Spenser's treatment of Venus and her wanton boy Adonis (i.34 ff., vi.46 ff.) and in the Venus-Cupid relation which is the paradigm for that between Cymoent and Marinell (vi.50); Spenser's associating Cupid with Adonis (both lost at vi.28–29 and secure at vi.49) sharpens our sense that Venus's possessiveness is not clearly distinguishable into maternal and erotic affection. When

Britomart's nurse, Glauce, tries to ease her lovelorn charge she displays normal motherly behavior, yet it is comically qualified by our having already seen Britomart in action as a strapping Amazon and by two passages of description, in the first of which Spenser echoes gestures he had attributed to Venus at i.36:

> And whilst he slept, she over him would spred
> Her mantle, colour'd like the starry skyes,
> And her soft arme lay underneath his hed,
> And with ambrosiall kisses bathe his eyes . . .

So Glauce to Britomart, though with somewhat different intentions:

> her twixt her armes twaine
> She straightly straynd, and colled tenderly,
> And every trembling joynt, and every vaine
> She softly felt, and rubbed busily,
> To doe the frosen cold away to fly;
> And her faire deawy eies with kisses deare
> She oft did bath, and oft againe did dry . . .
>
> *(ii.34)*

> upleaning on her elbow weake,
> Her alablaster brest she soft did kis,
> Which all that while she felt to pant and quake,
> As it an Earth-quake were . . .
>
> *(ii.42)*

The atmosphere of Book III is saturated with various kinds of confusion and ambiguity produced by eros in its early or regressive phases. Oceanic and chaotic matrices are ambiguously womb and tomb, benign and threatening, male and female. Desire is ambiguously martial and erotic, wounds ambiguously physical and psychic. At iii.i Spenser distinguishes between noble and base love, but at the same time in the cantos surrounding this distinction he describes Britomart's "sacred fire" for Artegal in terms which make it identical to the elemental affections "that move / In brutish minds." The various suitors of the false Florimell are unwittingly involved in a relation at once auto-erotic and homosexual (viii.5–8). Proteus's attitude toward Florimell slips from paternal care to tyrannical lust (viii.33–42). Malbecco's lust is directed with equal fervor toward two objects, his gold and his wife. A final example will lead into a discussion of the second aspect of eros: the Squire of Dames and his lady Columbell, whose courtship is turned farcically awry by the double meaning of *service:*

That gentle Lady, whom I love and serve,
After long suit and weary servicis,
Did aske me, how I could her love deserve,
And how she might be sure, that I would never swerve.

I glad by any meanes her grace to gaine,
Bad her commaund my life to save, or spill.
Eftsoones she bad me, with incessaunt paine
To wander through the world abroad at will,
And every where, where with my power or skill
I might do service unto gentle Dames,
That I the same should faithfully fulfill,
And at the twelve monethes end should bring their names
And pledges; as the spoiles of my victorious games.

So well I to faire Ladies service did,
And found such favour in their loving hartes,
That ere the yeare his course had compassid,
Three hundred pledges for my good desartes,
And thrise three hundred thanks for my good partes
I with me brought, and did to her present:
Which when she saw, more bent to eke my smartes,
Then to reward my trusty true intent,
She gan for me devise a grievous punishment.

To weet, that I my travell should resume,
And with like labour walke the world around,
Ne ever to her presence should presume,
Till I so many other Dames had found,
The which, for all the suit I could propound,
Would me refuse their pledges to afford,
But did abide for ever chast and sound.

(vii.53–56)

This presentation is so guarded—on Spenser's part—that it is impossible to tell whether the Squire misinterpreted his lady's will or whether Columbell's charge to him is itself confused by a morbid and ambivalent set of desires: to test his loyalty ("that I would never swerve") *and* his prowess ("how I could her love deserve"); to protract her own freedom from submission yet titillate her fantasy with vicarious enjoyment of his conquests. We cannot know whether his "trusty true intent" was fulfilled beyond or contrary to her expectations or whether his success aroused anger, jealousy, and frustration as the concomitants of her vicarious pleasure. Her name suggests her connection with Venus, and later, in IV.x, when Spenser has Scudamour describe his conquest of Amoret, he depicts in greater symbolic detail the virgin's desire to be a priestess of Venus without sacrificing her freedom or integrity to man's love. Briefly but densely Spenser's ambiguous treatment of the Squire's tale reveals the sexes working at cross-purposes, love as a warfare in which efforts at cooperation and *trouthe* break down, changing into lust and hate under the pressures of self-interest.

II

A second leading characteristic of eros in its early phases is its pain-giving quality. During the initial period of separation or differentiation, when elements and individuals emerge over against their environment and each other, when they strive blindly for an autonomy (or a union) which is absolute, the eros which drives them is manifested as hate, physical hostility, and war. This is the dominant tonality of the "histori-cal period" in which Britomart "lived," of the natural and psychic worlds rendered in III, and of the peculiar sequence of events which gives the book its narrative shape. I have already suggested the relation of this atmosphere to the antique image of woman and chastity, and I should now like to show some of the different ways Spenser renders the martial-erotic phase of experience. His basic method is to ring interest-ing changes on the manner in which the two sides of the conventional love-war ambiguity may be related: love as painful and warlike, and the desire to inflict pain and make war as a form of erotic pleasure, either simple or compensatory. This ambiguity gives point to the stanzas which introduce the third canto:

> Most sacred fire, that burnest mightily
>   In living brests, ykindled first above,
>   Emongst th'eternall spheres and lamping sky,
>   And thence pourd into men, which men call Love;
>   Not that same, which doth base affections move
>   In brutish minds, and filthy lust inflame,
>   But that sweet fit, that doth true beautie love,
>   And choseth vertue for his dearest Dame,
> Whence spring all noble deeds and never dying fame:
>
> Well did Antiquitie a God thee deeme,
>   That over mortall minds hast so great might,
>   To order them, as best to thee doth seeme,
>   And all their actions to direct aright;
>   The fatall purpose of divine foresight,

> Thou doest effect in destined descents,
> Through deepe impression of thy secret might,
> And stirredst up th'Heroes high intents,
> Which the late world admyres for wondrous moniments.
>
> But thy dread darts in none doe triumph more,
> Ne braver proofe in any, of thy powre
> Shew'dst thou, then in this royall Maid of yore,
> Making her seeke an unknowne Paramoure,
> From the worlds end, through many a bitter stowre . . .

The ambiguity centers not only on the difference between noble and base love, a difference which is not yet discernible and cannot emerge until later and more developed ethical phases of consciousness; it centers also on the relation between loving and fighting. Eros manifests itself in antiquity as high spirit—it is poured into *brests* and stirs up the *high intents* of heroes, among whom Britomart is numbered. Its might remains *secret* until the full dynamic of love is impressed on and partly guided by responsive human consciousness. Then the *late world* may "look back" on the *moniments* of early experience, seeing there both monuments of the past and admonitions for the present. The statement that Antiquity named eros a god seems to allude most directly to the *Symposium*, and we may recall that Socrates in that dialogue criticizes the preceding speakers for misconstruing a state of human consciousness as an objective deity: such a projection permits the soul to shift responsibility, yet Spenser (like Plato) allows some truth in the statement since consciousness in its early phases *is* determined primarily by external influence. The distinction of sources—what comes from "above" and what from the self—is part of the secret which cannot be revealed until one arrives at the kind of retrospective view Spenser is at pains to dramatize in these stanzas. And that "historical retrospect" is itself part of the fiction is affirmed in the next stanza when he invokes a Clio whose parents are Memory and *Phoebus*.

The retrospective view of an ancient warlike environment is amplified in the treatment of Merlin. Thus Spenser's introductory account of the conventional Merlin—everybody's Merlin—is amused and even condescending because it is presented in quotation marks as an example of the old mythology. We are shown a Merlin produced by the superstitious mind, the popular imagination which may once have been a fresh and significant cultural force but can no longer be taken seriously. Glauce and Britomart journey

> To *Maridunum,* that is now by chaunge
> Of name *Cayr-Merdin* cald . . .
> There the wise *Merlin* whylome wont (they say)
> To make his wonne, low underneath the ground,
> In a deepe delve, farre from the vew of day,
> That of no living wight he mote be found,
> Where so he counseld with his sprights encompast round.
>
> *(iii.7)*

Spenser could have found the antiquity stressed in Camden, who cites
the account given by Giraldus Cambrensis in the twelfth century, remarking that the original name, Maridunum, was given by Ptolemy.
Here as elsewhere in III the etymological play draws our attention to the
bond between ocean and war, and the sequence *Mari*dunum–Cayr-
*Mer*din–*Mer*lin allows some of this to rub off on Merlin; the echoes of
dune and *care* strengthen the ocean-war reference.

Spenser clearly locates this sophistication in his own revised versions
of the myth and separates it from the antique model, which stands beside
it in caricature form. As he continues to parody the tone of the old wives'
tale, he adapts the Mage of early legend more and more to his own
themes. The direct address to the reader (the old wife conjuring the
child) enforces the distance between the contemporary folk environment
of the speaker and the early world of the story:

> And if thou ever happen that same way
>   To travell, goe to see that dreadfull place:
>   It is an hideous hollow cave (they say)
>   Under a rocke that lyes a little space
>   From the swift *Barry,* tombling downe apace,
>   Emongst the woodie hilles of *Dynevowre:*
>   But dare thou not, I charge, in any cace,
>   To enter into that same balefull Bowre,
> For fear the cruell Feends should thee unwares devowre.
>
> But standing high aloft, low lay thine eare,
>   And there such ghastly noise of yron chaines,
>   And brasen Caudrons thou shalt rombling heare,
>   Which thousand sprights with long enduring paines
>   Doe tosse, that it will stonne thy feeble braines,
>   And oftentimes great grones, and grievous stounds,
>   When too huge toile and labour them constraines:
>   And oftentimes loud strokes, and ringing sounds
> From under that deepe Rocke most horribly rebounds.

The cause some say is this: A litle while
   Before that *Merlin* dyde, he did intend,
   A brasen wall in compas to compile
   About *Cairmardin*, and did it commend
   Unto these Sprights, to bring to perfect end.
   During which worke the Ladie of the Lake,
   Whom long he lov'd, for him in hast did send,
   Who thereby forst his workemen to forsake,
Them bound till his returne, their labour not to slake.

In the meane time through that false Ladies traine,
   He was surprisd, and buried under beare,
   Ne ever to his worke returnd againe:
   Nath'lesse those feends may not their worke forbeare,
   So greatly his commaundement they feare,
   But there doe toyle and travell day and night,
   Untill that brasen wall they up doe reare:
   For *Merlin* had in Magicke more insight,
Then ever him before or after living wight.

For he by words could call out of the sky
   Both Sunne and Moone, and make them him obay:
   The land to sea, and sea to maineland dry,
   And darkesome night he eke could turne to day:
   Huge hostes of men he could alone dismay,
   And hostes of men of meanest things could frame,
   When so him list his enimies to fray:
   That to this day for terror of his fame,
The feends do quake, when any him to them does name.
                                                          (iii.8–12)

The antics described in the final stanza may, as Todd put it, be "agreeable to the custom of classical magicians,"[1] but they also recall the powers Spenser and God gave to Fidelia at I.x.20, the faith which could
command the sun to stop, dismay great hosts of men, walk on water, and
move mountains to throw themselves into the "raging sea with roaring
threat." The point of the echo lies in the difference between the two passages rather than in their similarity: the difference between mystical and
magical power, between a theological virtue and a legendary Welsh ma-

---

[1] F. M. Padelford, ed., *"The Faerie Queene," Book Three,* vol. 3 of *The Works of
Edmund Spenser: A Variorum Edition,* ed. Edwin Greenlaw, C. G. Osgood, and F. M.
Padelford (Baltimore: Johns Hopkins Press, 1934), 225; this edition of the *Variorum* is
hereafter cited as *Var.*

gician, between biblical allusion and what may be a folk distortion or
reduction of scripture. The enumeration of Merlin's powers has little to
do with his function in Book III, which is limited to prophecy. Rather
it seems slanted toward the emphasis on warfare (as its differences from
the Fidelia passage suggest) and toward the theme of hostility between
the sexes: all Merlin's powers were of no avail in his encounter with the
Lady of the Lake, for *Spenser's* Merlin is a victim of the "historical"
phase of eros to which he belongs; his fate is like that of other male figures in the first half of III—Adonis, Marinell, and Timias.

The same warfare is evident in the genealogy which Spenser has con-
cocted for the present context:

> And sooth, men say that he was not the sonne
>   Of mortall Syre, or other living wight,
>   But wondrously begotten, and begonne
>   By false illusion of a guilefull Spright,
>   On a fare Ladie Nonne, that whilome hight
>   *Matilda*, daughter to *Pubidius*,
>   Who was the Lord of *Mathravall* by right,
>   And coosen unto king *Ambrosius:*
> Whence he indued was with skill so marvellous.
>
> *(iii.13)*

The names seem to allow translations which are thematically appropriate: War-Maiden, daughter of Youth (Puberty), lord of War-Tangle,
kin to Immortal. There is again an apparent distorted echo of Christian
myth and a direct reference to this phase of eros: the chaste maiden withdrawing from war to the nunnery during a "youthful" period of psycho-
history when opposites are at war; the possibility of love only through
force or deceit.

Merlin's relation to martial eros had been suggested in the second
canto when Spenser introduced the magic mirror through whose agency
Britomart fell in love, "as it in bookes hath written bene of old":

> In *Deheubarth* that now South-Wales is hight,
>   What time king *Ryence* raign'd, and dealed right,
>   The great Magitian *Merlin* had deviz'd,
>   By his deepe science, and hell-dreaded might,
>   A looking glasse, right wondrously aguiz'd,
> Whose vertues through the wyde world soone were solemniz'd.
>
> It vertue had, to shew in perfect sight,
>   What ever thing was in the world contaynd,
>   Betwixt the lowest earth and heavens hight,

>   So that it to the looker appertaynd;
>   What ever foe had wrought, or frend had faynd,
>   Therein discovered was, ne ought mote pas,
>   Ne ought in secret from the same remaynd;
>   For thy it round and hollow shaped was,
>   Like to the world it selfe, and seem'd a world of glas.
>
>   Who wonders not, that reades so wonderous worke?
>   But who does wonder, that has red the Towre,
>   Wherein th'Ægyptian *Phao* long did lurke
>   From all mens vew, that none might her discoure,
>   Yet she might all men vew out of her bowre?
>   Great *Ptolomæe* it for his lemans sake
>   Ybuilded all of glasse, by Magicke powre,
>   And also it impregnable did make;
>   Yet when his love was false, he with a peaze it brake.
>
>   Such was the glassie globe that *Merlin* made,
>   And gave unto king *Ryence* for his gard,
>   That never foes his kingdome might invade,
>   But he it knew at home before he hard
>   Tydings thereof, and so them still debar'd.
>
>   *(ii.18–21)*

Again we have the battle between the sexes; the one-sided and narcissistic eros of the woman who withdraws like Malecasta's Venus to feed her fantasy in furtive security (hence the voyeurism, which keeps its objects at eyebeam distance, and hence the name Phao); the vain wish-fulfilling attempt at total *maistrie* through magic rather than through the more difficult human efforts to sustain relations; the reference to "ancient Britain" as wartorn and treacherous—even friends *faynd*—and the appeal to magic to cope with violence or guile.

"Get thee to a nunnery": Hamlet's extremes, whorehouse or convent, aggressive lust or militant chastity, are feasible alternatives in a world dominated by *Mars* and *mare*. Spenser depicts an atmosphere of elemental strife in which, to use Glauce's words, "all Britanie doth burne in armes bright" (iii.52). Uther is fighting "the Paynim brethren, hight / Octa and Oza," Angela and her Saxons are fighting the Britons, Christians are in conflict with pagans, native tribes with foreign tribes, women with men. Glauce warns Britomart that if she is to seek her beloved in relative security she must become a *Matilda* and cope with men as a man:

>   That therefore nought our passage may empeach,
>   Let us in feigned armes our selves disguize,

And our weake hands (whom need new strength shall teach)
The dreadfull speare and shield to exercize:
Ne certes daughter that same warlike wize
I weene, would you misseeme; for ye bene tall,
And large of limbe, t'atchieve an hard emprize,
Ne ought ye want, but skill, which practize small
Will bring, and shortly make you a mayd Martiall.

And sooth, it ought your courage much inflame,
To heare so often, in that royall hous,
From whence to none inferiour ye came,
Bards tell of many women valorous
Which have full many feats adventurous
Performd, in paragone of proudest men:
The bold *Bunduca*, whose victorious
Exploits made *Rome* to quake, stout *Guendolen*,
Renowmed *Martia*, and redoubted *Emmilen*.

(*iii.53–54*)

This accords with the views expressed in the opening stanzas of cantos ii
and iv in which women are praised not for feminine virtues but for
being killers, conquerors, or emulators of men. Glauce urges Britomart
to arm for aggression and "greedy hardiment" rather than for love, and
at iii.57 Britomart responds in kind:

Her harty words so deepe into the mynd
Of the young Damzell sunke, that great desire
Of warlike armes in her forthwith they tynd,
And generous stout courage did inspire,
That she resolv'd, unweeting to her Sire,
Advent'rous knighthood on her selfe to don,
And counseld with her Nourse, her Maides attire
To turne into a massy habergeon . . .

In the ambiguous climate of Book III, this martial motive immediately
fuses with Britomart's erotic pain, as her encounter with Marinell reveals:

Her dolour soone she ceast, and on her dight
Her Helmet, to her Courser mounting light:
Her former sorrow into suddein wrath,
Both coosen passions of distroubled spright,
Converting, forth she beates the dustie path;
Love and despight attonce her courage kindled hath.

> As when a foggy mist hath overcast
>> The face of heaven, and the cleare aire engrost,
>> The world in darkenesse dwels, till that at last
>> The watry Southwinde from the seabord cost
>> Upblowing, doth disperse the vapour lo'st,
>> And poures it selfe forth in a stormy showre;
>> So the faire *Britomart* having disclo'st
>> Her clowdy care into a wrathfull stowre,
> The mist of griefe dissolv'd, did into vengeance powre.
>
> *(iv.12–13)*

She protects herself against aggressive male warfare by wearing armor, against aggressive male passion by wearing disguise, and against the assaults of eros within by using the forms of male aggressiveness as an outlet. I think it likely that Spenser means to present Britomart as *too* fierce and aggressive; here her effort to project her frustration into warfare and get rid of it may possibly be an effort at too violent and quick a relief. The episode follows Britomart's allegorical complaint to ocean, and this, together with the simile in stanza 13 above, contributes to the ambiguous climate which characterizes early experience: psyche is scarcely separable from nature, inscape from landscape; since ocean momentarily condenses into the figure of Marinell, it stands indifferently for male and female eros, because it embodies both human and cosmic eros. The model for Britomart's inner turmoil as for her head-on fight with Marinell is the warfare of elements. Therefore if we are asked to be somewhat critical of Britomart's masculine aggressiveness, we are also given reason to sympathize with her predicament: it is forced on her by the behavior of man in this phase of experience, by the strife of opposites, by the blind force of self-enclosed wills seeking to protect or ease themselves in violent, immediate, and physical action. It is not yet the time for woman to express herself as woman. For the nonce she must abjure feminine behavior and play the game a man's way.

The extreme instance of woman asserting autonomy by playing the man's role occurs significantly at the very beginning of III: in the name *Malecasta* we hear not only *unchastity* and an echo of *evil castle* but also an echo of *male castle*. This is a man's, not a woman's, image of the ideal courtly life for women—that is, if a man were to envisage the kind of courtly pleasure he should like to have as a woman, this would be it. The figure of the master-woman (*mi dons*) presiding over her court of love projects the one-sided culture, dominated by male imagination, which Spenser is about to revise. Spenser recalls this culture by having Britomart paraphrase Chaucer's Franklin:

> Ne may love be compeld by maisterie;
> For soone as maisterie comes, sweet love anone
> Taketh his nimble wings, and soone away is gone.
>
> *(i.25)*

Woman as master of man is the perverted form of the ideal to be exemplified by Britomart, woman as equal and companion of man. In Malecasta's fantasy world, men have no choice:

> every knight, which doth this way repaire,
> In case he have no Ladie, nor no love,
> Shall doe unto her service never to remove.
>
> But if he have a Ladie or a Love,
> Then must he her forgoe with foule defame,
> Or else with us by dint of sword approve,
> That she is fairer, then our fairest Dame,
> As did this knight, before ye hither came.
> Perdie (said *Britomart*) the choise is hard:
> But what reward had he, that overcame?
> He should advaunced be to high regard,
> (Said they) and have our Ladies love for his reward.
>
> *(i.26–27)*

> The first of them by name *Gardante* hight,
> A jolly person, and of comely vew;
> The second was *Parlante*, a bold knight,
> And next to him *Jocante* did ensew;
> *Basciante* did him selfe most curteous shew;
> But fierce *Bacchante* seemd too fell and keene;
> And yet in armes *Noctante* greater grew:
> All were faire knights, and goodly well beseene,
> But to faire *Britomart* they all but shadowes beene.
>
> *(i.45)*

These shadows are intended to guarantee the master-woman a controlled pattern of ritual foreplay which delays and thus intensifies her pleasure. Her castle is "plaste for pleasure" near a forest "whose hideous horror and sad trembling sound / Full griesly seem'd," and in which no living creatures were found "Save Beares, Lions, and Buls, which romed them around" (i.14). It is from this forest that Florimell first appears, fleeing in full career from its human embodiment, the "griesly Foster . . . / Breathing out beastly lust" (i.17). Spenser's transition from the fearful Florimell, helpless in a world of savage male lust, to Malecasta's efforts at

mastery represents a violent swing of the pendulum: the insecurity and
hysterical fear of Florimell may be seen as causally related to Malecasta's
equally hysterical drive toward control, domination (*daunger* in the male
sense), and total pleasure. The castle is in this sense protective, but it is
also a lure and a trap: "faire before the gate a spatious plaine, / Mantled
with greene, it selfe did spredden wyde" (i.20). She wants what Florimell
flees from, but she wants it domesticated, refined, and submissive to
her whim. It is between the extremes of Malecasta and Florimell that
Britomart, who has a Florimell within, must locate her course.

III

The third characteristic of eros appears in the backward or downward
pull exerted by the matrix or chaos on figures struggling to emerge
and break free. We see this most clearly in the relation of Cymoent to
Marinell: the mother will not let her son go, and his defeat by Britomart
in effect sends him back to the womb for a second chance. A similar
influence is exerted by the witch on her son (III.vii–viii) and by Venus.
The backward pull may manifest itself as an urge to escape from life's
difficulties and limitations, a longing to return to the paradisal or womblike situation from which one was ejected. This longing is represented
briefly and at the most general level in the early stanzas describing the
Garden of Adonis, where the emphasis is not on departure but on the
return to the ideal mythic place of origins:

> double gates it had, which opened wide,
> By which both in and out men moten pas;
> Th'one faire and fresh, the other old and dride:
> Old *Genius* the porter of them was,
> Old *Genius*, the which a double nature has.

> He letteth in, he letteth out to wend,
> All that to come into the world desire;
> A thousand thousand naked babes attend
> About him day and night, which doe require,
> That he with fleshly weedes would them attire:
> Such as him list, such as eternall fate
> Ordained hath, he clothes with sinfull mire,
> And sendeth forth to live in mortall state,
> Till they againe returne backe by the hinder gate.

> After that they againe returned beene,
> They in that Gardin planted be againe;
> And grow afresh, as they had never seene

Fleshly corruption, nor mortall paine.
Some thousand yeares so doen they there remaine;
And then of him are clad with other hew,
Or sent into the chaungefull world againe,
Till thither they returne, where first they grew:
So like a wheele around they runne from old to new.

Ne needs there Gardiner to set, or sow,
To plant or prune: for of their owne accord
All things, as they created were, doe grow . . .
(vi.31–34)

A different but related form of this attraction is embodied in Argante and Ollyphant, the monstrous brother and sister who, "whiles in their mothers wombe enclosd they were . . . in fleshly lust were mingled":

So liv'd they ever after in like sin,
Gainst natures law, and good behavioure:
But greatest shame was to that maiden twin,
Who not content so fowly to devoure
Her native flesh, and staine her brothers bowre,
Did wallow in all other fleshly myre,
And suffred beasts her body to deflowre:
So whot she burned in that lustfull fyre,
Yet all that might not slake her sensuall desyre.

But over all the countrey she did raunge,
To seeke young men, to quench her flaming thrust,
And feed her fancy with delightfull chaunge . . .
(vii.49–50)

Thus they pass their lives compulsively repeating, trying to recover and perpetuate, their prenatal pleasure. In contrast to this is the separation and development of another set of twins: the complex and dialectically articulated structures of response embodied in Belphoebe and Amoret are shown to emerge from a simpler, more incomplete matrix in the golden birth produced by the juncture of pure opposites—the nymph Chrysogone and the sun, water and fire, passive and active, the too help-less feminine and the too potent masculine principles. Chrysogone is the daughter of an even vaguer figure, only a name—*Amphisa*, which means, among other things, "undifferentiated" (both the same). That the twins are fostered by Venus and Diana adds another dimension to the developmental aspect of the myth, especially since the portraits of Venus and Diana in III.vi represent them as stock literary figures, the conventionally opposed feminine responses to eros. The traditional view of the feminine psyche based on the Venus-Diana model is simplistic and inadequate, a one-sided masculine caricature. A psyche composed of—or rather divided by—two such exclusive and antipathetic dispositions is not open to the kind of relation Spenser envisages as married love. His solution is to revise and complicate the traditional male view of woman, and the myth in III.vi is central to this revision. Each twin contains and is partly determined by a differently inflected mixture of Venerean and Artemisian elements. Together with Florimell, the twins are infolded into the more complete image of the feminine psyche of which Britomart is the exemplar in the *Faerie Queene*. Thus there are two quite different, yet interrelated, lines of development: the development of the feminine psyche from early phases which may be thought of as mythic or archetypal (female rather than feminine) and which are inadequate—too "close to nature"—for the complexities of human experience; and the development of man's image of woman from the traditionally limited views to the Spenserian revision, which more fully respects the complexities of human experience. Spenser presupposes not only a matrix of "nature" but also a matrix of convention.

The primal matrix is variously represented in Book III by Ocean, Night, caves, the Chaos under the Garden of Adonis, Chrysogone, Venus as Great Mother, Cymoent, and Glauce. Glauce, as her name suggests, embodies the ambiguous blue or green or gray of ocean, the undisciplined lore of old wives' experience. Benign but rude, she understands Britomart's predicament and moves her to do something about it, but she does not know how or in what direction to guide her. She simply turns Britomart round and round trying, in a parody of superstitious incantation, "to undoe her daughters love" (ii.51), and this turning also symbolizes the treadmill repetition of life lived close to its origins in chaos or ocean. To approach the ocean or to return to it or to be driven into it symbolizes a jeopardy which may come from within the self or from outside it or both. Britomart, Florimell, Marinell, the old fisherman, and Malbecco—in various degrees all come close to dissolution of the complex self; overwhelmed by erotic force (either as hate or as love), all are threatened with submission to a single compulsive urge. This *singleness*, being primitive, is ambiguous, a blurred mixture of different passions and motives: desire, fear, hate, jealousy, despair.

The pattern of return is schematically suggested in the figure of the earthly peer Dumarin, who fulfills his name by his casual undine encounter with Cymoent in which, as Spenser is careful to phrase it, he "was taken with her love." Later the oceanic state is metaphorically applied to Paridell, whose ancestor Parius sailed to the isle of Paros, which before

Hight *Nausa*, there he many yeares did raine,
And built *Nausicle* by the *Pontick* shore,
To which he dying left next in remaine
To *Paridas* his sonne.
From whom I *Paridell* by kin descend;
But for faire Ladies love, and glories gaine,
My native soil have left, my dayes to spend
In sewing deeds of armes, my lives and labours end.

(ix.37)

Like the old fisherman, Paridell is unwittingly out of control, in effect a floating island (named Ship) spending his days and ending his life and labor asea. He and his partner Hellenore (Helen-whore, Helen-over-again) are lesser versions of Paris and Helen. Effectually tyrannized by their ancient literary prototypes, they can only repeat over and over again what those lovers did. And where the original act had tragic and historical consequences, Paris's *idell* descendant has withdrawn from history to Faerie, to the unending repetition of the waves of love and war (love as war and war as love) which encompass him. Like Florimell, though without any consciousness of the similarity, he dramatically embodies the condition described by Britomart in her complaint:

Huge sea of sorrow, and tempestuous grief,
    Wherein my feeble barke is tossed long,
    Far from the hoped haven of reliefe,
    Why do thy cruell billowes beat so strong,
    And thy moyst mountaines each on others throng,
    Threatning to swallow up my fearefull life?
    O do thy cruell wrath and spightfull wrong
    At length allay, and stint thy stormy strife,
Which in these troubled bowels raignes, and rageth rife.

For else my feeble vessell crazd, and crackt
    Through thy strong buffets and outrageous blowes,
    Cannot endure, but needs it must be wrackt
    On the rough rocks, or on the sandy shallowes,
    The whiles that love it steres, and fortune rowes;
    Love my lewd Pilot hath a restless mind
    And fortune Boteswaine no assuraunce knowes,
    But saile withouten starres gainst tide and wind:
How can they other do, sith both are bold and blind?

(iv.8−9)

Paridell and Hellenore represent a psychic and cultural dead end, a kind of genealogical blind alley, a one-way tendency toward death and chaos which can never be reversed but can never be resolved. The simile Spenser applies to Paridell when he is unhorsed by Britomart (ix.15) encapsulates his condition:

> Tho hastily remounting to his steed,
>> He forth issew'd; like as a boistrous wind,
>> Which in th'earthes hollow caves hath long bin hid,
>> And shut up fast within her prisons blind,
>> Makes the huge element against her kind
>> To move, and tremble as it were agast,
>> Untill that it an issew forth may find;
>> Then forth it breakes, and with his furious blast
> Confounds both land and seas, and skyes doth overcast.

The tyranny of the primordial archetype and its antihistorical recurrence is manifested in a variety of ways in III. One of the more obvious manifestations is the salient recurrence of archetypal figures: the wizards, magicians (Merlin, Proteus, Busirane), and other more pathetic old men (the fishermen, Malbecco); the mothers; the sacrificial Adonis figures (Marinell, Timias, Adonis); the virgins, temptresses, monsters, prisoners, and lechers. Though individual archetypal figures differ from each other—often in significant and contrastive ways—their generic qualities are primary, and consequently as we move through Book III we encounter recurrent examples of a few archetypes varied by the pressures of new and changing contexts. This effect is reinforced by a patterned recurrence of symbolic landscapes (in cantos i–vi, forest–castles–ocean–forest–garden, and in vii–xii, forest–ocean–castle–forest–ocean–forest–castle) and by an Ariostan plot treatment which dissipates the force of chronological happening. The sequence of events is displaced by the sequence of cantos, of imagistic and symbolic patterns, and of significant juxtapositions which produce contrast and parallel rather than straight narrative development. In cantos ii–iii and vi Spenser flashes back to the geneses of Britomart's love and Chrysogone's daughters, while the plot line is further dislocated by the temporal obscurity of the Britomart-Marinell and Florimell-Marinell stories. Added to the recurrence of archetypal figures are the repeated narrative motifs (e.g., the rhythmic alternations of pursuit and flight) and the increasingly frequent return of night (i.57, ii.28, iv.52, viii.51, x.12, x.46, xi.55, xii.29). Most of the action during cantos ix–xii is nocturnal, and the particular qualities which Spenser rhetorically assigns to night are those which associate it with chaos and ocean or water—the humid element whose psychic and organic functions relate to the lower urges (desire and lust) and basic processes (generation, sleep, death); for example:

> By this th'eternall lampes, wherewith high Jove
> Doth light the lower world, were halfe yspent,
> And the moist daughters of huge *Atlas* strove
> Into the *Ocean* deepe to drive their weary drove.
>
> *(i.57)*

> Now whenas all the world in silence deepe
>   Yshrowded was, and every mortall wight
> Was drowned in the depth of deadly sleepe . . .
>
> *(i.59)*

> All suddenly dim woxe the dampish ayre,
>   And griesly shadowes covered heaven bright . . .
>
> *(iv.52)*

> Now gan the humid vapour shed the ground
> With perly deaw, and th'Earthes gloomy shade
> Did dim the brightnesse of the welkin round,
> That every bird and beast awarned made,
> To shrowd themselves, whiles sleepe their senses did invade.
>
> *(x.46)*

> chearelesse Night ycovered had
> Faire heaven with an universall cloud . . .
>
> *(xii.1)*

Night periodically inundates the world and soul, bringing with it a threat of the restoration of its ancient domain, strengthening all those elemental impulses which waking reason must coordinate and control.

The primacy of night during the last four cantos contributes to a larger pattern of regression and decline, a pattern in which Spenser parades before us—in all their ugliness and absurd inadequacy—one after another conventional model of love: the fabliau triangle in which Malbecco and Hellenore replay January and May while Paridell replays the courtly adulterer, the frustrated and helpless lover wallowing narcissistically in his misery (Scudamour), the Ovidian lovers in Busirane's tapestry and the Petrarchan sonnet figures in his masque. These episodes do more than merely allude to traditional literary genres and cultural institutions; they dramatize and exemplify them. Spenser presents them as flat, artificial, and archaic—not only cliché and perverse but also simplistic. They actualize one-sided masculine conceptions of love which Spenser and Britomart encounter and render obsolete. This atmosphere of literary artifice is conflated with a resurgence of elemental and inorganic imagery, one example of which has already been described above in the figure of Paridell. Another is provided by Malbecco, victim of a single obsessive humor and the literary stereotype based on that humor. Still others appear in the outbursts of fire, gold, and air which punctuate Britomart's adventure at Busirane's house:

> in the Porch, that did them sore amate,
> A flaming fire, ymixt with smouldry smoke,
> And stinking Sulphure, that with griesly hate
> And dreadfull horrour did all entrance choke . . .
>
> *(xi.21)*

> with pure gold it all was overlayd,
> Wrought with wild Antickes, which their follies playd,
> In the rich metall, as they living were:
> A thousand monstrous formes therein were made,
> Such as false love doth oft upon him weare . . .
>
> *(xi.51)*

> an hideous storme of winde arose,
> With dreadfull thunder and lightning atwixt,
> And an earth-quake, as if it streight would lose
> The worlds foundations from his centre fixt;
> A direfull stench of smoke and sulphure mixt
> Ensewd . . .
>
> *(xii.2)*

As the language of the second passage makes clear, these wild *antickes*, foolish and archaic, do not emerge from but are imposed on the material; they are the forms created by a mind fundamentally out of control. Erotic uncontrol and aesthetic control, chaos and art, primitive ends and overrefined means, converge in Busirane's decadence. Spurred to revenge by pain and jealousy, the male imagination's attempts at *maistrie*—the Busy-reign—become frenetic as the feminine will recoils in ever greater panic (Amoret and "wavering wemens wit"), and the orderly masque degenerates into a "rude confused rout / Of persons . . . whose names is hard to read" (xii.25).

Thus there is a return to a new and more sinister level of chaos as the recently distinguished sets of contraries fail to uphold each other. Ob-

sessively caught in relations of increasing repulsion, the opposites collapse, reviving or sinking back into polymorphous disorder. The last six
cantos of Book III—in their thematic and narrative movements from
the failure of the witch's pathetic son and diseased monster to the triumph of False Florimell, from the helplessness of Malbecco to the
"power" of Busirane—trace a single psychic pattern: The first response
of the thwarted psyche is violence, rape, intensified fury. When this
fails, when the true object is totally beyond attainment, the second attempt at gratification is withdrawal into, or substitution by, magic or art.
The emphasis throughout Book III on riches, hoarding, sumptuous in-
teriors, and artifacts is connected to this failure. Those who are frustrated in their misguided efforts to gain total power and pleasure are
much occupied with wealth and lavish living—Malecasta, Malbecco,
Busirane, the creators and lovers of False Florimell. Precious elements
may be more easily obtained and shaped to their owner's whim than may
women, who are alive and conscious and have wills of their own. Having
material possessions is a one-way relation in which the self may fulfill
itself with minimal resistance from the objects of desire. As Spenser shows
in the instance of Marinell, hoarding has something in common with
fighting, in which people are controlled by being reduced to corpses:
both are safer than loving insofar as they free the self from the bother of
personal relations. Thus wealth is only ironically a symbol of power; it is
actually a symbol of failure in the normal sphere of "adult" and personal
relations. It marks a revival of autistic impulses directed toward a world
of inorganic objects which may be safely vivified by projection. The
False Florimell reveals how attitudes toward women are modeled after
the attitudes toward dead things. She is a magico-mechanical robot made
to the specifications of the sonneteer's ideal and operated by an evil spirit
(viii.5−7): the witch "in the stead / Of life, . . . put a Spright to rule
the carkasse dead." The operator is a male demon, for men know best
what pleases men in feminine behavior. But the creatrix is female, for
women collaborate in this perversion which allows men to fulfill the desire to possess women who are basically male, who have no independence
or otherness, and who are therefore totally controllable machines of
stimulation and pleasure. The enemy is everything in feminine nature
which makes woman more than this. Book III thus ends with the absolute and mutual aversion of the two contraries—male and female—
which have emerged from the matrix of the pre-human, the presexual,
the prerational. These contraries are centered in the Garden of Adonis
and the House of Busirane. Each asserts wholly different claims, each
wants to be the whole, yet each betrays its lack of self-sufficiency.

Book III has therefore traced a process of distinction which has become too radical. Book IV will deal with new efforts and problems of getting together under the aspect of Concord. But the paradox of III is that the mutual hostility and aversion of opposites is a by-product of the mutual urge toward union. Again and again Spenser presents examples of one-sided and premature union, development or fulfillment which must be obstructed or destroyed so that they may be repeated in more adequate form at a later, more appropriate phase of relationship: poet and lady in *Amoretti/Epithalamion;* the recreative shepherds in the *Shepheardes Calender;* Clarion in *Muiopotmos;* Redcross and Una, Britomart and Artegal, Marinell and Florimell, Scudamour and Amoret. This motif is a special case of a more general category in which a first or instinctive form of behavior must be experienced, felt as insufficient, corrected, and revised. The second chance occurs at a later time, a more sophisticated or complex phase of a poem, or a career, or a relation, or a culture. This is the Hegelian dynamic of sublation (*aufheben*): the new context and usage confer on earlier, simpler forms a destiny more inclusive than their own, a more universal and organic function, so that they may transcend themselves in a manner not possible to them in their first isolated push toward fulfillment.

The Structure of Merlin's Chronicle in *The Faerie Queene* III.iii

AT *FAERIE QUEENE* III.iii.4 Spenser invokes Clio in preparation for Merlin's chronicle:

> Begin then, O my dearest sacred Dame,
>> Daughter of *Phoebus* and of *Memorie,*
>> That doest ennoble with immortall name
>> The warlike Worthies, from antiquitie,
>> In thy great volume of Eternitie:
> Begin, O *Clio*, and recount from hence
> My glorious Soveraines goodly auncestrie,
>> *Till that by dew degrees and long protense,*
> Thou have it lastly brought unto her Excellence.
>
>> > *(italics mine)*

Protense is a rare form of a rare word (Spenser's elliptical noun form is the only recorded instance in the *OED*), and it seems carefully chosen as a precise counterpoint to "by dew degrees": to protend is to protract, extend through time, stretch out a duration; the idea of continuing the same is opposed to the developmental implication of "by dew degrees." The chronicle itself demonstrates both aspects, for on the one hand it is ordered as a series of three recurrent cycles (III.iii.26–34, 35–42, 43–50) in which elemental, hostile, and animal tendencies are sustained

118

through history; on the other hand, each cycle differs in total character from its predecessor.

Merlin's prophecy offers a synoptic view of the developmental process which is immediately suggested by the language of his introductory exhortation to Britomart:

> It was not, *Britomart*, thy wandring eye,
>   Glauncing unwares in charmed looking glas,
>   But the streight course of heavenly destiny,
>   Led with eternall providence, that has
>   Guided thy glaunce, to bring his will to pas:
> Ne is thy fate, ne is thy fortune ill,
>   To love the prowest knight, that ever was.
> Therefore submit thy wayes unto his will,
> And do by all dew meanes thy destiny fulfill.
>
> *(III.iii.24)*

>   the fates are firme,
> And may not shrinck, though all the world do shake:
> Yet ought mens good endevours them confirme,
> And guide the heavenly causes to their constant terme.
>
> *(iii.25)*

Upton notes the echo of Virgil's *fata viam invenient* formula and refers to *Aeneid* III.395 (*Var.* 3:227), but a more relevant instance occurs at x.111–113 when Jupiter, frustrated, disclaims responsibility, saying "sua cuique exorsa laborem / fortunamque ferent" (to each man his beginnings will bring hardship or luck). The god himself will no longer favor any man, since he rules all alike. Thus the way the fates find, the web they spin, will depend partly on the framework laid by the human will. Merlin's emphasis shifts from "the streight course of heavenly destiny, / Led with eternal providence," which presided over the beginning of Britomart's experience, to "mens good endevours" *guiding* the heavenly causes, his advice concerning her future conduct. It is, as St. Augustine knew (*City of God* V.9), the interference of free will which transforms the *streight course* of fate to the less overpowering force of providence—*providentia*, with its stress on omniscience rather than omnipotence and with its implied request for cooperation from man.

Glauce had brought Britomart to Merlin to obtain both information and help, since she had found "nor herbes, nor charmes, nor counsell" effective in allaying Britomart's grief. Though their first view of Merlin suggests his older thaumaturgical character ("the dreadful Mage . . . /

Deepe busied bout work of wondrous end, / And writing strange characters in the ground," III.iii.14), he chides her for her intention:

> More need of leach-craft hath your Damozell,
> Then of my skill: who helpe may have elsewhere,
> In vaine seekes wonders out of Magicke spell.
>
> *(iii.17)*

Spenser lists Merlin's magical powers (iii.8–14) only to relegate them
to the archaic cluster of legends and superstitions which adhere to the
Merlin he is now revising for his own purposes. This Merlin will offer
aid through prophecy, a form of assistance appropriate to the phase of
experience described in III, since it is a compromise between magic and
the more natural sources of information. His relation to Britomart is
modeled after that of Anchises to Aeneas in *Aeneid VI:* he provides an
ostensibly comforting overview of the future, leaping beyond the painful
experience immediately ahead to make Britomart aware of her responsibility not only to herself and Artegal but also to the larger historical plan.

The mood of his utterance is admonitory as well as consoling and
instructive:

> Most noble Virgin, that by fatall lore
> Hast learn'd to love, let no whit thee dismay
> The hard begin, that meets thee in the dore,
> And with sharpe fits thy tender hart oppresseth sore.
>
> For so must all things excellent begin,
> And eke enrooted deepe must be that Tree,
> Whose big embodied braunches shall not lin,
> Till they to heavens hight forth stretched bee.
> For from thy wombe a famous Progenie
> Shall spring, out of the auncient *Troian* blood,
> Which shall revive the sleeping memorie
> Of those same antique Peres, the heavens brood,
> Which *Greeke* and *Asian* rivers stained with their blood.
>
> Renowmed kings, and sacred Emperours,
> Thy fruitfull Ofspring, shall from thee descend;
> Brave Captaines, and most mighty warriours,
> That shall their conquests through all lands extend,
> And their decayed kingdomes shall amend:
> The feeble Britons, broken with long warre,
> They shall upreare, and mightily defend
> Against their forrein foe, that comes from farre,
> Till universall peace compound all civill jarre.
>
> *(iii.21–23)*

Spenser may have intended Merlin's tree metaphor to pick up a phrase used by Glauce a few stanzas earlier when she was describing how long Britomart's "sore evil" persisted since it "first rooting tooke" (iii.16). At first glance its referent seems to be her own fulfillment as lover, and thus the local facts of the virgin's consciousness retain relevance even while being transformed by the dramatic shift of scale and context. The tree is a resolving image: it crystallizes the whole historical process in a single figure and under the double aspect of sexual and natural activity (with more emphasis on the second), as if the British future would grow toward some millennial fulfillment ("to heavens hight," "Till universall peace") as surely and fatedly and spontaneously as a plant. The tree image is a threshold, a transitional moment of *primavera,* at which Britomart briefly pauses before crossing from lovesick virgin to founding mother, from individual figure to historical symbol. But "the hard begin" is extended beyond her own situation to the historical future; her progeny will revive the fame of *warriors* and of that epic struggle noted here chiefly for its costliness; "most mighty warriours" will be necessary to amend the decayed kingdom and uprear the feeble Britons "broken with long warre." Lines 4–5 and 6–8 of stanza 23 are not in simple apposition; the positive meaning of the couplet is restated so as to produce a shift to the sense of weariness and defeat (*"mightily* defend" in this context connotes a certain desperation). And this makes the optimistic conclusion slightly inappropriate; it seems forcefully imposed, like a *deus ex machina,* on a narrative situation which moves from good to bad.

The tension revealed in these stanzas between the actual vicissitudes and the resolving tendency imposed by the overview (and demanded by the rhetorical situation) characterizes the chronicle as a whole. Of the three waves, or cycles, in terms of which it is organized (iii.26–34, 35–42, 43–50), the first two end with returns to chaos and the third with a resolving image uneasily imposed. Development from cycle to cycle is easy to show, but it is hardly millennial, and one may wonder why Britomart conceives "hope of comfort glad" from what she hears (iii.51). The accent of the first cycle, which covers the period of Britomart, Artegal, and their immediate heirs, is on physical size, force, and numbers. Britomart's life after marriage will not be a model of felicity: Artegal, the son of Gorlois and "brother unto *Cador* Cornish king," is famous "for his warlike feates":

> From where the day out of the sea doth spring,
> Untill the closure of the Evening.
> From thence [Faerie], him firmely bound with faithful band,
> To this his native soyle thou backe shalt bring,

> Strongly to aide his countrey, to withstand
> The powre of forrein Paynims, which invade thy land.
>
> Great aid thereto his mighty puissaunce,
>   And dreaded name shall give in that sad day:
>   Where also proofe of thy prow valiaunce
>   Thou then shalt make, t'increase thy lovers pray.
>   Long time ye both in armes shall beare great sway,
>   Till thy wombes burden thee from them do call,
>   And his last fate him from thee take away,
>   Too rathe cut off by practise criminall
> Of secret foes, that him shall make in mischiefe fall.
>
> With thee yet shall he leave for memory
>   Of his late puissaunce, his Image dead,
>   That living him in all activity
>   To thee shall represent . . .
>
>   *(iii.27–29)*

The rhetoric is penetrated not simply by the general awareness of human frailty but by the particular environment of the psychohistorical phase considered in Book III: the day springing out of ocean, Britomart's union with Artegal described as a feminine conquest, the theme of treachery (erotic, domestic, political) connected with furtive narcissism and instability of motive, the relation of mother to son described in terms which anticipate the problems of the oceanic trio Cymoent, Dumarin, and Marinell (iv.19–20, 36).

Artegal's "image dead" (Conan) is described in terms which blur the figure in the same way Artegal will be blurred in Book V—that is, he is announced with full honors as his parents' son, but the sort of virtue he demonstrates seems to us dated if not suspect. Spenser leaves the outcome of his achievements in doubt, then remarks the falling-off in Britomart's grandson: Conan

>   from the head
>   Of his coosin *Constantius* without dread
>   Shall take the crowne, that was his fathers right,
>   And therewith crowne himselfe in th'others stead:
>   Then shall he issew forth with dreadful might,
> Against his Saxon foes in bloudy field to fight.
>
> Like as a Lyon, that in drowsie cave
>   Hath long time slept, himselfe so shall he shake,
>   And coming forth, shall spred his banner brave
>   Over the troubled South, that it shall make
>   The warlike *Mertians* for feare to quake:

> Thrise shall he fight with them, and twise shall win,
> But the third time shall faire accordaunce make:
> And if he then with victorie can lin,
> He shall his dayes with peace bring to his earthly In.
>
> His sonne, hight *Vortipore*, shall him succeede
> In kingdome, but not in felicity . . .
>
> *(iii.29–31)*

Carrie Harper has described Spenser's departures from his sources: for obvious reasons he suppressed "the unpleasant aspects of Conan's career. No authority is known for Conan's wars with the Mertians. On the contrary, what the chroniclers say of Conan is uncomplimentary" (*Var.* 3:229). But there was no need for Spenser *to show himself* trying to accentuate the positive, and this is what makes his treatment interesting. (The reference to the Mertians seems included primarily for the sake of the warlike name.) Britomart's "hard begin" is also Britain's, and their fulfillment, which lies well in the future, depends on their experiencing and transcending the limits of early culture, its criteria, and its sensibility. The rhythm of Conan's career is uncertain: sudden violence, prolonged inactivity, renewed violence tapering into decline in the last four lines of stanza 30. It is like the rhythm of Marinell's career, and Scudamour's, and also Artegal's in its early confidence and fury, in its bad timing, and even in its wry illustration of the concord theme: "twise shall win, / But the third time shall faire accordaunce make."

More than a stanza of this cycle is devoted to a hero notable for his antique virtues and for his early unification of Britain—details which apparently led Spenser to make Malgo Britomart's great-grandson without any chronicle authority:

> Behold the man, and tell me *Britomart*,
> If ay more goodly creature thou didst see;
> How like a Gyaunt in each manly part
> Beares he himselfe with portly majestee,
> That one of th'old *Heroes* seemes to bee:
> He the six Islands, comprovinciall
> In auncient times unto great Britainee,
> Shall to the same reduce, and to him call
> Their sundry kings to do their homage severall.
>
> *(iii.32)*

I think the point of this accomplishment lies once again in its being a premature and deceptively complete reduction of many to one. Most of the six islands—Norway, Denmark, Ireland, Iceland, Gotland, and the

Orkneys—will shake off the yoke; the future unity of Britain will be less
extensive spatially but ethnically and politically a more complicated and
stable organization. But before this happens Britain will itself be reduced
to chaos by a bestial and oceanic force, bringing the first wave of British
history to an unpleasant "closure of Evening"; Malgo's son will be op-
pressed "with multitude" by "a straunger king from unknowne soyle":

> Great *Gormond,* having with huge mightinesse
> Ireland subdewd, and therein fixt his throne,
> Like a swift Otter, fell through emptinesse,
> Shall overswim the sea with many one
> Of his Norveyses, to assist the Britons fone.
>
> He in his furie all shall overrunne,
>   And holy Church with faithlesse hands deface,
>   That thy sad people utterly fordonne,
>   Shall to the utmost mountains fly apace:
>   Was never so great wast in any place,
>   Nor so fowle outrage doen by living men:
>   For all thy Cities they shall sacke and race,
>   And the greene grasse, that groweth, they shall bren,
> That even the wild beast shall dy in starved den.
>
>   *(iii.33–34)*

   The second cycle differs from the first, which featured brute force and
clear-cut moral issues (good Britons, bad enemies). The situation is
complicated by the introduction halfway through of a Christian enemy,
"the good king Oswald . . . indewd / With heavenly powre, and by Angels reskewd" (iii.38). But the cycle began by continuing the clash of
simple and equal opposites, of fury and counterfury: "Proude Etheldred
shall from the North arise" and "repulse the valiaunt Brockwell twise, /
And Bangor with massacred Martyrs fill." "But the third time . . .
Cadwan . . . shall stoutly him defeat, and thousand Saxons kill" (iii.35).
Cadwan's son Cadwallin continues the new onslaught until "the Britons,
late dismayd and weake, / From their long vassalage gin to respire"
(iii.36). The motive remains the same as in the first cycle: the Britons
"on their Paynim foes avenge[d] their ranckled ire," and Cadwallin
did not

> his wrath so mitigate,
> Till both the sonnes of *Edwin* he have slaine,
> *Offricke* and *Osricke,* twinnes unfortunate,
> Both slaine in battell upon Layburne plaine,
> Together with the king of *Louthiane,*

> Hight *Adin*, and the king of Orkeny,
> Both joynt partakers of their fatall paine:
> But *Penda*, fearefull of like desteny,
> Shall yield him selfe his liegeman, and sweare fealty.
>
> *(iii.37)*

Our sympathies are gradually redirected toward the Saxons by the excessive fury, by the unfortunate twins, and by Cadwallin's joining a cowardly traitor in a perverse concord of enemies.

The Christian paradigm in the next stanza contrasts with the wrath and bloodlust of the Britons, and also with the earlier perversion of miracles in "the wicked sorcery / Of false Pellite," a Saxon enchanter (iii.36): Cadwallin makes Penda "his fatall Instrument"—the phrase is deliberately set against the more providential terms of the following description—and Penda

> marching forth with fury insolent
> Against the good king *Oswald*, who indewd
> With heavenly powre, and by Angels reskewd,
> All holding crosses in their hands on hye,
> Shall him defeate withouten bloud imbrewd:
> Of which, that field for endlesse memory,
> Shall *Hevenfield* be cald to all posterity.
>
> *(iii.38)*

This early ingression of Christian influences seems premature—as if northern culture is not ready for it—and it does not last. Oswald's exceptional example diverges from the motive and fate more appropriate to the age, the Martyrdom to Mars of Brockwell's troops in stanza 35:

> Where at *Cadwallin* wroth, shall forth issew,
> And an huge hoste into Northumber lead,
> With which he godly Oswald shall subdew,
> And crowne with martyrdome his sacred head.
> Whose brother *Oswin*, daunted with like dread,
> With price of silver shall his kingdome buy,
> And *Penda*, seeking him adowne to tread,
> Shall tread adowne, and do him fowly dye,
> But shall with gifts his Lord *Cadwallin* pacify.
>
> *(iii.39)*

A third British defeat concludes the second cycle, and it differs from the end of the first wave in being imposed by heaven not by men. But the atmosphere reverts from the New to the Old Testament. Divine justice

is deterministic and retributional; the Britons are treated like Egyptians
in stanza 40:

> Then shall *Cadwallin* dye, and then the raine
>   Of *Britons* eke with him attonce shall dye;
> Ne shall the good *Cadwallader* with paine,
>   Or powre, be hable it to remedy,
> When the full time prefixt by destiny,
> Shalbe expird of *Britons* regiment.
> For heaven it selfe shall their successe envy,
> And them with plagues and murrins pestilent
> Consume, till all their warlike puissaunce be spent.

In the next stanza they resemble stiff-necked Hebrews whom the Heavens
have decreed to displace "for their sinnes dew punishment, / And to the
Saxons over-give their government." The third Briton leader in this
cycle, Cadwallader, is not defeated in battle but "by vision staid from his
intent" to resume the attack. The second wave concludes on the same
note as the first, but the new context lends it an absolutely different significance. The Britons' decline is attributed not to martial failure in an
age of force *ante legem* but to a failure of racial ethos in an early period
sub lege. Responding in the same manner as they did in the first cycle, the
Britons reveal themselves clearly inadequate to the more complicated
issues and demands of the later age and so are returned to the woods and
threatened (in apocalyptic tones) with historical extinction, or at least
obsolescence:

> Then woe, and woe, and everlasting woe,
>   Be to the Briton babe, that shalbe borne,
> To live in thraldome of his fathers foe;
> Late King, now captive, late Lord, now forlorne,
> The worlds reproch, the cruell victors scorne,
> Banisht from Princely bowre to wastfull wood:
> O who shall helpe me to lament, and mourne
> The royall seed, the antique *Troian* blood,
> Whose Empire lenger here, then ever any stood.
>
> *(iii.42)*

Here again we have the familiar Spenserian pattern: early ascendancy
followed by some kind of failure which leads to a phase of captivity, withdrawal, or exile (cf. Redcross, Artegal, Calidore, Satyrane, Marinell,
Timias, Amoret and Florimell). The epoch during which the Britons
held dominion both as a race and as a nation was subject to "the streight

course of heavenly destiny"; the irreversible changes of history and culture preclude this from happening again—in later times Britons will regain power not literally as a nation but symbolically in representative individuals, namely, the Welsh Tudors.

Thus the third cycle stresses the increasing divergence between the history of England and of Britomart's descendants. This is anticipated in Britomart's unhappy response to the second cycle, when she expresses her grief "for *her peoples* sake" and asks whether their name will "for ever be defast, / And quite from the earth their memory be rest" (iii.43). Merlin has to strain to offer Britomart a few crumbs of consolation:

> Nay but the terme (said he) is limited,
>   That in this thraldome *Britons* shall abide,
>   And the just revolution measured,
>   That they as Straungers shalbe notifide.
>   For twise foure hundreth yeares shalbe supplide,
>   Ere they to former rule restor'd shalbee,
>   And their importune fates all satisfide:
>   Yet during this their most obscuritee,
> Their beames shall oft breake forth, that men them faire may see,
>
>   *(iii.44)*

specifically, three times between the ninth and fifteenth centuries:

> For *Rhodoricke*, whose surname shalbe Great,
>   Shall of him selfe a brave ensample shew,
>   That Saxon kings his friendship shall intreat;
>   And *Howell Dha* shall goodly well indew
>   The salvage minds with skill of just and trew;
>   Than *Griffyth Conan* also shall up reare
>   His dreaded head, and the old sparkes renew
>   Of native courage, that his foes shall feare,
> Least back againe the kingdome he from them should beare.
>
>   *(iii.45)*

This catalogue has the effect of praising them for personal qualities and "nice tries" while relegating them to the back country. The exile may be construed as a purgative return to nature, during which the Britons prepare themselves for their fated return. But a less favorable construction may also be placed on these stanzas: the Britons as a nation have had their day in history, and their day was *timely;* that is, they represent the youthful and intuitive vigor of the English people as an ethno-natural quality.

Though Spenser associates them with the ancient Trojans, he treats them rather as Virgil treated the Italic peoples in *Aeneid* VI–VII: their positive force and beauty and virtue were undeniable but too closely tied to and determined by the soil, by natural locality and the intuitive infusion of its qualities into the collective ethos. In the catalogue concluding Book VII Virgil makes the various tribes seem autochthonous as their heroes rush from the mountains, coasts, groves, and streams of Italy. He prefaced the catalogue by asking the Muse to sing of the men, or manly forces, which blossomed from the mothering Italic soil—"quibus Itala iam tum / floruerit terra alma viris" (VII.643–44). The virgin land of Turnus, Diana, Camilla, and the noble stag resisted the irrevocable *fata*, striving to sustain its pristine character, lovely yet incomplete, against the threat of loss which was more immediate than the dim promise of fulfillment. The tempered elegiac atmosphere of Virgilian poetry affirms both the costliness and the necessity of historical process. The Italic *vires* must be uprooted, their determined innocence and intuitive splendor negated, if they are to be absorbed into the more self-conscious, thought-marked, and complex organization of the Roman ethos. And in the last-minute revision pressed by Juno on Jupiter in Book XII the uprooting and assimilating process is conclusively imposed on the Trojans as well, for they are not to rule as a pure strain over the peoples they conquered but are to be absorbed and sublated by the Latins.

This is undoubtedly the model for Spenser's treatment of the Britons and Britomart. In the third cycle Merlin describes two invasions: the Saxons, who "ruled wickedly," were overrun by the Danes, and the Normans under William rent "from the Danish Tyrants . . . / Th'usurped crowne" (*FQ* III.iii.46–47). Both forces are described as cruel, ferocious, and bestial to allow the implication that the native virtue of the Welsh would provide the redeeming element in the English character. All forces (Briton, Saxon, Danish, and Norman) are presented as primary elements (hostile, egocentric, and exclusive) unaware of the larger organic development to which they contribute, a development kept before us in Merlin's frequent references to fate. Against the recurrent cycles of emergence and decline, against the apparent treadmill pattern of continual invasion, is set the increasingly complex assimilation of racial elements into a political *concordia*. But this vital historical process, the emergence of new nations and combinations, cannot be appreciated from the limited perspective of the early heroine for whom *nation* is an ethnic and genealogical concept. Like all elemental forces, the Britons resist the very organic development which will ultimately fulfill them— or, if they do not actively resist it, they are not aware of its existence. As the *alma terra* of the Britons, Britomart's own character and sensibility symbolize both the virtues and limitations of the English ethos in its early psychocultural phase. Her chastity, though an "early" structure in the development of virtues, differs from the chastity of Diana, Camilla, or Belphoebe. She is as eager to open herself to the future as is Spenser to open himself to the past. If the dominance of the genealogical motif with its deterministic criteria indicates the limits of her consciousness, the episode as a whole contributes to the enlarging of her consciousness. *She* sees herself protended into the future, while *we* see the complementary development "by dew degrees" which depends on a continual return to, or tempered revival of, the native and antique Britomartian virtues.

But in the conclusion of the prophecy we also see something else:

> Tho when the terme is full accomplishid,
>> There shall a sparke of fire, which hath long-while
>> Bene in his ashes raked up, and hid,
>> Be freshly kindled in the fruitfull Ile
>> of *Mona*, where it lurked in exile;
>> Which shall breake forth into bright burning flame,
>> And reach into the house, that beares the stile
>> Of royall majesty and soveraigne name;
> So shall the Briton bloud their crowne againe reclame.
>
> Thenceforth eternall union shall be made
>> Between the nations different afore,
>> And sacred Peace shall lovingly perswade
>> The warlike minds, to learne her goodly lore,
>> And civile armes to exercise no more:
>> Then shall a royall virgin raine, which shall
>> Stretch her white rod over the *Belgicke* shore,
>> And the great Castle smite so sore with all,
> That it shall make him shake, and shortly learne to fall.
>
> But yet the end is not. There *Merlin* stayd,
>> As overcomen of the spirits powre,
>> Or other ghastly spectacle dismayd,
>> That secretly he saw, yet note discoure . . .
>
> *(iii.48–50)*

which greatly confused "the two fearefull women" until he recovered his "chearefull looks." As in stanza 23 (see above) the movement is downward from perfection to problems: from eternal union to the resolving image of the royal virgin, whose gesture seems purely symbolic and hieratic until the white rod suddenly becomes the emblem of a weapon and a war, and from this to the unrevealed ghastly spectacle. What Merlin conceals from Britomart and exorcises with the wish-fulfilling virgin image must surely consist of the international events detailed in Book V. Thus the *moniment* he presents to Britomart is first rounded to a panacea, then rendered *endlesse*, or *unperfited*—like the conclusions to the *Amoretti* and *Epithalamion* and all the books of *The Faerie Queene*. At the same time, the developmental process is clearly in view. The eternal union refers to the end of civil war and the concord of "nations different afore" in the new polity of England; the remaining lines adumbrate but do not spell out the larger area of international politics in which the recently unified England plays an elemental role and confronts a wholly new field of problems.

Spenser's Gardens of Adonis

Force and Form in the Renaissance Imagination

Behold now the hope and desire of going back to one's own country
or returning to primal chaos, like that of the moth to the light, of
the man who with perpetual longing always looks forward with joy
to each new spring and each new summer, and to the new months
and the new years, deeming that the things he longs for are too slow
in coming; and who does not perceive that he is longing for his own
destruction. But this longing is in its quintessence the spirit of the
elements, which finding itself imprisoned within the life of the
human body desires continually to return to its source.

—*Leonardo da Vinci*, Notebooks

There is one continuous attraction, beginning with God, going to the
world and ending at last in God, an attraction which returns to the
same place whence it began as though in a kind of circle. This single
circle . . . is identified by three names. Inasmuch as it begins in God
and attracts to Him, it is Beauty; inasmuch as, going across into the
world, it captivates the world, we call it Love; and inasmuch as it

This is a considerably revised version of a paper read in March 1959 before the Graduate English Club of Brown University at the invitation of Professor Leicester Bradner. I
should like to thank Richard B. Young for much helpful criticism.

returns to its source and with Him joins its labors, then we call it
Pleasure. In this way Love begins in Beauty and ends in Pleasure.

—*Marsilio Ficino*, De amore

These statements seem diametrically opposed not only in content but also
in tendency: Ficino looks back to Plotinus and the theory of procession;
Leonardo looks ahead to Freud and the theory of instincts. Yet we observe in both the same style of imagination, the same image of pulsing
dynamism intuited as the nature of the real. And we know that for both
thinkers, as for most of their contemporaries, whatever lay beyond or
beneath the perceived universe was felt to be charged with motion and
energy. It was not that the old and honorific formulas—eternal, stable,
immutable, and the like—were either abandoned or disbelieved. But the
objects of theological and scientific thought could no longer be ingenu-
ously identified with the enduring individual substances, the stable and
visualizable forms, of Aristotle's commonsense world. The forms of
human vision came more and more to be felt as creations of the human
mind in response to a God who manifested himself chiefly in process,
force, and relation.

The persisting question seems first to have been put in its new aspect
by Cusanus: not *what* to visualize, but *how* to visualize it—"no image
will so faithfully or precisely reproduce the exemplar, as to rule out the
possibility of an infinity of more faithful and precise images."[1] It is an
uncertainty not about the content of the ancient wisdom and belief, nor
always about the form, but primarily about the relation between them,
which gives the question its point. When in the proem to Book V of *The
Faerie Queene* Spenser unhappily compares "with state of present time,/
The image of the antique world," we must not ignore the importance of
the words *image of*. It may be that modern times are bad, but it may also
be that the inherited vision of the world, the forms bequeathed the
imagination, no longer suffice. The poet, trying to "reforme . . . the
ill" (V.x.2) he sees around him, finds his given mythological machinery—Christian as well as pagan—inadequate, and it is not until the second canto of Mutability that he re-creates the dynamism of the real into
what Sidney himself called "another Nature."

Such a doubt about the sources of perception, about the relation between the real in itself and in its images, leads to Sidney's emphasis on
creation, to Bruno's belief that poets are legislators, to Michelangelo's

[1] *Of Learned Ignorance*, I xi, trans. Germain Heron (New Haven: Yale University
Press, 1954), I.xi, p. 25.

anguish and Leonardo's often Pyrrhic victories, and also to Montaigne, Galileo, Hobbes, and Pascal. It leads to the problematical relation of cosmos to stage in Shakespeare's later plays, especially *Hamlet*, *Troilus and Cressida*, *The Winter's Tale*, and *The Tempest*. It seems to have something to do with the radical novelty of the artistic styles labeled Mannerism and Baroque: in contrast to Romanesque and Gothic, which are true group styles, these are distinguished precisely by their lack of homogeneity, by the factors of individual revolt from convention, eccentricity, the primacy of personal expression and experience, and—a negative sign—the new awareness of a need for academies. This last may remind us of the paradox embodied in Descartes: the assertion of the *cogito* coupled with the continual appeal to the forms of the scholastic tradition.

The very method of modern stylistic analysis must accommodate itself to these new requirements, for where analyses of Romanesque and Gothic may with some justice describe their objects in purely visual categories, the adequacy of such criteria becomes a question among writers who deal with the later period styles.[2] Wölfflin's famous analyses of form are

---

[2] An attempt to account for the differences between medieval and later concepts of style, and for the development from the first to the second, may be found in Erwin Panofsky's important essay, "The History of the Theory of Human Proportions as a Reflection of the History of Styles," in *Meaning in the Visual Arts* (Garden City: Doubleday, 1955), 55–108; see especially 88–99. Panofsky emphasizes the practical autonomy of schematic and decorative canons in Byzantine and Gothic—canons which are not only independent of "nature" but whose relation to dogmatic content is accidental. Two reasons may be adduced for this: (1) Medieval culture is dominated by a form of constitutive imagination, called analogical or allegorical, which clearly separates the sensible from the supersensible "levels" of existence. The sources of resemblance between levels are ascribed to the higher invisible forms which God incarnates in a cosmos whose perceptual and symbolic characters are given together in a single creative act; (2) yet perceptual information—especially that given by sight—provides the basic language of forms in terms of which the realities of spirit and thought are envisaged. The system of analogical relations, the hierarchic organization of visible and invisible worlds, the very attribution of this work to God—these are all, from a purely epistemological viewpoint, projections of imagination onto reality. Thus, for example, once the analogy is established between metaphysical and physical light, between spiritual and physical place, height, magnitude, and so on, investigation in each sphere may proceed according to its own formal requirements. Given the primacy of religious content, styles are free to develop according to their own practical and decorative needs (it was precisely this primacy which was *not* given during the Renaissance and which brought on the reforms and counterreforms). Given the primacy of perceptual form as a module for constructing reality, the purely visual qualities of any style will always be susceptible to complementary aesthetic and metaphysical interpretations. See J. Huizinga, *The Waning of the Middle Ages* (New York: Longmans, Green, 1949), 222–43; Richard Krautheimer, "Introduction to an 'Iconography of Medieval Architecture,'" *Journal of the Warburg and Courtauld Institutes* 5 (1942): 1–32; Meyer Schapiro, "On the Aesthetic Attitude in Ro-

squarely based on general principles of epistemology and psychology whose importance to his work has been recognized by critics from Roger Fry on—principles which, necessitated by the characteristics of Baroque, had never been demanded by the different needs of medieval art historians and which have as yet been applied to the Middle Ages only in a cautious manner or else with limited success.[3] A period style synthesized from diverse individual styles and diverse "schools," a style whose nature is to be sought either in individual manifestations[4] or else in the most general cultural assumptions about man's relation to the world (the New Philosophy which calls all in doubt), a style whose common factors are located in the particular psychological bases, the process and rationale of artistic creation[5]—such a style seems the natural outcome of an intellectual climate in which the visible forms of the real are no longer felt as external or given but are created and stabilized through the experience of the individual soul and the creative effort of the individual imagination. The contour and stability, the achieved shapeliness of a form, become more and more crucial as the belief in its objective or transcendent reality weakens. If the essence of the real is motion, force, ceaseless energy, and the essence of human perception is substantial form, palpable and enduring—if all forms are in a sense mind-made, so that what is unconsciously given in perception may be as subjective as what is consciously produced by imagination—then the forms created by the mind and the experience through which they are created assume a

---

manesque Art," in *Art and Thought*, ed. Bharatha Iyer (London: Luzac, 1948), 130–50. See note 4, below, for works dealing with the concept of Baroque.

[3] See, e.g., Panofsky, *Gothic Architecture and Scholasticism* (New York: World Publishing Co., 1958); and Otto von Simson, *The Gothic Cathedral* (New York: Pantheon Books, 1956). Panofsky, the more boldly speculative of the two, tends to lean precariously on merely verbal analogies in the second half, after opening with a brilliant description of the style of scholastic thought.

[4] On the problem of defining Mannerist and Baroque criteria, see the symposia in *Journal of Aesthetics and Art Criticism* 5 (1946): 77–128 and 14 (1955): 143–74; Nikolaus Pevsner, "The Architecture of Mannerism," in *The Mint*, ed. Geoffrey Grigson (London: Routledge & Kegan Paul, 1946), 116–39; Ernest C. Hassold, "The Baroque as a Basic Concept of Art," *College Art Journal* 6 (1946): 3–29; Otto Benesch, *The Art of the Renaissance in Northern Europe* (Cambridge: Harvard University Press, 1945), 127 ff.; Rudolf Wittkower, *Art and Architecture in Italy, 1600–1750* (Baltimore: Penguin Books, 1958), chaps. 1, 7, 15. Wittkower's account of the relations between Tridentine religion and art is especially relevant.

[5] The increasing quantity of theory and biography written during the late sixteenth through the seventeenth centuries is a sign of this emphasis. See Wittkower, *Art and Architecture in Italy*, 238–39; for a general treatment, see Denis Mahon, *Studies in Seicento Art and Theory* (London: Warburg Institute, 1947).

new and urgent reality of their own. Forms are the sole embodiments of force, and part of the energy they embody, part of the reality they express, must be that of the very human process, the course of experience, whereby they are created. This new relation of force to form may be seen as a precursor to the modern relation between energy and mass: "What impresses our senses as matter is really a great concentration of energy into a comparatively small space."[6] A particular form is now, so to speak, a quantum of spiritual energy, the compact center of the cultural field it generates.

The consequences for the historical and critical study of poetic style have not been recognized with sufficient clarity. What has been called Metaphysical poetry (the term again is symptomatic of the problems raised by Mannerist and Baroque styles) is manifestly related to the epistemological changes outlined above. All the characteristics ascribed to this style may be traced to a single historical fact: changing conceptions of self and experience at some time penetrated the practice of lyric poetry so that the poem was conceived not merely as a report of prior experience but as the unfolding experience itself.[7] This is not yet the case, for example, in Petrarch's *Rime*. His units of celebration, complaint, confession, and even self-analysis are statements about a situation existing outside the boundaries of the particular poem. In the act of poetic utterance the situation is recalled, described, and reflected on rather than changed or resolved. But poems like *Epithalamion, The Extasie, The Garden,* force us to concentrate on what happens to the poet as he utters the poem. The poem becomes a record of itself, a moment in which past experience is revived and revised—re-lived, re-seen.[8]

This revisionary play can only have come about at a time in history when the concept of *self* was in flux: disengaging from the more objec-

---

[6] Albert Einstein and Leopold Infeld, *The Evolution of Physics* (New York: Simon and Schuster, 1938), 258.

[7] For an excellent and concise description see Frank J. Warnke, "Jan Luyken: A Dutch Metaphysical Poet," *Comparative Literature* 10 (1958): 45–54. The relation of Metaphysical poetry to the formal disciplines of religious meditation has been treated at length by Louis L. Martz, *The Poetry of Meditation* (New Haven: Yale University Press, 1954).

[8] "Lyric expression now does not merely describe a completed interior reality which already has its own form, it discovers and creates this very reality" (Ernst Cassirer, *Individuo e Cosmo,* Italian trans. F. Federici [Florence: La Nuova Italia, 1950]). Cassirer applies this phrase to Petrarch and Dante's *Vita Nuova,* but I do not think interpretation would bear him out. Wallace Fowlie has described the poetry of Maurice Scève in similar terms, but though his general definition is suggestive—he draws it from Symboliste and modern theory and practice—his attempt to see Scève in this light seems rather suspect; see *Sixty Poems of Scève* (New York: Swallow Press, 1949), xii, xix.

tive concepts of *soul* and *person* and moving toward the notion of *experiencing subject*. Soul and person entail the idea of a determined actuality (a first *entelecheia*), a substantial form whose essence and power are always greater than its operation, whose substance is prior to its function. To the Greek idea of soul as individual (member of a species, part of the World Soul), Christian thought added the integrity and singularity of the person, created for temporal as well as eternal life and created in a single act in the image of the Creator.[9] But if this increases the value of self and personality, it does so by affirming the limits of consciousness, the mystery inherent in any *imago Dei* whose being is not fully its own. To affirm the limits of consciousness in this way is also to exalt the function of conscience: Christians "must learn to know the nature God gave them, and the place He marked out for them in the order of the universe, so that they in their turn might order themselves towards God" (Gilson, 214).

Personal experience is thus a discovery of what already is, of a created form and the immutable divine substance in which it participates. The person is a metaphysical and moral object, and in this connection it is interesting to note that the same Romance word usually does double duty for the now quite different ideas of conscience and consciousness. In the Christian person, the self is always bounded by—and merges into—that Otherness which is at once its limit and its source of freedom. This Otherness, part of the person, cannot possibly be known in the forms of consciousness. Temporal consciousness and perception, founded by St. Augustine on memory, can contemporize the flux of experience into a present, a now, but this form imposed on becoming is a defective imitation of eternity, which is "the possession, all at once (*total simul*) and perfect, of interminable life" (Boethius, *Consolatio* V.Pr.6).[10] And such a condition should be seen, according to Boethius, under the category of spatial form rather than that of temporal process or extension: not *praevidentia* but *providentia*—the prospect, as it were, from a mountain-top (ibid.).

The emergence of the self from the person; its disengagement from a mysterious and constraining Otherness; the gradual development of self-other and subject-object as dialectical terms created in and by consciousness; the change from substance to process, from an ethico-metaphysical

---

[9] See St. Augustine, *De Trinitate*, especially Book XV; and Boethius, *Contra Eutychen et Nestorium* II–IV; E. Gilson, *Spirit of Medieval Philosophy*, trans. A. H. C. Downes (New York: Scribner's Sons, 1940). Chaps. 9, 10, and 11 of Gilson contain a full discussion of Christian anthropology, personalism, and Socratism.

[10] "Aeternitas igitur est interminabilis vitae tota simul et perfecta possessio."

to a psychological definition of personality; the transfer of emphasis from memory, which records and discovers, to rational imagination, which creates—this familiar development in the history of thought, perhaps first outlined by Burckhardt, has been documented with increasing clarity and detail ever since. One has only to think of Montaigne, for whom existence was passage, not being, for whom the stuff of experience was not to be seen as issuing from but as culminating in a form which would fix it in its very dynamism: "nous allons conformément, . . . mon livre et moy . . . qui touche l'un touche l'autre." Or perhaps we recall Pico's man, whose creator placed him in the middle of the world and addressed him thus: "Neither a fixed abode nor a form that is thine alone nor any function peculiar to thyself have we given thee, Adam, to the end that according to thy longing and according to thy judgment thou mayest have and possess what abode, what form, and what functions thou thyself shalt desire." [11]

The glory of the soul now lies less in its ineffable and substantive mystery than in the indeterminateness which it is obliged to gather into the forms of consciousness. This notion has been the burden of Cassirer's brilliant studies of Renaissance thought, and in his essay on Pico he describes its importance to the theory and practice of art:

> [Man] is the "sculptor" who must bring forth and in a sense chisel out his own form from the material with which nature has endowed him. We can understand how such a view must have affected the aesthetics and the theory of art of the Renaissance. . . . For art . . . has found a different and a purely "spiritual" goal. It expresses in its own sphere what characterizes and distinguishes mankind as a whole. Beauty becomes, to express it in Kantian terms, the "symbol of morality": for in the capacity of man to produce from himself a world of forms, there is expressed his innate freedom. The artist in a sense possesses this freedom raised to a new power; from it and because of it he can bring forth a new "Nature." [12]

But although this influence of Neoplatonic thought has been exhaustively explored in the field of the visual arts, its effect on lyric poetry, and especially its culmination in Metaphysical style, has been largely ignored in the crucial realm of practical criticism and interpretation. Spenser seems to me to be perhaps the most important means through which this influence is transmitted into English poetry. Therefore I should like to offer the following interpretation of the Garden of Adonis (*FQ* III.vi.28–51)

---

[11] Trans. E. L. Forbes, in *The Renaissance Philosophy of Man*, ed. E. Cassirer et al. (Chicago: University of Chicago Press, 1948), 224–25.
[12] "Giovanni Pico della Mirandola," *Journal of the History of Ideas* 3 (1942): 333.

as a model which embodies the above ideas and brings them to life. Admittedly this is an extract, and no claims are made for the reading as a paradigm of Book III. The passage is sufficiently self-contained to be viewed in isolation. It has the additional virtue not only of exemplifying the poetic process whereby force becomes form but of being *about* that process.

The passages from Leonardo and Ficino with which this essay opened suggest two opposed sources of cosmic energy, one in chaos and the other in heaven. Though Ficino himself, in his dynamic anthropology, has distinguished two contrary but equally natural appetites in man (*Theologica Platonica* VI.6) and has elaborated the corresponding myth of the two Venuses (*De amore* II.7), he has left us no account of the lower cycle to compare with the fascination and the horror of Leonardo's vision. Just as almost a century later something akin to Galileo's vision of force and flux, the atomic swirl of a nature without man, is to be found in the Chaos at the end of Book II of *Paradise Lost,* so in Spenser's third book we feel the presence of a Leonardesque life force. Throughout the episodes of the first five cantos a single energy blindly rages: the force of eros flowing through all things, giving itself only momentarily to form. These cantos abound in the rhetoric and imagery of elemental motion: the fury of wind and water; the sudden burst of flame involved in smoke and sulphur, or spreading like a disease through the veins; the volcanic spasms of earth applied as a metaphor of passion; the onslaught of humid night, image of death, as it periodically inundates the world, blurring forms and relations. Though the poet hints in Neoplatonic fashion that there are two different kinds of love, the evidence of chaotic force given in the opening cantos makes us wonder: Are there really two totally different kinds of energy coursing through the universe and the soul? Is the energy of spirit in some strange way identical with the elemental force? Or is it possible that the Neoplatonic formula is itself a sublimation, perhaps only a metaphor which evades the sad truth about the source of cosmic eros?

The poem is nominally about chastity, and we become aware, as we read, that a similar problem confronts both heroine and poet. Both must impose some form on the welter of experience flowing in them and around them. Chastity is the response to love, and Britomart must learn not to suppress the force which impels her but to accept it, suffer it, understand it, build up a habit of will which enables her to direct this energy to a higher goal in the enduring love of human persons. Like his heroine, the poet himself seems at first hard put to impose form and meaning on the force he has so successfully portrayed. He continually digresses, interrupts an action in mid-career, introduces a new world or episode, expands a small germ into an adventure. The straight narrative line is deflected time and again by the apparent unruliness of a fecund imagination. And by canto vi little of positive value has been accomplished. The first half of the book develops an elegant panorama of frustrations: women are thwarted by men, men by women, women by women, sons by mothers. Virgins run after heroes afraid to love; squires feel the death for goddesses incapable of love.

With matters thus snarled, the poet interrupts his narrative at canto vi and takes us both in space and time to a totally different set of situations: the birth of Belphoebe and Amoret, the debate of Venus and Diana, the search for Cupid and the finding of the twins, the Garden of Adonis. It seems clear that Spenser directs his audience away from the particular romance problems of Book III not only for relief but also for clarification. The canto moves from chastity to love, from Belphoebe to Amoret, from Diana's wood to the Garden of Adonis; from the unconscious parthenogenesis by which the twins were conceived to the fully personal encounter of Cupid and Psyche. Escape becomes exploration. The poet wants to find out whether the frustrations of the first five cantos can be justified, whether it is worthwhile to endure. Why not fulfill every wish, submit to the first pang, assault the nearest object? If the aim of love is pleasure, why not please oneself immediately and perpetually? If it is generation, why not generate as soon and as often as one can? What is demanded, then, is a series of definitions—of love, of desire and pleasure, and above all of chastity. What the imagination seeks beyond this is a form, a vision, in which the previous broken narratives may be gathered up and in which the forces of life and love, time, passion, pain, and decay may be given their due, yet controlled.

The poet leads us to the Garden of Adonis after wandering through a strange world in which traditional and original characters freely mingle; a world of half-realized mythic echoes and episodes, of scenes dissolved in mid-motion, of figures who look suggestively meaningful but are left indeterminate. And yet beneath the confusing enjambment of discontinuous events, certain recurrent motifs begin to emerge. In Glauce, Cymoent, and Chrysogone (III.ii, iv, vi) we encounter versions of the nurse or mother which are all, in varying degrees, defective. Marinell and Timias (III.iv, v) are wounded lovers close to death—Adonis figures. We are prepared, then, for Venus's mythic place, which in its geographic vagueness suggests the kind of *topos* found only in the spirit:

> She brought her to her joyous paradize,
> Where most she wonnes, when she on earth does dwel.

So faire a place, as Nature can devize:
Whether in *Paphos*, or *Cytheron* hill,
Or it in *Gnidus* be, I wote not well;
But well I wote by tryall, that this same
All other pleasant places doth excell,
And called is by her lost lovers name,
The *Gardin* of *Adonis*, farre renowmd by fame.

In that same Gardin all the goodly flowres,
Wherewith dame Nature doth her beautifie,
And decks the girlonds of her paramoures,
Are fetcht: there is the first seminarie
Of all things, that are borne to live and die,
According to their kindes. Long worke it were,
Here to account the endlesse progenie
Of all the weedes, that bud and blossome there:
But so much as doth need, must needs be counted here.

(III.vi.29–30)

Yet a problem immediately arises about the figure of Venus, for she
has been presented, or represented, in a number of aspects which the
poet has not attempted to reconcile. Venus and Adonis first appeared on a
tapestry in Malecasta's House (III.i.34–38), and there, to translate the
myth, Beauty or Love was tyrannized by Desire (wounded by Cupid).
Ogling the dormant Adonis, artfully intensifying her own lust, Venus
concentrates more on foreplay than on fulfillment: it is the feeling she
cultivates, the surface or phenomenology of love—the real process outlined by Ficino (beauty to desire to pleasure) is suspended in mid-career.
The Malecastan Venus is a dead image, a motionless tapestry woven
by the perverse appetite. And the myth is given in its unsatisfactory Ovidian form: Venus frustrated, Adonis gored and transformed to a flower.
But when Venus reappears in canto vi she has descended from "her heavenly hous/ . . . of goodly formes and faire aspects." She comes to ask the
help of Diana in finding Cupid—Beauty enlists the aid of Chastity to
reclaim wayward Desire; the Artemisian *daunger* and independence of
the feminine psyche will be placed in a superior service. This Venus embodies the Ficinian principle, the divine energy radiating in mental and
visible forms through the world, attracting creatures to the "birth in
beauty."[13]

[13] This Venus is not totally identifiable with Ficino's heavenly Venus but seems rather a
Venus in flux, moving from *Mens* through *Anima* toward the *Natura* of the garden.
Compare *De amore* II.7, and see Panofsky's discussion in *Studies in Iconology* (New York:
Oxford University Press, 1939), 141–45.

There is yet a third aspect of Venus, the maternal figure mentioned above. Venus as mother of species is an unconscious love which knows nothing of desire and has little concern for the life of the individual psyche. Like Cymoent (who in effect devours her son so that his descent [III.iv] is like a return to the womb), her love is that of Ocean, mere life, *bios,* and its immortality is that of chaotic substance. Cymoent's form—like the wave from which she takes her name—is a mere shape under which the tidal flux surges and recoils without end, without direction, lending its substance to higher forms, then swallowing the forms.

This fragmentation of a complex mythic figure defines the poetic problem: to draw the different aspects of love together into meaningful relation, to see them whole, present in their diversity yet infolded.[14] So we move from the temporal succession of narrative to the lyric moment of the garden, a place in the imagination where the strands of fragments may be, as it were, organized into a simultaneous "spatial" unity. But at first, though the description is detailed, it is difficult to visualize the space or objects of this garden in any concrete manner:

> It sited was in fruitfull soyle of old,
>   And girt in with two walles on either side;
>   The one of yron, the other of bright gold,
>   That none might thorough breake, nor over-stride:
>   And double gates it had, which opened wide,
>   By which both in and out men moten pas;
>   Th'one faire and fresh, the other old and dride:
>   Old *Genius* the porter of them was,
> Old *Genius,* the which a double nature has.
>
> He letteth in, he letteth out to wend,
>   All that to come into the world desire;
>   A thousand thousand naked babes attend
>   About him day and night, which doe require,
>   That he with fleshly weedes would them attire:
>   Such as him list, such as eternall fate
>   Ordained hath, he clothes with sinfull mire,
>   And sendeth forth to live in mortall state,
> Till they againe returne backe by the hinder gate.

[14] The term infolding is borrowed from Edgar Wind, who uses it to translate Cusanus's *Complicatio: Pagan Mysteries in the Renaissance* (New Haven: Yale University Press, 1958), 168. The rhythm of procession and reversion ("unfolding" and "infolding") will come to be a formal principle in the Mount Acidale episode of *FQ* VI.x and more extensively in the *Mutabilitie Cantos,* where the gods are folded into Mutabilitie who is folded into Nature who is folded into the Sabaoth God.

>   After that they againe returned beene,
>   They in that Gardin planted be againe;
>   And grow afresh, as they had never seene
>   Fleshly corruption, nor mortall paine.
>   Some thousand yeares so doen they there remaine;
>   And then of him are clad with other hew,
>   Or sent into the chaungefull world againe,
>   Till thither they returne, where first they grew:
>   So like a wheele around they runne from old to new.
>   *(vi.31–33)*

Precisely what object is to be identified beneath the changing terms of *flower, thing, weed, men, babe?* At the outset—because there are echoes from the myth of Er, echoes also of the earthly immersion of souls described in the *Timaeus* and the soul-wheels in the *Phaedrus*—one would be tempted to call this a mystical garden. It seems to be saying something about the cycle of forms-as-souls: the seminary of life grows souls, which are then clothed in flesh and so committed to mortal existence. The very difficulty of visualizing this garden with any precision suggests that the images symbolize mystical objects.

But a garden metaphor requires that souls, or forms, or whatever they are, be seen under the aspect of plants. And in this connection we have to remember that it is a garden of *species*, a seminary of things "According to their kindes." This inherent limitation emerges in the next two stanzas when the garden becomes literal:

>   Ne needs there Gardiner to set, or sow,
>   To plant or prune: for of their owne accord
>   All things, as they created were, doe grow,
>   And yet remember well the mightie word,
>   Which first was spoken by th'Almightie lord,
>   That bad them to increase and multiply:
>   Ne doe they need with water of the ford,
>   Or of the clouds to moysten their roots dry;
>   For in themselves eternall moisture they imply.

>   Infinite shapes of creatures there are bred,
>   And uncouth formes, which none yet ever knew,
>   And every sort is in a sundry bed
>   Set by it selfe, and ranckt in comely rew:
>   Some fit for reasonable soules t'indew,
>   Some made for beasts, some made for birds to weare,
>   And all the fruitfull spawne of fishes hew

> In endlesse rancks along enraunged were,
> That seem'd the *Ocean* could not containe them there.
>
> *(vi.34–35)*

We meet with setting, sowing, planting, pruning, water of the ford, dry roots, beds, rows, and ranks. The shapes and forms are now put on by souls: where the term *form* seemed at first to be used in its Aristotelian sense, it is now equated with material shape or outline. Form is now less essential and active, more shadowy. The garden image has solidified; it is closer to matter; the image and the thing it represents are harder to pry apart.

By stanzas 36–38 the character of the garden has clearly changed. The "fruitfull soyle of old" is now shown as founded on "An huge eternall Chaos, which supplyes / The substances of natures fruitfull progenyes." All things are made of this substance, called *matter*, and the law of its conservation is asserted:

> All things from thence doe their first being fetch,
>   And borrow matter, whereof they are made,
>   Which when as forme and feature it does ketch,
>   Becomes a bodie, and doth then invade
>   The state of life, out of the griesly shade.
>   That substance is eterne, and bideth so,
>   Ne when the life decayes, and forme does fade,
>   Doth it consume, and into nothing go,
> But chaunged is, and often altred to and fro.
>
> The substance is not chaunged, nor altered,
>   But th'only forme and outward fashion;
>   For every substance is conditioned
>   To change her hew, and sundry formes to don,
>   Meet for her temper and complexion:
>   For formes are variable and decay,
>   By course of kind, and by occasion;
>   And that faire flowre of beautie fades away,
> As doth the lilly fresh before the sunny ray.
>
> *(vi.37–38)*

Where in the beginning what chiefly struck us was the concrete nature of the substantives—flower, weed, men, babes—here the nouns are vague, abstract: the image of the garden having moved from a symbolic to a literal state now gives way to a quasi-philosophical discussion of force. Verbs are more concrete and assertive than nouns; their repetitive pattern fixes on violence, change, and decay. Form is no longer the source of life's energy. Form has become passive; the force breaks loose and asserts itself, revealing its source in death and chaos. The love which is the energy from chaos does not flower in beauty; rather the form which is beauty flowers in the force which is death. This is indeed, as it has been called, a forcing garden.

But there is more at stake than a garden: the emphasis is not on the thing visualized but on the process of visualizing. The imagination itself, trying to form an image, is shown to be caught in this decay. As spirit gives way to matter and form to force, so art and myth give way to mere nature. Life as *bios* has triumphed over the forms of thought and culture. Wishing for an image of the fullness of life, the poet evokes it and finds his vision to be rooted in death. Is not the wish as well as the image so rooted? The vision, vegetative in form, shows the compulsion of nature to repeat. This is one way of explaining the function of love, but it is a way that bypasses the facts of pain and frustration, the burden of human consciousness, by reducing the problem to plants and species. At the end of stanza 38 the biological garden of species recedes; the poetic garden floats back into view in the vague half-abstract figure of "that faire flowre of beautie" and then plants itself solidly before us in the concrete image of the single lily. We are brought back to the sunlight world of living shapes and colors only in terms of their inexorable return to chaos.

Only by working through these stanzas does the poetic imagination come to recognize the pull of death beneath the dream of perpetual regeneration. The complaint against time is the logical outcome of this process:

> Great enimy to it, and to all the rest,
>   That in the *Gardin* of *Adonis* springs,
>   Is wicked *Time*, who with his scyth addrest,
>   Does mow the flowring herbes and goodly things,
>   And all their glory to the ground downe flings,
>   Where they doe wither, and are fowly mard:
>   He flyes about, and with his flaggy wings
>   Beates downe both leaves and buds without regard,
> Ne ever pittie may relent his malice hard.
>
> Yet pittie often did the gods relent,
>   To see so faire things mard, and spoyled quight:
>   And their great mother *Venus* did lament
>   The losse of her deare brood, her deare delight:
>   Her hart was pierst with pittie at the sight,

> When walking through the Gardin, them she spyde,
> Yet no'te she find redresse for such despight.
> For all that lives, is subject to that law:
> All things decay in time, and to their end do draw.
>
> *(vi.39–40)*

It must be emphasized that the poet does not simply continue his description of the garden: here he creates a new and different space, substituting a second garden for the first. Momentarily, however, there is confusion: it is as if Time had not left the stage when the scene was changed. Stanza 40 attenuates the terror of Time's aspect by making it legal. But if this allows a familiar plea for resignation, the poet cannot heed his own advice: he moves into higher gear and builds another escape garden:

> But were it not, that *Time* their troubler is,
>   All that in this delightfull Gardin growes,
>   Should happie be, and have immortall blis:
>   For here all plentie, and all pleasure flowes,
>   And sweet love gentle fits emongst them throwes,
>   Without fell rancor, or fond gealosie;
>   Franckly each paramour his leman knowes,
>   Each bird his mate, ne any does envie
> Their goodly meriment, and gay felicitie.

> There is continuall spring, and harvest there
>   Continuall, both meeting at one time:
>   For both the boughes doe laughing blossomes beare,
>   And with fresh colours decke the wanton Prime,
>   And eke attonce the heavy trees they clime,
>   Which seeme to labour under their fruits lode:
>   The whiles the joyous birdes make their pastime
>   Emongst the shadie leaves, their sweet abode,
> And their true loves without suspition tell abrode.
>
> *(vi.41–42)*

The forty-first stanza shifts from the conditional of wish to the eternal present tense of fulfillment: art, or dream, whose beautiful forms are insubstantial and whose pleasure is unearned, has begun to withdraw from time.

In the next two stanzas the vision progressively rids itself of mortal and imperfect things: the boughs are not cut by sharp steel, the buds not chewed by wicked animals; thick shade keeps out the hot sun and sharp wind. Finally, the ultimate illusion: the arbor is made not by art but by nature. This is the hope that inspires magic—the hope that the mind can re-create and identify itself with the order of nature. Yet the forms of this garden are not those of specific persons but of bird, flower, tree, and, in general, "lover," male and female. As the forcing garden presented a procession of nameless moments of the life in time, so the pleasure garden gives us equally anonymous paramours who merge now and forever in an ideal space. Death in the escape world is the Ovidian death of metamorphosis, something not taken seriously but made the occasion of a metaphor or a trope. An image of all-things-now, without want or pain, the escape garden has no need of generation, fills no purely natural or vegetable need. Its focus is the moment of animal consciousness, the single moment of relief from tension drawn out into an eternity.

A state of consciousness which walls out death and pain, which is unrelated to generation on the one hand or chastity on the other—such a state is a grasping at straw flowers, a despairing of real flowers which must (like the fair Florimell) expose themselves to the flux of experience, give themselves up for the sake of new life. So in Stanza 45 this pleasance spills over into the forms of pure art: into Ovidian varieties ("To which sad lovers were transformd of yore") and the symbolic flower amaranthus, which means unfading:

> Sad *Amaranthus*, in whose purple gore
> Me seemes I see *Amintas* wretched fate,
> To whom sweet Poets verse hath given endlesse date.

This is apparently Thomas Watson's Amyntas, and along with the allusion to Ovid it makes clear the basis of this world in a long tradition of literary *topoi*.[15] *Topoi* are the treasures of the Muses, the conventional schemata which provide the young poet with the raw material of meaning as well as expression. The *topos* is the opposite of the archetype: its artifice guarantees that it has been formed by some conscious act of mind rather than by the random process of nature, guarantees also that it is insulated from mutability and decay; but its timelessness is that of the library stack, for *topoi* are at the surface, not in the depths. They are merely blueprints, flat forms. Yet Renaissance thinkers called them hieroglyphs because they felt that the significance, the purpose and meaning extracted from past experience, had been transmitted in just such desiccated germs. A poet could acquire them by imitation, could plant

---

[15] I am grateful to Leicester Bradner, who supplied and confirmed this identification, correcting my previous assumption (and that of the editor of the *Variorum*, vol. 3) that Amyntas was Sidney.

them in the soil of his own experience, make them flower as the expressions of his own life and vision. The poet does not passively "receive" the archetypes of life or literature from the race or from his culture: by meditating and assimilating *topoi* he creates them; he is, in effect, his own iconologist.

The transformation of Venus and Adonis from the Ovidian surface of the tapestry to the living world of Spenser's garden exemplifies the development of the *topos* into the archetype in what seems a conscious and fully sophisticated manner. For the poet "finds" the lost Adonis (and ultimately the lost Cupid) not in the biological garden of decaying forms but in the poet's garden of endless verse. Venus and Adonis spring to life in what seems superficially a continuation of the static pleasance:

> There wont faire *Venus* often to enjoy
> Her deare *Adonis* joyous company,
> And reape sweet pleasure of the wanton boy;
> There yet, some say, in secret he does ly,
> Lapped in flowres and pretious spycery,
> By her hid from the world, and from the skill
> Of *Stygian* Gods, which doe her love envy;
> But she her self, when ever that she will,
> Possesseth him, and of his sweetnesse takes her fill.
>
> And sooth it seemes they say: for he may not
> For ever die, and ever buried bee
> In balefull night, where all things are forgot;
> All be he subject to mortalitie,
> Yet is eterne in mutabilitie,
> And by succession made perpetuall,
> Transformed oft, and chaunged diuerslie:
> For him the Father of all formes they call;
> Therefore needs mote he live, that living gives to all.
>
> *(vi.46–47)*

The second is an extremely difficult stanza not only because of its wealth of references, its explosive symbolic possibilities, but also because of its phrasing. It yields two meanings which directly contradict each other, depending on how the following phrase is inflected: "he may not/ For ever die, and ever buried bee/ In balefull night." The main meaning seems to be: "He cannot remain dead forever, or continually pass away. He must reappear periodically in new forms, taking life and rising from darkness." But it is possible to read it this way: "He cannot ever die or be buried, but is something eternal within mutability." Though subject

to the conditions of mortality—he must put on and produce new forms—
his transformations are ways of maintaining himself. Generating form
through time and death, he triumphs over them. Giver of life, he lives
forever.

This is no isolated ambiguity but the focus of a pattern running
through the poem. Adonis as father of forms is associated with the sun
(vi.9), the "father of generation . . . authour of life and light." But we
remember that the sun in the garden withers the "lilly fresh," and we
may also recall the emphasis on shade in stanzas 42–46 of the pleasure
garden: staying out of the sun is a way of avoiding time and process.
Adonis, furthermore, is linked by verbal echoes to the substance of
chaos: the description in stanza 47 is like that in stanzas 37–38. Both are
eternal, maintain themselves through transformation, become the species they produce.

Who, then, is Adonis? Is he a transparent figure of sun and substance,
an instrument of chaos, in the grip of the forces he symbolizes? To settle
on this as an answer would be to ignore the tone of the passage. The
Chaucer-like references to authority—"some say," "And sooth it seemes
they say," "For him . . . they call"—produce an interesting effect, the
sense of a "new idea," a change of mind which has slowly asserted itself
throughout the garden passage. Spenser seems almost to stumble upon
the Venus-Adonis image, and he does so by way of—as an extension
of—the pleasure garden. At the beginning of the garden passage, we
were told that this garden was called by her lost lover's name. Now the
lover is found, borrowed from the Ovidian myth depicted in Malecasta's
tapestry. The first "some say" indicates a slight hedging, an appeal for
support from tradition. As the speaker meditates on the image his cer-
tainty increases, and stanza 47 is primarily his explanation for the *sooth*
of what "they say." The explanation can be felt to proceed from the first
to the second of the two meanings locked in that ambiguous phrase—
from the death-oriented Adonis to the living Father of all forms. This
shift results in the apex of the vision beginning at stanza 48: "There now
he liveth in eternall blis." The formula is repeated in the next stanza:
"There now he lives in everlasting joy." "There now" has a triumphant
ring, the clear outcry of a *Eureka*. The labor of the imagination seems to
have been fulfilled; the image is fixed in all its lucidity as a *now*, a qualitative moment or state of vision which is bound by no particular time, is
in a sense out of time. We feel it as the immediacy of a psychic present, a
living form, which knows nothing of passage. But precisely what vision
is this? What does it mean? What will it tell us of Love?

Whatever this new vision is, it is qualified by a curious addition in stanza 48:

> There now he liveth in eternall blis.
> 　Joying his goddesse, and of her enjoyd:
> 　Ne feareth he henceforth that foe of his,
> 　Which with his cruell tuske him deadly cloyd:
> 　For that wilde Bore, the which him once annoyd,
> 　She firmely hath emprisoned for ay,
> 　That her sweet love his malice mote avoyd,
> 　In a strong rocky Cave, which is they say,
> Hewen underneath that Mount, that none him losen may.

The boar which gave death to Adonis and pain to Venus is not itself done away with or exiled to some remote place but is kept alive directly underneath the bower.[16] And the boar is part and parcel of this new vision; the mountain and bower of Venus are not fully concrete until we become aware of the cave hewn out within. The boar seems to be Spenser's metamorphosis, at this point, of Time-Death—the ache of mortality and pain of love, imprisoned yet alive and very close to the pleasure garden. Adonis, the life principle, and the boar, Time-Death (or, as Renaissance mythographers have called it, Winter), are simultaneously revived—the first from the Ovidian flower state, the second from the nonexistence into which death was willed by the pleasure-garden impulse. The terms of the vision are such that one cannot be revived without the other. With the boar, the whole import of time and death enters into the Venus-Adonis myth.

The boar image allows the poet to confront death on a favorable footing. Time is visualized, characterized, depicted as a dweller in the ideal place, imprisoned in a dream which will not exhaust itself in the service of death. The meaning of Time-Death as conferred through the image of the boar takes on a special quality: it is the enemy to be chastised, the beast to be hunted and captured; it bears the connotations of animal passion, the law of the jungle, the forces of violence and destruction. As a natural foe it must be contained, kept in mind, "firmely imprisoned for ay" within the rock on which the pleasure garden is founded. And here a strange ambiguity inserts itself. The first line of stanza 49, "There now

---

[16] This seems original with Spenser. In *The Dead Adonis*, an anonymous poem printed in *The Greek Bucolic Poets* (trans. J. M. Edmonds [London: W. Henemann, 1912]), Venus's cupidons shackle the boar but set him free because he repents.

he lives in everlasting joy," means literally Adonis, but a vagueness of reference lingers from the preceding lines, whose subject is the boar. Adonis is also in a sense the prisoner of Venus, "hid from the world . . . that none him losen may." It is not only that Adonis and the boar at moments seem two sides of the same thing but also that the place in which both are imprisoned is the place of myth, the imagination. The relation binding them together gives to each and to both their full meaning.

It scarcely seems possible to resolve the contradiction in stanza 47. Quite the opposite strategy is demanded: we are for the moment asked to see one situation from contrary perspectives, Adonis rising from Chaos and descending from heaven. There are two conflicting orders here, two opposed laws conjoined in the figure of Adonis: the law of the conservation of matter and the law of the conservation of spirit. The two forms of consciousness previously displayed—that of the forcing garden and that of the pleasance—merge in conflict. These two perspectives fade together and pull apart, continually turning the passage inside out. Shortly after, the enemy is imprisoned in the shape of the boar, and the boar is conquered. The cosmology of death, the forces of matter and chaos, are caught in a symbolic form and subordinated to the cosmology of life, spirit, eternity. The presence of the boar transforms the meaning of eros: no longer merely the unconscious force which drives species or the conscious escape to pure pleasure, eros works through time, death, suffering, and tension toward the development and fulfillment of a single human soul, toward the knowledge of true love whereby each soul recognizes the value and dignity of the other. It is because this must be understood that the boar is neither killed nor exiled but kept fast in the cave of consciousness as it is already in the cage of the body.

If we turn our gaze to the final tableau we may see what the poetic imagination has accomplished:

> There now he lives in everlasting joy,
>> With many of the Gods in company,
>> Which thither haunt, and with the winged boy
>> Sporting himselfe in safe felicity:
>> Who when he hath with spoiles and cruelty
>> Ransackt the world, and in the wofull harts
>> Of many wretches set his triumphes hye,
>> Thither resorts, and laying his sad darts
> Aside, with faire *Adonis* playes his wanton parts.
>
> And his true love faire *Psyche* with him playes,
>> Faire *Psyche* to him lately reconcyld,
>> After long troubles and unmeet upbrayes,

> With which his mother *Venus* her revyld,
> And eke himselfe her cruelly exyld:
> But now in stedfast love and happy state
> She with him lives, and hath him borne a chyld,
> *Pleasure,* that doth both gods and men aggrate,
> *Pleasure,* the daughter of *Cupid* and *Psyche* late.
>
> *(vi.49–50)*

Desire begets true pleasure on the soul only "after long troubles." That Venus which the soul apprehends in the passive and passionate response of first sight is the soul's enemy. The soul must go the long way around, through exile, through insight, through the labor of control, will, imagination, chastity. It apprehends the true amplitude of love and beauty only in the second sight which is *re-spect*, in that transfigured image, that embodied idea with which the mind returns from within itself to enhance the being of another. Here again one may compare Spenser and Leonardo:

> For soule is forme, and doth the bodie make.[17]

> You who speculate on the nature of things, I praise you not for knowing the processes which nature ordinarily effects of herself, but rejoice if so be that you know the issue of such things as your mind conceives.[18]

This is not, of course, the poet's final word: the garden appears only halfway through Book III and only at the very beginning of Britomart's quest. The garden is myth, and Britomart must move beyond myth, beyond the world of Faerie, into the historical world where she is destined to found and rule a nation. We may see that *myth*, as I have been using the term and as it is embodied in the symbolic form under discussion, has a meaning quite different from that of the ancient concept preferred by anthropologists. Here, for example, is Plotinos: "If myths are to earn their name . . . they must necessarily develop their stories under the category of time, and present as separate many things, that are simultaneous, though different in rank or power."[19] This is based on the older notion of the priority of substantial form over accidents and operations. But Spenser's myth of the garden is a gathering up of many separate things and processes into a single subsequent form which is their symbol

---

[17] Spenser, *An Hymne in Honour of Beautie* 133.
[18] Leonardo da Vinci, *Notebooks* 1:76, MS G 47r, Library of the Institut de France.
[19] *Enneads* III.v.10, in *Plotinus*, trans. K. S. Guthrie (Alpine, N.J., 1918), 4: 1138–39.

and which can hold them in meaningful relation only by virtue of its simultaneous or "spatial" unity. To this infolding of myth is opposed the unfolding of narrative time, historical adventure. In the systolic moment of myth the soul isolates itself from time, contracts itself to imagination, reforms experience as symbol. It creates a hypothetical world not only because its forms are mind-made and imaginary but also because they are hypotheses—attitudes or "mental sets" which confront, which are submitted to and tested by, the forces of history.

The stabilizing and "infolding" activity of Spenser's garden myth is apparent in the way the various aspects of Venus, fragmented in discontinuous and discontinued narratives, are united. We see, for example, how she comes to embody not only the Malecastan goddess lost in desire but also the earthly Venus of generation and the heavenly Venus of forms. The various maternal and erotic images of the first six cantos have been gathered up into a single form which controls and redefines the erotic force; yet this form is not static, not isolated in a surface outline, but understood only within the dynamic field of the tableau, in relation to Adonis, the boar, Cupid, and Psyche—a field in which each figure is in some sense part of all the others. Similarly, Adonis gathers together meanings not only generated in the poem but adhering to the traditional figure of the dying god. As an image of the male lover who pleasures the voracious mother of generation, he embodies all the nameless youths who are born and quickly die, like flowers, who must perpetuate their images to supply their places. Adonis is the succession of dying lovers, germinal principles, seen from the perspective of the female, imprisoned in the world of feminine experience of which the garden is mainly constituted. By themselves these principles are isolated creative moments, sudden thrustings and vanishings. Only in the imagination—in the form conferred by myth—are they bound together. Adonis stands for that which does not endure, that moment whose very act is an instantaneous spending of itself, a sharp point of creativity. Whatever he is, he maintains himself by losing himself in others. He endures only in this myth, on this mountaintop, at this moment of Spenser's creative life.

The final tableau is not an image of dissolving plants nor a picture of animal shapes but a place inhabited by mythic figures—figures whose form and history and meaning have been created not by nature but by human spirit. Here nature has become culture, dream has become poetry, force has been caught up in mobile form.[20] The mountaintop repre-

[20] See Northrop Frye, *Fearful Symmetry* (Princeton: Princeton University Press, 1947), 74–75, 228–29, 233–34. Frye, however, seems to leave Spenser at the end of

sents an ascent of the spirit to a firm plateau above the ocean of change, yet full of its meaning and motion. In the flickering and momentary resolution of a single complex image, the tableau holds a multitude of references, meanings, feelings, and suggestions together so that they continually act on each other, move and change as we look at the image. The tableau, which is itself a stillness, comprehends in tension the two opposed activities of pure art and pure nature: the tendencies embodied in the first two gardens. Poetry as myth, then, cuts between pure art (decoration, static convention) and pure dream, or chaos, or nature. It begins at the extremes of the rhetorical *topos* and the Jungian archetype—the inert shape and the unruly force—and it works toward some resolution which will bring life to the first and order to the second. Poetry as myth is a stillness of form beneath which the tension, the muscular activity of its life, persists.

---

the forcing-garden phase either because he sees Spenser's garden through Blake or because he reads it as an instance rather than as a creative transformation of the given archetype.

The Discarding of Malbecco

Conspicuous Allusion and Cultural Exhaustion in The Faerie Queene *III.ix—x*

THROUGH AN INTERPRETATION of the Malbecco episode, the present essay will explore three interrelated aspects of Spenser's style: The first is the peculiarly mixed tone in which Spenser narrates so much of the *Faerie Queene* and which is especially noticeable in the second half of Book III. It is a tone in which the comic and the serious, the playful and the contemptuous, may either blend together or follow each other in rapid succession. This tone is directly related to the second aspect, a disjunction characteristic of Spenserian narrative which I have discussed elsewhere and will only mention here: the disjunction between the playful or toylike or hyperliterary quality of his literal Faerie world and the immediate realistic issues which that world conveys by allegorical and other means.[1] I shall call the third and most important aspect the technique of conspicuous allusion: presenting stock literary motifs, characters, and genres so as to emphasize their conventionality; displaying both their debt to and their existence in a conventional climate—classical, medieval, romance, and so on—which is archaic when seen from Spenser's retrospective viewpoint.

These three features control our responses to most of the episodes in cantos vii through x. The local action, the literal sequence of episodes,

---

[1] See "Spenser's *Faerie Queene*, Book I," in this volume.

may feature an outlandish pageant of monsters, mishaps, and perversions; yet their resemblance to stereotypes and their exaggeratedly fantastic or literary character bathe even the most vicious figures and the most critical moments in a comic light. The poet encourages us to feel the extent to which he controls and manipulates the action even when it seems most incoherent in its hurried movement from one to another unresolved episode. From the standpoint of the main characters, this is clearly a world of beginnings and early phases, and from the reader's standpoint the narrator's Ariostan restlessness implies an ample conception whose patterns we have just begun to glimpse and whose complex unfolding will take place in its own good time.

That part of the story which follows the Garden of Adonis reveals a world not only *without* but also *before* Britomart and Artegal, and analogously a world Spenser presents as pre-Spenserian in its orientation toward earlier influences. Thus the *beginnings* which Spenser creates for himself and his new vision are also *endings,* since they involve acts of transcendence or supersession whereby the new either rejects and replaces or transforms and assimilates the old. Characters like Florimell and Satyrane are in different ways boundary figures revealing at once the older influences which limit them and the newer vision they herald. The pre-Spenserian world is adapted to the conventional False Florimell but not yet to the Spenserian real Florimell, who must consequently be withdrawn (to the house of Protean change) after her premature emergence. Satyrane's limited effectiveness in III.vii is probably because his service on behalf of woman is not motivated by erotic feeling. Here, as in Book I, his derivation from the satyrs (reemphasized by a change of shields at vii.30) suggests an early psychic phase in which purely erotic forces (satyr-reign) have been radically suppressed (sad-tyranny, cf. I.vi.26) and transformed into their simple opposite, high courage or "greedy hardiment" socialized in the form of benign chivalric activity.

Another sign of his limitations is his easy concourse with the Squire of Dames and Paridell, who represent older conceptions about to be replaced. The three are thematically linked by their skewed relation to the ambivalent term *service:* Satyrane and Paridell actualize its contrary meanings in simple opposition, while the Squire's courtship of Columbell is turned farcically awry by the term's ambivalence in her demand that he "do service unto gentle Dames" (vii.54); his punishment for serving three hundred women Paridell-style is to find as many who will resist his advances, and in the world he inhabits he can be reasonably sure of almost total failure. Thus he and Paridell wander through Faerie in unresolved and seemingly unresolvable careers. They are joined by

Satyrane, whose future is also constrained by the mold of a static or recurrent activity and who accepts without question the cynical worldliness
which colors the atmosphere of these cantos: he responds to the Squire's
narrative with locker-room guffaws, and his one contribution to the theory of sex is a typical piece of Ovidian or courtly advice about the skill
needed to control "a woman's will, which is disposed to go astray,"
namely, "gentle courteseyes, / And timely service to her pleasures meet"
(ix.6–7). All three display the pseudosophistication of older attitudes
associated with the various genres they embody: chivalry, courtly love,
and the fabliau. At the same time they are plainly ignorant of Spenser's
new vision of love, of the new literary world in which they exist as limited or defective anticipations, and of the new heroine who is about to
pass them by. None has penetrated the magic circle of more complicated
psyches in which chastity and love, or temperance and desire, are two
sides of the same disposition.

Although Paridell had been immediately identified "by the burning
hart, which on his brest / He bare" (viii.45), his true colors blend into
this atmosphere until they are brought out by the appearance of Britomart outside Malbecco's house, and from this point on Spenser discloses his nature and function with increasing depth. The Malbecco episode is introduced in all its conventionality as Spenser emphasizes the
climate of literary cliché surrounding the fabliau triangle in which Malbecco and Hellenore replay January and May while Paridell replays the
courtly adulterer. The miserly cuckold first appears to us with his familiar attributes as seen through the eyes of the Squire of Dames (ix.3–6),
which is entirely appropriate, since the Squire knows him as a stereotypical inhabitant of the same socioliterary milieu he himself occupies (a
milieu which includes the *Amores, The Adventures of Master F. J.*, and
the *Romance of the Rose*, where the husband is a Jealousy figure). But the
fabliau is soon complicated by its juxtaposition to the rape-of-Helen
motif. Paridell and Hellenore (Helen-whore, Helen-over-again) are
lesser versions of their ancient literary prototypes. The association makes
the husband in the old worn-out triangle an old worn-out Menelaus.

Paridell is effectually tyrannized by his ancestor: he can only reenact,
in a compulsively repetitive alternation of arms and love, what those
lovers did once, but fatefully. He has withdrawn from history to Faerie,
from the politically centered world of heroic antiquity to the self-
centered isolation of the courtly game,

> for faire Ladies love, and glories gaine,
>   My native soile have left, my dayes to spend
> In sewing deeds of armes, my lives and labours end.
>
> *(ix.37)*

Paris and Helen are spent and finished in these lovers; their images reproduced and preserved in shrunken stereotypes have reached a cultural dead end. Deprived of its functional if accidental value as the cause of a momentous event, the rape of Helen reappears as a tired courtly cliché in the diminished world of the medieval fabliau.

In tracing his genealogy, Paridell praises Paris and Helen as the first courtly adulterers and measures their fame by their ability to ruin Troy and make "many Ladies deare lament / The heavie losse of their brave Paramours" (ix.35). Paris's *idell* descendant sees Troy as no longer anything "but an idle name" (ix.33), a thing of the past whose only enduring significance was that it gave birth to courtly love. Britomart by questioning elicits from Paridell a view quite different from his own, a history whose British chapter he has heard from "Old *Mnemon*" but does not know firsthand. In this Virgilian perspective, ancient Troy (which had "raignd so many yeares victorious," ix.39) must be destroyed so that it may be resurrected and revised—sustained and transcended first by Rome, then by British Troynovant (ix.38–51). The example and influence of Paris ("Most famous Worthy of the world, by whom / That warre was kindled, which did *Troy* inflame," ix.34) suggests the extent to which its civilization has fallen off from its original estate and been cut off from its primal energies—a decline which Paridell and Britomart interpret in significantly different ways:

> angry Gods, and cruell skye
> Upon thee heapt a direfull destinie,
> What boots it boast thy glorious descent,
> And fetch from heaven thy great Genealogie . . .
>
> *(ix.33)*

> ensample of mans wretched state,
> That floures so fresh at morne, and fades at evening late.
>
> *(ix.39)*

The "antique *Troian* stocke" (ix.47) must be uprooted so that its seed may be scattered on new soil, its decadence washed away and vigor renewed by a return to the elemental matrix of ocean. The exiled race can only renew itself by confronting, fighting, and finally merging with its opposite, the native tribes who wish to conserve their pure savage or primitive state from the forces of change and history. Moving through war to concord, New Troy will finally assure its survival by taking into itself the youth or natural vigor of the conquered enemy. And as Britomart knows, the ocean is twice furrowed, Troy's seed twice resurrected from the watery grave and garden to which it was uncertainly committed in the hope of new beginnings: the voyages of Aeneas to Italy (ix.40–43) and Brutus to Britain (ix.48–51) are described as parallel courses of flight. In the second of the three stanzas on Aeneas, Paridell discusses an ancient model of the institution represented in its decayed form by the marriage of Malbecco and Hellenore:

> he with old *Latinus* was constraind,
> To contract wedlock: (so the fates ordaind.)
> Wedlock contract in bloud, and eke in blood
> Accomplished, that many deare complaind:
> The rivall slaine, the victour through the flood
> Escaped hardly, hardly praisd his wedlock good.
>
> *(ix.42)*

Paridell's choice of words, especially the thrice-uttered *wed-lock*, reveals his own general aversion to that unhappy state, but his insinuation that Aeneas was a fool of fate is balanced by our own different view of the hero's sense of obligation to history—a view conditioned partly by our knowledge of Merlin's chronicle in canto iii, partly by the obvious contrast (which Paridell no doubt misses) between the divinely ordained mingling of antique Trojan with primitive Italic blood and the sheer self-interest of Malbecco's contract.[2]

Paridell's account would have ended on his express and favorite subject, himself, had not Britomart redirected his narration toward her race and country. This conflict of interests echoes, amplifies, and explains her earlier triumph over Paridell in the armed encounter outside the castle. There he is first polarized as evil by his negative response to Britomart (ix.14) when she seeks shelter in the swine-shed protecting the three companions from bad weather. Spenser presents their argument as a comically inflated fuss over her effort to come in out of the rain (see especially stanzas 13 and 14). Paridell is not a significant obstacle for Britomart, and if he evokes a momentary counterfury in her, if she is forced into what seems an excessively masculine and aggressive posture, this is because the new heroine is still in an early phase of her own—as of the world's—development.[3] After their brief and casual collision (ix.16)

---

[2] See the acute remarks on Paridell's story by Thomas Roche in *The Kindly Flame* (Princeton: Princeton University Press, 1964), 62 ff.

[3] Having conquered Marinell and in the same act restored her own psychological equilibrium ("al was in her powre," III.iv.18), Britomart's chief danger during the remainder of Book III will be a tendency toward unnecessary aggressiveness. She gives herself a little too easily to her role as masculine warrior in part because her experience of lust leads her to repress her feminine and erotic impulses during this phase of her adven-

she recovers first, for in the natural contrariety between them it is not Paridell who threatens Britomart but she who threatens him. The reason for this reversal emerges most fully in the Trojan history dialogue, but it is glimpsed earlier in two complementary similes. In the first Spenser compares Paridell's angry charge to an earthquake or volcano; the imagery momentarily relocates him in a world of primal forces, epitomizing both his own unstable nature and the real character of the energies which drive him:

> Tho hastily remounting to his steed,
>   He forth issew'd; like as a boistrous wind,
>   Which in th'earthes hollow caves hath long bin hid,
>   And shut up fast within her prisons blind,
>   Makes the huge element against her kind
>   To move, and tremble as it were agast,
>   Untill that it an issew forth may find;
>   Then forth it breakes, and with his furious blast
> Confounds both land and seas, and skyes doth overcast.
>
> *(ix.15)*

Though the unruliness of his passions is suggested, the simile literally describes him as, and therefore reduces him to, the "boistrous wind." The phrase is certainly not epic in tone, and it is the kind of description which could as easily be applied to the *flatus* of Braggadocchio as to that of Earth. Yet despite the contempt for Paridell which the phrase implies, the wind has built up a fairly destructive capability by stanza's end. The courtly stereotype may not be the most heroic embodiment of these ancient elemental forces; yet he *is* an embodiment, and Spenser *does* convey a serious image more or less over Paridell's head: the archaic warfare of simple natural forces which have not been creatively channeled into higher forms of organization but have remained blindly imprisoned in their original state until they can only express themselves in destructive violence. If we are briefly reminded of the Garden of Adonis, we iden-

---

ture. Busirane, who plays on this tendency, conveys some of his own animus against the opposite sex into Britomart's psyche on the blade of his sword. The wound is superficial, but Amoret sees and indicates the danger (xii.33–35): in wanting to revenge herself on masculine nature, Britomart jeopardizes her own capacity for chaste affection and therefore its embodiment in, and as, Amoret. In the 1590 edition, Spenser had Bellona rather than Minerva in the first line of ix.22. Bellona loved war for its own sake, and the "impetuous rage and forse" with which Britomart and Paridell make contact, unhorsing both, suggests the excessive ferocity which besets Britomart at this moment.

tify this Paridell force not with the chaos which periodically lends itself
to new seasons of growth but with the imprisoned boar.

Seven stanzas later Britomart doffing her armor is described as the
opposing figure of militant reason:

> Like as *Minerva*, being late returnd
>   From slaughter of the Giaunts conquered;
>   Where proud *Encelade*, whose wide nosethrils burnd
>   With breathed flames, like to a furnace red,
>   Transfixed with the speare, downe tombled ded
>   From top of *Hemus*, by him heaped hye;
>   Hath loosd her helmet from her lofty hed,
>   And her *Gorgonian* shield gins to untye
> From her left arme, to rest in glorious victorye.

(ix.22)

Again, though Enceladus is too inflated a role for Paridell, the two have
something in common in being carriers of the fiery element which broke
forth from Paris's unruly soul to engulf Troy and which will again break
forth in the houses of Malbecco and Busirane. In casually disposing of
the burning and boisterous Paridell, Britomart is really fighting another
fight: as Minerva she has triumphed over the effort of the primeval
earth-forces to restore their ancient dominion; the association identifies
not only Paridell but also Argante and Ollyphant (vii.47–50) with powers overthrown long ago but always present and dangerous. By following
Natalis Comes and having Britomart-Minerva do the job more often assigned to Jove, Spenser emphasizes the idea of the triumph of the new
order over the old. The suggestions adhering to the Gorgonian shield
may remind us that Britomart's strength has been augmented by the
power of the enemy she had already defeated in cantos ii–iv: the oceanic
passion which she controlled and sublimated in overthrowing Marinell
(iv.12–18). Britomart has not had to draw her sword, which she does
only when she is personally, inwardly threatened—as by Gardante in
canto i and Busirane in canto xii.

The disparity between the insignificant squabble of knights and the
grand scale of the comparisons leads us to the particular use Spenser
makes of narrative disjunction in this episode: the distinction between
the local forms of disorder and the disorderly forces which—fundamental, universal, and recurrent—are by no means confined to these forms.
Britomart cannot, of course, finally dispel the threat of unruly erotic
forces, nor would she want to. She challenges not the forces themselves,
but their particular constellation in Paridell: so obvious a stereotype of

false love is not likely to pose serious problems for the devotees of true love. The force Paridell "borrows" temporarily will emerge in much subtler and more sinister forms in cantos xi and xii, where it confronts chaste women and faithful lovers who harm themselves and each other in spite of their good intentions. When Paridell, Malbecco, and Hellenore are replaced by Amoret, Scudamour, and Busirane, the problems which ensue are of an entirely different order of complexity and difficulty. Thus if Spenser laughs the first triangle out of court it is not because its perversions of marriage, seduction, and love are likely to have strong appeal for true lovers; on the contrary, the evils which threaten a real relationship are caricatured by straw men which make them seem deceptively clear and unattractive. The straw men are too familiar and too artificial to be taken seriously. The actual dangers to love must be liberated from the stereotypes and given new relevance, new immediacy, in more problematical representations.

This process of revitalization is epitomized in Spenser's treatment of Malbecco, most obviously in the way the situation draws out the various meanings which lurk in the name itself. *Becco* means not only "cuckold" but also "burner" (of a lamp), "he-goat," "beak," and "prow" of a ship—a series which compactly identifies the source of his lust, of his jealousy, and of his predetermined betrayal (in this context the prefix *mal-*, which here and in *Malecasta* yokes "male" together with "evil," also suggests "defective"). The nautical allusion is evoked not only by the ship-launching presence of Helen in the background but also by the ocean image which pervades the third book and by the frequent references—literal or metaphoric—to sailing and to drowning (ix.3, 36, 37, 40, 41, 48; x.6, 17, 56, 58). Malbecco has committed himself to a course he is not fit to navigate among the waves of passion. Like Paridell (who differs only in being more shipshape) he has doomed himself to spend his days and end his life and labors metaphorically asea. He may be contrasted to Aeneas (ix.40−43) and Brutus (ix.48−51), who return to the elemental matrix in parallel courses of flight and find new life on the thither shore for the "antique Troian stocke" (ix.47); to Marinell and Florimell, who are committed by Proteus's knowledge or power to the depth of the flux where time brings truth; and to Britomart, who in the fourth canto had developed an image more applicable to Malbecco than to herself:

> Huge sea of sorrow, and tempestuous griefe,
> Wherein my feeble barke is tossed long,
> Far from the hoped haven of relief,
> . . . .

> . . . my feeble vessell crazd, and crackt
> Through thy strong buffets and outrageous blowes,
> Cannot endure, but needs it must be wrackt
> On the rough rocks, or on the sandy shallowes,
> The whiles that love it steres, and fortune rowes.
>
> *(iv.8–9)*

For Britomart, who remains briefly on the edge of the "Continent" (iv.10), this is a moment of weakness during which she luxuriates in her helplessness and "sweet consuming woe" (xi.45); for Malbecco it is the chosen way of life. The literal or metaphoric proximity to ocean is the sign of return or regression to an archaic condition. And the difference between literal and metaphoric is important: characters like Britomart and Florimell who see the ocean near or around them know well what condition they are in and can do something about it; but the figurative ocean is at once revealed to readers and concealed from self-deceiving characters who think of themselves as safely inland—Paridell, for example, places the oceanic experience in earlier generations (ix.31–32).

Behind the cuckold is the shadow of the he-goat: animal lust not yet deprived of sexual vigor, a symbol which yokes together the compulsion and privation tormenting the old man. Malbecco's being is dominated by the goat rather than by the satyrs to whom Spenser finally consigns Hellenore. Husband and wife are sent along different paths in their regression from complexity to simplicity, from human to sub- or prehuman lives. Monogamy is unnatural for the kind of disposition embodied in Hellenore, who "does joy to play emongst her peares, / And to be free from hard restraint and gealous feares" (ix.4). If courtly adultery brings some relief from the captivity of arranged marriage, it is at best a risky and makeshift solution whose terms are set by, and chiefly for, the "learned lover" (x.6): Paridell's incendiary art is a warfare aimed as much against the object of desire as against the husband. His "deeds of armes" consist of "continuall battery" aimed at breaching the fort (x.10), destroying whatever resistances protect the feminine psyche, reducing woman to a False Florimell. Even Hellenore wants more than that: she finds her proper place and realizes her ideal of domestic bliss by withdrawing from civilization to the primitive and innocent pastoral world of the satyr community.

With their collective society and pastoral sufficiency, their free and joyful sexuality, the "jolly *Satyres* full of fresh delight" (x.44) express all the impulses perverted by the unserviceable lecher, the antisocial miser whose plenty makes him poor. As his antithesis, they provide a caricature which illuminates Hellenore's ideal of domestic bliss—an ideal denied by the monogamous (or adulterous) bondage imposed by civilized institutions on her freewheeling nature. Thus the satyrs "every one as commune good her handeled," but they also made her their housewife, dairymaid, and May queen, with the result that "shortly she *Malbecco* has forgot, / And eke Sir *Paridell*" (x.36–37). It is an outlandish solution, an archaic if benign fantasy of the sort of social idyll—no longer possible—where such impulses as Hellenore's may be liberated and "naturally" fulfilled. It is also Spenser's judgment on Helen and the centuries of male worship which have elevated her into a heroic institution. Hellenore is Helen *de*glamorized and returned to her proper place.

Malbecco's is a grimmer fate. He first joins and later is rejected by the satyrs' herd of goats (x.47, 52). Finally, "prickt forth with loves extremities, / That is the father of foule gealousy" (x.22), he degenerates into the abstracted passion of jealousy. It is here that Spenser lays bare the real psychic basis of the stereotype and—in that revelation—rescues it from its existence as a cliché:

> But through long anguish, and selfe-murdring thought
> > He was so wasted and forpined quight,
> > That all his substance was consum'd to nought,
> > And nothing left, but like an aery Spright,
> > That on the rockes he fell so flit and light,
> > That he thereby receiv'd no hurt at all,
> > But chaunced on a craggy cliff to light;
> > Whence he with crooked clawes so long did crall,
> > That at the last he found a cave with entrance small.
>
> Into the same he creepes, and thenceforth there
> > Resolv'd to build his balefull mansion,
> > In drery darkenesse, and continuall feare
> > Of that rockes fall, which ever and anon
> > Threates with huge ruine him to fall upon,
> > That he dares never sleepe, but that one eye
> > Still ope he keeps for that occasion;
> > Ne ever rests he in tranquillity,
> > That roring billowes beat his bowre so boystrously.
>
> Ne ever is he wont on ought to feed,
> > But toades and frogs, his pasture poysonous,
> > Which in his cold complexion do breed
> > A filthy bloud, or humour rancorous,
> > Matter of doubt and dread suspitious,
> > That doth with curelesse care consume the hart,

Corrupts the stomacke with gall vitious,
Croscuts the liver with internal smart,
And doth transfixe the soule with deathes eternall dart.

Yet can he never dye, but dying lives,
And doth himselfe with sorrow new sustaine,
That death and life attonce unto him gives,
And painefull pleasure turnes to pleasing paine.
There dwels he ever, miserable swaine,
Hatefull both to him selfe, and every wight;
Where he through privy griefe, and horrour vaine,
Is woxen so deform'd, that he has quight
Forgot he was a man, and *Gealousie* is hight.

(x.57–60)

As Malbecco *degenders* into this single and simple form, Spenser complicates the climate of allusion in which he is set. His situation with Hellenore is translated into an ancient and primitive equivalent: Just as he willfully imprisoned his wife and himself, so here he *resolves* to build in dreary darkness and continual fear. The odd reference to *that* rock suggests that he has chosen an already prepared environment, and indeed "that rockes fall" is not merely an analogue of Hellenore's fall but also a respectable antique torment. The circumstances of life which Malbecco had from the beginning unknowingly chosen reflect those of old Tartarean victims—Tityus, Tantalus, Ixion, the Lapithae—especially as they are described by Virgil (*Aeneid* VI.595 ff.), though with a crucial difference: pagans were victims of the gods, punished and deprived for aspiring to divine fulfillment and arousing divine *phthonos;* Malbecco's torments are not only self-inflicted but ultimately self-pleasing. As he changes before our eyes into a generic and elemental figure, the passion which feeds "it selfe with selfe-consuming smart" (xi.1), he assumes some of the characteristics of despair, traits earlier represented by Spenser in the "man of hell" who also dwelt "low in an hollow cave, / Farre underneath a craggie clift ypight, / Darke, dolefull, dvearie, like a greedie grave," and who also was unable to die (I.ix.33, 54).

Spenser does not reveal Malbecco's new name until the end of this metamorphic process. The effect is to suggest a more profound and resonant notion of jealousy, to make the surfaces of literary cliché seem to conceal the basic process of psychic self-destruction, and thus to convert the dead stereotype into a living archetype. The vigor and animus of Spenser's description, the energy with which he demolishes Malbecco, may surprise us into a new view of the relation between the familiar so-

cial comedy and the serious human problems which the comedy, in its
function as a recognizable literary *divertissement,* diminishes more than
it displays.

Having liberated jealousy from Malbecco, Spenser reintroduces it in
the new context of Scudamour and Amoret at the beginning of canto xi.
He does this in a deceptive manner, however, for he presents himself as
eager to leave the whole problem behind and to get on to more pleasant
matters:

> O hatefull hellish Snake, what furie furst
>> Brought thee from balefull house of *Proserpine,*
>> Where in her bosome she thee long had nurst,
>> And fostred up with bitter milke of tine,
>> Fowle Gealosie, that turnest love divine
>> To joylesse dread, and mak'st the loving hart
>> With hatefull thoughts to languish and to pine,
>> And feed it selfe with selfe-consuming smart?
> Of all the passions in the mind thou vilest art.
>
> O let him far be banished away,
>> And in his stead let Love for ever dwell,
>> Sweet Love, that doth his golden wings embay
>> In blessed Nectar, and pure Pleasures well,
>> Untroubled of vile feare, or bitter fell.
>> And ye faire Ladies, that your kingdomes make
>> In th'harts of men, them governe wisely well,
>> And of faire *Britomart* ensample take,
> That was as trew in love, as Turtle to her make.
>
> *(xi.1–2)*

The first stanza continues the subject of the previous canto and in fact
makes explicit the antique character of Malbecco's "balefull mansion."
But the context is subtly shifted from false love to true love, shifted
therefore from narrative retrospect to anticipation of Scudamour and
Amoret. The reference forward is a little more sharply focused in the
second stanza: sweet love with his golden wings anticipates "the winged
boy in colours cleare / Depeincted" on Scudamour's shield (xi.7), while
Amoret has been trained in the Garden of Adonis (vi.51–53) to make
her kingdom in the heart of one man. The first stanza touches on the
troubles which threaten true love, but the poet immediately recoils from
this prospect; the heightened tone and imagery of the second stanza reveal him overleaping troubles to imagine the happy ending. The poet
seems to allow himself a moment of weakness, as if he has had enough of

the pains and perversions of false love and longs for an easy, a no doubt premature, resolution. This tone effects a modulation into the more serious episode to follow and guides us into the more innocent and well-meaning sensibilities of his true lovers—Britomart, Scudamour, and Amoret—for it is their longing he imitates. In the case of Scudamour and Amoret, the longing for union and resolution is too intense, as the rejected first ending of Book III reveals, and is no doubt based on a pattern of expectations which gave rise to their dilemma. But since the poet himself expresses or "feels" this longing it appears more natural, more understandable.

Malbecco's metamorphosis was presented in the mode of literary wish-fulfillment: the evil was artificially isolated, condensed in a clear and distinct personification, and then discarded as if the poet could do away with it by sticking a pin in its image: "O let him far be banished away." At the same time he transferred jealousy from the local personification to the generalized metaphor of the snake, one of whose iconographic referents is envy (cf. I.iv.31 and V.vii.30). The snake of envy and jealousy appeared previously in the wake of the "griefe, and despight, and gealousie, and scorne" which dogged Malbecco on having been "so shamefully forlorne of womankind; / That as a Snake, still lurked in his wounded mind" (III.x.55). It will reappear as a metaphor applied to the stuff of Busirane's tapestries (xi.28) and, in amplified form, as the wounded dragon supporting Cupid in the gold statue of the first room (xi.48). As both these contexts suggest, the mind wounded first by desire, then by jealousy and/or envy, provides a backdrop and basic support to the condition embodied as Busirane's house.

Through the interrelated uses of the mixed tone, the disjunctive narrative style, and conspicuous allusion, Spenser has clearly labeled and discarded the antiquated form of Malbecco. Similarly Paridell's antiquated version of the Trojan War, a view sustained in degenerate form by the courtly love imagination, has been discarded and replaced. In both cases the technique of conspicuous allusion has been used to present the degenerate forms as medievalized versions of culturally earlier insights and motifs (*earlier* here means pagan, though it may include native Celtic lore—e.g., Merlin—and early Christianity, as in those sections of Book I which focus on Orgoglio and Despair). We have seen that Spenser's narrative and rhetorical as well as tonal devices enforce the disjunctive relation between the poem's "flat" characters, its fairy-tale atmosphere, and the serious problems of life beneath or behind the narrative surface. A figure like Malbecco emerges briefly as a *condensation* into human form of a set of conventional notions and psychological forces.

These notions and forces are "eterne in mutabilitie"; like Adonis and the chaos under the Garden of Adonis, or like Nature's mutability, they persist by continually trying on and casting off forms; this fluid process of condensation and evaporation or dissolution goes on at the level of culture and history, in the life of the individual psyche, and during the course of Spenser's poem itself. The mixed and varying tone controls our changing attitudes toward and distance from the condensations, it keeps us from taking these temporary figures too seriously, and it sustains our awareness of the underlying forces as distinct from the characters who temporarily and often defectively embody those forces.

The process of condensation affects positive as well as negative characters, and I should like to conclude with a discussion of the way the techniques described with reference to the Malbecco episode operate in the presentation of a more central set of characters, Spenser's new boundary figures. The limitations inherent in primitive archaism may but need not develop into the codified medieval perversions of antique—that is, antiquated—archaism. Thus Spenser opposes to the discards his own revised versions of pagan and Celtic primitives, among whom are Merlin, Proteus, Cymoent, Glauce, Venus, the satyrs, Satyrane, Belphoebe, Florimell, Marinell, Amoret, Scudamour, Britomart, Artegal, and Arthur. These figures tend to group and regroup according to various relational contexts. Belphoebe, Amoret, and Florimell, for example, are definable in different ways by their relations to their antecedents, to each other, to their consorts, and to Britomart. Belphoebe and Amoret are complicated revisions of Diana and Venus: though their natures are distinguished more or less in terms of the typical differences between the goddesses, each twin infolds characteristics of both goddesses. By contrast, Florimell combines aspects of two Venuses, Urania and Pandemos, the Neoplatonic goddess of beauty and (as her name suggests) the Lucretian goddess of generation; these aspects are in turn qualified by variants of Belphoebe's chastity and Amoret's helplessness, and Florimell is further defined by the similarity as well as by the contrast of False Florimell. Joined to their consorts, these three boundary figures embody forms of disposition and relation which Spenser coordinates with three different moments of culture and levels or domains of experience: Marinell and Florimell are classical figures closely involved in the world of nature and generation. Scudamour and Amoret are medieval figures active in the precarious and ambiguous mixing range of *courtship*, understood in its social as well as its sexual meaning. Timias and Belphoebe play out a refined version of certain aspects of the courtly love relation transformed to the ideals of the Renaissance sonnet: the lowly lover gives up everything, including the possibility of erotic fulfillment, to remain in the presence of his goddesslike beloved and to devote himself to worship and honorable service.

Each of these three levels and relations is one-sided and incomplete, and each excludes, yet is troubled by, the dominant characteristics of the other levels. The movement from the earlier to the later cultural moments is also a movement away from a relatively primitive and untamed natural milieu toward a sublimated, a highly sophisticated and artificially controlled, form of "nature" (and relation) conceived as a pastoral retreat from the threats and uncertainties of the other levels. Thus from the feminine standpoint the problems which confront Florimell and Amoret are ideally solved in the independence and radical immunity of Belphoebe; but in this form the solution is simplistic and is reached at the expense of the fulfillment of other equally valid needs of both the feminine and the masculine psyches. Similarly the difficulties inextricable from the particular masculine virtues of Marinell and Scudamour are ideally—unrealistically—resolved, again from the feminine standpoint, in the admirable but unsatisfactory service of Timias. The point Spenser makes in this interplay of characters and relations is that all three levels are equally valid and necessary, and all must be reconciled in a manner not possible so long as each is separately represented by, embodied in, a distinct boundary figure.

Therefore Belphoebe, Amoret, and Florimell are conceived as temporary embodiments who must themselves be superseded even though they represent improved versions of older cultural forms. The psychic elements they individually exemplify must be harmoniously concorded—interrelated but not totally interfused—in the ampler and more fully human psyche of a single character whose ultimate destiny lies not in the restricted and essentially traditional or conventional domain of Faerie but in the actual and historical world, the world of Britain looking forward to Elizabeth, to Spenser, and to us. This character is Britomart, and I should like to offer a brief example of her relation to one of the boundary figures, Amoret. At III.vi.51–52 we learn that Amoret was "trained up in true feminitee," "lessoned / In all the lore of love, and goodly womanhead," in the Garden of Adonis. "When she to perfect ripenesse grew, / Of grace and beautie noble Paragone," Venus

> brought her forth into the worldes vew,
> To be th'ensample of true love alone,
> And Lodestarre of all chaste affectione,
> To all faire Ladies, that doe live on ground.

The phrase "ensample of true love alone" indicates the singular as well as the privative character of the model. To point as Spenser does to her singularity is to remind us that Amoret is his own contribution: a new embodiment of woman's Venerean impulse, and in particular an ethically superior version of the Venus whose "delight is all in joyfulness, / In beds, in bowres, in banckets, and in feasts" (III.vi.52). She stands for a complex which may be defined as "the desire and consciousness of chaste affection, true love, and womanhood." The privative sense of the above phrase is associated with the ideal (therefore limited) nature of her upbringing: "trained up" and "lessoned" to a form of awareness wholly dedicated to the experience of *true* love, carefully shielded from any knowledge of false love or even from the sometimes frightening and unpleasant realities of true love, Amoret is unprepared for the problems raised by Scudamour's own insufficiencies and easily susceptible to the obsessive concern forced on her by Busirane.

She is explicitly brought forth into the world to model her new sensibility and replace all previous examples. But the world she enters is archaic; its denizens approach her—as they approach Florimell—in terms of earlier and less exemplary models. And the noble knight "To whom her loving hart she linked fast / In faithfull love" (vi.53) turns out to be unwittingly influenced by the archaic atmosphere of the courtly world, by the chivalric ethos and its self-oriented values. She must therefore be rescued not only from Busirane but also—as the 1596 continuation strongly implies—from Scudamour. But above all, true love must be liberated from its *ensample*, chaste affection from its *lodestarre*, the psychic disposition from its Faerie model. Located in a precarious intermediate zone between the old and the new, Spenser's boundary figures are temporary externalizations, or personifications, whose fixed exemplary purposes are directly responsible for the dramatic and psychological dilemmas they cause and suffer. What Amoret stands for—the desire and consciousness of chaste affection, true love, and womanhood—is jeopardized by the pure, exclusive, and separated figure of Amoret through which the complex is exhibited. It must be weaned away from Amoret and fully internalized by—or better, introjected in—Britomart. Amoret *as* chaste affection is headed toward coalescence with Britomart's chaste affection, a coalescence which can only occur after Amoret has been discarded.

This process of coalescence or introjection begins when Britomart replaces Scudamour as Amoret's protector in III.xi. The function traditionally assigned to man is here reassigned to woman, who is better able and motivated to shield her own impulses of chaste affection, woman-

hood, and true love. Busirane briefly and superficially threatens her protective ability at III.xii.33–34 when he wounds Britomart, causing her
to respond with a ferocity which jeopardizes Amoret. Amoret warns
Britomart not to kill him,

> else her paine
> Should be remedilesse, sith none but hee,
> Which wrought it, could the same recure againe.
> Therewith she stayd her hand, loth stayd to bee;
> For life she him envyde, and long'd revenge to see.

The wound arouses feelings of hate and revenge toward the male ag-
gressor, feelings available to her since her conquest of Marinell. And
these feelings jeopardize the capacity for chaste affection. Britomart is to
be bold but not too bold, for then she may too violently inhibit her "true
feminitee . . . and goodly womanhead," her ability to open herself to
Artegal. In finding, saving, and joining Amoret, she approaches this
goal, for Amoret's qualities are of special importance in the civilized and
social context of love appropriate to the Book of Friendship, which depicts a more advanced stage of relationship than the Book of Chastity.
The sequence of events culminating in the meeting between Britomart
and Artegal—a meeting brought about by her patronage of Amoret—
suggests the following allegory: Chaste affection was prematurely bestowed on, or won by, the masculine lover before either the man or the
woman was prepared for the communion of true love. It had therefore to
be withdrawn into feminine safekeeping, to be guided and husbanded by
the feminine mind until the later and more appropriate moment.

I believe that Spenser intended to have all three subsidiary pairs of
true lovers—Timias and Belphoebe, Marinell and Florimell, Scudamour and Amoret—discarded and introjected in Artegal and Britomart
by the time these last would have attained their consummation. The
boundary figures, all Elfin and Faerie—that is, nonhistorical—characters, embody relatively fixed and restricted elements of masculine and
feminine consciousness, elements temporarily abstracted from the *discordia concors* of the human psyche in which they normally exist. Spenser
explicitly presents them as revised forms of older conceptions and shows
them to be influenced by those conceptions in ways which limit their natures or threaten their fulfillment. At the same time, and with no less
explicitness, he presents them according to the logic of myth as qualitatively "prior to" the more complete and complex Britons who are capable of development and who embody Spenser's new images of man,
woman, and love. As analytical representations, the boundary figures

break the new images down into their elements, exemplifying the "moments" of transition and transformation, and in this sense they are sources as well as personified aspects of those images. But the process does not end with Britomart and Artegal, for these figures are also presented as early or primitive versions of human nature; their context is not myth or Faerie but history, and they are not simply exemplars for the modern age but historical prefigurations who are or ought to be transcended and fulfilled by such figures as Elizabeth.

Thus I suspect that Spenser's final aim, at least in one stage of his planning, was to discard not only the decadent forms—Malbecco, Paridell, Hellenore, et al.—but also the boundary figures, and perhaps even the antique Britons. In Books III–V we see the early phase of that process; this consists in the typically Renaissance technique of discarding the outworn forms while returning to the earlier forms to revise and justify them as both different from and relevant to the present. The cumulative and dominant effect of the three aspects of style or technique exemplified in this essay is the sense of historical consciousness in poet and poem, and it is this which produces the marked quality so often noted in *The Faerie Queene:* the ceaseless and dynamic flow of changes, both negative and positive, the force of mutability driving the fundamental system of Spenser's universe—the *discordia concors*—toward ever-new and never-permanent configurations.

Busirane and the War
between the Sexes:

An Interpretation of The Faerie Queene *III.xi—xii*

THE MASCULINE MIND wounded first by desire and then by jealousy and envy: this is the center of the emotional and psychological experience visualized by Spenser as Busirane's house and depicted in the concluding two cantos of Book III of *The Faerie Queene*. I shall discuss the episode in the light of the general approach to Spenser's poetry and the particular reading of Books III and IV which I have partially sketched out in previous essays.[1]

Britomart, the heroine of Books III—V, visits three rooms in the castle of the enchanter Busirane. In the outermost she finds Ovidian tapestries displaying Cupid's triumphs over the gods and a gold icon of a blindfolded Cupid standing on a blinded dragon and grasping arrows "which he shot at random" (III.xi.48). The walls of the middle room are decorated with "monstrous formes" (xi.51) of false love in gold bas-relief and with the spoils of "mighty Conquerours and Captaines strong" (xi.52)

---

[1] See my introduction in *Spenser: A Collection of Critical Essays* (Englewood Cliffs: Prentice-Hall, 1968), 1—12, and also the following essays in this volume: "The Spenserian Dynamics," "*The Faerie Queene*, Book III: A General Description," "The Discarding of Malbecco: Conspicuous Allusion and Cultural Exhaustion in *The Faerie Queene* III.ix—x," "Two Spenserian Retrospects: The Antique Temple of Venus and the Primitive Marriage of Rivers," and "The *Mutabilitie Cantos:* Archaism and Evolution in Retrospect." "The Discarding of Malbecco" is especially germane to the present essay, which is in effect a sequel to it.

172

who were driven by "cruell love" (xi.52) to commit suicide. In this room she sees the masque of Cupid which emerged from the inmost room where Britomart finally discovers Busirane alone with Amoret.[2]

In addition to the meanings suggested by Nelson, Roche, and Williams,[3] Busirane is simply *Busy-reign:* the male imagination trying busily (because unsuccessfully) to dominate and possess woman's will by art, by magic, by sensory illusions and threats—by all the instruments of culture except the normal means of persuasion. In a vastly more subtle manner than Paridell, Busirane displays before Britomart a slanted history, articulated into three rooms or phases—his phases. His message is that erotic experience must inevitably terminate in torment and breakdown; he charts the psychocultural development of this process from the mythic past of the first room to the latest and most immediate moment in the third room. Tapestry, sculpture, relief, theater, music, poetry, and magic are all put into play to convince Britomart of *Busy-reign's* power and to impress on her the sad range of possibilities offered male and female psyches by the centuries of erotic experience crystallized in pagan, medieval, and Renaissance institutions, as in the literature in which Spenser finds them reflected. "When Britomart rescues Amoret from this place of death she is ending . . . centuries of human experience, predominantly painful."[4]

I

The theme on which Busirane somewhat deceptively plays his variations may be brought into focus by lines from *An Hymne in Honour of Love*. Spenser has been tracing the genesis and uncertain progress of true love, and here he describes the effect of a beautiful image on the noble lover who "feeds his hungrie fantasy":

> Like *Tantale,* that in store doth sterved ly:
> So doth he pine in most satiety,

[2]Thomas P. Roche, Jr., places the masque Britomart sees in the third room in *The Kindly Flame* (Princeton: Princeton University Press, 1964), 86; but, as Alastair Fowler has pointed out in *Spenser and the Numbers of Time* (London: Barnes & Noble, 1964), 148, it is important to be precise when Spenser himself stresses the articulations of the experience. Britomart is an observer in the middle room and a participant in the inmost room; the final episode significantly condenses and revises the masque. Cf. A. C. Hamilton, *The Structure of Allegory in "The Faerie Queene"* (Oxford: Clarendon Press, 1961), 158.

[3]William Nelson, *The Poetry of Edmund Spenser: A Study* (New York: Columbia University Press, 1963), 229–30; Roche, 81–83; Kathleen Williams, *Spenser's World of Glass* (Berkeley: University of California Press, 1966), 109–10; also Fowler, 20 n, 150 n.

[4]C. S. Lewis, *The Allegory of Love* (London: Oxford University Press, 1936), 341.

> For nought may quench his infinite desyre,
> Once kindled through that first conceived fyre.
>
> *(200–203)*

"Infinite desyre" is the restless, dynamic, self-transforming force of eros driving both cosmos and psyche through phases of growth, change, development, and decay. In the cosmos, eros binds hostile elements into more stable and more highly articulated compounds; and in its primitive modes the manifestations are extensive, relatively crude, and physical; it must work by force and deterministic pressure to constrain the self-centered and self-destructive tendencies of elemental beings.[5] In its more advanced modes the manifestations of eros are social and psychic, intensive and relatively complicated. As the basic drive, or *conatus*, of the soul it may but need not be aroused, may but need not be satisfied, by a particular external object. In Britomart's attachment to Artegal, shadowed in the attachments of the more incomplete and restricted figures of Florimell and Amoret to Marinell and Scudamour, Spenser sketches infinite desire in its most developed form as a longing which can only be permitted and released if directed toward a particular individual, a longing which in fact is only aroused by a particular individual. This provides a "natural" basis for the institution of monogamy, though it does not preclude the continual threat of breakdown between lovers unprepared to navigate the perilous course of sustained intimate relationship.

But Spenser presents this most developed form as his new vision, a vision which justifies as natural and necessary all the phases of infinite desire, all the restlessness and discord potential in any stable concord, from their primitive origins in the cosmos to their presence in the virtuous and fully conscious soul. It is alongside this justifying vision that Spenser has Busirane set his older and perverse alternative. In his first two rooms he presents two corrupt forms of infinite desire which I shall distinguish as *lust* and *false love*. These forms are antithetical in character: infinite desire as lust seeks vainly to fulfill itself by possessing one object after another; as false love it is fixed on a single object and aims at absolute possession. The tyranny of lust leads to compulsive repetition of a momentary pleasure, to a restless flux of quests and conquests which yet fail to satisfy the inexhaustible appetite. The tyranny of false love produces obsessive fixation not on a mere body or series of bodies but on the total psychophysical being of the person chosen as object.[6]

The tapestries in the first room depict

---

[5] Cf. *An Hymne in Honour of Love* 57–112; *Colin Clouts Come Home Againe* 839–86; *FQ* IV.x–xi and the whole of Book V.

[6] Cf. the fine description of this obsessive state in Lewis, 341.

> Many faire pourtraicts, and many a faire feate,
> And all of love, and all of lusty-hed,
> As seemed by their semblaunt did entreat;
> And eke all *Cupids* warres they did repeate,
> And cruell battels, which he whilome fought
> Gainst all the Gods, to make his empire great . . .
>
> *(III.xi.29)*

The lines shift from the accent on the positive triumphs of love and "lusty-hed" through the qualifying "As seemed by their semblaunt" to the stress on wars and cruel battles. This pattern epitomizes the general drift in Busirane's house from sexual triumph to frustration and from the assertion of virile power to slavery, bitterness, and sadistic vengeance. The gods are assaulted by their desire as if it were a hostile force over which they have no control. Their efforts at relief drive them through various shapes—mostly animal—and toward objects of both sexes. The tapestries stress the extents to which they will go, the humiliations they will undergo, to ease their "scalding smart" (xi.30).

Yet of course the "scalding smart" is also a "sweet consuming woe" (xi.45). The triumphant freedom of the gods, the magical ease with which they rove the universe and overcome obstacles, is shown as fully as their subjugation to lust: "Passion or conquest, wander where they will, / Attend upon them still." Infinite desire is expressed by the tapestries in its primitive, or *whilome*, form as cosmic, extensive, mythic. Primitive also is the restlessness, the instability, of the gods which the tempo of narration conveys as well as the brute physical violence of their exploits and the simplicity of their motives, all of which are far from the psychological subtleties of the courtship game.

Thus Busirane presents the gods not merely as exemplars of lust, but as *early* exemplars which, woven in the fixed and flat medium of tapestries, are images of the past brought forward into the narrative present. The tapestries allow an ironic interpretation to play back over the following phrase in xi.1: "Fowle Gealosie, that turnest love divine / To joylesse dread." For their content is the product of a later phase; it is in the perspective of joyless dread already attained that Busirane presents and reinterprets the gods' "love divine." Thus the jealous mind of the artist reveals itself in the art:

> For round about, the wals yclothed were
>   With goodly arras of great majesty,
>   Woven with gold and silke so close and nere,
>   That the rich metall lurked privily,
>   As faining to be hid from envious eye;

> Yet here, and there, and every where unwares
> It shewd it selfe, and shone unwillingly;
> Like a discolourd Snake, whose hidden snares
> Through the greene gras his long bright burnisht backe declares.
>
> *(xi.28)*

As the tapestries yield to the statue and men replace gods, Cupid and his victims are denoted in more medieval terms,[7] while the god's hostility and power seem to increase:

> Kings Queenes, Lords Ladies, Knights and Damzels gent
>   Were heap'd together with the vulgar sort,
>   And mingled with the raskall rablement,
>   Without respect of person or of port,
>   To shew Dan *Cupids* powre and great effort:
>   And round about a border was entrayld,
>   Of broken bowes and arrowes shivered short,
>   And a long bloudy river through them rayld,
> So lively and so like, that living sence it fayld.
>
> And at the upper end of that faire rowme,
>   There was an Altar built of pretious stone,
>   Of passing valew, and of great renowme,
>   On which there stood an Image all alone,
>   Of massy gold, which with his owne light shone;
>   And wings it had with sundry colours dight,
>   More sundry colours, then the proud *Pavone*
>   Beares in his boasted fan, or *Iris* bright,
> When her discolourd bow she spreds through heaven bright.
>
> Blindfold he was, and in his cruell fist
>   A mortall bow and arrowes keene did hold,
>   With which he shot at randon, when him list,
>   Some headed with sad lead, some with pure gold;
>   (Ah man beware, how thou those darts behold)
>   A wounded Dragon under him did ly,
>   Whose hideous tayle his left foot did enfold,
>   And with a shaft was shot through either eye,
> That no man forth might draw, ne no man remedye.
>
> And underneath his feet was written thus,
>   *Unto the Victor of the Gods this bee:*

---

[7] A sense of removal of time and space is suggested by the last four lines of xi.45: "to declare the mournfull Tragedyes, / And spoiles, wherewith he all the ground did strow, / More eath to number, with how many eyes / High heaven beholds sad lovers nightly theeveryes."

> And all the people in that ample hous
> Did to that image bow their humble knee,
> And oft committed fowle Idolatree.
>
> *(xi.46–49)*

The gods of antiquity may have been enslaved by Cupid, but they did not willingly apotheosize their desire and pay homage to it. That "the people in that ample hous" *do* worship Cupid suggests a more advanced stage of perversion: sexual desire is consciously deified by minds locked into a purely erotic universe from which all other functions and all nonerotic concerns have been purged.[8] The tapestries celebrate the mythic moment when erotic monotheism or monomania overcame noneretic and cosmic polytheism: Jove, Phoebus, and Neptune are shown as diverted from the heavens, the sun, and the ocean (xi.30, 38, 40–41).[9]

The "hellish Snake" of xi.1, the *dis-colourd* snake of xi.28, is now an injured and blinded dragon: the jealous mind grown more monstrous because overcome by a desire whose sinister tendencies it yet supports— Cupid's left foot is enfolded by the dragon's tail, a gesture which argues continuing self-destructive devotion to the cause of pain. The statue represents desire uprooted from any of its functional contexts—cosmological, generative, interpersonal—which require either the symbolic or the literal cooperation of the feminine. He shares with the more orderly forms of desire the characteristics of pain and aggression; but he shares nothing else. Busirane's Cupid is desire solely as a *state of consciousness*, a course of feeling, which is its own goal. He is blind and shoots at random for these reasons, but also because the mind he possesses is turned inward ("with his owne light shone," xi.47), preoccupied and paralyzed by the monotonous recurrence of a pain which can never be quieted for long.[10]

The tapestries depict the primitive age of gods and myths from an obviously slanted viewpoint which makes Busirane's version of the archaic differ sharply from what *we* have seen or heard in the earlier cantos of Book III, for Spenser has already impressed on us the varieties and ambiguities of primitive experience in such figures as Merlin, Proteus, Cymoent, Glauce, Venus, Diana, the satyrs, and others. These figures have smoked edges, ambivalences which make them mysterious or

---

[8] Cf. again the general description in Lewis, 340–46.

[9] See Fowler, 154.

[10] For another interpretation which dovetails with mine, see C. S. Lewis, "Spenser's Cruel Cupid," in *Studies in Medieval and Renaissance Literature* (Cambridge: Cambridge University Press, 1966), 164–68, where we are reminded that dragons were guardians of chastity.

unreliable; only the test of time and subsequent experience will retrospectively establish the true functions and values of their behavior. But
Busirane's retrospect reduces all the gods to emblems of lust.[11] His
woven antiques are tyrannized not only by Cupid's arrows but also by the
spiderlike artist's obsessive singleness of purpose. This is his version of
the origins of courtly love, and it is a model of infinite desire which
conditions the mind to view as hostile, perhaps even "unnatural," any
recalcitrance, delay, or refusal on the part of the object of desire. Whatever the underlying motivations—whether the diffidence of a Belphoebe, a Mirabella, a Florimell, a False Florimell, a Hellenore, or an
Amoret—such behavior can only appear as the Petrarchan expression of
"cruell love."

The transition to the second room thus continues Busirane's history:
random lust gives way to its antithesis, false love; and false love, against
the background of the expectations visualized in the first room, quickly
becomes jealousy, envy, and revenge:

> Much fairer, then the former, was that roome,
>   And richlier by many partes arayd:
>   For not with arras made in painefull loome,
>   But with pure gold it all was overlayd,
>   Wrought with wilde Antickes, which their follies playd,
>   In the rich metall, as they living were:
>   A thousand monstrous formes therein were made,
>   Such as false love doth oft upon him weare,
> For love in thousand monstrous formes doth oft appeare.
>
> And all about, the glistring walles were hong
>   With warlike spoiles, and with victorious prayes,
>   Of mighty Conquerours and Captaines strong,
>   Which were whilome captived in their dayes
>   To cruell love, and wrought their owne decayes:
>   Their swerds and speres were broke, and hauberques rent;
>   And their proud girlonds of tryumphant bayes
>   Troden in dust with fury insolent,
> To shew the victors might and mercilesse intent.

> (xi.51–52)

After the leisurely description of the tapestries, this passage is rapid and
elliptical. It is as if the history encountered in the first room, with its

---

[11] In this respect Busirane is like Aragnoll and Arachne in *Muiopotmos* and like Acrasia
in *FQ* II.xii. Frederick Hard's remarks on the immediacy and reality of Busirane's art-
work are pertinent here (*Var.* 3:398).

wild antics/antiques, is summed up in a manically intensified burst of fantasy which reduces them to a chaotic profusion of follies. The second stanza varies the sense of "false love" from lust to the meaning I have assigned to it, for it identifies false love with "cruell love," which I take to mean the lady's recalcitrance and its effects. Deceived by past triumphs in another kind of warfare, perhaps misled also by the kind of expectations depicted in the tapestries, the captains were no doubt too eager for easy attainment and quick resolution. The same high spirit and urge to dominate which led to mastery in war and government led afterward to failure in love. Their heroic *zelos* was intensified and corrupted from strong passion and emulation to jealousy and envy;[12] their high spirit was honed to anger and introverted until they "wrought their owne decayes." They have in effect left the world or genre of classical heroism and entered that of medieval romance, no doubt by the agency of a *Trionfo d'Amore*, which is also a triumph of the Ovidian over the Virgilian vision. With their generalized references, the above lines seem to compress sad centuries of love and literature in murals in which Ovidian fools still animate Petrarchan gold.

It is against this mural background that the masque unfolds. Literal suicide is a canceled option here, causally associated with the symbolic murder by which it is replaced in the masque. Spurred to revenge by pain and jealousy, the futile and therefore *busy-reign* of the male imagination becomes busier and more frenzied as the feminine will recoils in greater disdain or panic. The masque of Cupid appears as the sophisticated development and antithesis of the pseudoprimitive content of the tapestries: the extensive, promiscuous, and physical pursuits of the gods are replaced by the measured, introverted, intensive, and solipsistic character of the masque. With its marching psychological personifications and its special social atmosphere, the masque brings us closer to the mind, and to a particular phase and state of mind. The movement from weaving through sculpture and relief to the magically induced pseudolife of Busirane's airy masquers, his insubstantial pageant, suggests an increase of effort and activity by the male imagination. So blatant a flourish of mumbo jumbo (especially at xii.1−3) and theatrical display amounts to a flaunting of power. But this intensified show of power dialectically entails an aggravated sense of desperation which is equally visible in the masque. The change from the first to the second room in this re-

---

[12] *Zelos* denotes both "jealousy" and "strong passion"—emulation in its positive sense. *Zeloon* means "to strive after, to emulate, to admire, to commend, to envy," while one of the meanings of the root verb *zeon* is "to boil with passion." This family of terms, which also yields *zeal*, epitomizes the interrelation of eros, heroics, and jealousy.

spect is apparent in the difference between the two Cupids (xi.47–48 and xii.22–23). The first is a statue, "an Image all alone," the second "the winged God himselfe." The first is blindfolded and shoots his arrows at random "without respect of person or of port" (xi.46). The second exercises his tyranny over one figure and lifts his blindfold for a sadistic thrill, "That his proud spoyle of that same dolorous / Faire Dame he might behold in perfect kind; / Which seene, he much rejoyced in his cruell mind" (xii.22). The first stands on the wounded dragon of jealousy and envy he has victimized, while the second rides on a symbol of wrath and fury, "a Lion ravenous, / Taught to obay the menage of that Elfe" (xii.22)—the jealous mind now ravenous from pain, furious for revenge, and actively supporting its rider.

The prologue and presenter of the masque is Ease, who issues forth "as on the ready flore / Of some Theatre" and is clad "in costly garments, fit for tragicke Stage" (xii.3). He bears "a branch of laurell" and precedes a band of minstrels, "wanton Bardes, and Rymers impudent," all singing "A lay of loves delight, with sweet concent" (xii.5). After this the "jolly company, / In manner of a maske, enranged orderly," moves quickly through the traditional tragic pattern from specious order to unhappiness and breakdown: Fancy and Desire lead the way, followed by Doubt and Daunger, Fear and Hope, Dissemblance and Suspect, Griefe and Fury, Displeasure and Pleasance. They precede Amoret, who is led by Despight and Cruelty and whose heart "transfixed with a deadly dart" (xii.21) lies bleeding in a dish. "Next after her" is Cupid, succeeded by Reproch, Repentance, Shame, and "after them a rude confused rout" of more serious consequences (xii.25).

Fowler remarks that the sequence of the masque is "clearly meant to convey the difference between earlier and later stages of a sexual relationship; the later stages showing the cruel and chaotic effects of Cupid at his most despotic" (p. 59). This distinction suggests that the earlier stages must somehow be happier because more orderly, whereas they are carefully controlled images of misery and mismatch. Whether male or female, the personifications parade before us a mind inordinately fascinated by its own states and therefore excessively distrustful of, but uncontrollably attentive to, the dangers and incitements of the surrounding world. It is an experience in which friendship is not possible and in which the characters address each other voyeuristically as objects or enemies. The masque is also a *masking*, as the participants use façades for concealment, espionage, protection, and calculated effects of flirtation or aggression. Fowler's references to *earlier* stages and to *sexual* relations are misleading. The earlier stages were depicted in the tapestries, statue, and reliefs. By this time the relations are more than sexual, yet the basic motive and feeling remains sexual, or rather sensual. Isolated from friendship or generation, obsessively diffused into states of mind and into an intellectualized fencing which aims at total psychophysical possession or else destruction of the object, the sensual motive has been beat to airy thinness until spread over the entire soul. The techniques of pursuit and flirtation, encouragement and delay, combined with the sadistic and masochistic pleasures of unassured love, have become the courtly mind's exclusive preoccupation.[13] Fowler notes that "sexual joy and the obstacles to sexual joy are preoccupations of this book" (p. 144), but he does not recognize Spenser's general message: that the mind must be at least partially freed from the tyranny of so narrow a concern before it can open itself to the fulfillment of sexual desire in generation and friendship.

With their artificially simplified and exaggerated poses, the masquers project an atmosphere histrionic in its character and literary in its basis, for they are acting out generalized roles which imitate literary models. The personified states of mind are learned rather than native, developed and refined through centuries of cultural or literary repetition; this accounts for Ease's branch of laurel and for the prominent position assigned to "wanton Bardes, and Rymers impudent" (xii.5).[14] The masque, in Nelson's words, is "a distillation of unhappy love stories" in which men have always suffered from their own inability to transcend lust and false love (p. 230). They have thus codified their roles as victims of feminine cruelty and despite; and these roles aggressively paraded before Britomart display—with an air of inevitability—the causes for which Amoret is being punished: the experiences culminating in Displeasure lead to male despite and cruelty, which in turn whet the sadistic edge of the furious desire tyrannizing the mind.

The presence and influence of poets indicate the extent to which the experience of false love is a self-generated product of male fantasy. It reveals itself to Britomart as having been created within the mind, protectively sealed off from the actual world. The progress of false love began in response neither to the casual promptings of lust nor to the wound inflicted by a real woman. It was introduced by idleness amid the elegant languor of a court insulated from normal political functions or from the "daily exercize" to which men elsewhere are called (xi.28).[15] Wanton

---

[13] Cf. the interesting discussion of this preoccupation in Roche, 78–79.

[14] Cf. Williams, 113, for a concise contrast between courtly self-consciousness and the "more deeply rooted" intuitive impulses and responses of figures like Florimell.

[15] Lewis, *Allegory of Love*, 341.

books diverting the mind from boredom gave rise to exotic fancies which stirred up desire. Thus the first two masquers differ from the next five couples in that they are emblems not of the conventional states of mind but of the psychic activity producing those states: Fancy is a homosexual object, a "lovely boy" compared to Ganymede and Hylas, waving "a windy fan . . . in the idle aire" (xii.7–8). "Amorous *Desyre*, / . . . seemd of riper yeares, then th'other Swaine, / Yet was that other swayne this elders syre, / And gave him being, commune to them twaine . . ." (xii.9). Desyre held sparks in his hand, "which still he blew, and kindled busily, / That soone they life conceiv'd, and forth in flames did fly" (xii.9). The emblems display a mind enamored of its power to devise airy phantasms, a power outlandish enough to produce in a jaded appetite the effort required to work up new passion. The logical outcome of this autogenesis of passion, and of the centuries of experienced pain built into the masque, is a sequence of cringing or aggressive responses (Doubt, Daunger, Feare) which express distrust of the outside world in general. These responses are then pointed by the appearance of Hope and Dissemblance toward the feminine object in particular and attain to a climactic focus in the central group (Despite, Cruelty, Amoret, and Cupid). At this point, as Roche (p. 79) has noted, the description stops and the orderly pageant gives way to a confusion in which mere names replace iconographically articulated figures. This pattern reproduces in condensed form the earlier rhythmic progression from the tapestries through the icon to the chaotic murals; it is an accelerated repetition of the movement from initial artistic control—or overcontrol—to loss of control, heightened in the masque because of the approach of Amoret. Such a breakdown is presented as inevitable. On the one hand, the mind cannot sustain itself on its airy feast of Barmecide, the game of false love which demands and evokes the participation of a real object, an *other*. Yet on the other hand, the mind cannot tolerate the pain of knowing that the real object—the woman to whom the role of object is offered—has a being, mind, and future of her own. The erotic and sadistic fascination of the game depends on her continuing existence and resistance; therefore she cannot be literally or finally killed. Although the sacrifice of a real victim is necessary to propitiate the angry god, it is not a real sacrifice but a magical illusion; the murder is ritual, symbolic, and psychological only.

The replacement of personifications by mere names, after Amoret, reflects a peculiar shift of perspective which leads toward the final episode in the inmost room. Beginning within the male mind and projecting a spatialized display of courtly attitudes as the ritual object approaches, the masque gradually moves toward and into the feminine mind. The figures following Cupid—Reproch, Repentance, Shame (xii.24)—are sketchily personified and seem more applicable to the plight of woman than to that of man.[16] The thirteen terms squeezed into stanza 25 are even less allegorical and therefore more immediately suggestive of mental actions, states, and conditions. Though their reference is ambiguous, the next stanza quite explicitly draws them into the feminine psyche and associates them "with that Damozell," Amoret:

> There were full many moe like maladies,
>> Whose names and natures I note readen well;
> So many moe, as there be phantasies
> In wavering wemens wit, that none can tell,
> Or paines in love, or punishments in hell;
> All which disguized marcht in masking wise,
> About the chamber with that Damozell,
> And then returned, having marched thrise,
> Into the inner roome, from whence they first did rise.
>
> *(xii.26)*

Thus in the narrative sequence of the episode it is only after Amoret's appearance that we are alerted to the possibility of the masque being imposed on her mind. This delayed shift of perspective reinforces the effect of temporal and qualitative progression which I have been tracing through the House of Busirane. From tapestries to icon to reliefs to masque, and from the beginning to the end of the masque, there is increasing inwardness, compression, and complication, correlated with increasing activity and motion, and, above all, with increasing proximity to the present moment of narrative.

That the masquers returned to "the inner roome, from whence they first did rise" (xii.26) prepares us for their connection to the final episode. When Britomart gains entry into that room, she looks about expecting to see "all those persons, which she saw without: / But lo, they streight were vanisht all and some, / Ne living wight she saw in all that

---

[16] Williams, 108, assumes too easily that the experience is all Amoret's fantasy. Roche discusses the different perspectives on the masque but fails to account for the developing sadism in Busirane's house and therefore reads the male viewpoint in too positive a fashion—"the mask of the triumph of love, in which Amoret, the prize, is about to surrender to her victor knight" (76). Roche's interpretation of the episode is in general vitiated by his eagerness to read the subsequent developments of Book IV back into Book III—a flaw acutely discussed by Roger Sale, "Spenser's Undramatic Poetry," in *Elizabethan Poetry*, ed. Paul J. Alpers (New York: Oxford University Press, 1967), 431–32.

roome" (xii.30) save Amoret, bound by an iron chain to a brazen pillar, and sitting before her "the vile Enchaunter,"

> Figuring straunge characters of his art,
> With living bloud he those characters wrate,
> Dreadfully dropping from her dying hart,
> Seeming transfixed with a cruell dart,
> And all perforce to make her him to love.
> Ah who can love the worker of her smart?
> A thousand charmes he formerly did prove;
> Yet thousand charmes could not her stedfast heart remove.
>
> *(xii.31)*

The substitution of this more condensed and dramatic scene for the expected masque strengthens the connection between them; and one is tempted to read the masque as an explication of what is happening here—or, conversely, to read this scene as the dramatic situation, previously unarticulated, which anchors the masque in the story of Britomart, Amoret, and Scudamour. The "straunge characters" of Busirane's art allude to the symbolic figures of the masque. Amoret's bleeding heart— her desire for Scudamour—is at once the medium through which he works his charms and the source of her resistance to the charms. Since the cruel dart may refer both to her passion for Scudamour and to the torment Busirane inflicts, the two male figures tend momentarily to converge, most explicitly in the stale lovers' paradox "who can love the worker of her smart?" If the dropping blood symbolizes what her painful wound costs her in terms of psychic energy and well-being, either or both male figures may be the cause.[17]

This transaction between Busirane and Amoret, and involving Britomart and Scudamour in ways which are not yet articulated, radically alters the meaning of the masque. Prior to this, its reference had been retrospective: the first two rooms had recapitulated in generalized form not only the past history of lust and false love, but also many of the motifs, characters, and incidents of the preceding ten cantos; the masque furnished the decadent end and climax of this history. But the final episode changes the direction of reference to the future. The masque is now resituated in the beginning of the experience of true love and friendship, where it points toward the threats which will materialize in Books IV and V.

[17] Busirane dips his pen in the wound of love to inscribe the charms which bind Amoret: I read this as an iconographic echo of the influence of bards and rhymers in the masque, an influence she was apparently protected from in the Garden of Adonis and which is therefore all the more terrifying now.

II

By itself, Busirane's masque of Cupid does not deal either with true love or with the personal problems which afflict lovers who have presumably become friends. Except in the most oblique manner and in a few symbolic details, its pageant gives us no information about the reason for Amoret's imprisonment or about the particular problems she and Scudamour face. We know she is being tortured because she will not transfer her love to Busirane, but the role forced on Amoret in the masque is that neither of a true lover nor of a truly beloved. She is in fact miscast: the feminine personifications preceding her—Hope, Dissemblance, Fury, and Pleasance—display modes of behavior and feeling which have little to do with her, though much to do with the conventional sonnet figure Spenser later epitomizes as Mirabella in Book VI (vii.28–viii.27), much also with the carryings-on of False Florimell and Hellenore. Cupid punishes her as if she were Mirabella because her effect on men is superficially the same: "To Faery court she came, where many one / Admyrd her goodly haveour, and found / His feeble hart wide launched with loves cruell wound" (III.vi.52). As an object of hate and revenge, it is irrelevant to the logic of the masque that she refuses love *because* she will not deny Scudamour; the refusal itself is all that matters.

Busirane's motives extend beyond revenge, beyond the masque's archaic presentation of false love, and beyond the merely generalized or symbolic treatment of Amoret as a scapegoat in man's war on woman. What he does in the third room is related not only to Scudamour but also to Britomart. This complex network of relations is not spelled out for us in Book III; it remains problematical. But this much seems clear: in showing Britomart what and how Amoret suffers, Busirane tries to dissuade both from their promised futures. The masque refers indifferently to relations in courtship and in marriage, the latter because of the echoes of the Malbecco episode. Either or both are presented as dramatic rituals in which the woman's role is determined by the male mind, rituals refined through centuries of practice and soured by centuries of hate. Busirane has already abused Amoret's mind by forcing on it an anticipatory image of herself as doomed by the very strength of her chaste affection, and this *abusion* is displayed as an exemplum before Britomart. His rooms depict the phases leading up to the advanced stage of disaffection which his house as a whole represents, and they depict them so as to suggest that the sequence of erotic phases is grounded *in* potential jealousy—the jealousy inherent in infinite desire—not merely productive *of* jealousy. He thus plays on the conflict in the loving virgin between her chastity and her desire, using the intensity of the latter to push the former toward fear, panic, and frigidity. He encourages her fear of losing independence, her dread of male possession, by flaunting the evil power of art and magic whereby masculine eros masters the world and woman.

Britomart's discovery of Scudamour early in canto xi provides a shadowy allusion to a network of erotic themes which will not become explicit until Book IV. She was in pursuit of Argante's twin brother, the giant Ollyphant "that wrought / Great wreake to many errant knights of yore, / And many hath to foule confusion brought" (vii.48), and who is himself "with hideous / And hatefull outrage" chasing a young man (xi.3). The giant, who "surpassed his sex masculine, / In beastly use," gave up his greedy chase of "the fearefull boy" (xi.4) because he feared

> *Britomart* the flowre of chastity;
> For he the powre of chast hands might not beare,
> But alwayes did their dread encounter fly:
> And now so fast his feet he did apply,
> That he has gotten to a forrest neare,
> Where he is shrowded in security.
>
> *(xi.6)*

> Faire *Britomart* so long him followed,
> That she at last came to a fountaine sheare,
> By which there lay a knight all wallowed
> Upon the grassy ground . . .
>
> *(xi.7)*

"As if he had bene slombring in the shade" (xi.8). That Scudamour materializes in place of the giant suggests a symbolic equivalence and transference. *Ollyphant* is spelled the same way in all three of its occurrences (vii.48, xi.*arg.*, and xi.3), and this spelling indicates something more than a Chaucerian analogue. It looks rather like an etymological cipher composed of the Greek *ollumi*—"to die, destroy, lose something"—and *phant*, that is, "destructive phantasy." The giant chasing the boy thus seems very lightly and briefly to condense Scudamour's problems during the next eleven cantos, for he too will be pursued by a destructive fantasy based in lust and infinite desire and variously displayed in the House of Busirane, the House of Ate, the House of Care, and, in a less evident manner, the Temple of Venus. Whereas Amoret's expectations derive from her too idyllic training in the Garden of Adonis, Scudamour's are induced by the conventions of Ovidian, romance, and courtly forms of quest, forms which appear also in Busirane's house. Though innocent and well-meaning, the lovers appear to be conditioned by mutually exclusive contexts of archaic experience which run a collision course in the Temple of Venus in Book IV: the primitive matrix of nature entirely free of lust and false love, and the antique matrix of convention dominated by the various masculine models of lust and false love.

The persistence and increasing complexity throughout Book IV of problems only touched on toward the end of Book III indicates the peculiar quality of Britomart's triumph over Busirane. It also explains, I think, the odd feeling we have that the entire Busirane episode hangs or floats before us deceptively: its surfaces seem at once too real (in the sense of being vivid, visual, immediate) and too unreal in that they appear to be concealing their precise function in the story. They are conspicuously digressive; they puzzle us with their dislocated quality, their unconnectedness; and they invite further interpretation—Spenser encourages this also by his heavy emphasis on seeing, appearing, seeming, and masking, an emphasis which simultaneously proclaims and hides meaning. As to Britomart's victory, it is too complete and easy. Once she forces Busirane to reverse his charms, Amoret is magically healed (xii.37–38) and the whole structure dissolved—"those goodly roomes . . . / Now vanisht utterly, and cleane subverst" (xii.42). The sentiment externalized in this happy conclusion recalls that expressed by the poet at the beginning of canto xi: "O let him far be banished away" (xi.2). If we remember the symbolic transference of jealousy from Malbecco (through Ollyphant-Scudamour) to the House of Busirane, we might feel that we are confronted with a more complicated version of the same technique, a complication arising partly because Spenser's character is now employing his author's technique. So complete and lucid a visualization, so radical a transposition of time into the sequenced forms of architectural space, invites quick and thorough disposal of the represented evil. And the evil presents itself as remote in a number of ways from the heroine, or from the relevant aspects of the inner life she may anticipate in her quest of Artegal: it is external, extraordinary, magical, and antique. Reified into a single form, it may be confronted and overcome in a single encounter.

But this is a typical Spenserian device: the resolution or reconciliation which is false in being premature, or too complete, or a distraction from the real locus of trouble. This device allows problems to be visualized and solved at the level of external and often of narrative action, while they continue and increase within the ongoing psychic life of the characters. The evils displayed in the House of Busirane will, in spite of Britomart, permeate Book IV: in the continuing problems of Amoret and Scudamour; the martial-erotic encounters of Britomart and Artegal; the episodes involving Lust, Slander, Corflambo, and the Temple of Venus. If Britomart's triumph provides a resounding conclusion to Book III, it also introduces the main issues and tensions of Books IV and V. In fact, the House of Busirane as a whole furnishes a kind of iconograph or dumb show which is only unfolded and explained through cantos of retrospective analysis: its causes, functions, and effects are not fully clarified until IV.x–xi. For, once again, values and meanings emerge not in the immediacy of action and vision but in the slow time-bound process of retrospective interpretation and revision. And in Books IV–VI this Spenserian device will become a central Spenserian theme—namely, the growing tension between the flatness of resolution typical of romance needed to exemplify themes or wrap up episodes, and the radically insoluble problems of psychic, social, and political actuality.

When Spenser discarded the figure of Malbecco, he forcibly *extrojected* jealousy from the stereotypical soul to Busirane's architectural environment. Should we not expect to find a similar act of symbolic transference when Busirane is discarded through the agency of Britomart? What we find is in fact a little different: the evil is *introjected* into the souls of true lovers, where—separated from its frozen and archaic structure—it may flourish anew, adapting itself to its new psychic environment. Spenser touches casually on both sides of the introjective relation, though in brief and widely separated formulas:

> ye faire Ladies, that your kingdomes make
> *In th'harts of men*, them governe wisely well . . .
>
> *(xi.2; italics mine)*

> Great God of love, that with thy cruell dart
>   Doest conquer greatest conquerors on ground,
>   And setst thy kingdome *in the captive harts*
>   Of Kings and Keasars, to thy service bound,
>   What glorie, or what guerdon hast thou found
>   In feeble Ladies tyranning so sore;
>   And adding anguish to the bitter wound,
>   With which their lives thou lanchedst long afore,
> By heaping stormes of trouble on them daily more?
>
> *(IV.vii.1; italics mine)*

We have already seen how the masque was symbolically transferred to Amoret's mind, and I have mentioned the possibility—suggested by a number of recent commentators—that Busirane's torture of Amoret may be in part a function of Scudamour's behavior and of the mental state only glanced at in the image of Ollyphant pursuing the boy. There are also hints which vaguely suggest, or at least anticipate, another introjective relation: the coalescence of Britomart's chaste affection and Amoret *as* chaste affection, a coalescence which can ultimately occur only after Amoret has been discarded. In Amoret's case, the introjective relation is formally announced when Britomart replaces Scudamour as her protector: at xi.18–19, both characters use phrases which allow the reader to register, however fleetingly, a significant change of roles. The function of protector traditionally assigned to man is now being reassigned to woman, who is better able and motivated to shield her own impulses of chaste affection, womanhood, and true love. Scudamour's functions will ultimately be distributed between Britomart *and* Artegal, but the very moment of his entry into *The Faerie Queene* is the moment when the process of supersession which will result in his being discarded begins. Though his experience at the Temple of Venus will show why this must be the case—briefly, he uses the shield to *win* the lady rather than to *protect* her—in Book III Spenser presents us only with facts and the vaguest hints of causes. The House of Busirane is by no means a picture of Scudamour's "unconscious mind" (whatever that means), yet it does suggest a developed and traditional structure of male presuppositions about courtship which tacitly influence him so that he tends to see his relation to Amoret as one of assault and conquest rather than one of persuasion, protection, and companionship.[18] Britomart's tour through the house is her formal initiation into this structure (the elements of which she had previously experienced and seen throughout Book III), while the very change signified by the tour, her replacing Scudamour, renders the existing form of the structure obsolete.

At the same time, something of that structure is symbolically introjected at xii.33, when Busirane communicates his influence inside Britomart on the blade of his knife. Though the wound is superficial, she responds with a ferocity which turns out to be excessive and to jeopardize Amoret's freedom: Amoret, who knows more than Britomart about Busirane, warns her not to kill him,

> else her paine
> Should be remedilesse, sith none but hee,
> Which wrought it, could the same recure againe.
> Therewith she stayd her hand, loth stayd to bee;
> For life she him envyde, and long'd revenge to see.
>
> *(xii.34)*

---

[18] Cf. A. Kent Hieatt, "Scudamour's Practice of *Maistrye* upon Amoret," *PMLA*, 77 (September 1962): 509–10; Graham Hough, *A Preface to "The Faerie Queene"* (New York: Norton, 1963), 175–76; Nelson, 230–31; Roche, 83, 128 ff.; Williams, 105 ff.

Britomart's wound is at once a miniature of Amoret's and the antithesis of a wound of Cupid's. It arouses feelings of hate and revenge toward the male mind, feelings which jeopardize the capacity for chaste affection. Britomart is to be bold but not too bold, for then she would too violently inhibit her "true feminitee . . . and goodly womanhead" (vi.51), her ability to open herself to Artegal. Hence in Book IV she has to get to know Amoret better, and her patronage of Amoret brings her together with Artegal in IV.vi. The sequence of events suggests the following allegory: Chaste affection was prematurely bestowed on, or won by, the masculine lover before either the man or the woman was prepared for the communion of true love. It has therefore to be withdrawn into feminine safekeeping, to be guided and husbanded by the feminine mind until a later and more appropriate moment.[19] Britomart's subsequent separation from Amoret in Book IV is intimately connected to the effect on her of her encounters with Artegal. It is not only desire, but also a deeper, more troubling emotion of "secret feare" which she feels again on seeing Artegal in person (IV.vi.29): the nightmare fear of her own lust as well as his, the fear of being captured and possessed in mind and heart as well as in body, the fear of collaborating with the male enemy in yielding control of herself and her destiny. To some extent this fear is blatantly acted out in the rape of Amoret by the figure Lust, who appears as a nightmare version of Artegal in the primitive guise which marked his appearance at Satyrane's tourney. Thus Britomart has not yet gained full control over the femininity embodied as Amoret—she has not yet, that is, fully internalized Amoret. And Spenser's technique of personification suggests that she will not until Amoret as a separate figure has been discarded. What Amoret stands for is jeopardized by the pure, exclusive, and separated figure of Amoret through which that particular psychic complex is exhibited. Spenser's earlier conception of the fate of the complex in its Faerie embodiment is suggested in the rejected 1590 ending of Book III, in which he effectually discards Amoret and Scudamour. I shall conclude with a brief discussion of those stanzas.

---

[19] Having been wounded by Busirane, Britomart hides her womanhood in IV.i–vi and becomes more martial; Amoret becomes concerned, as if she fears Britomart may violate and destroy (her) chaste affection. Amoret's virtues, developed as defenses against such dangers as Florimell encounters, are built up so that woman may court and draw man in security, may arouse desire and still remain aloof, independent, and chaste. The word *womanhead*, applied to Amoret in III.vi.51, fuses *maidenhead* and *womanhood:* in Amoret the two *are* fused, and these dual traits define and cause her particular range of problems and virtues.

III

When she leads Amoret from the ruined house, Britomart discovers that Scudamour has reassumed the prone position she first found him in beside "a fountaine sheare" (III.xi.7):

> At last she came unto the place, where late
>> She left Sir *Scudamour* in great distresse,
>> Twixt dolour and despight halfe desperate,
>> Of his loves succour, of his owne redresse,
>> And of the hardie *Britomarts* successe;
>> There on the cold earth him now thrown she found,
>> In wilfull anguish, and dead heavinesse,
>> And to him cald; whose voices knowen sound
> Soone as he heard, himself he reared light from ground.
>
> There did he see, that most on earth him joyd,
>> His dearest love, the comfort of his dayes,
>> Whose too long absence him had sore annoyd,
>> And wearied his life with dull delayes:
>> Straight he upstarted from the loathed layes,
>> And to her ran with hasty egernesse,
>> Like as a Deare, that greedily embayes
>> In the coole soile, after long thirstinesse,
> Which he in chace endured hath, now nigh breathlesse.
>
>> *(xii.43–44 [1590])*

The simile makes brief contact with the desperate figure of Fury in the masque, who "As a dismayed Deare in chace embost, / Forgetfull of his safety, hath his right way lost" (xii.17.8–9), but I think it primarily reminds us of Ollyphant pursuing his dear boy, of Britomart pursuing Ollyphant (who was "swift as any Roe," xi.5), and of Scudamour "wallowed" on the grass beside the fountain. After seven months of "dull delayes" he is quick to return to his wonted if "loathed layes." The echoes suggest a temporal protraction of the image through the Busirane passage; they encourage us to speculate on the ways in which Scudamour's being pursued and overcome by destructive fantasy might contribute to the torment of Amoret by the "annoyd" male imagination.

Scudamour "greedily embayes": bathes, drinks, shuts himself in the cool soil of his beloved whom he has longed for while (because?) pursued by his destructive fantasy. The happy ending thus blends the sense of sexual fulfillment with feelings of escape and death, sustained in the next stanza:

> Lightly he clipt her twixt his armes twaine,
>   And streightly did embrace her body bright,
>   Her body, late the prison of sad paine,
>   Now the sweet lodge of love and deare delight:
>   But she faire Lady overcommen quight
>   Of huge affection, did in pleasure melt,
>   And in sweete ravishment pourd out her spright:
>   No word they spake, nor earthly thing they felt,
> But like two senceles stocks in long embracement dwelt.
>
> (xii.45 [1590])

The oscillation from sad ravishment to its contrary is violent: completely separated from and alien to each other in the experience with Busirane, Scudamour and Amoret close as if the otherness dividing them could be entirely dissolved, and by the mere act of *physical* embrace.

Their urge to melt into unconscious union and freeze eternally into that posture is traced from the outpouring of life through the senseless stocks to the following image in which Spenser first names the actual figure and then turns it to marble:

> Had ye them seene, ye would have surely thought,
>   That they had beene that faire *Hermaphrodite,*
>   Which that rich *Romane* of white marble wrought,
>   And in his costly Bath causd to bee site:
>   So seemd those two, as growne together quite,
>   That *Britomart* halfe envying their blesse,
>   Was much empassiond in her gentle sprite,
>   And to her selfe oft wisht like happinesse,
> In vaine she wisht, that fate n'ould let her yet possesse.
>
> Thus doe those lovers with sweet countervayle,
>   Each other of loves bitter fruit despoile.
>
> (xii.46–47 [1590])

The direct reference may be to some actual patron and statue—some Lucullus, for example—about which Spenser had read. But there is also an oblique reference to the artistic riches, or richness, of Ovid and to the pool of the nymph Salmacis in whose clear water she and Hermaphroditus were fused by the gods in a manner not entirely accordant with her prayer for eternal union (*Metamorphoses* IV.285–388). Both references work with the apostrophe to the reader to produce an effect of sudden distance. As Spenser intertwines his lovers even more closely in their happy ending, he sends them back whence they came—back through romance toward ancient Rome, back into *Anticke* art where they inhabit and symbolize the enfeebling (*costly*) climate of Busirane's decadent forebears. Having reached their goal, their life in the poem is over and they are memorialized, antiquated, fixed in a pre-Spenserian region of literature and art as if, in this final moment, the older influences prevail and the new boundary figures gravitate back toward the source: "So flowing all from one, all one at last become" (IV.xi.43). The figure of the hermaphrodite reveals the gravitational pull of the primary source, the androgynous Venus, whose purposes are not entirely consonant with those of human persons and whose unifying pressure is deflected in the courtly consciousness from its basic generative function to the blissful release from pain. This hermaphrodite is neither a myth of spiritual union nor an icon of generative union; it is in a villa, not a temple; far from the fertile and primitive matrix of ocean, it laves in the filtered and purified enclosure of a man-made pool.

The lovers are involved in, yet remain innocent of, these darker suggestions. Unlike Salmacis and Hermaphroditus, they are neither punished by the gods nor diminished by the poet for failures which derive from the restricted psychic functions which it is their fate to personify and exhibit. To pursue the contrast with Ovid, Amoret differs from Salmacis in being a legitimate counter-Belphoebe, whereas the nymph is a defector from the *durus* Artemisian life, punished first for preferring narcissistic indolence to hunting, then for being too headlong in her desire. Amoret's desire is constrained until the end by an educated concern for her own image and dignity (cf. Salmacis's more superficial self-attention at *Metamorphoses* IV.311–19), and she accordingly demands more effort, skill, and activity from her lover.

The happy ending nevertheless does not solve the problems posed by Busirane; it gets rid of them by sweeping them under the rug. The lovers attempt to abolish the pain of separateness by headlong convergence, not by the slowly and painfully won knowledge of self and other. Their polymorphous reconciliation exemplifies the opposite of developed self-consciousness, for the experience of Busirane has made clear how much they do not know about themselves, how little each knows about the other. It is for this reason that the hermaphrodite, especially in its Ovidian context, provides so apt an image. As Ovid describes it, the image is an emblem neither of true love nor of natural union: "nec duo sunt et forma duplex, nec femina dici / nec puer ut possit, neutrumque et utrumque videntur" (378–79)—"they are not two and double in form, so that they could not be called either a woman or a boy, but seemed at once both and neither."

Spenser revises Ovid by converting the literal description of bodies to a figurative interpretation of psyches: he suggests the real meaning of what Scudamour and Amoret want as they press into each other, though it is a meaning not fully revealed until Scudamour has concluded his account of the Temple of Venus. That account reveals a basic misunderstanding and antipathy between him and Amoret, founded partly on his view of her as the reward for chivalric prowess, partly on her fear of being taken and possessed in a manner which threatens the very image of self she has been trained to cherish and display. Their straining together is thus not mere erotic self-abandon; there is an edge of conflict to it. In this framework Ovid's description applied to the lovers is an image of double narcissism: each lover desires a union which amounts to absolute possession, for each wants to assimilate the other—wants to become both—entirely on his/her own terms; and neither wants to surrender his/her sovereignty. Their dilemma is all the more insoluble for being the product of innocence rather than willfulness: neither knows the other's terms, since they approach the relations and roles of love from the narrowly conceived contrary viewpoints determined by their training and their very existence as literary *ensamples*. Britomart's triumph over Busirane has impelled them too quickly and forcibly from total otherness to total oneness, a violent oscillation characteristic of early psychic phases and elemental instability.

"Thus doe those lovers with sweet countervayle, / Each other of loves bitter fruit despoile" (III.xii.47 [1590]). *Countervayle* means "compensation" and "reciprocation," but it also means "resistance": the lovers equally matched, each self veiled from the other (*counter-veil*), the power of one counterbalancing and canceling out that of the other as they close together. *Countervail* describes the pendulum swing of the relationship as it moves from the radical hate and alienation of Busirane to the radical love and fusion of the hermaphrodite. If the lovers "despoil" each other of love's bitter fruit, the fruit must be useful. For Artegal and Britomart, as we know, there is much bitter fruit ahead.

Two Spenserian Retrospects

The Antique Temple of Venus and the Primitive Marriage of Rivers

IN THIS ESSAY I shall consider a mature or retrospective view of two extremes of archaic or "early" experience, primitive and antique, exemplified by the Marriage of Rivers and the Temple of Venus. The primitive extreme involves submission to the characteristic expressions of pure natural behavior, namely, (1) the kaleidoscopic swirl of chaos, ocean, elements, passions, and (2) the treadmill of eternal recurrence, the archetypal repetition of the same tyrannizing history and prohibiting growth or novelty. By contrast, the antique extreme involves the effort to escape from "nature" in that suspension or closure of activity, that circumscription by mind of an entirely autonomous world—self-generated, self-sustaining, and self-renewing—which Spenser often visualizes as magic, art, architecture, and court life. The individual psyche, because of its ontogenetic relation to culture, may revive these phases within itself, either in developmental sequence or in moments of regression. Primitive and antique responses are thus permanent and recurrent possibilities even though they represent particular historical phases of culture.

The two retrospects to which I now turn vividly exemplify the act of revision whereby the poet moves back in time to recapitulate the antique and primitive sources of his own vision. In the Temple—and especially the statue—of Venus, he presents a premature closing down on, or freezing of, experience; here "early" cultural forms have been protracted be-

yond the original context in which they were functional and useful. In
the Marriage of Rivers, his mind travels even further backward and
downward to release the living sources of energy frozen in the temple.

I

The idol in the Temple of Venus symbolizes three aspects of venerean
experience in sequential order. First, the matrix, the undifferentiated
and recurrent cycle of nature represented by the uroboric (tail-eating)
serpent:

> both her feete and legs together twyned
> Were with a snake, whose head and tail were fast combyned.
>
> *(IV.x.40)*

Second, the differentiated phase in which opposites separate, then unite
in generation; here the mother of species in her bisexual sufficiency represents the death or transcendence of self which occurs when two creatures surrender their separate identities, flow together like rivers, re-
plenish the earth, and disappear into Ocean:

> The cause why she was covered with a vele,
>   Was hard to know, for that her Priests the same
>   From peoples knowledge labour'd to concele.
>   But sooth it was not sure for womanish shame,
>   Nor any blemish which the worke mote blame;
>   But for, they say, she hath both kinds in one,
>   Both male and female, both under one name:
>   She syre and mother is her selfe alone,
> Begets and eke conceives, ne needeth other none.
>
> *(IV.x.41)*

Third, the play of erotic experience—desire, flirtation, pleasure—at the
level of culture and consciousness, a play which is irrelevant to Venus
Genetrix except as an instrument with which to lure human lovers to
fulfill her purposes:

> And all about her necke and shoulders flew
>   A flocke of litle loves, and sports, and joyes,
>   With nimble wings of gold and purple hew;
>   Whose shapes seem'd not like to terrestriall boyes,
>   But like to Angels playing heavenly toyes;
>   The whilest their eldest brother was away,

> *Cupid* their eldest brother; he enjoyes
> The wide kingdome of love with Lordly sway,
> And to his law compels all creatures to obay.
>
> *(IV.x.42)*

The description suggests the artificiality of this aspect of love, its tendency to become refined and gratuitous, an end in itself which may even justify itself as a form of "heavenly" love. These "little loves" are thus "younger" than Cupid, natural desire, because elaborated in later and higher phases of response. The context places them in an ironic light, for they have so little to do with the actual generative process. In *An Hymne in Honour of Love,* Venus Genetrix moves all living things

> To multiply the likenesse of their kynd,
> Whylest they seeke onely, without further care,
> To quench the flame, which they in burning fynd:
> But man that breathes a more immortall mynd,
> Not for lusts sake, but for eternitie,
> Seekes to enlarge his lasting progenie.
>
> *(100–105)*

That is, animals try only to relieve their desire while in fact they are fulfilling the purposes of the lower Venus. Men differ because they are also subject to and may become aware of a higher Venus. But from the perspective of IV.x, the notion of the "higher Venus" may itself be a lure and artifice, related to the mother of species as the "litle loves" to their elder brother. In the Lucretian hymn uttered by a tormented lover complaining at the altar (IV.x.44–47), the opening apostrophe to "Great *Venus,* Queene of beautie and of grace, / . . . that under skie / Doest fayrest shine" gives way to a description of the effects produced by the lower Venus mainly in birds and beasts; though included at the end of the hymn, human lovers are not treated as exceptions:

> So all things else, that nourish vitall blood,
> Soone as with fury thou doest them inspire,
> In generation seeke to quench their inward fire.
>
> So all the world by thee at first was made,
> And dayly yet thou doest the same repayre:
> Ne ought on earth that merry is and glad,
> Ne ought on earth that lovely is and fayre,
> But thou the same for pleasure didst prepayre.

> Thou art the root of all that joyous is,
> Great God of men and women, queene of th'ayre,
> Mother of laughter, and welspring of blisse,
> O graunt that of my love at last I may not misse.
>
> *(IV.x.46–47)*

The singer's emphasis is on pleasure, laughter, and bliss, and from his point of view generation has its primary significance as a means of relief. The mother of laughter is more important to him than the mother of species—which helps explain why her androgynous aspects were veiled and why her priests labored to conceal what lay behind the veil (that "all the Priests were damzels" [IV.x.38] also helps explain their efforts at concealment). Attention is displaced from the idol's function to the "litle loves, and sports, and joyes" playing about her smiling and apparently unveiled (x.56) face. Attention is also displaced from the forces and functions Venus symbolizes to the symbol herself. Described both as an *it* and as a *she* (x.39–42), coming to life at x.56, the idol is ambiguously statue and goddess. Its devotees project, see, and worship only what they want, namely, their own commitment to courtship as the totality of life. Thus they isolate her visible form with its self-contained "life" from the oceanic reality behind the appearance; they isolate love as a game from love as a function, love as a state of mind and a way of life from love as a natural process.

The emblems which, apart from the veiled body, most specifically refer to pure natural process indifferent to human sentience are those which are most stylized and artificial, and therefore most unlike what they represent—the uroboric serpent around her feet and the altar on which she stands:

> Right in the midst the Goddesse self did stand
> Upon an altar of some *costly masse,*
> *Whose substance was uneath to understand:*
> For neither pretious stone, nor durefull brasse,
> Nor shining gold, nor mouldring clay it was;
> But much more rare and pretious to esteeme,
> Pure in aspect, and like to christall glasse,
> Yet glasse was not, if one did rightly deeme,
> But being faire and brickle, likest glasse did seeme.
>
> *(x.39; italics mine)*

The increments and substitutions of "art" reveal an excessive refinement of motive, a wish-fulfilling avoidance of chaos, ugliness, and death (see also x.21–23). These unruly forces have been purged in being rendered into architectural, sculptural, and ritual forms; at the same time Spenser's diction reminds us *that* they have been purged and so works against the intentions of the worshipers. The wordplay of the italicized phrase suggests not only the strangeness of the "costly masse" but also perhaps a note of instability reinforced a few lines later by the word *brickle:* "Whose substance uneasily stood under [the idol]." The "masse" which really stands under the idol, under the enisled temple world, under the closed courtly consciousness, is the oceanic world of cosmic violence and fecundity presented in the next canto as the setting for the Marriage of Rivers.

Spenser's attitude toward all this is much like that of Lucretius, whose role in the canto (the song at x.44–47 is an adaptation of the beginning of *De rerum natura*) has often been noted but never understood—not that Spenser echoes the Roman poet's general or systematic skepticism but rather that in this particular episode he is concerned with the difference between the actual process at its primitive, unromantic level and the restricted human motives whose mythopoetic distortion signifies the courtly mind's flight from reality. In Scudamour's world of the temple, as in the worlds of Malecasta, Malbecco, Paridell, and Busirane, there is a variety of "litle loves, and sports, and joyes" but there are no babies. Thus if the symbolic union of the androgyne means one thing in the context of natural process, it means something entirely different in the courtly context of the erotic game, the chivalric context focused on fame, beauty, and social value, the psychological context of stimulus/response and pleasure/pain.

It would be wrong to see Venus Genetrix one-sidedly favored by Spenser in her conflict with the courtly consciousness. If the generative impulse necessarily operates throughout organic existence, its manifestations must be appropriate to the levels at which they appear. Spenser's mother figures range from Celia (I.x) and Sapience (*An Hymne of Heavenly Beautie*), whose progeny are theological and cosmological, to Cymoent in her undersea world; they include Concord, Natura, and Isis, who preside over various interrelated forms of organization, as well as the Venus of VI.x, connected both to the Graces and to the Muses. They do not, however, include the particular mother figure appropriate to the ultimate relation of Britomart and Artegal—the Venus Apostraphia whom Natalis Conti describes on the authority of Pausanias as the inventress of marriage.[1] The Venus of IV.x–xi is the mother of species and

---

[1] *Mythologiae* (Paris, 1583), 263.

has a single purpose: the perpetuation of life through the union of sexual opposites. She is interested only in those qualities of men and women which expedite this process. In her world, womanhood and its attendant virtues (x.49–52) are mainly a protective social structure—a civilized form of *daunger* (compare stanzas 17–20 with 49–58)—which guards woman against a Hellenore-like breakdown. Venerean womanhood is not a positive capacity for real love and friendship but rather a way of keeping the generative process from being undermined by obsessive lust and the pursuit of pleasure. Similarly the arts of love and courtship and chivalry are guises or disguises of Venus Genetrix. To win the shield, which will in turn win the woman, the knight need only be a good warrior. What the goddess requires from males is simply a token display of their "lustfull powres," the mark of Mars, the oceanic force of Marinell, the fury of lions, tigers, and raging bulls which "dare tempt the deepest flood, / To come where thou doest draw them with desire" (IV.x.46). High spirit or "greedy hardiment" is the harbinger of virility. Scudamour symbolizes that moment in the life of the male psyche when Venus for the first time converts hate to love, the aggressive pursuit of enemies to the aggressive pursuit of woman. The generative force begins with opposites—a martial Scudamour and a womanly Amoret— and tries to bring them together by converting both from their original dispositions. Like all creatures under the domination of this force, they can only move *toward* each other. They cannot move *beside* each other in parallel and mutual love. Their goal is union, not communion. If courtly interference displaces the center of the relationship from generation, and frequently even from sexual union, sexual union for the sake of generation is still the entire goal of the mother of species in the human as in other spheres. And this union is by no means an adequate model for human lovers; married love is jeopardized when the whole experience of love is understood as fulfilled, justified, and exhausted by the moment of androgynous merging.

Thus what we see in IV.x is by no means "a temple of cosmic harmony,"[2] a vision of "the reality and unity of love,"[3] or the "final state of lovers' bliss."[4] We see rather a dead end, a brilliantly articulated state of fragmentation in which all parties work at cross-purposes—Venus against human lovers, each lover against the other, both against Venus—and all

---

[2] Graham Hough, *A Preface to "The Faerie Queene"* (New York: Norton, 1962), 189.

[3] Thomas Roche, *The Kindly Flame* (Princeton: Princeton University Press, 1964), 133.

[4] A. C. Hamilton, *The Structure of Allegory in "The Faerie Queene"* (Oxford: Clarendon Press, 1961), 156.

engage in the single experience from within different, mutually exclusive, frames of reference. Clearly neither Scudamour nor Amoret seems to have any knowledge of the Great Mother's intentions, that is, of the generative impulse as the motive behind all their apparently nonerotic behavior ("it of honor and all virtue is / The roote," IV.Pr.2). This lack of awareness causes them to do violence to their own natures and also to make needless trouble for Britomart in her pursuit of true love and for Venus Natura in her efforts at promoting fruitful unions. Venus as an elemental cosmic force, Scudamour and Amoret as elemental and relatively determined forces of the psyche, produce not so much a concord as an amalgam of discrete, self-centered parts. This pattern also governs Scudamour's narrative and the particular images of concord or resolution he passes on the way. The narrative sequence as it stands is a fragmented and arbitrary collection of episodes; the particular moments of resolution are all partial and essentially unrelated—the two kinds of lovers in the garden (x.21–27), the porch of Concord (x.31–36), the interior of the temple centered on the altar and goddess, the vision of Amoret, and the final conquest. Whatever we have seen in Books III and IV is here at least by suggestion but is yoked together in an external unity, not organically intergrafted. What is absent is some controlled and controlling self-awareness, a more capacious mind in which these fragmented impulses—the natural, the sensual-courtly, and the social-courtly—may be reflected and coped with as facts of consciousness. (Perhaps the very exteriority of the temple, its physical actuality for Scudamour, is itself a sign of limitation.) These egotistical impulses must be guided by lovers mutually aware of themselves and of each other as human persons, separate but equal; lovers whose achieved insight and second sight (*re-spect*) frees them from both the tyranny of nature and the obsessive fascination of courtly eroticism. The mind which creates and then submits to the Temple of Venus closes down too quickly on experience; like its concords and resolutions, the temple itself represents a prematurely "final state of . . . bliss" which is at once archaic and regressive.

As Hamilton rightly points out, "the whole action of Books III and IV is carefully placed within Nature aroused by Venus" (p. 155), and I take this to be an "early" or rudimentary domain. The temple looks back on and summarizes the main drift of experience in Books III and IV, the movement from the problems of precourtship and chastity to those of courtship and concord. Spenser's synoptic presentation of the experience, his close interweaving of psychic and cultural phenomena, is reflected in the environment and architecture of the temple, with its eclectic assemblage of pagan, Near Eastern, and gothic motifs. As a particular, if complex, structure of mind and experience, it has been a long time abuilding. Its visual, ritual, emblematic, and narrative forms epitomize something of the sweep of eros through many minds, lands, centuries, poems, institutions, and modalities of response. But in this sweep an antique and defective form of idolatry, crystallized and codified too early, has been imposed on, sustained by, and diffused throughout civilization.

II

What Spenser feels as necessary at this point, and what he does in the next canto, is—to borrow a phrase from Donald Cheney—"return to the natural origins which lie obscured beneath the premises of court life."[5] In the retrospect of the civilized mind, natural or primitive experience has positive as well as negative features. It is true that Spenser delineates the life close to nature as defective, libidinal, violent, and subhuman. Early structures and products of mind are narcissistic, superstitious, and fabulous. In his own career his mature retrospect characterizes his early poetry as child's play, recreative and fantastic. But in all this there is something of value: in nature, the restlessly creative thrust of male force and the generative, conservative tendency (pairing and repairing) of female force; in imagination, the sensuous abundance (*copie*) of forms and the ease of visionary mythopoeia; in both, the vital and instinctive, therefore easy and uninhibited, surges of energy. But in its primitive state this energy is uncritical, undirected, and untested, and in its germinal form would merely go on reproducing more of the same, an eternal recurrence of archetypes without novelty, differentiation, or uniqueness. Spenser's attitudes toward the primitive are not exhausted by his treatment of it as either archaic (therefore to be left behind) or regressive (therefore to be avoided). The primitive is to be caught up, redirected, and reincluded in the mature structures of personal and social consciousness which are progressively elaborated through the phases of Chastity, Concord, Justice, and Courtesy. Periodic returns to the sources of energy—for renewals and new beginnings—are essential to psychocultural development.

If, then, the antique Temple of Venus looks back, the Marriage of Rivers looks forward toward Book V: toward a frame of reference which sets love in a historical, national, and political context alive with contemporary European problems; toward a new beginning, as Spenser changes

[5] *Spenser's Image of Nature* (New Haven: Yale University Press, 1966), 65.

from the perspective of Britomart and woman to the perspective of Artegal and man, going back this time to the early phases of male behavior. He also returns, as he himself indicates in IV.xii.1–2, to the original Venus myth and through his treatment in the Marriage of Rivers revives what the inventors of the temple had "obscured beneath the premises of court life":

> much more eath to tell the starres on hy,
>   Albe they endless seeme in estimation,
>   Then to recount the Seas posterity:
>   So fertile be the flouds in generation,
> So huge their numbers, and so numberlesse their nation.
>
> Therefore the antique wisards well invented,
>   That *Venus* of the fomy sea was bred;
>   For that the seas by her are most augmented.

This Venus operates not in terms of a single consciousness, or set of lovers, or even species. She symbolizes a cosmic force which can be apprehended only if the scope and scale of her domain are radically enlarged so as to embrace aeons, to suggest the evolving of life from oceanic prehistory to British history and to show at the same time the continuing though continually modified existence of the oceanic in the British. Thus the icon, static and fixed in place, is translated into a dynamic pageant whose visual surface flickers and changes as we view it. The pageant is cartographic in its place references, but focused on *rivers* which—though their waters perpetually change, flow, decay, and repair—have their courses firmly shaped by a continent at once natural and human; rivers, which are mythically the children of the earth-girdling stream Ocean, but also, because of the natural cycle, derived "from the skie" and "mountaines hie" (xi.20), so that they only flow through human space on their way to rejoin Ocean:

> All which long sundred, doe at last accord
>   To joyne in one, ere to the sea they come,
>   So flowing all from one, all one at last become.
>
> *(xi.43)*

Roche's characterization of the theme of the canto is probably acceptable if we distinguish more carefully than he does the difference between oceanic and spiritual forms of "eternity":

> The physical cycle describes a perfect circle: Ocean to cloud to rain to river and back to Ocean—"eterne in mutability." The ocean is the girdle of the

earth, the analogue to eternity. . . . The essential purpose of this procession
is to show the unity underlying the multiplicity of life, as symbolized by the
world of the sea. (pp. 177, 181)

But the perfect circle is the eternal recurrence of the same, the antihistorical perpetuation of ancient archetypes and primitive forms of behavior in the world whose creatures and phenomena are unified deter-
ministically from the outside. The river's tendency to return to the
source is not in its pure or abstract form an ideal for human imitation;
the actual river bears with it more than it knows—all the marks of cultural, military, economic, and political history, as well as all their detritus—and this interchange between geography and history, between
the eternally recurrent flow-through of water and the continually changing organization of society, is Spenser's theme.

Those central aspects of Venus which her virgin priests veiled and
labored to conceal are amplified in IV.xi in the two pairs of deities,
Neptune-Amphitrite and Ocean-Tethys. Neptune's is an imperious and
ambivalent energy which spawns both creators and destroyers, a rank
principle shooting upward from chaos to embody itself in higher forms
or to threaten established forms with rape and rebellion. His sons are
divided into two groups: first, sea-figures, giants, and monsters who are
enemies or victims of heroes (xi.13–14) and are essential to the careers
of heroes, who could scarcely be heroes without enemies and victims;
second, the heroes themselves, described not as single warriors or jus-
ticers but rather as "most famous founders . . . / Of puissant Nations"
(xi.15). Since the canto is primarily about rivers, not heroes, the activity
of heroic founders appears in Spenser's telescoped treatment as an archetypal moment, a kind of threshold from one to another level and aeon of
life, from prehistory to the new epoch of Man as it emerges from
Ocean. The virile and masculine emphasis in these stanzas suggests that
Neptune-Amphitrite and their sons are meant to personify the half of
Venus which is male, sire, and begetter. Their fighting leads to founding, their loving to generation. Spenser stresses their character as beget-
ters of societies rather than of individuals, and he lets them pass quickly
out of the picture at the beginning—not at the end or resolution—of
significant experience. They embody, in effect are reduced to, the very
nature of the creative act in Neptune's realm: restless, brutal, striving
toward new conquests, self-spending and self-transcending, concentrating and exhausting itself in an instant of relief, then repeating the whole
process.

The pair Ocean-Tethys are iconographically related to the uroboric serpent at the base of the icon, the great round whose end feeds its beginning. But their appearance and function in IV.xi suggest that they also represent the other half of the androgyne, Venus as female, mother, and conceiver. In "aged Ocean, and his Dame, / Old Tethys, th'oldest two of all the rest," we see a force subject to decay, needing new life, powerful in fertility but passive rather than aggressive. Ocean is "older" than Neptune and more primitive, in the sense that the ancient mythographic mind draws its personification of Neptune, as of Venus, "out of" Ocean. Neptune's parade of heroes comes first in the pageant because it is an antique construction, presented as such; it is presumptively a catalogue of mythic persons, and what Spenser at once suggests and suppresses is the physical or geographic origin of many of the names (Astraeus, Neleus, Caicus, Asopus, Ogyges, Inachus, Phoenix, and Belus are names of rivers or tutelary spirits; Aonia, Pelasgia, Ogygia, Phoenicia, Albion, and Phaeacia are names of countries, regions, or races). This patently naive mythopoeia is contrasted with the more elaborate and sophisticated treatment of rivers in content as well as in presentation: what comes first is martial, gigantic, and self-expansive, eros as the blind hostility of egocentric opposites. The first phase is appropriately concluded by Hercules' conquest of Albion, "father of the bold / And warlike people, which the Britaine Islands hold" (xi.16). Albion, in this context the most advanced and important of Neptune's sons, is described only to show his defeat by Hercules, who is the son of Jove and a figure of the imperfect justice to be practiced by Artegal in Book V. Hercules represents a rude civilizing force, a principle of order-through-repression appropriate only to early phases of civilization. The character of eros in this phase is underlined by Spenser's spelling: "*old Gall*, that now is cleeped France" (italics mine). The elemental motive of uncompromising self-assertion appears as the cause driving together the two opposites, sea-giant and land-giant, Albion to make "proofe of his great puissance" (IV.xi.16) and Hercules "to vanquish all the world with matchless might" (IV.xi.16). Spenser frames this first phase of the pageant with a stanza which reminds us of its antiquity, reminds us at the same time that we are reading his own selective revision of the old mythology, not merely an uncritical revival:

> But what doe I their names seeke to reherse,
>   Which all the world have with their issue fild?
>   How can they all in this so narrow verse
>   Contayned be, and in small compasse hild?
>   Let them record them, that are better skild,
>   And know the moniments of passed times:

> Only what needeth shall be here fulfild
> T'expresse some part of that great equipage,
> Which from great *Neptune* do derive their parentage.
>
> *(xi.17)*

Ocean and Tethys are introduced in the next stanza and with them both a new genealogy and a new image of the role of primitive venerean force: "all the rest of those two parents came, / Which afterward both sea and land possest" (xi.18). The syntactical ambiguity—"all the rest" and "sea and land" are interchangeable as subject and object of "possest"—heads us in the new direction: Ocean's rivers possess sea and land only by being possessed and contained within a more complicated system of organization to which they give themselves. Ocean is chaos conceived as reservoir; his children "possess" by giving themselves not only to new generations but also to later and higher modes of existence. The natural characters of rivers are enhanced and transformed by the actions of heroes, nations, and societies: they are described as boundary markers, sites and memorials of historical events, sources of raw material and food which play a critical role in the British economy (xi.29–44). After a preliminary excursion into mythic and heroic figuration (xi.18–22), Spenser concentrates on the cultural ecology of rivers.

As part of the human environment the river is not a separable entity; it belongs to an order whose physical center is the city, crown of civilization. As parts of the verbal pageant, river and city are in turn caught up into another more complicated order, that of the mind externalized in poetry. This nexus of relations is exemplified in the stanzas describing the Old Thame and his son Thames; the father, "full aged by his outward sight,"

> seemed to stoupe afore
> With bowed backe, by reason of the lode,
> And auncient heavy burden, which he bore
> Of that faire City, wherein made abode
> So many learned impes, that shoote abrode,
> And with their braunches spred all Britany,
> No lesse then do her elder sisters broode,
> Joy to you both, ye double noursery
> Of Arts, but Oxford thine doth *Thame* most glorify,
>
> But he their sonne full fresh and jolly was,
> All decked in a robe of watchet hew,
> On which the waves, glittering like Christall glas,
> So cunningly enwoven were, that few

> Could weenen, whether they were false or trew.
> And on his head like to a Coronet
> He wore, that seemed strange to common vew,
> In which were many towres and castels set,
> That it encompast round as with a golden fret.
>
> Like as the mother of the Gods, they say,
> In her great iron charet wonts to ride,
> When to *Joves* pallace she doth take her way;
> Old *Cybele*, arayd with pompous pride,
> Wearing a Diademe embattild wide
> With hundred turrets, like a Turribant.
> With such an one was Thamis beautifide;
> That was to weet the famous Troynovant,
> In which her kingdomes throne is chiefly resiant.
>
> *(xi.26–28)*

Thame is bowed down by the fair city he sustains, yet Oxford "doth Thame most glorify": something is imposed on nature which is alien to it and yet fulfills it. Human activity as *art*—education, culture, civilization—may be conceived as the apex of natural activity, a nursery shooting up from below. But a nursery is also planted—set down—so that it becomes a burden, and an apex is also a crown, and both may be imposed "from above" so as radically to change the character and destiny of lower nature. While the natural cycle sustains its recurrent pattern (from old Thame to new), metabolic interchanges may be taking place between different orders of existence. The basic cycle remains the same, but the emergence of new configurations imposes on it continual changes of function and significance.

The figure of Thames is a "cunningly enwoven" image whose waves seem as artificial as its crown. Here "art creates nature" in the simple sense that the poet is being pointedly fanciful, but the message of his fancy, supplied in part by the drift of the entire canto, turns it to imagination—the message, namely, that in the perspective of art the river is no less a product of the civilizing mind than is the city, no less an object shaped by the imagination than is a simile. The Cybele comparison fulfills the interchange by reversing the message: there the city appears in the perspective of nature and primitive myth. Cybele is mythologically a predecessor of Venus, more barbaric and—especially here—more closely associated with war than with love. "Turribant" (turban), with its echo of Corybant, suddenly weaves river and city into a dense and exotic network of connections—the Eastern origins of worship; Crete, the cradle of civilization; a mother figure referred by Lucretius to the invention of ancient poets and used more disingenuously by Virgil to symbolize the triumphs of Augustan Rome in the (for him) archaic mode of Homeric and mythic hyperbole.

The word *her* in the final line of stanza 28 refers logically to Troynovant, whose kingdom is Britain, but the weight of the stanza makes Cybele the more likely antecedent: Troynovant is the capital of Cybele's kingdom. Roche sees this in a positive light:

> Cybele . . . is the great mother of the gods and first taught men to fortify cities. . . . The principles of law and order and ancient fertility . . . are drawn together in this simile. Cybele is a symbol of ancient civilization and fertility, of which Troynovant is the latest example. Spenser is going beyond the patriotic zeal of the antiquarian poets to show that his nation partakes of the ancient order of civilization, that its youthful fertility, symbolized by the Thames, is the inheritance of the beginning of civilization, of Troy and Rome. (p. 182)

This is certainly half the story, but at the same time Troynovant is Cybele's "pompous pride" and crowns the abiding power of a ruthless as well as fecund goddess who is like the Night of I.v and who—like "old Styx the Grandame of the Gods" (IV.xi.4)—has her roots in death as well as in fertility. Spenser characteristically blends the antiquity of the goddess with the primitive state of culture and imagination her mythology reflects—a state of mind which projected its experience of intra-family rift and socionatural upheavals into cosmic fables, physically gigantic and bizarre images of local tensions. This sense of antiquity is conveyed partly by the distancing phrase "they say," partly by the catachrestic yoking of the ancient myth with a modern detail: the crown is the symbol of the chief city on maps of Spenser's time.

The name Troynovant is colored by its Virgilian context in a manner of which Roche and other commentators are apparently unaware: the various New Troys of the *Aeneid* are nostalgic revivals of the archaic way which has been physically destroyed and must be psychologically left behind. To transmit vital energy and to preserve achieved culture, the mind must undertake the painful weeding-out process of revision through which alone the past may be assimilated. Book V clearly shows what happens when contemporary civilization becomes merely "the latest example" of an archaic order: modern Europe unleashes and submits to the rude fury of the elements. The primitive revival is half-comically personified by one of the featured monsters, Geryoneo (V.x–xi), which may be roughly translated as the "New Archaism." The ancient pattern of force and counterforce, the mutual antipathy and exclusion of opposites, reappears at the beginning of Book V with another reference to the progress of ancient "justice" from east to west (Cybele to Jove, Troy to Rome to Britain):

> Such first was *Bacchus*, that with furious might
> All th'East before untam'd did overronne,
> And wrong repressed, and establisht right,
> Which lawlesse men had formerly fordonne.
> There Justice first her princely rule begonne.
> Next *Hercules* his like ensample shewed,
> Who all the West with equall conquest wonne,
> And monstrous tyrants with his club subdewed;
> The club of Justice dread, with kingly powre endewed.
>
> And such was he, of whom I have to tell,
> The Champion of true Justice *Artegall* . . .
>
> *(V.i.2–3)*

The synoptic quality of the Marriage of Rivers differs radically from that of the Temple of Venus. In the previous canto the reader's perspective is contrary to Scudamour's. The elfin narrator remembers and describes a single, literal, and visible episode perceived close-up from an involved and limited standpoint. The dynamic verbal texture of reference, allusion, and connotation is at once disclosed to us and hidden from Scudamour by being congealed into the architecture and episode he "sees." But in IV.xi this dynamism is released from the interlocked archaic structures of temple and narrator. Mythic, natural, and historical domains unfold in the interplay of the various functions of language, and this interplay most immediately affects the reader. The only "pageant" which can be said to have any continuity is the pageant of names. At moments the reference is transparently spatial and geographical, apprehending the map and countryside of Britain. At other moments we view a solid mythic procession of gods and heroes. Still other passages focus on physical rivers but describe them with half-personifying adjectives (xi.20–21) or with ornamental figures (xi.32–33, 37) which often echo themes and qualities of the first ten cantos. Occasionally Spenser introduces strange double images, like Thames and Medway (xi.27–28, 45–47), who are treated as both actual rivers and masque figures. Structurally, the pageant begins with the mythic processions, moves toward geographic and historical reference, then back to myth as Medway becomes Medua and yields to a catalogue of the fifty classical Nereids.

Most of the nymphs are described by a single adjectival term or phrase derived from the Greek name,[6] reminding us that the literary life of these sea nymphs, as of the entire pageant, is generated from the word and that Spenser is enacting the mythopoetic process before our eyes.

The effect of this verbal pageant is a panorama which is not merely spatial and temporal but also cultural and mental—a panorama which could only be rendered in the medium of language because its sole locus is the poetic imagination and its sole time of occurrence is the sophisticated modern *now* of poetic utterance:

> Helpe therefore, O thou sacred imp of *Jove*,
>   The noursling of Dame *Memorie* his deare,
>   To whom those rolles, layd up in heaven above,
>   And *records of antiquitie* appeare,
>   To which no wit of man may comen neare;
>   Helpe me to tell the names of all those floods,
>   And all those Nymphes, which then assembled were
>   To that great banquet of the watry Gods,
> And all their sundry kinds, and all their hid abodes.
>
>   *(xi.10; italics mine)*

The poem is set before us as itself the culmination of the continual process of revising which began aeons ago; here is the latest transformation of rivers, the latest reorganization and resignification of cosmic forces first emergent in chaos and ocean, the latest interchange between nature and mind, the latest form which the ancient reservoirs have nourished with their perpetual supply of vital energy.

One mark of its sophistication, and a major source of its odd panoramic quality, is that the pageant seems to be a meditation on a map of the British Isles. Scudamour's narrative act in IV.x was essentially passive in that he was "copying," that is, remembering, something previously seen. In IV.xi, however, the narrator works not from nature but from an artifact or schema which is itself a triumphant act of mind: the improvements over older methods of cartography introduced during the sixteenth century by Mercator and others produced new and justified respect for this activity in which the mind projected not what the eye saw but rather its own mathematical reorganization of the data. And Spenser does not simply "copy" a map. Though his visualization in effect asks us

---

[6]Cf. H. G. Lotspeich, *Classical Mythology in the Poetry of Edmund Spenser* (New York: Octagon Books, 1965), 89–90.

to be aware of this model, it leaves maps far behind; the principle of meaning and visualization is rhetorical, not cartographic:

> Pictures and recordings stand for things by possessing certain properties of the original itself. Images, reflections, pictures and maps duplicate the spatial properties of what they image, reflect, picture or map. . . . Sentences are not like this. They do not stand for things in virtue of possessing properties of the original; they do not *stand for* anything. They can state what is, or could be, the case. They can be used to make assertions, convey descriptions, supply narratives, accounts, etc. . . . Images, reflexions, pictures and maps in fact copy originals with different degrees of strictness. . . . The more like a reflection a map becomes, the less useful it is as a map. . . . Language copies least of all.[7]

The Marriage of Rivers seems indeed to be a profound revision of an earlier recreative effort which *was* a cartographic fancy, an exercise in transforming map images and information into quantitative meter:

> I minde shortely . . . to sette forth a Booke in this kinde [i.e., a specimen of "Englishe Versifying"], whyche I entitle *Epithalamion Thamesis* . . . very profitable for the knowledge and rare for the Invention and manner of handling. For in setting forth the marriage of the Thames I shewe his first beginning and offspring, and all the Countrey that he passeth thorough, and also describe all the Rivers throughout Englande whyche came to this Wedding, and their righte names, and right passage, &c. A worke, beleeve me, of much labour, wherein notwithstanding Master *Holinshed* hath muche furthered and advantaged me, who therein hath bestowed singular paines in searching oute their firste heades and sources, and also in tracing and dogging oute all their course til they fall into the Sea.[8]

The vectors of development are parallel: on the one hand, from nature, through maps and Holinshed, through versified maps-and-Holinshed, to poetry; on the other hand, from the relatively superficial play of verse and fancy in the early career to the revising play of poetic imagination, the mature poet knowing now what he did not then, seeing and using the idea now as he could not then.

In itself, in the larger context of Books III–V, and in its juxtaposition to the Temple of Venus, the pageant reveals both the sequential and the

---

[7] N. R. Hanson, *Patterns of Discovery* (Cambridge: Cambridge University Press, 1958), 27–28.

[8] Letter to Harvey, in *Elizabethan Critical Essays*, ed. G. Gregory Smith (Oxford: Clarendon Press, 1904), 1:100.

simultaneous relations of the early to the late. On the one hand, Spenser articulates an epochal process, a process which is "evolutionary" in a structural rather than an ethical sense—that is, the creative force of eros impels the phases of existence not from worse to better but from chaos through elements and composite organisms to animals and men. On the other hand, he depicts any phase of existence as an interaction between lower and higher, earlier and later, modes of activity. The evolutionary process is thus potentially present, ontogenetically condensed, in every organic phase, entity, or occasion. Thus the general process provides a model for the proper course of ethical development in the individual soul: from cosmos to psyche, outside to inside, the "unconscious" to consciousness, external law to conscience, passion to reason. When cosmic and primitive influences dominate, the forms of existence tend to be at once unstable and universal (i.e., recurrent, generic, or archetypal). When psychic and rational influences dominate, the forms tend to be personal, unique, and potentially more stable; at the same time, the forms of discord, evil, danger, and temptation are subtler and therefore less easily located and contained.

Primitive life and behavior are hardly immoral in themselves. Conversely, "rationality" can and does (in Book V) become tyrannical in its obsession with utopian solutions; in its rage for order it may indeed revert to primitive methods of force, striving to conform untidy life to its pure Idea, reducing individuals to universals or to recurrent instances of the archetype. The directive force of Astraea and Artegal is imposed "from above" like a repressive superego. Spenser significantly assigns this obsession to a *giant* in V.ii but reveals elements of it in Artegal as well as in himself (V.Pr.). Here the rage for order is born of premature despair, of an inability to accept or cope with the uncertainties and frustrations of actual life. The extremes of mental art and primitive chaos collapse: the giant's allies are the "lawlesse multitude," the vulgar who cluster around him "like foolish flies about an hony crocke" (V.ii.33) and who embody oceanic disorder at the level of psychosocial life.

Spenser conveniently summarizes the natural process of evolution in *Colin Clouts Come Home Againe* (839–70): Eros reconciles the elemental enemies until they begin to feel a little love for each other, and "so being knit, they brought forth other kynds / Out of the fruitfull wombe of their great mother." The "other kynds" are various, complex, and new: heaven, day, earth, living creatures—animals, birds, fish, man. Though at the primitive level of oceanic flux resolutions may occur and recur—moments of "Happy Ending" in conception or generation, in absolute union, in death, relief, or nirvana—at other levels wholly new orders are created with new kinds of problems and new fields of discord. The kind of resolution epitomized by the androgyne may not be applicable at those levels as a way to end pain or discord. Thus Spenser presents this model as the basis of one after another of the flawed and premature efforts at total union, pleasure, power, or knowledge. At the level of oceanic chaos, where nature runs its prodigal treadmill, the "longing" for union, form, and stability is the normal reaction to an environment dominated by flux and death. The Marriage of Rivers takes place in the House of Proteus (IV.xi.9). In the psychocultural phase dominated by this environment, the mind projects both its longing and its instability in its mythological figures: in Venus (see section I above); in Merlin, who is prophetic and can bind friends to his service but is betrayed by his love for the Lady of the Lake (III.iii.7–13); in Proteus, a prophet (III.iv.25) whose good intentions are easily dissolved into lechery (III.viii.29–42); in Nereus, "th'eldest, and the best" son of Ocean and Tethys, who is identical with Proteus in being prophetic and ethically unreliable, or at least ambivalent:

> none more upright,
> Ne more sincere in word and deed profest;
> Most voide of guile, most free from fowle despight,
> Doing him selfe, and teaching others to do right.
>
> Thereto he was expert in prophecies,
> And could the ledden of the Gods unfold.
> · · · · · · · · · · · · · · ·
> . . . So wise is *Nereus* old,
> And so well skild; nathlesse he takes great joy
> Oft-times amongst the wanton Nymphs to sport and toy.
>
> *(IV.xi.18–19)*

The mythological inconsistencies register the limits of archaic imagination: unable to coordinate its given powers and impulses, pulled apart by different and often contradictory impulses to fulfillment, it fragments and dissipates its energies. At III.viii.30 Spenser calls Proteus the "Shepherd of the seas *of yore*" (italics mine). The shepherd of yore and the seas of yore belong to the "image of the antique world" as products of ancient fantasy. Like Merlin, Venus, and others, they are in effect presented in quotation marks as the sophisticated poet's examples of "early" responses. His burlesque treatment of Merlin and Proteus—who emerge less as archetypes from the depths than as refugees from the Sunday comics— contributes to the effect: they are figures of the superstitious or popular imagination which may once have been a fresh cultural force but can no longer be taken seriously unless it is revised. The phrase which Spenser applies to Nereus ("th'eldest, and the best") seems an ironic echo of his teacher Mulcaster's "the eldest and not the best." Thus in each of the instances cited above, the sequence in which Spenser reveals their qualities and careers suggests a decline because it moves from success to failure, and from power to virtue to weakness or vice.

A Secret Discipline

The Faerie Queene, Book VI

Only skilled artists should draw from living bodies, because in most
cases these lack grace and good shape.

—Tintoretto, recorded by Ridolfi

We are told Tintoretto transmuted the gamin divers of the Venetian
canals into the angels of his painting. . . . the conquest, in form, of
fear and disgust means such a sublimation that the world which once
provoked the fear and disgust may now be totally loved in the fullness of contemplation. . . . that gazing . . . is, as Yeats puts it,
                    our secret discipline
          Wherein the gazing soul doubles her might.
The might is there for the moment when the soul lifts her head.

—R. P. Warren

I

THE HELLENISTIC SCHEME for the divisions of the literary treatise—
poesis, poema, poeta—might be put to rhetorical use as an approach to the
dominant movement evident in Spenser's *Faerie Queene. Poesis* adumbrates subject matter, what the poem is about; *poema* refers to questions

I would like to acknowledge the invaluable help given me by Richard B. Young, with
whom many of the general notions in this paper were telephonically worked out on a
two-party line.

of form, manner, style, and therefore to the imagination in its act of rendering subject matter; *poeta* names the category in which the poet and his conditions are discussed. The increasingly reflexive emphasis articulated by this simple scheme may be transferred to *The Faerie Queene* in the following manner:

First, Books I and II are self-contained, coherent narratives which focus quite clearly on the respective quests of Redcross and Guyon. The allegorical dimension of each book has its main purpose in illuminating the character and quest of the fictional hero—the holiness (wholeness) of Redcross and the temperance of Guyon.[1]

Second, if in the first two books our attention is directed to the nominal subjects, Books III and IV are presented so as to make us more aware of the act of rendering, the behavior of the poetic mind. In meandering through the places of the classical and courtly landscapes, the romance of Britomart explores both the mythopoetic and the erotic imaginations. The magnificent climaxes of IV.x and IV.xi reveal poetic activity in its most representative aspect, drawing the forms of the mind from oceanic chaos, creating its own symbolic Love and Nature.[2]

Third, Books V and VI, though strikingly different from each other, are both unfolded within the ambience of the poet's contemporary world. They reflect not merely the process of imagination as such but the problems of the Renaissance poet trying to make sense of the world around him, trying also to continue his interior journey through Faerie amid distractions which make this imaginative quest ever more difficult.

The subject of this essay will be the culmination of this development in the sixth book. Book VI is not, of course, Spenser's final word, but the limits of the topic do not extend to the *Mutabilitie Cantos*. The essential problem confronting Spenser in the third phase is defined in the proem to Book V: how to re-form poetically the corrupt spectacle of modern life in the ideal images of antiquity. The poet sees that the world around him is out of joint, and he feels that if he would discharge his obligation as man and citizen he must try to set it right. Since the actuality perceived offers no hints of order, no models of the reality desired, the poetic mind must confer upon the world its own mythic forms. Spenser's antique forms are those which he has created in his great poem. The life of his

[1] I have discussed this aspect of Book II at length in the *The Allegorical Temper* (New Haven: Yale University Press, 1957).

[2] The Temple of Venus is displayed as the product of human imagination. A good epigraph for these cantos may be found in the commonplace from Ovid's *Ars amatoriae* II.401–2:

> Si Venerem Cois nunquam pinixit Apelles
> Mersa sub aequoreis illa lateret aquis.

imagination is compacted into the lives of Artegal, Britomart, and the other creatures of Faerie. They have their own problems and passions and destinies; they impose their own claims on their creator. Although they are make-believe—or precisely *because* they are make-believe—they are more real to the poet than any of the fragmented forms he sees in the world outside his mind. And so, if he is going to make his creatures express that very different world, he will have to jeopardize their independence. Justice, as he remarks in the tenth canto, "Oft spilles the principall, to save the part." And the same holds true for an allegory of justice: the "principall" is the concrete world of adventure, the "part" the allegorical or exemplary meaning. But this is not merely a problem facing the poet: he makes it his theme—no doubt, if Josephine Bennett's chronology is right, his revision of Book V was governed by this reflexive awareness. The body of the poem is always threatened with the fate of Munera, the Lady Meed figure in canto ii. Munera has fair locks and a slender waist, but she also has gold hands and silver feet. Talus nails up her symbolic extremities and throws the rest of her in the river. Though Artegal is momentarily moved by her femininity, he does not interfere. The allegory of justice requires that when a particular episode is over, its apposite meaning be nailed up on the wall and its remaining details discarded.

Book VI should be understood as the logical result of these developments. It is an attempt at once to cope with justice at the personal and social levels and to give freer play to the stylistic reflexes of the poet's imagination. In accordance with these needs, the chivalric idiom must be more emblematic, the view of actuality more oblique. To move from justice to courtesy means to turn away from the direct and rigorous moral confrontation of Book V toward the more mannered and aesthetic perspective of Book VI. This accords with one of the poem's compositional rhythms: Books I, III, and V are mainly British books because they are, in different ways, approaches to the real or the actual—as theological, as natural, as social. But Books II, IV, and VI seem to involve corresponding withdrawals into Faerie. Book V presents the decay of antique norms, and the threatened subjection of Spenser's antique forms, before the darkness of the present. Book VI retreats from the plains, mountains, and rocky coast of Book V into the rich wood of Faerie forms and motifs.

Space does not allow a close inquiry into the effects of the transition on the sixth book. But a brief listing of its main features may suggest something of its quality. There is, for example, a deliberate casualness in Spenser's treatment of narrative and character. After the first canto almost every episode is left unresolved: the poet breaks off an incident promising further installments which never materialize;[3] or he presents a situation whose very nature is inconclusive, as in the case of Mirabella;[4] or he conclusively ends an episode before our narrative expectations have been fulfilled, as with Priscilla, Serena, and Pastorella.[5] This effect is impressed on us by the heavily stressed transition from one story to another.[6] At times he introduces details and motifs of romance which are left undeveloped, and made to flaunt their irrelevance, as in the story told by Matilda to Calepine.[7]

The characters are all flat and typical, and it is often hard to keep them straight. This is made worse by a similarity in names and situations: the same *kinds* of situations recur again and again, and the poet merely substitutes one set of figures for another. There is, however, a pattern in the substitutions, for the second group is always worse or more ineffective than the first—we move from Crudor to Turpine, from Calidore to Calepine, from the hermit to Melibee, from the noble savage to the cannibals to the bandits. As a result, we are aware of a progressive flawing in the romance world. Related to this pattern are the wounds inflicted by the blatant beast, which grow steadily worse and do not respond to physical treatment.[8] Physical action, in general, is played down. The problems posed by courtesy and slander pertain to the sting infixed in the name, not in the body. The physical action demanded by the chivalric idiom is revealed as inadequate—in both its narrative and its symbolic functions.

Though variety is stressed by the transitions and large number of episodes, the poet continually returns to a small number of motifs. There are the motifs of the nursery,[9] the gifts of nature,[10] the foundling;[11] the

[3] Thus we are left in the air about the future of Tristram, the Noble Savage, and Matilda's child (ii.40, v.1–2, iv.38).

[4] viii.17–18, 22, 29–30.

[5] At iii.18–19 Calidore leaves Priscilla with her father, and we never find out whether or not she is reunited with her lover Aladine, though this is the main point of the episode. Similarly the fate of Calidore and Pastorella is ignored (xii.22), though a reader might divine it without the help of the gods. Perhaps the most flagrant example of this motif comes at the end of canto viii, when Spenser abandons Calepine in the dark with the naked Serena, who nervously waits for daylight to "discover bad and good." The sudden shift from the problems of murder to those of modesty is characteristic of the disequilibrium Spenser maintains in this book. One might ask, incidentally, what the poet had in mind when he picked those good humanist names, Calepine and Aldus.

[6] See ii.40; iv.17; v.11; vi.17; vii.27; viii.4, 31, 51; ix.1, 46; x.1–3; xi.24; xii.1–2, 14, 22.

[7] iv.29–33.

[8] VI.iv.16; v.31; vi.1–15.

[9] Pr.3–4, 7; i.1; iv.11–14; v.1–2; vi.9–12; ix.20; x.22–23. *Nursery* simply refers to the concept of *source* in its various aspects.

[10] E.g., i.2; ii.2, 24; iii.1–2; v.1–2; vii.1–2, 28; viii.1–2; ix.20–23.

[11] iv.32–38; ix.14; xii.3–9.

motif of withdrawal and return, or of retirement;[12] the motif of primitivism, related to the nursery theme and diversely embodied in the savage, the cannibals, and the shepherds. There is the motif of the center and the ring, which appears in three progressively higher and more symbolic stages: Serena at the raised altar surrounded by cannibals; Pastorella on a hill surrounded by swains; and the unnamed figure on Mount Acidale surrounded by dancing graces. The most frequently repeated motif is, significantly enough, that of a character surprised in a moment of diversion.[13] Such moments are all perfectly natural or necessary—love, sleep, hunting, or merely a walk in the woods. These are the small but precious joys of everyday life, and they are not the ordinary subjects of the epic world. Yet to these moments the poet adds many touches which might be called homely or realistic—the care of babies, the adjustment of harness and pasturing of mounts, the gathering of food and other agricultural details.[14] This realistic texture keeps the actual world always before us, even in the heart of Faerie. Precisely here, where we feel most secure, where we momentarily turn our backs on the outside world, the danger is greatest. For the beast of slander is no chivalric figure. The hermit, who knows this, gives hard counsel to Timias and Serena: "Abstain from pleasure, restrain your will, subdue desire, bridle loose delight, use scanted diet, forbear your fill, shun secrecy and talk in open sight" (vi.7, 14). In other words, "Keep your eye always on the treacherous world around you; don't withdraw, don't relax, for a single moment."

The result of these features is curiously ambivalent. The poet is bemused, a little bewildered, by the rich variety of Faerie, its many paths, the lure of so many joys: the opening stanzas of the proem and the final stanza of the sixth book together suggest that he is like all the lovers in the woods, or Timias with Belphoebe, or Arthur distracted by thoughts of Gloriana (vii.6). At the same time, the hermit's advice embodies an element of awareness in the poet which is responsible for the stylistic traits just described. The contrivance of the narrative, the inconclusiveness of the adventures, the gradual flawing of the romance world, the failure of chivalric action—these dramatize the claims imposed by actuality on the life of imagination. They also reveal the poet's awareness that the problems of life cannot be solved by poetry, cannot even be adequately represented in the simplified forms of Faerie. J. C. Maxwell has

---

[12] ii.27–30; v.11–23; v.36–vi.4; ix.24–31; x.2–3, 9, 22; xii.19–21.

[13] ii.16–18; iii.20–21, 23–24; iv.17; v.10–11, 15; vii.6–7, 18–19; viii.34; x.18, 34, 39; xii.40–41.

[14] iv.14, 23–24, 38; v.10–11, 38; vi.19; vii.24; viii.35; ix.1–xii.4 passim.

remarked that Spenser's handling of certain episodes "betrays a mind not fully engaged by what it is doing."[15] This comment is meant as criticism, but it is likely that Spenser intended a poetic effect: he *shows* poetry facing the actual world to cope with the difficult social problems of slander and courtesy, but he *knows* poetry's true work and pleasure require detachment rather than involvement. Something of this attitude is written into his curious presentation of the blatant beast.

The beast is an emblem or symbol which is clearly distinguished from the thing symbolized, so that the complex relations of slander and courtesy are reduced to an artificial and ideographic fable. Calidore thinks he is chasing some sort of animal possessed of two unfriendly habits: it bites and it reviles.[16] The first is a shorthand version of the effects of the second, and it permits the evil to be expressed in physical terms so that chivalric action is possible. This is a radically reduced image of the social dangers disclosed toward the end of Book V, and of a profound spiritual evil with which Spenser was preoccupied throughout his career. The blatant beast, as I have suggested elsewhere,[17] embodies the social expression of the malice produced by despair and self-hatred—the despair of the have-not who hungers after the good of others, who sees himself deprived of place and function, totally dependent on the world outside him, stripped of any "daily beauty in his life." The words of Slander in Book IV, of Envy, Detraction, and the "raskall many" in Book V, are uttered to alleviate inward pain rather than to express meanings; their words become a form of rending, a spiritual cannibalism whose perverse and irrational music is aimed at the nerves and the affections:

> Her words were not, as common words are ment,
> T'expresse the meaning of the inward mind,
> But noysome breath, and poysnous spirit sent
> From inward parts, with cancred malice lind,
> And breathed forth with blast of bitter wind;
> Which passing through the eares, would pierce the hart,
> And wound the soule it selfe with griefe unkind:
> For like the stings of Aspes, that kill with smart,
> Her spightfull words did pricke, and wound the inner part.
>
> *(IV.viii.26)*

---

[15] "The Truancy of Calidore," in *That Soueraine Light*, ed. W. R. Mueller and D. C. Allen (Baltimore: Johns Hopkins Press, 1952), 68.

[16] For the double meaning of *blatant*, see Leslie Hotson, "The Blatant Beast," in *Studies in Honor of T. W. Baldwin*, ed. D. C. Allen (Urbana: University of Illinois Press, 1958), 34–38.

[17] See an early version of this paper, "The Prospect of Imagination," *Studies in English Literature* 1 (Winter 1961): 106–7. .

The emblematic descriptions of the blatant beast (i.7−9, vi.9−12, xii.26−28) adumbrate this evil and suggest the rich complexity of meaning packed into the image. The bite then brings all this to bear on a character so as to compare the peculiarly simplified existence of Faerie creatures with the difficulties of actual victims. Since slander in real life is not conveniently gathered together into the form of a single monster, and since—as the hermit points out (vi.6−7, 13−14)—the sting infixed in the name is not susceptible to physical remedies, Calidore's pursuit and conquest can hardly be anything but wish fulfillment.

This is in fact the way the final battle is presented: the affair is purely literal, and the beast is diminished not only from an emblem to an unsymbolic animal but also from a fearful monster to little more than a muzzled cur. Thus, after a terrifying prebattle bristle in which it bares a jaw crammed with significance (xii.26−28), the beast responds to Calidore's attack by "rearing up his former feete on hight" and ramping "upon him with his ravenous pawes" (xii.29). As Spenser cuts the contest down to size, hero and enemy are compared to a butcher and a bull in the abattoir (xii.30), and the beast then behaves like an angry girl: "almost mad for fell despight, / He grind, hee bit, he scratcht, he venim threw" (xii.31). Compared to this description, the epic similes look clearly oversized and are deliberately misapplied to stress disparity rather than likeness (xii.32, 35). While the Hydra's thousand heads increase in stanza 32, the tongues of the waning beast diminish from a thousand (i.9; xii.27) to the hundred he originally owned when he offered Artegal a glancing threat (V.xii.41; VI.xii.33). Finally, Calidore applies a muzzle and a "great long chaine" and draws him trembling "like a fearefull dog" through Faerie. The conclusion of the quest has nothing to do with slander, everything to do with an Elfin hero's dream: it is a ticker-tape parade through Faerie, whose crowds "much admyr'd the Beast, but more admyr'd the Knight" (VI.xii.38)—the most triumphant and ridiculous of all Elfin homecomings, exposed a moment later when the beast roars into the present and threatens the poet. Thus, as an allegorical creature, given a shape and a place in the poem, the complex evils summarized in the term *slander* can be understood and controlled. But they can only be controlled in the play world created by the mind. What the beast represents is still in the actual world, and not in a simply identifiable form but diffused among the corrupt, weak, and bitter spirits of civilization.

The importance of courtesy is dialectically illuminated by this danger. Maxwell has indicated the allegorical irrelevance of the beast's relation to its victims (pp. 68−69), and this irrelevance constitutes its meaning: attacks of slander are not made on the evil but on the virtuous; otherwise they would not be slander. Since the beast represents nothing whatsoever in the souls of its victims, its forays appear as sudden and inexplicable to us as they do to the sufferers. The armor of courtesy consists of "outward shows" which fulfill rather than deceptively conceal "inward thoughts." It is not simply *a* virtue, nor merely an ornamental polish distinguishing gentry from boors, but a technique of survival in a difficult world; courtesy makes virtue and virtuous behavior possible, maintains trust between men, keeps open the lines of civilized communication. Actuality, with its dangers, requires a movement out from the virtuous center to the circumference of the self where others are met. But—and this is the trouble for the poet who must exercise this technique even in poetry—such a movement diametrically opposes the poet's tendency to journey inward toward the mind's center, toward the source of his ravishing gift.

Thus the apparent inattention Maxwell notes seems deliberate and springs from a conflict which lies at the heart of Spenser's work. On the one hand, poetry is his supreme pleasure; on the other hand, he has to survive; especially if he is a professional dependent on patronage, his delight must be tempered to his needs and those of others. Circumstances force the poet as man to adapt his poetry to the actual environment. But the man as poet is concerned with his second nature, the world within the poem, a world of which he is creator and legislator. If poetry is play, it is deadly serious play, a way of life in which imaginary experience means more than actuality—Spenser is thoroughly Neoplatonist in his belief that the soul can turn inward and find a second world more perfect and real than the first. But he is also aware of the mind's limits: in a negative sense, the limits placed *on* the imaginary by the actual; in a more positive sense, the limits *of* the imaginary. For if the Muses transport him to an ideal world perfected by wish or perverted by nightmare, will they not reward him with a glimpse of the real? Will they render him defenseless against the threats of the beast, or deny the actual world its own rightful claims on a man's inner life? If they ravish him, are they sirens or something better?

Spenser raised questions of this sort as early as *The Shepheardes Calender*, and they are raised again in the proem to Book VI. They are implicit in the three modes of pastoral whose names were given, and distinctions blurred, by E. K.—*recreative, moral,* and *plaintive* may be understood more literally than his discussion indicates. Recreative pastoral is a poetry of escape in a holiday world free from care: its swains use the problems of life as excuses for indulging in song; delighting chiefly in rhetoric and the manipulation of *topoi*, they pursue their bent both for its own sake and for its social value as entertainment. In Colin's *Aprill* song of Eliza, for example, the mythic figures are nothing more than names—adjectives rather—applied as ornaments to the Queen. The richness of tradition and meaning which makes one mythic figure distinct from another has been rigorously screened out of the poetry; it appears only in E. K.'s gloss, where much of it (e.g., the Three Graces, *Apr.* 267–74) will remain until April is revisited on Acidale.

The moral eclogues are mainly about the inadequacy of the artless to verbalize or to reflect clearly on the problems of the great world— behind these eclogues one feels the force of the Ciceronian commonplace about wisdom and eloquence both being necessary to hold civilization together. The moral pastors, who live in the English countryside rather than in England's Helicon, lack control of thought and expression, are sadly wanting in the poetic, dialectical, and rhetorical disciplines neces- sary to proper communication. These eclogues argue the ethical function of poetic skill. The great world *is* corrupt, and this is the problem: someone has to deal with it. Someone needs the knowledge, the shrewd- ness, the sophistication, the command of expression to cope with the evils and articulate them with clarity. In the great world, knaves seize power by playing roles and practicing the arts of persuasion; therefore— since the moral pastor is too simple, perhaps too honest, certainly too lazy—poets are enjoined to fulfill their social obligations: the aesthetic pleasure must not be channeled into escape and mere recreation but placed in the service of the public good.

Thus the recreative and moral modes appear incompatible and incom- plete as displayed in the *Calender:* the former turns away from life to poetry, the latter from poetry to a sort of life. The plaintive eclogues are simply complaints. They center on Colin's skill and, with the exception of the *November* eclogue, on his love, though their rhetoric shades the meaning into a variety of other problems. As the title of Spenser's later volume suggests, the term *complaints* comes to cover any sort of frus- tration or disappointment with actual life and the human condition— "death, or love, or fortunes wreck" (*Epithalamion* 8). Colin is a recre- ative shepherd whose art has been cut short by a love which, since it keeps him from poetry, breaks all pastoral rules. He is unlike the moral pastors not only because he embodies rhetorical culture—his personality is compacted of *topoi*—but also because he was first moved by the joy of poetry; he is unlike the recreative pastors because his problem goes be- yond the limits of his poetry. Therefore he provides Spenser with a pos- sible way out of the recreative-moral dilemma. This way has two related characteristics: (1) it involves frustration, withdrawal, and the ideal recreation of life in imaginary forms; (2) it is committed to literary and cultural commonplaces—the treasures of the Muses—as the raw materials of poetic style, the traditional seeds which will germinate in the soil of personal experience. It is the way which, as we know, leads to Mount Acidale.

The proem to Book VI begins with an expression of the recreative impulse, though at a much deeper level than in the earlier work. The first two stanzas, after all, follow the moral and plaintive poetry of Book V:

> The waies through which my weary steps I guyde,
>   In this delightfull land of Faery,
>   Are so exceeding spacious and wyde,
>   And sprinckled with such sweet variety,
>   Of all that pleasant is to eare or eye,
>   That I nigh ravisht with rare thoughts delight,
>   My tedious travell doe forget thereby;
>   And when I gin to feele decay of might,
> It strength to me supplies, and chears my dulled spright.
>
> Such secret comfort, and such heavenly pleasures,
>   Ye sacred imps, that on *Parnasso* dwell,
>   And there the keeping have of learnings threasures,
>   Which doe all worldly riches farre excell,
>   Into the mindes of mortall men doe well,
>   And goodly fury into them infuse;
>   Guyde ye my footing, and conduct me well
>   In these strange waies, where never foote did use,
> Ne none can find, but who was taught them by the Muse.

The Muses make him forget his tedious "travell": not only the labor of art but perhaps also the straight and difficult path dictated by such a purpose as the allegory of Justice. They tempt him from the goal, lead him the long way round, and yet refresh the goal-bound spirit. The imagination recognizes both the risk and the privilege of so profound a holiday diversion: it cannot find this ideal place unless the Muse reveals, but it may lose its way in Faerie unless the Muse leads it out. The Muses are felt to be an independent and objective power, an ambiguous Other imposing on his will. The poet's problem is the same as Arthur's when he was lured into a new world by his dream of Gloriana: he has to find out "whether dreames delude, or true it were" (I.ix.14). The presence of the Muses within him demands a response of will: it is man who must put them to the test, whose experience or experiment will discover and articulate their divinity.

Spenser's response in stanzas 3 and 4 of the proem is an attempt to keep the Muses honest. He asks for moral illumination as well as pleasure: "Revele to me the sacred noursery / Of vertue." From the fourth to the sixth stanzas he poses, then rejects, the temptation to withdraw completely from the corrupt world around him, to go straight to "vertues seat . . . deepe within the mynd, / And not in outward shows, but inward thoughts defynd." At the end of the proem he acknowledges a source of virtue at the center of the social order in the person of the divinely appointed Queen: "Right so from you all goodly vertues well / Into the rest, which round about you ring." This is the first instance of the geometric motif which will be repeated three times in the poem, and it is the only case in which the dynamic image is discerned in forms which inhabit real nature; the others are Faerie rings discovered or devised "deepe within the mynd."

The significance of these two kinds of circles, actual and imaginary, becomes clearer if we recall a familiar element of Plotinian thought utilized by Ficino and other Renaissance Neoplatonists: the notion that when the objective Idea proceeds downward from the World Mind to the World Soul and Nature it may divide into two forms of existence, actual and mental. The Idea may be incarnated in the form of one human being and may exist as a form or concept in the mind of another. The mental form is purer than its incarnate analogue and may be aroused by it—this is the more or less utilitarian function of the beloved in Neoplatonist love psychology. In terms of Book VI, the geometric symbol represents an objective *harmonia* which God has embodied in the Queen and her order and which the Muses have implanted in the poetic imagination. Elizabeth's circle will be transfigured on Mount Acidale; when its full richness and meaning are unfolded it will be understood as one of many embodiments of that single form gathered together through the quest of imagination, through the reversion of the mind from the scattered particulars of experience to the Idea which is their formal source. Thus on Acidale the center is, so to speak, pushed upward so that it is the apex of a spiral or a mountaintop.

II

The episodes leading up to Mount Acidale center on Faerie figures drawn from the realm of literary conventions: Mirabella, the Proud Fair of Petrarchan fame; Serena, the Distressed Maiden of romance, whose name seems as deliberate an irony as her antiromantic encounter with the cannibals; Pastorella, the aristocratic foundling who presides over the idyllic community of recreative and moral pastors. Each of these episodes constitutes an evocation of an ideal (as opposed to actual) community, completely unified and controlled by the mind, and each is a self-contained environment, a circle focused on its conventional center. Mirabella, surrounded by "murdered" lovers, gives way to the antithetical image of Serena about to be murdered; the raw nature of the cannibals, remote ancestors of the rending beast, is replaced by the "raw" artifice of walking pastoral commonplaces. Mirabella projects the germinal form of frustration, Serena and her cannibals the germinal form of desire, Pastorella and her swains the germinal form of poetic recreation, all of which are infolded and transfigured by Colin's vision. Each, then, is a kind of beginning, an apparent but not a real nursery, a primitive version of that ravishing source finally discovered deep within the mind. And each is centered on a female figure who adumbrates the source or object of desire, the cause or effect of a certain mode of imagination. Each figure, that is, embodies claims on the male psyche which seem to be imposed by some outside force, some otherness working in or through the form of woman.

Like other incidents in Book VI, the Mirabella episode (vii.27 – viii.30) has the air of being a reprise: in a kind of miniature compass it recalls the erotic atmosphere of Books III and IV (especially Busirane's house), the Cruel Fair sonnets among the *Amoretti*, passages from *Colin Clouts Come Home Againe* and *An Hymne in Honour of Love*. This is the world of erotic narcissism and courtly love where, as C. S. Lewis has shown, all human activity is subordinated to the consciousness of desire. Love becomes art, war, religion, a way of life, and a form of death. In the Court of Cupid *topos* (vii.32 – 37) Spenser presents a totally artificial world which, with its carefully sustained legal metaphor, smacks of over-sophistication. Like Busirane's tapestry, the imagination, by displaying its gold thread, asserts the power of art over haphazard nature.

Mirabella is a typical projection of the Petrarchan lover's impatience, a scapegoat for his lust—not the image of a real woman so much as a single aspect of the feminine psyche abstracted and personified as a Faerie creature—like Belphoebe, Florimell, Amoret. The Mirabellan frustration produces a desire which gradually obsesses and paralyzes the will, so that the decadent refinements and rituals of Cupid are means by which the natural processes of love and life are suspended, the condition of lust fixated rather than sublimated. The source of this fixation which Spenser has so exhaustively explored is suggested in viii.28 – 29: Mirabella's "meane parentage and kindred base"—we think momentarily of Rosalind—are related to the "wondrous giftes of natures grace" which made all men admire her. This is simply her physical beauty, the first gift of nature. Since she lacks the second gift of spirit, her popularity reflects on the love entertained by her suitors: "Yet was she lov'd of many a worthy pere, / Unworthy she to be belov'd so dere." Theirs is the first undisciplined response to beauty; its aim is physical satisfaction, immediate union rather than sustained *com*munion. It is this longing which has produced Mirabella—all Mirabellas—and given her the power to tyrannize the male appetite. Her name means Beauty-look, Beautifullooking, or perhaps Beauty-mirror: not the true beauty but a physical image, not her own but a reflection of the beholder's passion. Like the Eros of Plato's *Symposium,* she is born of poverty and plenty—the poverty of lust and the plenty of nature's gifts.

This evil is connected to the more general theme of the need for alertness, the threat of actuality which led the hermit to warn the beast's victims, "First learne your outward sences to refraine / From things, that stirre up fraile affection" (vi.7). Lovers must be inwardly alert, their first sight demands temperance by insight if it is to lead to that second sight which is *re*-spect. And in *An Hymne in Honour of Beautie,* Spenser describes this insight in Neoplatonic terms which connect it to the poetic process:

> all that like the beautie which they see,
> Streight do not love: for love is not so light,
> As streight to burne at first beholders sight.
>
> But they which love indeede, looke otherwise,
> With pure regard and spotlesse true intent,
> Drawing out of the object of their eyes,
> A more refyned forme . . .
>
> *(208–214)*

First sight is the passive response to the gifts of physical nature, the sensory signals from actuality. In its context, the Mirabella episode connects her with the inability to transform first sight by insight. If we recall Colin's problem in the *Calender,* we may add to the charges against Mirabella that she even stops the recreative pleasure of poetry. True poetry, like true love, cannot proceed until Mirabella has been controlled or transformed by creative insight, and it is significant that Spenser visualizes, exposes, and exorcizes Mirabella before moving toward Colin's vision on Acidale. One may see the episode as the poet's way of taking his revenge on an image; but one may also see the whole movement from Mirabella to Acidale as a poet's progress reunderstood, a transition from the wound to the bow.

Serena's character and predicament are diametrically opposed to Mirabella's. Here the men are the aggressors, and what they project on the helpless object is a primitive confusion of hunger, lust, and ritual awe. Yet the cannibal and Petrarchan lovers are shown to have something in common:

> they hands upon her lay;
> And first they spoile her of her jewels deare,
> And afterwards of all her rich array;
> The which amongst them they in peeces teare,
> And of the pray each one a part doth beare.
> Now being naked, to their sordid eyes
> The goodly threasures of nature appeare:
> Which, as they view with lustfull fantasyes,
> Each wisheth to him selfe, and to the rest envyes.

> Her yvorie necke, her alablaster brest,
> Her paps, which like white silken pillowes were,
> For love in soft delight thereon to rest;
> Her tender sides, her bellie white and clere,
> Which like an Altar did it selfe uprere,
> To offer sacrifice divine thereon;
> Her goodly thighes, whose glorie did appeare
> Like a triumphall Arch, and thereupon
> The spoiles of Princes hang'd, which were in battel won.
>
> *(viii.41–42)*

Serena's "goodly threasures of nature" are detailed in a typical sonneteer's catalogue in which the Lady is parceled out as a number of valuable minerals or vegetables. More striking than the difference between primitive and civilized responses is the similarity: Cupid's poet-lovers have progressed far in ornamental refinements, little in true spiritual culture. Both primitive and civilized lovers respond to the same stimulus, for the savages are aroused by Serena's beautiful face "Like the faire yvory shining" (viii.37).

In the catalogue Serena becomes an anatomy of love, religion, and war, a cradle or epitome of civilization. This breadth of allusion suggests the continuity of urges and difference of expression between the two societies; the relation of the inarticulate Noble Savage to the courtly hero provides an analogy. Seen this way, culture is the only natural environment for man, the full flowering of mind into a social order redeemed from raw actuality. But if one thinks of Cupid's world, where love is a religion and warfare as well as a "soft delight," the restraints imposed by society may be seen to cause the most elaborate and widely diffused corruption of spirit. The female body becomes the source of all value, the object of all desires—we may recall the troubadour's *mi dons* and the kind of idolatry on which Mirabella capitalized ("What could the Gods doe more, but doe it more aright?").

Spenser's cannibals provide a physical image the very form of which exposes both the evils treated in the sixth book and the source of actual disorder which jeopardizes the poetic imagination. The savages do not take a stand within themselves or stay in one place to cultivate, to impose a form on experience; and like Mother Hubberd's knaves, they wander about on the borders, encroaching on the beings of others:

> There dwelt a salvage nation, which did live
> Of stealth and spoile, and making nightly rode
> Into their neighbors borders; ne did give
> Them selves to any trade, as for to drive
> The painefull plough, or cattell for to breed,
> Or by adventrous marchandize to thrive;
> But on the labours of poore men to feed,
> And serve their owne necessities with others need.
>
> *(viii.35)*

In their urge to rend and devour, to serve their own necessities, they reveal the evil of the blatant beast in its unsublimated character. Crudor, the Noble Savage, and the other artificial versions of the evil or the primitive give way to an image in which both manner and subject pretend to lack imaginative refinement. The episode appears as a kind of bedrock, an etiological account which strips away the veneer of civilization.

But as a myth of origins, the cannibals reveal something else. They are not entirely free of restraint, and the appearance of Serena produces a first response of withdrawal. The priest rebukes their lust, advising them

> not to pollute so sacred threasure,
> Vow'd to the gods: religion held even theeves in measure.
>
> So being stayd, they her from thence directed
>   Unto a little grove not farre asyde,
>   In which an altar shortly they erected,
>   To slay her on . . .
>
> . . . .
>
> Of few green turfes *an altar soone they fayned,*
> And deckt it all with flowres, which they nigh hand obtayned.
>
> *(viii.43–44; italics mine)*

It is an ironic, even a comic, withdrawal, yet "fayned" points the way from the body's altar toward the temple and the mind. Though Spenser remarks that they found Serena "by fortune blynde" (viii.36), the cannibals think, because of her beauty, that she was sent by "heavenly grace" (viii.37). Serena is still a thing and not a person, an object and not an Other, an It and not a Thou. But she has already begun to be a symbol for the cannibals, whose crude religion is shown to be no less indigenous than lust and hunger. They are confused by this adumbration of the divine, and they do not know how to respond to it. The priest, functioning in his Orphic role as an Ur-poet, directs them to an act of ritual imagination, namely, that it is better to murder Serena on God's behalf than to rape her on their own.

Spenser's cannibals strike all sorts of Freudian sparks, but they are better understood in the light of the Neoplatonic psychology elaborated by Ficino. It will be useful briefly to indicate the points of doctrine relevant to Spenser's erotic and poetic psychology: Beauty is the visible manifestation of God's goodness as it radiates outward from the divine center through the four cosmic circles of Creation; it produces Ideas in Mind, Concepts in Soul, Seeds in Nature, and Shapes in Matter.[18] Perception begins with shapes, the images of material objects; then, moving inward and upward, it corrects these by reference to Ideas (formulas), innate though germinal forms which the mind unfolds through experience and in the activity of thought.[19] "Since human thought rises from the senses,[20] we invariably judge the divine on the basis of what seems to us highest in physical bodies." Yet the shapes of bodies "neither sufficiently are divine things, nor adequately represent them to us, for the true things are the Ideas, Concepts, and Seeds."[21] The Neoplatonic quest is a reversion to the divine source, a recovery within the forms of human consciousness of the creative principle. Seen in this light, the love of Mirabella is regressive, for her beauty attracts neither to God nor to her soul but outward and "downward" to her body. Spenser's transition to the cannibal ring logically reduces the sophisticated evil to its confused origin and, in effect, allows him to begin all over again:

---

[18] *De amore* II.2–4, trans. and ed. Sears Jayne, in *Marsilio Ficino's Commentary on Plato's Symposium*, University of Missouri Studies, vol. 19, no. 1 (Columbia: University of Missouri Press, 1944), 133–40.

[19] See, e.g., *Theologica Platonica* XI.3 and the *Comment. in Plotin. Ennead.* I.6; *Opera omnia*, 241, 1574 ff.

[20] The Latin, *a sensibus oritur*, contains this ambiguity: thought may originate in the senses, as Aristotle and Aquinas held, but it fulfills itself only in rising above the senses, as Plato held. See P. O. Kristeller, *The Philosophy of Marsilio Ficino*, trans. Virginia Conant (New York: Columbia University Press, 1943), 234 ff.

[21] *De amore* II.4, in Jayne, 139–40.

> It happens that the passion of a lover is not quenched by the mere touch or sight of a body, for it does not desire this or that body, but desires the splendor of the divine light shining through bodies, and is amazed and awed by it. For this reason lovers never know what it is they desire and seek, for they do not know God Himself. . . . Hence it also happens that lovers somehow both worship and fear the sight of the beloved. . . . It also often happens that the lover wishes to transform himself into the person of the loved one.[22]

What the mind seeks is not what it finds in the actuality of Matter and Nature, but what it finds deep within itself, what it creates and expresses as culture in its attempt to envisage the divine as it can. The savages have nothing but a woman on which to project their primitive eros, and the Petrarchan catalogue describing Serena suggests that their eros demands new objects, different modes of expression, more refined forms. However obscure, the primitive eros is the response to God which the Neoplatonists call love, "the desire of beauty." It is a desire which involves not only passive pleasure, not only the urge for generation in nature, but also the urge to create, in Diotima's words, "that which is proper for the soul to conceive or contain," namely, wisdom and virtue. "And such creators are poets and all artists who are deserving of the name inventor" (*Symposium* 209, Jowett trans.). The soul is driven by its very confusion before the poverty of the actual—the mere gifts of nature—to create the symbolic forms which embody its desire and shadow its goal; objectifying these forms into an environment it may better understand its own energy by gazing at its diverse cultural images. Therefore eros produces a cultural dialectic between the soul and its environment: each soul is born into a world of institutions, traditions, and conventions which are external to it and impersonal, yet which are the work of previous souls; they supply the vocabulary through which the soul defines its desire, the forms through which it articulates its experience. The soul internalizes these forms, makes them personal, makes them new.

But if "making them new" proceeds by that sculptural Michelangelesque energy R. P. Blackmur has called the "inward mastery of experience," it is sustained by delight; its original motive is recreation and play. And this revisionary play accounts for the transition from the primitive to the rustic nursery in the ninth canto. The description of Pastorella and her circle echoes that of Serena and hers:

> Of few greene turfes an altar soone they fayned,
> And deckt it all with flowres, which they nigh hand obtayned.

[22] *De amore* II.6, in Jayne, 140–41.

Tho when as all things readie were aright,
   The Damzell was before the altar set,
   Being alreadie dead with fearefull fright.
                                        (viii.44–45)

Then gan the bagpypes and the hornes to shrill,
   And shrieke aloud, that with the peoples voyce
   Confused, did the ayre with terror fill,
   And made the wood to tremble at the noyce:
   The whyles she wayld, the more they did rejoyce.
                                        (viii.46)

A few stanzas later we meet Pastorella, wearing a crown

   Of sundry flowres, with silken ribbands tyde,
   Yclad in home-made greene that her owne hands had dyde.

Upon a litle hillocke she was placed
   Higher then all the rest, and round about
   Environ'd with a girland, goodly graced,
   Of lovely lasses, and them all without
   The lustie shepheard swaynes sate in a rout,
   The which did pype and sing her prayses dew,
   And oft rejoyce, and oft for wonder shout,
   As if some miracle of heavenly hew
Were downe to them descended in that earthly vew.

And soothly sure she was full fayre of face,
   And perfectly well shapt in every lim,
   Which she did more augment with modest grace,
   And comely carriage of her count'nance trim,
   That all the rest like lesser lamps did dim:
   Who her admiring as some heavenly wight,
   Did for their soveraine goddesse her esteeme,
   And caroling her name both day and night,
The fayrest *Pastorella* her by name did hight.
                                        (ix.7–9)

Pastorella is later revealed as an aristocrat, a true Faerie heroine. As the
center of rustic and recreative pastoral, she symbolizes the artificial desire on which it is based—the escape to the *Petit-Trianon*. It is an existence sustained by the act of naming, the pleasure of words and song.
Pastorella's fairy-tale return to her noble parents suggests the continuity
of Spenser's earlier and later, his lower and higher, recreative forms.

   In naming her, the swains reduce her from an aristocrat to a shepherd-
ess; in worshiping her, they exalt her from an aristocrat to a goddess,

identifying the symbol with the reality to which it refers. In this way the essential limits of the pastoral idyll are defined: a simplified paradise whose narrow confines are exalted by its inhabitants to a perfect world complete with incarnate divinity. Its philosopher gives low marks to aspiration and unfulfilled desire, preaching that very sufficiency of the first nature which the sixth book questions. Melibee's "morality" is in fact the same kind of excuse for laziness used by the moral pastors of *The Shepheardes Calender*; it is a recreative withdrawal from care.[23] In the recreative situation the manner, the manipulation of the medium, the present activity, becomes an end in itself, and what looks like symbolism may only be an excuse for indulging in the self-sufficient pleasures of play.

But it is precisely this pleasure which will lead to the triumph on Mount Acidale, for the recreative impulse is significantly different from the moral or plaintive. Its object is not social improvement or a woman but the activity of poetry itself, the play of the mind simply for its own sake—"the mind's delight in itself, in its power of excess and fantasy, in its ability to play the game of freedom, even freedom from law and the moral order."[24] The treasures of the Muses may supplant the objects sought by savages, lovers, and heroes; found nowhere in nature, they must be created and objectified by the human spirit before they can exist over against the soul, as pleasures to be pursued. The recreative interest is not in the originals which poetry imitates but in the models and model-making power through which originals are explored.

If Pastorella and her circle are a more refined form of Serena and the cannibals, if the object of desire is heightened and enhanced by inhibition, by withdrawal to more symbolic forms of action, then the second image is still not simply a revised version of the first. The two are also parallel: the savage ring is the nursery of the first nature, the starting point of culture as a whole; the pastoral ring is the nursery of the second nature, the deliberately reduced and purely artificial landscape of *topoi*, images, rhetorical figures, and phonetic structures which are the raw material of poetry. These first attract the poet simply as ornaments and jewels, or, to use a common Renaissance image, flowers.[25]

[23] See VI.ix.20–23, the essence of which is in the final lines: "when I wearie am, / I downe doe lay / My limbes in every shade, to rest from toyle." Melibee's counterpart in the pastoral spectrum of *As You Like It* (which dramatizes E. K.'s three modes) is Corin—see especially III.ii.11–85. Melibee, whom commentators have atrociously glamorized, spouts a philosophy partly based on sour grapes: he worked for ten years as a gardener at court without getting ahead (ix.24–25). For all his self-sufficiency, Spenser kills him off in a hemistich (xi.18).

[24] Lionel Trilling, "Dr. Leavis and the Moral Tradition," in *A Gathering of Fugitives* (Boston: Beacon Press, 1956), 105.

[25] Plato's *Ion* 533D is a familiar source for the figure of the poet as a bee in the Muses' garden. This may also have suggested Spenser's Clarion, in *Muiopotmos*, whose behavior

By reproducing the *Calender* world in all its flatness Spenser justifies the recreative delight in artifice. *Artifice*—as we understand the term when thinking of literary conventions, and as Renaissance thinkers certainly understood it—displays the shaping hand of spirit and guarantees that meaning lurks beneath the surface of the form. As the Neoplatonist term *hieroglyph* suggests, a symbolic object must indicate, by various simplifications, its symbolic nature if the reader is to look beyond it; to make the rustic actual, as Spenser did in the moral eclogues, is to dissipate its artificiality.[26] The conventional artifice may be nothing more than a sign, but it is the necessary blueprint or flat form on which the meaning is ultimately raised.

Thus in the ninth canto we return to the blueprint world, the polyglot landscape of borrowed conventions which Spenser assembled in *The Shepheardes Calender*. We come upon this place through a magical, a kind of Proustian, transformation: the blatant beast disappears and we are led with Calidore out of chivalric Faerie, back in time to Spenser's early poetry. All the space between vanishes—five books of Faerie, eight cantos of Book VI, the arduous questing, plaintive or moral, which led to this moment. The fullness of vision, the triumph of imagination, is suddenly sprung from the conventional platform as the description of Pastorella reappears in its refined form: on top of the mountain where "*Venus*, when she did dispose / Her selfe to pleasaunce, used to resort / . . . and therein to repose / And rest her selfe" (x.9) Calidore sees

> An hundred naked maidens lilly white,
> All raunged in a ring, and dauncing in delight.

> All they without were raunged in a ring,
>   And daunced round; but in the midst of them
>   Three other Ladies did both daunce and sing,
>   The whilest the rest them round about did hemme,
>   And like a girlond did in compasse stemme:
>   And in the middest of those same three, was placed
>   Another Damzell, as a precious gemme,
>   Amidst a ring most richly well enchaced,
> That with her goodly presence all the rest much graced.

---

in his garden recalls that of the young poet, the first gift of delight in the nursery of commonplaces. Like the poet of Book VI, Clarion is ravished by the variety of the garden, but *his* meander is aimless and uncontrolled, a picking at choice bits.

[26] In the *December* eclogue, Colin moves from literal rusticity back to the kind of metaphoric language with which he opened the *Calender*, thereby salvaging some symbolic possibilities from the wreckage left by the boors.

Looke how the Crowne, which *Ariadne* wore
 Upon her yvory forehead that same day,
 That *Theseus* her unto his bridale bore,
 When the bold *Centaures* made that bloudy fray,
 With the fierce *Lapithes*, which did them dismay;
 Being now placed in the firmament,
 Through the bright heaven doth her beames display,
 And is unto the starres an ornament,
Which round about her move in order excellent.

Such was the beauty of this goodly band,
 Whose sundry parts were here too long to tell:
 But she that in the midst of them did stand,
 Seem'd all the rest in beauty to excell,
 Crownd with a rosie girlond, that right well
 Did her beseeme. And ever, as the crew
 About her daunst, sweet flowres, that far did smell,
 And fragrant odours they uppon her threw;
But most of all, those three did her with gifts endew.

Those were the Graces, daughters of delight,
 Handmaides of *Venus*, which are wont to haunt
 Uppon this hill, and daunce there day and night:
 Those three to men all gifts of grace do graunt,
 And all, that *Venus* in her selfe doth vaunt,
 Is borrowed of them. But that faire one,
 That in the midst was placed paravaunt,
 Was she to whom that shepheard pypt alone,
That made him pipe so merrily, as never none.
                                                        (x.11–15)

Then comes a sudden flashback to the simple origin of this vision and an allusion to the plaintive experience, the frustration, which led to the sublime triumph and which is included as part of it:

She was to weete that jolly Shepheards lasse,
 Which piped there unto that merry rout,
 That jolly shepheard, which there piped, was
 Poore *Colin Clout* (who knowes not *Colin Clout?*)
 He pypt apace, whilest they him daunst about.
 Pype jolly shepheard, pype thou now apace
 Unto thy love, that made thee low to lout:
 Thy love is present there with thee in place,
Thy love is there advaunst to be another Grace.
                                                        (x.16)

Finally, after revealing the genesis and emblematic significance of the Graces, Colin describes the radiant center, the heart of light, into which Rosalind has been transfigured:

> But that fourth Mayd, which there amidst them traced,
> Who can aread, what creature mote she bee,
> Whether a creature, or a goddesse graced
> With heavenly gifts from heven first enraced?
> But what so sure she was, she worthy was,
> To be the fourth with those three other placed:
> Yet was she certes but a countrey lasse,
> Yet she all other countrey lasses farre did passe.
>
> So farre as doth the daughter of the day,
> All other lesser lights in light excell,
> So farre doth she in beautyfull array,
> Above all other lasses beare the bell,
> Ne lesse in virtue that beseemes her well,
> Doth she exceede the rest of all her race,
> For which the Graces that here wont to dwell,
> Have for more honor brought her to this place,
> And graced her so much to be another Grace.
>
> Another Grace she well deserves to be,
> In whom so many Graces gathered are,
> Excelling much the meane of her degree,
> Divine resemblaunce, beauty soveraine rare,
> Firme Chastity, that spight ne blemish dare;
> All which she with such courtesie doth grace,
> That all her peres cannot with her compare,
> But quite are dimmed, when she is in place.
> She made me often pipe and now to pipe apace.
>
> Sunne of the world, great glory of the sky,
> That all the earth doest lighten with thy rayes,
> Great *Gloriana*, greatest Majesty,
> Pardon thy shepheard, mongst so many layes,
> As he hath sung of thee in all his dayes,
> To make one minime of thy poore handmayd,
> And underneath thy feete to place her prayse,
> That when thy glory shall be farre displayd
> To future age of her this mention may be made.
>
> *(x.25–28)*

Here two voices merge into one, Colin as he speaks, Spenser as he writes, the man momentarily transformed into the pure poetic voice, the recreative voice re-created, the past leaping to new life in the present. It is the moment of second sight in which the poet returns to his early fragments of insight, inspiration, or mere sportive pleasure and revises them, *sees* them for the first time. The past and present are juxtaposed as promise and fulfillment in a single poetic form, and the oscillation between them is sustained by Spenser's keeping unworked pastoral elements in the later vision.

In this great passage there is not only the circling of thought which unites the parts of time, but the circling of words in rhythmic repetition, echoing and re-echoing, as they imitate the movement of the figures around a center beyond the reach of language, and at the same time the rising and cresting of vision as it moves from the dale to Ariadne's crown, then returns to Colin, Rosalind, and Calidore only to ascend once more, in Colin's explication, to the Sun of the world. Perhaps in that first lyric outcry of discovery, when the entire episode is momentarily grasped in the image of Ariadne's crown, we may best see the luminous compression of Spenser's thought.[27] The crown of a mortal placed high in the visible heavens is a ring round which the stars move in order excellent, and this movement is compared to the dance of the three Graces circled by the hundred auxiliary graces. The comparison unites the heavenly and imaginary dances, the physical and mental orders, the actual zodiac and the zodiac of the poet's wit.

But the subject of the simile is the imaginary rather than the actual cosmos, the dance rather than the constellation. Even in the comparison, the constellation appears as the result and symbol of a human experience; its meaning is referred not to its divine creator but to the man-made myth. As the crown gives way to the "rosie girlond" of the central figure, it embellishes the pastoral dance which, while remaining pastoral, resonates with the full amplitude of the cosmic harmony. The rosy garland of *The Shepheardes Calender* displays its glory throughout the universe visibly ordered now—after long pain—by the poet's "fayning." And in this movement it is not simply the described figures but the vision itself which seems stanza by stanza to shift and revolve, expand and contract, unfolding as if the poet does not know what he thinks till he

---

[27] For the various problems connected with this allusion see the *Variorum* notes to IV.i.23 (4:168–69) and VI.x.13 (6:251). If the battle of Centaurs and Lapiths was transferred from Pirithous's wedding to hint at a defect in Theseus and the consequent abandonment of Ariadne, this may point to the particular version of the myth Spenser had in mind: the one in which her pain was resolved in her second marriage to Bacchus, a love-death and apotheosis signified when the god enskied her crown. For the Neoplatonist motif, see Edgar Wind, *Pagan Mysteries in the Renaissance* (New Haven: Yale University Press, 1958), 130–31.

sees what he says. The landscape displays a mind negatively capable, an indeterminate and creative collaboration between the epic poet and his pastoral persona.

Thus our first view is of a place visibly emerging from, or involved with, certain typical Spenserian themes:

> It was an hill plaste in an open plaine,
>   That round about was bordered with a wood
>   Of matchlesse hight, that seem'd th'earth to disdaine,
>   In which all trees of honour stately stood,
>   And did all winter as in sommer bud,
>   Spreadding pavilions for the birds to bowre,
>   Which in their lower braunches sung aloud;
>   And in their tops the soring hauke did towre,
> Sitting like King of fowles in majesty and powre.
>
> And at the foote thereof, a gentle flud
>   His silver waves did softly tumble downe,
>   Unmard with ragged mosse or filthy mud,
>   Ne mote wylde beastes, ne mote the ruder clowne
>   Thereto approch, ne filth mote therein drowne:
>   But Nymphes and Faeries by the bancks did sit,
>   In the woods shade, which did the waters crowne,
>   Keeping all noysome things away from it,
> And to the waters fall tuning their accents fit.
>
> *(x.6–7)*

This is the second nature spun by human desire and art; the actual and ugly are excluded by fiat as the choice bits once sampled in the Muses' Elizium are collected in a new setting, deep within the mind; the aristocratic disdain is that of the second nature for the first. The essence of this place is that it is totally meaningful, human intention projected as image: "And on the top thereof a spacious plaine / Did spred it selfe, to serve to all delight" (x.8). The place was called Acidale *because* it seemed "to overlooke the lowly vale" of early pastoral, and also because the prospect is far from care and serves to all delight.

But Acidale is also the Graces' fountain and turns the mind toward a mythic possibility:

> They say that *Venus*, when she did dispose
>   Her selfe to pleasaunce, used to resort
>   Unto this place, and therein to repose
>   And rest her selfe, as in a gladsome port,
>   Or with the Graces there to play and sport . . .
>
> *(x.9)*

The parallel suggests a further meaning for Spenser's private place: the Queen of Beauty, whose "goodly formes and faire aspects" (III.vi.12) make her the Mother of Love, comes here not to exercise her creative powers but simply to delight in them. It is a second holiday, wayward yet rhythmic, amid the embodied Ideas produced by the mind's "tedious travell." The imagination looks at what it has made, sees that it is good, and hopes to attract something more real than itself, the universal symbol of that God which is the source of its energy. The Graces are not yet here and now, since the convergence is put off by the phrase "they say." The landscape is first solidified into something concrete and sensuous so that the recreative delight is seen and heard and felt but does not yet release its new meaning. Calidore hears "the merry sound" of Colin's pipe and "many feete fast thumping th'hollow ground" (VI.x.10), and then he sees the "hundred naked maidens lilly white." This pastoral image is immediately expanded and etherealized—the Ariadne comparison looks like a sudden inspiration, since it is an apostrophe in the present tense—and just as quickly contracted to the "rosie girlond." The Graces now appear in person; the vision is further contracted in the second apostrophe to Colin, after which it vanishes. Even without Calidore's intrusion, the descriptive rhythm anticipates this outcome, and one feels that however long Spenser's hidden recreative voice has invoked the vision it is unfolded only now, in the brevity of the present fulfillment.

The episode as a whole circles through three familiar emphases: first, the vision of delight, where the earliest recreation becomes the latest recreation; second, the plaintive moment in which the vision is interrupted and Colin again breaks his pipe; third, the moral emphasis when Colin converts the vision into an emblem. Here he has replaced E. K.; this would have been unthinkable in the *Calender,* where the amplitude of life and meaning was precisely what that first world of conventions excluded. But now Colin catches up the recreative and plaintive moments into the moral. Love, poetry, and morality converge—"Divine resemblaunce, beauty soveraine rare, / Firme Chastity"—all become eros, the latest gift and the earliest source. For it was eros that led him years ago to fall in love and moved him to confront the fox and ape, and above all impelled him to play with words, to become a poet long before he could know *why* he was so inclined—eros was the true source of even that mindless joy. What began in the realm of the Muses ends in the realm of the Graces. One thinks especially of the *Aprill* eclogue, the meaning of whose forms remained inert in the gloss taken from dictionaries and handbooks. But one is also reminded of the country lass who denied her love, and one realizes that when the poet's amorous insight finally yields its refined Acidalian form, the handmaids of Venus have in effect become Muses.

Colin's account does more than explain the vanished dance: it imports into Spenser's Acidale the rich iconographic tradition of Venus and the Graces elaborated by the human mind in its long cultural dialectic.[28] He begins again with the widest perspective: the Graces are daughters of "sky-ruling Jove" and Eurynome, "The Oceans daughter" (x.22); effects of cosmic force and fertility, justice and generosity, but in Spenser's variation effects produced only on Acidale in a moment of repose and gratuitous delight. The catalogue of their qualities leads to a new image of the Graces:

> two of them still froward seem'd to bee,
> But one still towards shew'd her selfe afore;
> That good should from us goe, then come in greater store.
>
> *(x.24)*

The dance is a diaphanous shimmer of meaning and image, turning and interacting, each modifying the other. The Graces are unfolded from Venus in their ancient and familiar poses, advance concretely before us, display their meanings, then fade into qualities as they are infolded by Colin's beloved: "Another Grace she well deserves to be, / In whom so many Graces gathered are." For a moment the beloved is poised alone in visionary splendor; in the next moment she recedes to make room for Gloriana, though with the words "Sunne of the world" the two Ideas make brief contact. The lyric Muse reveals her affinity to the epic Muse, and the vision gives way to the narrative of Book VI.

In that momentary poise, however, and in the circling dance, the vision resonates with harmonious echoes. We may recall the revelation on the mountaintop in Book I, and the other in the Garden of Adonis; the hundred virgins in the temple of Venus; the image of Amoret surrounded by her garland of virtues. The vision is the solution and resolution of all the problems, all the motifs, suggested in earlier parts of the book: the aristocracy and foundling motifs; the nursery, withdrawal, and retirement motifs; the motifs of love, of holiday and diversion, of being caught off guard, of turning inward—all these, along with the previous

---

[28] On the Graces, see Ernst Gombrich, "Botticelli's Mythologies: A Study in the Neoplatonic Symbolism of His Circle," *Journal of the Warburg and Courtauld Institutes* 8 (1945): 32; André Chastel, *Marsile Ficin et l'art* (Geneva: E. Droz, 1954), 146–47; D. T. Starnes, "Spenser and the Graces," *Philological Quarterly* 21 (July 1942): 268–82; Wind, passim.

circles, are now revealed as symbols and dim prefigurations of Acidale. And at the center of the ring of Graces is no single creature but a richly complicated knot of all the figures the poet has ever meditated on— Rosalind, Elizabeth, Amoret, Belphoebe, Florimell, Britomart, Venus, Psyche—"Who can aread, what creature mote she bee"? Unlike Pastorella, she has no name, is beyond names; though she has been in part generated from the fictional domain of names and images in the dance of meanings, she has, so to speak, been sprung from this domain, having been "enchaced" by his thought distilled from so much "tedious travell." He has never taken his eye off that first form, the simple country lass, but whoever she is in herself no longer matters. The form has been refined until the beloved has become love, the hieroglyph of eros—not an Other, but a vision or symbol or concept of whatever it is that draws us toward the Other.[29]

In its context and in its form the vision enacts the Neoplatonic idea that the soul is a foundling, an aristocrat long ignorant of its true source. It confuses its principle with primitive beginnings, with something temporally prior and externally simpler, like savagery or rusticity. The true beginning and principle is neither in time nor in space but always vivid at the center, deep within the mind. Only by turning inward, by self-creation, by tirelessly seeking and wooing and invoking the Muses, or eros, or what lies behind them all—only thus do we regain our long-lost heritage. By some process akin to anamnesis we withdraw, we retire, we return to the nursery, we close the circle of beginnings and endings, we come finally to that first Idea, that pure grace which has always moved us. And our point of contact with the real is the moving geometric form, the dynamism of thought itself. What is felt as divine is not the vision itself so much as the sense of having been given—the sense of a richness and variety, a copious world of forms and meanings which the mind produces *as if* by its own reflex activity, but really by the grace of God. The divine, the real, are now sought for only in their transfigured forms, and they are found not in the transfiguration but in the activity, the process of transfiguring. So *The Faerie Queene* swings on its great

---

[29] A passage in Wind, 168, describing the Neoplatonic dynamics of symbolic thought is worth quoting because of its applicability to Spenser's method in this poem: "It follows that all mystical images, because they retain a certain articulation by which they are distinguished as 'hedges' or *umbraculae*, belong to an intermediate state, which involves further 'complication' above, and further 'explication' below. They are never final in the sense of a literal statement which would fix the mind to a given point; nor are they final in the sense of the mystical Absolute in which all images would vanish. Rather they keep the mind in continued suspense by presenting the paradox of an 'inherent transcendence'; they persistently hint at more than they say."

axis from the objective reality of Dante's universe, to which Book I is closest, toward the symbolic form of *Paradise Lost*.

It is important to take into account the presence of Rosalind as a simple country lass and poor handmaid of Gloriana if one is to do justice to the realistic basis of Spenser's vision. The triumph of imagination is partly measured by the extent to which it has converted frustration, brute fact, the world of first sight and first nature, into a symbolic intuition of the real; the presence of the country lass and the early pastoral testify to this triumph. But the triumph is also measured by acceptance of what the mind cannot transform, by the awareness of limit which Clarion must learn the hard way. The complete self-sufficiency of the second nature, the total inward mastery of experience—this is no triumph at all, only delusion, if it takes itself seriously. For then it would have nothing to do with the poet *now*, a man still faced by life, fortune, malice, Providence. Thus poetry, having triumphed, must dissolve its triumph again and again to show that it is still engaged in the ongoing process of life where experience is not yet ordered. On Mount Acidale, when the play of mind realizes its vision, the poet dissolves it and moves on. In vision the mind objectifies its desires and intuitions so that it can see and respond; Colin's explanation is the response of the mind to the figure it has made and which it accepts as given. But just as the explanation acknowledges the persistence of the country lass, so the poem returns to the blatant beast and to its own dissolution. Spenser's poetic style is generated from the awareness that the poetic universe must be circumscribed as artifice and play; yet within the circumscribed place the poet must adumbrate the raw, the meaningless, so that we see it in the poem but outside the poetry. The secret discipline of imagination is a double burden, discordant and harmonious: first, its delight in the power and freedom of art; second, the controlled surrender whereby it acknowledges the limits of artifice. For Spenser, who is among the true poets, the vision must be bounded and shaped by the sense that it is not reality; and it must yield to reality at last.

The *Mutabilitie Cantos*

Archaism and Evolution in Retrospect

THE VIEW OF experience expressed in and as Spenser's poetry is shaped by a radically historical consciousness. It is historical in two reciprocal aspects: the objective character of Spenser's vision is *evolutionary*; its subjective mode is *retrospective*. The present essay will explore these terms in the specific context of the *Mutabilitie Cantos*, but I shall preface my interpretation with some remarks of a more general nature to clarify my use of these terms. By *evolutionary* I mean that we may find in Spenser's poetry an overall developmental pattern in which three vectors coalesce: from lower to higher, from simpler to more complex, and, of course, from earlier to later. These vectors run parallel courses in the history of the individual psyche and in that of culture or civilization. The relation between these two courses is reciprocal. Haeckel's discredited biogenetic formula, "Ontogeny recapitulates phylogeny," covers one side of it: the individual organism (the microcosm, the human or psychic *discordia concors*) manifests in compressed form the development of culture from its earler childhood phases to its later more sophisticated phases. The normal and normative growth of human consciousness and conscience is from a relatively narrow, simplistic, or elementally "pure" perspective to a broader, more complex, and more comprehensive perspective. In early or in regressive stages, for example, distinguishable areas tend to blur or overlap, as when the mind fails to perceive or re-

243

spect the boundaries between itself and the world, man and God, self and other, love and hate, heaven and earth, the divine and the chaotic or natural sources of energy. The other side of the reciprocity between psyche and culture is the effect of the microcosm on any phase of the larger order: here Spenser agrees with Plato, Virgil, and others in depicting the institutions and products of "early" culture as dominated by, expressive of, those tendencies of the psyche which are usually described as childlike, autistic, superstitious, sensuous.

The subjective mode of Spenser's historical vision is retrospective: he looks back into the past from his own *here and now.* In his early or archaic world, action is caused for the most part by the large-scale play of forces which, though psychic as well as cosmic, operate outside any individual will or consciousness. Book III of *The Faerie Queene* is especially ordered to suggest how entirely independent actions and episodes, occurring in widely separated places and moments of the Spenserian world, are triggered so as to produce a meaningful coalescence whose import could not possibly be grasped by any of the figures involved, except perhaps for gods and prophets (and even their perspectives are limited in ways to be discussed below). The driving purpose of this organic system of forces is beyond its conscious members because both system and purpose are retrospectively fashioned by the poet, and only tentatively, temporarily, fulfilled in his own time. The possibility of prophecy is founded on deterministic presuppositions, and a leading characteristic of Spenser's "primitive" age is the manifest domination of behavior by extra-human forces whose influence tends toward the conservation or restoration of an archaic state of affairs. As psyche and culture develop, this collective and determined mode of behavior gradually yields to the more active and original assertions of individual souls. When the center of will, decision, and activity is located in the individual consciousness, archaic determinism gives way to retrospective determinism as the dominant organizing mode.

When cosmic and primitive influences dominate, the forms of existence tend to be at once unstable and universal (that is, recurrent and generic or archetypal). When psychic and rational influences dominate, the forms tend to be personal, unique, and potentially more stable; at the same time, the forms of discord, evil, danger, and temptation are subtler and therefore less easily located and contained. Fundamental to this model is Spenser's conviction that no moment of union or reconciliation, of relief or triumph, is to be construed as absolute—absolute either in the sense of being final or in the sense of being totally one-sided. Every triumph or resolution at a lower level of existence or an earlier phase of experience releases new and different problems at a higher level or a later phase. This will be oddly demonstrated in the *Mutabilitie Cantos*, where the vision of cosmic harmony which triumphantly concludes canto vii in the medieval mode triggers a new brief lyric moment of anxiety in the closing stanzas.

The full vision of the pattern I have been describing is seldom attained by characters within the Spenserian world, while its complex and articulated unity is a condition attained by soul, state, or culture only in relatively advanced phases of its career. And only in such phases does the imagination double back to activate the tacit or latent elements—the primitive and palingenetic factors—of experience to set the present moment within its developmental context. As I suggested before, Spenser presents the latest form of experience both *in* his work and *as* his work. The historical sense which is the defining mark of that work asserts itself in his effort to locate the various elements of his poetic *discordia concors* at their proper temporal distances from the present. His poetry thus represents in its complex form all the phases which preceded it and which it, in effect, supersedes. This representation is achieved by means of the technique of *conspicuous allusion:* the depiction of stock literary motifs, characters, and genres in a manner which emphasizes their conventionality, displaying at once their debt to and their existence in a conventional climate—classical, medieval, romance, and so on—which is archaic when seen from Spenser's retrospective viewpoint.

The *Mutabilitie Cantos* provide the most concise and complete embodiment of Spenser's historical consciousness. Explicitly lyric or self-referential in mode, the poem not only directs our attention toward the "modern" narrator, but it also reveals the effect of his retrospective narrative on his own feelings. Spenser uses conspicuous allusion to organize the poem along evolutionary lines: its three sections—canto vi, canto vii, and the final two stanzas[1]—develop what is in effect an ontogenetic recapitulation of the phases of experience from pagan through medieval modes of imagination to the lyric (and Renaissance) present. Canto vii, the medieval phase, includes, infolds, and transcends the two simple pagan modes (epic and pastoral) of the comic sixth canto. The later moment is a more complex, more finely articulated revision of the earlier moment, which it redirects and transforms; but it is itself distanced and superseded in the poem's concluding stanzas.

If we look carefully at the opening six stanzas we shall see that all the

---

[1]Cf. the different triadic scheme in Donald Cheney, *Spenser's Image of Nature: Wild Man and Shepherd in "The Faerie Queene"* (New Haven: Yale University Press, 1966), 246; he divides canto vi into epic and pastoral sections, resolved in the "didactic synthesis" of canto vii.

themes, attitudes, and problems to be displayed throughout the work are
present here in a special and temporary form, that is, dominated by a
limited viewpoint which will change as Spenser moves through the
poem:

> What man that sees the ever-whirling wheele
>> Of Change, the which all mortall things doth sway,
>> But that therby doth find, and plainly feele,
>> How *MUTABILITY* in them doth play
>> Her cruell sports, to many mens decay?
>> Which that to all may better yet appeare,
>> I will rehearse that whylome I heard say,
>> How she at first her selfe began to reare,
> Gainst all the Gods, and th'empire sought from them to beare.
>
> But first, here falleth, fittest to unfold
>> Her antique race and linage ancient,
>> As I have found it registred of old,
>> In *Faery* Land mongst records permanent:
>> She was, to weet, a daughter by descent
>> Of those old *Titans,* that did whylome strive
>> With *Saturnes* sonne for heavens regiment.
>> Whom, though high *Jove* of kingdome did deprive,
> Yet many of their stemme long after did survive.
>
> And many of them, afterwards obtain'd
>> Great power of *Jove,* and high authority;
>> As *Hecaté,* in whose almighty hand,
>> He plac't all rule and principality,
>> To be by her disposed diversly,
>> To Gods, and men, as she them list divide:
>> And drad *Bellona,* that doth sound on hie
>> Warres and allarums unto Nations wide,
> That makes both heaven and earth to tremble at her pride.
>
> So likewise did this *Titanesse* aspire,
>> Rule and dominion to her selfe to gaine;
>> That as a Goddesse, men might her admire,
>> And heavenly honours yield, as to them twaine.
>> At first, on earth she sought it to obtaine;
>> Where she such proofe and sad examples shewed
>> Of her great power, to many ones great paine,
>> That not men onely (whom she soone subdewed)
> But eke all other creatures, her bad dooings rewed.
>
> For, she the face of earthly things so changed,
>> That all which Nature had establisht first

> In good estate, and in meet order ranged,
> She did pervert, and all their statutes burst:
> And all the worlds faire frame (which none yet durst
> Of Gods or men to alter or misguide)
> She alter'd quite, and made them all accurst
> That God had blest; and did at first provide
> In that still happy state for ever to abide.
>
> Ne shee the lawes of Nature onely brake,
> But eke of Justice, and of Policie;
> And wrong of right, and bad of good did make,
> And death for life exchanged foolishlie:
> Since which, all living wights have learn'd to die,
> And all this world is woxen daily worse.
> O pittious worke of *MUTABILITIE!*
> By which, we all are subject to that curse,
> And death in stead of life have sucked from our Nurse.

By the end of the poem Spenser will stand before us as a *man* in meditation, responding personally to what he has made and seen. But here he
introduces himself in a more detached stance as a *poet* who will use an
old story to exemplify and embellish the power of mutability. At first he
separates himself from the audience ("What man . . .") whose concern
he will delineate in fiction. His attention moves back to the pagan genealogy and its sources, mentioning not only Mutabilitie's ancient lineage
but also the antique account of the lineage. "Faery Land" seems to have
two references: to his own literary world or imagination, the myths and
fictions devised by the poet of *The Faerie Queene,* and to the "antique
rolles" in the "everlasting scryne" (I.Pr.2) of the Muses, the fictions,
myths, and legends recorded throughout history. The association of the
everlasting *scryne* (from *scrinium,* a chest or casket for manuscripts) with
antique rolls and of "records permanent" with "registred of old" suggests something fixed early in culture, and therefore permanent if not
necessarily adequate. This kind of permanence sets itself over against
that of "the ever-whirling wheele," and it therefore embodies the wish to
resist inevitable change, to memorialize for all time a particular vision
or solution that arose in response to a particular situation. As the ever-
whirling wheel is an early and defective view of the dynamic recurrence
that yields the constancy of Nature, so this archaic permanence is a defective prevision or imitation of that on which Nature and the poet meditate
at poem's end. In the second and third sections, these simple opposites,
whirl and permanence, will converge and interpenetrate, will move forward and inward from the reconciling cosmic symbolism of the medieval

mind to the lyric present in which the poet stands, altered yet still unreconciled—even more deeply divided, in fact, by what he has envisaged.

Something like this larger pattern of movement is condensed in the introduction, though it takes a different direction. Stanzas 2–4 comprise a relatively matter-of-fact rehearsal in the antique pagan mode of canto vi. Stanza 5 anticipates canto vii by introducing Nature and allowing Judeo-Christian echoes to filter in. As the poet lists Mutabilitie's evil effects in stanzas 5 and 6, the rhythm and feeling of his rhetoric build toward the exclamation "O pittious worke of *MUTABILITIE!*" and toward the final couplet which at once generalizes the curse and draws it close by the use of the first person plural. Like the blatant beast at the end of Book VI, Mutabilitie seems to rush from the remote past into the poet's present as her influence spreads throughout the universe and into the human domain where Justice and Policy have been abused. The introduction thus ends at a nadir. Having moved from the position of detached narrator, the poet now joins his mortal audience, plainly feels the effect of what he has found or invented, and actualizes the grimmest possibilities of the opening lines.

These lines imply a limitation of vision and response most explicitly glossed by the proem to Book V, which the sentiments expressed in stanza 6 echo in more condensed form. The man who sees the ever-whirling wheel may not see beyond it, and as a result he *plainly* feels mutability as entirely evil. In addition to *clearly* or *vividly*, the word *plainly* carries the sense of *directly, flatly, simply*. Spenser here depicts an objective attitude, a general frame of mind, and then adopts it as his own. It is nevertheless adopted with a degree of detachment as the *wrong* attitude, one that affects his view of life, that will affect his poem, and that is modified in the course of narration. In Book V and in the *Mutabilitie Cantos*, he locates this attitude in the poetic first person in order to dramatize it, give it play, and put it to the test. The attitude is the basic problem—the enemy, as it were—with which both poems deal. It is an attitude that in one form Spenser stated directly at the beginning of *A View of the Present State of Ireland*. Irenius reports the received opinion that it is Ireland's "fatall destinie" that no purposes "mente for her good" can succeed in reforming that miserable nation, perhaps because of "the *very Genius* of the soile, or influence of the starres, or that Allmighty god hath not yeat Appointed the tyme of her reformacion or that he reserveth her in this unquiet state still, for some secrete skourge, which shall by her Come into Englande." Eudoxus pooh-poohs this opinion as the "vaine Conceipt of simple men" and attributes the trouble rather to "the unsoundnes of . . . Counsells and Plottes." He then offers the commonplace criticism, perhaps most familiar to us in Edmund's famous soliloquy on Gloucester's self-deception, that "it is the manner of men that when they are fallen into anye Absurditye or theire accions succede not as they woulde they are ready allwaies to impute the blame theareof unto the heavens, soe to excuse their owne follies and imperfeccions. . . . [it] is the manner . . . of desperate men farre driven to wishe the utter ruine of that which they Cannot redresse. . . ."[2]—the manner not only of the egalitarian giant of *The Faerie Queene* (V.ii), for example, but also of the justice of Talus and Artegal and, to some extent, of Spenser's own vision of actuality in that book.

When Spenser dramatizes this "vaine Conceipt" at the beginning of the *Mutabilitie Cantos,* he immediately connects it with the "records permanent" of antiquity. It is the response "of simple men," the pessimistic fatalism of the vulgar mind "farre driven." At the same time it is characterized as regressive by being "historically" located in an archaic framework of pagan conceptions and images. The essence of this framework lies in the polarity between Mutabilitie and Nature as Spenser initially presents it—*initially,* that is, because the idea of nature in vi.5–6 will be radically altered in the figure of Natura, who dominates canto vii.[3] Nature in vi.5–6 has already succumbed to mutability, who *brake* her laws, *changed, did pervert,* and *alter'd quite* her original estate and the world's fair frame. Stanza 5 tends to push Nature back into Eden and to identify the reign of her enemy with the whole history of fallen man,[4] though the general pagan context diffuses the Edenic reference so that it suggests any conception of the first Golden Age. This idea of nature has already been outmoded because it projects unrealistic expectations; it is based on a longing for too perfect and fixed a state of nature. Under the pressure of actual life, so unguardedly sanguine a hope dialectically produces its opposite, that is, the despairing acceptance of negative mutability as life's ruling principle, which in turn generates the wish to escape back into the paradisaic state of nature. Wish fulfillment and nightmare are simple contraries, twinned and mutually intensifying im-

[2] *Var.* 9:43–44. The connection has been made by John Danby, *Shakespeare's Doctrine of Nature* (London: Faber & Faber, 1949), 35–38, and related to Spenser's description of Nature at vii.5–6.

[3] Noted by Sherman Hawkins, "Mutabilitie and the Cycle of the Months," in *Form and Convention in the Poetry of Edmund Spenser,* ed. William Nelson (New York: Columbia University Press, 1961), 86–87.

[4] In *Paradise Lost* Milton ascribes a similar attitude to the God of Book III. Cf. my essay "Archaism, Vision, and Revision: Studies in Virgil, Plato, and Milton," *Centennial Review* 11, no. 1 (Winter 1967): 46 ff.

pulses, neither of which is more realistic than the other. We may thus translate the fabled triumph of mutability over sublunary nature into its psychological equivalent: it is the triumph of a view of earthly life that "sees the ever-whirling wheele" of entropic change as the nature of things, having succeeded an inadequate and fragile view of nature as a pleasure garden where all things endure forever just as they were when "establisht first / In good estate, and in meet order ranged." In terms of the mythology of Book V, this radical counterswing from the golden to the iron age, from Saturn to Jove, is signified by the departure from earth of Astraea, whose virginity symbolizes classical disdain and self-withholding exclusiveness. Her desire to resist change, to retain in its purity her ruthlessly idealistic and aprioristic justice, is related to the feeling that the present decay of justice, politics, and ethics may have been determined from creation by the mechanics of physical change:

> Me seemes the world is runne quite out of square,
> From the first point of his appointed sourse,
> And being once amisse growes daily wourse and wourse.
>
> *(V.Pr.1)*

This is archaic determinism, whose premise of irreversible decline dissipates the possibility of second thoughts and second chances, of rebirth, redemption, and revision.[5] It encourages the violent repressiveness of iron-age justice in Jove, Hercules, Artegal, Talus, and the stoic censors.

The opposed visions of the ever-whirling wheel and the ever-abiding happy state are permanent possibilities for the mind, but they represent an archaic mode of seeing and feeling. Therefore they "may better yet appeare" in the *whylome* form recorded early in man's psychocultural history. In signaling his return to this mode, the poet dramatically enacts the urge to escape time, change, and history. During the remainder of the sixth canto this assumption of the archaic perspective is comically sustained by four parodistic devices that I shall now discuss:

First, to attribute all evil to mutability, "to impute . . . unto the heavens" the blame for human follies and sins and failures, is the first stage of a time-honored mode of evasion.[6] The next stage is to devise a way of producing an Ultimate Solution in a single encounter, and this is accomplished by condensing all evils into an allegorical or mythological scapegoat who may then be defeated by a more powerful divine embodiment

[5] Cf. "Archaism, Vision, and Revision," 26–28, 33–38.

[6] Cf. Cheney, 240–41; Hawkins, 84; Kathleen Williams, *Spenser's World of Glass: A Reading of "The Faerie Queene"* (Berkeley: University of California Press, 1966), 225–26.

of order. Helpless man may thus surrender both his responsibility and his power, may relieve himself of moral efficacy and effort, consigning the good fight to the cosmic forces of Darkness and Light. This is a return not only to a primitive, but also to a childlike, sensibility—thus the appropriateness of Spenser's recourse to an old fairy tale. From the total evil plaintively delineated in the first six stanzas he withdraws into a purely recreative world of ancient fable and into a comic portrait of the way antique genres—the high and low styles of heroic bombast and pastoral homeliness—render and cope with the problem of mutability.[7]

Second, the opposition between simple change and simple permanence, black mutability and golden nature, plaintive and recreative attitudes, high and low styles, points toward an attempt stylistically to imitate an archaic pattern mentioned in the beginning of this essay—the separation of elements into pure and mutally exclusive contraries. Such divisiveness is already the essence of the fable action in this canto, from the first mention of Mutabilitie's antique lineage through the facing-off with Cynthia and Jove to the new arrangement of these contraries in the pastoral digression. The action of the canto is so disposed as to emphasize the catabolic process of fragmentation, the breaking down of primeval and unstable compounds: chaos-earth-heaven; Uranus-Titan-Saturn and Saturn-Jove; Jove-Hecate-Bellona (the latter two being opposed principles of order and disorder); male and female, old and young, separating off from the primal family matrix; the members of the ruling Olympian pantheon set at odds among themselves by Mutabilitie's assault (vi.23); the hints of a composite goddess splitting into Hecate, Cynthia, and Diana; Mutabilitie by implication dividing into Faunus and Diana, the lustful voyeur and the Astraean destroyer of Ireland's "first . . . good estate"; the uneasy pastoral alliance between Ovidian mythic and Irish actual landscapes.

This pattern penetrates the division of the canto into high and low styles. The inherent contrariety between epic and pastoral perspectives is intensified by Spenser's comic exaggerations of the devices that characterize each mode: in the former, bombastic rhetoric, heroic vaunting and "flyting," Homeric formulas, cosmic muscularity, panoramic vistas, and in general the fusty, expansive, and broad-planed way of at once magnifying and simplifying problems;[8] in the latter, the problems reduced, lightened, dissipated in homely analogies, rustic minutiae, buf-

---

[7] Cheney, 241–42, remarks on the tone of "detached, ironic wit" informing the first third of the canto (i.e., the heroic episode).

[8] Examples in stanzas 3, 7, 10–12, 21; 20–21, 26–33; 3, 14, 18, 22, 30; 7, 10, 22; 8, 10, 14, 19, 23.

foonery, sylvan diversions, minor woodland metamorphoses that conspicuously evoke Colin Clout's pastoral in Ireland.[9]

The pastoral episode is not comic relief for the simple reason that it is no less serious than the heroic episode, in which the inflated presentation is continually punctured. The conflict between Mutabilitie and Cynthia, for example, is little more than a scuffle between over-sized schoolgirls (vi.13), and Jove ends five thundering stanzas in a wheedle: "ceasse thy idle claime thou foolish gerle" (vi.34). Both episodes are equally comic and recreative, equally acts of withdrawal into ancient fairyland from the grimmer vision of the opening stanzas. The more intricate and pressing human issues, the problems of justice and polity, are introduced at the beginning and then conspicuously ignored. Early epic and pastoral are portrayed from the standpoint of the present as pure contraries that fall on either side of real life; the poet climbs upward and backward to Jove's heaven until Jove is about to be passed by (vi.35–36), at which point he runs downward to make a new beginning in Cynthia's unfallen wood.

Third, in canto vi, Mutabilitie, Cynthia, Mercury, Arlo Hill, and to some extent the other gods, including Jove, all suffer the same ignominous fate at the hands of their author; they are *desymbolized*, for they are more cosmic, portentous, and epic at the beginning of the canto than at the end. Spenser first flashes the full range of symbolic references while converting the referents to mythic or allegorical personifications, then conspicuously ignores or abandons these references for the literal play of his story. Withdrawal into the recreative now of storytelling is heightened since most of the symbolic references that are present-as-excluded are plaintive. Mutabilitie begins as the ever-whirling wheel of entropic change, is personified before being blamed for the sum total of human vicissitudes, and, immediately after the introductory stanzas drops off these first two stages to become merely a large, aggressive, and upwardly mobile woman with some of the qualities of Britomart and Radegund. Spenser's obvious relish in heroic parody, the enjoyment with which he gratuitously elaborates details of dialogue and description, produce something like a cartoon world whose heroine is a version of Superwoman; but it is a world seen through the eyes of *Mad* magazine.

This recreative desymbolizing is historical in its implications, because Spenser directs us to the more recent identities of the gods as planetary forces before he moves back to animate their older mythological images as Ovidian dramatis personae. Cynthia and Mercury are introduced in astronomical guise (vi.8, 14) but are immediately converted to emblem-

[9] Examples in stanzas 47–48; 39, 48, 50; 46, 49; 41–42; 40–41, 51, 53.

atic or mythological figures. Mutabilitie climbs to the "Circle of the Moone" and Cynthia's "bright shining palace,"

> All fairely deckt with heavens goodly story;
> Whose silver gates (by which there sate an hory
> Old aged Sire, with hower-glasse in hand,
> Hight *Tyme*) she entred, were he liefe or sory:
> Ne staide till she the highest stage had scand,
> Where *Cynthia* did sit, that never still did stand.

> Her sitting on an Ivory throne shee found,
> Drawne of two steeds, th'one black, the other white,
> Environd with tenne thousand starres around,
> That duly her attended day and night;
> And by her side there ran her Page, that hight
> *Vesper*, whom we the Evening-starre intend:
> That with his Torche, still twinkling like twylight,
> Her lightened all the way where she should wend,
> And joy to weary wandring travailers did lend . . .
>
> *(vi.8–9)*

The puns lurking in *story* and *stage* pivot the scene from astronomical space and function to theatrical or emblematic fiction, and this process is completed in the symbolic reversal whereby Vesper's torch becomes the subject, and his twilight only the comparison, of the simile. By the time Mutabilitie has laid hold of Cynthia—"raught forth her hand / To pluck her downe perforce from off her chaire" and threatened to club her with "her golden wand" (vi.13)—the hieratic emblems have themselves given way to physical action that on the one hand is heightened by epic scale and rhetoric and on the other hand is comic, even pastoral, in its inconsequence. A multilevel stage set replaces the spheres, embellishing an action invented and controlled by the myth-making mind. This change of imagery reduces to pure visual and spatial terms a subject whose essential meaning is temporal.

Desymbolizing is a contrastive technique that, while dividing the surface narrative from its significant background, keeps both before us. We are encouraged to feel that the narrative obscures the themes that generate and organize the plot of the fable. We learn at the beginning of the canto that the superlunary world is about to be threatened by mutability. The heroine's ascent through the spheres therefore acts out some contemporary commonplaces in a pessimistic or apocalyptic vein. Perhaps it also alludes to current changes in astronomical and cosmological theory. Toward the end of the epic section we are given glimpses of the hidden order that will emerge in canto vii. Jove begins to use legal jargon (vi.33). Mutabilitie, whose ultimate ambition was presented earlier as a martial attempt to displace "highest Jove" from his palace in the "highest sky," aims beyond Jove (vi.34–36) and wants to plead her case before "the highest him," the "God of Nature." Jove is grudgingly forced to accede and bids "Dan Phoebus Scribe her Appellation ·seale." By this time Mutabilitie has become more beautiful, or at least her physical stature and beauty are noted by Spenser, the gods, and Jove (vi.28, 31–34) for the first time only after she has ascended to Jove's palace. This alteration will be clarified in the next canto, when the beauty of change is emphasized, but here it seems a purely gratuitous and ad hoc touch.

Finally, the three parodistic devices above point toward a purposeful disjunction between the underlying order apparent to the medieval Christian imagination of canto vii and the misguided, obscure anticipations of the pagan mythopoesis that dominates canto vi. This disjunction, the fourth and final aspect of canto vi to be discussed, reinforces the conspicuously digressive quality of the narrative. It sets off the instability of the characters and, occasionally, of the narrative. It heightens the comic effect of inflatedness and irrelevance that attends the posturing of the gods. For, looking back from stanzas 33–36, we see the episode in an entirely new light. Mutabilitie's real problem is procedural and falls within the legal domain of Right, not the martial domain of Might: she wants a hearing and apparently has to go through channels and attract the attention of the proper authorities to get one. This lends her previous wranglings the air of legalistic maneuvers. Her transactions with Cynthia, Mercury, and Jove retrospectively assume this character, whereas Jove's feeble effort at seduction (vi.34) seems motivated not solely by lust, but also, as she points out, by his desire to keep her from putting her case before the court. As the plot action moves closer to the higher and later system of forces disclosed in the next canto, it reveals the influence of that system with increasing clarity.

From this standpoint the heroic pagan gestures are at once more meaningless in themselves and more significant as expressions of limited responses. There is little real action or conflict in the episode, and even this is continually interrupted or deflected: the tussle with Cynthia, the interchange with Mercury, the military council of the gods, the assault on heaven, and the interview with Jove are all broken off (vi.17, 19, 24 ff., 35–36) for apparently arbitrary reasons before they produce any serious consequences. Plot and narrative therefore seem ruled by contingency and whim, by unforeseen occurrences and unexpected reactions. Against this pattern such resounding passages as the following are faintly

ridiculous, especially the final example, in which the advent of mutability reduces the ancient psychopomp to his Lord's legman:

> Eftsoones she cast by force and tortious might,
> Her [Cynthia] to displace . . .
>
> *(vi.10)*

> Fearing least *Chaos* broken had his chaine,
> And brought againe on them eternall night . . .
>
> *(vi.14)*

> Doubting least *Typhon* were againe uprear'd,
> Or other his old foes, that once him sorely fear'd.
>
> *(vi.15)*

> And there-with-all, he on her shoulder laid
>   His snaky-wreathed Mace, whose awfull power
>   Doth make both Gods and hellish fiends affraid:
>   Where-at the *Titanesse* did sternely lower,
>   And stoutly answer'd, that in evill hower
>   He from his *Jove* such message to her brought,
>   To bid her leave faire *Cynthias* silver bower;
>   Sith shee his *Jove* and him esteemed nought,
> No more then *Cynthia's* self; but all their kingdoms sought.

> The Heavens Herald staid not to reply,
>   But past away, his doings to relate
>   Unto his Lord . . .
>
> *(vi.18–19)*

The antique thunder, the fear of the recurrence of old catastrophes, the
portentous gesture with the caduceus—these items, all futile or beside
the point, contribute to Spenser's image of the archaic mind. Together
with the emergent influence of the medieval *concordia discors*—the process of gradual, ordered change silently moving and modifying these
"antickes"—they suggest that mind's inflated self-image, its tendency toward violent and headlong yet easily deflected impulses, its backward-
looking reliance upon ancient precedents, and its consequent ignorance
of or resistance to Nature's message that all things "by their change their
being doe dilate." [10]

---

[10] So Orgoglio's "auncient" porter and foster father Ignaro, "An old old man, with
beard as white as snow," who held "the keyes of every inner dore," but could not use
them, since "as he forward moov'd his footing old, / So backward still was turnd his
wrincled face" (I.viii.30–31).

Thomas M. Greene has described the "perpetual *becoming*" of Spenser's characters while their "status and meaning and concreteness . . . shift and fade and recombine,"[11] and this is exemplified in a pointedly contrapuntal manner by the *Two Cantos of Mutabilitie*. What unfolds in canto vii as cyclical and developmental change appears at the surface of canto vi as random motion and instability. The gods not only shift from planets to characters, but they suffer sudden changes of quality and whim, as when the stern titaness becomes beautiful and Jove is moved from anger to desire. Both Mutabilitie and Mercury experience, then *boldly* overcome, unexpected impulses of fear (vi.17–18, 25–26). When Mutabilitie and Cynthia face off, the latter is momentarily infected with her enemy's nature ("sterne countenaunce and disdainfull cheare," vi.12). Cynthia's demotion to her earthly domain, in the pastoral digression, seems to intensify this influence. She destroys her *locus amoenus* just as the titaness destroyed golden nature. As if in reaction to her closer involvement with mutable earth and lustful males, she waxes Astraean in her self-withholding disdain (vi.42) and her anger at folly and weakness (vi.51, 54–55).[12]

The pastoral digression is the most interesting example of instability, because it is the speaker himself who is affected: Spenser introduces Arlo Hill as a place of revelation "Where all, both heavenly Powers, and earthly wights, / Before great Natures presence should appeare," but presents himself as distracted immediately after by the thought of his own earlier pastoral portrait of that region of Munster ("my old father *Mole*, whom Shepheards quill / Renowmed hath with hymnes fit for a rurall skill," vi.36). He spends the next stanza vacillating:

> And, were it not ill fitting for this file,
>> To sing of hilles and woods, mongst warres and Knights,
>> I would abate the sternenesse of my stile,
>> Mongst these sterne stounds to mingle soft delights;
>> And tell how *Arlo* through *Dianaes* spights
>> (Beeing of old the best and fairest Hill
>> That was in all this holy-Islands hights)
>> Was made the most unpleasant, and most ill.
> Meane while, O *Clio*, lend *Calliope* thy quill.
>
> *(vi.37)*

---

[11] *The Descent from Heaven* (New Haven: Yale University Press, 1963), 330–31.

[12] Cf. Cheney, 245–47. Faunus has often been recognized as an allegorization of bestial man, but the gist of such an identification, if it is allowed, is that this is a pointedly biased and contemptuous estimate of man from the god's, and goddess's, angle of vision.

That the conditional is negative in force, that Calliope is more appropriate for great Nature's trial than for Faunus's minor tribulations—these suggest that Spenser has controlled the impulse to digress. But this effect of control only accentuates the about-face of the next lines, in which he appears to yield to his caprice in spite of himself.

As an alternative to the prospective trial, the pastoral episode may strike us even more sharply as reversion and diversion—reversion to an obviously fanciful mixture of outmoded Spenserian, Irish, and classical myths of the permanence-mutability conflict, and diversion from the glimpse of cosmic order to a playful explanation of the entropic change that still prevails on earth. The problems raised in the opening stanzas of canto vi re-enter in much diminished and localized form. Well-known metamorphic catastrophes are alluded to but averted.[13] The canto concludes with a black joke upon Ireland—Diana's "heavy haplesse curse" that specifies that wolves should

> all those Woods deface,
> And Thieves should rob and spoile that Coast around.
> Since which, those Woods, and all that goodly Chase,
> Doth to this day with Wolves and Thieves abound:
> Which too-too true that lands in-dwellers since have found.
>
> *(vi.55)*

Having looked through the archaic or youthful mind's anthropomorphic window on the world, Spenser ends on a Eudoxian note that makes light of that whole realm of explanation: "men fallen into any Absurditye . . . are ready allwaies to impute blame theareof unto the heavens, soe to excuse their owne follies and imperfeccions." It is the explanation, not the problem, that is parodied, for the canto, like its opening six stanzas, ends with a sudden return to the present and to the nearness, the actuality, of the dark "state of present time" in Ireland. It ends, furthermore, upon a more intensely pessimistic note: "desperate men farre driven . . . wishe the utter ruine of that which they Cannot redresse." The destructive wish flashing forth in the final stanza makes the Ovidian *pourquoi* story and "the image of the antique world" seem frivolous by contrast—a flight into the recreative mode of imagination, with its focus upon the pleasures of fancy and the ornaments of verse.[14] It is the mode most ap-

---

[13] Noted by Cheney, 246; see also Richard N. Ringler, "The Faunus Episode," *Modern Philology* 62, no. 1 (August 1965): 12–19, for a detailed study of these averted catastrophes.

[14] Unless one reads this topically and introduces Elizabeth in Diana's clothing. Even so, this could hardly cancel the atmosphere of play which bathes the earlier stanzas. The

propriate to the poet in his youthful phase, but when revived in its pure form in a later stage it is a function of the escape impulse.

This conclusion frames the next canto within the motivational context that will lead ultimately to the concluding two stanzas. For if things are still bad on earth, maybe they will work out more happily in heaven. If a grasshopper flight over Ireland touches down on bumpy terrain, maybe a higher flight, a more panoramic view, an increase in distance, an Astraean remoteness, will resolve the discords and ugliness into a satisfying pattern. I think it is important to keep this context in mind when reading canto vii. Otherwise the more obviously positive and triumphant aspects of the vision of order may appear to solve all problems in a real and unqualified manner, which certainly is not the case so far as Spenser is concerned. The opening stanzas of canto vii register with some delicacy the degree and kind of resolution we may expect, and they also stand dramatically as a reaction to the pastoral interlude.

> Ah! whither doost thou now thou greater Muse
>   Me from these woods and pleasing forrests bring?
>   And my fraile spirit (that dooth oft refuse
>   This too high flight, unfit for her weake wing)
>   Lift up aloft, to tell of heavens King
>   (Thy soveraine Sire) his fortunate successe,
>   And victory, in bigger noates to sing,
>   Which he obtain'd against that *Titanesse*,
> That him of heavens Empire sought to dispossesse.
>
> Yet sith I needs must follow thy behest,
>   Doe thou my weaker wit with skill inspire,
>   Fit for this turne; and in my feeble brest
>   Kindle fresh sparks of that immortall fire,
>   Which learned minds inflameth with desire
>   Of heavenly things: for, who but thou alone,
>   That art yborne of heaven and heavenly Sire,
>   Can tell things doen in heaven so long ygone;
> So farre past memory of man that may be knowne.

Except to classify the digression under a new and more general category (the mortal poet's insufficiency), he speaks as if it had not occurred and the woods had not been defaced. Looking forward, he describes Jove's

---

topical reference would enter only toward the end, abruptly, and its entry would intensify the contrast discussed here.

prospective victory as much more complete than it in fact will be. The language of the second stanza promotes a momentary blurring of pagan and Christian Muses and divinities, but insofar as we feel the presence of the pagan Muse we are allowed to suspect that she is capable of nepotism. The final couplet fills out the chronological relations in the poem. The happening on Arlo Hill occurred too long ago to be remembered by man; the contemporary poet must woo a Muse whose usefulness arises not only from her transcendence but also from her antiquity. "So farre past memory of man" refers to both and leaves temporarily unresolved the location of the event; as a vision of pagan-Christian concord, it is culturally "later" than the vision of canto vi, yet Nature's trial and judgment are pushed far back into the past and/or high up in heaven. We may feel that it is the image of a wished-for stabilization of order that occurred at the beginning of time, and this may lead us to see in canto vi an inadequate pagan version, in canto vii a more adequate medieval version, of the same mythical event.

The medieval account reflects more accurately than its predecessor the essential feature of that mythical event, namely, its promise of a cyclical natural order whose processes recur throughout the course of time. This superiority is made evident in a number of ways, though space does not permit more than a brief itemization.

First, canto vii reconciles the antique contraries of epic and pastoral, contracting the expansive and relatively vacant regions of canto vi into the narrow, densely packed confines of its middle ground (vii.3–4).[15] In canto vi, the poet's eye ranged through the ancient heaven and earth, going where the action was. In canto vii, the action and characters come to Arlo Hill.

Second, the desymbolized figures are, so to speak, *re*symbolized. The gods resume their planetary functions, and their influence is felt not only on earth but also in the zodiac. The literal reaches of the two-level pagan cosmos are infolded in Arlo Hill, which, desymbolized by the poet and Diana in canto vi, now regains its symbolic value as an apocalyptic height. Mutabilitie cannot be contained within her own personification; she stands for processes that are beyond her not only because they are diffused throughout the natural universe, but also because they have values diametrically opposed to those the titaness affirms. Although she is conveniently defeated and "whist" in the single action of the trial, this is the classic Spenserian feint: the defeat of an externalized and localized enemy diverts attention from the continuing and deepening effectiveness

---

[15] Cheney, 246; see n. 1 above.

of the enemy within; Mutabilitie is limited mainly by the rigid qualities and archaic personification to which "she" lays claim, and the disappearance of the titaness corresponds to the infiltration of all nature by mutability.

In this connection, it is significant that Mutabilitie talks so much. She is a real windbag, and Spenser's judgment upon Faunus is surely meant to rub off on her:

> He could him not containe in silent rest;
> But breaking forth in laughter, loud profest
> His foolish thought. A foolish *Faune* indeed,
> That couldst not hold thy selfe so hidden blest,
> But wouldest needs thine owne conceit areed.
> Babblers unworthy been of so divine a meed.
>
> *(vi.46)*

Had Faunus followed the example of the goddess Natura—stayed hidden and kept as still as possible—he would have seen what he wanted to see. The more Mutabilitie speaks, the more she imposes and expresses herself as a personality, the clearer her limitations become; if she only gets what she, as a titaness, claims, it will be much less than what mutability, as a process, covers. Her prosopopoeia is thus itself a primitive form of self-seeking and self-deceiving arrogance, as Nature points out: "thy decay thou seekst by thy desire" (vii.59). The ultimate stage of resymbolization would be *depersonification,* in which the referent breaks free from its containing symbolic form. Thus released, it is open to new forms and to new life in later times. This process is already under way as we move from the aggressive pagan individuals of canto vi to the impersonal concord of forces and functions shining more clearly through the figures and emblems of canto vii. More retrograde and stubborn than the others, Mutabilitie is almost the last to get the word.

Third, the organization of Nature's concord in canto vii is dominated by the form of the cycle, or round. This form appears not only in the obvious pageant of seasons and months but also in the stanzas on Nature (vii.5–13), discussed below, and in the larger unit of the canto as a whole, which moves from benign Christian Nature through Mutabilitie's older vision of negative elemental change (vii.17–26) and back to a benign nature that has dilated to assimilate mutability's influence. Both cantos together may also be viewed on this cyclical model in terms of the semantic pattern, symbolizing—desymbolizing—resymbolizing, that binds the movement of the whole poem into a single action.

Fourth, the cyclical pattern is not one of simple recurrence but rather one in which recurrence is part of a larger evolutionary movement. In this movement the older and simpler elements are at once negated and upheld (*aufgehoben*, Hegel's term for the one process divided into these two contrary moments). Mutabilitie and the gods persist in the same attitudes they held before, even while debating planetary influence. In his one stanza of rebuttal, Jove cites that influence as evidence for his previous claim: it is true, he admits, that all things under heaven are changed by Time,

> who doth them all disseise
> Of being: But, who is it (to me tell)
> That *Time* himselfe doth move and still compell
> To keepe his course? Is that not namely wee
> Which poure that vertue from our heavenly cell,
> That moves them all, and makes them changed be?
> So them we gods doe rule, and in them also thee.
>
> *(vii.48)*

His language is purged of the old heroic thunder, but the archaic resistance to change lurks in the legalism *disseise*, which usually connotes *wrongful* or forcible dispossession. Mutabilitie's discourse on the elements is similarly located between the old and the new: it is related to the mock-heroic business of canto vi much as the "philosophical" discourse in *Metamorphoses* XV is related to the metamorphoses of Ovid's first fourteen books, and as a piece of Lucretian materialism it aims at demythologizing the elemental processes; for example:

> So, in them all raignes *Mutabilitie;*
> How-ever these, that Gods themselves do call,
> Of them doe claime the rule and soverainty . . .
>
> *(vii.26)*

At the same time, the argument reveals its proponent's antique and limited viewpoint in reducing the principle of life to "unsteady ayre" (vii.22) and in selectively dwelling upon changes that reveal only instability, unpredictability, hostility, or decline. Her summation concisely recapitulates that early vision and early state of world order that the medieval concord passes by and upholds *as* early, as fulfilling necessary yet partial functions in an evolving universe of whose real nature those functionaries are scarcely aware:

> Thus, all these fower (the which the ground-work bee
> Of all the world, and of all living wights)

To thousand sorts of *Change* we subject see:
Yet are they chang'd (by other wondrous slights)
Into themselves, and lose their native mights;
The Fire to Aire, and th'Ayre to Water sheere,
And Water into Earth: yet Water fights
With Fire, and Aire with Earth approaching neere:
Yet all are in one body, and as one appeare.

(vii.25)

Echoing this stanza at the end, Nature corrects and reinterprets the process, thus emphasizing Spenser's evolutionary view that things sustain
and enrich themselves through self-surrender to the fated influences of
time—fated because communicated from whole to part. Nature finds

that all things stedfastnes doe hate
And changed be: yet being rightly wayd
They are not changed from their first estate;
But by their change their being doe dilate:
And turning to themselves at length againe,
Doe worke their owne perfection so by fate . . .

(vii.58)

At once dynamic and organic, cyclical and developmental, this explanation is in direct contrast to Mutabilitie's image (emphasized by her jag-
gedly disjunctive "Yet . . . yet . . . yet" construction) of the elements
fighting each other, becoming each other, and finally falling into the undifferentiated "one body."

In a rough way, the process of reinterpretation affects all the large-
scale relations between the two cantos. The discourse on elemental flux
may be linked to the earlier myth of the revolt of the titans by reference
to Natalis Conti's reading of that myth as a symbol of *elementorum mu-
tationes.*[16] Mutabilitie's ascent to the house of Jove is translated from image to argument (vii.49–55) when she describes, in Ptolemaic order,
changes in the planetary gods. Her beauty appears as the beauty of
change in Nature's pageant. Jove's attempt to make her his mistress finds
a parallel in his statement (vii.48) that although time and change rule in
the lower world, they are controlled by the *vertue* poured "from our
heavenly cell." The references to Astraea and Diana in the cycle of

---

[16] Suggested by Robert Kellogg and Oliver Steele in their edition of *Books I and II
of "The Faerie Queene"* (New York: Odyssey Press, 1965), 405. See Natalis Conti,
Mythologiae (Padua, 1637), VI.20, p. 342.

months (vii.37, 39) allude glancingly to the rigor and questionable justice of the golden-age sensibility that dominated canto vi. All these parallels dramatically exhibit Nature's message that things—in this case, conceptions or interpretations—"by their change their being doe dilate." The continuity of cultural ideas is guaranteed by demythologizing the older pagan version and resymbolizing it in the newer medieval context.

The various characteristics of canto vii are vividly present in the set of stanzas devoted to Nature—not only those, noted above, that make its vision "later" and more positive than that of canto vi, but also those arising from its deliberately imposed limits and exclusions. The latter are suggested by the sorting-out process that occupies the following stanzas:

> Now, at the time that was before agreed,
>   The Gods assembled all on *Arlo* hill;
>   As well those that are sprung of heavenly seed,
>   As those that all the other world doe fill,
>   And rule both sea and land unto their will:
>   Onely th'infernall Powers might not appeare;
>   Aswell for horror of their count'naunce ill,
>   As for th'unruly fiends which they did feare;
> Yet *Pluto* and *Proserpina* were present there.

> And thither also came all other creatures,
>   What-ever life or motion doe retaine,
>   According to their sundry kinds of features;
>   That *Arlo* scarsly could them all containe;
>   So full they filled every hill and Plaine:
>   And had not *Natures* Sergeant (that is *Order*)
>   Them well disposed by his busie paine,
>   And raunged farre abroad in every border,
> They would have caused much confusion and disorder.

> Then forth issewed (great goddesse) great dame *Nature*,
>   With goodly port and gracious Majesty;
>   Being far greater and more tall of stature
>   Then any of the gods or Powers on hie:
>   Yet certes by her face and physnomy,
>   Whether she man or woman inly were,
>   That could not any creature well descry:
>   For, with a veile that wimpled every where,
> Her head and face was hid, that mote to none appeare.

> That some doe say was so by skill devised,
>   To hide the terror of her uncouth hew,

From mortall eyes that should be sore agrized;
For that her face did like a Lion shew,
That eye of wight could not indure to view:
But others tell that it so beautious was,
And round about such beames of splendor threw,
That it the Sunne a thousand times did pass,
Ne could be seene, but like an image in a glass.

That well may seemen true: for, well I weene
That this same day, when she on *Arlo* sat,
Her garment was so bright and wondrous sheene,
That my fraile wit cannot devize to what
It to compare, nor finde like stuffe to that,
As those three sacred *Saints*, though else most wise,
Yet on mount *Thabor* quite their wits forgat,
When they their glorious Lord in strange disguise
Transfigur'd sawe; his garments so did daze their eyes.

(vii.3–7)

As Spenser's earlier tongue-in-cheek reference (vi.36) to Arlo—
"Who knowes not *Arlo-hill?*"—may have suggested, it is hardly a
mythic or literary landmark, and the contraction of the natural universe
to a somewhat eccentric locale works like a signature. Whatever vision
we are about to see will fit the modest scope of this poet's purposes and
may be expected to answer the previous episode. The visionary place
must not again be allowed to decline into a figure of contemporary actuality at its worst. The polarity between recreative and plaintive modes,
like that between epic and pastoral genres, must be reconciled in the synthesis of the later moral mode, as in the vision on Mount Acidale.[17] Thus
Spenser begins by reversing the pattern of decline and instability that
marked the previous canto and by opposing to the sad-brow complaint of
vi.1–6 a creative sequence that depicts something like an accelerated
cosmogony and theogony: first, the sharing out of the universe among
heavenly, earthly, and infernal gods and powers, described in descending order and logically followed by Pluto and Proserpina (logically,
because they carry us back from the depths to vernal earth and are admitted not only as seasonal gods, but perhaps also as pagan divinities sustained and revised by subsequent allegorization); next, the multitude of
natural kinds and creatures on whom order must be imposed just as, in
other Spenserian contexts, eros aligns the elements emergent from chaos

---

[17] Cf. "A Secret Discipline: *The Faerie Queene*, Book VI," in this volume.

(*An Hymne in Honour of Love* 71–91); third, the appearance not of the fecund source itself, but of its personification. Nature is described first as a goddess and then as greater than the gods, first as possibly mortal (male or female) and then as a transcendent mystery, first as the primitive form of Venus (the Magna Mater, goddess of lions and the law of the claw),[18] then as a later conception, the symbol of heavenly beauty (Sapience).[19] The image takes on added richness if seen to include and develop Spenser's own earlier images, especially the veiled Venus of IV.x–xi:

> So fertile be the flouds in generation,
> So huge their numbers, and so numberlesse their nation.
>
> Therefore the antique wisards well invented,
> That *Venus* of the fomy sea was bred . . .
>
> *(xii.1–2)*

In rejecting the lion-headed figure, preferring the sun-headed figure, and comparing himself to the biblical observers of the Transfiguration, Spenser at once moves Nature more definitely toward a Christian context and affirms his own selective and retrospective presence. His reference to Chaucer and Alanus (VII.vii.9) specifies the Christian context as medieval, but also as secular and literary: Chaucer, the "pure well head of Poesie," did not dare describe such radiance,

> But it transferd to *Alane,* who he thought
> Had in his *Plaint of kindes* describ'd it well:
> Which who will read set forth so as it ought,
> Go seek he out that *Alane* where he may be sought.

In following his *auctor's* example, he fixes the image of a certain historical distance from the present. At the same time, in stanzas 8 and 10, he establishes Nature in a *locus amoenus* reminiscent of the *Foules parley* as well as of his own ideal gardens: the earth "her self of her owne motion" produced a pavilion of trees that seemed to do homage to Nature and "like a throne did shew"—"Not such as Craftes-men by their idle skill / Are wont for Princes states to fashion"; flowers "voluntary grew / Out of the ground," and seemed richer "then any tapestry, / That Princes

---

[18] Cf. the reference to Cybele, *FQ* IV.xi.28.
[19] These two figures are in a way simple opposites: the primitive and the terrible earth mother under or within nature, and the Neoplatonic Heavenly Beauty, the hermetic Wisdom, above nature. Their extremes are mediated by the descending and rising god of incarnation and resurrection.

bowres adorne with painted imagery." Human art and government are together excluded from this idyllic order, whose ease and security are guaranteed by a transcendent power of nature. It is typical of this familiar pastoral logic that it blends subhuman and superhuman nature together to produce a model of sure spontaneous behavior in which the subjects (*natura naturata*) both automatically and voluntarily express the will of the ruler (*natura naturans*)—a model free of the pride and weakness of fallen human nature.

The infernal powers, the "confusion and disorder" that call forth the "busie paine" of Nature's Sergeant, the lion-headed goddess, the prideful luxury of princes—these are mentioned in order to be excluded. After a glance at his own earlier pastoral (the vernal renewal of Mole in vii.11), Spenser circles back to the epic marriage of Peleus and Thetis "On Haemus hill" (vii.12), a pagan prevision of "the *paradis terrestre* in which man lived before the apple thrown by Discord, that *diable d'enfer*, began our woe" (Hawkins, 87). From the unfallen nature on Haemus to the resurrected nature on Thabor and Arlo, and from the archaic god's-eye view of Phoebus ("that god of Poets hight" who, they say, "did sing the spousall hymn" of Peleus and Thetis) to the saintly vision and its analogues in the redactions of later poets, Spenser overleaps the valleys of fallen nature, synoptically compressing into Arlo's middle height a history of apocalyptic moments, summits of redeemed time and purged vision. Present-as-excluded are those sociopolitical problems that lead to the breaking of the laws "of Justice and of Policie." The prohibition of the infernal powers who administer the irreversible doom of Hell is a logical consequence of this exclusion.

The creatures on Arlo are specified in terms of "life or motion"; man, if he is included, is present only as a member of this organic domain. Later, when the pageant of seasons and months reaches out to embrace human activities—love, recreation, procreation, and labor—it absorbs them into the securely determined cycles of "the lawes of Nature," cycles whose upward swing from winter to spring and death to life is carefully emphasized. This benign pattern of continuity, positive change, and birth and rebirth is condensed into the familiar paradoxes of the brief concluding description of Nature:

> This great Grandmother of all creatures bred
> Great *Nature*, ever young yet full of eld,
> Still mooving, yet unmoved from her sted;
> Unseene of any, yet of all beheld . . .
>
> *(vii.13)*

The antithesis "unseene/beheld" is blunted because the latter term may mean "possessed." Nature is possessed by, held in the forms of, all its creatures and is therefore visible to its creatures, perhaps also it is viewed mentally as in a vision. This is a more dynamic, powerful, and beneficent figure than the goddess described at vii.5–6, and Spenser's circling back to the second passage from the first gives the effect of an advance, for he has shifted attention from her garments and visual presence to her operations and inner nature. The paradoxes are interpreted by the preceding stanzas so as to infold both the cyclical and developmental patterns, since the renewal is cultural and linear as well as seasonal and recurrent. The underlying matrix, "full of eld," gives rise not only to various living kinds but also to various human conceptions of nature. Thus great Nature may be the effect as well as the cause of all creatures—"of all creatures bred."

The ideal and idyllic qualities of this medieval vision derive from its dialectical relation to canto vi; it is *an* improvement over the pagan viewpoint, but not *the* final improvement. As a reaction to the golden-age pessimism underlying canto vi, it swings a little too far in the opposite direction, providing not a tentative *discordia concors* but a carefully purified *concordia discors* whose climax is the cycle of seasons and months. In its elliptically emblematic reference to—and coordination of—human, seasonal, and zodiacal phenomena, this pageant attains a cosmic synthesis sufficiently panoramic in scale to minimize the subtle yet fundamental problems of social life and human relations.[20] The vast network of psychosocial and psychocultural problems considered throughout *The Faerie Queene*, and especially in its last three complete books, is admitted in allusions, echoes, and oblique references. But it is present-as-excluded; it is either resolved into the limited context of nature's round, or muffled, pushed into the background, by the hieratic quality of the pageant. What the poet stresses, especially in the more vivid genre-life details, are natural problems—hunger, age, heat, and cold—and these are so closely observed that they tend to divert our attention from the symbols of the other, less simple, evils.[21] By these de-

[20] So Hawkins, 92 and passim; my reading, however, differs from his in assuming that Spenser means the very power and perfection of his pageant to be felt as *too* perfect.

[21] Examples: the crab compared to hypocrites (vii.35); the Nemaean lion and the implied death of Hercules (vii.36); Astraea's abandonment of "th'unrighteous world" (vii.37; stanzas 36 and 37, together evoking the world of Book V, remind us that the earlier attitude of golden-age pessimism is still alive); Diana's "doom unjust" (vii.39); echoes of various metamorphic deeds of rape and violence, here presented for the most part in benign form (vii.32–34); perhaps also a papist reference in the "Romane floud" (vii.42).

vices, the poet reminds us that his vision of nature has been selectively refined and idealized.

This is why we must not confuse Spenser's picture of the medieval mind with what are often thought of as Spenser's medieval habits of mind. Commentators frequently have noted the medieval texture of the canto in terms of the sources and traditions behind it, for example,

> for such images as the signs of the zodiac, the personification of the seasons and the months, the council of the gods, and the allegorical debate, dozens of analogues in medieval plastic and literary art make source hunting unnecessary. (Kellogg and Steele, 404)

> For centuries the months and their labors appeared over and over again in calendars and books of hours, above the portals of cathedrals, in handbooks and encyclopedias, signifying that the divisions of time . . . are part of the divine plan, and that by labor man works out his own place in it. The medieval man who paused to contemplate the great stone calendar over a church door found various meanings there, . . . and all of them apply to Spenser's Calendar. (Hawkins, 88)

If this vision is particularly attractive to Spenser, it is not because he is uncritically traditional or unconsciously medieval. The medieval mind may have believed in this vision as a divine and providential work, a panoramic picture of God's real order of nature. But Spenser employs the technique of conspicuous allusion in this canto not only to distance that vision in terms of cultural time, but also to emphasize its artistic and artificial quality. The essence of the order is so clearly dependent upon and communicated by its artistic organization, the whole harmony of the natural universe is so dramatically foreshortened and its rhythms condensed by Spenser's symbolic shorthand, that we are impressed primarily by the synoptic power of the human poet's imagination. This impression is heightened by the forms that comprise the network of allusion: literature, pageantry, emblematic imagery, ancient cosmological speculation, the arts of relief and illumination, judicial process, and debate.

The two cantos I have just discussed develop a cosmic rather than a microcosmic vision; their subject is the harmonious order of the physical and organic universe; the domain of the human psyche and society as such is not included as an object in that field; human attitudes have been externalized into pagan and medieval world views. The concluding stanzas move beyond the vision into the mind that has unfolded it and into the lyric moment evoked by that unfolding:

When I bethinke me on that speech whyleare,
  Of *Mutability*, and well it way:
  Me seemes, that though she all unworthy were
  Of the Heav'ns Rule; yet very sooth to say,
  In all things else she beares the greatest sway.
  Which makes me loath this state of life so tickle,
  And love of things so vaine to cast away;
  Whose flowring pride, so fading and so fickle,
Short *Time* shall soon cut down with his consuming sickle.

Then gin I thinke on that which Nature sayd,
  Of that same time when no more *Change* shall be,
  But stedfast rest of all things firmely stayd
  Upon the pillours of Eternity,
  That is contrayr to *Mutabilitie:*
  For, all that moveth, doth in *Change* delight:
  But thence-forth all shall rest eternally
  With Him that is the God of Sabbaoth hight:
O that great Sabbaoth God, graunt me that Sabaoths sight.

There is an uncertainty of tone reflected especially in the ambiguous syntax of the first stanza, lines six and seven: (1) "This thought makes me loathe this unstable life, and makes me (to) cast away the love of things"; (2) "I am loath to cast away this state of life and this love of things." As an adjective, *vaine* could modify either *love* or *things:* the love may be vain not because things are vanity, but because all such attachments are doomed; things are loved because they flower into brief beauty, perhaps in vain. In the adverbial position, *vaine* enforces the second alternative: the state of life and love of things may be vainly put off if no experience or vision can attain what lies beyond the mutable whirl. Similarly the often noted doubt about *Sabbaoth* (meaning either "rest" or "host") carries the unresolved feeling through to the end: (1) "Grant me the vision of that final rest," or, more forcefully, "Grant me its prospect, put it within reach"; (2) "Grant me a vision of that Host"—the armies of the saved, the children of the spirit, the Host assembled at the end of time. He wants to get beyond the clutches of change, and the first emphasis is simply upon escape. But he also wants to carry the variety up with him—"all things firmely stayd." The doubts of the first stanza suggest the added possibility that he may be asking to see this vision *now*, while alive, since he cannot be certain of what is to come. And though these stanzas have been described as moments of prayer, they express, as

Watkins has put it, "desire rather than affirmation." [22] The final line is not a great leap through faith; it is a slow and guarded turning *toward* prayer and faith, moving from mere indication ("Him that is . . .") through half-apostrophe ("O *that* great Sabbaoth God") to the final direct exhortation. It is as if, should he turn too quickly, too hopefully, too unguardedly, nothing would be there.

Though the conclusion may be called plaintive, this does not mean that—in Greene's words—if Spenser's faith "is indeed a refuge here, it is a lonely and bitter one" (p. 323). For we have moved, through the two cantos, from one sort of complaint to another, and from a plaintive attitude dramatically, impersonally, given play by the man-as-poet, to a plaintive attitude affecting the poet-as-man as he considers what he has made. The first complaint is based upon rejection, upon fear of life, upon disillusionment with the world, upon the desire to escape from the world as it is and to return to some pristine mythical state that the mind locates before time and change. The final complaint arises from so strong an involvement in and attachment to, such utter delight in, the changing world that the poet bemoans its fragility. "Spenser . . . has made the inevitable confession, that he loves all changing, mortal things too much, and they are betraying him. . . . the commitments to mortality have gone too deep to allow [the renunciation of earthly love]" (Arthos, 94–95). Having oscillated between the elemental divisions of pagan pessimism and the organic harmony of medieval optimism, he attains a more complicated and dynamic equilibrium at the end, still looking backward, still pressing forward, still revolving doubts.

Cheney has described as follows the "mixture of opposing attitudes with which Mutabilitie is being viewed":

> One pole of this opposition is the Christian *contemptus mundi*, the feeling of exhaustion and disdain for this world and intense longing for the combination of absolute delight and absolute rest to be found through death in the "Sabaoths sight" hinted by nature. At the other pole is the artist's delight in the inexhaustible variety of his creation. (pp. 246–47)

The first sentence needs some modification; the attitudes described here resemble those that reciprocally reinforce each other in canto vi (see above) and that are overcome by the shift in canto vii to the variety of natural and artistic creation. What is required after canto vi is a redistri-

---

[22] W. B. C. Watkins, *Shakespeare and Spenser* (Princeton: Princeton University Press, 1953), 72; see also John Arthos, *On the Poetry of Spenser and the Form of Romances* (London: Allen & Unwin, 1956), 198.

bution of values and a redirection of longing; earthly life must be enhanced, the absolute must be distanced or veiled, and the distinction between the mundane and the transcendent more rigorously honored. This theme is touched upon in two passages: At vi.32 Jove criticizes Mutabilitie for wanting "Through some vaine errour or inducement light, / To see that mortall eyes have never seene"; and at vi.46 Spenser chides Faunus for breaking out into laughter because he cannot contain his "great joy of some-what he did spy"—"Babblers unworthy been of so divine a meed." These are comic images of the "intense longing for . . . absolute delight" and vision, for the unveiled nearness of divinity, and for possession of the god's-eye view—a longing entailed by "disdain for this world."

The poem as a whole enacts a turning away from these conjoined opposites. Thus in canto vi the 'highest heaven" is identified with Jove, whereas in canto vii we find a higher celestial region (the zodiacal sphere of the fixed stars) and clues to the different spiritual heaven clearly disclosed only in the final stanza of the poem. The contrast of genres in canto vi intensifies the pastoral insignificance of the earthly episode; the perspective on both episodes, visually or qualitatively, is that of the gods (Mutabilitie, Jove, Diana), whereas their burden centers on the departure of a goddess from an unworthy and ruined earth, an earth seen by the uncomfortable ruling pantheon as the chief source of danger. The poet's initial gesture in canto vii is to move higher up for a more panoramic and harmonious view, then to settle into the middle region of Christian pastoral on Arlo. By the time he has described Arlo and Nature, this view has been further defined and "lowered"—located in terms of a particular cultural moment, a literary tradition, and his own limited, selective vision (his reliance on sources, his effort to make adequate comparisons, the weakness of mortal sight). This "descent" of viewpoint and desire is traced in the sequence of summits and seers: first, the easy mixture of mortal and immortal elements in the marriage on Haemus, whose singer was the god of poets himself; second, the more miraculous moment of transfiguration, seen by saintly mortals, symbolizing both the absolute transcendence of Christ and his promise to resurrect earthly nature; third, the literary vision on Arlo, a fable invented by the humanist poet who gives it historical distance by looking through medieval eyes and through a variety of traditional modes of expression.

This psychological movement of the point of view and of desire down into earth and history appears in other details. The second description of Nature is "lower" than the first, and though Mutabilitie calls her "Goddess" after this, the poet himself does not. The two specific references to Christian belief are both to Christ—his transfiguration and incarnation (vii.41). The pageant itself is centered on earthly activities as the focus of cosmic motions. In all these ways, then, the seventh canto reverses the upward- and outward-bound thrust of the pagan sensibility with its unguardedly childlike anthropomorphism. Canto vii places in high relief the archaic impulse to unify heaven and earth on earthly terms that presume to raise men closer to gods while actually lowering heaven to put it within the finite reach of man. The Christian answer to this centers on the paradigm of the Incarnation. Whereas the pagans envisaged their deities as human in form and behavior but remote from man in attitude, the three-personed God is mysterious and remote from man in terms of behavior but much closer to man in the manifestations of his love. The unbridgeable gap between man and a God who is Wholly Other requires God to descend. The descent, in enhancing fallen nature by expressing God's love for it, urges man to cherish not disdain it.

But from the standpoint of the sixteenth-century poet, this good news, along with its medieval edition, was delivered long ago; man's problems and attitudes were changed but not automatically resolved thereby. Although Spenser opens himself to the consoling harmony of the medieval world view, his stylized presentation is itself a way of lowering and limiting that view, since it declares its origins in the mind and art and culture of man. The Nature of canto vii is less easily identified with those aspects of divine providence to which it ostensibly refers than with the creative process of poetic imagination. This is suggested by Cheney's phrase "the artist's delight in the inexhaustible variety of *his* creation" (italics mine). The organization, emblems, images, *topoi,* and personifications (including Nature herself) are generated by the intercourse between nature as underlying matrix and the poet's mind. Toward the end of the canto, after the processes of nature have been unfolded in the discourse on elements, the pageant, and the passage on planetary gods, Natura is even more closely linked to the poet. Firmly personified at vii.57, she speaks for the first time, then vanishes "whither no man wist," concurrently with the canto's last words. "Her doome" sets forth in a plain statement what the entire canto has already enacted: the poet's moral, or argument, is simply placed in her mouth, and immediately thereafter he gives the phrase "turning to themselves at length againe" a new direction by turning to consider his own state of mind as affected by the argument.

Such an identification of nature with art places a heavy burden and a high value upon the work of the human mind and the function of man's art and vision. For where else if not here is the summit and fulfillment of created nature to be found? If, as many Renaissance and Reformation thinkers suspected, the forces of reality both transcend and differ in character from their equivalent forms in the mind, how else can they be even obscurely adumbrated? If God makes the world, it is His collaborator, man, who makes world views. However insubstantial the pageant of human forms in nature, culture, art, and play, it may yet be the only token, the only record and impress, of a power that may not find expression after man has had his day: "If it be now, 'tis not to come; if it be not to come, it will be now."[23] But the poet cherishes at the end of the poem the hope that "if it be not now, yet it will come; the readiness is all. Since no man has aught of what he leaves, what is't to leave betimes? Let be."

Yet these assertions of man's shaping power can be taken seriously only if they do not claim too much, only if made tentatively and experimentally, placed in quotation marks or in the presumptive fiction of play and poem. The magic and triumph of art reside in its ability to indicate the reality before which all art fails. When this happens, make-believe becomes "unrealistic," its tissue grows artificial, diaphanous to the point of vanishing. To be closed within the poet's secure second nature, to substitute *a world view* for *the world*, to long for solutions and resolutions not found in life, is to confuse the true *contemptus mundi* with "the feeling of exhaustion and disdain for this world." Thus Spenser shifts and opens his prospect throughout the poem, discloses new depths and distances continually emerging and continually receding. In the final moment the furthest depth is touched, but only lightly touched, for the poet's long brooding, his slow turning, his tone of reaching and beseeching, express a Sabbaoth God still moving away from man approaching.

---

[23] So also Prospero:

> like the baseless fabric of this vision,
> The cloud-capped towers, the gorgeous palaces
> The solemn temples, the great globe itself,
> Yea, all which it inherit, shall dissolve,
> And, like this insubstantial pageant faded,
> Leave not a rack behind.

PART TWO

The Shepheardes Calender

Introduction to
The Shepheardes Calender

SPENSER'S *SHEPHEARDES CALENDER* is self-amused pastoral, a critical and comically squint reenactment of attitudes, topics, and norms characteristic of a traditional literary mode. If it is "about" the limits of conventionally defined pastoral assumptions and points of view, it is equally "about" forms of sensibility and responses to life restricted enough to fit within those narrow bounds. The fundamental object of Spenser's criticism is the longing for paradise as the psychological basis of the pastoral retreat from life. He presents this longing in dialectical form, inflected either toward wish-fulfilling fantasy or toward bitter rejection of the world that falls short of such fantasy. These two inflections are causally interdependent and mutually intensifying: the mind schooled to expect a perfect world of gold or green responds to actuality by painting it pure black and running back to paradise. The longing for paradise is thus expressed in disappointed as well as in unrealistic expectations. I shall borrow some terms from E. K., the speaker whose dedicatory letter, arguments, and glosses frame the eclogues, and call these two inflections the *recreative* and *plaintive* attitudes. The recreative attitude is voiced by those speakers who have found paradise or who are in it and see no reason for leaving it. The plaintive attitude is voiced by those speakers who have lost it, either through thwarted love or through experience of the actual world and its vicissitudes. These attitudes often wear moral disguises—that is, the idyllic is set up as the ideal, what *could* be is converted to what *should* be—and this mystification provides the model compared to which actuality is found wanting.

I shall refer to this recreative/plaintive dynamic as the "paradise *principle*." I do this partly to highlight its kinship to the more familiar pleasure principle, partly to suggest its motivating character as the shaping cause of what appears as a structure, when the *Calender* is approached in synchronic perspective, and as a process or sequence, when it is viewed in diachronic perspective. The structure is a polarity of recreative and plaintive attitudes that may in any instance take the disjunctive form of a conflict or the conjunctive form of ambivalence. The sequence may be variously viewed as an obsessively repeated alternation between paradisal expectations and bitterness, or as a "fall" from the first to the second followed by an effort to return. My reading of the *Calender* will avail itself of both perspectives, but since (as will gradually become clear) the structural view of the paradise principle is closer than the sequential view to recent interpretive trends, I shall generally focus on synchronic polarities before turning to the various aspects of diachronic organization.

We often encounter in both *The Faerie Queene* and the minor poems figures who display various aspects of Spenser's psychology of the have-not. Some examples are Clarion's foe Aragnoll, Mother Hubberd's Fox and Ape, the tearful Muses, Alcyon (the diminished Halcyon of *Daphnaida*), Malbecco, Busirane, Ate, Slander, Radegund, Envy, Detraction, the Blatant Beast, Dame Mutabilitie, and the speaker (not necessarily the author) in several poems, including Book V and the *Mutabilitie Cantos*. Spenser depicts the plaintive condition of the have-not as self-willed submission to Tantalean bitterness and pain in response to loss, deprivation, and the inability to appease the "infinite desyre" of eros. Some offered prospect or hope of paradisal bliss arouses a longing for quick and complete possession that is marked as self-defeating in its hybristic excess, a premature and unrealistic compulsion to assimilate (and so to destroy) the desired other. This longing for what is unattainably beyond and for what has been irretrievably lost furrows the have-not's spirit with parallel competing impulses: to re-create, worship, replace, disparage, oppress, repress, violate, devour, destroy the loved and hated other or the deprived self. Behind all his have-nots, Spenser traces the lineaments of the paradise principle.

I propose to show that the spirit of the have-not is dramatized in the *Calender* as the plaintive condition. Furthermore, I shall argue that Spenser locates this condition not merely—not even primarily—in his pastoral speakers but in the tradition of received opinion that shapes their culture, norms, and expectations. Few readers now seriously challenge the thesis that the *Calender* is a critique of the great variety of literary traditions and conventions it imitates, and I shall demonstrate that this critique draws much of its power from the *Calender*'s preliminary sketch of the profound and complex portrayal of human motives we tend with greater ease to associate with Spenser's "mature" work. Thus the two basic premises of my argument are (1) that the paradise principle as the source of both the have-not response and the futile attempts to restore and return to the lost paradise is the organizing motif of the *Calender* and (2) that the paradise principle so conceived is the organizing motif of the literary tradition that Spenser's first complete published work imitates, sums up, and deconstructs. These premises are so closely related to the particular view I take toward Spenser's pastoral speakers, their obligation to and divergence from positions developed by other commentators is so problematical, and their applicability to other pastoral poets is so important to demonstrate to reinforce the present reading that consideration must be given to all these topics. The remainder of this introductory section will be devoted to this task.

The account of the paradise principle with which Renato Poggioli begins the earliest of his three classic studies of pastoral, *The Oaten Flute*, is paradigmatic of a view of pastoral that has prevailed until fairly recently:

> The psychological root of pastoral is a double longing after innocence and happiness, to be recovered not through conversion or regeneration, but merely through a retreat. By withdrawing not from the world, but from "the world," pastoral man tries to achieve a new life in imitation of the good shepherd of herds, rather than of the Good Shepherd of the Soul. . . . [Contrary to the Christian ideal] the pastoral ideal shifts on the quicksands of wishful thought. Wishful thinking is the weakest of all moral and religious resorts; but it is the stuff dreams, especially daydreams, are made of. Mankind had not to wait for Freud to learn that poetry itself is made of that stuff. . . . it is easier to reach moral truth and peace of mind . . . by abandoning the strife of civil and social living and the ordeal of human fellowship for a solitary existence, in communion with nature and with the company of one's musings and thoughts.[1]

Insofar as Poggioli is judging rather than merely describing the pastoral mode and its practitioners, his account is a little unfair to those poets

[1] *The Oaten Flute* (Cambridge: Harvard University Press, 1975), 1–2. This view has recently been reaffirmed by John D. Bernard in "'June' and the Structure of Spenser's *Shepheardes Calender*," *Philological Quarterly* 60 (1981): 305–22.

who share his critical insights and make the dangers or limits of the pastoral ideal their subject. Had it been voiced unambiguously as a paraphrase of a critical tradition *in* pastoral—as a set of themes dramatized by Virgil, Chaucer, Spenser, Shakespeare, Cervantes, Marvell, Milton, Pope, Yeats, and others—Poggioli's statement could hardly be improved.

Poggioli makes it clear that the pastoral impulse is entertained *in absentia* by minds encumbered with "the world"—that, as Frank Kermode put it, "the first condition of Pastoral is that it is an urban product."[2] Other writers make it equally clear that escapism is not the only motive, and Peter Marinelli has concisely summarized this view:

> To arrive in Arcadia . . . is merely to have one's problems sharpened by seeing them magnified in a new context of simplicity, by seeing Art against Nature and . . . being forced to conclusions about them. The issues of the great world or of adulthood are transported into Arcadia or into the magic gardens of childhood as to a place and time in which they may be better scrutinized . . . and the process may result in a clarification of the motives that bred the desire for escape in the first place. . . . Those who complain of the vitiation of pastoral by the introduction of . . . foreign or extraneous elements that cloud its pristine loveliness, fail to realize that a note of criticism is inherent in all pastoral from the beginning of its existence. It is latent in the form in its very desire for movement away from an unsatisfactory time and place to another time and place that is imagined to be superior. Satire, moralizing and allegory are merely the inborn tendencies of pastoral rendered overt and explicit.[3]

When Marinelli speaks of clarifying the motives "that bred the desire for escape," he makes a move toward recognizing a type of pastoral that is reflexive in critically examining its own basis. This differs from the type the passage centers on, that is, pastoral that criticizes the extrapastoral world. Writers on pastoral have tended to identify the reflexive critique with post-Renaissance developments in the mode. Thus Marinelli begins his study with Wordsworth's elegiac farewell to traditional pastoral in the eighth book of *The Prelude.* Harold Tolliver, who isolates some interesting moments of reflexive criticism in older pastoral and who is extremely sensitive to reflexive pastoral in general, reserves to "modern versions of pastoral" the suggestion "that the distance between fictional idylls and the daily world precludes any genuine transformation of reality except an imagined one." The modern pastoralist "is likely to take a skeptical view of the pastoral tradition and use it primarily as a

[2] *English Pastoral Poetry* (London: George G. Harrap, 1952), 14.
[3] *Pastoral* (London: Methuen, 1971), 11–12.

device for gaining perspective on the nature of the imagination itself."[4] But Tolliver finds that in English pastoral "from 1579 to about 1610 and again in Marvell and Herbert," the imagination is the locus rather than the object of the perspective. It is the poet's "own imaginative enclosure that provides the ground on which discordant values could be reconciled," and the "association between poetry and pastoral enclosures where ideal harmony reigns timelessly is common" in this period. Nevertheless, "the pastoralist's impulse to withdraw into the world of his own ornamental song is checked in most pastoralists by an equally strong urge either to spread the dream abroad, as a socially relevant ideal, or to project it as a final reality" (pp. 39–42).

That pastoral has its own peculiar powers that modern critics have insufficiently appreciated is a leading theme in Paul Alpers's earlier studies of the mode. In "The Eclogue Tradition and the Nature of Pastoral," Alpers notes that the "soft" view (e.g., Poggioli's) that mistakenly identifies "pastoralism with a simple lyricism" tends to generate its equally misleading "polar opposite—a 'hard view.' . . . The soft and hard views of pastoral, antithetical though they are, have one thing in common. Neither takes pastoral nature seriously as a home for the human spirit."[5] Alpers goes on to argue that Spenser does take "both 'soft' and 'hard' views of nature seriously, because he takes literally . . . the idea that there is a proportion between man and nature." He asserts that this idea "is basic to Renaissance pastoral and represents a fundamental point of difference between it and ancient pastoral, where life in nature is an ethical alternative, one possibility for the good life. In Renaissance pastoral, with its Christian perspective, man's life has an inherent relation to nature" (p. 364). But Renaissance pastoral shares with its classical predecessors at least one important characteristic:

> The eclogue tradition shows us that the pastoral is not merely, or even primarily, a matter of projecting worlds, real or imaginary, golden or savage. At the center of pastoral is the shepherd-singer. The great pastoral poets are directly concerned with the extent to which song that gives present pleasures can confront and, if not transform and celebrate, then accept and reconcile man to the stresses and realities of his situation. (p. 353)

While I agree with Alpers on many points and find his critique especially valuable, my view of pastoral differs from his in its general orientation, and the differences are sharper when we come to *The Shepheardes*

---

[4] *Pastoral Forms and Attitudes* (Berkeley: University of California Press, 1971), 14.
[5] *College English* 34 (1972): 352–53.

Calender. I am more inclined than Alpers to see Spenser as a "meta-pastoralist," that is, as a poet who dramatizes the limits of traditional pastoral because he is attracted to the mode and wants to revise rather than to discard it. Consequently my judgment of Spenser's achievement in the *Calender* is more positive than that of Alpers, for whom Spenser fails where Virgil and Milton succeed (pp. 366 ff.). Furthermore, I would argue against the position that "the skeptical view of the pastoral tradition" had to wait for romantic or modern pastoralists. I have learned from Alpers, however, that reflexive criticism is a property of Virgilian pastoral. I think pastoral that criticizes itself rather than (or as well as) the great world is an enduring element of the mode, and I shall try in this essay to substantiate the assertion that reflexive criticism is fundamental to Spenser's pastoral. The assertion itself is by no means original, and a summary of some of the recent commentators to whose work I am indebted will suggest the extent and the limits of the debt.

William Nelson was one of the first to establish the principle that the debates in the *Calender* were not one-sided, a principle implying that the author is not easily identified with any particular speaker or position: "As Spenser uses it, the dialogue of a pastoral poem is not a Socratic demonstration but a valid disagreement in which the speakers explore what may best be said on either part."[6] Nelson argued convincingly that the debates center on a small cluster of contraries, centered on the youth-age antithesis, each of which "recurs often enough to give unity to the whole." Subsequent criticism may occasionally have questioned the assertion that the speakers explored "what may *best* be said," but Nelson's reduction of the diversity of matter and mode to this principle of balanced antithesis has largely been accepted, especially since the principle he casually sketched out was later developed in considerable detail by Patrick Cullen (as Alpers, 365, points out).

Cullen's assessment of the *Calender* speakers and their polemical achievements is substantially more negative than Nelson's. He developed perhaps the first full-scale defense of the argument that Spenser was to be praised rather than blamed for the speakers' inadequacies, since the poet used them to criticize the two pastoral perspectives or traditions that dominated the Renaissance versions of the genre available to him—the soft and the hard, or Arcadian and Mantuanesque, perspectives:

> Whereas the Arcadian tradition creates, or attempts to create, a world in
> which man's instincts and desire for *otium* can be satisfied, Mantuanesque

[6] *The Poetry of Edmund Spenser: A Study* (New York: Columbia University Press, 1963), 39.

pastoral creates a largely predatory world from which only religion and eternity promise relief: the city, the court, Eros, all are instruments of the devil preying upon man, luring him to the loss of his soul; and against these vices there can be no ambivalence. . . . This division in pastoral is . . . the proper starting point for any analysis of the *Calender*. The work is . . . a critique of pastoral, through a confrontation of conflicting pastoral perspectives.[7]

Cullen argues that although the tension between these perspectives is sustained throughout the eclogues, Spenser uses the calendrical scheme to illustrate the ideal complementarity or equilibrium holding these "seemingly conflicting principles" in balance: "The natural year in the *Calender* . . . represents the mutable world that man must adapt to and yet ultimately triumph over, and it symbolizes in its own precarious balance of winter and spring the balance-in-opposition necessary for man and pastoral society within the natural world" (p. 123). Insofar as Spenser dramatizes the weaknesses as well as the limited virtues of both perspectives, he tolerates ambivalence like a true Arcadian. Cullen nevertheless finds the *Calender*'s synthesis precarious enough to opine that Spenser probably "sympathizes more with the Mantuanesque than with the Arcadian" viewpoint (p. 33).

Cullen's general view of the *Calender*'s polar and critical or ironic nature is roughly in accord with the one I advanced in an earlier essay[8] and shall develop in this study, but beyond that my approach differs from his in several respects, two of which I shall mention here: First, he identifies the two perspectives more closely with individual speakers than I think the text allows, and this ethico-dramatic emphasis leads him to reduce such speakers as those in the February debate to single-valued exemplars of their positions, that is, Thenot with Mantuanesque Age and Cuddie with Arcadian Youth. I shall argue that the two perspectives must be more cleanly dissociated from their proponents (1) to establish at an abstract level the complex interplay in which the two perspectives are engaged under the influence of the paradise principle and (2) to explore the effects of the interplay on the speakers through whom Spenser exhibits it—to explore, for example, the infiltration of the Arcadian perspective

---

[7] *Spenser, Marvell, and Renaissance Pastoral* (Cambridge: Harvard University Press, 1970), 25–26. Partial anticipations of this view had appeared in A. C. Hamilton's "The Argument of Spenser's *Shepheardes Calender*," *ELH* 23 (1956): 171–83 (reprinted in my *Spenser: A Collection of Critical Essays* [Englewood Cliffs: Prentice-Hall, 1968], 30–39), and in my "Mode and Diction in *The Shepheardes Calender*," *Modern Philology* 67 (1969): 140–49. The large number of references to Cullen's book in this and the following chapters documents not only my disagreements but also my profound obligation to his work. I have learned much from this encounter.

[8] "Mode and Diction" (see note 7).

of Youth into Thenot's Mantuanesque critique of Youth's Arcadian values. Second, Cullen's sharp division of perspectives logically precludes the possibility of an overarching paradise principle governing their relationship. For him anything that smacks of paradise is subordinated to the Arcadian perspective. He cannot therefore envisage a genuinely dynamic and dialectical interaction, nor can he appreciate the self-generating and self-perpetuating character of the conflict of opposites. His study of the *Calender* consequently remains locked within the fundamentally static and repetitive terms of that conflict, and this leads him finally to question Spenser's achievement. Searching for unity and resolution, he is forced to fall back on the idea of balanced structure, and the calendrical "balance-in-opposition" he finds remains too precarious to meet his criteria for a "reassuring synthesis."

A more genuinely dialectical view of the conflict between soft and hard pastoral is set forth in Isabel MacCaffrey's "Allegory and Pastoral in *The Shepheardes Calender*."[9] For MacCaffrey Spenser implies that the "naive [or soft] version of the pastoral metaphor inadequately expresses reality" because it posits an idyllic congruence between man and nature, microcosm and macrocosm, which experience belies (p. 94). The natural cycle in its literal form is an inadequate model because it is either false or unsatisfying—false in that "the orderly cycle of human life is [often] turned awry, its promise blasted" (p. 95), and unsatisfying in that "submission to the seasonal round" leads "only to death" (p. 93). To presuppose a benign or paradisal congruence of the natural and human cycles produces false expectations because "man must suffer inevitable outrage from the forces released in nature at the Fall"—passion, corruption, death—"and against these forces there is no remedy within nature itself" (p. 105). The *Calender* thus moves from soft to hard pastoral and beyond: while it teaches us to abandon our condemnation by sin "to live in an unsheltered world, hostile and uncongenial" (p. 97), it does not advocate rejecting either pastoral or temporal pleasures. "Rather those pleasures are defined and confirmed with relation to an ultimate religious sanction" (p. 100). Hence for MacCaffrey Spenser's sophisticated pastoral transcends both soft and hard versions in shifting the reference of soft pastoral from earth to heaven and from nature to spirit, that is, from literal to metaphoric signification: "the power of the pastoral paradigm is reaffirmed as having *metaphorical* validity"; in other words, its meaning "concerns the need for us to accept a nonliteral invisible reality as the one most relevant to us as human beings" (p. 100).

---

[9] *ELH* 36 (1969): 88–109. Reprinted in *Essential Articles for the Study of Edmund Spenser*, ed. A. C. Hamilton (Hamden, Conn.: Archon Books, 1972), 549–68.

John Moore gives the MacCaffrey argument a more uncompromisingly religious turn in a reading of the *Januarye* eclogue using the same dialectical scheme.[10] He defines Colin's "spiritual odyssey" as a progress "from allegiance to Pan, the nature God, to the real Pan, the real All, Christ." As a pagan nature god Pan presides over values and expectations that are out of touch with the realities of the fallen world and that leave his devotee unprepared to cope with pain and loss. Colin "must seek his values not in the temporary and fragile beauty of nature's spring, but in the enduring beauty of heaven's eternal springtime, the nonvisible world of the infinite. By doing this he will not define human happiness in terms of an earthly harvest but will seek a heavenly harvest free of mutability" (pp. 22–23). Moore's argument is structured according to the same three-stage model as MacCaffrey's: (1) a naive or soft or pagan or idyllic view of the man-nature relation precedes (2) a fall into hard actuality for which stage 1 left the neophyte unprepared, but in the crucible of bitter experience (3) the mind may yet find "transcendence and escape from . . . disasters" by soaring on "the uplifting powers of the human imagination" (MacCaffrey, 99) toward the heavenly harvest and a "spring-like birth of a better set of values" (Moore, 23). Both critics see the *November* eclogue as a critical moment in which nature's imagery is metaphorically turned against itself and transcendentalized.

Readings of this sort prompted Alpers to call much recent commentary "portentous" and to censure allegorical critics for overlooking "what Hallett Smith calls 'the verve of the poetry'" (Alpers, 363). Alpers applies to Spenser the lesson he learned from Theocritus and Virgil: pastoral speakers and singers are "men who fully 'realize their own natures,' while still bound, and accepting their bondage, to the earth" (p. 362). His view of nature consequently differs from that exemplified by MacCaffrey and Moore: since in Renaissance pastoral "man's life has an inherent relation to nature," poetry can answer "to permanent realities of nature and human nature," and "the severities and disappointments" expressed by "the pastoral of winter" can be taken to "register a coming to terms with reality and not merely a negative process of disillusionment" (Alpers, 364). When Colin hangs up his pipe, for example, "he is neither expressing despair nor confessing failure," for "this is the traditional act of an old shepherd who submits to the nature of things" (pp. 365–66). On this basis Alpers criticizes the allegorists not only because they are "serious at the expense of poetic surface" but also because, identifying pastoral "with naive idyllicism," they assume that the poet

---

[10] "Colin Breaks His Pipe: A Reading of the 'January' Eclogue," *English Literary Renaissance* 5 (1975): 22.

intended pastoral nature to be transcended in the reader's search for more serious messages (pp. 361–62).

I think something can be learned from both sides in this argument by isolating positive insights from those that seem less tenable. MacCaffrey's is, as Alpers noted, one of the more forceful and intelligent statements of the position he criticizes. The link she draws between the theme of false expectations and the limits of "naive idyllicism" strikes me as an important connection, one that can be further developed by separating it from her somewhat inconsistent emphasis on the role Spenser assigns to nature.[11] The account is inconsistent because the accent on fallen nature as a source of the problem conflicts logically with any attempt to root the negative consequences of the naively idyllic attitude within the attitude itself. In her account nature per se is thematized by the *Calender*, and the various senses she assigns to the term compose a set of imaged places and processes, a "macrocosm" (p. 94), "the world of nature" (p. 103), all of them inadequate to the human spirit's desire for transcendence and the imagination's preference for metaphor, which is never "found in nature."[12] Alpers objects to her emphasis on allegory as a visionary mode that adumbrates invisible reality through metaphorical fictions: "The notion that poetry serves human needs only by transcending nature comes from thinking of pastoral solely as a matter of images and projected worlds" (p. 362).

This criticism seems justified to me, for if it is the case—as I maintain—that the *Calender* dramatizes the causal relation between soft expectations and an excessively pessimistic or defeatist reaction to problematical aspects of nature (*and* culture), then in positing the Fall as the cause of nature's hostility, MacCaffrey's argument digresses from the dramatic point. It illustrates that the visualizing or topographic tendency Alpers criticizes has often encouraged serious-minded readers of the *Calender* to take two further steps: (1) to assume that something called "nature" exists "in" the "world" of the poem, that the speakers are to be imagined as "in" that preexisting natural world, and that it can be described apart from their descriptions of it; (2) to assume that nature exists in two forms, unfallen and fallen, and that the Golden Age is a prelapsarian state identical to Eden. The eclogues proper, however, contain few unmediated references to nature as setting or process. Since all but twenty-five lines are assigned to pastoral speakers, these assumptions

---

[11] See note 16 in "Re-verting to the Green Cabinet," below.

[12] See MacCaffrey, *Spenser's Allegory: The Anatomy of Imagination* (Princeton: Princeton University Press, 1976), 25 and Introduction (passim).

make it difficult to focus steadily on—or rather to listen carefully to—the speakers' responses to what they take to be "nature." This is why Alpers's insistence on the primacy of speakers and song in pastoral is a useful corrective. It shifts our attention "to such topics as voice, *tradition*, self-representation, self-reflexiveness, and the community implied by song," as he himself puts it in *The Singer of the "Eclogues."*[13] I have italicized the term *tradition* because of its importance to my reading. I shall try to demonstrate that the paradise associated with the paradise principle has nothing to do with the original pleasance created by God. Rather it is the product of the Muses—that is, of the literary elders, the tradition—and what it delineates is not the prelapsarian state but a set of paradisal expectations implanted by tradition in the pastoral mind. This thesis leads me to uphold against Alpers MacCaffrey's emphasis on the limits of naive idyllicism, but only as corrected by Alpers's emphasis on the representation of pastoral speakers and singers.

Alpers's brilliant insight into the soft and hard views of pastoral—that the former both precedes and generates the latter—uncovers the presence of the paradise principle in recent criticism. In denying the same insight to Spenser, however, he deprives himself of a valuable guide to interpretation of the *Calender*. He agrees with the commentators he criticizes that the *Calender* moves toward a positive resolution, though his sense of that resolution differs substantially from theirs. This marks the point of departure for the reading I shall give in these essays. I shall argue that Spenser does *not* take "pastoral nature seriously as a home for the human spirit," and that although he does take soft and hard pastoral seriously, it is to suggest their limits and show why they make traditional pastoral a home from which a pastoral adequate to the needs of the human spirit must be weaned. In other words, I shall defend the position that Spenser's view of soft and hard pastoral is the same as Alpers's and therefore that Alpers's conclusions about the *Calender*, and his evaluation of it, are represented in the *Calender* and have been targeted in advance. There is plenty of evidence in the eclogues to support the idea that their dominant theme is the power of the paradise principle—the power, that is, of the self-perpetuating dialectic between soft and hard perspectives—to promote disillusionment and to inhibit "a coming to terms with reality." Mantuanesque (or any other) bitterness is produced not by the limitations of the "fallen" world but by those of the golden-world attitude. It may therefore be inadvisable to continue thinking of the rec-

---

[13] *The Singer of the "Eclogues": A Study of Virgilian Pastoral* (Berkeley: University of California Press, 1979), 6; italics mine.

reative and plaintive attitudes as "soft" and "hard" pastoral, since the adjectives seem to have attached themselves firmly to nature. I propose replacing them by the terms *sweet* and *bitter* to distinguish them as attitudes that speak only secondarily to nature as such but primarily to the paradisal expectation and disillusionment of Spenser's pastoral speakers.

Though I plan to discuss many eclogues not directly or explicitly about poetry and poets, my thesis is that such reflexive issues are central to *The Shepheardes Calender* as a whole, that problems about "art" and problems about "life" are handled together under the same set of ethico-psychological premises, and that these premises are articulated primarily in the presentation of what may be called Spenser's drama of literary imitation. At the heart of the drama is the dialogue, or convergence, or collision, of old with young, ancient with modern, past with present. The literary withdrawal the poet depicts as prompted by paradisal influence is characteristically a "return to"—that is, an imitation of—a set of *topoi*, of "places" as well as conventions, authenticated by their durability. The new poet treasures the beauty or value of these ideal "places" as much as he fears their dangers and temptations. The aesthetic power of his literary models threatens to reduce him either to silence or to the status of an epigone, an ape not of nature but of art. He must criticize and reject the received form of the art he would embrace; otherwise, trying to revise the form, he will succeed only in repeating it. The problematic of imitation and that of the paradise principle converge in the new poet's dramatization of belatedness. His way of breaking free of what he constitutes as his tradition is to encapsulate it in a critical profile, to activate its conventions and to reenact its characteristic "moves" so as to bring out the complexity of attitude implicit in but flattened under the conventional surface. In thus showing how an attitude toward art implicates an attitude toward life, he doesn't merely criticize the tradition; he gives it new energy and meaning.

A clue to the particular form this sympathetic criticism takes in the great metapastoralists may be drawn from Humphrey Tonkin's distinction between the satiric and the romantic functions of pastoral:

> Its first function is satiric: it serves as a device for criticism. It distances the writer from his own milieu and forms a base from which to attack its standards or lack of standards. The eclogue is its special vehicle. Its second function is as a means of articulating moral or spiritual aspirations. It creates a world where the conflicts and pettinesses of ordinary life are eliminated, where all investments have returns, and where actions have desired results. Love is untrammelled, and belief suffers no contradiction. . . . These two devices are not mutually exclusive. Pastoral satire depends on an awareness

of the virtues of the pastoral existence, while pastoral romance at least presupposes the existence elsewhere of urban and courtly corruption. Most pastoral works involve a combination of satiric and romantic ingredients, some leaning towards the former and some towards the latter.[14]

By rejoining these two functions, directing them back toward each other, we may effect a more complete closure of pastoral's reflexive critique than Tonkin's account suggests, one that will allow us to capitalize on his illuminating remark that "the pastoral *world*" is to be distinguished from "pastoral *works*, which are often concerned with the disintegration of this world" (p. 283). This world, "this country of beautiful landscape and simple emotions" which "often has an air of fantasy" and is "a retreat into the imagination rather than an escape to the country" (p. 283), is generated and integrated by the romantic function. And the object of the *Calender* poet's criticism (whether satiric or, more genially, parodic) is precisely this function. Tonkin suggests that the disintegration of which he speaks involves the transition from childhood and sexual innocence to manhood and sexuality, and his discussion implies what other scholars have stated—that love is an outside intruder separating us from idyllic nature and the Golden Age (pp. 283–84). But I think that the pastoral criticism is inflected differently: it asserts that the disintegration of the golden world and the plaintive response to love and experience are consequences of the very "retreat into the imagination" that produced that world. Romantic expectations are the source of failure and premature bitterness. And since poetic conventions are in turn the source of romantic expectations, the pastoral critique is first and foremost a critique of pastoral.

[14] *Spenser's Courteous Pastoral: Book Six of the "Faerie Queene"* (London: Oxford University Press, 1972), 282–83.

The Moral Eclogues

Introduction

THE *SHEPHEARDES CALENDER* is notable for the conspicuous variety of conventional perspectives it puts into play, and any effort to find some single psychological motive or basis must begin by taking these into account. The obvious starting point is in E. K.'s distinctions of mode:

> These xii Æclogues every where answering to the seasons of the twelve monthes may be well devided into three formes or ranckes. For eyther they be Plaintive, as the first, the sixt, the eleventh, and the twelfth, or recreative, such as al those be, which conceive matter of love, or commendation of special personages, or Moral: which for the most part be mixed with some Satyrical bitternesse, namely the second of reverence dewe to old age, the fift of coloured deceipt, the seventh and ninth of dissolute shepheards and pastours, the tenth of contempt of Poetrie and pleasaunt wits. ("Generall Argument," 29–39)

In general, older critics either ignored these distinctions of mode or accepted them without question, perhaps emphasizing one or another group.[1] To my knowledge A. C. Hamilton was the first critic to use

[1] See, for example, Edwin Greenlaw, "*The Shepheardes Calender,*" *PMLA* 19 (1911): 427 ff., and Paul McLane, *Spenser's "Shepheardes Calender": A Study in Elizabethan Allegory* (Notre Dame: Notre Dame University Press, 1961), 315 ff.

them seriously and imaginatively as aids to interpretation. Hamilton sees the poem's argument controlled by the subjects, relations, and sequence of the three modes. The logical first position is occupied by the recreative mode:

> The pastoral world which provides the poem's setting is traditionally identified with Arcadia, the state of innocence before the Fall. This "unreal" world, seen in the poem's deliberate artifice with its conventions of the shepherd's life, provides the subject of the Recreative eclogues: March with its story of Cupid, April's hymn of praise, and the contest of the shepherds in August. These eclogues exist in the poem as fragments of an earlier pastoral tradition, the idyll, that serve to "test" the poet's skill. In each he seeks to "overgo" the traditional form.[2]

The other modes branch out in different directions from this starting point:

> The pastoral world of innocence circumscribed by the "real" world of fallen nature becomes the subject of the moral eclogues with their allegory of the political and religious conditions of England. The simple pastoral life of enjoyable ease must then be rejected for the dedicated life where man does not live according to Nature but seeks escape out of Nature. . . . In the moral eclogues the pastoral conventions become radically allegorical; simple lyricism is replaced by satire, irony, and open denunciation. The poet's relation to the simple pastoral world of innocence becomes the subject of the plaintive eclogues. Within the pastoral world he is the melancholy shepherd dominated by the elusive and faithless Rosalind. (Hamilton, 34)

To this or any employment of E. K.'s divisions, the following objections may be made: The unfallen state of innocence is an ideal or reality in nearly all the eclogues, and the recreative eclogues are by no means the only ones that are "fragments of an earlier pastoral tradition," since the elegy, political comment, and religious satire all have precedents in earlier pastoral. "Overgoing" can just as easily be imputed to Spenser in these cases as in those Hamilton lists, especially if we accept as a comic or perverse form of overgoing Spenser's pleasure in fracturing rustic speech more than earlier English pastoralists did—"rhimes more rumbling than rural," as John Gay put it, reaching a climax of splendid verbal obfuscation in *September*. Furthermore, complaining about love is

---

[2] Hamilton, "Argument," in *Spenser: A Collection of Critical Essays*, ed. H. Berger (Englewood Cliffs: Prentice-Hall, 1968), 34. Future citations of Hamilton's essay refer to this edition.

not restricted to E. K.'s plaintive eclogues (which, incidentally, include a complaint about death). Hamilton hedges on Colin Clout's *August* sestina (p. 38), the inclusion of which may have postdated E. K.'s commentary. But even the simpler shepherds of *March* and *August*, though they whine more merrily and less articulately than Colin, "conceive matter of love." And many of the moral pastors contribute more than their share of complaint, though it is not about love. Hamilton seems aware that Spenser's image of "the simple pastoral life of enjoyable ease" is not restricted to the recreative eclogues; the recreative mode as he defines it must include otiose complacency in the simple life as well as the "simple lyricism" of traditional literary artifice. Since he is also aware that an otiose or recreative speaker carries one side of most of the moral debates, his statement would be more accurate if it read "simple lyricism is *opposed*" rather than "*replaced*" by satire, irony, and open denunciation."

Although Hamilton submits too easily to E. K.'s crude attempt to sort the eclogues out by subject matter—an attempt that, as we shall see, is not entirely devoid of merit—his descriptions are genuinely suggestive and become useful if we separate the modes from particular eclogues and apply them to impulses running through the *Calender* and often existing side by side. The basis for this application may be discerned in Hamilton's own analysis, for he sees the plaintive and moral impulses as antithetical developments of or responses to the recreative impulse. E. K.'s distinction between plaintive and moral categories derives from the differences between Colin, who complains chiefly about his love and his own miseries, and the speakers whose subjects of complaint are the conventional topics of ethical, social, and political satire. The distinction is sharpened by the sustained stylistic contrast between Colin's flair for the artifices of rhetoric and prosody and the often arrhythmic, anti-rhetorical rumblings of the moral speakers. These two aspects of the distinction are important in view of Spenser's obvious commitment to the Ciceronian commonplace that wisdom and eloquence are both essential to the health and integrity of public life. His moral pastors, who live in the English countryside rather than in England's Helicon, are short on mental and verbal subtlety. Simplicity, earnestness, and barnyard pragmatism will not guarantee success in either understanding or dealing with the artful and persuasive knaves who flourish in the corrupt great world; the ways of sheep are not the ways of men. Morality needs more articulate advocates, and this means that rhetorical skill such as Colin Clout commands must be brought to bear on social problems. Colin must therefore be drawn out of himself, made to face life and to place his art in the service of the public good.

There is thus one striking similarity between the moral and plaintive attitudes as depicted in the *Calender*, and to bring this out I shall shift and narrow the reference of these two terms before exploring their meaning in the eclogues: Let *plaintive* refer to attitudes Spenser presents as deficient—the title of his second volume of minor poems, *Complaints*, has the same negative force. Let *moral* refer to attitudes present in the *Calender* only by default, that is, let it denote criteria not met by the pastoral speakers, unachieved standards by which we measure the limits of the pastoral conventions on display. If we shift from (E. K.'s) descriptive to evaluative grounds, we can formulate the following hypothesis: neither the responses of Colin nor those of the moral pastors are sufficient for life; though the objects about which they complain differ, the tone and motive are identical. Hamilton describes as moral those speakers who uphold the dedicated life against the life of *otium*, implying that their antagonists are immoral (p. 34). But the following examples will suggest that this is not the case: Spenser shows that these so-called moral attitudes are fundamentally plaintive because they are dominated no less than the idyllic attitudes by the psychology of retreat and by the inability or unwillingness to face or to cope with the actual world.

As I noted before, the *Calender* is dominated by a single restrictive ideal, the paradise principle, and the eclogues reveal two essential relations to that ideal, recreative and plaintive. The class of recreative speakers covers a range of attitudes from careless or carefree enjoyment of the present, as in the *March* shepherd's "let be, as may be, that is past: / That is to come, let be forecast" (58–59), to the more expansive and reflective utterances of Hobbinol in *June* and *September:*

Lo Colin, here the place, whose pleasaunt syte
From other shades hath weand my wandring mynde.
Tell me, what wants me here, to worke delyte?
The simple ayre, the gentle warbling wynde,
So calme, so coole, as no where else I fynde:
The grassye ground with daintye Daysies dight,
The Bramble bush, where Byrds of every kinde
To the waters fall their tunes attemper right.
(June 1–8)

Content who lives with tryed state,
Neede feare no chaunge of frowning fate:
But who will seeke for unknowne gayne,
Oft lives by losse, and leaves with payne.
(Sept. 70–73)

Similar arguments are voiced by Palinode in *Maye* (63–67) and Morrell in *Julye* (75–92). This paradise embraces literary as well as rustic, political, and moral ideals: the perpetual and perfect state of nature, self, and society includes among its most important diversions the pleasures of song and poetry; it is a garden of Muses and Graces, where art is as effortless as birdsong (compare *Aprill* 35–36 and 100 ff. with *June* 7–8 and 57 ff.) and where divinities are easily persuaded to attend the rustic fetes.

In the debate poems the plaintive position is upheld by Thenot in *Februarie*, Piers in *Maye*, Colin in *June*, Thomalin in *Julye*, Diggon in *September*, and Cuddie in *October*. These debates are complicated in a manner Hamilton misses when he calls the second group of speakers "good" and the idyllic speakers the "antagonists" (p. 34). William Nelson rightly argues that the debates are not one-sided, though their complexity does not arise from the reason he gives: "the dialogue . . . is a valid disagreement in which the speakers explore what may best be said on either part."[3] The virtues on both sides are usually outweighed by the weaknesses, since the speakers in the second group also have their hearts in paradise. They are differentiated from the first group primarily because they look back in desire toward a condition the other speakers do not feel they have lost. In the following section I shall try to demonstrate this thesis with a reading of the moral eclogues. I begin with *Maye* because my discussion of *Februarie* is included in a later chapter.

Four Moral Eclogues

The contrast between idyllic and plaintive modes is sharply etched in *Maye*. In the woodcut the two speakers stand off to one side, slightly higher than the revelers, and look on reflectively. In the *Februarie* woodcut, by contrast, Thenot and Cuddie gesture with some vehemence, obviously in heated discussion. This difference between Cuddie and Palinode is dramatized in their respective styles of discourse: Cuddie's has more bounce and bite, his speeches take the form of insults flung at Thenot with coarse good humor, and in general he responds more spontaneously to the rising of the sap.[4] Palinode begins in a calmer and more thoughtful manner; his nostalgia tends to distance the green world:

> PALINODE.   PIERS.
> Is not thilke the mery moneth of May,
> When love lads masken in fresh aray?

---

[3] *The Poetry of Edmund Spenser: A Study* (New York: Columbia University Press, 1963), 46.

[4] See the discussion of *Februarie* in "Hore Heed and Grene Tayle."

How falles it then, we no merrier bene,
Ylike as others, girt in gawdy greene?
Our bloncket liveryes bene all to sadde,
For thilke same season, when all is ycladd
With pleasaunce: the grownd with grasse, the Woods
With greene leaves, the bushes with bloosming Buds.
Yougthes folke now flocken in every where,
To gather may buskets and smelling brere:
And home they hasten the postes to dight,
And all the Kirke pillours eare day light,
With Hawthorne buds, and swete Eglantine,
And girlonds of roses and Sopps in wine.
Such merimake holy Saints doth queme,
But we here sytten as drownd in a dreme.

PIERS.

For Younkers Palinode such follies fitte,
But we tway bene men of elder witt.

As Cuddie followed Colin with a rustic and naturalized attitude toward love, so Palinode rusticates the extremely literary landscape of the *Aprill* blazon: the themes of masking, dressing-up, and decorum extend the *Aprill* atmosphere into the first eight lines, after which Palinode abandons his vaguely metaphoric speech for a direct report in plainer style. The "moral" topic is set up in the reference to church and saints and becomes explicit in Piers's use of the word *Younkers*, which surrounds the term *youth* with connotations of worldliness, gaiety, and the idle rich. From *March*, with its innocent rustics, through Colin's *Aprill* extravaganza to *Maye* there has been a brief flowering of the simple recreative attitude unhampered by plaintive criticism. But the recreative speaker is now an older shepherd, and his age allows Piers to point the theme of decorum in a new direction: "Haven't you outgrown that nonsense?" Palinode apparently has not, for in the next interchange he is more involved in and excited by the scene he describes, and Piers responds by converting the green world from a literal situation to a symbol:

PALINODE.

Sicker this morrowe, ne lenger agoe,
I sawe a shole of shepeheardes outgoe,
With singing, and shouting, and jolly chere:
Before them yode a lusty Tabrere,
That to the many a Horne pype playd,
Whereto they dauncen eche one with his mayd.
To see those folkes make such jovysaunce,

Made my heart after the pype to daunce.
Tho to the greene Wood they speeden hem all,
To fetchen home May with their musicall:
And home they bringen in a royall throne,
Crowned as king: and his Queene attone
Was Lady Flora, on whom did attend
A fayre flocke of Faeries, and a fresh bend
Of lovely Nymphs. (O that I were there,
To helpen the Ladyes their Maybush beare)
Ah Piers, bene not thy teeth on edge, to thinke,
How great sport they gaynen with little swinck?

                                    PIERS.

Perdie so farre am I from envie,
That their fondnesse inly I pitie.
Those faytours little regarden their charge,
While they letten their sheepe runne at large,
Passen their time, that should be sparely spent,
In lustihede and wanton meryment.
Thilke same bene shepeheards for the Devils stedde,
That playen, while their flockes be unfedde.
Well it is seene, theyr sheepe bene not their owne,
That letten them runne at randon alone.
But they bene hyred for little pay
Of other, that caren as little as they,
What fallen the flocke, so they han the fleece,
And get all the gayne, paying but a peece.
I muse, what account both these will make,
The one for the hire, which he doth take,
And thother for leaving his Lords taske,
When great Pan account of shepeherdes shall aske.

                                    (19–54)

    W. L. Renwick's comment on the word *faytours* in line 39 summa-
rizes the semantic mismatch in terms of which Spenser projects the debate: "The change from reality to metaphor is rather violent."[5] Piers
opposes to Palinode not only a different attitude toward life but also a
different kind of pastoral and a different style of poetic reference. Seeing
all images as *exempla*, the moralistic sensibility views the green world as
grist for an allegorical mill. At the semantic level Palinode and Piers are

    [5] *The Works of Edmund Spenser: A Variorum Edition, Minor Poems*, ed. C. B. Osgood
and H. G. Lotspeich (Baltimore: Johns Hopkins University Press, 1943), 1:295 (hereafter cited as *Variorum, Minor Poems*).

thus at odds about the way to interpret the terms *shepherds* and *sheep*, but since they are unaware that they disagree, they talk past each other. In the above speech Piers intends priests and their pastoral charge, but in Palinode's reply *shepheards* may also mean humankind in general and may even refer to the rustics of his opening speech; he does not address himself to Piers's criticism of the immoral practices of clergymen because he does not appear to be taking account of the particular allegorical level at which Piers philosophizes.[6]

Piers in turn, and for the same reason, fails to deal with the roughly Epicurean sentiments of Palinode's reply.[7] We might have expected some Stoic commonplaces from him, but in fact he begins a new argument, based again on the distinction between clergy and laity, that answers more directly to Chaucer's Reeve (*Canterbury Tales*, A3977–86) than to Palinode:

> shepheards (as Algrind used to say,)
> Mought not live ylike, as men of the laye:
> With them it sits to care for their heire,
> Enaunter their heritage doe impaire:
> They must provide for meanes of maintenaunce,
> And to continue their wont countenaunce.
> But shepheard must walke another way,
> Sike worldly sovenance he must foresay.
> The sonne of his loines why should he regard
> To leave enriched with that he hath spard?
> Should not thilke God, that gave him that good,
> Eke cherish his child, if in his wayes he stood?
> For if he mislive in leudnes and lust,
> Little bootes all the welth and the trust,

[6] What shoulden shepheards other things tend,
Then sith their God his good does them send,
Reapen the fruite thereof, that is pleasure,
The while they here liven, at ease and leasure?
For when they bene dead, their good is ygoe,
They sleepen in rest, well as other moe,
Tho with them wends, what they spend in cost,
But what they left behind them, is lost.
Good is no good, but if it be spend:
God giveth good for none other end.
(63–72)

[7] A glance at Palinode's previous speech will show that he also fails to answer to the point, for Piers was discussing the immoral practices of clergymen, whereas Palinode totally disregards the theme of the pastoral charge by disregarding the allegory.

That his father left by inheritaunce:
All will be soone wasted with misgovernaunce.
(75–90)

"Men of the laye" in line 76 may vaguely suggest the other shepherds
who sing songs, since recreative versus moral attitudes is one of the
issues involved. But because Piers tends to spray his bullets in all directions, his targets include the viciousness following the age of pastoral
gold, the evils of unsound inheritance, and the need for thrift (102 ff.).
Moreover his underlying agreement with Palinode lurks in the following lines, whose basic message is that vice is bad because it dissipates the
plenty of the former age and leads to poverty: after the shepherds had
been corrupted through "tract of time and long prosperitie,"

> Tho gan the shepheards swaines to looke a loft,
> And leave to live hard, and learne to ligge soft:
> Tho under colour of shepeheards, somewhile
> There crept in Wolves, ful of fraude and guile,
> That often devoured their owne sheepe,
> And often the shepheards, that hem did keepe.
> This was the first sourse of shepheards sorowe,
> That now nill be quitt with baile, nor borrowe.
> *(124–31)*

The reference to wolves is of course a signal to the reader to look
through the pastoral image toward contemporary affairs about which, in
Piers's plaintive view, nothing can be done. But Palinode either ignores
or misunderstands these lines when, after criticizing Piers's foolish talk,
he answers, "How shoulden shepheardes live, if not so? / What? should
they pynen in payne and woe?" (148–49). If not how? This can only
refer back to Piers's paean on dairy products or to Palinode's own earlier
praise of pleasure (63–72). They are not arguing about the same thing,
since Palinode fends off a future that to Piers is already present:

> If I may rest, I nill live in sorrowe.
>   Sorrowe ne neede be hastened on:
> For he will come without calling anone.
> While times enduren of tranquillitie,
> Usen we freely our felicitie.
> For when approchen the stormie stowres,
> We mought with our shoulders beare of the sharpe showres.
> *(152–57)*

Palinode says, "Let's enjoy our Golden Age while we may," and Piers says, "But the fools have already gone and lost it." They express two dialectically related phases of a single attitude. The substance of their polemic lies less in its content than in its tone and emphasis, and especially in its perspective. The discourse of the paradise principle speaks through both of them equally, but for Palinode the Golden Age is in the present and for Piers it is in the past and is therefore absent. This difference between its presence and absence is represented by the different semantic registers of the two speakers, Piers looking allegorically through the pastoral surround and Palinode looking at it. But if they obfuscate the issues they raise by their inability to make contact, those issues are recognizable to the reader—who could not otherwise be in the position to judge *that* they are being obfuscated. We have only to squint our eyes and blur out the pastoral semantics to bring the issues into clear focus: the different dispositions of the speakers, labeled Protestant and Catholic in the argument; ascetic and moral versus worldly and recreative; Christian versus pagan; Stoic versus Epicurean; puritan reform versus the ecclesiastic hierarchy and policy of the Church of England. These possibilities and others flow freely into each other because only at the general level—where the moral issues are childishly simple—is the conflict articulate.[8]

For most commentators the ecclesiastical allegory makes the debate coherent. Spenser anchors it to history by mentioning Algrind (Grindal), and it seems safe to say that various aspects of the reform issue account for the vagaries of Piers's argument. The easiest way to make sense of the eclogue is to go straight through it to Elizabethan England to identify the historical problem. Readers are encouraged to do this not only by the paraphernalia appended to Singleton's edition of the *Calender* but also by the conspicuous allusiveness that makes the moral eclogue *look* allegorical. Clues to a critique of the establishment are broadly hinted at, but potential censors might well be disarmed by the cloudy fulminations of Mantuanesque rustics. (See the afterword to this chapter for further comment.)

Palinode seems more alive to the failure of communication than Piers because his perspective is more firmly rooted in the immediate pastoral situation, the *here and now* of the argument. Thus he accuses Piers of being a pastoral wet blanket: "a fooles talke to beare and to heare" (141)

[8] See *Variorum, Minor Poems* 1:290–95, 600–609, 727 ff. See also W. L. Renwick, ed., *The Shepherd's Calendar* (London: Scholartis Press, 1930), 193–94.

is outrageous. This sentiment qualifies the passage cited above (152–57) and also the closing lines of the same speech:

> nought seemeth sike strife,
> That shepheardes so witen ech others life,
> And layen her faults the world beforne,
> The while their foes done eache of hem scorne.
> Let none mislike of that may not be mended:
> So conteck soone by concord mought be mended.
>
> *(158–63)*

These lines refer to the arguing itself rather than to the themes under discussion. Palinode objects that Piers's foolish talk and fault-finding are making them put on a bad show "the world beforne." But his objection, half of which is expletive (132–47), is an example of the fault-finding and railing he criticizes. Together with his uncompromisingly self-assured tone, it reinforces the reader's feeling that the *Maye* speakers are in no danger of changing each other's minds, of apprehending—much less resolving—their differences. The only thing they can readily change is the subject: "Let none mislike of that may not be mended: / So conteck soone by concord mought be mended." Piers would prefer to go on arguing, but, after extending their particular opposition to the universe, he offers a way out:

> Shepheard, I list none accordaunce make
> With shepheard, that does the right way forsake.
> And of the twaine, if choice were to me,
> Had lever my foe, then my freend he be.
> For what concord han light and darke sam?
> Of what peace has the Lion with the Lambe?
> Such faitors, when their false harts bene hidde.
> Will doe, as did the Foxe by the Kidde.
>
> PALINODE.
> Now *Piers*, of felowship, tell us that saying:
> For the Ladde can keepe both our flocks from straying.
>
> *(164–73)*

Foxily tempting Palinode with an offer no puerile *senex* could refuse— the chance to hear a story—Piers takes control of the discourse and continues his attack.

The sudden drop from mighty opposites to an Aesopic Disneyland somewhat illogically transforms "light" and "the Lambe" to a hapless

"Kidde . . . too very foolish and unwise" (174–75), the gullible son of
a gullible father who has already gone the way of all goats. The mother
in Piers's tale isn't much help, for after warning "her youngling" to be-
ware the fox she leaves him alone in the house and ignores a bad omen to
go "abroade unto the greene wood, / To brouze, or play, or what shee
thought good" (178–79). Along comes the sly "maister of collusion"
(219) disguised as a poor ailing peddler who easily arouses the kid's
sympathy and tempts him with an offer of popish trifles—"bells, and
babes, and glasses" (240)—no youngling could refuse. The fox tells a
few stories, unpacks some toys, shows "his ware" to "kiddie unawares"
(287, 275), and in no time Palinode's surrogate is "popt . . . in" the
pack and run home for dinner.

This brief abstract of the fable scarcely does justice either to Spenser's
delight in mimicking the art of sinking or to the effect of his mimicry on
the hapless Piers. As Piers warms up to his task he untrusses his rhetorical trifles with such exuberance as to divert attention from his moral.
The following scene, for example, speaks to us less of puritan, Anglican,
or antipapist themes than of the teller's commitment to the pleasures of
bathetic fabulation:

> Shee set her youngling before her knee,
> That was both fresh and lovely to see,
> And full of favour, as kidde mought be:
> His Vellet head began to shoote out,
> And his wretched hornes gan newly sprout:
> The blossomes of lust to bud did beginne,
> And spring forth ranckly under his chinne.
>   My sonne (quoth she) (and with that gan weepe:
> For carefull thoughts in her heart did creepe)
> God blesse thee poore Orphane, as he mought me,
> And send thee joy of thy jollitee.
> Thy father (that word she spake with payne:
> For a sigh had nigh rent her heart in twaine)
> Thy father, had he lived this day,
> To see the braunche of his body displaie,
> How would he have joyed at this sweete sight?
> But ah false Fortune such joy did him spight,
> And cutte of hys dayes with untimely woe,
> Betraying him into the traines of hys foe.
> Now I a waylfull widdowe behight,
> Of my old age have this one delight,
> To see thee succeede in thy fathers steade,

And florish in flowres of lusty head.
For even so thy father his head upheld,
And so his hauty hornes did he weld.
    Tho marking him with melting eyes,
A thrilling throbbe from her hart did aryse,
And interrupted all her other speache,
With some old sorowe, that made a newe breache:
Seemed shee sawe in the younglings face
The old lineaments of his fathers grace.
At last her solein silence she broke,
And gan his newe budded beard to stroke.

                                    (182–214)

We are touched by this affecting moment, never more than when we
visualize those lineaments of his father's grace, the haughty horns and
the heroic blossoms of lust that dangle from his chin.

The speaker's delight in portraying the wiles of the fox is closer to the
playful or impious spirit of popular beast fable than to the reform voice:

A Biggen he had got about his braine,
For in his headpeace he felt a sore payne.
His hinder heele was wrapt in a clout,
For with great cold he had gotte the gout.
There at the dore he cast me downe hys pack,
And layd him downe, and groned, Alack, Alack.
Ah deare Lord, and sweete Saint Charitee,
That some good body woulde once pitie mee.

                                    (241–48)

    he, that had well ycond his lere,
Thus medled his talke with many a teare,
Sicke, sicke, alas, and little lack of dead,
But I be relieved by your beastlyhead.
I am a poore Sheepe, albe my coloure donne:
For with long traveile I am brent in the sonne.

                                    (262–67)

The insistence on the animal image and on the physical silliness of the
goat ("creeping close behind the Wickets clinck, / Previlie he peeped out
through a chinck") enforce the discrepancy between manner and matter.
Is the simple animal surface of the tale an allegorical disguise through
which Spenser warns of recusants or dubious Anglicans? Or is it an innocent form of poetic play whose point lies in that very proliferation of
ornament that a puritan allegorist would consider wicked or irrelevant,

or at best a concession to the vulgar mind? The fable wavers uncertainly between its two targets: the allegorical emphasis turns on the falseness of the fox, but the kid's folly answers chiefly to Piers's eagerness to put down the recreative impulse of younkers defended by Palinode. Since its bathos serves neither function, and since we can't ignore the effect of topicality that makes this an "issue-oriented" poem, the attempt to extract a message runs up against the hilarious flowers of the poet's mawkish description. If we take this as characterizing the speaker, it suggests a recreative impulse in Piers himself—a weakness for poetic blossoms, and therefore a chink in his moral armor.

It is thus easy for Palinode to impose his recreative perspective on the fable, stressing its promise as holiday entertainment and reducing Piers's attempt at a message to the bromide that will provide a homiletic pre-text:

> Such end has the Kidde, for he nould warned be
> Of craft, coloured with simplicitie:
> And such end perdie does all hem remayne,
> That of such falsers freendship bene fayne.
>
> PALINODIE.
> Truly Piers, thou art beside thy wit,
> Furthest fro the marke, weening it to hit,
> Now I pray thee, lette me thy tale borrowe
> For our sir John, to say to morrowe
> At the Kerke, when it is holliday:
> For well he meanes, but little can say.
> But and if Foxes bene so crafty, as so,
> Much needeth all shepheards hem to knowe.
>
> PIERS.
> Of their falshode more could I recount.
> But now the bright Sunne gynneth to dismount:
> And for the deawie night now doth nye,
> I hold it best for us, home to hye.
>
> *(302–17)*

On the face of it Piers's moral has an air of plausibility: he wants nothing to do with recreative fools like Palinode because they don't take evil and knavery seriously enough.[9] Yet the fable makes little contact

---

[9] From the moral standpoint, as Herford points out (*Variorum, Minor Poems* 1:306), Palinode is no doubt portrayed ironically, but his comment remains double-edged.

with the themes articulated in his two major speeches (37–54 and 73–131): it touches only superficially on the topic of wolves in shepherd's clothing who, "ful of fraude and guile, / . . . often devoured their owne sheepe"; the topics of inheritance and childrearing are barely visible in the references to the kid's father and mother. Piers loses control of his categories from the start. In saying he would rather have Palinode as a foe than as a friend, he seems to classify him with darkness against light, the lion against the lamb, and the fox against the kid. But the tale switches Palinode to the kid's position, and Piers himself soon becomes a "kiddie unwares" when he succumbs to the recreative delight of telling a fable and scoring against Palinode, who outfoxes him at the end by offering to appropriate the tale for holiday uses. There is thus some justice in Palinode's statement that Piers has missed the mark. By the time he concedes that shepherds should learn about foxes, those figures have been safely desymbolized and restored to their provenance in the rustic world. This profound insight into the perils of animal husbandry comes as an afterthought, for Palinode's main interest is in robbing Piers to pay "our sir John," who needs help on the entertainment front. Given the idyllic world postulated by Palinode, churchgoing is simply another holiday diversion. Piers's final remarks might have been construed as symbolic, in view of his earlier reference to the antipathy between light and dark, but I think Spenser excludes that possibility by insisting on the immediate pastoral context and the standard pastoral conclusion. The shepherds have passed another afternoon in pleasant debate; Piers has eased himself of his griping burden and is now prepared to withdraw, if not to paradise, at least to bed.

As I noted above, various aspects of the reform issue may account for some of the vagaries of Piers's argument. The issue's notoriety sets in greater relief the conspicuous awkwardness of manner, sending the reader's attention back from Elizabethan England to the verbal and semantic infelicities, needless ambiguities of meaning, failures of communication, and deflections from the straight line of argument that Spenser imposes on his poor rustic speakers. If his motive for these was to provide himself with allegorical camouflage, he hit on an engaging method of diversion by making a central theme of the moral eclogues the inadequacy of the artless to verbalize or to reflect on the problems of a world about which they, in their pastoral confines, can know little.

The relation between the limits of pastoral expression and pastoral sensibility receives greater—or at least more explicit—emphasis in *Maye* than in *Februarie*, as we have just seen, and it is even more central in *Julye* and *September* than in *Maye*. This change is effected by a deliberate stylistic maneuver: though the moral issue in *Maye*, *Julye*, and *Sep-*

tember is singly and simply that of corruption in high places, the last two differ from the first in that Spenser solidifies the rustic topography and places it in direct contrast to the great world localized in Rome. It is not clear that Piers and Palinode are looking at the same literal scene, but the rustic landscape of *Julye* and *September* is taken for granted by all parties and is geographically rather than allegorically distinguished from the great world.

Along with this change, a central pastoral motif implied from the beginning becomes explicit: that of aspiration versus retirement. And this motif takes peculiar turns. Though Piers in *Maye* does not actually recommend aspiration except in a negative fashion ("Don't abandon yourself to pleasure, folly, vice"), one gets the *impression* that he does, since Palinode advocates the opposite ("What shoulden shepheards other things tend . . ."). In *Julye*, however, the motif is the nominal theme of the eclogue, and Thomalin, with whom commentators seem to sympathize, equates aspiration with pride.[10] *September* dramatizes the return of the native from a foolish attempt on the great world. But the Piers of *October* argues for poetic aspiration in a manner that looks forward to Spenser's epic poem. The values attached to low and high shift as the pastoral scene gets more concrete and the *low* becomes equated with rustic simplicity, with a range of experience more severely limited to agriculture and husbandry.

The *Julye* low-high debate revisits the dales and hills of the *June* opening: Hobbinol's paradisal dales and Colin's wasteful hills do not simply become the humble versus the proud, though Thomalin may think so:

THOMALIN. MORRELL.

Is not thilke same a goteheard prowde,
    that sittes on yonder bancke,
Whose straying heard them selfe doth shrowde
    emong the bushes rancke?

MORRELL.

What ho, thou jollye shepheards swayne,
    come up the hyll to me:

---

[10] The difference from *Maye* may be seen by comparing the golden-age speeches of Piers and Thomalin. Thomalin's exclusive concern is given only nine lines in Piers's presentation (*Maye* 117–25) and is directly related to the latter's emphasis on the impracticality of vice. Thomalin's criticism is more clearly a matter of outraged principle (*Julye* 125–204). Piers somewhat obscures his point by the wavering surface, the uncertain metaphoric level, of his presentation. But from line 169 on, when Thomalin's tone gets sarcastic, his is a perfectly comprehensible analogy: the great world of Rome is the tenor, and the rustic terms of his own life provide the ironic vehicle. The confusion in this eclogue lies elsewhere, as we shall see.

Better is, then the lowly playne,
    als for thy flocke, and thee.

THOMALIN.
Ah God shield, man, that I should clime,
    and learne to looke alofte,
This reede is ryfe, that oftentime
    great clymbers fall unsoft.
In humble dales is footing fast,
    the trode is not so tickle:
And though one fall through heedlesse hast,
    yet is his misse not mickle.
                    (Julye 1—16)

The moral pose is merely the husk of a practical attitude. Thomalin's real concern is ease and security, and Morrell's reply takes this into account: "Syker, thous but a laesie loord, / and rekes much of thy swinck" (33—34).

Morrell goes on to assert that hills are not bad places since they are holy, beloved of the saints, and—as his examples suggest—places of vision and vigil (37—52). But Thomalin replies with the kind of statement that helped cause the Counter-Reformation in Italy some years before:

The hylls, where dwelled holy saints,
    I reverence and adore:
Not for themselfe, but for the sayncts,
    Which han be dead of yore.
                    (113—16)

The real issue between the shepherds in *Julye* is not ethical but semantic or epistemological: they are quibbling over which symbolism best fits the pastoral locale. There is no need to repeat the kind of analysis applied to *Maye*, since the argument here clearly wavers in the same way between literal and metaphoric statement. If the argument involves Protestant and Catholic viewpoints, it is at a fairly deep level that has to do with modes of thought rather than with immediate dogmatic or political matters.

That the two lines of argument are not contradictory but simply out of phase is made clear in the emblems, Thomalin's "*In medio virtus*" and Morrell's "*In summo fælicitas*."[11] Thomalin's interpretation of *virtus* is

---

[11] Edgar Wind relates this to "the union of balance and transcendence" which Spenser "knew from his study of Italian Neoplatonists" and cites a possible or typical source from

succinctly caught in the gloss: "being both hymselfe sequestred from all ambition and also abhorring it in others of hys cote, he taketh occasion to prayse the meane and lowly state, as that wherein is safetie without feare, and quiet without danger . . . whereto Morrell replieth . . . that albeit all bountye dwelleth in mediocritie, yet perfect felicitye dwelleth in supremacie" (341–48).

The gap between manner and matter is comically manifested by the fable that concludes the eclogue. When Thomalin launches his criticism of corrupt Rome he leaves the physical hills for a purely metaphoric height where shepherds are clearly not shepherds (169–204). Morrell gives the standard response of the moral pastor:

> Here is a great deale of good matter,
>   lost for lacke of telling,
> Now sicker I see, thou doest but clatter:
>   harme may come of melling.
>   *(205–8)*

He then sets up the fable by asking who Algrind is:

> THOMALIN.
> He is a shepheard great in gree,
>   but hath bene long ypent.
> One daye he sat upon a hyll,
>   (as now thou wouldest me:
> But I am taught by Algrins ill,
>   to love the lowe degree.)
>
> For sitting so with bared scalpe,
>   an Eagle sored hye,
> That weening hys whyte head was chalke,
>   a shell fish downe let flye:
> She weend the shell fishe to have broake,
>   but therewith bruzd his brayne,
> So now astonied with the stroke,
>   he lyes in lingring payne.
>
> MORRELL.
> Ah good Algrin, his hap was ill,
>   but shall be better in time.

Pico (*Pagan Mysteries in the Renaissance* [New Haven: Yale University Press, 1958], 53). Here, as on pp. 171–72, Wind's analysis of intellectual content is vivid and suggestive, but his interpretation of Spenser's poetry is relatively crude and imprecise. The emblems assert not a Neoplatonic paradox but a failure of communication.

> Now farwell shepheard, sith thys hyll
> thou hast such doubt to climbe.
>
> *(215–32)*

Shepherds, the moral goes, want to avoid stray objects dropped from the sky. The local hill, which during the eclogue comes to symbolize a number of different things, is once again only a local hill. And the allusion to the death of Aeschylus enforces the comic irrelevance holding between great themes and rude wisdom, between culture and rusticity, between the former age of golden Greece and the simple wit of local farmers. The allusion, which makes the point of the joke, is utterly beyond the rustic speaker. But this tension between serious themes and rustic sensibility is obvious throughout the eclogue, sustained as well as imitated by the verse rhythm with which the shepherds jog in merry rote fashion through the various commonplaces that fit the hill-emblem.

Rustic morality comes to its plaintive demise in *September*. To Hobbinol Spenser assigns a variant of the recreative attitude previously represented by Palinode and Morrell ("Content who lives with tryed state," 70), but the good season is now in the past, not before his eyes; he has grown "so stiffe, and so stanck, / That uneth may I stand any more" (47–48), and his *otium* is a shrunken version of Palinode's. Diggon differs from the other "moral" complainers in being the first speaker to have had firsthand experience of the great world and to bring back the bad news to paradise (at *Julye* 181–83 Thomalin mentions that Palinode has been to Rome and gives his criticism as a secondhand eyewitness report).

Like Hobbinol's, Diggon's sensibility is idyllic; he is of but no longer in the paradise that Hobbinol never left. But Hobbinol's praise of pastoral self-sufficiency is perforce more modest and defensive than it was in *June:*

> Sitte we downe here under the hill:
> Tho may we talke, and tellen our fill,
> And make a mocke at the blustring blast . . .
>
> *(52–54)*

> were Hobbinoll, as God mought please,
> Diggon should soone find favour and ease.
> But if to my cotage thou wilt resort,
> So as I can, I wil thee comfort:
> There mayst thou ligge in a vetchy bed,
> Till fayrer Fortune shewe forth her head.
>
> *(252–57)*

The loss of Colin, which upset Hobbinol in *Aprill*, is mentioned here (176–77) and augmented by the decay of his green world. His viewpoint has been consistently identified with the innocent yet hubristic assumption of eternal paradise in which there is closeness and free intermingling between gods and humans. This assumption characterizes the mind in its garden matrix; it induces unguarded trust both in the gods and in one's own ability, and it is now belied by the inevitable failings of nature and society. Spenser's use of the calendar provides a changing background that throws different mixtures of light and shade on the otiose philosophy to which Hobbinol has too fixedly committed himself. Through his name Spenser pipes the *topoi* of an idyllic discourse, the bearer of limited ideals toward which youth aspires and toward which the culture transmitted from earlier times predisposes the mind. Though Spenser presents these ideals throughout the *Calender* as out of phase or out of date, they are allowed gradually to burgeon and to flourish in the idyllic speakers from *Februarie* to *June*, and they are now on the verge of being newly outmoded as the pastoral year draws to a close.

The significant aspect of *September* is that the winds of corruption blend with the winds of autumn; the geographic distance of the great world—the West—is established only to be negated, for Hobbinol's pastoral retreat is beleaguered both by the western wind "that nowe is in his chiefe sovereigntee, / Beating the withered leafe from the tree" (50–51) and by the bitter blast of Diggon's invective. This pressure makes Hobbinol insecure, both in attitude and in his use of language; as we shall see, he has a hard time keeping Diggon's style at the right level, which means keeping Diggon's disclosures at a proper distance. His gestures of withdrawal are touched by a tendency to shrink or recoil.

This uncertainty is comically asserted in Hobbinol's opening lines: "Diggon Davie, I bidde her god day: / Or Diggon her is, or I missaye." *Missaye* is a key term; both in subject and in style, *September* is the eclogue most directly concerned with failure of communication. So, for example, when Diggon makes a perfectly lucid statement about worldly corruption, Hobbinol scratches his head: false shepherds

> kindle coales of conteck and yre,
> Wherewith they sette all the world on fire:
> Which when they thinken agayne to quench
> With holy water, they doen hem all drench.
> They saye they con to heaven the high way,
> But by my soule I dare undersaye,
> They never sette foote in that same troade,
> But balk the right way, and strayen abroad.

They boast they han the devill at commaund:
But aske hem therefore, what they han paund.
Marrie that great Pan bought with deare borrow,
To quite it from the blacke bowre of sorrowe.
But they han sold thilk same long agoe:
For thy woulden drawe with hem many moe.
But let hem gange alone a Gods name:
As they han brewed, so let hem beare blame.

HOBBINOLL.

Diggon, I praye thee speake not so dirke.
Such myster saying me seemeth to mirke.

DIGGON.

Then playnely to speake of shepheards most what,
Badde is the best (this english is flatt.)

$(86-105)$

What seems to perplex Hobbinol is the abandoning of the pastoral metaphor. To speak plainly would no doubt be to speak of shepherds' "most
what," keeping the level of discourse closer to home. Diggon obliges
with one of the more incomprehensible moments in the history of English poetry and speech (though Spenser, as always, makes the basic
meaning penetrate the verbal fog):

Their ill haviour garres men missay,
Both of their doctrine, and of their faye.
They sayne the world is much war then it wont,
All for her shepheards bene beastly and blont.
Other sayne, but how truely I note,
All for they holden shame of theyr cote.
Some sticke not to say, (whote cole on her tongue)
That sike mischiefe graseth hem emong,
All for they casten too much of worlds care,
To deck her Dame, and enrich her heyre:
For such encheason, If you goe nye,
Fewe chymneis reeking you shall espye:
The fatte Oxe, that wont ligge in the stal,
Is nowe fast stalled in her crumenall.
Thus chatten the people in theyr steads,
Ylike as a Monster of many heads.
But they that shooten neerest the pricke,
Sayne, other the fat from their beards doen lick.
For bigge Bulles of Basan brace hem about,

That with theyr hornes butten the more stoute:
But the leane soules treaden under foote.
And to seeke redresse mought little boote:
For liker bene they to pluck away more,
Then ought of the gotten good to restore.
For they bene like foule wagmoires overgrast,
That if thy galage once sticketh fast,
The more to wind it out thou doest swinck,
Thou mought ay deeper and deeper sinck.
Yet better leave of with a little losse,
Then by much wrestling to leese the grosse.

HOBBINOLL.
Nowe Diggon, I see thou speakest to plaine:
Better it were, a little to feyne,
And cleanly cover, that cannot be cured.
Such il, as it forced, mought nedes be endured.
(106–39)

Diggon is as much concerned with missaying as with misdoing and introduces a primitive forebear of the blatant beast. The effect Spenser seems to be after is that of a verbal smokescreen: the facts of the matter are obscured first by the moral evil of false report, then by Diggon's honest but poor rhetoric. Actually the false report consists of opinions that not only appeared in previous eclogues but that Diggon gave as his own in previous statements (cf. 30–46, 80–101). Hobbinol's response is consistent with his program for pastoral escape—the evil that cannot be cured is better suppressed—thus restating in stronger terms Palinode's "Sorrowe ne neede be hastened on: / For he will come without calling anone" (*Maye* 152–53).

Diggon's fable exemplifies the same theme, for it tells how a facile wolf, a true master of style, turned the shepherd's establishment upside down by dressing like a sheep, barking like a dog, and calling like the shepherd. Spenser's feeling for hayseed gullibility is sharply conveyed in this portrait of the dog: the wolf

oft in the night came to the shepecote,
And called Lowder, with a hollow throte,
As if it the old man selfe had bene.
The dog his maisters voice did it weene,
Yet halfe in doubt, he opened the dore,
And ranne out, as he was wont of yore,
No sooner was out, but swifter than thought,

> Fast by the hyde the Wolfe lowder caught:
> And had not Roffy renne to the steven,
> Lowder had be slaine thilke same even.
>
> *(216–25)*

But the dog, whose thought is not overly swift, tends to symbolize the
speaker. Like the *Maye* and *Julye* fables, the local and literal surface of
Diggon's anecdote shifts the center of attention from the great world to
the more reassuring limits of farm life. The semantic uncertainty of the
discussion leading up to the fable emphasizes the shift, so that we feel the
speakers are trying to console themselves by recoiling from symbol to
letter. After Hobbinol asks Diggon to cloak his complaint in pastoral
terms, the latter obliges by speaking of shepherds, sheep, and "ravenous
Wolves" (141–49), and Hobbinol then objects that there have been no
wolves in Kent or Christendom "sith the Saxon king." The dialogue that
follows careens uncertainly between symbol and letter. Hobbinol continues, "the fewer Woolves (the soth to sayne), / The more bene the
Foxes that here remaine," and Diggon takes this as an allegorical reference to knaves who practice fraud and hypocrisy, "prively prolling two
and froe, / Enaunter they mought be inly knowe" (160–61). But Hobbinol moves the reference back more firmly to animals, forcing Diggon
to distinguish the planes of discourse, after which he himself tells a fable
at the level Hobbinol prefers:

> HOBBINOL.
> Or privie or pert yf any bene,
> We han great Bandogs will teare their skinne.
>
> DIGGON.
> Indeede thy ball is a bold bigge curre,
> And could make a jolly hole in theyr furre.
> But not good Dogges hem needeth to chace,
> But heedy shepheards to discerne their face.
> For all their craft is in their countenaunce,
> They bene so grave and full of mayntenaunce.
> But shall I tell thee what my selfe knowe,
> Chaunced to Roffynn not long ygoe?
>
> *(162–71)*

Because the ills of the great world encroach upon the pastoral microcosm, because the natural and social, or rustic and topical, planes of
reference are uncomfortably mingled, neither Hobbinol nor Diggon
can find much consolation in the recreative situation of tale-telling.

In *September* the cathartic function of poetry and dialogue fails for the first time. "I pray thee," says Diggon, "gall not my old griefe" (12) by asking for an account of the unfortunate journey. But Hobbinol presses him:

> Nay, but sorrow close shrouded in hart
> I know, to kepe, is a burdenous smart.
> Eche thing imparted is more eath to beare:
> When the rayne is faln, the cloudes wexen cleare.
>
> *(15–18)*

Yet the comforting analogy from nature fails to apply. At the end Diggon complains that "all this long tale, / Nought easeth the care, that doth me forhaile" (242–43). The recreative assumption "Poetry whiles your cares away" no longer holds true, not only because the problems of actuality are more insistent here, but also because rustic speech is not the best therapy. The *August* sestina has already shown a better way: Colin's attention is equally divided between his woe and his verse, and almost half the lines are devoted to the subject of decorum (150–59, 159–60, 165–67, 172–75, 182–88). The explicit effect of the *November* elegy is that the singer's woe is wasted. In both cases catharsis has to do with the poet's command of the medium, and in the case of *August* making poems is presented as a surrogate for the frustrated desire to make love:

> Thus all the night in plaints, the daye in woe
> I vowed have to wayst, till safe and sound
> She home returne, whose voyces silver sound
> To cheerefull songs can chaunge my chereless cryes.
>
> *(179–82)*

With its emphasis on saying and missaying, *September* paves the way for the *October* discussion of poetry. The speakers of the moral eclogues are hardly rhetoricians, much less poets. Since the knave manipulates style and therefore seizes power in the great world, it is not enough for the good shepherd to be simple and honest. His sheep

> nill listen to the shepheards voyce,
> But if he call hem at theyr good choyce,
> They wander at wil, and stray at pleasure,
> And to theyr foldes yead at their owne leasure.
> But they had be better come at their cal:
> For many han into mischiefe fall . . .
>
> *(Sept. 142–47)*

The great world *is* corrupt, and this is the problem: someone has to deal with it. Someone needs the knowledge, the shrewdness, the sophistication, and the command of expression to confront the evils and to articulate them with clarity. Where the moral complainer has tried and failed, the idyllic Hobbinol has avoided the confrontation. Like Palinode, he is a little wide-eyed about foxes and wolves: "If sike bene Wolves, as thou hast told, / How mought we Diggon, hem be-hold" (228–29). And when Diggon prescribes perpetual watchfulness, he replies:

> Ah Diggon, thilke same rule were too straight,
> All the cold season to wach and waite.
> We bene of fleshe, men as other bee.
> Why should we be bound to such miseree?
> What ever thing lacketh chaungeable rest,
> Mought needes decay, when it is at best.
>
> *(236–41)*

There is a particle of truth in the statements of both speakers, but they tend toward extreme positions of black-world invective and green-world idyllism. Hobbinol's medical insight can easily provide an excuse for such behavior as that of the shepherd in *Virgils Gnat,* who can scarcely walk two steps without sinking exhausted into a profound slumber. The same regimen is prescribed by old Melibee in *Faerie Queene* VI.ix.23: "when I wearie am, I downe doe lay / My limbes in every shade, to rest from toyle." Spenser shows how the topic "vain aspiration" can function as a euphemism for laziness, and Melibee is the final example of the recreative or plaintive pastor posing as moral.

October is not so much a fifth "moral" eclogue as a consequence of the process I have been tracing. It is a response to the vacuum that must be filled by truly moral, truly committed poets and rhetoricians. But it is a tentative and unsatisfactory response, not a final answer, in keeping with Spenser's critical attitude. Though both speakers are in substantial disagreement over the relations of poets and poetry to the actual world, both are influenced by the same golden-age sensibility. Cuddie sees poetry as controlled by the poet's external conditions, while Piers sees actual conditions as ideally subordinate to poetry and the life of the poet's mind. Yet neither wants to deal with corruption in the actual world; both shrink from confrontation. Cuddie withdraws in defeat while Piers converts to a gesture of escape, the Neoplatonic preference for aspiration beyond the mundane world.

For the plaintive Cuddie the poet receives nothing from within himself. Poetry is neither economically nor imaginatively self-sufficient: the poet must rely on patrons to supply his wants, heroes his subjects, and wine his inspiration. The example of Colin suggests to him that even the common personal theme—love—provides more of an obstacle than a subject: "The vaunted verse a vacant head demaundes, / Ne wont with crabbed care the Muses dwell" (100–101). In his view the exemplary older poet Tityrus (Vergil) owed his success mainly to the luck of having Maecenas behind him and Augustus before his eyes. But that was long ago and the world is old. For Piers, meanwhile, everything comes from within (or above) the poet: heaven and love inspire him; the moral and pleasurable influences of his art radiate into society, which rewards him with glory; the shape of the poet's career is determined not by success or patronage but by the rhythm his own interests impose. Piers seems to make a gesture in the direction of poetry's didactic power: "O what an honor is it, to restraine / The lust of lawlesse youth with good advice." But the next two lines reveal a broader interest that includes pleasure no less than profit: "Or pricke them forth with pleasaunce of thy vaine, / Whereto thou list their trayned willes entice" (21–24). The following stanza entertains an idyllic fantasy of poetic domination modeled on the dream or myth of Orphic power, a concept that ignores such difficulties as those indicated in the introductory verses to the *Calender* ("To His Booke") as well as in the reference made by other moral pastors to the unresponsiveness of the great world. A sign of this avoidance is the conspicuous exclusion of Orpheus's failure to save Eurydice:

> Soone as thou gynst to sette thy notes in frame,
> O how the rurall routes to thee doth cleave:
> Seemeth thou dost their soule of sence bereave,
> All as the shepheard, that did fetch his dame
> From Plutoes balefull bowre withouten leave:
> His musicks might the hellish hound did tame.
> *(25–30)*

The *October* debate leads Piers to turn his back on the world:

> O pierlesse Poesye, where is then thy place?
> If nor in Princes pallace thou doe sitt:
> (And yet is Princes pallace the most fitt)
> Ne brest of baser birth doth thee embrace.
> Then make thee winges of thine aspyring wit,
> And, whence thou camst, flye back to heaven apace.
> *(79–84)*

The motif of the return to heaven has a special significance for Spenser, parallel to the return—or longing to return—to paradise. In the mythology of *The Faerie Queene*, Book V, the radical counterswing from Saturn's golden to Jove's iron age is signified by the departure from earth of Astraea, whose virginity symbolizes classical disdain and self-withholding exclusiveness. Her desire to retain in its purity a ruthlessly idealistic and aprioristic justice is related to the feeling entertained by the speaker of the proem—that the present decay of justice, politics, and ethics may have been determined from creation by the mechanics of physical change, so that nothing can be done about it:

> Me seemes the world is runne quite out of square,
> From the first point of his appointed sourse,
> And being once amisse growes daily wourse and wourse.
>
> *(FQ V.Pr.1)*

Astraea left the world as soon as it fell from perfection "into all filth and foule iniquitie" (V.i.5):

> Now when the world with sinne gan to abound,
> Astraea loathing lenger here to space
> Mongst wicked men, in whom no truth she found,
> Return'd to heaven, whence she deriv'd her race;
> Where she hath now an everlasting place . . .
>
> *(i.11)*

Astraea's return to heaven is also mentioned at the beginning of *Mother Hubberds Tale,* where it suggests the poet's urge to escape from the corruption of the world and from the unspecified "wicked maladie" infecting him and many others—"that manie did to die, / Depriv'd of sense and ordinarie reason" (10–11)—a "common woe" suspiciously echoed in the "paine and inward agonie" (a sort of generalized *accidia* or *anomie*) of which the fox complains in lines 52–70. Embodying, and in effect exorcizing, this urge to escape in the figure of the pure classical virgin, the poet stays in the world and tries to cope with the disease by adopting the mask (*prosopon*) of "a good old woman . . . / Hight Mother Hubberd, who did farre surpas / The rest in honest mirth" (33–35), but who was no poet (43–44). She was among the friends who tried to console him in his illness with "pleasant tales": some "of Ladies, and their Paramoures," some "of brave Knights, and their renowned Squires," others of Faeries and giants (17–32), and finally Mother Hubberd's tale of honest mirth. This range of topics closely resembles that ascribed to Tityrus (tales of truth, youth, love, and chivalry in *Februarie,* "mery tales" in *June*), and it suggests once more the need for a new "Chaucerian" art to reinforce the humane impulses of those whose courage and sympathy and patience keep them in the troubled world: the selection of pleasant though literary tales delighted and relieved the ailing poet, but Mother Hubberd's "base . . . and . . . meane" fable was more adequate to the sad occasion.

Within the *Calender* the moral mode degenerates into the plaintive mode when dominated by the recreative desire for paradise. To present this critically, as Spenser does, is to reveal the true moral bias underlying the poem in its totality. But this bias is primarily manifested by his pleasure in his art. The poet's recreative or meta-recreative mode is a function of literary self-delight and aesthetic detachment. Gratuitous interest in the poetic activity, the play of imagination, and the exploration of his chosen medium is an end in itself to the fledgling poet, who became an artist because "he was more deeply moved by his . . . experience of works of art than by that of the things they represent. . . . Artists . . . stem . . . from their conflict with the achievements of their predecessors . . . their struggle with the form which others have imposed on life." [12] As Robert Frost has suggested, the artist is initially more fascinated by technique and medium than by the world's problems:

> There is a time of apprenticeship to texture when it shouldn't matter if the stuff is never made up into anything. There may be scraps of repeated form all over it. But form as a whole! Don't be shocking! The title of his first book was *Fragments*. The artist has to grow up and coarsen a little before he looks on texture as not an end in itself. [13]

The Shepheardes Calender is Spenser's second book, *Fragments Reconsidered*, the moment of revision in which the poet looks back from a standpoint of greater experience to reconstruct his literary innocence and to record his youthful fall or progress from the recreative garden. Colin Clout is Spenser's image of the fledgling imagination in its purest form, disporting itself in the Muses' garden of conventions and reluctant to pass through the gate into the world. Spenser himself, now evaluating the achievements of his predecessors from the other side of the garden wall, has discarded Colin's idyllicism but not his delight in artifice.

This meta-recreative pleasure is no less clear in Spenser's treatment of the moral speakers than in such obvious instances as the *Aprill* blazon. The deliberateness of his experiment in simulating rustic speech has often been remarked, but its particular contribution to the themes I have

[12] André Malraux, *The Voices of Silence*, trans. Stuart Gilbert (Garden City: Doubleday, 1953), 281.
[13] "The Constant Symbol," in *The Poems of Robert Frost* (New York: Random House, 1946), xv. On the poet's early career, see my "Biography as Interpretation, Interpretation as Biography," *College English* 28 (1966): 114–15.

been exploring remains to be discussed. Here again I shall begin by re-
shuffling some of E. K.'s observations. In his remarks on diction in the
epistle to Harvey he plods with his usual heavy-footed gait through two
familiar fields. The first is the theory of literary imitation, and the following passage is clearer if we bear in mind that he is speaking of earlier
English, not classical, authors:

> having the sound of those auncient Poetes still ringing in his eares, he mought
> needes in singing hit out some of theyr tunes. But whether he useth them by
> such casualtye and custome, or of set purpose and choyse, as thinking them
> fittest for such rusticall rudenesse of shepheards, eyther for that theyr rough
> sounde would make his rymes more ragged and rustical, or els because such
> olde and obsolete wordes are most used of country folke . . . they bring great
> grace and . . . auctoritie to the verse. For albe amongst many other faultes it
> specially be objected of Valla against Livie, and of other against Saluste, that
> with over much studie they affect antiquitie, as coveting thereby credence
> and honor of elder yeeres, yet I am of opinion, and eke the best learned are
> of the lyke, that those auncient solemne wordes are a great ornament both in
> the one and in the other; the one labouring to set forth in hys worke an eter-
> nall image of antiquitie, and the other carefully discoursing matters of gravi-
> tie and importaunce. (45–62)

What is notable for my purpose is the learned irrelevance of the closing
analogy, for it is not easy to see how we are to reconcile the praise of
rustic decorum with the reference to ancient solemn words and the eternal image of antiquity. The problem is that Spenser knows two quite
different kinds of antiquity: one is classical, learned, and symbolic of the
Golden Age of civilization; the other is primitive, rude, and symbolic of
the green origins of culture. The first form of antiquity is *senex* and the
second *puer* or *virgo*.

E. K. has in mind only the second form both in the above passage and
in the attack on borrowing that follows:

> This Poete . . . hath laboured to restore, as to theyr rightfull heritage such
> good and naturall English words, as have ben long time out of use and al-
> most cleane disherited. Which is the onely cause, that our Mother tonge . . .
> hath long time ben counted most bare and barrein of both. Which default
> . . . some endevoured to salve and recure [by borrowing] . . . of other lan-
> guages. . . . Other some not so wel seene in the English tonge as perhaps in
> other languages, if they happen to here an old word albeit very naturall and
> significant, crye out streight way, that we speak no English, but gibbrish, or
> rather such, as in old time Evanders mother spake. . . . of their owne coun-
> try and natural speach, which together with their Nources milk they sucked,

they have so base regard and bastard judgement, that they will not onely themselves not labor to garnish and beautifie it, but also repine, that of other it shold be embellished. (90–119)

Antiquarian and nativist, E. K. adheres faithfully to the criterion of decorum.[14] But in his practice the author of Spenser's poetry reveals, at the levels both of diction and of general thought, the historical consciousness of a modernist and eclectic who knows that the *discordia concors* of any system—whether poem or world—changes and develops through the continual combining and recombining of simple elements into new forms. His attitude toward native purity of the old language does not seem to differ from that of his teacher, Richard Mulcaster, who says of the objection to borrowings:

> If this opinion had bene allwaie maintained, we had allwaie worn old Adams pelts, we must still have eaten, the poets akecorns, & never have sought corn, we must cleve to the eldest and not to the best.[15]

It is therefore not sufficient to attribute Spenser's rustic impersonation to antiquarianism or to mere respect for decorum. These might characterize the intention of a poet like Turbervile, who remarks that "as ye conference betwixt Shephierds is familiar stuffe & homely: so have I shapt my stile and tempred it with suche common and ordinarie phrase of speech as Countreymen do use in their affaires." But Turbervile also praises the wisdom of these shepherds of old Mantua: "They were not in that age such siellie sottes as our Shephierdes are nowe a dayes."[16] Spenser, who no doubt read Turbervile's Mantuan, would have found there something to parody, not to imitate. For by the time we have moved through the four strictly "moral" or satirical eclogues to *September*, it might occur to us that Spenser's view of such shepherds as Thenot and Cuddie, Piers and Palinode, Morell and Thomalyn, and Diggon Davie, is no different from Dr. Johnson's: "Surely, at the same time that a shep-

---

[14] E. K.'s view has persisted. See, e.g., H. S. V. Jones, *A Spenser Handbook* (New York: Appleton-Century-Crofts, 1930), 48–49. Jones cites with approval the following statement by C. H. Herford: "Spenser as the disciple of the old poet and the lover of his archaic speech, defends the reverence for antiquity, of which all his own poetry is a monument."

[15] *The Elementarie of Richard Mulcaster*, ed. E. T. Campagnac (Oxford: Oxford University Press, 1925), 276. Quoted from Veré Rubel, *Poetic Diction in the English Renaissance from Skelton through Spenser* (New York: MLA Publications, 1941), 105.

[16] Quoted from Rubel, 112–13.

herd learns theology, he may gain some acquaintance with his native language." [17]

Satirical invective in the *Calender* is always to some extent genuine and "moral" because Spenser directs the conventional topics of criticism through pastoral mouths toward what he means us to understand as actually corrupt states of affairs. Having thus established the need for reform, he shows that the need will not be met by rural complainers who flee the future by withdrawing into the past or who flee the great world by consoling themselves with the simpler and more controllable government of the barnyard community. But it is obviously no tragedy to Spenser that a potentially moral response degenerates into plaintive withdrawal. For the controlling tone and attitude embodied in and as *The Shepheardes Calender* is recreative—or, to distinguish it from the more limited recreative sensibilities of idyllic shepherds, meta-recreative. Since the *Calender* produces its effect by critically miming features of the genre it claims simultaneously to revive and to revise or overgo, we might emphasize its deconstructive motive by calling it *strong pastoral* or metapastoral and opposing it to the *weak pastoral* of the traditional modes its mimicry evokes and, in the act of evocation, destroys. Metapastoral depends on a genre, a tradition, a victim that, if not already existing, it would create. Metapastoral consists, first, of the motivational critique of the system of values embedded in the psychology of withdrawal or escape; second, of the intertextual critique of the way pastoral conventions idealize their literariness along with the psychological experience they represent; third, of the reflexive critique, by any particular work, of its own commitment to the genre.

Metapastoral explores the dangers of the desire of literariness and—I hesitate to add—of the literariness of desire, and it explores the dangers of its own power to encourage misanthropy and escape under the justifying banner of Art. Poets in the great metapastoral tradition—Theocritus, Virgil, Spenser, Shakespeare, Marvell, Milton, and Pope, to name a few—critically or ironically portray states of mind through the "mouths" of fictional "speakers." But the speakers are clearly the embodied representatives of the cultural discourses or language games—including the game of poetry—conspicuously reduced in the pastoral form of life. The psychology of pastoralism is anonymous; it is a cultural construction discernible in—and discerned as active in—particular conventions. The states of mind involved are sedimented, preserved, re-

[17] *Variorum, Minor Poems* 1:575; from *Rambler*, 24 July 1750, no. 37.

produced, modified, in those discursive practices. It is the practice, discourse, or language game that "speaks through" the pastoral speaker, brings him into being as a puppet modeling states of mind, and often displaces him from the metapastoral *text* as the focus or scapegoat of the critique it levels at pastoral states of mind.

Afterword (1987)

The preceding chapter was written well before the others in this study of *The Shepheardes Calender*. It was part of a projected book on the *Calender* that I began in 1959, worked on periodically until 1965, and tinkered with in 1967–68 before being dissatisfied enough with it to put it on the shelf. The remainder of that draft was thoroughly overhauled when I next had the nerve to look at it, which was between 1979 and 1982. Some of the revisions have appeared piecemeal in various publications, but the chapter on the moral mode festered inert until I decided that I couldn't publish the present study of the *Calender* without some account of that topic and of the eclogues relevant to it. Owing perhaps to a slackening of standards that comes with age or second childhood, I decided that the errors of my misspent youth were less abominable than I once thought. And owing to a decline in energy that comes from spending the better part of thrice twenty years straining over a tepid typewriter, I decided to include the chapter on the moral mode pretty much as it was when I hid it away in 1968. A few pages have been touched up: the section on *Maye* has been shortened and partly rewritten, much of the *October* discussion has been transferred from material produced during the 1979–80 revision, and the brief concluding remarks on metapastoral were written for a different essay in 1985.

The occasion that prompted me to add this afterword was my encounter with a recent essay by Annabel Patterson, "Re-opening the Green Cabinet: Clément Marot and Edmund Spenser."[18] Patterson's thesis is that "in the *Calender* . . . Marot stood for Spenser as an intermediary between himself and Vergil" (p. 44):

We can safely assume that Spenser accepted Marot as a model for how to proceed in writing the pastoral of state, or, more precisely, in adapting to the needs of a modern European nation the Vergilian strategy of address to those in power. . . . But we must also now recognize that Marot represented a

[18] *English Literary Renaissance*, 16 (1986): 44–70.

more problematic example of that process than even Vergil himself, one that considerably extended the terms of confrontation within the forms of accommodation. . . . By citing a French poet as one of his major models, . . . but by choosing one whose ideology set him retroactively more clearly among the victims than the protegés of the French monarchy, Spenser placed himself in a position with respect to the pastoral of state that was not uncomplicated, but consistent with his own choice of patron (Sidney) and his connections (through Singleton [his publisher]) with the oppositionist press. (pp. 58–59)

Patterson concedes Louis Montrose's point that the *Calender* "has as one of its subjects the poet's power 'to create illusions which sanctify political power,' and his natural ambition to be rewarded for doing so," but she insists on the importance of "its *other* subject, to which Spenser gave more than equal time," namely, "the poet's responsibility to suggest *latenter* what is wrong with the system, and the dangers he may incur by doing so" (p. 70). Noting that one of the meanings of *cabinet* is "a place of secrets" and that E. K.'s gloss is conspicuous for its lack of "any satisfactory account of the meaning of the different eclogues, or of the intentions of the work as a whole"—she finds him "deliberately evasive" and consistently "provocative" in his refusals to explain—she argues that one "function of E. K.'s apparatus is . . . to reveal *by failing to reveal* the mysteries of the text" (pp. 67, 69). This argument is in line with her more sustained study of "the hermeneutics of censorship" in early modern England, the thesis of which is that in this period "'literature' . . . was conceived in part as the way round censorship," as the medium in which "the institutionally unspeakable makes itself heard inferentially, in the space between what is written or acted and what the audience, *knowing what they know*, might expect to read or see." She views "the prevailing codes of communication, the implicit social contract between authors and authorities, as being intelligible to all parties at the time, as being a fully deliberate and conscious arrangement." [19]

Patterson's is in part a polemic against what is variously called the aestheticism, idealism, or humanism of the New-Critical practice that I to some extent pursued and that Montrose has justly criticized in the introduction to this volume. The preceding section on the moral eclogues is a fairly good example of the limits of that practice. In it I write diffusely of the problems of "the great world," "corrupt states of affairs," the need

[19] *Censorship and Interpretation: The Conditions of Writing and Reading in Early Modern England* (Madison: University of Wisconsin Press, 1984), 63, 17.

for a "moral" poetry that engages questions of reform, and so on. But I pay little or no attention to the identification of specific political issues such as those, for example, that concerned Paul McLane, whose "systematic attempt to uncover the topical significance of the *Calender*" was available to me at the time.[20] Patterson's studies have taught me that I could have greatly reinforced my reading of the moral eclogues by taking those issues into account. But I could have done this without changing what I wrote. For neither McLane nor Patterson engages in a close reading of the eclogues. From my standpoint their studies have, like doughnuts, a hole in the middle where interpretation ought to be.

I can indeed profit from Patterson's hypothesis of "a fully deliberate and conscious arrangement" in which both reading and writing were undertaken "with suspicion" and in which censorship encouraged conventions of duplicity. The hypothesis supports the idea that Spenser's topical allusions would be easily identified and that E. K.'s evasive gestures would direct attention to them. But the hypothesis doesn't in any way engage or obviate the textual data on the basis of which I have tried to characterize Spenser's meta-recreative critique of his moral speakers. On the contrary, it supports the idea that Spenser ingeniously added a third subject to the two Patterson itemized above: if the poet has a responsibility "to suggest *latenter* what is wrong with the system," one way to do this is to show speakers who try to suggest but lack the skill to suggest *latenter* what is wrong, and to motivate the failed latency by inscribing it in breakdowns of communication due in part to the speakers' commitment to the dominant discourse of traditional pastoral, the discourse of the paradise principle. The more specific and recognizable the topical issues are, the more conspicuous the *effect* of failed latency.

When this third subject is factored in, the critique of the politico-religious system is glimpsed darkly through the veil of another critique, whose target is the failure of the Mantuanesque tradition to supply adequate moral and expressive means to articulate the first critique. This view decisively shifts the center of the *Calender*'s overall subject from the topical and political focus to one that is intertextually reflexive (meta-pastoral) and, in that respect, "aesthetic." It is not, however, an aestheticized reading but one that fixes on the intersection of and tension between aesthetic and political concerns. If critics of such a reading are to argue against it, they must begin by demonstrating the results of their

---

[20] The quotation (from Patterson, "Re-opening the Green Cabinet," 60) refers to Spenser's *"Shepheardes Calender."*

own close reading and must meet the challenge by offering counterinterpretations on the same level. It is foolish to argue, as many recent critics have, for a moratorium on close reading and an end to New-Critical practice. Practitioners of close reading must continuously modify their assumptions and methods to open up the green cabinet to a form of interpretation that is ideologically and politically more sensitive. But neither they nor their critics can afford to give up the practice.

The Mirror Stage of Colin Clout

COMMENTING ON Colin Clout's wintry analogizing in *Januarye*, Isabel MacCaffrey writes that "a sympathetic Nature offers ready emblems for the human psyche. It is the basic justification for pastoral, and as numerous Renaissance texts testify, the reciprocity of inner and outer worlds was based on something more solid than what Ruskin later termed the pathetic fallacy."[1] This way of putting it raises questions that place us directly before the chief problematical aspects of the eclogue. Why does MacCaffrey herself employ pathetic fallacy in personifying Nature? Is it to suggest the pastoral paradox that *nature* is really a synonym for *art*? Since she argues in her essay on the *Calender* that Spenser shows the inadequacy of Nature's ready emblems,[2] does she mean to imply that this "justification" and "reciprocity" may be characteristic of the naive versions of pastoral that Spenser criticizes? MacCaffrey does not confront these issues because the above passage is an aside that gives way immediately to a discussion of Britomart's employment of the ocean-passion analogy in *Faerie Queene* III.iv. But the questions implicit in her statement may profitably be submitted to the arbitration of the eclogues them-

[1] *Spenser's Allegory: The Anatomy of Imagination* (Princeton: Princeton University Press, 1976), 292–93.
[2] "Allegory and Pastoral in *The Shepheardes Calender*," *ELH* 36 (1969).

selves; hence I use them to frame the doorway leading over the dedicatory lintel and into the eclogue named after Janus.

I

Since *nature* in the *Calender* means primarily a set of references to their
environment by imaginary speakers, the semantic problem about the
status of references to nature is inseparable from the rhetorical or dramatic problem about the ethical status of those speakers. For how can the
aspects of nature they mention be any more "real," "three-dimensional,"
or (above all) autonomous and autotelic than the speakers themselves are?
From the outset their status is placed in question by the coy manner in
which Spenser adopts the mask of Immerito and then duplicates this act
when he, or Immerito, gives way to Colin Clout.

The dedicatory poem that performs the first of these two conventional
reductions is a parodic display of *sprezzatura*. Spenser flaunts his artful
facility in striking artless poses and shows his mastery of the convention
in which claims to worthlessness, anonymity, inadequacy, and so on, are
stated to be discounted.[3] The modesty *topos* is deployed along two fronts
at once, political and literary. He plays the humble suitor seeking Sidney's protection against the blatant beast of envy so as to imply that his
book contains matter interesting enough to make him hide his identity
(which only adds to the interest). At the same time he evokes and stands
in the legitimizing shadow of the two poets he aspires to emulate and
overgo, the two traditions—native and classical—he draws on and combines (Cain, 30). The opening words of the poem remind us of Chaucer
and of the pastoral image of Virgil:

> *Goe little booke: thy selfe present,*
> *As child whose parent is unkent:*
> *To him that is the president*
> *Of noblesse and of chevalree,*
> *And if that Envie barke at thee,*
> *As sure it will, for succoure flee*
> > *Under the shadow of his wing,*
> *And asked, who thee forth did bring,*
> *A shepheards swaine saye did thee sing,*
> *All as his straying flocke he fedde:*

---

[3] Cf. Thomas H. Cain, "Spenser and the Renaissance Orpheus," *University of Texas
Quarterly* 41 (1971): 30; Spenser's use of the "inability-topos" makes it "a protestation of
modesty and at the same time an advertisement."

> *And when his honor has thee redde,*
> *Crave pardon for my hardyhedde.*
> *But if that any aske thy name,*
> *Say thou wert base begot with blame:*
> *For thy thereof thou takest shame.*
> *And when thou art past jeopardee,*
> *Come tell me, what was sayd of mee:*
> *And I will send more after thee.*
>
> *Immeritô.*

The tetrameters and triple rhymes lend an air of simplicity visually enhanced, in the first edition, by large, well-spaced italic print filling a page that faces the much smaller and more crowded roman print of E. K.'s pedantic epistle. The combination of triple rhyme and tetrameters itself makes the simplicity hyperbolic, and it is marked as pretense or caricature not only by subtly varied patterns of enjambment but also by the vigor and fluency of diction.

Spenser's *sprezzatura* thus extends to his easy control of prosody and beyond that to the wit and rhetoric that signal mastery of the tonal etiquette of courtiership. The puns on *unkent* ("unknown" and "unkempt") and *president* testify to this, as does the reference to envy, which is a boast thinly masked as apprehensiveness. Similarly the professions of low status are phrased so as to seem false—mere defenses against envy. The directions to his book, which are simultaneously performatives addressed to Sidney, are confidently voiced, revealing a knowledgeable worldliness that belies as another pretense the innocent's need "for succoure." Finally, the playful archness and aggressiveness of the concluding tercet belie the signature humbly prostrate at the bottom of the page. Louis Montrose, from whose essays on pastoral and courtiership I have greatly profited, notes that "this conjunction of humility and pride exemplifies the pastoral poet's capacity to strike ambivalent poses."[4] Montrose goes on to state that "Spenser articulates a tense relationship to literary and social patriarchy," and at least in the case of Immerito's little poem I would argue that the tenseness is mimed rather than dramatized. Spenser refers to the existence of envy as a predictable response to his work but scarcely seems anxious about it; he all but commands its appearance. The reference is witty and high-spirited, it has (as I suggested) the force of a disguised boast, and it is used with a certain *brio* to justify the necessity of adopting the conventional mask of humility.

---

[4] "'The perfecte paterne of a Poete': The Poetics of Courtship in *The Shepheardes Calender*," *Texas Studies in Language and Literature* 21 (1979): 36.

When we turn from Immerito to Colin Clout we shall find that Spenser's handling of these two reductions differs, and the difference throws considerable light on the way he conceives the "mode of existence" of his pastoral speakers. Neither is an autonomous character to whom an interpreter may apply ethical criteria, but Immerito has even less fictional substance than Colin—as little, in fact, as that possessed by the subject of the following lines: "A shepheards swaine saye did thee sing, / All as his straying flocke he fedde." The lines glance toward a story, a setting, an implication of "nature," but "saye" aborts these possibilities. Immerito is a mere passing tone mediating the transition from Spenser to what Richard Helgerson has nicely called the "melodious self-pity" of Colin Clout.[5] Immerito, "the persona of the poet who has written the *Calender*" (Montrose, 36), is as transparent as the pastoral image he uses, and if all the *Calender*'s speakers were equally transparent the reader would be encouraged to be more energetic in his allegorical labors, diverting the references to sheep, shepherds, and song more quickly from the objects they name to secondary referents in the world not of the personae but of the poet.

II

Spenser begins *Januarye* by distancing and lowering Colin even as he establishes a link to him and uses phrases that recall Immerito:

> A Shepeheards boye (no better doe him call)
> When Winters wastful spight was almost spent,
> All in a sunneshine day, as did befall,
> Led forth his flock, that had bene long ypent.
> So faynt they woxe, and feeble in the folde,
> That now unnethes their feete could them uphold.
>
> All as the Sheepe, such was the shepeheards looke,
> For pale and wanne he was, (alas the while,)
> May seeme he lovd, or els some care he tooke:
> Well couth he tune his pipe, and frame his stile.
> Tho to a hill his faynting flocke he ledde,
> And thus him playnd, the while his shepe there fedde.

Immerito's pastoral image is echoed and amplified, and the parenthetical phrase in the opening line is an inelegant variation of *Immerito*. In the

---

[5] "The New Poet Presents Himself: Spenser and the Idea of a Literary Career," *PMLA* 93 (1978): 899.

dedicatory poem it is not clear whether we are meant to distinguish between Immerito as "swaine" and Spenser as the shepherd (thus interposing another pastoral mask), but here the distinction is less casual, more marked, so that we assume Colin to be Spenser/Immerito's "boye." The connection between them is maintained in the second line: on the one hand the alliterative stressing and the incipient personification of winter anticipate Colin's standard procedure, but on the other hand "Winters," while capitalized, is not italicized, and unlike Colin his author minimizes winter's "spight," punctuating his optimism with a reference to the sunny day. This presages "the return of spring and the renewal of life," and by the same token prepares us to view as excessive Colin's feeling "that his spring once lost can never be recovered."[6]

The continuity binding Colin to Spenser/Immerito is also stressed by two putatively different speakers' sharing the same stanza form and the same penchant for alliteration. When Colin begins to speak, the effect of the change of voices is comparable to what would happen if an actor, after speaking in his own voice, spoke through an ancient theatrical mask equipped with a megaphonic amplifying device—a *prosōpon,* or better, a *persona* (etymologically linked by Boethius to *per-sonando*). Miming Colin, Spenser exaggerates the prosodic and pathetic features of his introductory stanzas so that while his pleasure in artifice merges with Colin's, he also lets us distinguish his pleasure in mimicry from Colin's pleasure in the arts of singing and savoring pain. Hence it is difficult to isolate Colin and view him as an autonomous or "round" character. Framing a style he identifies as his own, Spenser/Immerito hands it to the "boye" into which he "folds" himself. Colin becomes his fold and his pipe, a kind of pastoral and prosodic enclosure built "of lighter timber cotes" (*Dec.* 77) within whose narrow lines the poet pens his voice. Or perhaps we could liken Spenser-playing-Colin to the wolf in sheep's clothing.

After comparing Colin to his forlorn flock, Immerito marks his detachment from Colin's personal affairs with a conjecture ("May seeme he lovd, or els some care he tooke") the tone of which casually understates Colin's most pressing concerns, and he follows this with a more assured opinion in line 10, the verdict of a professional on a colleague's skill.[7]

---

[6] John W. Moore, Jr., "Colin Breaks His Pipe: A Reading of the 'January' Eclogue," *English Literary Renaissance* 5 (1975): 16. See Bruce R. Smith, "On Reading *The Shepheardes Calender*," in *Spenser Studies I,* ed. Patrick Cullen and Thomas Roche (Pittsburgh: University of Pittsburgh Press, 1980), 86–87.

[7] Nancy Jo Hoffman thinks this line indicates that the narrator "is as much in the dark as we" about the source of Colin's woe, which would be odd if (as I believe) there is truth

Though the second response seems unrelated to the first, the two are separated, or joined, by a colon rather than a full stop, and they converge two lines later in the phrase "thus him playnd," for we see *play* in *playnd* and feel the force of a conventional motif: the metamorphosis of pain into poetry, sorrow into song, with the implication that pain and sorrow are part of the *playing*. *Playning* combines *play* with *payne*, and the ethical dative (*"him* playnd") signifies that Colin is no less part of his own audience than the gods he invokes. Complaint is expected to give pleasure, and pain may therefore be cherished as well for the artfulness with which it can be amplified as for the art into which it is sure to be transformed. These introductory lines, then, enable us to infer Spenser/Immerito's view of some of the expectations generated by the pastoral paradigm. They are at most implied, not in any way evaluated, but they provide a backdrop against which Colin's performance may be judged. The expectations are more clearly focused when Colin in the next stanza singles out Pan for special attention, alluding to his encounter with Syrinx.

While locating the relevant thematic features of the many-sided Pan, such an allusion is not particularly reverent, and John Moore has remarked a "note of ambivalence" in Colin's invocation. Moore sees it as "both a petition for divine pity and a test of the gods' loving relationship to him," and he connects this mixed tone with a departure from convention:

> Where the conventional amorous pastoral eclogue begins with a complaint to the reluctant mistress, "January" does not begin by imploring Rosalind for pity; it begins by appealing to the gods for pity. In the first stanza, the gods of love and Pan appear as the source of the comfort he seeks and, like the conventional mistress, they are presented as aloof and indifferent, withholding the perfect happiness he wishes them to share with him. By this revision of the conventions Spenser makes the gods the reluctant mistress of Colin's song and not Rosalind. (p. 9)

> Ye Gods of love, that pitie lovers payne,
> (If any gods the paine of lovers pitie:)

---

in her previous assertion that Spenser's "single characters are merely convenient vehicles for expressing emblematic human moods and circumstances" (*Spenser's Pastorals: "The Shepheardes Calender" and "Colin Clout"* [Baltimore: Johns Hopkins University Press, 1977], 44). This remark detracts from the novelty of Spenser's approach: they are indeed vehicles but at the same time they have enough autonomy to model attitudes from which the author at least partly dissociates himself. The understated conjecture has the effect of a stage direction suggesting that we not take too seriously what Colin is about to take terribly seriously: "he seemed troubled about something or other." Furthermore, "some care he tooke" conveys more willfulness than, e.g., "some care him tooke" (see below).

> Looke from above, where you in joyes remaine,
> And bowe your eares unto my dolefull dittie.
> And *Pan* thou shepheards God, that once didst love,
> Pitie the paines, that thou thy selfe didst prove.
>
> *(13–18)*

Moore inaccurately conflates "the gods of love and Pan" and soon ignores the former to concentrate on the latter, arguing that Colin serves the wrong god in serving "Pan, the amorous nature god," that he must choose "between divine love and erotic" and "seek his values not in the temporary and fragile beauty of nature's spring, but in the enduring beauty of heaven's eternal springtime" where he will find a "harvest free of mutability" (pp. 12, 22–23). Moore detects a glimmer of hope under Colin's bushel of January despair: "Colin's false values have revealed their inadequacy and prepared him for a possible spring-like birth of a better set of values" (p. 23). *Januarye* is the first step in a "spiritual odyssey" that takes him "from allegiance to Pan, the nature God, to the real Pan, the real All, Christ" (p. 22).

My own view is that if Colin makes an odyssey through the *Calender* it is not so much toward increasing spirituality as toward increasing petulance, which by *December* attains to heaven only in the sense that it assumes cosmic proportions. Moore's emphasis on the problematical and central significance of Pan nevertheless strikes me as an important insight, and to expropriate it from the high road of Christian wayfaring I shall return to consider Colin's January petulance at closer range. It makes its first appearance in the parenthetical second line of his invocation and is sharpened by the contrast to his own sad case implied in the next line—"where *you* in joyes remaine." Whoever these gods are—and that there are more than one rules out Christianity—their high altitude, joy, and success will probably keep them from appreciating the intense pain and failure reverberating from the "barrein ground" where a mere shepherd's boy makes rural music.[8] Hence Colin turns to address a god who dwells below, and with less deference he imposes a claim on Pan by reminding the goat-god of *his* past failure: "that once didst love" carries the implication that the Ovidian *amator* may have retired from the field in defeat and now, presumably, consoles himself with his (and his devotees') music. Colin rejects Pan's example: he will give up music and remain, defeated, in the field.

---

[8] Colin's reaction to the gods will be echoed by another subject of Spenser's critical portraiture, Alcyon in *Daphnaida* (183 ff.), and Alcyon, whose plight is more drastic, is correspondingly more explicit in his negative view of the gods.

III

Lovelorn and lovelocked in the January frosts of unrequited love, his rural suit and "Shepheards devise" contemned by fair Rosalind, Colin Clout shivers through five stanzas while turning winter's "waste," the "barrein ground," the "naked trees," and his "feeble flocke" into reflections of his woe. The first two stanzas, and especially the two lines of fustian that introduce them, deserve close attention:

> Thou barrein ground, whome winters wrath hath wasted,
> Art made a myrrhour, to behold my plight:
> Whilome thy fresh spring flowrd, and after hasted
> Thy sommer prowde with Daffadillies dight.
> And now is come thy wynters stormy state,
> Thy mantle mard, wherein thou maskedst late.

> Such rage as winters, reigneth in my heart,
> My life bloud friesing with unkindly cold:
> Such stormy stoures do breede my balefull smart,
> As if my yeare were wast, and woxen old.
> And yet alas, but now my spring begonne,
> And yet alas, yt is already donne.

> *(19–30)*

There is something comically redundant in the fervor with which Colin announces what the convention has already prepared us to take for granted. The pastoral semantics put into play by the eclogue context give the imitation of literature priority over that of nature, and this means we are encouraged to take Colin's utterances to refer to other utterances of the same kind and not merely to the objects his utterances designate. Since pastoral is a kind of literary metalanguage, the natural objects or processes signified by Colin's terms are themselves signifiers of the countless poems in which such references and images have characteristically appeared. The tree lovelier than any poem refers me more directly to Joyce Kilmer's poem than to God's tree.

At second glance, however, and in spite of their conventionality, these two lines yield considerable insight into the complicit relations between tradition and the individual talent: "Thou barrein ground, whome winters wrath hath wasted, / Art made a myrrhour, to behold my plight." This is either an evasive passive construction—"made" by whom, if not by Colin?—or else an active construction in which *Art* is a noun in agentive relation to *made*. Perhaps the necessities of the syntactical pun call for the sense of completed action ("Art already made you a mirror";

"you are already made a mirror") that strains against the apparent force of the complaint, since Colin seems to be making his mirror now. This sense makes us notice that the illocutionary force of the phrase ("with my art I now make a mirror") is suppressed and displaced to the literary precedents that have already prepared the ground ("Art *made*") for Colin to embroider on.

"To behold" is another focus of significant troping. If we take it in its familiar sense it feels like an ellipsis: "to enable me—or anyone else—to behold my plight." The infinitive shifts back and forth between "in order to behold" and "in which to behold"; the first stresses the speaker's own purposiveness in making the mirror while the second connects more easily with the past tense of literary preparation, implying that the mirrored plight already exists for Colin to imitate, in which case he himself becomes a mirror transmitting a reflected semblance of conventional despair. But *behold* also has more aggressive meanings—"keep hold of," "contain," "signify"—that reflect into the speaker's words a certain pride in achievement: his plight is preserved, amplified, rendered significant by being externalized and mirrored in the barren ground. This enables him not only to keep despair alive and publicize it but also to naturalize it, give it legitimacy by invoking the man-nature correspondence.

John Moore has sternly taken Colin to task for relying too much on "the book of nature, Pan's book," and as a result basing "his life on a set of inadequate and therefore false analogies" (pp. 15–16). But of course it literally *is* a book he relies on, a book written not by nature but by Colin in collaboration with his literary predecessors. It is convention rather than nature that supplies the false analogies. That Colin and convention mirror each other signifies his commitment to the literary and extra-literary norms embedded in the genre of the pastoral love lyric (with Petrarchan trimmings). Spenser's critique of Colin is thus one with his critique of the genre, and it is through his portrayal of Colin's response that he reanimates the ethico-psychological attitudes that give rise to the genre and sanction its continuing influence.

"Art made a myrrhour, to behold my plight": the line takes on Orphean implications resembling those explicitly indicated in the undersong of *Epithalamion:* "The woods shall to me answer and my Eccho ring." And as the presence of "Eccho" suggests, the artist's power to make nature his echo and mirror conflates Orpheus with Narcissus.[9] The two together preside as Ovidian proxies over the metamorphosis taking

---

[9] See Calvin R. Edwards's fine essay, "The Narcissus Myth in Spenser's Poetry," *Studies in Philology* 74 (1977): 63–88.

place. For even as *Colin* moves to naturalize his plight, *we* perceive his language to conventionalize it in distortions that denaturalize nature. Personification is merely the surface of this denaturalizing process, that is, the apostrophe to the ground, the attributes *wrath* and *prowde* assigned to winter and summer, and the image of the ground cloaking its barrenness in a flowery mantle. Less superficial is the "philosophy of nature" embedded in Colin's rhetoric: if "sommer prowde with Daffadillies dight" is a "mantle" worn in a masque,[10] then this artificial masking conceals the real or "natural" condition of the ground, which is barrenness. According to this logic the sweeter seasons inspire false pride and illusory hopes. It is as if the anti-erotic animus of such critics of youth as E. K., Thenot in *Februarye,* and Piers in *Maye* had displaced to nature the "follies fitte" for "love lads" who "masken in fresh aray" (*Maye* 17, 2). Nature is indeed at this very moment being "made a myrrhour" that serves the function of a scapegoat: it be-holds human folly so that the seasonal round may be blamed and man absolved for, say, falling in love.

Colin's image implies that behind the mask life's real face is the face of winter, "for ever the latter end of joy is woe." Like the rage of the spider in *Muiopotmos,* winter's destructive wrath is the spite of an embittered have-not—a seasonal counterpart to the "Envie" predicted by Immerito—who lies in wait to punish summer's pride and self-love by stripping it of its finery. This view of nature is thus the familiar sadbrow obverse and consequence of golden-age idyllicism. It makes interesting contact with the "spight" of old men, "Stoicke censours," and others who "ill judge of love, that cannot love, / Ne in their frosen hearts feele kindly flame" (*FQ* IV.Pr.2); as Patrick Cullen has noted, this resemblance suggests that Colin's premature senility—his "life bloud friesing with unkindly cold"—has already begun to have its effect.[11]

In the "barren ground" stanza, earlier commentators have noted one detail that adds to the sense of conspicuous artifice. Palgrave, for example, remarked sternly that "a poet who had his eye closely on natural fact" would not have assigned to summer the daffodils that, as Shakespeare knew, "come before the swallow dares, and take / The winds of March with beauty" (*Variorum, Minor Poems* 1:245). But whether intentional or not, the mistake works to enhance the fragility, and therefore the folly, of summer's pride—compare the "wandring wood" of

---

[10] See below on these anomalous daffodils.

[11] *Spenser, Marvell, and Renaissance Pastoral* (Cambridge: Harvard University Press, 1970), 82–83.

Faerie Queene, Book I, "Whose loftie trees yclad with sommers pride, / Did spred so broad, that heavens light did hide" (i.7). Perhaps also the pride receives a peculiar inflection if "Daffadillies" is taken as a slant rustic allusion to Narcissus. It is an appropriate instance of the metamorphosis theme lurking in the previous reference to Pan and in the figurative arborealization of Colin that occurs two stanzas later, and it appears in the vicinity of Colin's reference to the mirror in which he beholds his plight.

Though E. K. does not get around to mentioning the metamorphosis of Syrinx until *Aprill* and the related tale of Argus and Io until *Julye* and *October*, this Ovidian network hovers over the *Calender* as a whole. A moment's reflection will suggest how relevant Ovidian metamorphosis is to any inquiry into the constitution of pastoral "nature." Ovid's is not the simple reforestation project Marvell wittily proclaimed it to be in "The Garden." His flora and fauna are simultaneously reminders of failure, danger, or loss, and figures expressing the magical wish-fulfilling escape from pain, which is dissolved in the loss of consciousness but memorialized by the transformation of natural forms to symbols. So Mercury tells Argus how Syrinx, weary of fleeing from satyrs, found peace and plaintive immortality among the watery reeds (*Metamorphoses* 1.705 ff.). And so, in the wonderful lines about Myrrha, Ovid speaking through Orpheus imagines her impatience as the tree rises to her neck:

> non tulit illa moram venientique obvia ligno
> subsedit mersitque suos in cortice vultus.
> quae quamquam amisit veteres cum corpore sensus,
> flet tamen, et tepidae manant ex arbore guttae.
> est honor et lacrimis, stillataque robore murra
> nomen erile tenet mulloque tacebitur aevo.
>
> *(10.497–502)*

but she could not endure the delay and, meeting the rising wood, she sank down and plunged her face in the bark. Though she has lost her old-time feelings with her body, still she weeps, and the warm drops trickle down from the tree. Even the tears have fame, and the myrrh which distils from the tree-trunk keeps the name of its mistress and will be remembered through all the ages.[12]

With its displaced populations haunting the wood, the *Metamorphoses* is a mythological *Origin of Species* not in nature but in the imagination, and

---

[12] Trans. F. J. Miller, Loeb Classical Library (Cambridge: Harvard University Press, 1946), 2:99.

whether we think of it as the projection of human affairs into nature or the expropriation of natural forms, the idea of metamorphosis interprets the process by which pastoral nature is created. It is hard to resist the reflection that the myrrh is a "myrrhour" of Myrrha.

The second of the two stanzas under discussion only makes clear what was already implicit in the first: Colin does not compare himself to nature; he compares nature to himself. Though he appears to complete the analogy by internalizing the wintry landscape, what he actually internalizes is a projected distortion of nature congruent with his self-pity.[13] He begins with commendable restraint to describe his relation to the barren ground as one merely of likeness, not identity: "Such rage *as* winters," "*As if* my year were wast, and woxen old." But in "*my* year . . . woxen old" and "*my* spring begonne" the natural terms take on metaphoric shading and press away from the recurrent annual cycle toward the unique life cycle. The finality of the last line, "And yet alas, yt is already donne," completes this shift. The figurative result is neither an analogy between the two cycles nor an identification of the man's "season" with the year's. Rather the two are conflated to produce a hyperbole of premature aging; the lifetime is contracted to a year, but by the same distortion the annual cycle assumes the irreversibility of the life cycle.

Nancy Jo Hoffman remarks the humanization of nature in this passage but ignores the possibility of an ironic relation between Spenser and Colin:

> Nature loses its material referent, and becomes a language. . . . An analogy that does not make pictorial sense turns out to be a skillful and deliberate metaphor for the change and disorder that characterize Colin's love. Furthermore, meaning does not derive from what Colin sees but from what he thinks and feels *when* he sees. . . . Although winter's barren ground is called a "mirror," what Colin beholds is not a realistic image but an evaluative metaphor given meaning by the responsive poet's mind. . . .
> . . . By the time Spenser returns to winter landscape with its marred mantle, he has entwined nature and human nature to such an extent that no truly visual quality or precise analogy remains. (pp. 45–46)

Whose is the "skillful and deliberate metaphor"? And if it does not matter whether it is Spenser's or Colin's, does this mean that both evaluate Colin's "disorder" in the same way? If Colin is substantial enough to see, think, and feel, in what sense does he, or can he, behold "not a realistic image but an evaluative metaphor"? It would be more promis-

---

[13] This projection can be seen by substituting first- for second-person pronouns in the first stanza: "my fresh spring," "my sommer prowde," etc.

ing if Hoffman meant that what Colin sees as a realistic image we read as an evaluative metaphor given meaning, and so on. Then she would be in a better position to sort out what Colin sees, how he interprets it, and how we interpret his interpretation. As the final sentence shows, these distinctions are not entertained, and the consequence is that if we discern in the passage the Stoic censor's attitude toward nature, life, and love, we must ascribe this view to Colin's author as *his* sentiment.

IV

Continuing the project of naturalizing his plight in the following stanzas, Colin's bathos increases together with his increasingly grotesque metamorphosis—or better still, anamorphosis—of nature and man into distortions each of the other until he seems on the verge of ending his race in a tree:

> You naked trees, whose shady leaves are lost,
> Wherein the byrds were wont to build their bowre:
> And now are clothd with mosse and hoary frost,
> Instede of bloosmes, wherwith your buds did flowre:
> I see your teares, that from your boughes doe raine,
> Whose drops in drery ysicles remaine.
>
> All so my lustfull leafe is drye and sere,
> My timely buds with wayling all are wasted:
> The blossome, which my braunch of youth did beare,
> With breathed sighes is blowne away, and blasted
> And from mine eyes the drizling teares descend,
> As on your boughes the ysicles depend.
>
> *(31–42)*

Like Orpheus, Colin is trying to "learne these woods, to wayle my woe, / And teache the trees, their trickling teares to shedde" (*June* 95–96). Tree-person analogies are so common in Ovidian and Petrarchan traditions that the first thing we recognize about these stanzas is their aggressive claim to the status of literary cliché. The primary message is not "my trouble is like a tree's" but "my plight is like a poet's." Such a message, conveyed by the poet's plethora of dainty devices, ought to control our reaction in a manner that makes his tree trope less intrepid by directing us to classify it as the intertextual trope of allusion rather than as a species of iconic similitude. But even while flashing this signal, Spenser neutralizes it by a pictorial emphasis that diverts us from literary to arboreal emulation.

The bathetic effect owes partly to Colin's insistence on spelling out the analogy in visual images that are merely redundant. In her account of the stanzas Hoffman tries to blink this insistence away (pp. 45–46), but "lustfull leafe," "timely buds," and "blossome" confuse a simple commonplace by forcing us to visualize (we ask, do they figure parts of the body?), and if this effect is momentarily mitigated by the metaphoric "braunch of youth" it is revived by the bizarre *enargeia* of the concluding eyes-boughs equation. And it is reinforced by Colin's emphasizing the exactness of the visual comparison—reading "all so" with the first three Quartos; the "Also" of the Folio and fourth and fifth Quartos weakens this emphasis but accentuates the impression of redundancy. The clear difference between descending tears and hanging icicles impels us to challenge the claim to exact resemblance; we note and resist the straining toward convergence conveyed by steady alliteration and the cluster of internal rhymes ("sighes," "eyes," and "ysicles").

These details move the passage into the realm of literary parody, and yet at the same time the complex implications of the theme of narcissistic metamorphosis resonate in the imagery, providing a critical analysis of the self-indulgent motives, the "melodious self-pity," that inform it. For the image of icicles, like the effect of redundancy, indicates the "frozenness" of the emotion locked within the poet and "beheld" by the frigid fire of his rhetoric. If Colin's "All so" ultimately prevails it is because we decide the real flow of his grief is not only congealed but also concealed in the icy glitter of his images. The image then turns on the imagist: visually the tree does not resemble the man, for it "weeps" but does not weep; figuratively the man may resemble the tree in "weeping" rather than weeping. In this connection it is interesting that line 41 reads like a free translation of the line describing Myrrha's tears (*Metamorphoses* 10.500) quoted above—Myrrha's *warm* tears turning into "tears" of myrrh.

V

Colin's final stanza of comparison extends the pattern of conspicuous redundancy from vegetable to animal life:

> Thou feeble flocke, whose fleece is rough and rent,
> Whose knees are weake through fast and evill fare:
> Mayst witnesse well by thy ill governement,
> Thy maysters mind is overcome with care.
> Thou weake, I wanne: thou leane, I quite forlorne:
> With mourning pyne I, you with pyning mourne.
>
> *(43–48)*

A confession of misgovernment by Colin! Enough to make any attacker or defender of his character prick up ears. R. A. Durr, who generally found Colin depraved, thought this proved he was bad; John Moore thought it showed him "being responsible in a difficult situation" and was therefore an earnest of superior virtue in the future; and Patrick Cullen—holding his Aristotelian fire for bigger game, the Tragic Flaw—argued against Durr that any delinquency caused by Rosalind's wintry effect on her lover bothers the shepherd as much as his sheep. Cullen cites the opening two stanzas of the eclogue to prove that it is "real winter" rather than "bad shepherding" that tatters the flock, and he responds to the gravamen like a private investigator reporting to the counselor for the defense: "There is no substantial evidence to indicate that Colin fails to discharge his obligation to his sheep."[14] But perhaps by this time in the eclogue we don't find bad weather any more troublesome to Colin than—comparing small things to great—it is to King Lear. Both appreciate its seminal power to legitimize self-pity and to supply the imagery of barrenness. The bad weather real to Colin is only as real to us as his suffering body. And since the voice and mind projected into a puppet by his ventriloquising author may be taken more seriously than his body ("his" body, therefore his "body"), our attention is diverted from the dummy's grief to his enjoyment of winter's fitness to serve as his mirror. To this the counselor for the defense may object, "That's what the sheep are for—to revive the reality of winter." But like the barren ground and naked trees, the ragged sheep seem to be the symbols rather than the objects of the shepherd's care. Cullen so much as says this when he suggests that the case against Colin can be dismissed on grounds of insignificance: "Colin's self-accusation here is less moral reprobation than it is a conventional pastoral assumption of correspondence between the mood of the master and the condition of the sheep" (p. 80).

The ethical debate must have taken place in an environment specially designed to cut down the noise of alliteration, which reaches a deafening level as assonantal contrast and variation are played off against the steady beat of echoing consonants. Colin's flock is less weatherproof than his rhetoric, which leads one to wonder how he found time to pay any more attention to their misery than did Herbert Rix, who uncovered an apostrophe, an anaphora, a double parison, and an antimetabole all within the space of six lines (*Variorum, Minor Poems* 1:246). There may well be

---

[14] R. A. Durr, "Spenser's Calendar of Christian Time," *ELH* 24 (1957): 271; Moore, 14; Cullen, 80–81.

sermons in sheep, but since by this time in the eclogue we have a fairly good idea of "the mood of the master" we are perhaps more impressed by the scrupulousness with which he summons every item in the pastoral inventory to witness that the master's mind is overcome with tropes. Colin's sheep are scarcely more durable than the poor lamb that follows Una across the plain in one line ("by her in a line a milke white lambe she lad") only to be analogically sacrificed to her in the next ("So pure an innocent, as that same lambe, / She was . . . ," *FQ* I.i.4–5).

VI

Colin's stanzas of apostrophe sacrifice the pastoral inventory to the despotism of an art that deprives "things" of their otherness and reduces them to expressions—however elegantly or inelegantly varied—of a single plaintive theme. But this gives rise to a question: does such redundancy manifest primarily an erotic or a poetic obsession? The question receives an equivocal answer in the concluding section of his complaint:

> A thousand sithes I curse that carefull hower,
> Wherein I longd the neighbour towne to see:
> And eke tenne thousand sithes I blesse the stoure,
> Wherein I sawe so fayre a sight, as shee.
> Yet all for naught: such sight hath bred my bane.
> Ah God, that love should breede both joy and payne.
>
> · · · · · · · · · · · · · · ·
>
> I love thilke lass, (alas why doe I love?)
> And am forlorne, (alas why am I lorne?)
> Shee deignes not my good will, but doth reprove,
> And of my rurall musick holdeth scorne.
> Shepheards devise she hateth as the snake,
> And laughes the songes, that *Colin Clout* doth make.
>
> Wherefore my pype, albee rude *Pan* thou please,
> Yet for thou pleasest not, where most I would:
> And thou unlucky Muse, that wontst to ease
> My musing mynd, yet canst not, when thou should:
> Both pype and Muse, shall sore the while abye.
> So broke his oaten pype, and downe dyd lye.
>
> *(49–72)*

The shepherd's "good will" and "love" are less evident than the sense of injured merit "beheld" by his rhetoric. What seems most to rankle him is that his pipe, the "Shepheards devise" (emblem, mask, and art) that all his country cousins praise, is not merely ineffective in moving Rosalind but is unappreciated as art. Rosalind's response is close enough to Nysa's in Virgil's eighth eclogue to suggest by allusion that "Shepheards devise" is of ancient pedigree: despising all men, Nysa hates Damon's pipe, goats, shaggy brows, and scraggly beard ("tibi est odio mea fistula, dumque capellae / hirsutumque supercilium promissaque barba," 33–34). Spenser significantly shifts the emphasis from Colin's person to his music.

This combined emphasis on Colin's music and on the antiquity and conventionality of the situation focuses the poetic motive in a manner that makes it conflict with the erotic motive. As there is a difference between the two motives, so there is a difference between the respective audiences of lover and poet, that is, between the participant(s) primarily addressed by the poet as lover and the auditors or spectators addressed by the lover as poet. To which audience was Colin's "rurall musick" primarily directed? His response shows him to be stung by literary as well as erotic rejection. It is as if the conventional "myrrhour" of art that "beheld" and foreordained Colin's plight confused the fledgling poet-lover with its own demand for attention. Perhaps, to speculate idly, this confusion of literary and erotic motives informed the poetry addressed to Rosalind and affected her adverse reaction; perhaps she questioned the poet-lover's sincerity as well as his taste. Some evidence may be adduced from another quarter for this fantasy. The reaction Colin reports resembles that reported by the lover-poet in *Amoretti* 18 and 54:

> But when I pleade, she bids me play my part,
>   and when I weep, she sayes teares are but water:
>   and when I sigh, she sayes I know the art,
>   and when I waile she turnes hir selfe to laughter.
>
> Of this worlds Theatre in which we stay,
>   My love lyke the Spectator ydly sits
>   beholding me that all the pageants play,
>   disguysing diversly my troubled wits.
>
> Sometimes I joy when glad occasion fits,
>   and mask in myrth lyke to a Comedy:
>   soone after when my joy to sorrow flits,
>   I waile and make my woes a Tragedy.
>
> Yet she beholding me with constant eye,
>   delights not in my merth nor rues my smart:
>   but when I laugh she mocks, and when I cry
>   she laughes, and hardens evermore her hart.

What then can move her? if nor merth nor mone,
  she is no woman, but a sencelesse stone.

But of course her spectatorship seems appropriate to the theatrical pleasure his language betrays: playing all the pageants and disguising "di-
versly" in a one-man *tour de force*, he inflates his joy and sorrow into
their formal dramatic equivalents. His delight in artifice, interfering
with the more genuine impulses of love evident in other sonnets, reverses the Pygmalion story and turns his Galatea back into a statue. The
obvious fitness of her response, however, testifies to the reflexive irony
that animates the sonnet. We sense this irony in the reference to her
"constant eye": unmoved, unwavering, she provides a contrast to his
rapid and histrionic changes of mood; the constancy that makes him feel
and play the fool is a promise of stability and steadfast devotion.[15] The
same irony vibrates in the concluding couplet: the rhetorical question
and the disparaging hyperbole manifest the very staginess he knows she
scorns. Even as he blames her, he persists in humoring his penchant for
striking the literary poses that maintain her in, and justify, the role of
critical spectator.

In this manner the *Amoretti* poet knowingly persuades us to accredit
and share his beloved's response and therefore to feel the interaction of
two self-aware human persons behind the literary charade. Although this
is precisely what Spenser denies us and Colin Clout in the *Calender*, he
nevertheless depicts in flatter or more stenographic terms the same crossing of erotic and literary motives. E. K.'s delight in finding "a pretty
Epanorthosis . . . and withall a Paronomasia" in line 61 directs our attention to it by its very pedantry. "I love thilke lass, (alas why doe I
love?)": why love a lass rather than someone or something more trac-
table—for example, Hobbinol or the "refyned forme" of the woman as
Idea—and more susceptible to the allure of Epanorthosis and Paronomasia? Yet if Colin is less a person than the *Amoretti* lovers, the response
he models is not entirely predictable. He does not say he will stop loving, or even stop trying to persuade Rosalind; he says he will stop trying
to do it with his pipe. He feels snubbed chiefly for serenading her with
music that suited Pan's more countrified taste. I find it surprising that
Colin hybristically passes Rosalind's contempt for him on to his god in
the epithet *rude*. Something resembling a pastoral Peter Principle may
be discernible here: a touch of restlessness on Colin's part with the limits

---

[15] He conveys the sense that she is patiently waiting him out—waiting for the nonsense to stop.

of "Shepheards devise," a touch of ambition, a desire to promote himself beyond the level of his pastoral competence.

VII

Colin's reaction is emphasized, rendered more dramatic and sudden, by his failure to complete the penultimate stanza. Spenser/Immerito steps in with a direct and laconic stage direction. Although its rhythm enforces the sense of a predictable and unremarkable conclusion, the gesture it indicates is mannered; it is a comic hyperbole, amplified by conspicuous alliteration, assonantial in the first clause and consonantial in the second, with an alliteratively (and orthographically) induced trace of "dyd dye" behind "dyd lye." The poet flattens his puppet in a single line. Yet this is far from the whole story, for he picks him up again and sends him home with a certain sympathy:

> By that, the welked *Phoebus* gan availe,
> His weary waine, and now the frosty *Night*
> Her mantle black through heaven gan overhaile.
> Which seene, the pensife boy halfe in despight
> Arose, and homeward drove his sonned sheepe,
> Whose hanging heads did seeme his carefull case to weepe.

Hoffman, who stresses the conventional character of this ending, notes the continuity: "the mood of melancholy" is carried into "an emblematic nature" as Spenser takes over "Colin's now-familiar vocabulary of grief. . . . Independent of Colin, Spenser affirms the proportion between man and nature. The poem has defined a conventional pattern of experience and thought that is confirmed in the conventional pattern of nature just at the moment when Colin seems to have 'broken' pastoral possibility." She thinks the chronographic phrases "set us at a distance from Colin because, ultimately, the linear flow of human life is less capricious and more dependable than he is. Nature intrudes, not to end song, but to establish a ritual of order and poetic harmony" (p. 52). This perception of continuity between Spenser and Colin is important, but the terms of that continuity need some restatement to bring out the complexity of the relation.

It is Spenser, not Nature, who intrudes with imagery that scarcely betokens order or harmony; however conventional the *chronographia* is in itself, there is a touch of menace in the rhetoric through which the failing sun with its rustic "wain" is contrasted to the powerful epic ges-

ture ("through heaven gan overhaile") of "frosty *Night*."[16] It is a hyperbole implying the correspondence of day's and season's end to life's end.
And since "mantle black" echoes the earlier reference to the ground's
"mantle mard," the figure may be felt to project Colin's mental state into
the amplifying mirror of the cosmos. If so, the poet momentarily shares
his mood. Setting the "boy" against this background makes him more
rather than less sympathetic. He and his woe are diminished in scale,
subdued by "pensife" and "*halfe* in despight," while his dependability is
asserted in the word *sonned* as it was earlier in the reference to his feeding
sheep (12). The extra foot of the hexameter accentuates the poet's commitment to at least the semblance of pathetic fallacy and thus withdraws
from the onslaught of cosmic night to the more comforting pastoral
enclosure.

Yet this return to pastoral only emphasizes by contrast the momentary
transcendence centered in the word *heaven* (not *sky*) and in the energy of
"gan overhaile." The menace carried by the vague and comprehensive
economy of the phrase composes into a glancing allusion to powers and
dangers beyond the pastoral confine. This is a device Spenser could have
found in Virgil's *Georgics*.[17] Viewed with the hindsight afforded by
knowledge of Spenser's other poetry, it takes on the character of an unspecified prolepsis into which we may read an emblematically mediated
glimpse of real "despight" and "Envie," of "mighty Peres displeasure,"
of the "mishaps" of "death, or love, or fortunes wreck," of "idle hopes,
which still doe fly away." Sharing Colin's mood, the poet carries its emblem beyond his enclosed mind. But *Anchora speme:* if one reads the
night figure in this manner, then one also feels that Spenser anticipates
the ulterior darkness only to exclude it from the present scene as the
world he and Colin cannot yet, but must at some point, confront with
their art. The concluding image reminds us that Colin's life is still proportioned, as E. K. might put it, to the care and feeding of sheep: "All
Colin's skills cannot make him other than a shepherd. Fully to confront

[16] Montrose, 39, stresses the conjunction of "rude *Pan*" and "welked *Phoebus*" and
sees the transition from the first to the second as an "oblique allusion to the singing contest between Pan and Apollo," a reminder that "Colin's Apollonian aspirations are frustrated." But I fail to comprehend the logic of this reading. Phoebus, who defeated Pan,
is here on the verge of being overhailed by Night. If Phoebus equals the god of poetry as
well as the sun-god, then what is the "Night" that threatens it? Colin's frustration, at any
rate, is explicitly Panic rather than Apollonian.

[17] Cf. my "Archaism, Vision, and Revision: Studies in Virgil, Plato, and Milton,"
The Centennial Review 11 (1967): 24–52.

in poetry the problems he encounters in his progress through the *Calender*, problems of unrequited love and unredeemed time, he would have to deny his pastoral nature."[18]

This sympathetic closure, in which the poet joins with his puppet, nevertheless takes another turn in the final line, a turn reinstating the ambivalence of the relation between them. For "carefull case" may refer either to Colin's grief or to his art: the flock seemed to beweep either his woeful condition or the carefully constructed "case" he made for it, that is, the rhetorical grounds on which he rests his claim to nature's sympathy.[19] And the sheep only *seemed* to weep: the poet flags this as an interpretation with the same counterfactual quality as the teary icicles on Colin's naked trees. Perhaps Colin's tears are also no more than a semblance of tears: "May seeme he lovd, or els some care he tooke." The disjunctive phrase and its verb will now bear closer scrutiny: "or, if he didn't love, if he only seemed to love, he took some care"—not merely suffered or experienced some care ("some care *him* tooke"), but actively took it. At least some of his care went into tuning the pipe and framing the style with which he dresses the barren ground in flowery tropes to amplify his woe. Does he also take care in cherishing his care, drawing it out—like the poetic "honey Bee" in *December*—through the "formall rowmes" (*Dec.* 68) of verse so as to be-hold it in the Narcissan mirror?

The conclusion of the eclogue moves us to ask the questions about love and poetry that were gathering force through Colin's careful stanzas of complaint. How real—how genuine or authentic—are the love and grief that can be proportioned to the demands of poetry and displayed in the mirror of art? Can they be any more authentic than a "nature" so proportioned and so viewed? Isn't the disappearance of nature into art accompanied by a parallel disappearance of genuine love and grief? And is the love or grief that seems to be oriented toward another person, Rosalind, only a semblance of that which the poet-lover directs toward himself as he admires "the mirror of his owne thought" and "feeds his hungrie fantasy" with images whose "plenty makes me poore"?[20] On the other side of the equation, how authentic or adequate is an art that mirrors only the endless love and grief that fit conveniently (conventionally)

[18] David R. Shore, "Colin and Rosalind: Love and Poetry in the *Shepheardes Calender*," *Studies in Philology* 73 (1976): 186.

[19] I owe this reading to my former student, D. S. Manning.

[20] *An Hymne in Honour of Beautie* 224; *An Hymne in Honour of Love* 198; *Amoretti* XXXV; cf. Edwards, 71ff.

into its "formall rowmes" and have their end, like Ovid's *amatores* and *nymphae*, in the poet-tree? Andrew Marvell's wry interpretation of these themes makes explicit the essence of Spenser's sympathetic critique:

> When we have run our Passions heat,
> Love hither makes his best retreat.
> The Gods, that mortal Beauty chase,
> Still in a Tree did end their race.
> Apollo hunted Daphne so,
> Only that She might Laurel grow.
> And Pan did after Syrinx speed,
> Not as a Nymph, but for a Reed.
>
> *("The Garden," 25–32)*

Pan and the Poetics of Misogyny

I

"NOT AS A Nymph, but for a Reed": the marvelous idea that Pan was from the start strictly a music lover in search of a new instrument sends us rollicking back to the real story conspicuously excluded with such consummate glee. The importance of that story to the *Calender* has recently been pointed out by Louis Montrose, who links Pan closely with the positive if limited achievements of recreative pastoral:

> Pan is an archetype of the creative power of the human spirit, for he accomplishes his own transformation of what the Olympian gods have already transformed. Syrinx is metamorphosed into reeds; Pan makes a musical instrument from the reeds, turns nature into art, creates culture. Pan brings forth music from the artifact he has made; he is able to transform erotic frustration into the consolation of an art that can recreate the senses and the spirit, that can turn the plaintive into the recreative and turn sorrow into celebration.[1]

Given my view of the paradise principle I would prefer to place a stronger and more consistent accent on the escapism that colors the *pas-*

[1] "'The perfecte paterne of a Poete': The Poetics of Courtship in *The Shepheardes Calender*," *Texas Studies in Language and Literature* 21 (1979): 38.

toral mode of which *Pan* is the eponymous symbol, and the remainder of
the present section will be devoted to this task.

The idyllic closure of Pan is created and threatened by a double displacement: first, from the transcendent thrust of infinite desire to the
more compassable scope of sexual desire that chases mortal beauty and
ends its race in a body; second, from the cruel flame of bodily desire to
the still more compassable ardors of pastoral art. Pan's words and music
try to reincarnate themselves, recapture the absent body they simultaneously signify and displace. Laurel and syrinx stubbornly retain their ambivalence as symbols. In the absence that gives them meaning, words
bear the traces of unappeasable desire urging them doggedly on toward
the naked Diana who would destroy them as, in the *Mutabilitie Cantos*,
she almost destroyed "foolish God Faunus." But luckily for them, the
more they try to embrace what they mean in a picture, an *eidyllion*, the
more it recedes from view and thus preserves both meaning and desire:

> By absence this good means I gain,
>> That I can catch her
>> Where none can watch her,
> In some close corner of my brain;
>> There I embrace and kiss her,
> And so enjoy her, and so miss her.
>
> *([John Hoskins?], "Ode," 19–26)*

Pan's dilemma is nicely caught by the ambiguity of "and so miss her"
("and therefore fail to catch her," "therefore feel her absence," "miss her
so much"): his victory has Pyrrhic undertones.

Against this general background we may set the characterization of
Pan's poetry implied by Colin and Hobbinol's remarks in the *Calender*
and amplified in such other Spenserian *loci* as *Muiopotmos* and *The
Teares of the Muses*. The poetry of the "greene cabinet" (*Dec.* 17) may be
lowly, but it is not merely "rude." Pan *deigns* to hear "Rude ditties tund
to shepheards Oaten reede," he is pleased by "sonet song so clear" (*Dec.*
13–15), and he occasionally risks arousing Apollo's *phthonos* by having
the Muses down in the dell for a moonlit dance (*June* 25–32). The
range and resources of Pan may embrace those of Parnassus because the
Muses also ply their golden art in a green paradise. It is their "silver
song" and borrowed finery that Colin invokes in *Aprill* to help him celebrate Pan's daughter, who—through a double reduction and idealization, Elizabeth to Eliza to Elisa—becomes "a personification of pastoral
poetry. . . . The lowly pastoral deities, shepherd-poet and muse, have
engendered a great goddess" (Montrose, 40–41). But it should not be

forgotten that the nobler Muses, Calliope and her sisters, also shone on Elisa's nativity.

From these reflections I conclude that what the *Calender*'s Pan presides over is not pastoral as a formal genre but recreative pastoral in the specific sense I am giving it in this essay—recreative against meta-recreative, weak against strong pastoral, life and poetry dominated by the paradise principle. Elisa is, after all, the namesake of *Elisium,* which is not necessarily identical with pastoral. "Shepherd" is not so much the name of the pastoral poet as the pastoral name of the poet, and the shepherds' god presides over a realm that includes all the Muses, although as followers of Pan they operate under a particular restriction. The point Spenser makes in *Teares of the Muses* applies here: the "learned sisters" are antique figures, the voices of convention, and their tears are plaintive, not merely elegiac, because their vision of the golden past and black present is too absolute and pure.[2] The flowery perfection and idyllic purity of their state testifies to their insulation from life. The Golden Age to which they appeal exists "in the past" only in that it has been transmitted from the past and imprinted by tradition on the fledgling mind (making the poetic *puer senex*). Spenser's Muses complain that time has passed them by, but this is poetic retribution for their effort to annul time in "timeless" and "eternal" visions, the endless "monuments of unageing intellect." In their nostalgia for the artifice of eternity, they dance after Pan from life to art, from change to fixity, from death to immortality, from sorrow through Lethe to the green cabinet of Elisium.

Conventions implanted in the mind become expectations, and the expectations sown by the siren song of Pan and the Muses yield bitter fruit. In *December* Colin finds that "The eare that budded faire, is burnt and blasted" (99), "The flattring fruite is fallen to grownd before, / And rotted, ere they were halfe mellow ripe" (106–7), and "The fragrant flowres, that in my garden grewe, / Bene withered" (109–10). Montrose remarks of these lines that the punning images make

> the fates of husbandman and poet, crops and poems, merge. The lost harvest includes the disappointed hopes of material and spiritual sustenance, of patronage and verbal efficacy.
>
> Although Colin's final emblem appears to be missing from the printed texts of the *Calender,* E. K. provides its gloss: "The meaning whereof is that all thinges perish and come to theyr last end, but workes of learned wits and monuments of Poetry abide for ever." Colin's emblem has perished with its speaker but Immerito's *Calender* remains. (p. 60)

---

[2] See "Archaism, Immortality, and the Muse in Spenser's Poetry," above.

E. K.'s conventional gloss distorts the relation between mortality and poetic immortality, and it does so, appropriately, on behalf of the convention. No doubt Colin has worked "to overcome his alienation" and "has rightfully expected a return" for his creative labor (Montrose, 59), but his disappointed hopes should not be blamed on the fact or fiction that the world is dominated by Fox, Ape, Slander, and the blatant beast. The speaker of *Prothalamion* attributes his "sullein care" not only to his "long fruitlesse stay / In Princes Court" but also to "expectation vayne / Of idle hopes, which still doe fly away, / Like empty shaddowes": the redundancy ("vayne," "idle," "empty," "expectation," "hopes") places the accent of bitterness on persisting "idle hopes" the very nature of which is to fly away, since they are shadows cast on earth from within the mind—shadows of "golden plumes" mounting "above the native might / Of heavie earth, up to the heavens hight" (*An Hymne in Honour of Love* 178, 188–89), shadows of "infinite desyre" reaching vainly upward and backward toward "that first conceived fyre" (202–3), shadows of "Poesye's" eternal Astraean return to its source: "Then make thee winges of thine aspyring wit, / And, whence thou camst, flye backe to heaven apace" (*Oct.* 83–84). If Colin lost his harvest and was spoiled for the life in which "all thinges perish," it was because Pan's Muses deceived him with a Garden of Adonis where shortlived flowers whispered their flattering fragrance into his budding ear: "abide for ever"—"What wreaked I of wintrye ages waste, / Tho deemed I, my spring would ever laste" (*Dec.* 29–30).

Colin is distinguished from his silver-winged counterpart in *Muiopotmos* by little more than the two letters it takes to change him to Clarion. Both are carried by their "unstaid desire" into careless flights of predation, and the language describing both suggests that their hunting-gathering expeditions are aggressive tests of manhood that endanger the pastoral environment. Clarion, armed like a heavy tank (*Muiopotmos* 57–58), sallied forth "with vauntfull lustie head" (54)

> And with good speed began to take his flight:
> Over the fields in his franke lustinesse,
> And all the champion he soared light,
> And all the countrey wide he did possesse,
> Feeding upon their pleasures bounteouslie,
> That none gainsaid, nor none did him envie.
>
> *(145–52)*

Reaching the "gay gardins" his tender tasting gives way to "glutton sense": "he turneth to his play, / To spoyle the pleasures of that Paradise"

(185–86), and "tastes at will, / And on their pleasures greedily doth pray" (203–4).

Colin was even more of a threat to the peace of the green world:

> Whilome in youth, when flowrd my joyfull spring,
> Like Swallow swift I wandred here and there:
> For heate of heedlesse lust me so did sting,
> That I of doubted daunger had no feare.
> > I went the wastefull woodes and forest wyde.
> > Withouten dreade of Wolves to bene espyed.
>
> I wont to raunge amydde the mazie thickette,
> And gather nuttes to make me Christmas game:
> And joyed oft to chace the trembling Pricket,
> Or hunt the hartless hare, til shee were tame.
>
> .   .   .   .
>
> How often have I scaled the craggie Oke,
> All to dislodge the Raven of her neste:
> How have I wearied with many a stroke
> The stately Walnut tree, the while the rest
> > Under the tree fell all for nuts at strife:
> > For ylike to me was libertee and lyfe.
>
> *(Dec. 19–36)*

Colin in spring seems more discreet than the shepherd in Marot's *Eglogue au roy* after which he is modeled—Robin hunts the wolves he doesn't fear—but also more meanminded: he pesters "trembling" and "hartless" victims, manhandles a stately tree, is happy to watch the strife he caused from his secure perch.[3] His "libertee" has the privileges of a "hurtlesse pleasaunce" (*Dec.* 51) in the sense that he can hunt without being hunted, hurt without being hurt.

If this was how he passed his time "whylst youth, and course of carelesse yeeres / Did let me walke withouten lincks of love" (*June* 33–34), "When choise I had to choose my wandring waye" (*Dec.* 62), then we can see that—like Clarion—he was asking for trouble, never more than

---

[3] Colin's phrase "Withouten dreade of Wolves to bene espyed" recalls his remark in *June* that in Hobbinol's paradise flocks may wander "Withouten dreade of Wolves to bene ytost" (12). The *December* phrase might be construed to mean that paradise is like England (and unlike Marot's France) in having no wolves. While wolves are mentioned in *Maye* by a moral pastor speaking darkly, Diggon's reference to their presence in *September* touches off a heated denial by Hobbinol (150–54), which E. K. supports in his pedantic fashion (249–99). But E. K. fails to object in *November* when Colin mentions wolves in, presumably, Kent (136). It is nevertheless tempting to see the *December* reference as a joke: not, as in Marot, fearlessness of wolves, but absence of wolves.

when he exercised his competitive instincts in the special talent that old Wrenock made "by arte more cunning" (*Dec.* 42). According to Hobbinol, his music either reduced the birds to being his *epigoni* or else made them "hold theyr peace, for shame of thy swete layes," and when Colin showed his skill to the Muses, "They drewe abacke, as halfe with shame confound, / Shepheard to see, them in theyr art outgoe" (*June* 55–56, 63–65). The upshot of Wrenock's instruction was to send him running around the neighborhood to compete "in derring doe . . . / With shepheards swayne, what ever fedde in field" (*Dec.* 43–44). It was only to be expected that at some point he would be foolish enough to bite the apple and the hand that fed him and to challenge Pan himself (45–55). But even here a precedent had been established and he was only following his leader, since "*Pan* with *Phoebus* strove" (*June* 68).

From this contest it appears that the *otium* of Pan's green cabinet includes the harmony of the bow as well as that of the lyre or pipe. There is a definite place in the Muses' garden for the "vauntful lustie head." Competition is among its conventions, and just as the *Calender* eclogues consist of debates, so the garden encourages both georgic and literary derring-do as healthy contributions to its contest system. This would seem to prepare the dwellers in Elisium for participation in the actual world. But as the example of Colin shows, the contest system is carefully controlled so that danger is minimized, cooperation and reconciliation emphasized. The rhythm of Pan introduces strife only as a prelude and means to concord, sorrow to celebration, complaint to recreation. On the one hand, the harmless and functional nature of the contests legitimizes the honing of aggressive impulses or skills. But on the other hand, the relative security of the game situation, with its low-risk guarantee, and the poor quality of Colin's human competitors induce false expectations of easy victory.

Montrose offers a beautiful example of this in the *August* eclogue and appends a perceptive comment:

> What the "Argument" calls the "delectable controversie" of their singing match is the sublimation of the political, intellectual, and emotional strife of the moral and plaintive eclogues into harmonious counterpoint. Enchased on the mazer that Willye pledges is a shepherd saving a lamb from the jaws of a wolf: the scenario of the moral eclogues is re-created in the happy stillness of art. The singing contest between rude Pan and great Apollo—Colin's myth of vocational anxiety—is replaced by a game between youthful rustic equals. Cuddie is a delighted auditor whose appreciation is gracefully manifested in his refusal to disrupt the present harmony by a partial judgment. The interplay of songs is concluded in the exchange of gifts; this is a model of perfect reciprocity, in which there are no losers. (p. 43)

In this respect both "Poesye" and the pleasures of the Muses are doubly "pierelesse" (*June* 32; *Oct.* 79): they lull Colin and Clarion into the belief that they have no peers while at the same time their flowery prospects are unmatched by anything in the world beyond the garden.

The limits of Pan are sometimes traced to his classical roots in nature. For example:

> Originally an Arcadian god of hills and woods, the protecting deity of flocks, herdsmen, and hunters, Pan was also regarded as a god of prophecy. In addition, Pan was associated with love and became revered as an amorous nature god. . . . As a worshipper of Pan, Colin . . . appears in the opening eclogue as a worshipper of nature who seeks meaning from nature and fulfillment in nature. . . . He has sought his values by reading in the book of nature, Pan's book, but events have not transpired as that book indicated they would and he concludes that a wrong has been done to him. . . . By relying on it and Pan he has based his life on a set of inadequate and therefore false analogies and has derived expectations which are false, misleading, and incapable of being realized.[4]

This extends to Pan the argument put forward by Isabel MacCaffrey,[5] and although I agree with both authors that Spenser stresses the limits of the soft pastoral over which Pan presides, I think they wrongly ground those limits in nature. It isn't merely that "nature" is a cultural category and an abstraction selectively defined according to the norms of any particular culture, nor that soft and hard versions of nature are abstractions from that abstraction, but that the primary referents of nature terms in pastoral are literary conventions and contexts. The false analogies and expectations of which Moore speaks derive from the flowers of the Muses through the apian influence of the tradition constituted by E. K.'s "Poetes." What results is not a "fall" into hostile "nature" or Mantuan's "predatory world" (Patrick Cullen's phrase) or any other external environment, but a fall into an inadequate response to the environment.

It is not, then, the book of nature that causes the fall but the nature of books. The culture of Pan and the Muses is too anthological. Not that it banishes the activities and values of the world where men, with "uncessant Labours," "themselves amaze / To win the Palm, the Oke, or Bayes," or the laurel, or the rose—on the contrary, it includes them, but it does so in distorted form, reducing them to green thoughts in green shades. Because of their anthological nurture Colin and Clarion fell prey

---

[4] John W. Moore, "Colin Breaks His Pipe: A Reading of the 'January' Eclogue," *English Literary Renaissance* 5 (1975): 8, 15–16.
[5] "Allegory and Pastoral in *The Shepheardes Calender*," *ELH* 36 (1969): 88–109.

to "the bondslave of spight" and their aspiring wings were entangled in the "lymie snares" of spider love or hate (*Muiopotmos* 245, 429). But Clarion's foe was a skilled craftsman lurking within the garden, and his degendered "hideous shape of dryrihed" was the consequence of a prideful challenge to the gods similar to those of Colin and Pan. As conceived by Spenser, the bondslavery of spite is an inherent potentiality of the green cabinet, engendered together with "idle hopes, which still doe fly away." It seems of less moment in Spenser's poetry whether the spite in question is one's own or another's, or whether, in the first case, it is directed toward oneself or toward others. The poetry displays more interest in the complex structure of anthological innocence and in the consequent self-deception, the scapegoating and unacknowledged complicity, that dominate the garden sensibility when it "falls."

Between Spenser-E. K. and Ovid the intertextual network of allusions surrounding the Pan-Syrinx myth casts interesting lights and shadows on the relation of the paradise principle to poetry and music. Here is a rough guide to the relevant loci:

1. Ovid, *Metamorphoses* I.668–723. On orders from Jupiter, Mercury assumes a shepherd shape in order to free Io from her equally bucolic form and from the hundred-eyed herdsman assigned by Juno to guard her. He tries to lull Argus with stories and the music of his panpipe, and what succeeds is the story of the origin of his instrument, which Argus out of curiosity asked to hear. The poet-singer in this instance is a trickster who sings about his own art to make his auditor nod, drop his guard, and betray the charge entrusted to him. Of course the auditor is complicit in Juno's wicked doings, but the telling of the Pan-Syrinx myth may still be a skewed parodic reflector of the Ovidian speaker's relation to his audience.

2. There are thirteen references to Pan in the eclogues proper and nine in E. K.'s glosses. In a few of these "Pan" names God, Christ, the Pope, and even, according to E. K., Henry VIII. The most important references to the Ovidian Pan and his relations to other figures of classical myth are in *Aprill* and *June*, while the shepherds' god's relation to Colin is featured in *Januarye* and *December*.

3. E. K. is not forthcoming in his presentation of the Ovidian context, and Theodore Steinberg, who noticed that "one of the controlling myths of the *Calender* is told in bits and pieces," observes that

> E. K. does not mention Argus and Io until "July" (l.154) and it is not until "October" (l.32) that he tells their story, never mentioning that "Mercury wyth hys Musick lulling him aslepe" used the very story which Spenser has

used throughout the *Calender*. Although the whole story is necessary for understanding Spenser's references to it, E. K. only explains the parts which he feels are relevant in the particular eclogues, so that the reader must somehow put all of his glosses together to understand this aspect of the poem. And even then he leaves out the key step in the connection between Pan-Syrinx and Mercury-Argus—which any educated sixteenth-century reader would probably have known.[6]

The references to Argus are in fact interesting both in their own right and because of some of their neighbor glosses:

a. Thomalin's comment in *Julye* makes it clear that Argus has shifted to the side of the angels:

> But shepheard mought be meeke and mylde,
> well eyed, as *Argus* was,
> With fleshly follyes undefyled,
> and stout as steede of brasse.
>
> *(153–56)*

Perhaps we are to question Thomalin's pretension to learning, since the classical contexts (Ovid, and possibly Glaucon's tale of Gyges' ancestor in *Republic* II, where the brass steed may come from) strain against his ethical intent. But Diggon treats Argus the same way in *September:* "(For Roffy is wise, and as Argus eyed)" (203).

b. In *October*, after Piers compares the poet's musical power to that of Orpheus, who with "His musicks might the hellish hound did tame" (30), Cuddie responds, "So praysen babes the Peacoks spotted traine, / And wondren at bright *Argus* blazing eye" (31–32), whereupon E. K. tells the story, including the detail about Juno's transfer of the eyes to her peacock's tail (172–76). The point seems to be that the babes, who praise but do not repay the poet, admire the beauty of what they are seeing (read "hearing") but do not understand or profit from it and are as blind to its value as is the blazing eye. Presumably if they knew the story they would be more alert to the message of pride and failure compressed in the symbol of the Argus-eyed peacock.

c. Orpheus's musical conquest of Cerberus parallels that of Mercury over Argus. E. K.'s long and pedantic explanation of "the secrete working of Musick . . . in the myndes of men" (153) is applicable also to Mercury. Music in the Phrygian mode can inspire courage and military

---

[6] "E. K.'s *Shepheardes Calender* and Spenser's," *Modern Language Studies* 3 (1973): 51.

spirit (158–62), but "the Arabian Melodie . . . is of great force to molifie and quench the kindly courage, which useth to burne in yong brests" (165–69). Mercury's song of Pan and Syrinx must have been in the Arabian mode.

What emerges from this network of allusions is a diffuse uneasiness, permeating the *Calender* as a whole, about the uses of poetry and music, the motives of poet-musicians, and the ignorance and susceptibility of their auditors. One is tempted to attribute this attitude to the bitter or Mantuanesque view of poetry's Arcadian sweetness. The triumph of Pan and his art is embedded in this uneasiness. Like "bright Argus blazing eye" it stands out against the shadow cast by his amatory failure, and its lifeless lulling beauty, its power to "bereave the soule of sence" and "quench the kindly courage," speaks to the cost and the limits of Pan's melodious resolution of his problem. The *Calender's* Panic subtext informs Spenser's critical portrait of the attitude embodied in all his pastoral speakers, and preeminently in the figure of Colin Clout. Under the guidance of the paradise principle they approach life and relationship first as a zero-sum game in which the object of desire appears as a prey, a spoil, a "goodly scope," and second as a game in which success is assured. In this context the position of the object is assigned most often, and most significantly, to women.

II

The repetitiveness and hyperbole, and the insistent alliteration, of which critics have complained, powerfully impose Spenser's mood on the reader's or listener's response.

—*Peter Bayley,* Edmund Spenser: Prince of Poets

Colin's obsessive love leads to the tragedy of his self-destruction. . . . [His sestina] reflects the same tragically self-destructive obsession found in the Colin of "January." The sestina is little more than an elaborate invocation to nature to wail Colin's woes.

—*Patrick Cullen,* Spenser, Marvell, and Renaissance Pastoral

Literary repetition and psychological obsession do not seem intimately related beyond the one thing they have in common: redundancy. The formal and the psychological critic seem to be speaking past each other. Yet I think their discourse may be made antiphonal by a closer inspection of the common feature to which both respond. As their responses indicate, redundancy in the *Calender*, especially in the case of Colin Clout, may be framed in the two different contexts of behavior and poetry. On the one hand, it may signify the obsessive character of the response to thwarted love. But on the other hand, the lover's delight in self-pity may be reinterpreted as the poet's obsession with *copie*, his delight in self-expression and invention, in finding as many ways as possible to say the same thing. The lover may loose a teary flow of words to persuade his beloved or, failing that, to console himself and to glorify his grief. But for the poet the matter of love provides an excuse to flaunt his skill. He freezes the flow to credentiate himself as a Bachelor of Art and to compete with other poetic bachelors in the ingenious manipulation of *topoi*.

The anthological culture over which Pan presides organizes the *Calender*'s two major tendencies, the recreative and the plaintive, into what may be called the Panic cycle. These tendencies correspond to two fundamental relations, which converge most sharply on the interaction between love and poetry. In the first relation, love precedes poetry; in the second, poetry precedes love. That is, in the first, love is "real" and (whether terminable or interminable) it terminates in art. In the second, love is imaginary matter devised for the sake of song. In the first, the lover in his wilderness aspires to one or another paradise, that of his beloved or that of the Muses. In the second, the emparadised young poet imbibes a view of love as an excuse for song, which leaves him unprepared for any actual encounter, making it highly probable that he will experience the encounter as a wilderness. I have of course reversed the expected order of these relations, since it is logical to assume that the innocence of the lover as poet should precede the experience of the poet as lover. I do so to suggest that the recreative innocence of the young poet is a product of the plaintive experience of the literary fathers who constitute the tradition that initially shapes his individual talent.

I shall christen the two relations with names appropriated from the eclogues. Let the one that privileges erotic experience be called the Wandering Mind model and the other the Vacant Head model. The first is named in honor of Hobbinol, who opens *June* with these words: "Lo Colin, here the place, whose pleasaunt syte / From other shades hath weand my wandring mynde." *Weand* focuses an unexpected reversal from experience to innocence and from world back to womb, and I shall argue later that the state of the Wandering Mind is not only the "fallen" consequent of the state of the Vacant Head but also, in a different context, its antecedent. Hobbinol's inversion of weaning reminds me, perhaps arbitrarily, of a similar reversal in the myth the Eleatic Stranger proposes in Plato's *Statesman* as a solution to the unhappy state of the world—a reversal the outlandishness of which marks the speaker's disenchanted sense of the impossibility of such cures. In this reversal men were born out of the earth fully mature, after which they aged and weakened into the dotage of youth, shrank through boyhood to tiny infancy, and finally disappeared to seed new autochthonous generations (270d–e). This myth provides a perfect solution to all the problems that offend the Stranger's despotic logic and his utopian (i.e., paranoid) impatience with the world—the problems caused by intractable youth, the abuses of marriage, and the internal and external faction produced by the jealousies and loyalties of the family. The myth of cyclic reversal is essentially a fantasy of exorcism, a technique for wishing away the undesirable aspects of life, a magical recipe for fleeing its wilderness and running back to paradise. Hobbinol preaches a similar withdrawal from the actual world darkened by "other shades" to the garden of verses, where rustic and classical mythology mingle in the moonlit play of the child's imagination (*June* 25–32). That this is an attempt to turn back—indeed, to abolish—the clock and to escape from time and history is acknowledged in Colin's response: "O happy Hobbinoll, I blesse thy state, / That Paradise hast found, whych Adam lost" (9–10).

Cuddie succinctly articulates the essence of the Vacant Head model in some *October* remarks on Colin's dilemma: poets cannot be lovers,

> For lordly love is such a Tyranne fell:
> That where he rules, all power he doth expell.
> The vaunted verse a vacant head demaundes,
> Ne wont with crabbed care the Muses dwell.
>
> *(97–101)*

We can adopt Cuddie's terminology without committing ourselves entirely to his narrowly construed either/or position. For obviously the Vacant Head can pretend to be in love and can write love poetry without knowing anything about love except what is written in other love poetry. Literature has much advice to offer concerning the proper way to play the role of "lover," to feel and communicate the "pains" of love, and to respond to successful or unsuccessful courtship. Above all else it instills in the Vacant Head the assumption that such experience is fictive and that however seriously the young poet plays at love, he is still only playing. That is, he learns to love primarily in terms of the relation between the poet and his audience, only secondarily in terms of the relation between lover and beloved. These priorities might lead him to assume that since his audience viewed love and pain as imaginary topics for the exercise of art, they would be more interested in being delighted than in being taught or moved (i.e., persuaded), more interested in him as a per-former than as a lover. The love that was proportioned to the demands of poetry would have to provide occasions for *copie* and conceits, redun-dancy and elegant variation, schemes and tropes, invocation and closure. His real beloved may not be the one he complains *of* but the one he complains *to*—the pastoral listener who "lyke the Spectator ydly sits" and either applauds or deplores his verse. Perhaps all this partly explains why Colin Clout's first conquest was Hobbinol. But there is another and more important explanation.

These two models—the poetry of the Wandering Mind and of the Vacant Head—are given in the *Calender* as the paradigms of love that the literary tradition makes available. The similarity between the two models is not hard to make out: whether love is fictional or real, whether it begins in the love of verse or in the love of Venus, it disappears—like Pan's love for Syrinx—into art. But the art that enshrines the image of the lover as amatory hunter and enshrines itself as the refuge if not in-deed the objective of erotic failure, a failure understandably predictable given such premises, has more than a touch of misogyny about it. Fun-damentally the community of the eclogues is a branch of the Young Men's Pastoral Association. Women at best serve instrumental functions in the YMPA. Whether they are idealized or monsterized, worshiped or chased, whether they are sources of artistic inspiration, entertainment, or manly honor, their job is to contribute to the male bonding which poetry celebrates. For even in its pastoral refuge, the community of poets continues—like Duke Senior's company in the Forest of Arden—to affirm inherited patriarchal values in its attitude toward the ladies. Woman appears in pastoral as Idea, Grace, Goddess, Muse, fairy, Queen, tormentor, victim, trophy, or commodity, but not as a person. The kind of love depicted in *Amoretti and Epithalamion* and in the ro-mance of Britomart is excluded from the *Calender*. The male bond be-tween Hobbinol and Colin that Rosalind disrupted in *Januarye* is, if not restored, reinstated in the sympathetic dialogue of *June*. Rosalind's con-tempt for the "Shepheards devise" enables the appreciative Hobbinol to rejoin Colin as the confidante with whom losses are shared.

The relative insignificance of the pastoral nymph as a feminine person is traceable to the peculiarly limited origins of love in the Vacant Head. The Muses and their Elysium are inventions of the literary fathers, and like the False Florimell, they are created and operated by and for men. In spring they turn a young man's fancy to poetry rather than to "na-ture," and to desire rather than to woman. Cupid is the first object of the Vacant Head's pursuit, and Spenser dramatizes this originary moment in the *March* tale of Thomalin. In the recreative microsphere of the Vacant Head the vicissitudes of the Wandering Mind may be foreshadowed as the forms of play supervised by little winged Cupid or his younger brother Sport. Syrinx may be pursued as a nymph *and* for a reed. But the close relation of these two pursuits, their complementarity, reduces the scope and seriousness of each. If nymphs can be won by a song, and if song can fully compass love's victories and defeats with equal though contrary rewards—crowns of flowers or of thorns—then the nymph, the love, and the song are all diminished to the same manageable proportions. They are functionally equivalent entertainments of the pastoral microsphere. In *The Shepheardes Calender* the point of greatest diminution occurs in the *March* eclogue.

III

"In this Æglogue," the argument of the *Calender*'s third eclogue begins, "two shepheards boyes taking occasion of the season, beginne to make purpose of love and other plesaunce, which to springtime is most agreeable." One of them, Willye, is ready to stir up trouble by awakening "little Love . . . / That nowe sleepeth in *Lethe* lake," but he lags behind Thomalin, a latterday Sir Thopas who has already given rein to his holiday humor by flushing the "little God" out of a bush when he

> cast to goe a shooting.
> Long wandring up and downe the land,
> With bowe and bolts in either hand,
> For birds in bushes tooting.

Closing in on a noise in an "Yvie todde / (There shrouded was the little God)," our hero

> Might see the moving of some quicke,
>   Whose shape appeared not:
> But were it faerie, feend, or snake,
> My courage earnd it to awake,
>   And manfully thereat shotte.
> With that sprong forth a naked swayne,
> With spotted winges like Peacocks trayne,
>   And laughing lope to a tree.

Cupid at first did not take the tail-rhyming Nimrod any more seriously than we do, but when Thomalin persisted, first with bolts and then with "pumie stones," his genial prey deftly picked off the stones:

> Therewith affrayd I ranne away:
> But he, that earst seemd but to playe,
>   A shaft in earnest snatched,
> And hit me running in the heele:
> For then I little smart did feele:
>   But soone it sore encreased.
> And now it ranckleth more and more,
> And inwardly it festreth sore,
>   Ne wote I, how to cease it.
>
>   *(63–102)*

Nancy Jo Hoffman adeptly characterizes "the tone of nursery rhyme or fairy tale" prevailing in verse which, "full of small movements," is "sympathetic rather than satirical. . . . Removed from the usual stylized sonnet setting, the poet makes the love wound convention yield its unexpected perspective on youthful naiveté."[7] But glimmering through "the thicke" of the verse, shrouded within it like Cupid, lurk a host of ivy-covered allusions that have stimulated brave scholars to manful targetry, inspired by the example of Spenser's own hunter, E. K., who translated Cupid's wings into "flying fancies," his weapons into the "glaunce of beautye," and Thomalin's hurt foot first into the fatal wound of Achilles and then into "lustfull love," which—according to "the best Phisitions"—travels from the heel to "the previe partes" by "certaine veines and slender synnewes." More recent sallies into the iconographic bush have uncovered dormant lust in the ivy-shrouded Cupid, in Thomalin the ambivalent venery of the hunter of love, and in both together the complex interplay between Anteros and Eros; it would be as easy to find the prideful Fall from innocence (with Cupid as "feend, or snake"), or the ambush of manly heroism by effeminate lust. The *March* view of "youth's initiations into the rites of love and manhood," as one commentator phrased it, also features the clichés of homoerotic narcissism, since what the hunter pursues is not a woman but (presumably his own) desire as a god.

Thus behind the simple surface of the eclogue lies a network of varied allusions to the complex psychology of love. The problem is to establish the relation between surface and depth, and judging from much modern commentary it has not been an easy problem. It is evaded rather than confronted by such statements as the following: Thomalin is "love-wounded"; he is "surprised by the pains of love"; his last words reflect "a

---

[7] *Spenser's Pastorals: "The Shepheardes Calender" and "Colin Clout"* (Baltimore: Johns Hopkins University Press, 1977), 82–83.

first discovery of *nonphysical* hurt in a formerly benign world" (italics mine); he is "suddenly faced with a supernatural ancient force . . . older than civilization which we may call by its ancient name Eros."[8] These statements fail to distinguish *Love* as a proper noun from *love* as a common noun. Is Thomalin aware of the "allegorical" meanings as well as the personifying reference? He is, after all, wounded in the heel, and however important this part of the body is as a symbol of fatal weakness within strength, its connotations are less figurative than are those of the heart.

Thomalin suffers a *physical* hurt, and if Spenser wanted to suggest a nonphysical hurt more directly he could easily have written "And hit me running in the heart: / For then I felt but little smart." The displacement from heart to heel may only be skin-deep: "For then" may mean either "during that time" (i.e., of the hunting episode) or "therefore at that time";[9] the former does not suggest that Thomalin himself makes the heel-heart connection, but the latter does ("because I received my heart-wound in the heel it took time for it to fester *inwardly*"). Yet that the two shepherd boys mention love only as the referent of a name, never as the meaning of a term, supports the idea that the eclogue wants us to distinguish what Thomalin intends by his words from what we can read into or out of them. Perhaps Leo Spitzer is right to think of little Cupid as an ancient supernatural force (pp. 499–500). Perhaps also, remembering that Spenser elsewhere writes of love that "well did antiquitie a God thee *deeme*" (*FQ* III.iii.2; italics mine), we may think of him as an even more ancient psychological force subsequently externalized and apotheosized by classical tradition. Reading the convention as metaphor tells us Thomalin has been wounded by his own desire rather than by the "glaunce of beauty," that he is in love with love rather than with any particular love-object, and so we can understand why the lover does not know "how to cease it."

Thomalin, however, may not know "how to cease it" for other reasons. In *March*, unlike *Januarye*, it is not the speaker who has made nature a mirror of his mind or Cupid a mirror of his desire. Both the speaker and his desire, his pain and its cause, already exist as separate, contiguous elements in the *March* landscape. Since the transfer of the winged boy from metaphoric to metonymic status is the poet's responsi-

---

[8] MacCaffrey, 97; Paul Alpers, "The Eclogue Tradition and the Nature of Pastoral," *College English* 34 (1972): 364; Hoffman, 82; Leo Spitzer, "Spenser, *Shepheardes Calender, March* ll. 61–114, and The Variorum Edition," *Studies in Philology* 47 (1950): 499.
[9] Can it also mean "*before* then"?

bility, his speaker's wound is happily mitigated. It is not incurable; it is merely undiagnosed. Its full allegorical diapason remains inaccessible to Tom Piper's rustic stops and starts. Cupid's apparent purpose in aiming low was not to afflict Thomalin with infinite desire but to inoculate him against it, to keep him from that hopeless pursuit, to protect him from its Tantalean torments. Unexpectedly "affrayd" and lamed by his quarry, our tiny Achilles is rendered psychologically and physically *hors de la chasse*. Thomalin's injury sends him limping away from love and back to his sheep, and so in this instance the heel wound adds armor to innocence, fortifies the blessed ignorance preserved in the lively bounce of his tail rhyme. The dire consequences of the disease are displaced from the fields of love and war to a greener field:

> For sithens is but the third morowe,
> That I chaunst to fall a sleepe with sorowe,
>   And waked againe with griefe:
> The while thilke same unhappye Ewe,
> Whose clouted legge her hurt doth shewe,
>   Fell headlong into a dell . . .
>
> *(46–51)*

Where Colin's sheep in *Januarye* mirror his wounded mind, Thomalin's ewe only mirrors his wounded leg.

Willye responds to Thomalin's tale with a little idyll of his own:

> Thomalin, I pittie thy plight.
> Perdie with love thou diddest fight:
>   I know him by a token.
> For once I heard my father say,
> How he him caught upon a day,
>   (Whereof he wilbe wroken)
> Entangled in a fowling net,
> Which he for carrion Crowes had set,
>   That in our Peeretree haunted.
> Tho sayd, he was a winged lad,
> But bowe and shafts as then none had:
>   Els had he sore be daunted.
>
> *(103–14)*

If we add to this Willye's earlier remark that he has at home "A step-dame eke as whott as fyre" (41), his narrative teasingly points beyond itself and arouses the E. K. in all of us to a thought of Cupid's parents trapped by Vulcan. William Nelson entertained that possibility and also

thought the pear tree—which D. C. Allen called "the lecherous perch"—
might remind the reader "of the tree of Eden or the one into which May
climbed in Chaucer's tale."[10] The Vulcan-Venus-Mars motif is in good
form with respect to allegory and decorum because it suggests that a personified force (desire) has replaced the substances whose property it is
(Venus and Mars) under the net and also because it honors the modest
confines of pastoral art by substituting the "winged lad" for his more
august parents, who may indeed still be present in appropriate emblematic disguise, Mars in the carrion crow and Venus in the pear tree. Since
March is at once the name of the war god's month and of Cupid's eclogue, the allusion seems reasonable. The eclogue thus hints at problems
devolving from the vagaries of Cupid as male desire, problems of jealousy and adultery, and the hint may serve to remind us of the fears and
dangers the Anteros figure defends against. But since the allusion is undeveloped it has the effect of a feint or a false trail, just as the association
of Thomalin with Anteros seems at once iconographically correct and
dramatically irrelevant. And inasmuch as the eclogue by these devices
defends against fuller representation of the erotic dangers it hints at, it
may be said to take on the Anteros function dissipated in the portrayal of
Thomalin.

March illustrates a characteristic Spenserian practice whose basic pattern is produced by the action and reaction of two antithetical conventions. The first specifies that if, for example, bird, bush, grass, weather,
sheep, and god are mentioned with appropriate pastoral markers, they
will be understood to refer primarily to the *topoi* and symbols of previous literature and only secondarily to objects and figures in "nature."
That is, when poetic statements contain references to natural or other
objects the intent is to imitate and signify poetry in which such references have characteristically appeared and in which those objects have
become elements of a code using "nature" to signify moral, political, or
psychological meanings. In pastoral semantics the normal direction of
reference may be reversed so that things become the signs of words.[11]
The second convention specifies that if a proper name or direct discourse
indicates the presence of a fictive speaker, and if he refers ostensively to
birds, bushes, grass, weather, sheep, gods, and other speakers, these referents will have the same relation to the referrer that birds, bushes, and

---

[10] Nelson, *The Poetry of Edmund Spenser: A Study* (New York: Columbia University
Press, 1963), 42; Don Cameron Allen, *Image and Meaning: Metaphoric Traditions in
Renaissance Poetry* (Baltimore: Johns Hopkins University Press, 1960), 18.

[11] Kenneth Burke, *Language as Symbolic Action: Essays on Life, Literature, and Method*
(Berkeley: University of California Press, 1966), 366–79.

so on, in the actual environment of readers have to them. As figures in the *March* landscape, shepherds, sheep, Lethe lake, and the winged god are objects of sight to the fictional speakers who inhabit that landscape. The first convention is *intertextual* or generic, while the second may be called *pictorial* because it promotes a tacit agreement to emphasize the function of referentiality and to keep it distinct from intra- and intertextual complexities; it directs the reader cinematically toward the "pictures" that lie, so to speak, on the other side of the language. Since the second convention conspicuously excludes from the speakers' awareness meanings to which the first convention just as conspicuously alludes, a one-way window of structural irony is interposed between the scene of idyllic action produced by the pictorial convention and the intertextual scene of erotic mythology.

A glance at Willye's second speech will suggest how this interplay between intertextual and pictorial conventions is established:

> Seest not thilke same Hawthorne studde,
> How bragly it beginnes to budde,
>   And utter his tender head?
> *Flora* now calleth forth eche flower,
> And bids make ready *Maias* bowre,
>   That newe is upryst from bedde.
> Tho shall we sporten in delight,
> And learne with Lettice to wexe light,
>   That scornefully lookes askaunce,
> Tho will we little Love awake,
> That nowe sleepeth in *Lethe* lake,
>   And pray him leaden our daunce.
>   *(13–24)*

It may seem that Willye is the more poetic of the two speakers and more privy to the *feyning* of E. K.'s "Poetes." Except for Thomalin's two fleeting similes (80, 87) and Willye's concluding "periphrasis of the sunne setting" (E. K.)—"stouping Phoebus steepes his face"—all the significant figurative phrases occur in the above speech. But there they are arranged in a sequence that enacts the gradual naturalization of metaphor, the displacement of figures from language to landscape. Willye begins with an image that recalls the Briar, the flowery rhetorician of Thenot's *Februarie* fable, and characterizes the hawthorn's early blooming as boastful utterance (13–15). Hoffman comments on "the delicate energy of beginnings" conveyed by this image, in which "nature speaks the language of human nature and demonstrates the poet's appreciation of male sexuality" (p. 81). But the troping at this point is Willye's, not nature's; the *Februarie* echo adds a warning about the innocent's unwary pride that causes the fall Thomalin (but not Willye) has already experienced, and that echo touches "the poet's appreciation" with irony. Hoffman's observation nevertheless nicely foreshadows the semantic displacement by which the language of love is transferred from verbal to vernal acts and figures. This displacement modestly begins to "utter his tender head" when Willye in his next lines mentions Flora and Maia. I say modestly because it isn't yet clear whether these mythic personifications are meant as verbal or as vernal (i.e., landscape) figures, and our decision is delayed by a similar uncertainty a few lines later when Willye speaks of awakening "little Love . . . / That now sleepeth in *Lethe* lake."

It is only when Thomalin amplifies his remark that "lustie Love" is "abroad at his game" that we retroactively opt for a displacement of Willye's reference to love and decide that the *March* shepherds inhabit a world in which "Love" is a proper noun. The roman type, which associates "Love" with "Hawthorne" and "Lettice" as local names, dissociates it from the three italicized mythic names. At this point we may still wonder whether *Lethe* is simply the name of a lake in the neighborhood or a poetic reference to Cupid's dormant state. Though Spenser's change from river to lake may only reflect the necessities of rhyme, it contributes to the naturalizing effect, and, as Spitzer notes (p. 501), a lake provides a more "sluggish" bed than a river. Flora and Maia remain similarly poised between rhetorical and rural, or tropical and topographic, existence. Is Flora a divine presence or the personified process of vernal awakening, the female cause and complement of the hawthorn's pride? Is "Maias bowre" reducible to E. K.'s "Maye bushes," or does Willye refer to the newly arisen Pleiad? We may assume that in either case, whether he speaks in periphrases like a poet or of persons like a reporter, he is innocent of the network of allusions surrounding those two names— E. K.'s gossip about the harlot Flora, and the story Spenser will later tell about Maia, whom Jove took "on the flowry gras, / Twixt sleepe and wake, after she weary was" (*Epithalamion* 308–9). But if we reflect that the knowledge motivating our assumption is denied Willye, we throw into high relief the idyllic quality of an innocence from which the darker complexities of love are concealed.

Spenser produces the effect of idyllicism by leading with the intertextual convention and countering with the pictorial convention. The technique of conspicuous allusion gives his fable a distinctly literary flavor and sets it in a network of myths and motifs that have already been invested with allegorical values by established interpretive traditions. Reducing those myths and motifs by the pictorialization governing Thomalin's tale from line 31 on conspicuously excludes allegorical values and erotic complexities from the speakers' awareness, while the use of tail rhyme further diminishes the scope of the episode to that of idyllic miniature. The basic unit of the pictorial convention, the unit by which this effect is achieved, may be called the *figure of sight*, illustrated in Thomalin's first description of Cupid:

> No, but happely I hym spyde,
> Where in a bush he did him hide,
> With winges of purple and blewe.
>
> *(31–33)*

The figure of sight is a visual condensation contextually marked so that it represents itself as simplifying a more complex set of ideas and thus not only produces the *eidyllion* ("little picture") but also makes possible the metapastoral critique of its reductiveness. It may take the form of personification, as it does here; but personification is not inevitably a figure of sight, since what it symbolizes may be put into play and affect the meaning of its context, whereas the figure of sight, because it is conspicuously *de*symbolized, both alludes to its referent and indicates that the referent is not in play.

Figures of sight are important to the economy of Spenser's "literary pictorialism," which John Bender has explored in a notable study. Bender objects to "Lessing's idea that words, in their proper function, have little to do with pictures and are capable of far more sophisticated psychological effects than visual imagery: that word pictures somehow limit poetry and violate its true nature."[12] But Spenser's pastoral deployment of figures of sight and the pictorial convention suggests that in one important respect he would agree with Lessing—or, to put it more forcefully, his use of figures of sight *thematizes* Lessing's criticism of word pictures, for he represents them as transformations of more complex into simpler codes, of signs or symbols into percepts, and by this device dramatizes the escape from obscurities and uncertainties to the vivid cartoon world of the *eidyllion*. Paul Alpers has long criticized the tendency to think of pastoral primarily "as a matter of images and projected worlds" instead of recognizing its central concern with "human singers and speakers," yet I think that Spenser not only encourages the tendency but does so (like Alpers) to criticize it (p. 362).

---

[12] *Spenser and Literary Pictorialism* (Princeton: Princeton University Press, 1972), 22.

The essence of the criticism the pictorial convention produces is directed toward poetic self-delight, the poet's vulnerability both to the seduction of poetic craft practiced for its own sake and to the self-contained imaginary worlds this practice engenders. In "The Eclogue Tradition" Alpers notes that Virgil's "*Eclogues* are less concerned with creating an autonomous world than they are with creating and evaluating styles of speech and song" (p. 357), and he extends this assertion to the eclogue tradition that includes Spenser. More recently, however, he has defended the autonomy of the pastoral singer's domain against the claim of what Annabel Patterson terms the "post-modernist theory of pastoral," namely, that pastoral is "primarily a discourse of the relations of power": [13]

> By writing a book of eclogues, conceived as the performance of pastoral roles, Spenser created what I would like to call a "domain of lyric." In using this term, I am trying to meet Louis Adrian Montrose's argument that when critics speak of Spenser's work in terms of "aesthetic space," they ignore what is specifically historical and cultural about his or any Elizabethan writer's poetic project. The way to avoid this charge . . . is not to oppose the historical and the aesthetic but to recognize that the claim to relative autonomy, by means of something that looks like aesthetic "space," was Spenser's historical (and therefore, indeed, problematic) aim in *The Shepheardes Calender*.[14]

Again I would add that the recognition of this claim, and especially of its historically problematical character, is shared by the author of the *Calender*. To put it in terms I have used in the past, the *Calender* shows itself aware of the difference between the self-enclosed green world constructed by the escapism of the paradise principle and the more open, always precarious and permeable, boundedness of the text produced by the second-world attitude, a text whose constant negotiation and conflict with the first world are everywhere evident. In *March* the dialectical play of the intertextual and the pictorial conventions focuses this difference. What remains to be explored is the extent to which the intertextual convention of *March* implicates a discourse, if not precisely of "the relations of power," then of the social pressures that shape the conventions of poetry and love the *Calender* represents with affectionate but critical self-amusement.

As Alpers notes, the *Calender* dramatizes "two of the main cultural

[13] "Re-opening the Green Cabinet: Clément Marot and Edmund Spenser," *English Literary Renaissance* 16 (1986): 45, 69.

[14] Alpers, "Pastoral and the Domain of Lyric in Spenser's *Shepheardes Calender*," *Representations* 12 (1985): 94.

pressures on the mid-Tudor lyric": "the disparagement of love and the moral conflict between youth and age" ("Domain of Lyric," 96). Thus *Januarye* parodies the adverse effects of poetry and love on each other in the genre of erotic complaint, while *Februarie* assimilates the discourse of love to that of generational conflict. *Januarye* shows how the plaintive *puer* is *senex* in being imprinted with conventional expectations derived from the culture of the literary elders he imitates, while *Februarie* shows how the moral *senex* is *puer*—how the so-called wisdom of the elders thinly veils the bitterness born of nostalgia for lost youth. *March*, which celebrates the year's first month in the pagan calendar, seems on the face of it to cast off that bitterness and return to the recreative moment at which "the seasonable spring refresheth the earth, and the pleasaunce thereof being buried in the sadnesse of the dead winter now worne away, reliveth" ("Generall Argument," 49–52). The dialogue opens with a feint toward the return of the paradise lost in *Januarye* and *Februarie*. But although the censorious elder's voice represented by Thenot in *Februarie* may be absent from the dialogue it is still present in the eclogue as a whole, where in fact the two pressures Alpers mentions are most explicitly registered as a contradiction within the literary tradition.

Leo Spitzer adverts to the youth-age conflict when he remarks that Willye's tale discloses the influence of Bion's fourth Idyll. He suggests that Spenser "perhaps felt constrained to repeat the diptych of young lad and graybeard found with Bion," and that the old ploughman in Bion's poem is replaced by Willye's father (p. 505). If we accept this, then we must admit that the source has been subjected to a certain amount of skewing in the direction of "the simplicitye of shepheards opinion of Love" (*March* 193–94), for Bion's old man—unlike Willye's father— knew that the boy hunted no ordinary bird but a wicked beast that would one day turn on its pursuer. There is, however, a better candidate for the role of graybeard and a more adequate replacement for *Februarie*'s Thenot, though he has been transposed from the eclogue proper to the gloss. The class of elders can be extended without strain beyond Willye's father and Thenot to include Bion and E. K.'s "Poetes"—to "the whole literary tradition" that according to Allen (p. 14) fathered the *March* eclogue. This tradition also includes E. K. But in order to appreciate this we have to shift from the category of influence dominating the approaches of Spitzer and Allen to that of allusion and quotation. "The whole literary tradition" is not merely imitated, not merely resonant within the eclogue as a harmonic enrichment; it is quoted with amusement: its claim to wisdom and its vision of love are sympathetically mocked. In particular, certain familiar features of the tradition come in for playful scrutiny in the eclogue's text, gloss, and allusive structure: the anti-erotic attitude, the figure of Cupid, and the motif of the hunt.

March, then, gives us a comic portrait of the tradition. Its values are well embodied in E. K., who is the subject rather than the painter of the portrait. He remarks that in Willye's tale "is sette out the simplicitye of shepheards opinion of Love." The question this comment simultaneously raises and begs, the question lurking in some of E. K.'s other comments, is whether the opinion is simple because shepherds underrate love's power or because they think love is "a winged lad" rather than the affection that, as he puts it, "tofmenteth the mynde." Willye and Thomalin begin—but only begin—to learn the "truth" about love taught by Bion, Ronsard, E. K., and other elders, including Thenot and Piers in the *Calender:* "The change of love from honey to gall reflects a change in the god himself. . . . Love, who once upon a time went about without weapons, in all innocence, now is armed with a venomous sting." And Nelson, whose words these are, cites Spitzer's reading of "the moral of the tale, 'Rejoice not in spring, be not young!—for this is hybris, and nemesis must follow!'" (pp. 42–43).

I don't think this is Spenser's moral. In my view he presents it as the wisdom of the literary elders, their vision of love as folly, and he shows what is wrong with it. For the same elders who criticize youth and love have transmitted to succeeding generations precisely that limited conception that leads inevitably to the change from honey to gall. Mars, or cruel Cupid, lurks always behind the dimpled and iridescent figure of the winged *putto* because the traditional understanding of love, desire, courtship, and, in general, relations between the sexes is dominated by such aggressive and unilateral models as those of the hunt or military conquest. This Cupid is a creation of the very elders who rancorously condemn "all the delights of Love" as "follye mixt with bitternesse" not only because of the torment infinite desire causes young minds but also because of the pain caused by the loss and memory of those delights "when yougthes flowre is withered" (*March* 197–98, 205). *March* thus presents both sides of the experience: in the idyll the Arcadian perspective of youth barred from knowledge of the cankered future and in the gloss the Mantuanesque perspective of age exiled from youth and surrounding its bright green with a penumbra of bitterness. The traditional debate between Youth and Age is implicit in this opposition, which carries on the theme introduced in *Februarie,* but since the role of Thenot is assigned to E. K., actual debate is forestalled. Unlike Cuddie, Thomalin and Willye have no access to their critic. This change of structure produces a more radical distinction of semantic modes between the recreative innocence of the shepherds and the moral-plaintive sophistication of the commentator: what the shepherds see as single-valued phenomena are duplicitous allegorical signs to E. K., who therefore criticizes the youths for misinterpreting their experience. The metapastoral text in turn supplies the motivation behind this criticism, suggests how the two opposing viewpoints contaminate each other, and inscribes their apparent simplicity and blindness in the traditional discourses it parodies.

Spenser obviously enjoys exploring and sending up the misadventures produced when love is viewed under the aspect of the hunt with the man as hunter, hero, predator, or captor and the woman as victim, enemy, spoil, trophy, or prey. He frequently puts the hunt model into play to dramatize the self-subverting expectations it generates in lovers: the excitement of the quest guaranteed by surmountable difficulties and obstacles; the anticipation of a definite outcome that if successful will resolve the issue in a single climax conclusively terminating all difficulties; the security of an experience that is ritually controlled, like a game or sport, so that the techniques are easily learned and the moves predictable. He shows how the logic of the model demands women to take defensive measures but at the same time narrowly constrains the range of possibilities open to them, so that the roles of the sexes may be reversed and women may choose or be forced to react in the mode of Diana, Penthesilea, Belphoebe, or Radegund. Each party to the predator-prey relation may be forced into both roles. Each may engage unwittingly in the ambivalent venery of hunting and erotic possession. Each may see the other either as prey or as a potential predator who must be reduced to prey. Each projects on the other full blame for the desire she/he is partly responsible for arousing. This model provides the recipe for frustration and bitterness whether the hunter fails or succeeds, though the deferred bitterness of success-induced failure is the more interesting of the two possibilities.

March, Aprill, and the *August* roundelay are the *Calender*'s idylls of the Vacant Head. In different ways the first two contain within themselves the seeds of the Vacant Head's downfall and, partly through the agency of the gloss, the eclogues show how those seeds are embedded in the paradisal soil transmitted by the elders from one generation to the next. In *March,* where love remains recreative sport, Cupid saves Thomalin from going as far as poor Colin did. But Cupid himself is a creation of the very elders who rancorously condemn "all the delights of Love" as "follye mixt with bitternesse" not only because of the torment infinite desire causes young minds but also because of the pain caused by their loss and memory "when yougthes flowre is withered" (*March* 197–98,

205). Why the *Calender*'s elders present the Vacant Head with a paradisal version of experience they at the same time condemn, with honey
they know will turn to gall, is a story to which I shall return in the last
two chapters of this study.

IV

The presence of these two factions in the *Calender* complicates the notion
of *puer senex:* the young poet is *senex* in being imprinted with the culture
of an antiquity he imitates, but at the same time ancient culture preserves
and transmits its own experience of youth. It offers the new poet the
opposing values and different phases of the life cycle. Yet the signals
these factions give are only superficially contradictory, and I shall argue
in the final two chapters that they are united by their common subordination to the paradise principle. The effects of this union are registered with special force in Spenser's representation of the theme of anti-
eroticism. Since this theme continued to interest him throughout his
career, I shall digress to *The Faerie Queene* to place the *Calender*'s treatment in perspective.

   E. K.'s comment in the *March* argument started the *Calender* discussion of anti-eroticism:[15] "in the person of Thomalin is meant some secrete freend, who scorned Love and his knights so long, till at length
him selfe was entangled, and unwares wounded with the dart of some
beautiful regard, which is Cupides arrowe." This comment suggested to
D. C. Allen that Thomalin "assumes the role of the Renaissance Anteros. . . . His purpose is clear; he is the avenger of the martyrs of love; he
will strike Eros down" (p. 18). Allen finds that "an antieroticism stains
all the love eclogues" (p. 15). But the case for Thomalin's anti-eroticism
is flimsy, since the venery of the hunt metaphor is ambivalent. That the
winged god replaces a feminine prey could well mean that the pursuit
signifies the huntsman's desire to capture love and to make it his. And
the figure can reverse itself in a variety of ways: the hunter may fear his
prey and pursue to avoid being pursued; the pursued may desire the pursuer he/she fears and be in flight from that desire. Feminine *daunger* is
motivated as much by the fear of feminine desire as by the fear of masculine domination. Spenser's portrayal of such rebels to love as Marinell
and Artegal shows the anti-erotic attitude based on the fear of being conquered by love's attractive power.

----

[15] I mean preventive rather than reactive anti-eroticism. Colin's in *Januarye* and
Thenot's in *Februarie* are reactive.

Since these complexities are packed into the age-old convention of the erotic hunt, the reader of *March* may well be prompted to think of them. But at the same time the literalization of the metaphor and the bounce of the verse should keep the reader from applying them interpretively to Thomalin. They are, so to speak, miniaturized by his exuberant narrative. Whether one or the other sense of venery—or both, or neither—is intended cannot be formally determined. And that may be Spenser's point: to remind us of potentialities inherent in the convention but not actualized in this recreative form, the form of the folk sensibility that generates around itself an ambience at once imaginary and unimaginative, since its "real" fairies and elves (to which Cupid is easily assimilable) obviate the need for imagination and their facticity precludes its exercise.

The instability of the Anteros or Troilus motif is of course fully exploited in *The Faerie Queene*, where the anti-erotic hero's fear of yielding to love only makes him submit more violently to Cupid's power. Such a reversal is briefly described at IV.ix.21:

> *Druons* delight was all in single life,
>> And unto Ladies love would lend no leasure:
>> The more was *Claribell* enraged rife
>> With fervent flames, and loved out of measure . . .

The syntax implies that Druon's delight is the cause of Claribell's contrary rage. This little scenario enacts the return of the repressed. As his name implies, Druon is oaklike, "sterne" (ix.20), and martial. The repressive temperance of these self-withholding and self-embracing figures of power ironically produces the very loss of self-control they dread.

The same pattern is dramatized on a larger scale in Books I and II. Under Archimago's influence Redcross projects his fear of sexuality, woman, entrapment by the other, onto Una. Una, who as Princess is the hero's passport to glory and the potential spoil or trophy of his conquest, is metamorphosed by his waking lust into the Whore and replaced by Duessa. A little "too solemne sad," Redcross yearns "To prove his puissance in battell brave / Upon his foe, and his new force to learne" (I.i.2–3), but because the "new force" is eros or "pride," the source of both martial and erotic fire, his embracing the former inevitably leads to the advent of the latter. Guyon in Book II provides the counterexample: the reflux of sexual energy intensified by repression supplies the fuel that further intensifies the angry and destructive rigor with which he continues to repress it.

The sexual basis of anti-eroticism is stressed by the rhetoric with which Spenser opens the twelfth canto of Book II:

> Now gins this goodly frame of Temperance
>   Fairely to rise, and her adorned hed
>   To pricke of highest praise forth to advaunce,
>   Formerly grounded, and fast setteled
>   On firme foundation of true bountihed;
>   And this brave knight, that for that vertue fights,
>   Now comes to point of that same perilous sted,
>   Where Pleasure dwelles in sensuall delights,
> Mongst thousand dangers, and ten thousand magick mights.

Such anti-eroticism is also antifeminism. Even a virtuous feminized structure—Alma's frame or castle of temperance—receives the displaced imagery of phallic pride. The stanza effectively places Guyon at the crossroads between Temperance and Pleasure, Alma and Acrasia, as if they possess the powers and dangers for and against which he fights. Their status is typographically enhanced by the use of uppercase, and since it is Arthur, not Guyon, who saved the foundation of temperance in canto xi, the ambiguous sixth line throws its weight in one direction: the brave lowercase knight fights not so much to defend uppercase Temperance as to acquire his rightful portion of it against difficult odds. Against Phaedria's blandishments, Spenser had told us earlier, Guyon "was wise, and warie of her will, / And ever held his hand upon his hart" (II.vi.26). This gesture indicates that the crazy-quilt phrase appearing four lines later, Guyon "fairly tempring fond desire subdewd," may reflect more than a touch of self-distrust, as if he does not feel fully immune to the fate of a profligate like Cymochles and must himself guard against the loss of "sovenaunce" that haunts even the most temperate of knights. Cymochles abandoned "care of vow'd revenge, and cruell fight," and

> to weake wench did yeeld his martiall might.
>   So easie was to quench his flamed mind
>   With one sweet drop of sensuall delight,
>   So easie is, t'appease the stormie wind
> Of malice in the calme of pleasant womankind.
>
>   *(vi.8)*

A more complex presentation of the same theme occurs in the proem to Book IV, which depicts two apparently different forms of anti-

eroticism. In one the narrator exhorts Cupid to liberate "the treasures of
true love enlocked" in his Queen's breast: "From her high spirit chase
imperious feare, / And use of awfull Majestie remove." The phrasing
allows us to read the "use of awfull Majestie" as a defense against love,
a defense perhaps prompted by fear that is imperious (and not only by
the empress's fear). No matter how specifically Spenser may refer to the
political implications of Elizabeth's marrying or not marrying, these
implications, insofar as they are in the air, complicate the position of a
poet who advocates marriage seemingly on behalf of love. For love is
now a political as well as a private matter. This advocacy sets the poet in
opposition to another faction Spenser alludes to in describing the second
form of anti-eroticism:

> The rugged forhead that with grave foresight
> > Welds kingdomes causes, and affaires of state,
> > My looser rimes (I wote) doth sharply wite,
> > For praising love, as I have done of late,
> > And magnifying lovers deare debate;
> > By which fraile youth is oft to follie led,
> > Through false allurement of that pleasing baite,
> > That better were in vertues discipled,
> Then with vaine poemes weeds to have their fancies fed.
>
> Such ones ill judge of love, that cannot love,
> > Ne in their frosen hearts feele kindly flame;
> > For thy they ought not thing unknowne reprove,
> > Ne naturall affection faultlesse blame,
> > For fault of few that have abusd the same.
> > For it of honor and all vertue is
> > The roote, and brings forth glorious flowres of fame,
> > That crowne true lovers with immortall blis,
> The meed of them that love, and do not live amis.
>
> > > > > > > *(IV.Pr.1–2)*

The reference to "thing unknowne" could be taken to mean either that
their frozen hearts have never felt the "kindly flame," that is, that they
were born frozen-hearted, or that they repressed their own desire in re-
pressing that of others. In either case the intensification of Guyon's
"rigour pittilesse" to the degree approached in parts of Book IV and
reached in Book V implies a paranoid fear both of the ease with which "affaires of state" may be disrupted and also of love's power to disrupt them.
Stoic censors cannot afford to know love any more than they can afford to

countenance it; they must hold their hands upon their minds and eyes as well as upon their hearts. Hence the censor's frozen heart may be the result of a self-refrigerating process.

In a perverse way the censor has succeeded in recovering Vacancy of Head. But the situation has changed radically since Cuddie inveighed against love's tyranny in *October:*

> The vaunted verse a vacant head demaundes,
> Ne wont with crabbed care the Muses dwell.
> Unwisely weaves that takes two webbes in hand.
>
> *(100–102)*

Now "affaires of state" replace "The vaunted verse," while the emphasis of the second line undergoes a subtle dislocation: the censor's "crabbed care" cannot tolerate the ambiguities and seductions of the Muses. The defense of civilization entails the suppression of the very culture that gives it value for individual life and experience. Since the censor views the political organism as perpetually on the brink of breakdown, his crabbed care reaches its claws into every corner of the realm so that poetry unavoidably becomes a political act. No matter how Vacant his Head, the poet cannot help being a *font* for good or evil: his *doings* are a well-head, a *fountain* pouring his words over the polity, and the parable of Mercilla's victim suggests that even if the poet was originally a *Bon Font* the nature of his activity is such that his poetry cannot remain gratuitous or autonomous or Vacant-Headed for long; it is bound to submit to the contrary pressures of the fell incensed points of mighty opposites, and in trying to preserve his own interests the poet is more than likely to degender into *Malfont* (V.ix.26).

Occasionally in Book IV and consistently in Book V Spenser dramatizes the censor's moralistic perspective either by assigning it to his narrator or by superimposing it on the surface of a narrative structure that belies it at its depths. The censor's is fundamentally a vision of discord. Its germinal image is that of the figure of Ate, whose tongue and heart are each divided into two contending parts and whose eyes, ears, feet, and hands are oddly matched pairs working against each other. The strict moral imagination produces a poetry divided between simplistic *exempla* of good and bad behavior and excludes anything ambiguous or problematical. Duplication replaces complication. All the evil knights are reducible to a single generic image. Identical figures and episodes multiply and duplicate in a manner that scarcely seems accidental. The redundancy marks both the poverty and the ideological insistence of a poetry dominated by the imperatives that drive the censor's imagination. Different knights appear, and the same knights reappear, doing the same things again and again, never at rest, compulsively urged on by the society whose values or disvalues they repetitively display. Such compulsive repetition projects the censor's unappeasable anxiety.

When Spenser suddenly turns to the Chaucerian tale of Cambell and the three brothers in IV.ii and iii, he shifts from purely bad to purely good figures—another dichotomy, with more redundancy. Created in reaction to Ate, the world of Cambell and Triamond slowly squeezes her out until she does not exist at all. The tale is founded on bitter golden-age assumptions—that real life is essentially beyond human control, that history is dominated by the force of *Atē*, and that wicked time, pain, frailty, death are the human lot. Hence to fulfill one's wishes it is necessary either to perfect the utopian machinery of repression—which happens in Book V—or else to withdraw into a substitute world created by art or magic. In both cases, repression and withdrawal, the effort to preserve safety and power entails acts of creation that make a space for themselves by destroying what stands in the way as a source of danger or seduction.

In the retrospect provided by this larger view of Spenser's *oeuvre*, the dichotomy generated in the *Calender* by the paradise principle falls into place, and conversely we see that Spenser extends his concern with that principle to *The Faerie Queene*. The censor's simplistic vision aligns poetry with love and sharply rebukes the "looser rimes" that praise love and magnify "lovers deare debate." Spenser allows this rebuke to be deserved if the love they blame is characteristic of the Vacant Head—love under the aspect of the hunt, or of warfare, or of sport, or of any other model that enables lovers to eschew the committed and difficult relation of friendship. But he also shows that the censor's blame may reflect the fear based on his own experience of lordly love's power and that it may not do justice to the quality of the love he perceives.

Re-verting to the Green Cabinet

A Modernist Approach to the Aesthetics of Wailing

I

In trying to determine what "Marot as a model meant to Spenser," Annabel Patterson points to the French poet's meditation on Virgil's first eclogue, "with its opportunities for insight into the ethical problems of dependency and privilege," his "grasp of pastoral as the language of exile" with emphasis on "the inevitable predicament of the intellectual," and "his fix on the ontology of imitation . . . , his sense of the memorial and reflective function of quotation as echo." Patterson notes that Marot's *Eglogue au roy* is echoed in *Januarye* as well as in *December*, "framing the poem in a cold wind blowing from the Continent," and she suggests that Spenser's references to Pan are affected by Marot's identification of Pan with Francis I in his "vert cabinet," or by his ambiguous use of the eclogue as a vehicle for "promoting a new French Augustanism while annotating . . . its deficiencies."[1] Spenser followed Marot in positioning the *Calender* "between the poetics of accommodation and the poetics of dissent" (p. 63). Thus as the *Calender* moves through the seasonal cycle if it leaves the "springlike optimist" of *Aprill* behind and returns to Marot's eclogue in *December*, "accepting from it only what is unrelievedly

---

[1] "Re-opening the Green Cabinet: Clément Marot and Edmund Spenser," *English Literary Renaissance* 16 (1986): 44, 57.

depressing" (pp. 61–62), the unhappy conclusion can't be contained within the explicit terms of Colin's complaint: "Spenser demanded from his readers an ability to translate one metaphorical system into another, a personal explanation of Colin's melancholy into a national one" (p. 63).

Even as I find myself attracted by Patterson's argument, I feel compelled to resist it in the name and interest of the very "Modernism" she criticizes—of the kind of reading she finds to have been "on the whole hostile to, or at least depreciatory of, any version of pastoral that takes valence from sociopolitical cause and content" (p. 67). It must be clear by now that I have no objection to reopening the green cabinet at least enough to admit into it the politics of sexual and generational conflict as well as the political implications for poetry of the failure of topical criticism in the moral eclogues. But I am inclined to stay in the cabinet longer than Patterson and to spend more time rummaging about among Colin Clout's effects; and this may be because I distinguish Colin's effects from Spenser's more sharply than Patterson does. I don't deny that a translation from "one metaphorical system into another" is possible, but I think it would have to respond to a more detailed "personal explanation of Colin's melancholy." In what follows I shall touch on some of the details that should affect any such translation.

Thomas Cain argues that Colin Clout's is the story of the gradually increasing power of the "poet who will consummate Orpheus' line," and Patrick Cullen maintains the opposite in his view of Colin as the figure of a person whose career through the *Calender* is a steady downhill slide. As I see it, each of these two views is partly right if combined in a certain way with the other—but not in a way its author would approve. The increasing power is that of the paradise principle, while the decline of Colin Clout is less a subject for fulminations about Aristotelian flaws and "tragic waste" of talent than an occasion for pastoral amusement and metapastoral critique: it enacts the irony and entrapment of a mode in which love and life, the lover and his grief, disappear into art.[2] Colin activates and displays this mode with the same expectations as his pastoral auditors, who confuse technical excellence with literary excellence, verse with poetry. His literary aspiration survives into *December,* where his reductive view of poetry as verse is suggested by his claim to have been "Somedele ybent to song and musicks mirth" in his "looser yeares" and

[2] Thomas H. Cain, "Spenser and the Renaissance Orpheus," *University of Texas Quarterly* 41 (1971): 30; Patrick Cullen, *Spenser, Marvell, and Renaissance Pastoral* (Cambridge: Harvard University Press, 1970), 81 ff.

to have received his early lessons from a shepherd with a bird's name (Wrenock). Small wonder that his peers applauded the outpouring of his Wandering Mind as if it were the product of the Vacant Head.

At the same time he blames his plight on Pan's envy and on the whole Arcadian conspiracy that encouraged his "pryde" and made him think his spring "would ever laste":

> And if that *Hobbinol* right judgement bare,
> To *Pan* his owne selfe pype I neede not yield.
>   For if the flocking Nymphes did folow *Pan,*
>   The wiser Muses after *Colin* ranne.
>
> But ah such pryde at length was ill repayde,
> The shepheards God (perdie God was he none)
> My hurtlesse pleasaunce did me ill upbraide,
> My freedome lorne, my life he left to mone.
>   Love they him called, that gave me checkmate,
>   But better mought they have behote him Hate.
>
> *(45–54)*

Colin begins with a modest but legitimizing appeal to someone else's judgment. But naming his challenge "pryde" does not diminish the obvious pride inscribed in the verse he speaks—in the condescending reference to the "wiser Muses," for example, or in the shading of "ill," which may mean not only "harshly, painfully," but also "inappropriately, unfairly," as if Pan acted out of envy. Colin gives "pryde" more positive connotations by associating it with "derring doe" and suggesting that at worst it was "hurtlesse pleasaunce." Had Pan been a more honorable loser he would have rewarded Colin with a prize rather than a punishment.

Owen Reamer has observed that in the final couplet above "Colin somehow casually blends" Pan with Cupid, though Cupid remains unnamed except by E. K.[3] Instead of being personified as the cruel archer, the "raging fyre" of Love/Hate is ascribed to astrological causes (57–60) as if Pan had mobilized the forces of the cosmos against his poor victim. The metamorphosis of Pan into Love/Hate affirms the continuity between Colin's garden state and his present attitude. Colin has reason to reject Pan, who, after all, pursued Syrinx "Not as a Nymph, but for a Reed." Perhaps the god's failure as a lover affects the music of retirement over which he presides in his "greene cabinet," disenabling its per-

---

[3] "Spenser's Debt to Marot—Re-examined," *Texas Studies in Language and Literature* 10 (1959): 522.

suasive power precisely to perpetuate itself at the expense of the musician: by helping the singer fail as a lover it keeps him singing, since fewer songs would be sung if there were less woe to be wasted. The appreciation for Pan's pastoral art and care expressed in *Aprill, November,* and the beginning of *December* is now balanced by Colin's competitive and critical desire to emulate Pan, to surpass him, and to blame his own bad luck in love on the god. Colin invokes Pan in *December* not merely as "thou Shepheards God" but, more inflatedly, as "thou God of shepheards all," protector both of flocks and "their maisters" (7–12). This double invocation intensifies by contrast the Panic totality of his subsequent rejection at line 50: "The shepheards God (perdie God was he none)."[4]

The next stanza appears to rationalize as well as to naturalize this "checkmate" with a seasonal and astrological explanation:

> Tho gan my lovely Spring bid me farewel,
> And Sommer season sped him to display
> (For love then in the Lyons house did dwell)
> The raging fyre, that kindled at his ray.
>   A comett stird up that unkindly heate,
>   That reigned (as men sayd) in *Venus* seate.
>
> *(55–60)*

But the rationalization begins to wear thin when Colin harnesses it to an echo of his *August* wail in the woods:

> Forth was I ledde, not as I wont afore,
> When choice I had to choose my wandring waye:
> But whether luck and loves unbridled lore
> Would leade me forth on Fancies bitte to playe,
>   The bush my bedde, the bramble was my bowre,
>   The Woodes can witnesse many a wofull stowre.
>
> *(61–66)*

Beneath the bathos of the skewed musico-equine trope lies the hint of a more complex explanation: to make music on Fancy's bit is to hurt oneself with poetry, and whether the horse in question is the speaker or "loves unbridled lore," if the bit is unbridled, the self-wounding and self-pity must be gratuitous. They continue, however, in the next stanza, where they are once again targeted, this time by conspicuous hyperboles:

---

[4] The force of this parenthetical rejection is increased by the echoes in the eclogue of Marot's many bland tributes to Pan/Francis I.

> Where I was wont to seeke the honey Bee,
> Working her formall rowmes in Wexen frame:
> The grieslie Todestoole growne there mought I see
> And loathed Paddocks lording on the same.
>   And where the chaunting birds luld me a sleepe,
>   The ghastlie Owle her grievous ynne doth keepe.
>
> *(67–72)*

Of this stanza Patterson observes that Spenser has taken Marot's "suitably ironized" version of "Tityrus' idyll as conceived by Meliboeus" and "translated the dream into nightmare." She uses this Virgilian intertext to place Spenser in the Meliboean exile's position and to read the stanza as a kind of political prophecy: "In the English winter, poetry is effectively discontinued"—the winter that will send Spenser to Ireland (pp. 62–63). But there are two problems with this reading. First, the context and language of the stanza offer considerable resistance to Patterson's translation principle. Given the vividness of the *August* allusion, one has to discard too many details to translate "a personal explanation of Colin's melancholy into a national one." If the political tenor of the Virgil-Marot framework is felt at all at this point, the effect may be contrary to the one Patterson describes. If, that is, we assume that *Spenser* is speaking darkly of the political future, the effect is dissipated by Colin's playing on Fancy's bit, and if we take note of this dissipation we may be inclined to change the terms of any prophecy we read in the lines: the art and motivation embodied in the figure of Colin will have to be transcended or revised to produce a more persuasive poetry of political complaint. Second, Patterson's reading ignores the effect of bathetic hyperbole: the "loathed Paddock lording" on the "grieslie Todestoole" *may* be an allusion to those in power and thus a foretaste of political nightmare, but if it is, the reductive scale of the figure is so inappropriate as to trivialize it. Colin's worm's-eye view of the danger pitches it at the fairy level of, say, *A Midsummer Night's Dream*.

Having reviewed his victimage to love, Colin seems to change the subject. He recalls the period after "spring gives place to elder time" (73) when he applied himself to "thinges of ryper reason,"

> And learnd of lighter timber cotes to frame,
> Such as might save my sheepe and me fro shame.
>
> To make fine cages for the Nightingale,
> And Baskets of bulrushes was my wont:
> Who to entrappe the fish in winding sale
> Was better seene, or hurtful beastes to hont?

> I learned als the signes of heaven to ken,
> How *Phoebe* fayles, where *Venus* sittes and when.

> And tryed time yet taught me greater thinges,
> The sodain rysing of the raging seas:
> The soothe of byrds by beating of their wings,
> The power of herbs, both which can hurt and ease:
>> And which be wont t'enrage the restlesse sheepe,
>> And which be wont to worke eternall sleepe.
>
> *(77–90)*

The sequence moves rapidly from defensive to offensive skills, from building to trapping and hunting to learning how to read and to use nature's secrets. This passage obviously resonates with displaced echoes of his still-rankling love wound. The reference to caging the nightingale recalls the *August* lament (183–86) and thus suggests aggressive self-despite; the references to fishing and hunting are equally aggressive displacements. Line 84 transparently displaces the sources of erotic failure to astrological influences, figuring in Venus and Phoebe a world that conspires to make men feel lust and women fail to resist it. The mention of Phoebe looks back to Hobbinol's paradisal fantasy of "pierless pleasures" in *June*—Pan "Will pype and daunce, when Phoebe shineth bright" (31)—and freshly registers the loss of that careless time. These allusions color lines 86 and 88–90 with erotic bitterness and anger, a mood underscored by the following lines when Colin complains that all the knowledge gained in "elder time" is of no avail in curing himself (91–96).[5]

Finally, there seems to be a change from *Januarye* in his attitude toward Rosalind. There he described himself as victimized by her rejection, but in *December* she is the victim: "Ah who has wrought my *Rosalind* this spight / To spil the flowres, that should her girlond dight?" (113–14). The answer implicit in his preceding lines is that the culprit was whoever or whatever deprived him of his harvest of "grain" (99) and "fruit" (104) and caused his garden of "flowres" to wither "for lacke of dewe" (111); whoever or whatever was responsible for blasting "The eare [his ear?] that budded faire" (99) by denying him the reward ("dewe") he hoped for. By this time in the eclogue the culprit could be

---

[5] Reamer, 524, notes that while "Marot has Robin mention learning about how to 'avoid the dangerous plants'" Spenser "manages not only to extend the detail but to give it almost sinister overtones as he talks about plants which 'enrage the restlesse sheepe' and 'worke eternall sleepe.'"

Pan, Love, Hate, Venus, and the other astrological forces whose conjunctions frustrate "husbandry." But Colin cranks these cosmic causes of woe so energetically into his complaint machine as to make one suspect they are surrogates for the real culprit, Rosalind, victimized by her own stubborn resistance and thus justly deprived of poetic praise. Yet that suspicion immediately gives rise to another, the speaker's evasion of which is rendered conspicuous by all these displacements: the real culprit is the speaker himself, self-victimized by his continuing allegiance and submission to the paradise principle. The referential diffuseness of his georgic metaphors seems calculated to conceal the specific causes and character of the complaint, making them signify disappointed hopes at the most general level: erotic, literary, political, and social failure dissolve into a universal blur whose metaphoric charge is then transferred into the dominant analogy of winter and age (127–50).

This transference reverses the projective direction of the tropes Colin employed in *Januarye*, for the pastoral landscape is now retracted into the solitary singer to signify his defeat at the hands of the All governed by Pan. But the obsession concealed by his metaphoric smokescreen is restated with enough frequency to mark its presence and to reveal the smokescreen for what it is. The final stanza makes it clear that even the "natural" aging process has been appropriated as a figure of rejected love:

> Winter is come, that blowes the balefull breath,
> And after Winter commeth timely death.
>
> Adieu delightes, that lulled me asleepe,
> Adieu my deare, whose love I bought so deare:
> Adieu my little Lambes and loved sheepe,
> Adieu ye Woodes that oft my witnesse were:
>   Adieu good *Hobbinol*, that was so true,
>   Tell *Rosalind*, her *Colin* bids her adieu.
>
> *(149–56)*

E. K.'s comment shifts the emphasis of the stanza in a paraphrase whose misdirection is blatant enough to accentuate by contrast the speaker's focus on Rosalind:

> Where in sixe verses he comprehendeth briefly all that was touched in this booke. In the first verse his delights of youth generally. In the second the love of Rosalind, in the thyrd, the keeping of sheepe, which is the argument of all Æglogues. In the fourth his complaints. And in the last two his professed frendship and good will to his good friend Hobbinoll. (217–22)

As I shall try to show in the concluding chapter, this shift of emphasis conforms to the preferences and aversions inscribed in the portrait of E. K.: his praise of Colin, his delight in the traditional tropes and conventions of poetry, the uneasiness about love already noted in my account of *March*. Here he passes quickly over "the love of Rosalind," dwells on the centrality of the good shepherd theme, mentions complaints without connecting them to the theme of the second verse, and defuses the double message of the conclusion by ignoring the final verse: Hobbinol's truth implicitly measures Rosalind's falsity, and this contrast stresses the magnanimous and sportsmanlike gesture with which Colin rises above it to send the cause of his undoing the nasty message that he is undone.

Since I view Colin Clout less as Spenser's mouthpiece than as his target, I find it difficult to go along with Patterson's translation of Colin's problems into Spenser's. For me when Colin pronounces himself tired of complaining—"My Muse is hoarse and weary of this stounde" (140)—it is an occasion for the reader's "merry glee" (139): Colin's plaintive defeat is assimilated to Spenser's meta-recreative triumph. Hence I can't accept Patterson's account of the relation between Marot and Spenser. In her brief discussion of the *Eglogue* she names the pastoral speaker, Robin, only once because she premises that he is a Clementine transparency or mouthpiece, and the same premise underlies the thesis that Colin's pastoral of thwarted love translates into Spenser's pastoral of state. But this assimilation of the two poems ignores the difference that Owen Reamer pointed out in his earlier essay: Marot's Robin is worried about the future but Colin's complaint is fixed on the effects of past injury (Reamer, 525). On the face of it, therefore, Robin is easier to identify with Marot than Colin with Spenser, and although Patterson tries to neutralize this difference with her translation principle she can do so only by occluding the sort of detail produced by the "Modernist" interpretation she criticizes. The translation principle is necessary because Spenser departs from Marot in emphasizing not only the specificity and complexity but also the hilarity of the traditional discourse of complaint that speaks through Colin—the self-deceiving and self-justifying rhetoric of the victim's discourse.

Reamer comments on the near absence of the love theme in Marot's eclogue:

> Marot's Robin, much concerned with his singing and composing ability, his musical contests, and his relations with Pan, discusses those subjects at great length. Blond Helen gets only two lines. Spenser's Colin, on the other hand,

devotes more than half of his [summer] passage to his truly bitter love complaint. The few details pertaining to his education are tossed in almost indifferently, for even as he is listing them he is swept back into morbid grief. (p. 525)

Suppose we detect a strong allusion to Marot's eclogue. Then the effect of this difference is radically to alter the meaning of the recreative emphasis on skill and education, for (1) Spenser shows it to be rooted in the love complaint it displaces, and (2) the portrait of Colin as a whole shows how failure in love is in turn motivated by the recreative interests dominated by Pan and the paradise principle. In this light, an allusion to Marot could be construed as a critique of an insufficiently analytical representation of the recreative impulse, one that represses the erotic motive reciprocally bound up with it. This may not be a "pastoral of state," as Patterson calls it, but it is by no means apolitical; it implicates a pastoral of sexual politics and, by the same token, a political critique of paradisal poetics. It is in that respect a cultural critique of motivational patterns inscribed in and reproduced by dominant literary genres and conventions.

In Reamer's view the *Eglogue* is no more than "an entertaining autobiography" aimed at pleasing Marot's sovereign, who is thinly disguised as Pan (p. 526). Patterson goes beyond this in arguing that it is not only "an expression of gratitude to a royal patron" but also an appeal "to Pan to protect him from the coming of a winter of discontent. . . . For poetry's continuance the poet needs to be assured that the favor he now enjoys will not be taken from him" (p. 54). Because it would take a lot of translation to turn Colin's Pan into Elizabeth—especially since she is represented in *Aprill*—the gap between Colin and Spenser is wider than that between Robin and Marot.[6] Perhaps the confusion between author and pastoral speaker, the wavering boundary between actual and imaginary states of affairs, is something Spenser finds to criticize in the literary discourses he represents and alludes to. Perhaps he would defend the proposition that the truest political poetry is the most feigning. At any rate, in transferring political anxiety about the future to erotic complaint about the past, he redirects "the Vergilian strategy of address to those in power" (Patterson, 58) from the monarch to the Cruel Fair of the Petrarchan tradition and thus reformulates the conditions of "poetry's continuance." Colin's poetry, emulating Pan's, assures that the favor he de-

---

[6] Patterson refers to Elizabeth as "Spenser's Augusta," but this identification can't be extended with any conviction to Colin's Pan, and she has to strain to give Elizabeth a more central role than the one focused in *Aprill:* "her relationship to English culture must be inferred from the relationship of Spenser's pastoral practice to Marot's" (p. 64).

sires to enjoy will be taken from him so that he can go on writing about it: "lovers are given to poetry, and what they swear in poetry may be said, as lovers, they do feign."

Reamer remarks the redundancy and stasis of the plaintive mode in distinguishing the "care" Spenser ascribes to Colin from that of Marot's Robin: Spenser's "is but a figurative reference to the melancholy, dejected state of mind which the shepherd has harvested as a result of his pursuit for a lifetime of a fruitless love. Marot's is a temporary annoyance (if the cause be removed); Spenser's, a permanent condition which can no longer be alleviated" (p. 525). But from this contrast and others Reamer draws some odd conclusions:

> Colin, at the close of his song (ll. 130–56), is thoroughly an old man. . . . Robin never really grows old. . . . Colin . . . emerges more than ever as the rather real individual (despite his conventional trappings) who is concerned only with recounting the story of his life and who is now ready for death. . . . Marot was patently trying to write . . . in conventional pastoral style. . . . Spenser . . . wanted to create at least a quasi-realistic figure in Colin, whose erotic story binds the twelve months together. To do so he . . . infused into the conventional figure of the shepherd a convincing spirit of melancholy old age approaching the grave. (pp. 526–27)

The opening contrast is misleading: Robin is already old ("Mais maintenant que ie suis en l'automne," *Eglogue* 1.199), while Colin, since he is described at the beginning of *December* as making "of love his piteous mone" (6), is presumably to be thought of as no older than he was when moaning in *Januarye* and *June*. If by the end of *December* he has become thoroughly old and approaches the grave, he is less quasi-realistic than bizarre, "a rather [sur]real individual." Spenser transforms Marot's motif of the older shepherd's retrospect into a trope, a hyperbole expressing the pathological pleasure in the rhetoric of self-pity that marks the victim's discourse. Colin's "spirit of melancholy old age" *is* convincing as parody—convincing, that is, as a send-up of the resources of self-deception, self-justification, and blame shifting that such well-formed language games as the victim's discourse make available. It is the discourse, not the speaker, that is "realistic." Stressing the conventionality of the speaker and of the rhetorical self-indulgence that provides the site of the discourse is essential to this particular "effect of the real."

When Colin reviews the activities of his lost innocence he sees them deceptively mantled by the soft Arcadian tradition that promoted the illusion of unending youth: "What wreaked I of wintrye ages waste, / Tho deemed I, my spring would ever laste" (29–30). This couplet speaks to the one that occupies the corresponding place in *Januarye:* "And yet alas, but now my spring begonne, / And yet alas, yt is already donne" (29–30). The instant senescence that follows, prompted by the January landscape, is an obvious hyperbole, and though the comments on "ryper age" in Colin's *June* complaint (33–48) are less obviously hyperbolic, the remainder of the eclogue hardly encourages the thought that senescence is anything more than a state of Wandering Mind. No speaker in pastoral fiction has a body, grows old, or dies of natural causes unless it serves a discursive function, and it is the conventionality of the speaker, the literariness of his language, that renders this service conspicuous. The *Januarye* hyperbole shows that the function of senescence is to measure the folly of illusory expectations sown by the paradise principle in the Vacant Head and to express the bitterness that is its dialectical consequence.

On this point E. K. is a reliable guide to the character of Colin's senescence. In the argument to *Januarye* he says that Colin is "but newly (as semeth) enamoured of a countrie lass called *Rosalind:* with which strong affection being very sore traveled, he compareth his carefull case to the sadde season of the yeare." And in the argument to *December:* "Wherein as weary of his former wayes, he proportioneth his life to the foure seasons of the yeare . . ." This is a comic instance of the pastoral conversion of great things to small. To pass a lifetime in a year is to treat a year as if it were a lifetime and to make mountains of molehills. Colin is not in fact simply "recounting the story of his life," as Reamer puts it, but using that device to inflate the consequences of rejection. He relishes so much in his fantasy of himself as a winter wonderland that—in what for me is the eclogue's finest comic touch—his metaphors become insanely real:

> The carefull cold hath nypt my rugged rynde,
> And in my face deepe furrowes eld hath pight:
> My head besprent with hoary frost I fynd,
> And by myne eie the Crow his clawe dooth wright.
>
> *(Dec. 133–36)*

For such interpretive reasons I am skeptical of the specific terms of Patterson's claim that "Spenser demanded from his readers an ability to translate one metaphorical system into another, a personal explanation of Colin's melancholy into a national one." Unless one slides quickly past the detail of Spenser's rhetorical buffoonery at the expense of his pastoral puppet, the risibility factor is likely to be as high as it is when the critic by earnest castigation or commiseration brings the melancholy puppet, like Pinocchio, to life as a "rather real individual." If the *Calender* "is unmistakably dominated by the unhappy, and not the fortunate shepherd," and if that shepherd is Colin Clout, then I don't see how the "national" explanation can reach the promised land of "the first significant English pastoral of state" (Patterson, 64) without sinking into the cold river of "My head besprent with hoary frost I fynd." This bath, however, can be refreshing if we emerge from it to follow Patterson's formula in a different direction by translating the personal explanation of Colin's melancholy not into a national one but into a metapastoral one. During the remainder of this chapter I shall explore Spenser's mimicry of plaintive conventions by passing quickly through *August* and more slowly through *November.* For there, as in *December,* Spenser shows how the idyll of the Vacant Head persistently influences, or contaminates, the laments of the Wandering Mind.

II

For practical purposes there may finally be little or no difference between a model in which real love is destined to end in song and one in which love and pain are fictions dramatized by the Vacant Head "whylst youth, and course of carelesse yeeres" prevail. One who is "really" in love is likely to find himself unprepared for it by either model. Thus Colin, winningly surprised, responds to the stale paradox as if he had just discovered a blinding new truth: "Ah God, that love should breede both joy and payne." The bifold character of the *August* eclogue shows how difficult it is to distinguish one model from the other. Spenser makes this clear by assigning the pastoral auditors similar responses to both the roundelay and the sestina, despite the obvious tonal contrast.

Patrick Cullen has hammered home this contrast as an example of the polarity "between the comedy of normal human experience" and Colin's "tragedy of human waste and unnatural disorder" (p. 111). Cullen insists they are not parallel, but although he devotes several pages to the poetic construction of the roundelay he says nothing about Colin's sestina except that its "function" is to testify "to Colin's great talent"; he emphasizes Colin's life rather than his art and ignores Perigot's response ("How I admire ech turning of thy verse"), which, as Louis Montrose observes, "is not empathy with Colin's anguished spirit but awed delight in his skill."[7] Another critic follows Cullen's lead in arguing that "Colin's lament ought to alarm us as we apprehend the depths to which he has

[7] "'The perfecte paterne of a Poete': The Poetics of Courtship in *The Shepheardes Calender,*" *Texas Studies in Language and Literature* 21 (1979): 43.

plunged in self-absorption" since *Januarye*, and he thinks that while the
verse is technically "of a high order" its "ironic relevance to the state of
Colin's mind" should lead us beyond Perigot's praise toward recognition
that "his 'turning' . . . is vain and self-regarding."[8] I find it hard to
imagine that Spenser expects me to work up much alarm over the plight
or pathology of Colin Clout or to spend much time judiciously castigat-
ing his pastoral puppet's flawed character; "the state of . . . mind" Colin
models is a consequence of the logic of the literary tradition Spenser parodies. Something could be made in social terms of the difference between Amoebaean dialogue and the solo sestina, but since both are performances, and since Perigot is no less lovelorn than Colin, the salutary
hey-ho's Willye directs at the former are applicable to the latter as well.

So long as a poet can convert his despair into a sestina he is better off
than he claims. But there are different ways to read both this conversion
and its contribution to the eclogue and the *Calender* as a whole. Commentators who remain cool about Colin respond variously to the meaning of his recreative triumph. David L. Miller, for example, treats the
sestina as "an open assertion of Colin's preeminence (or a thinly veiled
assertion of Spenser's)"; "an exemplary tour de force, a pure sign of its
author's skill" at the conclusion of which Perigot "holds up an AP-
PLAUSE sign to the reader." But the applause is for Spenser's art, and
this art defines its triumph by making contrastive use of the figure of
Colin, whose "failure in the *Calender* is precisely a failure to reenact
Pan's sublimation of natural desire in the making of harmony." For
John D. Bernard, on the other hand, the eclogue does not represent
Spenser's personal bid for Virgilian preeminence so much as his celebration of pastoral's ability to reconcile classical complaint and Renaissance
moral debate in a recreative harmony that restores "an ideal order in
which human purposes are at one with nature's." Bernard claims that
both *August* songs

> deal with love . . . in a recreative manner: the roundelay by its joyous patter,
> the sestina with its erotic sublime. In this contrast they represent different
> modes of the Arcadian spirit, both implicit in the genre from the outset. But
> in their diverse ways both achieve the same end: to repair in the dimension of
> music the rent fabric of human experience. Thus Spenser reaffirms the tradi-
> tional function of pastoral song.[9]

---

[8] Richard Mallette, "Spenser's Portrait of the Artist in *The Shepheardes Calender* and
Colin Clouts Come Home Againe," *Studies in English Literature* 19 (1979): 29.
[9] David L. Miller, "Authorship, Anonymity, and *The Shepheardes Calender*," *Mod-*

Where Bernard emphasizes the *Calender*'s commitment to the ideal of withdrawal, Miller acknowledges that project but subordinates it to a return to action and history, stressing its "didactic purpose" and its attempt to establish, "in Elizabethan culture, a special public role for its author" (p. 229). But for both the *Calender* celebrates the special if limited virtues of traditional pastoral, and this is the position I have been contesting.

The question is whether the reconciliation and resolution Bernard finds is merely that or is marked in a more complex manner *as* escapism—whether, that is, "Pan's sublimation" is represented as sufficient or is problematized by conspicuous displacements and exclusions. I think this question may best be explored by examining the ecphrasis of the mazer Willye pledges. Bernard, Miller, and Montrose all agree that this passage, like Willye's response to the sestina, emphasizes the triumph of recreative concerns. Montrose remarks of the mazer's image of "a shepherd saving a lamb from the jaws of a wolf" that "the scenario of the moral eclogues is re-created in the happy stillness of art" (p. 43). Bernard notes that Spenser "has added to the customary *discordia concors* of the motif a touch of pastoral heroics in the manner of Sidney" (p. 318). Miller finds "a familiar aesthetics" implied by the scenes on the mazer: "art acquires the power to draw harmony out of conflict by removing itself from the world, but this withdrawal must be followed by a renewed commitment to action" (p. 229).

The two stanzas devoted to the ecphrasis show that even as the accent shifts from the moral to the recreative aspect, from the evil of wolves to the maker's skill, the "happy stillness" vibrates with aesthetic displacements of the violence it seems to distance:

> Then loe *Perigot* the Pledge, which I plight:
> A mazer ywrought of the Maple warre:
> Wherein is enchased many a fayre sight
> Of Beres and Tygres, that maken fiers warre:
> And over them spred a goodly wild vine,
> Entrailed with a wanton Yvie twine.
>
> Thereby is a Lambe in the Wolves iawes:
> But see, how fast renneth the shepheard swayne,
> To save the innocent from the beastes pawes:
> And here with his shepehooke hath him slayne.

ern Language Quarterly 40 (1979): 229, 234; Bernard, "'June' and the Structure of Spenser's *Shepheardes Calender*," 317, 305, 318–19.

Tell me, such a cup hast thou ever sene?
Well mought it beseme any harvest Queene.

(25–36)

What the language as picture domesticates, the language as text de-
familiarizes. *Enchased* puns on the idea of pursuing or hunting fair
sights, enjoying the "fiers warre" of savage beasts in voyeuristic safety.
The homonymous repetition of *warre* retrojects into the second line the
notion of the craftsman's war with the knotty burl ("warre") of the ma-
ple. The verb *spred* creeps away from the passive voice to suggest the
active splay of entangling vine either within the image or over the surface of the cup—a netlike figure of entrapment over the beasts (cf.
March 107–11) or else a token of wild nature (artificial? real?) embracing the cup and "entrailed" with an emblem of erotic desire. The first
stanza thus glances in a cautious, even insidious, way toward heroic venery in the far-off world of "Fierce warres and faithfull loves," while in
the second stanza the homebred hero seeks Happy Ending in rustic war
and love. This mazer becomes mazelike in its meaning, both embodying
and depicting the virile skills of the shepherd, implying a pledge of
manhood fit to amaze "any harvest Queene." Within the miniaturized
field of recreative fantasy, it speaks of passion, conquest, the competitive
spirit. And so too does the ecphrasis. E. K. reminds us of the intertextual scope of the ambition and conflict "enchased" in it when he mentions
Virgil's two Amoebaean eclogues in his argument and refers to the mazer's precedents in his gloss:

> So also do Theocritus and Virgile feigne pledges of their strife. . . . Such
> pretie descriptions every where useth Theocritus, to bring in his Idyllia. For
> which speciall cause indede he by that name termeth his Æglogues: for
> Idyllion in Greke signifieth the shape or picture of any thyng, whereof his
> booke is ful.

Recursively embedded in the ecphrasis is an anamorphic representation
of the *Calender* poet's own recreative "warre" with his precursors ("such
a cup hast thou ever sene?") and of his impressment of moral and plaintive topics to serve in the campaigns of art.

The mazer effect extends to the singing match that deflates Perigot's
"griefe" and to Cuddie's mediation, which at once distances Colin's grief
and contributes his sestina to the songfest. Borrowing Colin's art is a discreet and efficient way for Cuddie to trade the role of judge for that of
competitor. E. K. points this out in glossing the emblem and once again
directs attention to the recreative displacement of conflict: "Perigot by

his poesie claming the conquest, and Willye not yeelding, Cuddie the arbiter of theyr cause, and Patron of his own, semeth to chalenge it, as his dew." The mazer effect extends further, to the sestina itself and the auditors' response to it. Spenser's variation on Arnaut Daniel's sestina order swings it through a circle (1-2-3-4-5-6, 6-1-2-3-4-5, 5-6- . . . -n) back to its starting point, enacting a prosodic version of the Wandering Mind's return to the very equilibrium its singer rejects. And as Paul Alpers insists, Colin's "concern is continually with song": it centers on "carefull cryes," that is, on the proper sprinkling of cries, plaints, tears, shrieks, and the other gestures in the conventional repertory.[10] Colin's concluding call to universal insomnia is ignored by the shepherds as they in effect put a picture frame around the sestina and pipe their way home to bed (190–95).

Montrose comments that the singing match sublimates "the political, intellectual, and emotional strife of the moral and plaintive eclogues into harmonious counterpoint" and that the exchange of gifts that concludes it "is a model of perfect reciprocity in which there are no losers" (p. 43). All the more interesting is the additional counterpoint provided by Colin's sestina, which models the perfect nonreciprocity of the complete loser whose avowed project is to make the world share his pain by pub-licizing both Rosalind's misdeed and his victimization. Since Colin, be-fore he lost, participated in the Arcadian harmony and won notable vic-tories on the field of song, the two parts of the eclogue may be viewed in a before-after relation with respect to the paradise principle: the expecta-tions enchased on the mazer produce the bitter response inscribed in the sestina. But the turning of the verse and the troping of the whole struc-ture viewed under the aspect of the mazer reverses the normal relation of the two sources of redundancy: erotic obsession is the means to poetic expression. Misogyny is the dark side of recreative narcissism.

The *August* singing match and sestina evoke echoes of *March* and *Ap-rill* as well as of *Januarye, Maye,* and *Julye* to dramatize the growing power of the recreative mode—the return of the Wandering Mind to the desired Vacancy of Head—as it gains confidence, opens itself to moral and plaintive themes, and subordinates them to the immediate pleasures of song and verse. *September* then suggests the limits of this recreative triumph: metaphoric wolves in the great world are harder to control than literal wolves on the farm, but even the latter give more

---

[10] "The Eclogue Tradition and the Nature of Pastoral," *College English* 34 (1972): 362. On the sestina and its peculiar form, see Marianne Shapiro, *Hieroglyph of Time: The Petrarchan Sestina* (Minneapolis: University of Minnesota Press, 1980), 182–87.

trouble than the wolf happily concluded on the mazer. In the series of reductive displacements from the great world to the rustic world to the mazer we mark both the darkening shadows of real difficulties and the correspondingly more energetic appropriation of these by the art of Pan. The most striking example of this process occurs in Colin's next and final song, the *November* elegy, to which I now turn.

III

The primary consideration motivating the choice of song in *November* is not the death of Dido but Thenot's general desire to hear Colin sing— sing anything, even a pleasant song—and Colin's response that a sad song is best for the onset of winter. Thenot's reaction to the elegy, like that of the *August* shepherds, is directed toward the *dolceamaro* effect of Colin's verse (203–8). But critical opinion of *November* has been less firmly centered, wavering back and forth between the *dolce* and the *amaro*, and between attention to the verse and attention to the subject matter. On the one hand:

> As every alert reader of the *Calender* observes, *November* provides the source and end for all lesser visions. The transposition of pastoral imagery into a transcendental key, deriving as it ultimately does from *Revelation,* confers upon this mode of imagining the sanction of the divine artist. "Fayre fieldes and pleasaunt layes there bene" in Heaven (188); as a result, fields and lays are reinvigorated for us as metaphorical anticipation of bliss.[11]

On the other:

> The "heavie herse" section acknowledges the presence of death in the "hard" pastoral world, while the "happy herse" ending transforms the reality of death into a transcendental replica of the "soft" pastoral world infused by the apotheosis of Dido with consolatory Christian hope. . . . Is Spenser entirely serious in Colin's elaborate eulogy of Dido . . . with its merger of pastoral elegy and hagiography? . . . Spenser's humor seems calculated when Colin, after describing St. Dido's joys in heaven, celebrates the pleasures of daily dying and urges all the shepherds to die immediately in order to join her.[12]

---

[11] Isabel MacCaffrey, "Allegory and Pastoral in *The Shepheardes Calender,*" *ELH* 36 (1969): 104–5.

[12] Waldo F. McNeir, "The Drama of Spenser's *The Shepheardes Calender,*" *Anglia* 95 (1977): 52–53.

On the one hand:

> The strategy of the elegy is to transform the "earthlie mould" of a literal
> Dido into a symbolic vehicle of the poet's own aspiration. . . . Colin now
> sings in a visionary, prophetic mode that leaves the courtships of Rosalind
> and Eliza behind. . . . At the outset of the *November* eclogue, Colin keeps
> his *Januarye* vow: he will sing neither of Rosalind nor Pan. Through his
> power to enact symbolically a myth of sacrifice and apotheosis that *transcends*
> the pastoral world, he demonstrates his progression toward a higher kind of
> poetry and his emulation of a higher poetic genius. (Montrose, 51–52)

And on the other:

> "November's" elegy for Dido is significant not only for what it is, a lament
> for the death of Dido, but also for what it tells us about Colin, his obsession
> with death, his nostalgia for and yet increasing alienation from the pastoral
> world. Amplifying the personal significance of the elegy for Colin is the fact
> that Dido is, in part, a foil to Rosalind. . . . For Colin, the loss of Dido is
> emotionally charged with the loss of Rosalind. To be sure, the lament for the
> lost Dido does not deal primarily with Colin's own love, but we would be
> mistaken to think that his feelings for Rosalind and his sense of unjust dep-
> rivation do not carry over into his feeling for Dido. The November elegy is
> an elegy not only for the lost Dido but also for the lost Rosalind. (Cullen,
> 91–92)

Somewhere between these two positions we find Paul Alpers, who objects
on the one hand to MacCaffrey's emphasis on transcendence and on the
other to Cullen's emphasis on Spenser's ethical treatment of Colin, partly
because both distract the reader from the Spenserian emphasis on human
singers and song, on "verbal and modal pleasures" and their moral functions. The *November* elegy, he writes, "is most appropriately characterized by Thenot's words of thanks to Colin," in which he praises its
"doolful pleasaunce":

> The "doolful pleasaunce" of the song indicates a paradox that attends any
> aesthetic treatment of distressing realities. When Thenot says he does not
> know whether to rejoice or weep, he is referring not simply to his double
> feeling about Dido's death, but to his reactions to Colin's poem. Its power as
> a technical performance is essential to its spiritual use—which is to enable
> men to endure, accept, celebrate, not to transcend. (Alpers, 363)

In my opinion the interpretive evidence favors the Cullen-McNeir
view of the elegy, and consequently I am not persuaded that it has very

much "spiritual use" nor, if such use is intended (by Spenser? by Colin?), that it enables anyone to endure, accept, celebrate. Paradoxically this is why I find Alpers's focus on verse and song so salutary as a general thesis, considered apart from the particular readings it generates. It speaks to what seems to be the primary concern of Colin's audience. Thenot does not immediately confront Colin with a teary-eyed request to help him get over Dido's death. He begins by mourning Colin's Muse and asking him to dust off one of the old "songs of . . . jovisaunce"—a blazon of "thy loved lasse," a hymn "of higher vaine" to Pan—silenced "through loves misgovernaunce." It is Colin who prescribes the sad mood, on grounds of seasonal decorum; only then does Thenot propose a particular subject, and he does not mention Dido until he has appealed to Colin to instruct and inspire him with his art.

The terms of Thenot's request are worth noting in that he conditionally promises Colin a greater reward than he actually gives at the end of the performance:

> And if thou wilt bewayle my wofull tene:
> I shall thee give yond Cosset for thy payne:
> And if thy rymes as rownd and rufull bene,
> As those that did thy *Rosalind* complayne,
> Much greater gyfts for guerdon thou shalt gayne,
> Then Kidde or Cosset, which I thee bynempt . . .
>
> *(41–46)*

> Ay francke shepheard, how bene thy verses meint
> With doolful pleasaunce, so as I ne wotte,
> Whether rejoyce or weepe for great constrainte?
> Thyne be the cossett, well hast thow it gotte.
> Up *Colin* up, ynough thou morned hast,
> Now gynnes to mizzle, hye we homeward fast.
>
> *(203–8)*

If one wanted to press subtle distinctions of an ethico-dramatic sort, one could construe Thenot's failure to give greater gifts as an index to his opinion of Colin's priorities, namely, that Colin's lament over real death and another shepherd's loss was less "rownd and rufull" than his own loss and the merely metaphoric death of rejected love. Such distinctions depend on our taking the fictional autonomy of Thenot and Colin seriously. If this is problematical for Colin it is even more so for Thenot; hence we may test the limits of ethical interpretation by seeing what kind of a case might be made for his fictional status. "Thenot" names a speaker who participates in *Februarie*, *Aprill*, and *November*, and some critics have assumed without question that all three speakers are the same even though the Mantuanesque old man of *Februarie* appears to have little in common with the other two Thenots, who are auxiliary interlocutors.[13] To test their assumption I should like to adopt it as a hypothesis and make the argument they failed to make on its behalf.

The evidence for this hypothesis is as follows: The old man in *Februarie* fondly remembers the tales of youth, love, and chivalry he heard when he was young (98–99), though now he is a bitter critic of youth's erotic folly. In *Aprill* Thenot berates Colin for letting love blind him and impair his art (17–20, 154–57). In *November* his "light virelayes" and "looser songs of love" deserve "Poetes prayse," according to Colin, but his "Oaten pypes" have long been asleep (21–24), and he once again mentions Colin's disorder ("loves misgovernaunce," 4). Although there is some inconsistency here, especially in view of Colin's description of Thenot's poetry, we are encouraged by two relatively superficial indicators to wrest a pattern from the evidence. The first is the famous case of the misplaced zodiacal sign. Phoebus, Colin says, has "taken up his ynne in Fishes haske" (17), which, if this means the sun is in Pisces, he could do more easily in February than in November; whether or not this was an error on Spenser's part, it serves to link *November* with *Februarie*. Second, *November* and *Aprill* are linked by close thematic and rhetorical echoes, a linkage I shall discuss later. Thus connections are drawn among the three eclogues in which Thenot appears.

The pattern I mentioned may be extrapolated from Patrick Cullen's remark that in *November* "Colin, ironically, is older than Thenot" (p. 91). While the evidence for this assertion is inferential—nothing is said about their respective ages in *November*—it suggests a way to deal with Thenot. Just as Colin repeatedly portrays himself in the throes of the accelerated aging process, so Thenot seems to grow younger because his youthful attachment to poetry receives more emphasis in each succeeding eclogue after *Februarie: Aprill* displays his command of literary clichés (5–8), his appreciation of skill in making (19), and his eagerness to hear one of Colin's "ditties . . . so trimly dight" (29); in *November* we learn that he himself has been a practitioner of love poetry and goes so far as to justify love if, as in Colin's case, it improves one's verse. In *Februarie* Cuddie told Thenot his anti-erotic attitude would change if he

---

[13] E.g., McNeir, 51; Cullen, 95; S. K. Heninger, Jr., *Selections from the Poetical Works of Edmund Spenser* (Boston: Houghton Mifflin, 1970), 93.

could recover his youth (61–66), and Thenot's response makes it clear that the source of his bitterness is not simply ethical disapproval but nostalgia for pleasures he is deprived of by age: "Thou art a fon, of thy love to boste, / All that is lent to love, wyll be lost" (69–70). Thenot's image of "breme winter with chamfred browes, / Full of wrinckles and frostie furrowes," reminds us not only of himself but also of an aged embittered Cupid, "Drerily shooting his stormy darte, / Which cruddles the blood, and pricks the harte" (43–46). By *December*, then, he and Colin will have changed places: in the first the triumph of Youth in Age, in the second the triumph of Age in Youth. And since *November* and *December* return us explicitly to the source of the two names—namely, the poetry of Marot—we may view this as the triumph of the older literary generation over the younger, the triumph of tradition over the new individual talent. Thus the Panic cycle is transmitted: Colin's fall from the paradise of youth is a mirror inversion (and perhaps a consequence) of the elder's return to it.

To those who still insist that the *November* Thenot cannot be the same figure we met in *Februarie* one could reply either (1) that his erotic Muse has been sleeping since youth, (2) that he admits love as one of the standard subjects of poetry while remaining constant in his disapproval of actual love (the Vacant Head model), or (3) that his praises of Colin's love complaints and elegy are both faintly qualified by the withholding of "greater gyfts" at the conclusion of the elegy. The third alternative would imply that in Thenot's opinion Colin's "rymes" could have been even more "rufull" and "doolful," more pleasant and "rownd," had Dido's death meant as much to him as Rosalind's rejection. Given such postulates, the identity of Thenot throughout the *Calender* could be maintained and the consistency of the portrait justified in terms of the larger pattern that he, as a pastoral elder (one of the three in the *Calender*), exemplifies: the mind divided by its adherence to the paradise principle between the blandishment of the poets who glorify youth and love, and the resultant bitterness of discovering that "all that is lent to love, wyll be lost."

This line of argument is clearly hypothetical, and though I suspect it involves too much special pleading, I find it attractive. Even if, in spite of the argument, it would simplify matters to abandon the thesis that "Thenot" in the *Calender* names a single consistent figure, one insight generated by this inspection of the hypothesis seems worth retaining: the aesthetic quality of Colin's lament for Dido is in some way affected by his entanglement with Rosalind. This notion accords with the idea that Colin stops singing because he cannot fully transform or transcend his personal involvement, because his Wandering Mind cannot attain or re-attain the Vacancy of Head that is the goal of the paradise principle. Viewing the *Calender* within the context of Spenser's *oeuvre* as a whole, I see this refusal to sing as, in the long run, the positive sign by which Spenser distinguishes Colin from the other shepherds, associates him with himself, and suggests his ultimate promise: the paradise principle can be transcended only by dissociating love from poetry and poetry from love, by taking each seriously on its own terms in a manner unconstrained by the influence, needs, or interests of the other, and by establishing bases in both actual and imaginary experience for their eventual reunion.

In the short run, however, the paradise principle prevails, and we may see it at work in *November* by making another run, more modest this time, at the difference between Thenot's promise and his award of gifts. Even if the difference is accidental, even if the conventionality of the passages renders it trivial, it nevertheless indicates the priorities and expectations of the pastoral auditor for whom Colin frames his verse: a cosset for Colin's efforts in bewailing Thenot's "wofull tene," "greater gyfts" for "rymes as rownd and rufull" as those devoted to his love complaints. Thenot's emphasis is on "rymes." The alliterating phrase that subordinates the matter (ruth) to the manner, along with the link between Rosalind and Dido, may remind us of the partiality of response to the *August* sestina, which I discussed earlier in elaborating on Montrose's idea that "the shepherds' response is not empathy with Colin's anguished spirit but awed delight in his skill" and in arguing that the subordination of grief to art and its disappearance into art are the logical outcome of "the recreative expectations and responses of its fictive audience" (Montrose, 43; see above). The metamorphosis of grief into art is pleasurable in different ways to different parties to the performance. For the singer both aspects of the metamorphosis give pleasure if he delights in his pain. But for the listeners "pain" is noted only as an arabesque adorning the pleasures of song. The recreative logic produces an expression of love or grief, an image of the lover, that the fictive audience does not take seriously. Similarly we may distinguish between what the pastoral audience hears and what we hear. If Thenot attends primarily to "rymes," and if Colin likewise begins the elegy with a Vacant Head undaunted by his own "crabbed care," we soon become aware that a running invective underlies the elegy and that although it receives its impetus from Rosalind it gradually extends to a general complaint against life. But, as we shall see, the generality of complaint is not chargeable solely to Colin Clout as a fully autonomous fictional person. It is matched by a generality of reference to the pastoral tradition that speaks through Colin's mouth.

Colin's "carefull verse" will impress Thenot more by its careful construction than by its sorrowful care. Thenot's dismissal of Colin is brisk— "Up Colin up, ynough thou morned hast"—and it echoes the equally brisk line with which he urged him to begin mourning: "Then up I say, thou jolly shepeheard swayne" (47). The same note is carried into the opening line of the elegy proper when, as Alpers nicely puts it, Colin "proceeds to belt out the grandest poem in the sequence": "Up then Melpomene thou mournefulst Muse of nyne" (53). *Then* transfers Thenot's pep talk from Colin to the Muse in what is virtually a giddap, tripping over the unstressed triple cluster, "(Mel)pómĕnĕ thŏu," with rustic verve and slowing down immediately by means of a modulation through the spondaic "mournfulst" into high-serious elegiac formality. Colin dutifully takes up Thenot's challenge: "Up grieslie ghostes and up my rufull ryme" (55). Alpers cites the modulation as an instance of Spenser's inability to "establish continuity or interaction between what we may call speaking and singing voices" (p. 366), but surely there is no reason to conflate Spenser with Colin at this point. Colin's "inability" simply accentuates what Montrose describes as the "disjunction between poet and poem," and it serves to isolate the elegy's "power as a technical performance" from any personal motive that might be connected with "spiritual use" (p. 363). And, as I suggested earlier, this disjunction informs only the beginning of the elegy, which is soon contaminated by personal motives.

Yet "personal motives" is perhaps an inaccurate or inadequate way to put it: if Spenser is not reducible to Colin, he maintains the connection between them, maintains Colin's translucency as a persona, in an obvious manner and for an important reason. He assigns Colin Marot's emblem, *La mord ny mord*, as well as an elegy modeled on a poem by Marot. Thenot and Colin are also Marot's shepherds. The source is close to the surface. This conspicuous allusion momentarily lulls us into adopting the extreme recreative stance of the pastoral audience. Listening to Colin run through a series of elegiac and pastoral commonplaces, we may feel that the real theme of the poem is not death but "rymes"—the new poet's facile versification and handling of timeworn topics, his skill in Englishing Marot, the fluent control of invention enabling him to be copious without violating poetic decorum. All this is emphasized by the varied undersong, for example, "O heavie herse, / Let streaming teares be poured out in store: / O carefull verse" (60–62). *Herse* is not only a bier or catafalque (i.e., *catafalco*, a canopied framework to which epitaphs or short poems were affixed) but also—as E. K. points out—a funeral service. Additionally *herse* is the noun form of the verb *to hery*, "to praise," which Colin used in line 10. *Herse* is therefore nearly identical with *verse*, which simply rehearses its meaning. The elegiac movement from "heavie herse" to "happy herse" and "carefull verse" to "joyfull verse" is already compressed into the meanings of *herse* itself, which enacts the logic of recreative metamorphosis: the birth of verse is the burial of death and the death of grief.

This could be merely my fantasy rather than Spenser's message, in which case I have the choice of responding positively if what I fancy is "rymes" and technique or critically if I am out for deeper meanings. But such a possibility is precluded on a number of grounds. Marot's emblem is one. *La mord ny mord* bears a double significance in the context of the elegy: it emphasizes that this is not so much personal expression as poetic exercise or experiment, and it reminds us that in recreative metamorphosis death has no bite because life has disappeared into art. The intimate connection between these two senses validates my fantasy as Spenser's message, for it constitutes the elegy not only as an experiment *in* the tradition but also as a critique *of* the tradition. Spenser's relation to Marot is reflected and generalized within the poem as Colin's relation to the tradition that fathered the eclogue. *November*, as Richard Mallette puts it,

> is the most patently "literary" eclogue in the collection. As a pastoral elegy, whose forebears stretch with great distinction from Theocritus and Virgil to Marot and Petrarch, "November" asks to be measured against a redoubtable tradition. It abides virtually every convention of its mode, from the invocation of the Muses, to the questioning of the rural deities and the final consolation. (p. 31)

But *November* is more aggressive than that: the elegy *measures* the tradition and questions its redoubtability by illustrating the tendencies of escape into artifice that make it redoubtable. While Spenser shares with Colin the delight in testing his "tender wyngs," he diverges from Colin in making him exhibit the motivational effects of those tendencies. Hence it is neither accurate nor useful to conclude, as Mallette does, that Colin's persona in *November* "is relatively colorless, unobtrusive of idiosyncracy or 'character'" and that "we are relatively unaware of him as the lover of Rosalind" (p. 30). Only by measuring his motives can we measure the tradition he embodies. ___

It is easy to demonstrate Cullen's thesis that the elegy is "not only for the lost Dido but also for the lost Rosalind" (p. 92). The linkage is produced chiefly by echoes of *Januarye*. Even the misplaced zodiacal sign contributes to this thesis, apart from its obvious verbal echoes of the *Januarye* conclusion ("sadde Winter welked hath the day, / And Phoebus weary of his yerely taske," 13–14), since it inserts *November* into a January-February sequence. But the other examples are far less recondite:

> Breake we our pypes, that shrild as lowde as Larke . . .
>
> *(71)*

> The songs that *Colin* made in her prayse . . .
>
> *(78)*

> Yet soone as spring his mantle doth displaye . . .
>
> *(85)*

> She while she was, (that was, a woful word to sayne)
> For beauties prayse and plesaunce had no pere:
> So well she couth the shepherds entertayne,
> With cakes and cracknells and such country chere.
> Ne would she scorne the simple shepheards swaine,
>
> · · · · · · · · · · · · · ·
>
> Als *Colin cloute* she would not once disdayne.
>
> *(93–101)*

> Where bene the nosegayes that she dight for thee:
> The colourd chaplets wrought with a chiefe,
> The knotted rushrings, and gilte Rosemaree?
> For shee deemed nothing too deere for thee.
>
> *(114–17)*

> The faded lockes fall from the loftie oke,
> The flouds do gaspe, for dryed is theyr sourse,
> And flouds of teares flowe in theyr stead perforse.
>   The mantled medowes mourne . . .
>
> *(125–28)*

> The feeble flocks in field refuse their former foode,
> And hang theyr heads, as they would learne to weepe . . .
>
> *(133–34)*

These passages bear out Cullen's point that Dido "is, in part, a foil to Rosalind," an "image of Rosalind as Colin would have liked her to be" (p. 91). But since the insight serves Cullen only as another nail to drive into the case against Colin's obsession, he does not unfold its implications.

In doing double duty, reminding us of Rosalind and *Januarye* (with echoes also of *June* and *August*), the above passages suggest that for Colin rejected love and death converge; they have the same value. This equation could indeed be positively read as a form of sublimation, and if we take into account the *Aprill*-Elisa echoes, we could defend such a reading of *November* against Cullen's thesis; for example: "The problematic carnal and political complexities of Rosalind and Eliza are separated out from the pure spirit of Dido through the sacramental symbolism of death and rebirth" (Montrose, 53). The "immortal mirrhor" theory introduced by Piers in *October* supports this view. I cite Montrose's version of the positive reading, however, because he turns it as he proceeds and gradually admits the darker side of the elegiac triumph:

> Colin's elegy for Dido is a displacement of the Rosalind-Eliza problem in which Spenser attempts a radical solution by symbolic means: kill the lady, thus sending her spirit to heaven, where the lover's spirit might hope eventually to join her in a communion free from the accidents and constraints that characterize earthly life—life within the body and the body politic. . . . Dissatisfactions with the way things are can be assuaged by the artistic generation of pastoral counter-worlds. But the act of imaginative transformation is always suspect—potentially dangerous, escapist, or regressive. The "transcendence" achieved by Colin's *November* elegy is an ambiguous, melancholic, and symbolic remedy for actual problems. To make poetry a vehicle of transcendence is tacitly to acknowledge its ethical and political impotence. (p. 54)

Montrose takes the name *Dido* seriously and sees in "Spenser's pastoral elegy a conspicuous allusion to and revision of the critical episode of recreative truancy in Vergil's epic": whereas Virgil's Dido spurns Aeneas and rejoins her first husband, remaining in the *Lugentes Campi* where not even death can free unhappy lovers from their obsessive *curae* (*Aeneid* VI.441–44), "Colin's Dido has found her own rightful place in the field of heroes" (Montrose, 50–51). But a conspicuous allusion of this sort is also a conspicuous *ex*clusion. Reminding us of what it excludes, it conveys the pressure of exclusion, the meaning of that pressure, by asking us to resist it and to explore the excluded material. We know how and why Virgil's Dido died.[14] "Drent" in passion (cf. *Aeneid*

---

[14] The effect of the homonymous play on Dido/Died-O is that while the Virgilian name gives us a handle on a particular literary source and the psychological state the figure of Dido instantiates, the homonym tends to stress the anonymity and generality of the figure so named. She has as much ethical substance as *Elisa* insofar as the latter transparently embodies Elisium. Dido and Elisa are projective idealizations of elegiac and

IV.531–32), she failed to find release in suicide, remaining obdurate as "hard flint or Marpesian Rock" (VI.471) in sorrow for herself and enmity to Aeneas. If that side of Dido is "separated out from the pure spirit" of Colin's revised figure, its resemblance to Colin's unhappy love yet keeps it alive as a kind of subtext in the elegy.

This subtext is nourished by the presence of Philomela:

> The Turtle on the bared braunch,
> Laments the wound, that death did launch.
>   O heavie herse,
> And *Philomele* her songs with teares doth steepe.
>   O carefull verse.
>
>   *(Nov. 137–42)*

E. K. supplies the reason for Philomela's tears (257 ff.), and we have already learned the subject of her song at the conclusion of the *August* sestina:

> Hence with the Nightingale will I take part,
> That blessed byrd, that spends her time of sleepe
> In songs and plaintive pleas, the more taugment
> The memory of hys misdeede, that bred her woe:
> And you that feele no woe, | when as the sound
> Of these my nightly cryes | ye heare apart,
> Let breake your sounder sleepe | and pitie augment.
>
>   *(183–89)*

As in *June*'s bitter closing, Colin would inflict his pain on the world, publicizing both Rosalind's misdeed and his victimization. The exchange of genders hyperbolizes Rosalind's active aggression and his helpless passivity, both of them perpetuated, or so he hopes, in the metamorphosis to music.

The reference to Philomela in *August* suppresses the aspect of the story on which Ovid focuses at the end of his version: what Philomela's plumage commemorates is not Tereus's monstrous behavior but her monstrous revenge. In *Virgils Gnat* Spenser singles out this theme for emphasis:

---

recreative sentiment respectively. Retaining their allusive value, they are transferred by homonymy to imaginary *subjects* which may be "filled" with various contents—Rosalind, for example.

> There also those two *Pandionian* maides,
> Calling on *Itis, Itis* evermore,
> Whome wretched boy they slew with guiltie blades;
> For whome the Thracian king lamenting sore,
> Turn'd to a *Lapwing,* fowlie them upbraydes,
> And fluttering round about them still does sore:
> There now they all eternally complaine
> Of others wrong, and suffer endless paine.
>
> *(401–8)*

The ambiguity in the final couplet is equally applicable to Virgil's Dido and Spenser's Colin: "eternally complaine / *Of others wrong*" prompts us to measure the viewpoint selected by the victims ("of wrong done *by* others") against the viewpoint they eschew ("of wrong done *to* others"). The order of phrases further suggests that their endless pain is the effect not only of what they suffered at the hands of others but also of their own eternal complaining. Thus also Colin in the *August* sestina draws out his "melodious self-pity" in order "taugment / The memory of hys [her] misdeede." Here in *November* his linking the mourning dove with Philomela helps confuse different objects of wrong as well as different kinds of grief. Is the dove's "wound" its own or that of its departed mate? Is there any difference between mourning "the wound, that death did launch" and mourning the wound that love did launch—as in the last of the *Amoretti,* where the same image and the same exchange of gender produce the same hyperbolic effect?

If there is no difference between Lobbin's loss and Colin's, if mourning for another dissolves into mourning for oneself, then the person mourned ceases to exist or matter as an *other* and is, as Montrose argues, symbolically killed by the narcissistic withdrawal into the self. What is imaginative creation in the perspective of art is imaginary murder in that of love. Shakespeare's Troilus, waxing poetic in rapt anticipation, comically raiding the garden of romantic clichés that poetry has sown in his febrile brain, cries out, "I do fear . . . / That I shall lose distinction in my joys" (III.ii.24–25). Similarly Colin loses distinction in his griefs as the otherness of their objects fades from view. In complaining of the loss of Rosalind in *Januarye* and *June* and of the loss of Dido in *November,* he loses them again—but "loses" in the idiomatic active sense, as one "loses" one's pursuers. This performative or illocutionary dimension of elegy makes it paradoxical: elegy is a death-dealing action that re-creates, confirms, makes conclusive the loss it mourns for. And in *November* Spenser shows how the elegiac circle, to give this action a name, blends into the more general and diffuse plaintive circle. Spenser uses the title *Complaints* advisedly to express this loss of distinction in griefs, and his literary complaints are best viewed as critical mimes, or mimetic critiques, of poetic traditions that are not ethically neutral but, on the contrary, structured by the domination of the paradise principle. Complaints are the tears of the Muses for the ruins of time:

> And when ye list your owne mishaps to mourne,
> Which death, or love, or fortunes wreck did rayse,
> Your string could soone to sadder tenor turne,
> And teach the woods and waters to lament
> Your dolefull dreriment.
>
> *(Epithalamion 7–11)*

As "learned sisters" the Muses personify the received tradition, and what they "inspire" is not merely a self-interested delight in verse but also an attitude toward life. The repeated "or" in line 8 specifies indifference rather than disjunction, an indifference that arises partly from the primacy and constraints of delight in verse and partly from the tendency to generalize mishaps by "losing" the particularity, the otherness, of mourned objects. The plaintive circle "with teares doth steepe" its objects, as Philomela steeps her song, blotting them out until they are reduced to the blurred proximate causes of "endless paine," the root cause of which is the primal Mishap, paradise lost.

The Muses' *November* gift to Colin thus consists of elegiac conventions enabling the singer to redirect attention from death to loss and from loss to Loss. The name Dido, taken as a homonymous pun ("Died-O"), may by its redundancy serve this anonymizing function: "deade is Dido, dead alas and drent"; "Dido my deare alas is dead." But in this poem the elegiac circle is shown to produce an odd but telling illogic. The loss Colin mourns is untimely and unnatural, yet when he turns to question its divergence from nature's model he shifts to a more general concern:

> Whence is it, that the flouret of the field doth fade,
> And lyeth buryed long in Winters bale:
> Yet soone as spring his mantle doth displaye,
> It floureth fresh, as it should never fayle?
> But thing on earth that is of most availe,
>   As vertues braunch and beauties budde,
>   Reliven not for any good.
>   O heavie herse,

> The braunch once dead, the budde eke needes must quaile,
> O carefull verse.
>
> *(83–92)*

Nancy Jo Hoffman notes the shift when she comments that Spenser's question "refers to death in nature, Dido's death, and to other deaths as well," but she then goes on to obscure its significance in remarking that the "difference between nature and human nature . . . is not as sad as one might suppose"—presumably because of the perspective of "philosophical realism" in which "the impact of death is neither softened nor accommodated." [15] The point is, however, that a consoling model of natural process fails to accommodate human death in general. This is hardly philosophical realism or any other kind of realism. It is radical pessimism: measured by the consoling model, the difference is *sadder* because the implication is that death per se is *unkindly*—not only cruel but also unnatural. Dido's accidental or premature death is thus illogically converted to a paradigm of the hopelessness of the human condition. Colin's sentiment, "even the best of us must die," will later be restated in more negative terms when he laments the "trustless state of earthly things."

The unnaturalness of human death is soon imposed by pathetic fallacy on all of mourning nature:

> Ay me that dreerie death should strike so mortall stroke,
> That can undoe Dame natures kindly course:
> The faded lockes fall from the loftie oke,
> The flouds do gaspe, for dryed is theyr sourse,
> And flouds of teares flowe in theyr stead perforse.
>   The mantled medowes mourne,
>   Theyr sondry colours tourne.
>   O heavie herse,
> The heavens doe melt in teares without remorse.
>   O carefull verse.
>
> *(123–32)*

Here, Hoffman observes, "human death has power over a personified, sympathetic mother earth" (p. 89). Again the generality of the sentiment loses and disseminates the unusual death of Dido among the normal an-

---

[15] *Spenser's Pastorals: "The Shepheardes Calender" and "Colin Clout"* (Baltimore: Johns Hopkins University Press, 1977), 58–59.

nual "deaths" of natural objects. One death stroke is as mortal as any other, and it is "dreerie death" without further qualification that undoes the kindly course. This is why the heavens, and not merely their tears, are remorseless. The kindlier view of grief and nature is present by conspicuous exclusion in the trite play on tears, which figuratively veils and alludes to life-giving rain. But Colin affirms its limited power in centering on the darker view. Two extreme and antithetical models of nature threaten to pull apart from the precarious calendrical balance in which they are stereoptically integrated. At line 64 Colin calls on Kentish shepherds to wail "this wofull waste of natures warke," and *warke* alerts us to the war in nature's work.

It is here that Isabel MacCaffrey's thesis in "Allegory and Pastoral" proves helpful: soft pastoral, the "naive version of the pastoral metaphor" (p. 94) that uses nature in its literal form as a model for the human condition, is inadequate because it is either false or unsatisfying— false in that "the orderly cycle of human life is [often] turned awry, its promise blasted" (p. 95) and unsatisfying in that "submission to the seasonal round" leads "only to death" (p. 93). This thesis can be improved by distinguishing more carefully (1) between the putatively actual Fall at the beginning of history and the pastoral "Fall" from the Muses' garden, the nursery of the Vacant Mind, and (2) between "inevitable outrage from the forces . . . in nature" and the outraged response to it generated in the Wandering Mind by the paradise principle.[16]

What is nature to Spenser's shepherds is art to us and, more important, a special kind of art, since the artist is the paradise principle. As E. K. goes to great lengths to point out, there are two calendars, two natures, and we may think of the one that begins in and returns to

---

[16] MacCaffrey's argument is adversely affected by an unstable use of the term *nature*, which shifts casually about from one to another of five different senses:

a. A cluster of unimproved *loci*—the "archetypal hills, valleys, woods, and pastures" (p. 88) which, whether fallen or unfallen, compose the *Calender*'s rural locale.

b. A sequential process, "the cycle of nature," "the seasonal round" (p. 93).

c. Fallen nature as a cluster of unpleasant *places*, "an unsheltered world, hostile and uncongenial" (p. 97).

d. Fallen nature as a cluster of unpleasant *forces* "released at the Fall" (p. 105).

e. The implied contrary of "nonliteral, invisible reality" (p. 100), therefore literal, visible reality, the tangible and perishable setting for the too brief enjoyment of "the shows of things" and "the pleasures of the temporal world" (pp. 106, 100).

Each of these is described as inadequate or bad for a different reason: *a* in its idyllic or paradisal form is unrealistic; *b* is a closed system which frustrates the longing for transcendence and leads only to death; *c* is a threat to human security; *d* expresses and reinforces the effects of sin; *e* offers an invalid model of the spiritual realm unless properly apprehended as an imperfect analogy.

March as the kindly, soft, or Arcadian nature of naive pastoralists, while the January model is unkindly, hard, and Mantuanesque and requires a much more drastic technology of repair. Kindly old Dame Nature can handle her problems without outside assistance when the calendar begins in March, for "the plesaunce thereof being buried in the sadnesse of *the dead winter now worne away,* reliveth," but the January calendar calls for "our mighty Saviour" to renew "the state of *the decayed world*" ("Generall Argument," 50–52, 60–61; italics mine).

MacCaffrey sees the *Calender* as moving from the soft pagan consolations of the first model to the harder Christian consolation of the second. I have been arguing that both "natures" are works of art dialectically interactive in the pastoral mind and that what MacCaffrey calls "transcendence" is really a failure to transcend the dialectic—is, on the contrary, a desire to close the plaintive circle and return to paradise. Colin's complaint that the kindly March model leaves us unprepared for such tragedies as Dido's death gives way to a more radical pessimism in later stanzas: all forms of death, decline, or loss are equally unkind. Measured against the illusion of a paradisal nature that either never fades or perpetually regenerates itself, even the process of aging appears unnatural enough to be deemed a "mishap" on a par with untimely death, unrequited love, "or fortunes wreck." Anything touched by time becomes a ruin. In the Garden of Adonis, where one of Venus's roles is that of "great mother" (*FQ* III.vi.40) whom kindly "dame Nature doth . . . beautifie" (vi.30), Time appears as an alien intruder—"wicked Time, who with his scyth addrest, / Does mow the flowring herbes and goodly things"—but after he has gratified "his malice hard" by wreaking havoc with "his flaggy wings" (vi.39) and after we have been told that "such despight" is a law ("All things decay in time," vi.40), the narrative exorcises time. The poet returns to paradise by shifting through a counterfactual to an indicative assertion of "continuall spring" leading toward the climax of Adonis's "eternall blis" and "everlasting joy" (vi.41–42, 48, 49).

The same radical alternation and closure shapes the *November* elegy.[17] The dynamic receives added force from the contrastive allusion to *Aprill,* and Hoffman aptly points out how "the third mourning stanza in 'November' speaks directly to the April eclogue, undoing its festivities before our eyes" (p. 90):

---

[17] The connection between *Aprill* and *November* was made on political grounds by Paul McLane in *Spenser's "Shepheardes Calender": A Study in Elizabethan Allegory* (Notre Dame: Notre Dame University Press, 1961), 47–60.

I see *Calliope* speede her to the place,
    where my Goddesse shines:
And after her the other Muses trace,
    with their Violines.
Bene they not Bay braunches, which they doe beare,
All for *Elisa* in her hand to weare?
      So sweetely they play,
      And sing all the way,
That it a heaven is to heare.

                  (Apr. 100–108)

The water Nymphs, that wont with her to sing and daunce,
And for her girlond Olive braunches beare,
Now balefull boughes of Cypres doen advaunce:
The Muses, that were wont greene bayes to weare,
Now bringen bitter Eldre braunches seare,
    The fatall sisters eke repent,
    Her vital threde so soone was spent.
      O heavie herse,
Mourne now my Muse, now morne with heavie cheare.
      O carefull verse.

                  (Nov. 143–52)

The Orphean power of *Aprill* may be hopefully invoked in the reference to the Fates (*cf.* Ovid, *Metamorphoses* X.31, 40 ff.), but the contrast between the two eclogues only reveals the deeper continuity that links them in dialectical relation. Colin invoked the nymphs and Muses together in *Aprill* (37–45), and there the crown of olive branches was borne by the chief nymph, Chloris (122–23), whose name, E. K. writes, "signifieth greenesse"; of Chloris it "is sayd, that Zephyrus the Westerne wind being in love with her, and coveting her to wyfe, gave her for a dowrie, the chiefdome and soveraigntye of al flowres and greene herbes, growing on earth" (291–95). Also "the word Nymphe in Greeke signifieth Well water, or otherwise a Spouse or Bryde" (289–90). *Aprill* shimmers with the paradisal lore of the "learned sisters" who fill the Vacant Head with pleasures that, lovely and innocent in themselves, may cast their green shadows over the future. Nor is this future absent from the penumbra surrounding the Elisa who centers and embodies Elisium: love and brides, sovereignty and government, may be pushed to the edges of the green clearing or consigned to E. K.'s gloss, but they are not absent: "Olives bene for peace," but only "When wars doe surcease" (124–25). Among the flowers Colin names, "Coronations," "Kingcups," and "the Chevisaunce, / Shall match with the fayre flowre Delice" (138–44). Itself a brief return to the paradise Colin lost, the *Aprill* "myth of Elisa's generation from the Union of Pan and Syrinx is a re-creation of the original Ovidian myth, in which the desire for sexual union was first frustrated, then sublimated" into art (Montrose, 41). It moves cautiously from this green fastness *toward* actuality: "Spenser qualifies a visionary conception of poetry by placing it within the context of his own historical and social existence and by expressing it as the erotic idealization of a power relationship" (Montrose, 42). But it veers away at the end and closes the recreative circle when, as Montrose observes, Elisa is separated from Eliza: "Spenser emphasizes Elisa's status as an ideal image created by the poet, rather than her status as a poetic reflection of Elizabeth" (p. 41).

November not only shows that the same Muses who inspire the *Aprill* song also preside over the elegy; it goes further in implying a causal relation between the two moments. What was held back, conspicuously excluded, from the vision implanted in the Vacant Head now assaults the Wandering Mind with a vengeance. It may be stretching a point to see in Spenser's spelling of *Cypres* an evocation of the Cyprian—Venus as a goddess of death bearing "balefull boughes," with *balefull* suggesting not only "evil" but also "full of fire," the fire perhaps of desire, anger, or the funeral pyre, the fire that waits to consume the dry branches of the "bitter Eldre." Nevertheless, the two figures together *do* suggest a relevant *metalepsis:* Venus, who as queen of beauty kindles the love that cannot last, is the original source of *November*'s woe. This familiar anti-erotic sentiment immediately flares up into the elegy's most heated expression of the bitter elders' view:

> O trustlesse state of earthly things, and slipper hope
> Of mortal men, that swincke and sweate for nought,
> And shooting wide, doe misse the marked scope:
> Now have I learned (a lesson derely bought)
> That nys on earth assuraunce to be sought:
>   For what might be in earthlie mould,
>   That did her buried body hould,
>   O heavie herse,
> Yet saw I on the beare when it was brought
>   O carefull verse.
>
> *(153–62)*

Conspicuous triteness is an important aspect of the stanza. The sense of truism should keep us from responding too specifically. To say of this "series of aphorisms" that they are "Chaucerian in tone and sentiment" or that "Spenser is speaking his own language of pastoral" (Hoffman, 60, 58) is to overlook the important relation between "what oft was thought" and Colin Clout's expression of it. He has learned his lesson as much from the tradition as from experience. And it is only the second of two lessons. The first, taught by the "learned sisters" and practiced by Colin in *Aprill,* presented a "slipper hope" and a "marked scope" (a sight or vision, a target or prey, an object of desire or pursuit) that by its very paradisal nature could not but be missed. Hence to learn that "nys on earth assuraunce to be sought" is really the second part of the first lesson. The lightly voiced rusticity of *Aprill*'s "forswonck and forswatt" swain with his easy access to the beautiful and the good ("Bellibone") embodied as Elisa leads to its own subversion in the grave pronouncement on mortal men "that swincke and sweate for nought."[18] For in the fall from paradise Elisa turns out to be a kind of "nought" like Dido (Died → 0).

Colin's exile from paradise is in many respects like the self-imposed exodus of Yeats's traveler to Byzantium, torn between the blandishments of the poets who sing eternally of youth and the bitterness of the elder who cannot censure their sensual music without at the same time mocking his own self-justification:

> That is no country for old men. The young
> In one another's arms, birds in the trees
> —Those dying generations—at their song,
> The salmon-falls, the mackerel-crowded seas,
> Fish, flesh, or fowl, commend all summer long
> Whatever is begotten, born, and dies.
> Caught in that sensual music all neglect
> Monuments of unageing intellect.
>
> An aged man is but a paltry thing,
> A tattered coat upon a stick, unless
> Soul clap its hands and sing, and louder sing
> For every tatter in its mortal dress,
> Nor is there singing school but studying
> Monuments of its own magnificence;
> And therefore I have sailed the seas and come
> To the holy city of Byzantium.

This is the rationalization of "ryper age" and "stayed steps," of one for whom time "in passing weares / (As garments doen, which wexen old

[18] Cf. David Richardson's discussion of *Bellibone* in "Duality in Spenser's Archaisms," *Studies in the Literary Imagination* 11 (1978): 86.

above) / And draweth newe delightes with hoary heares." [19] The Byzantine traveler strains his hoary hearing toward the new delights of ancient singing masters but knows, even as he invokes them, that it is not transcendence he longs for but a return to the country of the young:

> Consume my heart away; sick with desire
> And fastened to a dying animal
> It knows not what it is; and gather me
> Into the artifice of eternity.

What he desires is eternal youth, eternal happy consciousness, the eternal body, eternal song and poetry, eternal Vacancy of Head, the tedium of endless happiness. But as he passes through the looking glass of gold mosaic into the salvation and resurrection of art he can only imagine with sad irony a world touched by Midas, the fate of a new Tithonus who asked for eternal youth but forgot to ask for life. His unaging audience will value the access his thin piping gives to the secrets of the underworld (for them the country of the living) and will confirm his own nostalgia for the sensual music of time:

> Once out of nature I shall never take
> My bodily form from any natural thing,
> But such a form as Grecian goldsmiths make
> Of hammered gold and gold enamelling
> To keep a drowsy Emperor awake;
> Or set upon a golden bough to sing
> To lords and ladies of Byzantium
> Of what is past, or passing, or to come,

—whatever is begotten, born, and dies.

It is only to the *artifice* of eternity that Colin consigns Dido when he harrows hell like Orpheus or Christ and successfully installs her in "heavens hight," where she walks "in Elisian fieldes so free" (*Nov.* 162–82):

> Unwise and wretched men to weete whats good or ill,
> We deeme of Death as doome of ill desert:
> But knewe we fooles, what it us bringes until,
> Dye would we dayly, once it to expert.
> No daunger there the shepheard can astert:
>   Fayre fieldes and pleasaunt layes there bene,

---

[19] *June* 36–40. *Stayed* may mean either "staid" or "supported" (as by a crutch).

The fieldes ay fresh, the grass ay greene:
    O happy herse,
Make haste ye shepheards, thether to revert,
    O joyfull verse.

Dido is gone afore (whose turne shall be the next?)
There lives shee with the blessed Gods in blisse,
There drincks she *Nectar* with *Ambrosia* mixt,
And joyes enjoyes, that mortall men do misse.
The honor now of highest gods she is,
    That whilome was poore shepheards pryde,
    While here on earth she did abyde.
    O happy herse,
Ceasse now my song, my woe now wasted is.
    O joyfull verse.

                                    (183–202)

In these stanzas the complicity of age and youth and the "marked scope" that unifies the sweet and bitter visions stand forth most clearly. Thenot had expressed his desire to hear Colin "honor Pan with hymnes of higher vaine" (8), and although Colin responded that this was not the time "to herye" Pan, there is a sense in which the elegy *has* honored Pan—Pan thinly disguised as Christ—and *does* become a hymn of "higher vaine," that is, higher vanity or futility. Colin urges the shepherds "thether to *revert*." To ascend is to return, and the return is to the green fields of Elisium, which, as E. K. tells us, "be devised of Poetes to be a place of pleasure like Paradise" (281). In the vicinity of the phrase "grass ay greene," *revert* becomes "re-green." This makes the misplaced zodiacal sign significant even if it was accidental. To place November in the February position is to make it precede March and April rather than December and January. "Phoebus weary of his yerely task" performs a minor miracle of acceleration and joins the shepherds in making haste "to revert" to spring.

Some commentators have seen the apotheosis of Dido as a critical moment in the *Calender*, the moment in which nature's imagery metaphorically turns against itself and is transcendentalized, the moment of heavenly harvest and Christian comfort. Even Montrose, who carefully spells out the dangers of *November*'s "transcendence," briefly lets down his guard at one point and remarks that "in turning from Rosalind-Eliza to Dido, Colin turns from Pan to Apollo-Christ, a greater Pan," and that Dido's translation signifies that "the poet's spirit is liberated from the lure of the mutable earthly things that have held it in its ceaseless cycle of desire and frustration" (pp. 52–53). But my interpretation of the elegy leads me to the opposite conclusion: the poet's spirit is still *not* liberated from the lure, is still held, still "beheld," in the Panic cycle. I am therefore more in sympathy with Waldo McNeir's opinion, quoted earlier, that "the reality of death" is transformed "into a transcendental replica of the 'soft' pastoral world." Colin's message is hardly a call to transcendence, and Paul Alpers is to that extent correct when in objecting to Isabel MacCaffrey's stress on transcendence he insists that the "spiritual use" of the *November* elegy "is to enable men to endure, accept, celebrate, not to transcend" (p. 363). But if transcendence is not its goal still less does it advocate endurance, acceptance, celebration. Rather it advocates escape, rejection, contempt for the "trustlesse state of earthly things."

The poetic spirit cankered by this cycle is not Colin's alone. He stands as an exemplum of the poet's spirit, and behind him stands E. K.'s "perfect paterne of a Poete," which gave Montrose his title. But let us complete E. K.'s description, given in the argument that prefaces *October:* "whiche finding no maintenaunce of his state and studies, complayneth of the contempte of Poetrie, and the causes thereof." This is the perfect pattern of the poet as have-not, the son of the tearful Muses by the paradise principle. Colin's career through the *Calender*—from the mythical moment of the *Aprill* lay through his *August* sestina, *Januarye* complaint, and *June* dialogue to the end of *November*—dramatically charts the operation of this principle as it plants in the Vacant Head a garden of green expectations that, when life fails to match them, wither like the plants in a forcing garden and leave the Wandering Mind confronting what appears to it by contrast to be a "wofull waste of natures warke." Having generated the bitter view the sweet vision does not fade but persists beside the other and exacerbates it until the mind is sorely tempted to flee the wicked world and recover Vacancy of Head. Colin's career displays a gradual diffusion of the bitter view from the narrow focus of love with which it began until it embraces the *cosmos* in *December*. His rapid senescence is at once a part-for-whole metonym symbolizing his converging complaints and a hyperbole conveying the premature and excessive quality of the fall—not from paradise into nature but from the sweet to the bitter phase of the paradise principle.

"An Hoor Heed and a Grene Tayl"

The Aging Boy Network in Februarie *and* June

> They fed him up with Hopes and Air
> Which soon digested to Despair.
> — *Marvell, "The Unfortunate Lover"*

COLIN CLOUT IS justly notorious for having passed from youth to old age in the space of Spenser's twelve *Calender* months, and as I noted in the last chapter the rhetorical effect of this achievement is to give *Age* (and *Youth* as well) a particular symbolic range. My thesis has been that this range may be expressed as a function of the paradise principle: Age and Youth signify two versions or phases of the have-not condition. In Age the plaintive mode is encoded as moral; in Youth it is encoded as recreative. Since the elders bemoan their lost youth and try to project it into the next generation, youthful and aged speakers hold the same values in spite of their apparent antipathy. Both the love of youthful pleasures and the bitterness at their loss are sedimented into the tradition, which is handed down from one generation to the next in a pattern of cyclic recurrence dominated by the paradise principle. In the next two sections I shall try to show how this theme informs the *Februarie* and *June* eclogues and how they animate it.

I

Februarie is a debate poem, and my overall view of Spenser's way with this genre both derives and departs from the readings of William Nelson and Patrick Cullen.[1] Cullen argues that the other shepherds are "comic foils" to Colin Clout; they represent the one-sided but still healthy values of each of the two perspectives, Arcadian and Mantuanesque. For example, the *Februarie* debate between young Cuddie and old Thenot "is not unnatural; it is not only expected, it is also necessary and desirable." The two positions, "neither sufficient unto itself," complement each other to provide "the balance-in-opposition of the natural year." In this conflict of limited contraries Cuddie "identifies winter with parental discipline, with age's dampening of youth's desire," and his aged opponent, Thenot, "identifies spring with carelessness, the lack of discipline of youth. The debate over winter and spring is thus symbolic of the psychological power struggle between youth and age." Both are partly right, partly wrong, and being incomplete, each needs the other. Thenot's emphasis on restraint and self-control is good practical wisdom, but there is "bias" in his

> contention that old age is "the lusty prime" man should live his life for, bias in his unwillingness or inability to see that spring and procreative love are as much the function of youth and life as restraint is the function of age. . . . There is an obvious aphoristic truth in the aged Thenot's contention that "All that is lent to love, wyll be lost," but there is no less wisdom in Cuddie's instinctive knowledge of the function and value of spring and youth, fertility and procreation. . . . The ideal here is a balance, lest age becomes sterility and youth be vainly spent. (Cullen, 127, 41, 34, 38)

Perhaps because he unaccountably finds "obvious aphoristic truth" in Thenot's "contention," Cullen misses its value as an index to the source of the old man's bias, namely, his membership in the devil's party of youth. Cuddie taunts Thenot with his remark that "such an one" as Phyllis "would make thee younge againe," and it is to this that Thenot replies, "Thou art a fon, of thy love to boste, / All that is lent to love, wyll be lost" (69–70). Behind the aphorism is a direct response: "I'll never be young again, and you won't be young for very long." Since

[1] See Nelson, *The Poetry of Edmund Spenser: A Study* (New York: Columbia University Press, 1963), 30–63, esp. 38 ff., 45–46; Cullen, *Spenser, Marvell, and Renaissance Pastoral* (Cambridge: Harvard University Press, 1970).

Cuddie's boast had been reasonably modest—"Phyllis is myne for many *dayes*," not months or years—Thenot's tart reply smacks more of "bias" than of truth. The bias had already been flagged in his earlier statement affirming the Philosophy of Waste: the common course of the world— and so, presumably, of the life cycle—is "from good to badd, and from badde to worse, / From worse unto that is worst of all," after which it returns not to its "former spring" but ironically to "his former fall"; death precedes another fall and long decline from paradise. The way Thenot sees it, he has "*worne out* thrise threttie yeares," only "*some* in much joy," but "*many* in many teares" (12–18). Do joys precede tears in life as they do in this line? Do the many sad years follow *because* the joys lasted too short a time?

Thenot's attachment to the Philosophy of Waste and his Stoic counsel seem intimately associated with his attachment to the joys of youth, his bitterness at their early, perhaps unexpected, loss. We do not seriously question Cuddie's insight that envy and the loss of virility make Thenot a killjoy:

> Ah foolish old man, I scorne thy skill,
> That wouldest me, my springing youngth to spil.
>
> . . . .
>
> Now thy selfe hast lost both lopp and topp,
> Als my budding braunch thou wouldest cropp:
> But were thy yeares greene, as now bene myne,
> To other delights they would encline.
>
> *(51–60)*

"*Other* delights" is interesting because it implies that railing at Cuddie's youth affords "rusty elde" the only pleasure of which it is now capable, the only way Thenot can keep in touch with what he has lost. To Cuddie's disparaging puns he responds in kind—"thou kenst little good, / So vainely tadvaunce thy *headlesse hood*"—and with equal rhetorical verve:

> For Youngth is a bubble blown up with breath,
> Whose witt is weakenesse, whose wage is death,
> Whose way is wildernesse, whose ynne Penaunce,
> And stoopegallaunt Age the hoste of Greevaunce.
>
> *(85–90)*

After these lines the tone of the debate temporarily mellows as Cuddie agrees to hear a tale from Thenot's youth and agrees also on the "well thewed" and "wise" quality of the tales devised by "that good old man," Tityrus. It becomes clear that keeping in touch with youth (or age) is as important as putting it down, that putting it down is a way to stay in touch.

This of course conforms with Cullen's view that youth and age represent complementary attitudes in healthy conflict, but his effort to bring them into calendrical balance keeps him from appreciating the complex self-dividedness Spenser depicts in Thenot if not in Cuddie. For example, the four lines of invective quoted above are confused by the divergent claims of two different arguments: First, "Greevaunce" is the consequence of misspent "Youngth." Here Thenot implicitly detaches "Youngth" from his own more prudent and patient youth (cf. 19–24) and assigns it to Cuddie. Because youths like Cuddie are heedless, self-indulgent, soft, and presumptuous, they become victims of "stoope-gallaunt Age." Second, "Youngth" is youth per se, and youth as a general condition, a stage of the life cycle, is more short-lived and frangible than the young know; their folly is to scorn the wisdom of those who have lived through the loss and want to prepare them for the harder life ahead. Here age is not the consequence of misspent youth, as it is in the first argument, but merely the natural sequel to spent youth; it is not youth that is reprehensible but age, that is, the common course of life ending in death "that is worst of all."

The second of these two lines is the one E. K. follows in the argument to the eclogue, and his way of associating it with the seasonal cycle is instructive: "The matter very well accordeth with the season of the moneth, the yeare now drouping, and as it were, drawing to his last age. For as in this time of yeare, so then in our bodies there is a dry and withering cold, which congealeth the crudled blood, and frieseth the weatherbeaten flesh, with stormes of Fortune, and hoare frosts of Care." Because the first sentence presents the annual cycle on the model of the life cycle, the phrase "this time of yeare" is metaphorically colored by "his last age," with the result that the "dry and withering cold" in the body is not merely that of seasonal winter but also that of wintry old age. If from the standpoint of the paradise principle the courses of world and individual life are both downhill, then the recurrence of literal spring-time should be minimized as a model for larger patterns of change. As I have noted in earlier chapters, this is the message Isabel MacCaffrey attributes to Spenser: the soft or "naïve version of the pastoral metaphor inadequately expresses reality" because it posits an idyllic congruence between man and nature, microcosm and macrocosm, that experience belies.[2] But the example of E. K. suggests that the analogical interchanges between seasonal and life cycles are more flexibly nuanced and that they can imply several ideologies. Since all of them reveal the influence of the paradise principle, none of them is directly attributable to Spenser as *his* message. E. K. and Thenot in these passages project the declining life cycle onto the annual cycle to produce a congruence that is hardly idyllic.

Furthermore, Thenot is capable of semantic diversity, as when he dissociates the metaphoric and the literal versions of the seasonal cycle:

> From worse unto that is worst of all,
> And then returne to his former fall?
> Who will not suffer the stormy time,
> Where will he live tyll the lusty prime?
> *(13–16)*

The figure of return is negatively skewed by its reference to the common course of the world and the life cycle, but when "lusty prime" replaces "former fall" as the point of return the reference shifts consolingly to actual spring as the happy conclusion of the cycle.[3] The shift is strategically useful to Thenot. His accent on "lusty prime" enables him to accuse Cuddie of making an unnecessary fuss over relatively minor discomforts thus showing himself unprepared for the bigger challenges to be posed by metaphoric winter.

Cuddie feels Thenot makes too much of the metaphoric sense and compares his sadbrow rhetoric to the fast day preceding Resurrection and holiday:

> And as the lowring Wether lookes downe,
> So semest thou like good fryday to frowne.
> But my flowring youth is foe to frost,
> My shippe unwont in stormes to be tost.
> *(29–32)*

For youth the cycle swings upward from fall to prime, from "lowring" to "flowring," and the old man's pessimism can be dismissed as the natural expression of those in the older generation looking with envy at what they have lost. To the annual and life cycles Cuddie's arguments add

---

[2] "Allegory and Pastoral in *The Shepheardes Calender*," *ELH* 36 (1969): 94.

[3] I can't agree with Cullen's reading of this passage (p. 38, quoted above). I see no sign of Thenot contending "that old age is the 'lusty prime' man should live his life for." On the contrary, Thenot seems if anything to be "biased" toward the lost pleasures of youth.

a third context: the passage from winter to spring figures the passing of the old generation and the advent of the new; Thenot's "lowring" is symptomatic of his loss of power, it presages the rising of the new "Lords of the yeare," and Cuddie can therefore endure—indeed enjoy—Thenot's storms more easily than those of winter. But it is the coupling of the annual with the generational contexts that gives the seasonal model its power to deceive the young as Colin was deceived: "What wreaked I of wintrye ages waste, / Tho deemed I, my spring would ever laste."

Thenot speaks to this deception with more animus than it would seem to call for in a passage that betrays the divergent pressures of his two arguments (youth is heedless and throws its life away on trifles; youth is foolish to cling to joys it must lose):

> The soveraigne of seas he blames in vaine,
> That once seabeate, will to sea againe.
> So loytring live you little heardgroomes,
> Keeping your beastes in the budded broomes:
> And when the shining sunne laugheth once,
> You deemen, the Spring is come attonce.
> Tho gynne you, fond flyes, the cold to scorne,
> And crowing in pypes made of greene corne,
> You thinken to be Lords of the yeare.
> But eft, when ye count you freed from feare,
> Comes the breme winter with chamfred browes,
> Full of wrinckles and frostie furrowes:
> Drerily shooting his stormy darte,
> Which cruddles the blood, and pricks the harte.
> Then is your carelesse corage accoied,
> Your carefull heards with cold bene annoied.
> Then paye you the price of your surquedrie,
> With weeping, and wayling, and misery.
>
> *(33–50)*

The illogicality of the opening couplet is something Thenot seems willing to risk for the pleasure of countering Cuddie's "My shippe unwont in stormes to be tost" with a tart proverb of his own: "Don't blame the sea god for knowingly and unnecessarily exposing yourself to storms you've experienced before." It is not at all clear how "so [in this manner] loytering" and its consequent follows from these lines, but Thenot goes on to criticize the young for pasturing their herds among the budding bushes, for prematurely celebrating their triumph over winter, and finally for being unable to withstand it when it comes. He uses the model of seasonal change in a fluid if not sophistical manner, and the shiftiness of this passage is worth noting: what seems at first to be a deceptive and fleeting harbinger of spring—one laugh of the sun—turns out to be spring itself, succeeded by the following winter.

Thenot thus rhetorically enhances both the insubstantial brevity of "lusty prime" and the folly of youth's "crowing." Spring quickly gives way to the recurrence of the "former fall," and as he proceeds, the rising intensity of his rhetoric transforms winter to "winter," that is, it works to detach the seasonal model from the annual cycle and to associate it with the declining course of life. He personifies "breme winter" as an archer who, despite his age, vigorously and aggressively attacks his foe. The archer is a Panic figure used to frighten Cuddie with a prospect of his grim future. But it is also a figure of Thenot, who stands before Cuddie as the agent of Elde giving an earnest of that retribution while the wintry dart of his rhetoric allows him to assert his own Nestorian vigor and savor his own revenge. Thenot wants it both ways: "some day you'll be as wrinkled and furrowed as I am; but when you are, you won't have my virile and hardy 'corage'; you'll be an easy target for the old bowman." Spenser ironically points this theme by having Cuddie begin his response with a contemptuous assessment of Thenot's virility and go on to speak of the pleasures of young love.

In terms of this theme the figure of the old archer takes on depth, suggesting the cause of Thenot's animus and the basic ambivalence of his attitude toward youth. Although at first glance it is a self-portrait, the dart is tell-tale. The preeminent dart shooter in the *Calender* is Cupid, who materializes in *March* and whose arrows make wounds that are felt in *Aprill* (22), *August* (93 ff.), and *December* (93–96). I find compelling the notion that Thenot's archer is a wintry Cupid, that is, a figure of the persistence of desire in old age, the thorn in the flesh, the ghost or after-image of young Cupid. It is as if this is what the "other delights" of youth inevitably become in the bitter afterwash of so brief a "flowring," as if desire ages with the body and the darts it keeps shooting replace the wounds of love with the "breme" memory of its loss after it has burst the bubble of "Youngth."

However speculative this reading may be, the sentiment is itself a commonplace that Spenser could have found in many sources and that informs his general treatment of the effect of the paradise principle on the mind "drawing to his last age." The rationale is perfectly expressed, for example, by Castiglione in the dedicatory preface to the second book of *Il libro del Cortigiano*. He finds it "contrary to reason and a cause for wonder that a ripe age, which in all other respects is wont to make men's judgment more perfect," should make them "praise bygone times and denounce the present," as if "fathers were generally better than their children" and all things were "continually going from bad to worse." The reason for this unreasonable attitude is that

> in old age the sweet flowers of contentment fall from our hearts, as in autumn the leaves fall from their trees, and in place of bright and clear thoughts there comes a cloudy and turbid sadness attended by a thousand ills. So that not only the body but the mind also is enfeebled, and retains of past pleasures merely a lingering memory and the image of that precious time of tender youth in which . . . the sweet springtime of happiness seems to flower in our thoughts as in a delightful and lovely garden. . . .
>
> Since the senile spirit is thus an unfit vessel for many pleasures, it cannot enjoy them; . . . to old people in their indisposition (in which, however, there is still the desire) pleasures seem insipid and cold and are very different from those which they remember enjoying once, although the pleasures in themselves are still the same. Hence, feeling themselves deprived of them, they complain and denounce present times as bad, not perceiving that the change is in themselves and not in the times. . . . For our minds in fact hate all things that have accompanied our sorrows, and love those things that have accompanied our joys.[4]

Chaucer's Reeve provides another precedent:

> But ik am oold, me list not pley for age;
> Gras tyme is doon, my fodder is now forage;
> This white top writeth myne olde yeris;
> Myn herte is also mowled as myne heris,
> But if I fare as dooth an open-ers,—
> That ilke fruyt is ever lenger the wers,
> Til it be roten in mullok or in stree.
> We olde men, I drede, so fare we:
> Til we be roten, kan we nat be rype;
> We hoppen alwey whil the world wol pype.
> For in oure wyl ther stiketh evere a nayl,
> To have an hoor heed and a grene tayl,
> As hath a leek; for thogh oure myght be goon,
> Oure wyl desireth folie evere in oon.
> For whan we may nat doon, than wol we speke;
> Yet in oure asshen olde is fyr yreke.
>
> *("Reeve's Prologue," 3867–82)*

---

[4]Trans. C. S. Singleton (Garden City, N.Y.: Anchor Books, 1959), 89–91.

The *Calender*'s most direct descendant of the Reeve is Palinode in *Maye*:

> To see those folkes make such jouysaunce,
> Made my heart after the pype to daunce.
>
>   *(25–26)*

>   (O that I were there,
> To helpen the Ladyes their Maybush beare)
> Ah Piers, bene not thy teeth on edge, to thinke,
> How great sport they gaynen with little swinck?
>
>   *(33–36)*

> Sicker now I see thou speakest of spight,
> All for thou lackest somedele their delight.
>
>   *(55–56)*

Thenot is superficially more like Piers than Palinode: "For Younkers Palinode such follies fitte, / But we tway bene men of elder witt" (17–18). But Cuddie's insight is justified by the response that betrays the lurking presence of both Cupids, young and old, in Thenot's "elder witt":

> But were thy yeares greene, as now bene myne,
> To other delights they would encline.
>
>   *(Feb. 59–60)*

> Thou art a fon, of thy love to boste,
> All that is lent to love, wyll be lost.
>
>   *(69–70)*

Cullen finds "obvious aphoristic truth" in Thenot's response (p. 38), but it may only seem true because it sounds obvious and aphoristic—a point to which I shall return in a moment. It may be true of a certain form of love, in which case it speaks to the limits of that love or of those who conceive love in that way; it is not true of the love dramatized in *Amoretti and Epithalamion*, nor of Britomart's love in *Faerie Queene* III–V. How arbitrary and cankered Thenot's "truth" is can be seen by contrasting it to the alternative view expressed by the Wife of Bath:

> But, Lord Crist! whan that it remembreth me
> Upon my yowthe, and on my jolitee,
> It tikleth me aboute myn herte roote.
> Unto this day it dooth myn herte boote
> That I have had my world as in my tyme.
> But age, allas! that al wole envenyme,

Hath me biraft my beautee and my pith.
Lat go, farewel! the devel go therewith!
The flour is goon, ther is namoore to telle;
The bren, as I best kan, now moste I selle;
But yet to be right myrie wol I fonde.

("Wife of Bath's Prologue," 469–79)

Thenot's utterances certainly have, as Cullen insists, the *ring* of truth. But that is one of the rhetorical and ideological functions of aphoristic style, and it derives from another, which is to signify the distillation of truth from long experience, time-honored age, and tradition. As Cullen notes at one point, if Thenot's "argument is an old one," Cuddie's is "no younger" (p. 35). Cullen stresses "the typicality of character and situation" in *Februarie:* "we have seen this confrontation [between youth and age] before; there is no need to mourn or moralize." But he ignores this insight and goes on immediately to moralize: "Spenser is portraying the comic absurdity underlying one of the common situations of human experience, the human comedy with its contradictions and conflicts, as natural as the conflict of winter and spring traditionally associated with the month of February" (p. 37). Such conspicuous aphorism of style and conspicuous truism of sentiment as *Februarie* displays should not head us directly toward nature, human nature, and the human comedy as the object of Spenser's portrayal. Rather they should head us toward the *literary* comedy, human *traditions,* and *artifice.* What Spenser is portraying—miming, or perhaps I should say mimicking—is the voice and "wisdom" of received opinion sedimented into the institution of literature operative in his time. Colin Clout's speech and sentiments are studded with literary clichés and Thenot's with "bromidic aphorisms" (Cullen, 37) that represent not only the forms but also the values enshrined in the traditional genres and conventions of poetry.

Thenot's apparently stoic response *to* life is actually a cynic's view *of* life. His argument is superficially ethical: youth is imprudent, arrogant, self-indulgent, and (taking the moral of his tale into account) ambitious as well as dishonest and malicious in its pursuit of pleasure or power. But at bottom his argument is practical: the pleasures of youth are folly not because they are evil but because they are short-lived and it is painful to lose them. His blanket rejection of youth smacks of the disappointment Cuddie attributes to him, measuring the force of his youthful attachments and the bitterness of his loss. The sense of loss is conveyed by the tale he tells and even by the details he gives in introducing it. For he dwells fondly on his recollection of Tityrus, from whom "I cond . . . in

my youth" not only the "tale of truth" he recites but also "many meete
tales of youth . . . / And some of love, and some of chevalrie" (*Feb.*
98–99). The tale of the oak and the briar betrays the deeper source of
his animus against Cuddie. His anxiety over the declining power and
authority of age translates into a diatribe against the "surquedry" of up-
start youth. The tale expresses his fear of the "Lords of the yeare" with
their parricidal impatience to wrest lordship from the elders, who find
themselves cast aside because their "witt is weakenesse" and their "wage
is death."

In the tale the oak is a bathetic distortion of Thenot, the briar an
abusive distortion of Cuddie. The oak, that "Whilome had bene the
King of the field," could find no words to answer the briar's insults and
"yielded, with shame and greefe adawed, / That of a weede he was over-
crawed" (108, 141–42)—again Thenot's focus is on the loss of his
former power, size, status, and nurturant fertility (103–10) and on
his present miserable remains: "His toppe was bald, and wasted with
wormes, / His honor decayed, his braunches sere" (113–14). Passages
that express loathing for physical decrepitude are thus assigned not only
to the briar (169–82) but also to the aged speaker himself. At the same
time the speaker's description of the briar is—in spite of his denun-
ciatory portrait—no less admiring than that which he assigns the briar:

> Yt was embellisht with blossomes fayre,
> And thereto aye wonned to repayre
> The shepheards daughters, to gather flowres,
> To peinct their girlonds with his colowres.
> And in his small bushes used to shrowde
> The sweete Nightingale singing so lowde . . .
>
> *(118–23)*

> Seest, how fresh my flowers bene spredde,
> Dyed in Lilly white, and Cremsin redde,
> With Leaves engrained in lusty greene,
> Colours meete to clothe a mayden Queene.
>
> *(129–32)*

Thenot delights not only in the flowers of spring but also in those of
speech: the inarticulate oak is never directly quoted, whereas the briar's
hated rhetorical colors fly high throughout the tale, and the anti-briar
sentiment with which the tale ends gives Thenot another opportunity to
indulge his proclivity for briar rhetoric. Hence he shows his attachment
to what he professes to scorn; while disparaging the devious but persuasive language of youth he lards his narrative with it.

The same ambivalence frames his account of the druidic practices that
marked the oak's early career. The "auncient tree" had been

> Sacred with many a mysteree,
> And often crost with the priestes crewe,
> And often halowed with holy water dewe.
> But sike fancies weren foolerie,
> And broughten this Oake to this miserye.
> For nought mought they quitten him from decay . . .
>
> *(208–13)*

Cullen uses this passage to illustrate one of the dangers of the arguments
on behalf of age: "Even Thenot, who can hardly be considered partial to
the ambitions and vitality of youth," shows how "age's reverence for tradition has been perverted by the Oak into superstition" (p. 40). But this
is only another example of Thenot's *persistent* partiality toward youth—
the youth he has lost—and his mixed feelings toward "antique age yet in
the infancie / Of time" (*FQ* IV.viii.30) are brilliantly inscribed in his
diction: though the first four lines are mainly positive, the fifth line
brings out the bitterness lurking in *sacred . . . crost . . . crewe. Dewe*
becomes a pivot—from *owing, appropriate,* to nature's fresh but fugitive
early-morning radiance. The force of the implied counterfactual wish in
the final line explains why *miserye* is the diminished echo of *mysteree*.

The fable is more than the wintry dart Thenot shoots at Cuddie, for
reviving the tale heard long ago enables him to relive his own youth
while criticizing Cuddie's. Cuddie cuts off the tale at the appropriate
word, forestalling the imminent *sentence:*

> Such was thend of this Ambitious brere,
> For scorning Eld
>
> CUDDIE.
> Now I pray thee shepheard, tel it not forth:
> Here is a long tale, and little worth.
> So longe have I listened to thy speche,
> That graffed to the ground is my breche:
> My hartblood is welnigh frorne I feele,
> And my galage growne fast to my heele:
> But little ease of thy lewd tale I tasted.
> Hye thee home shepheard, the day is nigh wasted.
>
> *(237–46)*

The tale has had an Ovidian effect on Cuddie: the "bitter blasts" of
Thenot and cold weather have "graffed" him to the ground—rooted

him like a tree, and indeed like a rapidly aging and twisted one whose "hartblood is welnigh frorne." He objects to the tale on youth's recreative grounds: "we are not amused." The shortfall of *otium*, and not merely the night, has "nigh wasted" another day, but at least it will bring him closer to the "lusty prime" while Thenot, who has briefly recaptured it in the only way he could, will move on "From worse unto that is worst of all."[5]

Cuddie's brusque interruption shows that he remains unmoved by Thenot's effort to "cruddle" his blood and "pricke" his heart. But this dismissal only means that paradoxically he and Thenot represent different phases of the same dialectical attitude. His *ad hominem* contempt of the Mantuanesque arguments, evident throughout the eclogue, reveals the lurking influence of the paradise principle openly expressed in Colin's "tho deemed I, my spring would ever laste." To have taken Thenot more seriously might have protected Cuddie from precisely the cynicism Thenot's arguments betray. And even though his description of youth's delights is relatively temperate, giving us cause to suspect Thenot's bitter response, his conception of love is also motivated by the paradise principle. The modest scale and playful sense of his approach to love provide a foil to Colin's plaintive excesses, but he shares with Colin the assumption that love involves pursuit, possession, and poetry, that woman is a trophy to be won, that she can be won by gifts or song, and that the conquest is a matter for further song:

> Tho wouldest thou learne to caroll of Love,
> And hery with hymnes thy lasses glove.
> Tho wouldest thou pype of *Phyllis* prayse:
> But *Phyllis* is myne for many dayes:
> I wonne her with a gyrdle of gelt,
> Embost with buegle about the belt.
>
> *(61–66)*

This economic view of *la chasse* is hardly heroic, but it reflects one kind of pastoral convention, reducing love to a game that has little or nothing to do with the difficulties of sustained personal commitment. Its recreative expectations are the same as those shortly to be expressed by Willye in *March:*

---

[5] Of course if the name *Thenot* found in *Aprill* and *November* refers to the same speaker, he has been saved from this fate by magical rejuvenation. See the preceding chapter.

> Tho shall we sporten in delight,
> And learne with Lettice to wexe light,
> That scornefully lookes askaunce.
> Tho will we little Love awake,
> That nowe sleepeth in *Lethe* lake,
> And pray him leaden our daunce.
>
> *(19–24)*

"Scornefully lookes askaunce" describes the expected challenge that sweetens an expected victory that may last as long as "many dayes." Cullen aptly characterizes such an attitude as the "naiveté of one who expects to realize his idealized conception of love as a rose without thorns" (p. 101), and he argues persuasively that genuine love is the mean excluded from the "comic" and "tragic" extremes represented respectively by the recreative tendency to minimize "little Love" and by Colin's plaintive exaggeration. Ironically the recreative love of Cuddie and Willye is informed by Thenot's attitude—"All that is lent to love, wyll be lost"—and it protects itself from that danger by not lending very much. But on the same principle not very much will be kept or returned. A diet of Phyllises and Lettices is too light to be sustained or sustaining beyond the recreative salad days of youth, so that a love reduced to these terms is bound to be lost when "Gras tyme is doon," "The flour is goon," and the mind "retains of past pleasures merely a lingering memory and the image of that precious time." Hence the effect of the paradise principle is to transform "little Love" into the wintry archer "Drerily shooting his stormy dart."

Such minikin pleasures as those of Cuddie and Willye are foils to Colin's plaintive excesses, but as I noted they seem to share the same assumptions. The function of woman in this basically misogynist view is to provide the kind of entertainment and test of masculinity that will enhance the cooperative and competitive activities by which the male pastoral community promotes its solidarity. A love thus governed by the dictates of the paradise principle is bound to be lost when the "breme winter," like an aged embittered Cupid, shoots its dart. No doubt because it *has* been lost "breme" Thenot shoots his dreary dart at Cuddie. Thus Cuddie and Thenot are more in agreement than they know.

The *Februarie* debate presents the surface of a simple opposition between Youth and Age that generates a conflict of commonplace arguments. Spenser shows how these arguments give the illusion of rising from more fundamental or "philosophic" polar differences of position, and recent commentary has concerned itself with the character of the polarity and with the evaluation of the two poles, the antithetical attitudes symbolized in this eclogue by youth and age. But this interpretive concern does not go far enough because both positions are dialectically inter-involved in a single complex attitude, and the limitations of both positions derive from their common source in the paradise principle.

In his programmatic statements Cullen affirms the relation between characters and impersonal attitudes or perspectives but subordinates the latter to the former:

> The comedy in the debates is . . . a comedy of character and misperception, of talking at cross-purposes on different wave-lengths, of naïve literal-mindedness, and of exaggerated argument. This is not to say that the issues are unimportant. Obviously that is not so; the point is that the debates are *debates between personalities as well as perspectives,* and that Spenser employs comedy to point to the limitations of *both the disputant and his perspective.* (pp. 33–34; italics mine)

As a corrective to the overemphasis on topical issues evident in much previous criticism, this is a salutary and balanced view, but Cullen's actual practice and rhetoric tend toward too extreme a counteremphasis. Consequently the disputants often appear to be the sole proprietors of their perspectives even though Cullen insists that Spenser is using them to characterize the Arcadian and Mantuanesque perspectives as they appear in the traditions available to him. That this ethical focus derives from Cullen's two main interests, the first in the polar conflict of Arcadian and Mantuanesque perspectives and the second in the *Calender's* liberal or pluralistic view of the conflict, is clear from the following passages:

> Even the characters who are often taken to represent Spenser's own opinions, like Thenot, Piers, and Diggon Davie, are not immune to seeming naïve, stuffy, literal-minded, or quaint. Thinking himself the possessor of the whole truth, no character is immune to Spenser's irony and its insistence on the limitations of our vision. The poem's technique is thus an extension of its recurring emphasis on the recognition of a plurality of values, a necessity for discrimination: the medium illustrates the message. (p. 34)

> From their confrontation emerges an ambivalence in which neither perspective can claim the whole truth. In "February," Thenot's Mantuanesque restraint and Cuddie's youthful *otium* are both limited, the one running the risk of sterility, the other running the risk of overweening pride and ambition. (pp. 31–32)

The pluralism and the polar conflict Cullen astutely picks out themselves need further explanation. I see both as the surface manifestations
of a deeper unity, a different kind of ambivalence, which may be located
in the dominance of the paradise principle. The *Calender*'s variety of
modes and plurality of values make it not merely a pastoral microcosm
of literary modes and values but a continuous allusion to them. The vector of influence internally mirrored as a vector of allusion brings Latin,
Alexandrian, Italian, French, and native sources into the *Calender* as objects of its attention along with satire, elegy, anacreontic lyric, panegyric,
Aesopic fable, and so on, so that, in Grosart's words, Spenser's poem
"must be studied less as Pastoral-proper than as Poetry framing itself in
rural scenery and rural human experience" (*Variorum, Minor Poems*
1:590). This is a first reduction—the literary cosmos reduced to the pastoral microcosm "where each kind / Does streight [straitened] its own
resemblance find." A second reduction may be located in E. K.'s classification of the range of subjects into the recreative, plaintive, and moral
modes. Cullen's distinction of Arcadian and Mantuanesque perspectives
cuts across these modes as a third reduction, and a final reduction inte-
grates the two perspectives as twin shoots of the paradise principle,
carrying its bifurcating influence throughout the range and diversity of
the represented literary cosmos.

So unified, characterized, and criticized, the poetic traditions that fathered the *Calender* become its child and stand within its readers' pur-
view as The Poetic Tradition—to be more precise, as The Paradise of
Poetic Tradition, or The Paradisal Poetic Tradition. This is the *Calender*'s main character, and it is fundamentally abstract, impersonal, collective. Its various aspects, such as Age and Youth, are also best viewed
as abstractions dissociable from any speaker who argues in their name.
What Age and Youth "belong to," what they are part of, is the paradise
principle, not this or that speaker. This perspective makes it easier to
approach the paradisal tradition as a pressure exerted on the speakers
who exhibit its influence. Thus I think it is important to reverse Cullen's
emphasis on the primacy and opacity of the pastoral speakers and to emphasize their translucency with respect to the attitudes they model. By
positing Age and Youth as symbols of attitudes that are the dialectical
components of the paradise principle Spenser represents as the organizing force of literary tradition, we are better able to explore their interaction in the language of a single speaker without overstating the speaker's
singularity. I have tried to demonstrate this thesis in my reading of
Thenot's language and will now do the same for Colin Clout in *June*.

II

Uncoupled from the sequence in which it is represented, Colin's career moves chronologically from the mythical moment of the *Aprill* lay through his *August* sestina, *Januarye* complaint, *June* dialogue, and *November* elegy to the end of his *December* retrospect. This movement dramatically charts the operation of the paradise principle as it plants in the Vacant Head a garden of green expectations that, when life fails to match them, wither like the plants in a forcing garden (known as a garden of Adonis) and leave the Wandering Mind confronting what appears by contrast to be as much nature's war as nature's work: a "wofull waste of natures warke" (*Nov.* 64). Having generated the bitter view, the sweet vision does not fade but persists beside the other and exacerbates it until the mind longs to escape from the wicked world and to recover the lost paradise by reinstating Vacancy of Head. Colin's career displays more than the coexistence and interaction of these twin shoots of the paradise principle, however. It displays a gradual diffusion of the bitter view from the narrow focus on love with which it began until in *December* it embraces the cosmos. This process is most fully explicated in *June*, and the present section will deal primarily with that eclogue.

In *Januarye* Colin managed to divert his anger and blame from Rosalind to himself, his pipe, his muse, and his "rude" god. When we meet him again in *June* after traversing Hobbinol's performance of the *Aprill* panegyric, his bitterness at first appears more widely and blandly diffused, expressing itself in a rueful rejection of his earlier pleasures and in a cautiousness of address toward those in high pastoral places. By the end of the eclogue, however, we learn that his animus remains targeted on Rosalind, having been sharpened by her "discurtesee" into a "poynt of worthy wight" aimed at "her heart" (97–100)—that is, a dart of deserved blame sent by a worthy man more sinned against than sinning.

Before this outburst Colin's remarks betray a general malaise about his position in the pastoral world. In *Januarye* it was Rosalind who scorned his rural music. Now the high-born Muses "holden scorne of homely shepheards quill," Colin remembers the folly of Pan's challenge to Phoebus, and his brief memoir of Tityrus resonates with elegiac sentiment (*June* 66–69, 81–93). Death, competition, hierarchy, ambition, the *phthonos* of the mighty and the hubris of the low: Colin's perception of paradise seems to have been informed by sobering experience and by the "ryper age" he claims to have reached.

This perception is in sharp contrast to the period of *Aprill* innocence surveyed by Hobbinol, and the point of the following lines would seem to be to recall that pleasance, which now appears to Colin as remote as the Paradise "whych Adam lost" (10). Hobbinol works up to his climax slowly, beginning with homely landscape details which, whatever their literary provenance, are Englished by the language that conveys them:

> The simple ayre, the gentle warbling wynde,
> So calme, so coole, as no where else I fynde:
> The grassye ground with daintye Daysies dight,
> The Bramble bush . . .
>
> *(4–7)*

He moves more rapidly through the dales, with their "shepheards ritch" and "fruictfull flocks" (21–22), and finally draws the veil from the higher pastoral mysteries:

> But frendly Faeries, met with many Graces,
> And lightfote Nymphes can chace the lingring night,
> With Heydeguyes, and trimly trodden traces,
> Whylst systers nyne, which dwell on *Parnasse* hight,
> Doe make them musick, for their more delight:
> And *Pan* himselfe to kisse their christall faces,
> Will pype and daunce, when *Phoebe* shineth bright:
> Such pierlesse pleasures have we in these places.
>
> *(25–32)*

This vision gathers into a bouquet the flowers of vernal myth scattered through *March* (13–24), the *Aprill* song (especially 64–126), and *Maye* (9–36). It selectively features the egalitarianism and the cooperation-*sans*-competition of the ideal community. The august Parnassans deign to harmonize for English country dances, Graces consort with (and may, as E. K.'s gloss suggests, be aspects of) Faeries who dance with nymphs, even the notorious *amator* appears as a guest rather than as an interloper, and under the chastening influence of Phoebe, whose light blanches away eroticism, he is allowed to kiss crystal.

Yet like crystal the vision shimmers with the hints of its fragility. Phoebe's is the domain of the changeable moon, of dreamtime, perhaps also of virginal *daunger*. The dancers try to chase away the night, which is their prime dancing time. The light feet of the nymphs, unwonted pursuers, bear traces of Pan's vaunted venery. Finally, E. K.'s sour antipapist and antigallic gloss on Faeries and Elves dispels the harmony, reminding us that "Elf" is a name to frighten children with (146–60).

When Colin claims to have passed these pleasures by, Hobbinol reminds him that he shamed the Muses by excelling them in their art (62–64), a remark that recalls the light-hearted hubris with which Colin addressed the Muses and gods in *Aprill* (cf. *Apr.* 100 ff. and *June* 57 ff.). Colin responds with increased wariness, speaking of the scornful Muses and jealous Phoebus in a way that brings out the lurking dangers briefly suspended by conspicuous exclusion in Hobbinol's moonlight vision of the happy community, which in retrospect provides the measure of Colin's disenchantment. His modesty is rhetorical and self-protecting, and at least for three stanzas (*June* 65–88) it conveys the discretion of riper age. But even here the emphasis slips from the inability *topos* to something a little more tendentious: the undertone of petulance in "I play to please my selfe, all be it ill" (72) increases in "Enough is me to paint out my unrest, / And poore my piteous plaints out in the same," that is, in rude rhymes fit "my carefull case to frame" (77–80).

Throughout the *Calender* Colin remains a literary competitor who appreciates his preeminence at least over his human peers and occasionally over the gods as well, and his sense of his own achievement is perhaps most clearly stated, its full confusion most apparent, in his memoir of Tityrus in *June:*

> The God of shepheards *Tityrus* is dead,
> Who taught me homely, as I can, to make.
> He, whilst he lived, was the soveraigne head
> Of shepheards all, that bene with love ytake:
> Well couth he wayle hys Woes, and lightly slake
> The flames, which love within his heart had bredd,
> And tell us mery tales, to keep us wake,
> The while our sheepe about us safely fedde.
>
> Now dead he is, and lyeth wrapt in lead,
> (O why should death on hym such outrage showe?)
> And all hys passing skil with him is fledde,
> The fame whereof doth dayly greater growe.
> But if on me some little drops would flowe,
> Of that the spring was in his learned hedde,
> I soone would learne these woods, to wayle my woe,
> And teache the trees, their trickling teares to shedde.
>
> *(81–96)*

Colin confines personal grief within parentheses and on the word *passing* turns quickly from elegiac feeling to a more interested and emulative sentiment: not merely grief for the passing away of Tityrus's skill but admiration for the posthumous fame that could conceivably accrue to a worthy successor who could equal Tityrus's surpassing skill and go on to match his skill in surpassing. He would like to place Tityrus's "soveraigne" and "learned hedde" on his own shoulders, but with different and more restricted intentions. Unlike the musicians Pan and Mercury, Tityrus sang "to keepe us wake" and "our sheepe" safe. Colin acknowledges this but does not himself seem eager to tell "mery tales" to advance the security and solidarity of the pastoral community. The "little drops" he asks for are distinctly of the wet variety, and they are in addition *learned* drops, drops of Orphic music giving him *expressive* power. He would particularly appreciate some drops of invective, for after this passage he returns with a vengeance to the "losse of her, whose love as lyfe I wayd," concluding the eclogue with a tirade indicating that bitterness rather than "mature" discretion (cf. Cullen, 88 ff.) underlies his withdrawal from aspiration to humble self-sufficiency.

Colin's reactions in *June* present the reader with the problem of reconciling this invective with his claim to have reached maturity. Otherwise we confront a situation in which, several "years" after being rejected, he is still piping obsessively on that note, and in fact has had his obsession recently stoked by another "discurtesee." Paul Alpers no doubt had in mind discrepancies of this sort when he complained that "Colin's dramatic speeches in 'June' and 'December' are full of inconsistencies of rhetoric and attitude."[6] And indeed the conflict between the themes of senescence and unrequited love is not the only inconsistency. Nancy Jo Hoffman found another in "Spenser's assertion that when he walked 'withouten lincks of love' . . . he also piped plaintive pleas for Rosalind, who presumably he *did* love."[7] I quote in full the stanzas to which she refers, since I shall return to consider them more closely later:

> And I, whylst youth, and course of carelesse yeeres
> Did let me walke withouten lincks of love,
> In such delights did joy amongst my peeres:
> But ryper age such pleasures doth reprove,
> My fancye eke from former follies move
> To stayed steps: for time in passing weares
> (As garments doen, which wexen old above)
> And draweth newe delights with hoary heares.

---

[6] "The Eclogue Tradition and the Nature of Pastoral," *College English* 34 (1972): 367.
[7] *Spenser's Pastorals: "The Shepheardes Calender" and "Colin Clout"* (Baltimore: Johns Hopkins University Press, 1977), 65.

> Tho couth I sing of love, and tune my pype
> Unto my plaintive pleas in verses made:
> Tho would I seeke for Queene apples unrype,
> To give my *Rosalind,* and in Sommer shade
> Dight gaudy Girlonds, was my comen trade,
> To crowne her golden locks, but yeeres more rype,
> And losse of her, whose love as lyfe I wayd,
> Those weary wanton toyes away dyd wype.
>
> *(33–48)*

Hoffman, whose reading of Spenser is avowedly indebted to Alpers, uses his rhetoric-versus-narrative approach to try to explain why "we should not and, appropriately, cannot logically reconcile" this inconsistency. Her theory is that Spenser explores "several pastoral rhetorics" and that in *June* these generate "not primarily a series of chronological narrative acts . . . but, rather, a series of poetic moments" in which Colin's "autonomous" mind "must struggle at each moment with changing but self-created landscapes" (pp. 61–62). The virtue of this theory is that it orients us toward the poet's relation to the various resources (pastoral rhetorics) that literature makes available to him, but since Hoffman doesn't sufficiently dissociate Colin from Spenser she tends to dismiss too easily the negative aspects both of conventional influence and of Colin's response. Conflating their two voices, she writes that Spenser's voice "acknowledges aphorism and convention as the formulations of basic human truths" and that he rejects the conventional styles of rhetoric "not because they are meaningless" but because, though he can reproduce them with facility, "he cannot perform them with the skill necessary to create an adequate place for the June season's restlessly wandering mind" (p. 69).

The inconsistency that troubles Hoffman is more apparent than real. The two stanzas quoted above lead upon closer reading to a different view of the relation between conventional formulations and the rejected lover's restlessness. In fact they open up on the larger prospect of Colin's career as he is importunately tumbled from Vacancy of Head into the pathways of the Wandering Mind. Let me begin by summarizing the postulated inconsistencies: it seems inconsistent of Colin to assert that (1) when he walked "withouten lincks of love" he (2) knew how to "sing of love," and further that (3) he made "plaintive pleas in verses" during what must have been roughly the same time that (4) he was courting Rosalind and had not yet lost her. The solution is simple as soon as we apply to the passage the rationale of the Vacant Head. Colin's lines about singing of love and tuning his pipe are appositional to "such delights" in line 35, and these words in turn refer back to the "pierelesse pleasures" of dance, song, and poetry Hobbinol describes in the previous stanza. This reference indicates that his early love songs and complaints had no connection to his being in love or being rejected. He wrote poetry about love because love is what one who aspires to literary fame writes poetry about. He may well have written plaintive pleas to amuse Rosalind because that is among the conventional ways poet-lovers amuse themselves, their loves, and their neighbors.

The Colin who looks back on his careless years communicates his retrospect in tones dominated by the ambivalence and uncertainty of the Wandering Mind. The first of the two stanzas combines simplicity of statement with shifting nuances of sense produced by syntactical and verbal figures. It describes the departure from old (i.e., young) delights and the turning toward new delights so as to make us wonder whether the turning is not also a returning, whether the new delights of age are not replicas of the old delights of youth; the idea of *re*turn and of reverse weaning is prosodically reinforced throughout the eclogue by the chiasmically reversing rhyme scheme (*a b a b b a b a*).

Though his careless years are over Colin caresses them fondly in the first three lines. Since the delights he refers to are Hobbinol's "pierelesse pleasures" of poetry and song, the "lincks of love" that would fetter him in care need not be links of *rejected* love: to the emparadised mind love per se may appear as bondage. Even after Colin has fallen his sentiments are clearly shaped by the lingering pressure of the paradise principle. Marvell would later suggest that *peerless* in the vocabulary of the paradise principle extends beyond *compareless* to include *pairless:* "Such was that happy Garden-state, / While Man there walk'd without a Mate." This golden retrospect seems related to the "Garden's" earlier image of the self-preening soul-bird that sits on a tree and "Waves in its Plumes the various light"—the light, no doubt, of the Muses filtering through the poet-tree into the bard's unencumbered freely waving plume: "Two Paradises 'twere in one / To live in Paradise alone."

Colin's turn to riper age in the fourth line of the first stanza signals a change in his perspective—though not without a struggle, since the line is invertible: the obvious sense secured by the adversative "But" is momentarily challenged by its contrary, "such pleasures reprove riper age." When this challenge is overcome and "such pleasures" decline to "former follies" then the sense of "carelesse" slips from "carefree" to "heedless." "Ryper Age" is abstract enough to signify a generalized role or personification, so that at first we may think Colin is speaking of his elders, in which case the piece of *sentence* that concludes the stanza has the comic ring of a youth's effort to justify and assimilate their wisdom. Dutifully and pretentiously he repeats the catechism of the Stoic censors: youth is unripe folly; to age is to ripen into wisdom. "Ryper" is honorific; as Colin intones the consolations of senior citizenship, Marvell's "Garden" gives way to "Rabbi ben Ezra." This change of perspective reaches another stage in the next stanza when Colin refers to his own "yeeres more rype." It appears that he is not merely imagining senescence but actually experiencing it, not merely internalizing the censor but becoming one. It takes him only two stanzas to move into the next generation.

As he continues, however, a different mood disturbs the complacency with which the catechumen pledges allegiance to the pleasures of ripeness. Colin returns to a closer view of his former follies and lingers over them with language in which affection tempers but does not dissolve reproof; I quote the stanza again:

> Tho couth I sing of love, and tune my pype
> Unto my plaintive pleas in verses made:
> Tho would I seeke for Queene apples unrype,
> To give my *Rosalind*, and in Sommer shade
> Dight gaudy Girlonds, was my comen trade,
> To crowne her golden locks, but yeeres more rype,
> And losse of her, whose love as lyfe I wayd,
> Those weary wanton toyes away dyd wype.
>
> *(41–48)*

"Tho couth I" expresses pride in his accomplishments, but the echoing anaphora of the third line is more tentative. "Tho would I seeke for Queene apples unrype" at once epitomizes and judges his pleasures with beautiful economy: "unrype" easily slips its tie to "apples" and qualifies the whole phrase; the words describing the gift ("Queene apples unrype") symbolize the immature or premature and excessive devotion of the giver; the pastoral modesty of the gift, which would normally have positive significance as a mark of humble but devoted attention (as in Virgil's second eclogue, cited by E. K. as source), is here dismissed as one of the "weary wanton toyes" by which the idle and idolizing shepherd wasted his youth inflating small things to great. The stanza thus shifts from something close to fond recollection toward something close to contempt in the final line, where the bitter rejection appears general enough to include Colin's music and verse among the wanton toys.

The last three lines of the stanza center our attention on the problematical relation of unrequited love to premature senescence. The weight of those lines is not on natural ripening but on unnatural loss; the cause briefly stated in the second half of the sixth line is more than counterpoised by the different cause self-pityingly bemoaned in the seventh. If the Rabbi ben Ezra viewpoint gives one value to "weary wanton toyes"—outlived, now tiresome and "tired"—the loss of Rosalind gives another: wearing, consuming, obsessive; love "wayd" as life. The subsequent invective and self-pity that occupy the closing stanzas of *June* make it clear that "yeeres more rype" play a small role in shaping Colin's present attitude. The equanimity taught in the catechism of Ryper Age, along with the bland maxim about "newe delightes," appears by the end of the eclogue to be a rationalization. It justifies a bitter disillusionment that seems superficially to have little connection with the aging process or the wisdom of the elders.

But this lack of connection turns out to be no more than superficial. Rewriting the previous stanza to explore the last four lines more closely, we find that as Colin shifts from the voice of youth to the voice of age he reveals in his own divided attitude the continuity, and indeed the complicity, between the two opposing pastoral parties. He contains within himself the perspectives of Youth and Age that interact not only intergenerationally, as in *Februarie*, but also intragenerationally, as in the *Maye* elders. Cullen has persuasively argued that the wintry and vernal pastoral visions are coupled Janus-like in Colin's mind, where "there is a suggestion of 'February's' contest between the old man and the youth, both of whose representative principles are exaggerated by Colin not just in 'January' but in all of his appearances in the *Calender*" (p. 124).

In the stanza in question Colin tells Hobbinol that riper age reproves his garden pleasures and moves his fancy from former follies to "stayed steps." In the *OED* entry for *staid* this phrase illustrates the following sense: "Settled in character; of grave or sedate deportment; dignified and serious in demeanor or conduct; free from flightiness or caprice." But as a participle *stayed* can also mean either "supported," as by a staff or cane, or "held back," "detained," that is, "slowed down." The sedateness of riper age may be a virtue of the crutch. This possibility opens up several lines of interpretation that lend Colin's tone an unexpected richness: First, Ryper Age revaluates "such pleasures" as "former follies" because although it still finds them attractive it is no longer capable of enjoying or experiencing them. They are follies not in being flighty or capricious or evil but in being short-lived—"former"—and painful to lose. That is, "they" are follies only in that *we* were foolish enough to give ourselves to pleasures that could not last. Second, Ryper Age reproves Youth for sowing "carelesse yeeres" whose only yield was a harvest of "stayed steps." The delights were transitory because they wore down and wearied the body, which, like time and garments, "in passing weares." Third, since "time in passing weares," Ryper Age has had its fill of the pleasures it once enjoyed, finds them wearisome, and turns sedately to "newe delightes."

The first two versions mix their reproof with an acknowledgment of loss, nostalgic in the first case and bitter in the second. In this context the reference to new delights seems less comfortable, more like a rationalization, than in that of the third, where the Rabbi ben Ezra outlook prevails. But that outlook is confirmed in lines whose bland complacency is slightly ruffled in two places.[8] First, the qualification in the garment simile is strange enough to demand attention: if "above" refers to the exposed surface, does that mean that on the inside they "wexen old" more slowly, stay "young" longer? And is this idea transferable to "time in passing," or to whatever that evasive phrase signifies? Does it imply that the mind remains young while the body ages? Second, the final line contains three ambiguous terms: "And *draweth newe* delightes with hoary *heares*." If *heares* means "hearing" as well as "hairs," then this construction is possible: Time attracts new delights with its hoary hearing; the ears of Ryper Age selectively pick out the pleasures that suit them, those they can tolerate with least pain. These pleasures, it should be noted, may well include the prerogative of impugning former pleasures, denouncing youth for its folly, and advocating the wisdom and virtue of "stayed steps," or of what Yeats called "slippered contemplation."

But *draweth* may mean "portrays" as well as "attracts," and *newe* may mean "young" or "unripe" as well as "novel" or "different." As it grows older, does the Wandering Mind portray to itself—imagine—delights that *conform* to newly acquired "hoary heares" or delights that *compensate* for them? Does it portray hoary-headed new delights in the mode of *puer senex*, delights of a second childhood, or of an aged child—rebirth and rejuvenescence either in the next world or in the next generation? The answers Thenot gives in *Februarie*, E. K. in the *March* gloss, and Palinode in *Maye* are similar, and they compose into a message that the rapidly aging Colin shows he has mastered in *June, November,* and *December.* Superimposed on this pessimistic golden-age view is a more benign view that occasionally leans, as in *June,* toward the consolations of

[8] The lines in question, 33–48, are quoted on pp. 345–36 above.

Rabbi ben Ezra. But what is the relation between the one view ("the best is yet to be") and the other ("the worst is yet to be")?

What I have tried to show in my reading of *Februarie* and *June* is that the bromides of Ryper Age may be useful and attractive but are not very credible to the speakers with "hoary heares." They may be used, as Patrick Cullen has rightly argued, to justify age's condition and to legitimize its authority, but at bottom Spenser's elders cannot ignore their "hoor heed" or the nail that "striketh" in the will; hence they are never fully persuaded by Rabbi ben Ezra's consoling sermon. Spenser uses the figure and career of Colin to show why this is so. The paradise principle expressed in such phrases as "Tho deemed I, my spring would ever laste" engenders bitterness not only at dramatic losses but also at the natural course of life itself—engenders the inability to accept aging, engenders hatred of one's aging body and the desire to recover old delights in some new form. But the presence of the *Februarie* and *Maye* elders in the eclogues, and of E. K. in the glosses, extends the significance of this process beyond Colin Clout. *Through* Colin Spenser models the genesis and structure of traditional contradictions and shows how they influence the new poet. But Colin is a translucent figure. The *Calender* displays in the body of sources it constitutes as its tradition the same division it dramatizes in Colin's mind.

Poets and Stoic Censors

E. K. and the Conflict of Generations in the Calender

LIKE OVID'S MERCURY, the *Calender* poet is a trickster whose art lulls asleep those auditors who fail to heed the subtextual warnings about the limits of its pastoral enterprise. And like Mercury telling of Pan, he sings of his own art and gives us a myth of its origins. The *Calender* is a reading of the collective sources, the tradition, that fathered it, and it thus provides a model of readership, or perhaps several models, for us to consider in our own readings. It is both hermetic and mercurial in its designs on us. Shifting rapidly and thievishly from one mode to another, it sings old songs we have heard before and speaks old wisdom we have heard before, yet at the same time it teases us with at least a semblance of meanings hidden or half-withheld. My personal *Calender* offers me the model of a genially parricidal young reader of a body of poetry it makes me question by so clearly labeling that body "old." It resists the blandishments of Pan as well as the sweet and bitter bromides of pastoral. Yet it does not discard them. Its temper is finally no more Mantuanesque than it is Arcadian. It reads them with pleasure, recites them out loud, mimes them, mimics them, but always with new inflections and in its own tones of voice. Above all, it resists the co-optation of paternity. Lovingly but firmly it stands up to the tradition and promises to preserve it, but only by weaning it from its anthological enwombment in the paradise principle.

Beyond its countless literary echoes, references, and allusions stands the profile of what I have just called *the* tradition. And this is clearly a reductive profile. It is as if, to borrow Harold Bloom's terms, Spenser cleared a space for himself by a combination of "revisionary ratios" that perform a brilliant misreading of the precursor traditions, re-creating and unifying them in the antithetical image of the paradise principle. In this concluding chapter I shall try to describe some of the central features of this misreading. I begin with a question: Why do the *Calender*'s elders present the Vacant Head with a paradisal version of experience they at the same time condemn, with honey they know will turn to gall? For as Patrick Cullen has so cogently shown, the tradition the *Calender* dramatically constitutes is divided against itself into sweet and bitter, Arcadian and Mantuanesque, recreative and plaintive factions.[1] But this is to be expected. For even the venerable elders were once young, and the monuments of unaging intellect they handed on included the poetry of youth and "matter of love" as well as the wisdom of age "mixed with some Satyrical bitternesse," along with eclogues urging "reverence dewe to old age" and "contempt of Poetrie and pleasaunt wits" (E. K., "Generall Argument," 33–39).

This polarized tradition brings together two sets of predecessors, one socio-political and the other literary:

Spenser articulates a tense relationship to literary and social patriarchy shared by many in his literary generation: poetic progenitors have shaped a literary tradition within which the new poet must find a place by creative imitation; the elder Tudor generation has shaped and still controls the social institutions and cultural values within which the young, educated gentleman or would-be gentleman must live and write and try to advance himself.

Colin's pattern of prodigality and misfortune has its origin precisely in his successful embrace of the Renaissance poet's pastoral role; the literary shepherd's otiose environment of eroticism and poetry is being viewed through the stern spectacles of Tudor patriarchal morality. . . . The Vergilian progression puts pastoral at the beginning of the poet's career. . . . Pastoral is persistently associated with new poets and with poets who are young.[2]

Petrarch's description of himself in his *Epistle to Posterity*, as led astray by youth but corrected by maturity, established a paradigm that would be repeated again and again, for it continued to serve the purpose for which it

[1] *Spenser, Marvell, and Renaissance Pastoral* (Cambridge: Harvard University Press, 1970), passim.

[2] Louis Montrose, "'The perfecte paterne of a Poete': The Poetics of Courtship in *The Shepheardes Calender*," *Texas Studies in Language and Literature* 21 (1979): 36–37.

was designed. It marked out a space within which the poet and his poetry might enjoy a certain autonomy—though an autonomy based on rebellion and even . . . idolatry.[3]

The presence of these two factions in the *Calender* complicates the notion of *puer senex:* the young poet is *senex* in being imprinted with the culture of the literary elders he imitates, but at the same time the elderly culture preserves and transmits its experience of its own youth. It offers the new poet the opposing values and different phases of the life cycle. Yet the signals these factions give are only superficially contradictory and are, as I have argued, united by their common subordination to the paradise principle. We may call these two factions the Poets and the Stoic Censors. The Poets are the tradition's party of Youth, sweet pastoral, and Arcadia; the Censors are its Mantuanesque party of Age and bitter pastoral. The Censor is censorious *because* his youth was dominated by the idyllicism of the Poets and was spent in paradisal Vacancy of Head. The Poets dominate youth *because* the Wandering Mind of the Censor still affects the paradise it has lost and reinstates its own youthful fantasy in the minds of its successors. Because the Censor is a closet Poet, the Poet is a budding Censor. The Poet is the larva, the Censor the *imago,* and they continually reproduce each other under the influence of their common parent, the paradise principle.

Spenser's originality is to have reproduced the parent within the child, to have made the *Calender* an ironic portrait of the tradition it claims for itself. The characteristics of the divided tradition are present not only in the speakers paired by debate in the so-called moral eclogues, not only in the senescent youth of Colin Clout, not only in the heavy floral scent of literary allusion and imitation, but also—perhaps unexpectedly because so obviously—in the chief contributor to that flowery ambience, E. K. himself. For E. K. is both Poet and Censor. Whether or not one accepts the interesting hypothesis, recently revived by T. L. Steinberg and Bruce R. Smith, that Spenser created E. K. as a pompous and bumbling persona who (in Steinberg's version at least) models the sins of the Pléiade, he undoubtedly provides a coherent epitome of the traditional attitudes toward love that the *Calender* cautiously criticizes.[4] E. K. is the

---

[3] Richard Helgerson, "The New Poet Presents Himself: Spenser and the Idea of a Literary Career," *PMLA* 93 (1978): 895.

[4] Theodore L. Steinberg, "E. K.'s *Shepheardes Calender* and Spenser's," *Modern Language Studies* 3 (1973): 46–58; Bruce R. Smith, "On Reading *The Shepheardes Calender,*" in *Spenser Studies*, ed. Patrick Cullen and Thomas P. Roche, Jr. (Pittsburgh: University of Pittsburgh Press, 1980), 1:87–89.

Calender's voice and wisdom of the elders come to life, and he embodies their dilemma in his commentary.

On the one hand, he is an avid if pedantic follower of the poets, and the expression "the poets feign" is always on his lips. On the other hand, he is a good Bible-reading Protestant, a confirmed antipapist and critic of idolatrous superstitions, and a proponent, in *March*, of the anti-erotic view. "The poets feign" occasionally seems to serve an apologetic function—the poets only feign; they affirm nothing and therefore never lie—enabling him to pursue scholarly delights that might be suspect to the Stoic Censor within him. At the end of his *Februarie* gloss he remarks that old men incline more than youth "to such fond fooleries" as the "Idolatrous regard of false Gods." He also has a hard time swallowing Hobbinol's fairies and elves in *June:* "the truth is, that there are no such things, . . . but onely by a sort of bald Friers and knavish shavelings so feigned." He explains that the poets feign the home of the Muses to be "on Parnassus, a hill in Grece, for that in that countrye specially florished the honor of all excellent studies" (*Apr.* 209–10); shortly thereafter he pleasures himself with an animated account of the Pan-Syrinx myth that fills more than five lines, only to conclude that the poet did not simply mean "those Poetical Gods" but also Henry VIII and to remind us further that Pan sometimes means Christ.

When E. K. pulls Christian rank on the learned pagans he nevertheless cites their reasons with respect and sometimes with feeling, as in explaining why they, lacking knowledge of the incarnation, make March the year's first month: "For then the sonne reneweth his finished course, and the seasonable spring refresheth the earth, and the plesaunce thereof being buried in the sadnesse of the dead winter now worne away, reliveth" ("Generall Argument," 48–52). The same ambivalence appears in the argument that prefaces *March*. E. K. there introduces one of the eclogue's main characters, "Cupide the Poets God of Love," and glosses "Cupides arrowe" as "the dart of some beautifull regard." This comment is amplified in the *March* gloss:

> For so he is described of the Poetes, to be a boye .s. always freshe and lustie: blindfolded, because he maketh no difference of Personages: wyth divers coloured winges, .s. ful of flying fancies: with bowe and arrow, that is with glaunce of beautye, which prycketh as a forked arrowe. He is sayd also to have shafts, some leaden, some golden: that is, both pleasure for the gracious and loved, and sorow for the lover that is disdayned or forsaken. (162–68)

E. K. clearly enjoys working the image over, but as he unpacks it his emphasis shifts slightly from the undeniable charm of the *putto*, who is not very threatening, to the less pleasurable features of love that the image displaces and chastens. At the end of the *March* gloss, as if sensible of having dallied too long over his erotic *scholia*, he amplifies the cautionary emblems in a burst of anti-erotic sentiment:

> Hereby is meant, that all the delights of Love, wherein wanton youth walloweth, be but follye mixt with bitternesse, and sorow sawced with repentaunce. For besides that the very affection of Love it selfe tormenteth the mynde, and vexeth the body many wayes, with unrestfulnesse all night, and wearines all day, seeking for that we can not have, and fynding that we would not have: even the selfe things which best before us lyked, in course of time and chaung of ryper yeares, whiche also therewithall chaungeth our wonted lyking and former fantasies, will then seeme lothsome and breede us annoyaunce, when yougthes flowre is withered, and we fynde our bodyes and wits aunswere not to suche vayne jollitie and lustfull pleasaunce.

In this passage E. K. gives two different reasons for bitterness, and they do not quite square with each other. The first is that the affection of love is folly because what lovers perversely call delight is nothing but mental and physical torment. But the vexation of later life has a different basis: the mind is tormented when "we fynde our bodyes and wits aunswere not to suche vayne jollitie and lustfull pleasaunce." Thus the absence of love's former pleasure, not of its former pain, causes bitterness. This clarification retrospectively adds a touch of poignancy to his earlier comment on Willye's proposal to awaken "little Love . . . / That nowe sleepeth in Lethe Lake" (*March* 23–24):

> Lethe is a lake in hell, which the Poetes call the lake of forgetfulnes. For Lethe signifieth forgetfulnes. Wherein the soules being dipped, did forget the cares of their former lyfe. So that by love sleeping in Lethe lake, he meaneth he was almost forgotten and out of knowledge, by reason of winters hardnesse, when al pleasures, as it were, sleepe and weare oute of mynde.

It would be easier for the Stoic Censor if the "winter hardnesse" of later life were a Lethe, if the love cares of his former life could be forgotten, and especially if "our wonted lyking and former fantasies" could be laid to rest "and weare oute of mind."

Montrose argues that E. K.'s epistle offers a way "to read the relation between Immerito and Colin in terms of the moral eclogues' dichotomies: the sage, serious, and mature moral poet confronts and condemns the image of his own unstayed youth, turning the unfortunate folly of his past to the public good and redeeming poetry from wantonness" (p. 37). But the stern morality of the Tudor fathers is imitated or glanced at in statements by E. K., as well as in other corners of the *Calender,* not only to anticipate and disarm it but also to expose its roots in motives that are not reducible to a concern for virtue and public morality. The Panic cycle contributes to E. K.'s moral stance. The kind of love Pan's venery slanderously images is justified only as a self-transcending prelude to the more socially acceptable Art and Learning it produces, but even in this form its allure remains to threaten E. K.'s composure. E. K.'s Wandering Mind remains divided between the pleasures of the Vacant Head and the patriarchal impulse to put childish things away.

The limits of the *Calender* world are defined in terms of this conflict, and the conflict is dramatized at both the intra- and intergenerational levels. I conclude my study with a brief glance at passages from Books III and IV of *The Faerie Queene* that encapsulate this dialectic, articulating its basic structure and revealing its abiding interest for Spenser. In Book III there is a nursery that testifies to the same escapist pressure as the poets' nursery of pastoral—testifies to the same fear of mortality, the same bitterness over the human condition, the same desire for eternal return:

> It sited was in fruitfull soyle of old,
>   And girt in with two walles on either side;
>   The one of yron, the other of bright gold,
>   That none might thorough breake, nor over-stride:
>   And double gates it had, which opened wide,
>   By which both in and out men moten pas;
>   Th'one faire and fresh, the other old and dride:
>   Old *Genius* the porter of them was,
> Old *Genius,* the which a double nature has.
>
> He letteth in, he letteth out to wend,
>   All that to come into the world desire;
>   A thousand thousand naked babes attend
>   About him day and night, which doe require,
>   That he with fleshly weedes would them attire:
>   Such as him list, such as eternall fate
>   Ordained hath, he clothes with sinfull mire,
>   And sendeth forth to live in mortall state,
> Till they againe returne backe by the hinder gate.
>
> After that they againe returned beene,
>   They in that Gardin planted be againe;
>   And grow afresh, as they had never seene
>   Fleshly corruption, nor mortall paine.
>   Some thousand yeares so doen they there remaine;

> And then of him are clad with other hew,
> Or sent into the chaungefull world againe,
> Till thither they returne, where first they grew:
> So like a wheele around they runne from old to new.
>
> *(vi.31–33)*

Old Genius, the Janus guarding the gates of Venus's Garden of Adonis, is endowed with his etymologically denoted function, birth-giver. An elder presiding over the birth and rebirth of the young, his double nature is thus complementary to that of *puer senex*. But he is double-natured because a birth-giver is also a death-giver, and the sad antithesis of stanza 31—"faire and fresh" versus "old and dride"—prejudices the viewpoint of the describer and presumably also that of Old Genius, bound by his epithet more closely to the "old and dride" than to the "faire and fresh." The phrase "All that to come into the world desire" seems at first positive and expansive but is framed in rhetoric that stabs with increasing force at the folly of this desire: from "fleshly weedes" to "sinfull mire" to "fleshly corruption," and from "mortall state" to "mortall paine." The naked babes who long for mortality do so only because their heads are vacant—because the promise of new life is coupled with the eradication of old knowledge. Replanted, "they had never seene / Fleshly corruption." As in Plato's myth of Er and Virgil's revision of it in the sixth book of the *Aeneid*, old souls become new, parents become children, only by passing through the Lethe that alone (the elders feel) will protect the young from the truth and delude them into carrying on the burden of mortal life.

In Book IV Spenser personifies the censorious have-not as Slander, who rails "Gainst all, that truth or vertue doe professe" to relieve her own bitterness and privation (viii.23–28, 35–36). Her abuse of Arthur, Amoret, and Aemylia for spending the night under the same roof is juxtaposed to the following comment:

> Here well I weene, when as these rimes be red
> With misregard, that some rash witted wight,
> Whose looser thought will lightly be misled,
> These gentle Ladies will misdeeme too light,
> For thus conversing with this noble Knight . . .
>
> *(viii.29)*

"Looser thought" is here associated with the Censor's response as well as with Slander's "grudgefull discontent" (viii.28). In the next line the poem does a turnabout as the narrator justifies that "misregard" by telling the golden-age story from the Censor's standpoint:

> Sith now of dayes such temperance is rare
> And hard to finde, that heat of youthfull spright
> For ought will from his greedie pleasure spare,
> More hard for hungry steed t'abstaine from pleasant lare.

> But antique age yet in the infancie
>   Of time, did live then like an innocent,
>   In simple truth and blameless chastitie,
>   Ne then of guile had made experiment,
>   But voide of vile and treacherous intent,
>   Held vertue for it selfe in soveraine awe:
>   Then loyall love had royall regiment,
>   And each unto his lust did make a lawe,
> From all forbidden things his liking to withdraw.

> The Lyon there did with the Lambe consort,
>   And eke the Dove sate by the Faulcons side,

> . . . .

> But when the world woxe old, it woxe warre old
> (Whereof it hight) and having shortly tride
> The traines of wit, in wickednesse woxe bold,
> And dared of all sinnes the secrets to unfold.

(viii.29–31)

This view of "antique age" conspicuously and selectively ignores two features of the narrative that convey the image of antiquity: the presence of patently wicked figures—Ate, Lust, Slander, Paridell, et al.—and the more subtly redistributed complicities produced by the rhetorical and allegorical techniques with which Spenser tells the stories of the "good" characters. The first group can be accounted for in fairy-tale terms, for if there are to be heroes in the peaceable kingdom there must also be monsters and villains. But the second group contradicts the narrator's vision of the paradise of virtue. The narrator offers the reader an example of a reading based on "misregard," a reading that dramatizes the dialectic of the paradise principle. How, from what source, and when does one learn about "the infancie / Of time" and the peaceable kingdom of yore? In one's own infancy. These are the old tales the elders tell us and their elders told them, the moral tales for a winter's night, tales gleaned from the tearful Muses about a storied world that never was. Infant time is story time. Spenser shows us that it was not necessarily that way in story time; in his reading of romance he reintroduces the ethical and psychological complexities of actual relations into the storied world. But against his revision, his interpretation, he places another, the idyllic interpretation, and by means of this contrast outlines the latter's selectivity. The elders tell us what they want us to hear and believe: cautionary tales to prepare us for a wicked world, *exempla* of virtue to emulate, visions of a better time before corruption set in, finally—as a spur to reverence and obedience—praises for the one remaining source of virtue, "Princes Court" (viii.33).

The elders in Spenserian gerontology also tell us what *they* want to hear and believe. Their view of contemporary life is darkened by the impossible idyllicism of the lost paradise that the Wandering Mind longs to recover, is slandered by the "grudgefull discontent" occasioned by the loss. The specious determinism of the golden-age thesis is produced by mapping onto history the model of physical aging—from the "infancie of time" to the "warre old" world. The elders make themselves microcosms and establish a perverse harmony between the patterns of organic life and history. The tales they tell the young reflect both their bitterness and their desire for some fairy-tale magic, some equivalent of Nepenthe, since no weaker antidote could pacify their desire for the bliss time or affairs of state have compelled them to renounce. So in Book IV when Priamond and Cambell "wearie both of fighting had their fill, / That life it selfe seemd loathsome" (iii.36), Cambina rides in and pacifies them *ex machina* with a wand in one hand

> Like to the rod which *Maias* sonne doth wield,
> Wherewith the hellish fiends he doth confound.
> And in her other hand a cup she hild,
> The which was with Nepenthe to the brim upfild.
>
> Nepenthe is a drinck of soverayne grace,
> Devised by the Gods, for to asswage
> Harts grief, and bitter gall away to chace,
> Which stirs up anguish and contentious rage:
> In stead thereof sweet peace and quiet age
> It doth establish in the troubled mynd.
> Few men, but such as sober are and sage,
> Are by the Gods to drinck thereof assynd;
> But such as drinck, eternall happinesse do fynd.
>
> Such famous men, such worthies of the earth,
> As *Jove* will have advaunced to the skie,
> And there made gods, though borne of mortall berth,

> For their high merits and great dignitie,
> Are wont, before they may to heaven flie,
> To drincke hereof, whereby all cares forepast
> Are washt away quite from their memorie.
> So did those old Heroes hereof taste,
> Before that they in blisse amongst the Gods were plaste.
>
> *(iii.42 – 44)*

The happy ending of the episode, with its return to perfect love and friendship, to paradisal Vacancy of Head (iii.49 – 52), exactly parallels the conspicuously unreal conclusion of *An Hymne in Honour of Love,* which turns violently around from the self-induced hell of unassured love to the paradise

> Of all delight, and joyous happie rest,
> Where they doe feede on Nectar heavenly wize,
> With *Hercules* and *Hebe,* and the rest
> Of *Venus* dearlings, through her bountie blest,
> And lie like Gods in yvorie beds arayd,
> With rose and lillies over them displayd.
>
> There with thy daughter *Pleasure* they doe play
> Their hurtlesse sports, without rebuke or blame,
> And in her snowy bosome boldly lay
> Their quiet heads, devoyd of guilty shame,
> After full joyance of their gentle game,
> Then her they crowne their Goddesse and their Queene,
> And decke with floures thy altars well beseene.
>
> *(281 – 93)*

The paradisal fantasy is naturally most intense when the mental disease it answers to is most extreme, and the imagery suggests that the fantasy does not easily distinguish eternal bliss from eternal rest. Those striking phrases "quiet heads" and "quiet age" are associated not merely with pacified desire but with the need for self-esteem and easy conscience. The Nepenthe passage asks for a disenchanted reading: apotheosis is presented as an illusion produced by the psychedelic agency of the drug. And the comparison of Cambina's rod to Mercury's may remind us of the Mercury-Argus-syrinx myth. Cambina's drug replaces Mercury's panpipe.

The inherited culture of the Vacant Head is the product of an attempt to flee from the lessons of experience by forgetting them; the forgetfulness is built into the legacy bequeathed by the elders to their children.

The green world is the lost "place"—the past—which the older generation can recover only by playing themselves anew in the minds of their
children. So Lévi-Strauss observes, in *Tristes tropiques,* that "it is not
only to deceive our children that we keep up their belief in Father
Christmas: their enthusiasm warms us, helps us to delude ourselves and
to believe, since they believe it, that a world of one-way generosity is not
absolutely incompatible with reality"[5]—that is, a world in which parents give without demanding returns and in which nature gives life
without taking it away. But the contradictions that perpetuate this dialectic convert the delusion to its antithesis; the proffered exemption from
reciprocity and death generates the false consciousness of childhood, and
the subsequent disenchantment of the naked babes only reproduces in
their generation the bitterness from which the elders tried vainly to escape: "So like a wheele around they runne from new to old." And the
elders, growing old and dried, eternally demand returns. Having constituted the "pierlesse pleasures" of soft pastoral as the norms of childhood, having trained their children to live out the parental fantasies of
youth, they exact the expected price for this gift. The young are made
their scapegoats for obediently enacting those fantasies. Thus the elders
can validate and vicariously enjoy lost illusions, but at the same time they
can validate their own judicious transcendence of the illusions. Yet their
wintry spite increases as they watch "the young / In one another's arms,"
and their one consolation is that they can blame youth's folly on their
children rather than on themselves.

[5] Trans. John Weightman and Doreen Weightman (New York: Athenaeum, 1974),
245.

AFTERWORD

I

The essays in this volume were written over a period of thirty years—
from 1958 to 1987. All except one of the studies on *The Faerie Queene*
were published during the 1960s. Of the chapters on *The Shepheardes
Calender* all except one were written since 1979. Much of part II had not
yet been published, and the published portions were in many instances
revised or repositioned during 1986 and 1987 when I tried to pull the
various pieces together into something resembling a monograph on the
Calender. I tuned out of Spenser from the late 1960s to the late 1970s
because what was going on "at that point in time"—as they used to say in
Washington at that point in time—persuaded me that the kind of New-
Critical close reading and the kind of cultural "history" I was then doing
were out of touch. I had always been interested in exploring complex
representations of ethico-psychological patterns, but I considered them
apart from the institutional structures and discourses that give them
historical specificity. So I started over and spent several years trying to
learn how to make my practice more responsive to the interplay between
texts and institutions, agents and structures, literary conventions (e.g.,
genres) and social reifications (e.g., gender). I went far afield for a while,
giving myself basic lessons in anthropology, political and social theory,
and the history of institutions and pursuing two interests I had had since
the late 1950s, one in art history and the other in the general theory of
culture change. The idea behind these projects was not to leave close
reading behind, since that was what I best liked doing and in the final
analysis the only thing I felt I knew how to do. Rather the idea was to de-
aestheticize New-Critical practice, to change its terms of reference so
that the representations of what Foucault has called "the micro-physics of

power" could be made more discernible in texts submitted to the micro-physics of interpretation. During this time I cut my micro-physical teeth on studies in several media—Shakespeare, Plato, Vermeer, and Rembrandt—and continued the work on pastoral begun in the 1960s.

Several of the developments that marked literary studies in the next decade and a half played a major role in my reeducation. They have in common a particular transgressive dynamic: all of them facilitate the breaching of those boundaries that New Criticism drew around interpretation and its "object" to distinguish the specifically literary or aesthetic transaction from others. Not surprisingly this transgressive approach picks out its mirror image, an analogous dynamic, in the picture it constructs of the transactions between art and society in early modern Europe. So, for example, in his powerful essay on the social production of English pastoral discourse, Louis Montrose attacks the tendency of academic criticism of the last generation to canonize literary texts "as compelling embodiments of timeless truths" and "exemplary instances of a distinctively aesthetic mode of experience," thereby suppressing "the specific social and historical conditions within which writing is produced and consumed."[1] He then goes on to argue that although Puttenham, in *The Arte of English Poesie*, stresses poetry's "ludic essence" and is preoccupied "with the complexity of poetry's formal features and the pleasures of its aesthetic effects," *The Arte* "at every turn . . . contaminates the purity of its own aestheticism" and "undoes itself" by disclosing "the basis of poetic disinterestedness in social self-interest" (p. 450). In this move the questioning of the autonomous status of "the work" in Renaissance literary discourse (even the use of *literary* begs the question) goes hand in hand with the questioning of Kantian or New-Critical postulates of autonomy privileged by academic humanists in our time. My only objection—not so much an objection as a qualification—is that Puttenham could not have "effaced the putative distinction between courtship and poetry, courtiers and poets, life and art" (p. 451), had it not preexisted its effacement. As Puttenham's transgression presupposes the practice and conceptualizing of fiction that marks the discourse of what I have called the second world, so Montrose's transgressive move presupposes its New-Critical precursor, indeed gives it new and revised life as his partner in sublation.

In developments of this sort I found a much fuller and more sophisticated elaboration of the notion of second-world discourse than I was ca-

---

[1] "Of Gentlemen and Shepherds: The Politics of Elizabethan Pastoral Form," *ELH* 50 (1983): 448.

pable of in the 1960s. In those years I came to an impasse because I was unable to connect my formulation of the second world with two other projects that seemed intimately bound up with it in ways I didn't then understand: studies of the kind of work done by the reflexive features of texts and efforts to explore the relations between those features and the "cultural ecology" of the first world. I had to wait for others to show me a path, and what initially made it possible for me to go on were the contributions of Roy Strong, Stephen Orgel, Stephen Greenblatt, Jonas Barish, Jonathan Goldberg, and Montrose to a revisionary view of the interactions between the politics of theater and the theatricality of politics. Their studies of the theatricalization of culture during the Renaissance opened the door to an interpretive practice that could more sensitively register not only the textual indices or symptoms of transgression but also their textual representation within fiction—register not only what Frank Lentricchia, paraphrasing Kenneth Burke, has recently referred to as "the political work of the aesthetic" but also its representation *within* the aesthetic.[2]

The effect of these studies was sharpened by a second set of influences, a cluster of interrelated and often conflicting lines of inquiry into the structural characteristics of and differences between speech and writing: the burgeoning field of comparative media study (McLuhan, Ong, Eisenstein, et al.), the hermeneutic approach to discourse and the textual dialectic (Benveniste and Ricoeur), the political implications of speech-act theory, and the critique of many of these approaches included in Derrida's analyses of the logocentric view of writing. I have been trying not so much to assimilate these lines of inquiry as to make them converge in a dialectical appropriation that would allow me to look *at* rather than *through* theatrical and literary media, to take account of the message of the medium or, as Hayden White puts it, the content of its form. It is no longer possible to ignore the categorical differences between *genre* and *medium* in dealing with literary and theatrical texts. The older classification that treated tragedy and comedy along with epic, lyric, pastoral, romance, and the novel as members of the same system, genre, obscured

---

[2] *Criticism and Social Change* (Chicago: University of Chicago Press, 1983), 156: "Burke would have us read the myth of Perseus as a tale of the political work of the aesthetic. It is a tale that tells us . . . that literature makes something happen, that the literary is always the taking of position and simultaneously the exercising of position with and upon the social field." If, like Perseus's mirror, representation "represents with a difference," it may also represent itself representing with a difference. If representation is "an act of power" that "makes something happen," it may represent this capability, and it does so even when, as in the moral eclogues of *The Shepheardes Calender*, it dramatizes its political incompetence.

the radical differences among diverse media of representation. The same can be said for the difference between rhetoric, with its connection to public speech, and poetics, with its connection to writing.

Recent criticism has been more responsive to the historically significant differences between or among conditions of mediation and to the awareness of those differences inscribed in early modern texts. For me the most important contributions in this area have come from studies by Margaret Ferguson, Victoria Kahn, and Maureen Quilligan. To all the critics mentioned so far I feel grateful because they opened a door that was once shut and that blocked the access I sought between second- and first-world discourse, or between the "aesthetic" and the "historical" or "political" approaches to texts. They gave me a better grasp of the transgressive power peculiar to each medium, literary and theatrical, a power actualized and enhanced as literature and theatrical drama attained more fully to the status of *instituted* processes (that is, public and culturally recognized discourses), the former through the agency of printing and the latter through the establishment of professional companies in playhouses.

A third set of influences emerged from the wave of new interest and studies in the politics of gender, generational conflict, and the family. No one working on Spenser's minor poems and *Faerie Queene* III and IV could avoid the themes of sexual politics, but until the late 1960s there was little public discourse or theorizing about that topic. My efforts in that area were as crude as those of other Spenserians. The new wave made things that were previously invisible to me magically materialize in the space between text and interpretation: well-formed patterns of motivation that transcend the individual speakers (or writers) who give them utterance and that inscribe those speakers at the poles of more or less structured sets of differential relations—for example, relations between woman and man, parent and child, senior and junior, outsider and insider, superior and inferior.

When I returned to Spenser in the late 1970s, I was better able to understand the complex intersection of gender conflict with generational conflict that constitutes the politics of the family romance in societies whose institutional orders were patriarchally organized and whose cultural orders were dominated by the male imagination. But I didn't see how to extend this understanding to pastoral until I encountered Montrose's essays and Richard Helgerson's *PMLA* essay on Spenser, subsequently included in his outstanding study of the Renaissance literary system, *Self-Crowned Laureates*. This book appeared in time for me to consult it during the last phase of rewriting, and anyone familiar with it will see its influence in my *Calender* chapters. It deserves special mention here because Helgerson opened up another line of transgressive interpretation by mapping generational conflict onto the thematics of genre, the politics of poetic self-representation, and the shaping of the poetic career.

Critics should feel grateful for the interpretive gifts they receive from—and the generosity they thereby create in—their precursors, but we all know that the convergence of two logics, that of the gift and that of belatedness, can press between what we ought to say and what we feel. A deeper gratitude, yet one more soothing, easier to acknowledge, is generated by or toward those critics whose benefactions spur the appropriator (as I have been called) to struggle with them in search of interpretive differences that enable him to clear a little space and go on. These two gratitudes, one simple and painful, the other complex and bracing, color my responses to Montrose's essays, to *Self-Crowned Laureates* and Helgerson's earlier *The Elizabethan Prodigals*, to the two studies by Greenblatt that helped Helgerson formulate and develop his thesis (*Sir Walter Ralegh* and *Renaissance Self-Fashioning*), and to much of the work that goes by the name of new historicism. My recent encounters with this criticism have strengthened an earlier suspicion that between my interests and those of its practitioners lies a difference in the direction of transgressive reading: while some have focused on the art of self-fashioning by which writers and others transformed literary conventions into behavioral and career patterns, my focus has been on the way certain motivational structures underlying those patterns are represented and analyzed within poetic fictions; while some have explored the way literary and theatrical performances functioned not only as reflectors and symptoms but also as acts within the political discourse of the first world, I have explored the (often critical) representations of those intended first-world functions within the textual confines of the second world. So, for example, in my account of the *Calender*'s moral eclogues I have tried to show how Spenser's metapastoral devices foreground the failure of rustic pastoral to participate meaningfully in the moral and political discourses it aspires to convey.

In sum, I have found it necessary to resist a variety of transgressive approaches to which I was—and remain—powerfully attracted and from which I am still learning. The flags of "cultural poetics" (Greenblatt's phrase), "new historicism," and "cultural materialism" fly over wide variations in practice that make common cause in an overlapping set of critiques—of formalism, aestheticism, essentialism, naive or mimetic historicism, idealist intellectual history, exclusivist canon formation, and the cultural hegemony of interpretive elites. Central to the common project has been the effort to counter the aestheticizing force of New Criticism and formalist criticism by moving from the second world to the first. My project, at once parallel and opposite, has been to counter that force by appropriating the methodological and substantive insights of new historicists and others and bringing them back alive from the first world to the second. I have always endorsed the challenges directed at New Criticism—or at the profession's inertial, unthinking commitment to it—in the name of methodologies that were politically and historically more responsible and theoretically more self-aware. But I couldn't imagine how to accomplish the critical objective behind the challenges without continuously testing the effects of new ideas on interpretive practice to determine the difference they made both to particular readings and to the activity that produces them. I wanted to see whether new orientations defining and integrating themselves into a kind of movement by taking a stand against New Criticism could help me improve and reconstruct a practice I still thought of as a version of New Criticism. Though I consider the new-historicist project complementary to mine, and though as a self-proclaimed parasite I would gladly play host if that could lead to symbiosis, the strains between the two projects may be difficult to overcome. Of the differences in practice the one that most concerns me is variability in the attitude toward and reliance on close reading, and the next section of this afterword will address that issue.

II

Close reading, formalism, and New Criticism are sometimes indiscriminately lumped together and consigned to the classroom or the back burner of literary discourse in the interest of more socially responsible, politically sensitive, and theoretically reflexive inquiry. Even a temperate judgment such as the following from Jean E. Howard's admirable critical survey of new historicism betrays the touch of impatience with reading that characterizes current trends in literary theory and practice:

> Readings remain, after all, the dominant form of scholarly production in the discipline. . . . There is nothing inherently wrong with doing readings, but if those readings are based on untenable or unexamined assumptions about literature and history, then they are merely a form of nostalgia and not a serious attempt to explore what it means to attempt an historical criticism in a postmodern era.[3]

[3] "The New Historicism in Renaissance Studies," *Elizabethan Literary Renaissance* 16 (1986): 19.

I'm happy to pledge allegiance along with everyone else to the cause of the examined assumption, but I question Howard's statement. Can good or interesting or responsible readings be based on tenable but unexamined assumptions, or does *unexamined* equal *untenable?* It isn't clear to me that such readings always presuppose acts of self-examination. Why can't they rely more or less unthinkingly on prevailing assumptions about literature and history, assumptions unquestioningly picked up from others, and assumptions that might well be based on what Howard would consider sound principles? Conversely, is it absolutely certain that good readings cannot be based on unsound interpretive principles or that critical self-reflection cannot yield diverse if not contradictory criteria of soundness within the framework of a "postmodern" practice? And further, is there any guarantee that critics who have examined their assumptions produce more interesting or responsible readings than those who do not? No one makes a show of examining assumptions—their own and everyone else's—more vigorously than neo-Marxists and self-styled cultural materialists writing about Shakespeare, but the interpretive practice that emerges from their critical self-reflection seems to me to produce thin results. I see no necessary connection either between tenable and examined assumptions or between the quality of the reading and the degree of self-reflection preceding it. Is any reading—whatever its quality—that is not explicitly accompanied by a critical credo "merely a form of nostalgia"? Again one finds frequent instances in current practice of the interpretation of snippets cut from texts to make a methodological or theoretical point. Snippetotomy was a standard and justifiably criticized operating procedure of the old historicism. One also finds "postmodernist" critics relying on others' interpretations to make their point, and sometimes—in using literature they are not familiar with (usually older literature) to illustrate the point—borrowing interpretations generated from principles they themselves would not sanction.

These reflections lead me to take issue with Howard's vaguely patronizing phrase, "There is nothing inherently wrong with doing readings," because I think there is something inherently wrong with not doing readings, one's own readings, especially since in the new dispensation the high-intensity reading formerly reserved for Literature and Art has spread to all forms of inquiry. The textualization of cultural and institutional life means that close reading becomes a primary source of evidence across the whole field of humanistic and social study, and this poses obvious problems at both the practical and the theoretical level: the demands on interpretive scholarship become enormous and call for the development of new forms (perhaps also a new spirit) of cooperation or collaboration; the aporetic character of interpretation can't but affect and destabilize the evidentiary base so that different interpretive approaches and different readings of texts may produce different or conflicting bodies of evidence and therefore different "pictures" of what used to be, but can no longer be, taken for granted as the background for any text or interpretive act.

I think the uneasiness with reading that marks contemporary practice springs from the tendency to confuse close reading, formalism, and New Criticism. Not every close reading is formalist and not every formalism is New-Critical. I consider myself a reconstructed old New Critic; that is, I claim to practice a form of close reading that avails itself of certain features of the New-Critical interpretation I learned in the 1940s and 1950s but that discards its basic commitment to the ideology of *the work* as a self-contained fictive representation, a representation to be prized not only for its aesthetic complexity and unity but also for the superiority to "life" of the complex moral statement it makes about the experience it represents. I view New Criticism as a system the sum of whose parts is greater and more promising than the whole. I have elsewhere sketched out an analytical model of the system, depicting it as a structure composed of six interrelated postulates, each of which has been challenged, revised, or radicalized in subsequent literary practice.[4] For my purposes here, it will be enough to identify the postulates and allude to their fate:

1. The *structural* postulate of *organic unity* underwrites the integrity of *the work* as a well-wrought urn or an organism, the different parts and functions of which contribute to the welfare, complexity, and so on, of the Unified Whole. Subsequent criticism turns this into a Unified Hole, melting the work down into the text and intertextuality.

2. The *aesthetic* postulate of *self-sufficiency* underwrites the autonomous and autotelic character that makes the work the proper object of a "cognitive" "disinterested" attention, thereby protecting it against the intentional and affective orientations of the older criticism. But this move becomes vulnerable to the reconstructed forms of those orientations in theories of text production, reception theory, and reader-response theory, among others.

3. The *deictic* postulate of *the dissociation of speaker or "point of view" from the author* underwrites the interpretive pursuit of "unbound" or "surplus" meaning—unbound by the author's intention and exceeding the speaker's or narrator's.

---

[4] "Reconstructing the Old New Criticism," *Journal of Comparative Literature and Aesthetics* 9 (1986): 1–14.

4. The *rhetorical* postulate of the *complexity, irony, and ambiguity* of the work provides the touchstone for determining what works are lucky enough to be the beneficiaries of the practice of close reading.

Postulates 3 and 4 haven't been challenged so much as radicalized: the third by extension to theories of the subject and the discourse of the other, the fourth by the intensification of ambiguity or "duplicity" to undecidability and by the extension of the postulate to all discourse.

5. The *cosmological* postulate of *the work* as in some sense (the evasion is useful) *a fully meaningful world* underwrites the notion that the work embodies a coherent world view, or ethical vision, or ontology. This adds to the structural and aesthetic postulates the implication that the work as a complex self-sufficient whole is also a microcosm, and this in turn sneaks in a relation to, a "statement" about, the macrocosm.

6. The *epistemic* postulate of *the fictiveness or imaginariness of the work* constitutes the work as a second world distinct from the first and elicits "disinterested" interpretation but also presents itself as a representation, an image, of the first world and offers knowledge of it—offers a kind of playground or staging ground for the *serio ludere* rewarded by fuller insight into "the human predicament" than is possible in the hustle of the iron cage.

Postulates 5 and 6 have been subjected to several kinds of abuse, all of them largely justified and many of them deriving from the root objection that New Criticism has neutralized the fictiveness of the actual world.

Without detailing the systematic organization of these postulates, let me simply assert, first, that the system of New Criticism has arguable theoretical coherence and, second, that this coherence constricts the range of interpretive possibilities latent in the individual postulates. Some of these possibilities were more fully realized when, in what amounts to a decomposition of the inhibiting structure, the constitutive and regulative power of individual postulates was extended from "work" to "world," from literary text to "social text," from literature to criticism, from speakers to readers, and so on. Howard touches on some of the consequences of this movement when she complains of the "binarism we casually reinforce every time we speak of literature and history, text and context," for the literary text is "as much a context for other aspects of cultural and material life as they are for it. Rather than erasing the problem of textuality, one must enlarge it in order to see that *both* social and literary texts are opaque, self-divided, and porous, that is, open to the mutual intertextual influences of one another" (p. 25). Here, in spite of her complaint, Howard still finds it necessary to distinguish between social and literary texts, although their figure/ground or inside/outside relation has been relativized. I think the distinction is important and has to be sustained as long as one can show that it is recognized by the set of texts in question and not merely superimposed by the critic. In other words, however porous the boundaries and however undifferentiated the method of reading, such texts may be simultaneously circumscribed as literary and treated as sites transgressed by "other aspects of cultural and material life." If the genres and media of literary—or, more generally, fictional—discourse are themselves forms of social practice, they also represent putatively extrafictional forms of discourse and practice. And if the latter can now be read the way New Critics used to read works of literary fiction, they can also be read *within* literary works as transgressions that their texts either betray or represent. In the next, and final, section of this afterword I cross back into *The Faerie Queene*, revisiting some of my old haunts in Book III to sample some of the changes produced by my reeducation to post-New-Critical practice.

III

One reason Spenser is the poet's poet is that his poems are discourses of discourses, which is to say that they are discourses about the discourses they represent. The represented discourses include both the traditional genres—romance, pastoral, epic, lyric, elegy, satire, hymn, and georgic, along with their various combinations and their more elusive modal extensions—and such historically specific actualizations of genre as the Virgilian, the Ovidian, the Ariostan, the Petrarchan, the Arthurian, the Neoplatonic, and the Mantuanesque.[5] We owe much to the critics who have sensitized us to the presence and operation of these forms in Spenser's poetry—Frye, Alpers, Nohrnberg, Fletcher, Fowler, and Quilligan, among others. Their work has helped us realize not only that the forms are present *in* his text but also that they are represented, indeed fore-

---

[5] See Alastair Fowler, *Kinds of Literature: An Introduction to the Theory of Genres and Modes* (Cambridge: Harvard University Press, 1982). In *The Prophetic Moment: An Essay on Spenser* (Chicago: University of Chicago Press, 1971) Angus Fletcher surveys five "typological matrices" in *The Faerie Queene*, the biblical, Vergilian, Ovidian, Galfridian, and Hermetic (pp. 55–132). These are, he writes, "the five large banks or matrices of myth" the poem "draws on," and its stability comes from the "multiplication of sources" that overdetermine individual incidents (few of which "have a discursive interest of their own") and from "their continual giving way to each other unexpectedly" (p. 56). Fletcher's language makes it unclear whether he views the status of these matrices primarily as influence or allusion. For me they become significant only when they appear unequivocally as products of conspicuous allusion and are therefore represented in the poetry as dominant literary or cultural discourses. I think of them less as matrices than—to borrow Spenser's pun—as *paternes*.

grounded, *by* it; not only that they are strongly marked discursive structures and, as such, systems of values and interests but also that they receive citational status through Spenser's techniques of conspicuous allusion. Conspicuous allusion makes them the object or target of imitation rather than merely its medium: what appears at first to be an Ovidian moment in *the Faerie Queene* or a Mantuanesque moment in *The Shepheardes Calender* turns out on closer examination to be (in the currently fashionable formula) an *effect of Ovid* or an *effect of Mantuan*. Furthermore, inasmuch as Spenser's intertextual citations direct the reader to the values and interests embedded in the discourse of any genre, they transgress the boundaries of literary institutions and implicate the extraliterary "texts" of social, political, and cultural discourse: discourses of gender, generation, statecraft, law, hierarchy, religious controversy, and courtiership.[6]

Spenser's metadiscursivity is something I only dimly perceived when I was writing the essays on *The Faerie Queene* that appear in this volume. Were I to recast those efforts I would—to give one example—return to the figure of Archimago, the *Old Man*, or *vetus homo*, whose metamorphic magic and image making in Book I are ascribed in antipapist terms to the religious idolatry and self-damning despair of the unregenerate nature. His name authorizes a cultural imagination corrupted by its own impossible aspiration toward "wholeness"/"holiness," toward godlike autonomy and tyrannical power, and thus torn by deprivation, anger, and the perpetual fear of impotence. I would now take more seriously that Archimago, who hates Una "as the hissing snake" (I.ii.9), is mentioned in Book III just as Britomart gives way to Florimell, who is replaying Una's flight through the woods (III.iv.45). And I would go on to explore the intricate network of contrasts and resemblances linking him to Merlin, Proteus, and Busirane, the sequence of whose appearances registers increasing impotence and aggressiveness.[7] Archimago is

---

[6] Included among these are historical, biblical, and prophetic discourses, such as Spenser's familiar excursions in the domain of *translatio imperii*. See Frances Yates, *Astraea: The Imperial Theme in the Sixteenth Century* (London: Routledge & Kegan Paul, 1975). For Spenser's ambivalent, revisionary, and at times parodic treatment of the translation-of-empire discourse, see the abstract of Elizabeth J. Bellamy's "Pagan Prophecy and Christian Revelation: A Reassessment of Virgilian Parody in *The Faerie Queene*, I.v," along with John D. Bernard's critical response, in *Spenser at Kalamazoo, 1984*, ed. Francis G. Greco (Clarion: Clarion University of Pennsylvania, 1984), 21–29.

[7] Compare I.i.34–37, III.iii.7 and 14, and III.xii.31–36; also compare I.ii.9–10 with III.viii.41. James Nohrnberg traces the analogies between Una and Florimell, discusses the more explicit linkage of Archimago to Proteus, and suggests a connection between Archimago and Merlin in *The Analogy of "The Faerie Queene"* (Princeton: Princeton University Press, 1976), 114, 444, 570. Kenneth Gross notes the analogy between

my candidate for the fictionalized source of the discourses parodically represented in *The Faerie Queene:* his avatars haunt Book III in specifically male form and exhibit powers sometimes associated or confused with poetic discourse. They are androcentric and gerontocentric practitioners of the arts of image making—prophetic vision, the play of "double senses" (III.iv.28), shape shifting, and thaumaturgical illusion. The major activity of each is an effort to persuade or force a chaste—that is, true-loving—virgin to submit her "wayes unto his will" (III.iii.24). Proteus's will is that of Ovidian discourse and Busirane's that of a more comprehensive Ovidian-courtly-Petrarchan discourse. Merlin, who utters the quoted phrase, refers ambiguously to the will of Artegal and of "eternall providence," the heroic and patriarchal will of national epic and politico-historical myth that Angus Fletcher calls Galfridian discourse, which is articulated in Book III with the *translatio imperii* discourse (III.ix).

The apparently benign figure of Merlin is the most interesting of the three because he most fully represents the dilemma of the discursive tensions energizing the third book. His ambivalence is hinted at not only in the associations that connect him with Archimago, Proteus, and Busirane but also in the strange contradictions that crisscross Spenser's portrayal, hatching Merlin's prophetic power within the shadows of his sinister birth, his magical fiend binding, and his enthrallment to the Lady of the Lake (III.iii.7–14). That his prophecy inscribes Britomart's love in a political myth illustrates the power and value of the virgin's chastity: whether erotic or anti-erotic, it is a virtue prized by and necessary to male control of the institutional cornerstone, marriage, on which the preservation and continuity of patriarchal order are founded. Merlin's own demise reinforces the lesson that since men are weak they need to inseminate strong women with the fidelity and the capacity for chaste love required to guarantee the "transmission of the phallus." This lesson will be illustrated in Book V when Britomart, as if remembering the injunction to "submit thy wayes unto his will," saves Artegal from the gynarch Radegund and reestablishes him in his andrarchy. After repealing "The liberty of women" and restoring them "To mens subjection,"

Merlin and Busirane, both of whom—like Archimago—use or consult magical writing, in *Spenserian Poetics: Idolatry, Iconoclasm, and Magic* (Ithaca: Cornell University Press, 1976), 152–53. These analogies make the single reference to Archimago at III.iv.45 seem less anomalous. The momentary blurring together of Britomart, Una, and Florimell at that juncture, the earlier appearance of Redcrosse at Malecasta's house in an episode that bears some resemblance to his bad night at Archimago's (I.i), and the mention of "Duessaes traines" in the argument prefacing III.i compose a strong allusion to the problems and dangers of Book I.

she defers to "his honor, which she tendred chiefe," and quietly, dutifully vanishes from Book V, surrendering the remaining adventures to "her noble Lord" (V.vii.37–45). The Amazon episode pathologically recapitulates the sexual thematics of Book III. With its celebration of virgin power, its varied repetitions of the *pietà*, its emphasis on the dangers of engulfment by overpowering mothers and lovers, the third book winds its readers through episodes whose turnings again and again expose the precariousness of male identity, generating an ingenious diversity of threats to male power that motivate the *busy reign* of terror.

Merlin's injunction to Britomart assumes ironic force against the background of his fatal susceptibility to the Duessan wiles, the "false Ladies traines," that will seduce him "to forsake" his demonic "workemen" and their apparently endless work of wall building (III.iii.10–11). His predicament precisely figures that of the poet of Book III. Although his prophetic discourse outlines the matter of the national epic celebrating Elizabeth's genealogy, it remains no more than "an imaginative groundplot of a profitable invention."[8] Its very origin, the alliance of Britomart and Artegal, is deferred beyond the compass of *The Faerie Queene*, while the poet dallies among the solicitations of Ovidian, Petrarchan, and courtly discourses. Book III is about the origin of this origin—about the onset of desire, the formation of gendered identity, the early stages of a quest destined to end in marriage. But it is also about an origin of another kind: the emergence of a new idea of chastity, one that derives its meaning within the project of desire rather than in opposition to it, from the reactionary framework of discourses that threaten to block or divert it. Those discourses endanger the new idea by locking up traditional forms of desire in a chase that imprints gender relations with the language games of warfare and conquest, gaming and hunting, idolatry and iconoclasm, voyeuristic dismemberment and sadomasochistic fantasy. These are the tropologies of discourses that are at once literary and cultural practices, at once conventions of poetry and attitudes toward—or strategies of—sexual politics. Since they not only *represent* but also *organize* relations between genders and between generations as struggles for power, it may be more accurate to follow Foucault's example and call them *discursive regimes*. They dominate the literary culture Spenser aspires to rewrite and the literate rhetorical culture of the elite readers (aristocratic, courtly, mercantile) he writes for, and to, and about, and against.

The fifty-two years of criticism since the appearance of C. S. Lewis's

---

[8] Sidney, "An Apologie for Poetrie," in *Elizabethan Critical Essays*, ed. G. Gregory Smith (London: Oxford University Press, 1904), 1:185.

The Allegory of Love place us in a better position not only to appreciate the partial justice of his striking claim that *The Faerie Queene* "is 'like life'" but also to supply the revision necessary to save the claim. Lewis insisted that what "we have before us . . . is not so much a poet writing about the fundamental forms of life as those forms themselves spontaneously displaying their activities to us through the imagination of a poet," and, he added, this makes us "feel that his poetry has really tapped sources not easily accessible to discursive thought."[9] Today we give a different value to *discursive*, one that prises it away from conscious "thought" and slides it under the apparently spontaneous display of those language games Wittgenstein called "forms of life." The imagination through which those forms of life, or discursive regimes, display themselves is not that of the poet of *The Faerie Queene*. Rather Spenser writes about the forms of life displayed through the imaginations of other poets whose strong readings of their respective cultures authorize their versions of collective discourses.

For example, James Nohrnberg argues that in the story of Florimell and Marinell "Spenser is consciously re-creating the marine motifs of the Mediterranean epyllion" and "is showing us that the power of love extends to the kingdom of the sea. . . . The flux of analogies and comparisons makes a related point as well: love takes many forms. As Ovid says . . ." (p. 592). In my lexicon, "consciously re-creating" becomes "representing," and since I believe that "as Ovid says" is part of what Spenser represents, I would raise this to a higher power: the poet is showing us what poets have shown us about the power of love. Reading the story of Florimell one is struck not merely by the pastiche of Ovidian motifs and allusions but by the effect of Ovid. This extends beyond the Ovidian plot and theme to the storyteller's urbane amusement, and here one might also want to describe it as the effect of Ariosto, the representation of the poet as a virtuoso storyteller and literary *régisseur*, himself a voracious if skeptical reader of the Great Texts of his culture.

The skepticism is evident in the comic play of episodic visualization that frames Ovidian art in the critical perspective of a counter-Ovidian art serving the moral ends of heroic discourse and dynastic epic. That is, Spenser's technique of discontinuous narrative produces a flow of isolated, sharply visualized, but highly conventional episodes whose modern theatrical counterpart is the musical comedy or variety show—an art that diverts and debunks, that delights in its witty disenchantment, that

---

[9] *The Allegory of Love: A Study in Medieval Tradition* (London: Oxford University Press, 1936), 358.

flags its commitment not to the portrayal of Life, Society, and so on, but to the portrayal of the portrayal of Life, Society, and so on in the Literature it emulates or parodies. Thus *The Faerie Queene* is not merely "influenced" by that Literature. It exhibits a range of techniques (rhetorical, structural, intertextual) that contain and criticize it, conveying the message that the Ovidian, Ariostan, or Petrarchan artist was seduced by his material and failed to get all he could out of it—a message reaching beyond the aesthetic domain into cultural, social, and political "art." So, for example, the narrativization of Petrarchan tropes works to parody the self-serving, self-subverting character of the androcentric fantasy inscribed in the lyric genre represented by the episode of Timias and Belphoebe. And the Ovidian figure of Florimell is depicted as no less a male invention than the False Florimell. Both equally project and reflect male desires, and their effects sometimes converge, just as Neoplatonist fantasies easily slide into Petrarchan fantasies. From this standpoint the False Florimell is truer insofar as she is more explicitly an engine built from parts invented by "ydle wits" for whom "beautie is nought else, but mixture made / Of colours faire" (*An Hymne in Honour of Beautie*, 64–66).

What I now find most interesting about Spenser's metadiscursive project is its conspicuous ambivalence toward the discourses it represents. Commenting on his treatment of the *translatio imperii* theme, Elizabeth Bellamy argues that "in the process of rewriting the penultimate dynasty, Spenser becomes increasingly and ironically entangled in the remnants of the very empires he is seeking to surpass."[10] Substituting *discourses* for *empires* gives us a precise characterization of the general effect I am trying to convey. Book III, for example, flaunts its susceptibility to the discursive regimes it presents itself as "seeking to surpass," shows itself not only wary of but also diverted by their literary blandishments, dramatizes their resistance *and its own* to the project of expropriating their language in the service of a "purer" discourse of love and dynastic celebration. Thus the poet who invents and narrates the Florimell-fisherman-Proteus episode in III.viii represents himself succumbing to Ovidian pleasures and giving the tale its head. No one manhandles the hapless heroine with more gleeful disrespect than he does in making her unwittingly stir up the old fisherman with the kind of double-talk one would expect from a Malecasta or Hellenore (III.viii.24). And when, after sending the mighty Proteus to the rescue, he reduces the

[10] Abstract of "Pagan Prophecy and Christian Revelation," *Spenser at Kalamazoo*, *1984*, 21.

Old Man of the Sea to another "old leachour," the poem reaches new heights of hilarity. Proteus goes the way of all Florimell's would-be saviors; first cajoling and then threatening, he exercises his mythic privilege, dances out his Ovidian principle, in a frenzied but futile display of shape shifting (viii.39–41). At such moments the poem, reveling in its voyeuristic play, promotes the very atmosphere—of dirty jokes in the men's locker room of Western civilization—that it is elsewhere at pains to dispel. It is difficult to keep the ear attuned to the grand mythic resonances of the Florimell story and "the Mediterranean epyllion" when the narrator so clearly enjoys the rhetoric with which he converts her darkest moment to a Monty Python episode. If a poem that mocks traditional fantasies about love and gender relations at the same time exploits them for their entertainment value, it remains parasitic on—and testifies to—their continuing influence.

Northrop Frye notes that in Spenser's day "*The Faerie Queene* was regarded as pandering to a middlebrow appetite for stories about fearless knights and beauteous maidens and hideous ogres and dragons." Since he assumes that Spenser knowingly appealed to this taste because "he was trying to get imaginative support for the Protestant revolution of his time," Frye considers the poem to exemplify what he calls "kidnapped romance, that is, romance formulas used to reflect certain ascendant religious or social ideals," the ideals of a "more uncritical kind" of "social mythology . . . founded on prejudice and unexamined assumptions."[11] Though I endorse the insight encoded in Frye's metaphor, I question the implication that Spenserian kidnapping was undertaken solely as an undercover police initiative on behalf of the Reformation state. For me Spenser is a second-order kidnapper, a double agent who rekidnaps kidnapped romance in a poem that is not a quest romance *tout court* but a representation of the way quest romances have been used or represented and, by implication, of the readerships whose tastes and values they appeal to. The "middlebrow appetite" for stories of knights and maidens, not to mention stories about Ovidian hunts, gynarchic pastoral, and Petrarchan sadomasochism, is an appetite the poem represents by its mimicry of those genres, by its critique of the motives, interests, and values sedimented in one or another mode of what Fredric Jameson calls "collective narrative fantasy."[12] And just as the kidnapper's project is

---

[11] *The Secular Scripture: A Study of the Structure of Romance* (Cambridge: Harvard University Press, 1976), 28–30, 168.

[12] *The Political Unconscious: Narrative as a Socially Symbolic Act* (Ithaca: Cornell University Press, 1981), 115.

often complicated by some unaccountable attraction to the kidnappee, so the poem does not always maintain its critical distance but frequently weakens, melts, embraces the kidnapped forms. The fluid variations between distance and embracement are, however, consistently sustained within the perspective of analysis and critique, and this means that whenever embracement dominates, the critique becomes reflexive; the narrator archly performs his mimicry for our amused contempt, displays the susceptibility his mastery of the forms allows, shares with us his delight in being seduced by his endless inventiveness and improvisatory surprises.

For such a complex and ambivalent enactment to succeed, the poem must in some manner persuade readers both to embrace the kidnapped discourses and to reestablish the critical distance that acknowledges— and questions—their appeal. One device Spenser uses to encourage this divided response is, as I have suggested, the occasional comment on the story that promotes the narrator from the role of teller to that of reader and interpreter of the tale he tells. I subscribe to a currently prevailing opinion that the narrator's expressive and interpretive interventions are not authoritative guides to reader response. And to this opinion I add my own: the reason they aren't authoritative is that Spenser uses the commentator as the voice of the discourses, the voice of the kidnapped genres parodied in *The Faerie Queene*. This idea came into clear focus only after I had worked through the implications of the concept of metapastoral that informs my more recent readings of *The Shepheardes Calender*. At that point I realized that the function I ascribed to E. K. in the *Calender* could be extended to the narrator of *The Faerie Queene*. I conclude this afterword with an example drawn from the fifth canto of Book III.

In the opening stanzas of cantos iii and v the narrator voices the conventional pieties of romance reinforced by Neoplatonizing sentiments. Here, as in cantos ii and iv, he plays the advocate of chivalry and courtesy who joins with his protagonists in the effort to redress the wrongs done to women.[13] As a courtier he stresses the long view leading to

---

[13] Consider, for example, the opening stanza of canto iii:

> Most sacred fire, that burnest mightily
> In living brests, ykindled first above,
> Emongst th'eternall spheres and lamping sky,
> And thence pour into men, which men call Love;
> Not that same, which doth base affections move
> In brutish minds, and filthy lust inflame,
> But that sweet fit, that doth true beautie love,
> And choseth vertue for his dearest Dame,
> Whence spring all noble deeds and never dying fame.

Artegal, Gloriana, and Elizabeth but conspicuously evades what the text just as conspicuously reveals in its treatment of the discourses being staged in fairyland. The incompatibility between what the narrator says and what the text of his narrative shows is most striking when he registers his admiring response to Belphoebe's chastity and exhorts women to follow her example:

> That dainty Rose, the daughter of her Morne,
>   More deare then life she tendered, whose flowre
>   The girlond of her honour did adorne:
>   Ne suffred she the Middayes scorching powre,
>   Ne the sharp Northerne wind thereon to showre,
>   But lapped up her silken leaves most chaire,
>   When so the froward skye began to lowre:
>   But soone as calmed was the Christall aire,
> She did it faire dispred, and let to florish faire.
>
> Eternall God in his almighty powre,
>   To make ensample of his heavenly grace,
>   In Paradize whilome did plant this flowre,
>   Whence he it fetcht out of her native place,

The sacred fire is dissociated from lust and described in terms that are sufficiently Neoplatonic in tone to make us wonder whether the feminine reference is purely metaphoric and the "sweet fit" some contemplative prelude to heroic action. But the context belies the narrator's attempt at purification, for canto ii centered on Britomart's violent love pangs, the description of which made them seem less like a "sweet fit" than like the bitter wounds of Cupid so often associated with "base affections."

The narrator begins canto v with a statement that differs from iii.1 in presenting love as the root of base no less than noble affections:

> Wonder it is to see, in diverse minds,
>   How diversly love doth his pageants play,
>   And shewes his powre in variable kinds:
>   The baser wit, whose idle thoughts alway
>   Are wont to cleave unto the lowly clay,
>   It stirreth up to sensuall desire,
>   And in lewd slouth to wast his careless day:
>   But in brave sprite it kindles goodly fire,
> That to all high desert and honour doth aspire.

"Baser wit" and "brave sprite" may refer either to different parts or impulses of a single psyche or to different kinds of individuals. Though the language may hesitate between these options, it seems to commit itself more firmly to the second, more simplistic, reading because this echoes the burden of Arthur's complaint to night in the immediately preceding stanzas of canto iv. Yet the action of the poem, the language of the text, and the behavior of the characters all encourage us to resist the narrator's conventional pieties. The pieties are those of the traditional ethos of romance discourse reinforced by Neoplatonizing sentiments.

And did in stocke of earthly flesh enrace,
That mortall men her glory should admire:
In gentle Ladies brest, and bounteous race
Of woman kind it fairest flowre doth spire,
And beareth fruit of honour and all chast desire.

Faire ympes of beautie, whose bright shining beames
Adorne the world with like to heavenly light,
And to your willes both royalties and Realmes
Subdew, through conquest of your wondrous might,
With this faire flowre your goodly girlonds dight,
Of chastity and vertue virginall,
That shall embellish more your beautie bright,
And crowne your heades with heavenly coronall,
Such as the Angels weare before Gods tribunall.

(v.51–53)

The *effect* of a narrator struggling to impose a preferred interpretation against the grain is evident in the often-noted ambivalence of the opening phrase. "That dainty Rose" echoes two demonstrative phrases in the previous stanza, "that sweet Cordiall" and "that soveraigne salve" that Belphoebe "did envy" to Timias "and to all th'unworthy world forlore" (v.50). By synonymy, therefore, the Rose at first signifies virginal chastity less directly than the erotic "salve" or "cordiall" chastity denies. This impression is enhanced by the concrete but ambiguous adjective *dainty* (pleasant, choice, delicate, rare, precious, fastidious) and by the spelling of *chaire*, which adds a French meaning to its obvious sense (charily), that is, "her most fleshly silken leaves." If "Rose" glances at the discourse of courtly love and the *Roman de la rose*, the narrator's response carefully muffles the subversive implications his rhetoric activates. Even as he verbally caresses the Rose, his nature metaphors are referentially obscure enough to diffuse the impact of the erotic image. His weather report is at once so evasive and so detailed as to be funny. "Lapped up her silken leaves" and "did it faire dispred" clearly denote actions. But just what actions do they denote? There is something oddly voyeuristic in these displacements. They are, one might say, "chaire," as if his fleshly desire is occasioned by her fleshly beauty, her chariness by his desire, his chariness by hers.

The Actaeonic danger hinted at in all Belphoebe's appearances is here affixed to the narrator's viewpoint. As the first reader of his story, he dramatizes the temptations of Ovidian entrapment and signals the danger by following the voyeuristic innuendo of the "dainty Rose" stanza with four stanzas of fervent praise and exhortation. Like Timias before

Belphoebe and Arthur diverted by Florimell, he recoils from the erotic
glimpse and attraction of the virgin's sexuality into a Neoplatonizing
mode that spiritualizes the flower, then goes on in stanza 53 to make
amends for his lapse by paying the Ladies a chivalrous compliment and
enthusiastically recommending the advantages of the virtue Belphoebe
models. Yet the particular way he defines and endorses that virtue betrays
a more complex reaction to Belphoebe's Rose than is acknowledged by
his impassioned sweep through the stanza.[14]

In the subtext of the stanza erotic skills are political skills: "chastity
and vertue virginall" is a euphemism for sexuality displayed and with-
held to subdue men. Maureen Quilligan sees this passage as one of
Spenser's many addresses in Book III to "female" or "woman" readers,[15]
but here at least the class of addresses is more restricted: these are
"Ladies" and "Faire ympes of beautie," women who—being desirable—have something men want and who are presumed to be socially
well placed and politically ambitious. Their adviser speaks as a courtly
and Petrarchan insider. He knows from bitter experience, the experience of Timias or Arthur, what it takes for a woman to become a Lady,
that is, to dominate men while playing by the rules of a man's game in a
man's world. The message his speech conveys under its Neoplatonizing
rhetoric is that women should use their power judiciously, should learn
when it is profitable to "faire dispred" the Rose and when to withhold it.
The message undermines the narrator's rhetorical investment in the pattern of descent and ascent (from "Eternall God" to "Gods tribunall")
that characterizes Neoplatonic discourse: it converts the discourse to a
smokescreen that mystifies an appeal to political interest as an appeal to
ethical and religious aspiration. At the same time, the strategy of sub-

---

[14] Commenting on the narrator's response to the plight of Timias in III.v.42–43,
Jerome Dees notes "the extent of the narrator's emotional involvement in the story he is
recounting" and suggests that the passage reflects "in the narrator's own words the mental
processes by which Timias struggles against, rationalizes, and finally acquiesces in his
'love' for Belphoebe." But the narrator's involvement in the story is hilarious because it is
set off by his equally intense involvement in a battery of alliterating antitheses, internal
rhymes, and puns ignited by phonetic repetition ("hole"/"whole," "Mayd"/"dismayd,"
"Malady"/"a Lady"). If, as Dees asserts, the vocabulary in these stanzas "is a fairly
conventional mixture of Petrarchism and Platonism," it is so with a vengeance ("The
Narrator of *The Faerie Queene*: Patterns of Response," *Texas Studies in Language and
Literature* 12 [1971]: 548). The speaker of these lines is clearly sending up the conventional mixture, enjoying his display of verbal wit, flaunting his recreative skill and pleasure in the histrionics of erotic complaint, and pretending with some relish to be emo-
tionally involved in the story his mimicry targets.

[15] *Milton's Spenser: The Politics of Reading* (Ithaca: Cornell University Press, 1983),
188–89.

limation marking his retreat from his encounter with the Rose reveals his own interestedness. He makes a bid to regain power over women by speaking as their disinterested servant, admirer, advocate, and counselor, one who knows and is willing to share the secret that will help them advance their careers and dominate such men as himself.

In these comments on the narrator I have been trying to suggest the way Spenser uses this figure to dramatize the limits, contradictions, evasions, and self-deceptions inscribed in the different literary versions of the traditional discourse of gender. The narrator speaks the familiar literary language and expresses the familiar sentiments of the more "refined" or polite traditions of love lore. His response to the story minimally registers its textual complexities and uncritically endorses an ideology of gender that the text again and again places in question. His falsifying simplifications, his pious clichés appealing to the *bien pensant* among Spenser's readers, throw the critique of that ideology in high relief. Like E. K. in the *Calender*, the narrator is the first reader and interpreter of *The Faerie Queene*. That his interpretation is at once conspicuously inadequate and conspicuously conventional drives the wedge deeper between the radically revisionary discourse of Spenserian romance and the maze of interpenetrating discourses it revises. The narrator is there to state the claims of those discourses, and the statement fails to persuade. By showing us how not to read *The Faerie Queene*, he opens up another way to read it.

INDEX